The Microsoft Antitrust Cases

The Microsoft Antitrust Cases

Competition Policy for the Twenty-first Century

Andrew I. Gavil and Harry First

The MIT Press
Cambridge, Massachusetts
London, England

MIT Press books may be purchased at special quantity discounts for business or sales promotional use. For information, email special_sales@mitpress.mit.edu.

Set in Stone Sans Std and Stone Serif Std by Toppan Best-set Premedia Limited, Hong Kong. Printed and bound in the United States of America.

Library of Congress Cataloging-in-Publication Data

Gavil, Andrew I., 1957– author.
The Microsoft antitrust cases : competition policy for the twenty-first century / Andrew I. Gavil and Harry First.
    pages cm
Includes bibliographical references and index.
ISBN 978-0-262-02776-2 (hardcover : alk. paper)
1. Microsoft Corporation—Trials, litigation, etc.   2. United States—Trials, litigation, etc.   3. Antitrust law—United States—Cases.   4. Software industry—Law and legislation—United States—Cases.   I. First, Harry, 1945– author.   II. Title.
KF228.U5G38 2014
343.7307'21—dc23
2014003842

10 9 8 7 6 5 4 3 2 1

Contents

Acknowledgments

When work began on this book, we hardly thought it would be so many years before we would be penning the acknowledgments. As time went on, however, the story we wanted to chronicle continued to unfold, and the project grew as each new facet of the collective "*Microsoft* cases" captured our interest. The result, we think, is a unique volume that covers more than two decades of public and private investigation and litigation, as well as academic thought about the role of the antitrust laws in the digital age. The story tells us much about the competition policy system's strengths and weaknesses in the near future, especially for global consumer-technology firms such as Microsoft. The book may be done; the story surely is not.

First and foremost, we would like to thank each other. Our friendship and our mutual respect have grown during this collaboration, spurred on by our shared and firm conviction that the information and perspectives contained in these pages had not been fully captured elsewhere, despite the extensive commentary on various aspects of the *Microsoft* cases.

We also deeply appreciate the support of our respective law schools and colleagues. Andy would, in particular, like to thank Howard University's School of Law for summer research grants, and Deans Kurt L. Schmoke and Okianer Christian Dark for their unwavering commitment to support him in bringing the project to fruition. Andy's long-time colleague Andrew E. Taslitz provided years of encouragement, helpful suggestions, and, most important, his own example; Andy says "I will miss you, my old friend, and I wish you could have seen the book in print so we could have celebrated together." Patricia V. Sun gave generously of her time to provide very helpful comments on early drafts of the first chapters. Andy would also like to acknowledge the many helpful conversations he had about the *Microsoft* cases with Professors Jonathan B. Baker, William E. Kovacic, and Steven C. Salop.

Harry would like to thank the Filomen D'Agostino and Max E. Greenberg Research Fund at the New York University School of Law for financial support. He would also like to acknowledge the very helpful discussions he has had with Stephen Houck and Jay Himes, respectively his predecessor and successor at the New York State Attorney General's Antitrust Bureau.

Both Andy and Harry had many conversations with a number of the participants in the various *Microsoft* cases. Some of those conversations are cited in the book; others were off the record. We thank all the participants for their generous help.

Many research assistants worked with us, over the years, on various aspects of the book. Andy would like to thank Reshaun Finkley, Joseph Gasper II, Michelle Yost Hale, Josephine Nelson Harriott, Kara Hoffman, Kirsten Nelson, Kapil Vishnu Pandit, and Varnitha Siva. Harry would like to thank Pascal Berghe, Ralph Eissler, Peri Schultz, Matthew Trokenheim, and Melissa Wasserman, and the students who participated in two seminars on the *Microsoft* cases.

In addition to our home institutions, we thank Professor Spencer Weber Waller and the Loyola Institute for Consumer Antitrust Studies. Spencer invited us to present earlier versions of several of our chapters at the Tenth Annual Midwest Antitrust Colloquium, held in April 2010. We benefited from comments from Professor Waller and from the other participants in the colloquium.

Finally, we must acknowledge the support of our families and friends, who listened patiently to us as we optimistically announced deadline after deadline that we would surely meet … this time! If they doubted that the book would ever be completed, they carefully (and thankfully) kept that thought to themselves. Andy would like to acknowledge the support of his wife, Judith H. Veis, and their children, Justin, Noah, and Zoe Ruth. Harry thanks his wife, Eve, and their daughters, Devra and Miryam, all of whom helped him maintain his enthusiasm for this project.

A few disclaimers: While serving as Of Counsel to Sonnenschein Nath & Rosenthal LLP between 2003 and 2004, Andy worked with the team prosecuting Sun's antitrust suit against Microsoft. All discussions of that case in the book, however, are based on public records. No confidential information was used. Also, in 2010 Google Inc. provided a research grant to the Howard University School of Law to support Andy's antitrust research. By mutual agreement with Google and Howard University, none of those funds were used in connection with the preparation of this book, which was already well under way at the time the grant was awarded. Since September 2012, Andy has been serving as the director of the Federal Trade

Commission's Office of Policy Planning. The views expressed in this book are solely his own and do not necessarily reflect the views of the FTC or those of any commissioner. No FTC resources were used in the completion of the book. Harry was the chief of the Antitrust Bureau of the New York State Attorney General's Office from May 1999 to May 2001, during which time he was responsible for supervising New York's efforts in the *Microsoft* litigation. The views he expresses in this book are solely his own and do not in any way reflect the views of the Office of the Attorney General.

1 The *Microsoft* Antitrust Cases

Microsoft Corporation's origins are legendary in the world of technology firms. Microsoft was founded in 1975 by Bill Gates and Paul Allen. Its most significant early product breakthrough came in the early 1980s, when it spearheaded the development of the first operating system for the IBM PC: the Microsoft disk operating system (MS-DOS). Late in 1985, building on the success of MS-DOS, Microsoft launched the first version of Windows. In 1989 it launched its first "suite" of office-productivity software, which it marketed under the name Office. The collective success of MS-DOS, Windows, and Office, fueled by advances in microchip technology and memory technology, was extraordinary. The personal-computer revolution propelled Microsoft to a position of preeminence in the computer world in little more than a decade, making it one of the most successful firms of the early information age.[1]

With that preeminence, however, came scrutiny by government antitrust enforcers in the United States and Europe. In 1990, Microsoft became a subject of extensive investigations that focused on its alliance with IBM and its use of restrictive licensing practices for Windows, which had already become its flagship product. Although these early investigations concluded with the entry of a consent decree in 1994, they fostered some of the principal story lines that would persist through years of legal challenges to Microsoft's practices. Whereas Microsoft's rivals and government prosecutors painted Microsoft as a ruthless predator abusing the power it had acquired in the market for PC operating systems to suppress competition, Microsoft countered that it was a victim of overzealous government prosecutors, who were too easily swayed by the lobbying efforts of its disgruntled rivals. Less clear at that time was that the firm's entanglement with the antitrust laws would persist and expand to include a multitude of public and private legal challenges in the United States and elsewhere in the world.

This book provides a comprehensive account of Microsoft's encounter with the global competition policy system (which now has spanned more than twenty years) and explores its lessons and its durable meaning. The enforcement effort directed at Microsoft—the collective "*Microsoft* cases"—provides a unique opportunity to study the strengths, the weaknesses, and some of the features of that system, which today includes federal, state, and private enforcers in the United States and more than a hundred public enforcement authorities around the world. That system, as revealed through the *Microsoft* cases, is institutionally and substantively intricate. Remarkably for a single group of related cases, the *Microsoft* cases illustrate virtually all of the richness of the antitrust tradition and the tensions inherent in it, from its origins through the emergence of today's global system.

Although we chronicle the most significant cases directed at Microsoft since 1990, specific emphasis is placed on the complementary public prosecutions of Microsoft initiated by the U.S. Department of Justice, twenty states, and the District of Columbia in May of 1998 and on the objections to its conduct initiated in Brussels by the European Commission. The U.S. actions were prompted by the imminent release of Windows 98, the next generation of Microsoft's operating system for desktop personal computers, which included Microsoft's latest version of a browser called Internet Explorer (IE). When those cases were filed in May of 1998, the Attorney General of the United States, Janet Reno, and representatives of the state government plaintiffs accused Microsoft of pursuing a wide-ranging campaign to destroy its principal browser rival, Netscape Communications, in order to obstruct competition in the emerging market for browsers and to perpetuate its monopoly of operating systems.[2] In a prepared statement, Joel Klein, the Assistant Attorney General in charge of the Antitrust Division, called on the federal district court "to put an end to Microsoft's unlawful campaign to eliminate competition, deter innovation, and restrict consumer choice."[3]

In investigating and eventually prosecuting their claims against Microsoft, federal and state prosecutors weren't assuming any novel role as government enforcers. Since July 2, 1890, when the first federal antitrust law—the Sherman Act—was signed into law, the federal government has frequently served as the policeman of national markets, dispensed to rein in overbearing private corporate power. Federal power, wielded in the public interest, was conceived by Congress as the antidote to such private power when it threatened to hinder competition.[4]

In important ways, however, the government's prosecution of Microsoft was unprecedented. It pitted the century-old Sherman Act against the volatile business practices of the information age. As the most significant monopolization case brought by the government since the litigation against International Business Machines (IBM) and American Telephone & Telegraph (AT&T) thirty years earlier, the prosecution also was unique in the degree to which it attracted immediate and continued attention outside the antitrust community. The notoriety of Microsoft and the ubiquity of its products guaranteed that the case would captivate the legal, business, and technology communities, as well as the public at large. With more than 90 percent of users of personal computers dependent on Microsoft's Windows operating system (on which the controversy centered), consumers, businesspeople, academic and corporate customers, and industry observers and investors all sought daily reports of the case's progress. For perhaps the first time in modern antitrust history, an antitrust case became a true cause célèbre. The press followed the case's daily progress with rapt attention.

Moreover, as the *Microsoft* cases expanded to engross the full range of public, private, domestic, and international institutional actors that today are responsible for enforcing the antitrust laws, they tested the capacity of the antitrust system to efficiently reach consistent, reasoned, and economically sound judgments about markets and competition. By 2001, the 1998 prosecutions had triggered a far wider engagement with the U.S. antitrust system as the proceedings against Microsoft multiplied throughout the country. Producers of complementary software, Microsoft's rivals, consumers, and customers (including government customers such as school districts), initiated scores of antitrust claims directed at Microsoft. In all, Microsoft was sued more than two hundred times in the United States, in both state and federal courts, as a consequence of the conduct highlighted by the government cases. Potential recoveries in the billions of dollars were sought by rivals and millions of consumers. Microsoft not only had to defend itself; it also had to manage numerous cases, many of them brought as class actions, with overlapping claims in multiple jurisdictions. And the courts had to do the same, coordinating the cases both formally and informally given the procedural tools available.

Microsoft's encounter with the antitrust system, however, wasn't confined to the United States. A global competition policy system was emerging. Reflecting that changing regulatory landscape, Microsoft's antitrust troubles expanded beyond the borders of the United States. Simultaneously with the U.S. cases, the investigation and prosecution of Microsoft on related grounds proceeded outside the United States, most importantly in Europe. Early in 2004, after a five-year investigation and lengthy negotiations with Microsoft, the European Commission, which is charged with enforcing the European Union's competition laws, concluded that Microsoft had indeed violated those laws by tying its Windows Media Player to the Windows PC operating system and by refusing to give its rivals in the market for operating systems for workgroup servers the interface information that would enable their products to interoperate with Windows. This proceeding was followed by a second case, filed and settled in 2009, charging that Microsoft was unlawfully tying its Internet browser, IE, to its dominant Windows PC operating system.

Taken together, the public and private *Microsoft* cases in the United States and elsewhere in the world thus illuminate many of the most pressing challenges to policing competition in the global marketplace of the twenty-first century, especially in technology industries.

Goals of the Book

This book has three primary goals. The first is to provide a comprehensive account of the decades-long effort to police Microsoft, emphasizing the government-led efforts in the United States and the European Union but also examining the extensive private litigation in the United States. What were these cases about? What were their goals? What did the evidence show? Were the cases ultimately successful in securing their goals? Did they serve the broader public policies of competition law? With respect to the private cases, we will ask whether consumers were indeed harmed by Microsoft's conduct and, if so, whether they were adequately compensated. In answering these questions, we detail the theories behind the cases and the facts as revealed by the evidence; we will also examine the legal principles and economic analysis that were used to resolve them. As we will see, these elements became plot lines in complex and competing narratives woven together and advocated by Microsoft and its adversaries. Which narratives proved to be most consistent with the evidence, and thus most persuasive?

In chapter 2 we examine Microsoft's early encounters with U.S. and European competition authorities—the "pre-history" of the major battles that commenced in 1998. In chapters 3 and 4 we take an in-depth look at the cases commenced by the federal government and the states in 1998. In chapter 5 we turn to the private litigation that followed in the United States during the subsequent decade. In chapter 6 we discuss the proceedings in Europe that began in late 1998.

To assess the durable meaning of the *Microsoft* cases, however, it also will be necessary to locate them in their broader institutional and political context. As was noted above, the government cases filed in the United States in 1998 triggered a far broader effort to constrain Microsoft from abusing its market power and to remedy the consequences of its conduct. This institutional complexity led to political complexity. Through three successive administrations in Washington, federal and state antitrust agencies sought to coordinate their efforts while Microsoft and its rivals sought to persuade the various and changing government officials of their respective views of Microsoft's conduct.

A second major goal of the book, therefore, is to use the *Microsoft* cases—public, private, domestic, and international—to illuminate and evaluate the institutional and remedial dimensions of contemporary antitrust enforcement. Two federal agencies, a multiplicity of states, numerous private parties, and a number of foreign antitrust enforcement agencies all pursued Microsoft. Courts and (at least in theory) juries in the United States were charged with sifting through often complex economic and technical evidence to resolve the various claims and defenses of the parties. Expert witnesses, especially economists, also emerged as critical players in this system, influencing the framing and presentation of the key issues in the cases.

What reasons could there be for constructing such a multi-layered, arguably overlapping, global "antitrust system" in which a single U.S.-based firm can be subject to investigation by multiple government enforcement institutions and exposed to years of private suits by the victims of its conduct? Is it sensible public policy to subject successful firms to the scrutiny—and uncertainty—of investigation and possible legal action by so large and so diverse a group of potential challengers? How can multiple public enforcers with overlapping enforcement authority—and potentially with different judgments about the nature of any given case—readily cooperate or sort out differences of opinion when they arise?

Third, and related to the first two goals, the *Microsoft* cases sparked a continuing and intense debate among ardent critics and supporters of antitrust enforcement about the standards to be applied in judging the conduct of large firms, referred to as "monopolists" in the United States and as "dominant firms" in most other parts of the world. The international scope of that debate confirmed the coming of age of the "global" competition policy system. Whereas enforcers and commentators in the United States had for decades presumed to take a leading role in discussions of competition policy, their counterparts abroad emerged with greater confidence as equals in this debate, initiating cases of their own and issuing public guidelines and guidance statements detailing their enforcement priorities. Notwithstanding sometimes vocal and public criticism of their efforts from

U.S. antitrust enforcement officials, they often concluded that the increasingly non-interventionist views of U.S. officials and courts were inconsistent with their own assessments of sound policy.

This debate about substantive and remedial standards has revealed not only differences of opinion among economists and lawyers, but also significant and continuing ideological divisions. Those divisions often flow more from political judgments than from economic judgments about the ability of markets to self-correct in response to abusive conduct by dominant firms, the competence of government agents to police their conduct, and the probable effect of specific legal judgments on the innovation incentives of dominant firms and those who would challenge them. Often expressed as presumptions about the likely incidence and consequences of error by decision makers and the comparative virtues and efficacy of markets and the rule of law, they can profoundly influence policy makers' preferences for alternative institutions, legal standards, burdens of proof, perceptions of evidence, and remedies.

In chapters 7–9, assessing these institutional, substantive, and remedial issues, we seek to answer some of the most important questions raised by advocates and critics of the *Microsoft* cases: Were the institutions charged with enforcement of their respective national competition laws up to the challenge of evaluating the effects of Microsoft's conduct? Were the laws themselves up to the task of accurately judging Microsoft's conduct? Were the tools of antitrust analysis suited to the economics of the computer software industry? Were the remedies imposed on Microsoft through negotiated settlements and court orders adequate? Did they halt Microsoft's anticompetitive conduct? Did they appropriately deter Microsoft (and other large firms) from engaging in similar conduct in the future? Did they effectively restore the competition that Microsoft suppressed? In chapter 7 we assess the range of remedies that were proposed and imposed on Microsoft globally and offer a set of "lessons learned" from the *Microsoft* remedy experience. In chapter 8 we focus on the challenges and virtues of institutional diversity, showing how the *Microsoft* case benefited from today's diverse and decentralized antitrust enforcement system. In chapter 9 we return to the central questions of our study of the *Microsoft* litigation and the implications their answers have for competition policy in the twenty-first century.

A study of the *Microsoft* cases remains timely and important for a number of reasons. After more than two decades of public, private, domestic, and foreign investigations and lawsuits, the *Microsoft* cases collectively provide a unique opportunity to study the integrity and operation of the still-evolving global competition policy system. It is now more possible than ever before to seek answers to the many questions we have posed—to identify and assess the lessons learned from the cases from institutional, remedial, and substantive law perspectives.

In the remainder of this chapter, we provide a general overview of the federal antitrust laws in the United States that were invoked to judge Microsoft's conduct, especially Section 2 of the Sherman Act. Since its enactment in 1890, Section 2 has prohibited three offenses: "monopolization," "attempt to monopolize," and "conspiracy to monopolize." It has been invoked against some of the most storied names in American business history, including Standard Oil, Alcoa, DuPont, AT&T, and IBM. Through these and other cases, standards for judging the legality of single-firm conduct have evolved and significantly influenced the legal and economic analysis of Microsoft's conduct.

Antitrust Laws and Monopoly in the United States: A Brief History

To begin our examination of the *Microsoft* cases, it is first necessary to appreciate the basic legal framework of U.S. antitrust laws. As the oldest set of contemporary competition laws in the world, they have influenced other jurisdictions, sometimes by their specific letter but more often through the economic concepts that have developed to guide their interpretation and application, especially since the 1970s. This is true in the analysis of cartels and mergers, as well as with respect to the acts of single, powerful firms.

At the federal level, the principal prohibitions are contained in three statutes: the Sherman Act of 1890, the Clayton Act of 1914, and the Federal Trade Commission Act of 1914. There are also individual state antitrust laws in nearly all of the fifty states and in the District of Columbia, and there are complementary federal and state consumer-protection laws that can be invoked in conjunction with or as alternatives to federal antitrust laws.

The federal antitrust laws are enforced by two federal agencies (the Federal Trade Commission and the Antitrust Division of the Department of Justice), by the attorneys general of the states, and by private parties. The "private right of action," an original feature of the Sherman Act, is now codified in Section 4 of the Clayton Act. It has often been referred to as empowering "private attorneys general" who by pursuing their own self-interests also serve the public interest.[5] As we discuss in chapter 5, the U.S. private right of action, uniquely in the world, permits the victims of antitrust violations to recover treble damages—that is, three times their actual damages—and, in addition, their attorneys' fees and litigation costs. When integrated into the federal system of litigation, which authorizes class actions and broad discovery of evidence, this right of action can provide a formidable deterrent to anticompetitive conduct and a means of securing compensation. Critics have argued, however, that it provides so great an incentive to bring suit that weak cases are inadvertently encouraged and unwarranted settlements may result simply to avoid the costs of typically complex and protracted antitrust litigation. These concerns have also been expressed by the U.S. Supreme Court, which has invoked them to constrain the scope of both the private right of action and the substantive antitrust law.[6]

As we have already noted, the antitrust system of the United States operates today in the far wider context of a global system of "competition laws." This expansion of antitrust into a global enterprise is a direct consequence of two developments: the maturing of the European Union since its inception in 1957 and, more recently, the dissolution of the Soviet Union in 1991 and the consequent redirection of many countries in Eastern Europe and elsewhere away from centrally planned economies and toward greater reliance on market principles. Although the laws of other jurisdictions often have features in common with U.S. laws, they are increasingly modeled on the somewhat different laws and institutions of the European Union.[7]

The principal allegations in the governments' cases against Microsoft in the United States arose under the first two sections of the Sherman Act, which contain its principal prohibitions. Section 1 of the Act prohibits "contracts, combinations in the form of trust, or otherwise, and conspiracies" that unreasonably "restrain trade." A violation of Section 1, therefore, has two elements. First, there must be "concerted action"—that is, coordinated action by more than one person or firm. Second, the conduct challenged must have an unreasonably adverse effect on competition. Since the Supreme Court's 1911 *Standard Oil* decision, the standard for judging concerted action's effect on competition has been the "rule of reason."[8] Under the rule of reason, adverse competitive effect sometimes can be presumed, as with the most obvious kinds of anticompetitive conduct—for example, the formation of a cartel to fix prices rather than compete. In such cases, the courts have traditionally applied a *"per se"* approach to applying the rule of reason that presumes that the conduct in question is unreasonably anticompetitive and precludes evidence of any defenses. The presumption is therefore irrebuttable. Often, however, the effects of concerted action are less obvious. In such cases, courts and enforcement agencies have relied on a range of relatively more comprehensive methods of applying the rule of reason that involve shifting but rebuttable presumptions. Using a sliding scale, the courts evaluate the relative strength of the evidence of both anticompetitive and procompetitive effects, especially efficiencies, to reach a judgment about a particular restraint's reasonableness.[9] Section 2 of the Sherman Act complements Section 1 and prohibits three distinct offenses: monopolization, attempt to monopolize, and conspiracy to monopolize. In contrast to Section 1, Section 2 can reach the actions of a single firm—what is sometimes referred to as "unilateral" or "single-firm" conduct.[10]

The bulk of the legislative history of the Sherman Act explores its first section, which most directly addressed the principal concern of the day: the "trusts." It was these trusts—formed in, for example, the oil, sugar, railroad, whiskey, and tobacco industries—that most preoccupied the Congress in 1890.[11] Through collusion, sometimes overt and sometimes tacit, rivals in these and other industries coordinated their pricing and their production in lieu of competing. Consumers were the losers and literally paid the price.

The trusts were feared, however, not only for their power over price but also for their willingness to protect and effectuate that power by engaging in "exclusionary" or "predatory" conduct.[12] Such conduct might be directed at barring the entry into the market by would-be rivals of the trusts, or at punishing members of the trust who deviated from its agreed-upon prices and practices. Often the targets of exclusionary conduct by the trusts were smaller businesses, and it has long been evident that the Sherman Act and the later Clayton Act were viewed in part as vehicles for protecting such smaller businesses from the exclusionary tactics of their larger rivals. But that was understood as an intermediary purpose. The ultimate goal was to protect consumers from the consequences of the diminished rivalry that followed from exclusion.[13] Yet for the Sherman Act's drafters there was no distinction between protecting competitors and protecting competition—to protect competition, rivals had to be shielded from the exclusionary strategies of dominant firms. As we shall learn, however, the Supreme Court, in its recent interpretations and applications of the Sherman Act, has viewed these two complementary purposes as distinct and has prioritized the protection of "competition" over the protection of individual "competitors." It has reasoned that it is necessary to do so lest the law be used to shield unworthy rivals from healthy though aggressive competition. This argument was frequently advanced by Microsoft in response to charges that it had harmed its rivals.

Today, the economic relationship between collusion and exclusion that was implicitly acknowledged in Sections 1 and 2 of the Sherman Act is better understood than it was in 1890. In order to exercise what economists call "market power"—the ability to charge prices above the competitive level or to otherwise restrict other dimensions of competition, such as service, quality, or innovation—a single firm or a group of colluding firms may have to impair or totally preclude rivals from responding through entry or expansion. Without some control over entry, the effort to exercise market power may well fail, because it will attract new or expanded entry by firms willing to provide customers better products, services, and/or lower prices. This imperative to control entry as a means of facilitating the exercise of market power is as true for a single dominant firm as it is for a group of rivals who have formed a trust or a cartel. For the monopolist bent on raising or maintaining price, it must be true that entry by new firms or expansion by firms already in the market is very difficult or that cost-effective strategies are available for the monopolist to make it so. In fact, the monopolist might well be willing to invest significant resources in such strategies, provided the payoff in power over price is sufficiently promising. This conduct—undertaken primarily in the hope that it will facilitate the collection of supra-competitive profits[14]—is sometimes referred to as "rent-seeking." "Barriers to entry" are often viewed, therefore, as a prerequisite to the successful exercise of market power, whether it is exercised by a coordinated group of rivals or by a single firm. And under the antitrust laws conduct that creates, raises, or fortifies barriers to entry can be suspect when it facilitates the exercise of market power. Such barriers impair the ability of actual or potential rival firms to respond to the monopolist's high-priced goods and hence reduce consumers' ability to switch their allegiance.

In recognition of the relationship between power over price and entry into the market, Section 2 of the Sherman Act is directed at exclusion. It was added late in the legislative process, but it is essential to the operation of Section 1. It was viewed as a complement to Section 1, intended to catch any firms that somehow slipped past Section 1's prohibition of concerted action, successfully reaching the status of "monopoly," but only when they acted to prevent competition by some illicit means.[15] Sections 1 and 2 acknowledged collusion and exclusion, therefore, as the twin foundations of modern antitrust policy.[16]

Prohibiting the conduct of a single firm that excludes rivals, however, can be tricky. The Sherman Act's requirement of exclusionary or predatory conduct manifests an intuition about competition that was evident even in the legislative history of 1890: that competition will always have winners and losers. Monopoly may be the consequence of a successful battle for supremacy in a field. From the points of view of both the victor and the vanquished, the results of successful competition and exclusion or predation may even look the same in many cases—some businesses will thrive whereas others will fail. "Monopolization" as a legal term of art in the United States has long been understood to draw a line between monopolies secured honestly through skill, which should be untouched, and those obtained or maintained through exclusionary conduct or predation, which are condemned. This approach to monopoly presumes the acceptance in some cases of the evils of monopoly (higher prices and the inefficient distortions they can create), leaving the cure to the forces of the market. The approach can be justified on the ground that the incentive to compete and win may be weakened if genuinely industrial victors are denied the enjoyment of the fruits of their efforts. "Many people believe," Judge Learned Hand remarked in his 1945 decision in *United States v. Aluminum Co. of America*, "that possession of unchallenged economic power deadens initiative, discourages thrift and depresses energy; that immunity from competition is a narcotic, and rivalry a stimulant, to industrial progress; that the spur of constant stress is necessary to counteract an inevitable disposition to let well enough alone." Yet he also recognized that the promise of monopoly is a spur to competition, and that to condemn the mere possession of it without ascertaining whether the monopolist has acquired its position through means other than superior skill would erode the very incentives that drove it to compete in the first place. He concluded, therefore, that "the successful competitor, having been urged to compete, must not be turned upon when he wins."[17] Hand's observations have guided U.S. antitrust policy toward single firms ever since.

From these general principles, the courts have developed two defining characteristics of Section 2. First, "mere size" in and of itself has never been viewed as a violation of the Sherman Act. "Monopoly" isn't the offense defined by Section 2; "monopolization," the active verb, is.[18] Reflecting this fact, the Supreme Court has long adhered to a two-part formula for monopolization that requires proof of both power and conduct: "It is settled law that this offense requires, in addition to the possession of monopoly power in the relevant market, 'the willful acquisition or maintenance of that power as distinguished from growth or development as a consequence of a superior product, business acumen, or historic accident.'"[19] To be "big" isn't enough; the firm accused of a violation of Section 2 must also be "bad."[20] "Conduct" that isn't industrious thus is a prerequisite to the active offense of "monopolization" or "attempt to monopolize."

Second, from its inception Section 2 presented the challenge of deciding what kind of conduct warrants condemnation. How can judges and juries differentiate between aggressive but wholly legitimate competition (that is, what Judge Hand described in *United States v. Aluminum Co. of America* as "superior skill, foresight, and industry") and "predatory" or "exclusionary" conduct (which warrants condemnation) if both can result in success for some firms and failure for others?[21] The standard refrain, recently restated by the Supreme Court, distinguishes between "superior product, business acumen, or historic accident" and "willful acquisition or maintenance," but this articulation of the distinction leaves unanswered the question of how courts are to draw the line between the two.

Courts and commentators have grappled with this Section 2 puzzle for nearly a century, and it remains a topic of intense debate in antitrust circles. The common goal is to develop a standard that strikes a reasonable balance between over-deterrence (that is, a tendency to discourage aggressive but efficient conduct) and under-deterrence (that is, failure to condemn illegitimate conduct that hobbles or destroys competition and harms consumers, which could inadvertently encourage additional, unjustifiable aggression). "Over-deterrence" is associated with a concern for false positives or false convictions—mistaken decisions to condemn conduct that is competitive. "Under-deterrence" is associated with a concern for false negatives or false acquittals—mistaken decisions to permit conduct that is anticompetitive.

The standard also must provide firms with some degree of predictability about the permissible scope of single-firm conduct and must be reasonably administrable by the enforcement agencies and courts charged with applying it. An added complication is that even though some kinds of conduct can harm rivals through exclusion and consumers through higher prices, they can also provide efficiency benefits to the monopolist—for example, lower costs of production or sale. Lower costs may reflect a more efficient allocation of resources and eventually may lead to lower prices for consumers. How should the law address conduct that produces such mixed results? Commentators and courts have been divided on this question because of variations in the relative weight placed on harm to consumers and benefits to producers and because of the assumptions they make about the likely incidence and likely consequences of errors (that is, about false positives and false negatives) and about the efficacy of the antitrust system in making sometimes subtle economic judgments. Those more concerned that less demanding liability standards may diminish the incentives of monopolists and their rivals to compete and innovate prioritize concerns for false positives and tend to advocate a less interventionist policy with respect to single-firm conduct. By contrast, some view these fears as overstated and worry instead that more demanding standards of proof will tend to protect monopolists, lead to a greater incidence of false negatives, and diminish the incentives of their rivals to challenge their dominance.

By the mid 1980s, this schism had reached the Supreme Court and had produced two rival lines of cases, one rooted in traditional confidence in the ability of courts to correctly identify anticompetitive conduct and the other giving greater voice to the growing concern for false positives and their assumed adverse consequences. Although both sought to define the line between conduct fairly characterized as superior skill and conduct warranting condemnation as exclusionary, they diverged by reflecting different assumptions about the likely incidence and consequences of over-deterrence and under-deterrence.[22] Navigating between these two lines of cases was a challenge that faced the courts of the United States in the *Microsoft* cases. As we shall explain, however, they firmly and comfortably viewed the case as falling within the former line of cases because the imposition of liability on Microsoft, in view of the facts found in the case, didn't present legitimate concerns about inhibiting competition on the merits.

Two of the more influential cases expressing concern for harmful exclusion of competitors after *United States v. Aluminum Co. of America* were *Lorain Journal Co. v. United States* (which challenged a dominant local newspaper's decision to refuse to publish advertisements from customers who also sought to advertise with a new neighboring radio station) and the Supreme Court's 1985 decision in *Aspen Skiing Co. v. Aspen Highlands Skiing Corp.* (a private Section 2 challenge by Aspen Skiing's smaller rival, Aspen Highlands). The evidence in *Lorain Journal* established that the *Journal's* effort was successful and that it reduced the number of advertising customers available to the radio station, potentially depriving it of the revenue necessary to operate profitably. The Supreme Court concluded that the challenged conduct "strengthened the *Journal's* monopoly" and "tended to destroy and eliminate" competition for advertising revenue from the new radio station.[23]

The enduring value of *Lorain Journal* derives in large part from its intuitive grasp of the economics of exclusion, which is also what made it relevant to the analysis that came out of the *Microsoft* cases. Faced with a new competitive threat to its monopoly of what the Court described as "the mass dissemination of news and advertising," the *Journal* adopted a strategy that would disrupt its rival's access to the very revenues that could make it profitable. It couldn't have done so successfully but for its own monopoly position, and it was unable to offer a credible efficiency-related justification for its conduct. Although this is less clear, the *Journal's* campaign might have enabled it to maintain higher advertising rates in the absence of competition from the radio station or perhaps merely enabled it to preserve the rates it was already charging from erosion through competition.

Aspen Skiing contributed more directly to the establishment of a modern legal and economic framework for evaluating claims of exclusion. After a careful review of its own previous Section 2 decisions, the Court offered the following formulation of a test for unlawful conduct:

> The question whether Ski Co.'s conduct may properly be characterized as exclusionary cannot be answered by simply considering its effect on Highlands. In addition, it is relevant to consider its impact on consumers and whether it has impaired competition in an unnecessarily restrictive way. If a firm has been "attempting to exclude rivals on some basis other than efficiency," it is fair to characterize its behavior as predatory. It is, accordingly, appropriate to examine the effect of the challenged pattern of conduct on consumers, on Ski Co.'s smaller rival, and on Ski Co. itself.[24]

In reaching this point of synthesis, the Court sought to integrate not only its previous decisions but also the efforts of several prominent commentators who had sought to define the line between permissible and condemnable single-firm conduct. The Court drew the phrase "impairing competition in an unnecessarily restrictive way" from the work of Philip Areeda and Donald Turner: "Thus 'exclusionary' comprehends at the most behavior that not only (1) tends to impair the opportunities of rivals, but also (2) either does not further competition on the merits or does so in an unnecessarily restrictive way." From the work of Robert Bork it drew the idea of "attempting to exclude rivals on some basis other than efficiency."[25]

The Court also was suggesting a legal framework in which these various ideas about "bad" and "good" conduct could be evaluated—a more process-oriented approach to structuring the evaluation of conduct under Section 2. The final sentence of the Court's synthesis in *Aspen Skiing* directs lower courts to examine the effects of the conduct on rivals, on consumers, and on the alleged predator to reach a conclusion as to whether the conduct is fairly characterized as "exclusionary." This invites inquiry into the conduct's immediate effects on a targeted rival and into its ultimate effect on consumers and arguably constitutes an implicit rejection of any artificial separation of effects on "competitors" from effects on "competition"—both are relevant, although effects on rivals alone would be an incomplete analysis. Under *Aspen Skiing*, consideration also must be given to any business justifications offered by the alleged predator. The Court didn't undertake, however, to assign weight to any particular factor. Its suggested approach, therefore, arguably has features in common with the rule-of-reason approach long followed under Section 1, in that it requires an evaluation of both effects and justifications. But it is a structured framework guided by an assessment of effects and justifications, an assessment that integrates economic inquiries into a process-oriented legal approach.

As we discuss at greater length in chapter 4, the principal opinion on the merits of the U.S. Court of Appeals for the District of Columbia Circuit in *Microsoft* would reach these same conclusions about the state of the U.S. law of monopolization.[26] Building on the Supreme Court's decisions in *Aluminum Co. of America* and *Lorain Journal* and on the structured analysis of *Aspen Skiing*, the court of appeals openly recognized a kinship between the approach used to judge monopolization under Section 2 and the rule of reason under Section 1. In doing so, it made potentially important contributions to the development of Section 2 standards, although in a number of respects it has proved controversial.

Debates about monopolization standards implicate issues that go to the heart of American antitrust law and policy. Many of antitrust law's most celebrated prosecutions under Section 2 involved challenges to the largest, most publicly visible, and most successful firms of their times. Often those firms were leading participants in industries that were considered to be on the cutting edge of industrial development. Antitrust law as an expression of the American aspiration for competitive opportunity is often judged by these cases, which influence public perception of the capacity of government to serve as a counterweight to private power. The federal government's formative cases against Standard Oil, American Tobacco, United States Steel, Alcoa, and DuPont, and later the controversial prosecutions of IBM and AT&T in the 1970s, are illustrative. All have commanded popular attention and sparked substantial legal and economic commentary.[27] Although the image of the empowered public policeman of markets thwarting abusive private power has been romanticized (in reality, relatively few government monopolization cases are brought and their effectiveness has often been questioned), it is a powerful and enduring image that probably promotes popular support for antitrust enforcement and that remains relevant to other areas of antitrust law.[28] What is really at stake in the debate about the standards for judging the conduct of dominant firms, therefore, is the capacity of government to challenge private power when it is abused and the availability of effective public and private remedies to terminate and redress the competitive effects of the offensive conduct.

Conclusion

The antitrust enforcement efforts directed at Microsoft are at once traditional and groundbreaking. In pitting the public power of the government against the private power of Microsoft, and in channeling the traditional conflict of image between the predator and the skilled and resourceful competitor, the cases presented some of the most persistent and traditional themes of past government prosecutions of monopolists. Yet the actions also showcased some of the most advanced doctrinal, economic, and institutional facets of modern antitrust enforcement. They spawned a global debate about the standards to be used in judging the conduct of large firms such as Microsoft, and about the remedies that should be imposed when they violate the proscriptions of competition laws. In the pages that follow, we will examine both the old and the new, emphasizing the institutional framework in which the various issues of the cases—legal, factual, economic, and political—had to be developed and resolved.

Much of this book is devoted to exploring Microsoft's varied encounters with the antitrust system. In the appendix, to help readers to follow the development of those various stages of the Microsoft cases, we present a chronology.

2 Microsoft's Early Encounters with the U.S. Antitrust System: The FTC Investigation and the Antitrust Division's Licensing Case

Microsoft's engagement with the U.S. antitrust system didn't begin in 1998 with the commencement of the Windows 98 cases mentioned in chapter 1. Eight years earlier, the Federal Trade Commission opened a non-public investigation of the company that went on for more than three years before stalling when the FTC twice deadlocked on votes to issue complaints (once in February and once in July of 1993). When it became clear that no majority could be assembled either to initiate a case against Microsoft or to drop the matter—and after a change of administrations in Washington brought in an eager new head of the Antitrust Division—responsibility for the investigation was transferred to the Department of Justice, where it remained.

The Justice Department's initial investigation culminated in 1994 in a consent decree that prohibited some of Microsoft's licensing practices and appeared to place significant constraints on Microsoft's ability to bundle additional software with Windows. Within a year, however, the Justice Department received new complaints about Microsoft's bundling practices. More investigation ensued, eventually culminating in the initiation of the "Windows 98" case in May of 1998.

In this chapter we discuss (1) what is publicly known about the Federal Trade Commission's investigation in the years 1990–1993, (2) the Justice Department's first investigation (which was opened in 1993 and which concluded the following year with a controversial consent decree that was challenged and appealed to the federal court of appeals), and (3) the Justice Department's subsequent effort to enforce the decree against Microsoft through contempt proceedings that were commenced in 1995 and concluded in 1998. In a variety of ways, the principal themes later advocated by prosecutors and by Microsoft in the United States and in Europe first took shape in these earlier cases. But the story of the FTC's investigation and the transfer of the case to the Justice Department does more than provide the prologue to the Windows 98 case. It also offers insights into the institutional and political characteristics of the federal antitrust enforcement system. Shared public regulatory power is an essential institutional feature of the U.S. competition policy system, and the early history of Microsoft's encounter with that system illustrates its complexity.

The FTC's Investigation of 1990–1993

Microsoft's early success in developing operating systems was linked to the emergence of the IBM Personal Computer (PC). IBM's first PC was introduced in 1981. At the invitation of IBM (which had developed the hardware for the PC), Microsoft developed its "disk operating system," called Microsoft DOS or MS-DOS. MS-DOS 1.0 was shipped with the first IBM PCs and quickly became the operating system of choice for the IBM PC and for compatible computers. This hardware-software cooperation between IBM and the young Microsoft produced one of the great success stories of the early "Information Age."

Microsoft continued to evolve MS-DOS for use on the PC, but it also developed Windows, a graphical user interface (GUI). Windows was introduced in late 1985 as a distinct product designed to run in tandem with MS-DOS. It provided a less arcane interface than MS-DOS running alone, and it facilitated more user-friendly access to the PC's functions. It also supported early multi-tasking. With help from Microsoft, IBM had developed its own operating system, called OS/2. Also designed specifically for the IBM PC, OS/2 was released in 1987. While still working with IBM on refinements to OS/2, Microsoft was also developing Windows 3.0, a more advanced GUI that was eventually released in May 1990. By 1990, therefore, Microsoft and IBM appeared to be simultaneously cooperating and competing—a difficult dance to choreograph without inviting attention under the antitrust laws.

On November 13, 1989, at the annual Comdex trade show in Las Vegas, Microsoft and IBM issued a joint press release detailing their future product strategies. The press release, titled "IBM and Microsoft expand partnership; set future DOS and OS/2 directions," directed "[c]ustomers with high-powered machines and sophisticated needs" to OS/2 and "[u]sers of less-powerful machines" to Microsoft's Windows. According to press reports, it went on to state that "the majority of their [IBM and Microsoft] application and systems development sources will be applied to OS/2 solutions."[1]

From the perspective of antitrust law, the joint press release was immediately suspect. One of the oldest and most traditional concerns of antitrust is collusion by direct rivals. The worst offense is price fixing, in which competitors agree on prices rather than permitting them to be set by the market. A variant of price fixing is "division of markets," in which rivals agree not to compete with each other in a certain arena of competition, usually by dividing the geographic areas in which they compete or by dividing their customers (for example, on the basis some characteristic of the users). Because the November 1989 press release could be read as suggesting that IBM and Microsoft had agreed to channel different categories of customers toward OS/2 and Windows, respectively, it raised some immediate concerns at the Federal Trade Commission. In particular, the FTC was asking whether Microsoft had agreed to restrict the development of Windows in order to support OS/2, as the press release seemed to suggest. FTC file 901-0117 thus was opened, not as an inquiry concerning monopolization, but as an investigation of possible collusion between Microsoft and IBM.

FTC investigations are typically not made public unless the parties choose to reveal them, and the FTC investigation of the Microsoft-IBM relationship remained non-public for almost a year. That changed on March 12, 1991, when Microsoft publicly announced that it was the subject of an investigation by the FTC. According to the statement—delivered by William (Bill) Neukom, then Microsoft's Vice President for Law and Corporate Affairs—the investigation began in June of 1990 and had been triggered by the press release issued by Microsoft and IBM at Comdex on November 13, 1989. It was focused on (1) whether Microsoft and IBM had divided their respective customers and agreed to restrict the future functionality and features of Windows and (2) whether Microsoft had misled developers in order to gain an advantage in applications software developed for Windows 3.0 by interfering with the compatibility of other applications written for OS/2. Neukom also reported that in August of 1990 the FTC had requested a substantial number of documents. IBM, for its part, publicly stated only that it had been contacted by the FTC "about a year ago," but declined to provide any details of the nature of the investigation.[2]

It was quickly apparent to the FTC that Microsoft's behavior wasn't wholly consistent with any agreement to restrict the development of Windows and of the applications programs that would run on it. To the contrary, despite the announcement at Comdex, in May of 1990 Microsoft released Windows 3.0, its most ambitious effort yet to provide PC users with a multi-tasking graphical user interface modeled on that of Apple's successful Macintosh. Microsoft appeared to be aggressively pursuing its own competitive strategy with Windows despite its cooperation with IBM. Indeed, software applications developers at the time accused Microsoft of a "head fake" that misdirected them to prepare applications for OS/2 even as

Microsoft poured its own development efforts into Windows and into Windows-compatible applications such as word processors and spreadsheets.[3] Whether or not that is an accurate portrayal of Microsoft's motivations and conduct at the time, it does seem clear that Microsoft was perceived that way by IBM and by some of the largest and most successful software companies of the day (including Novell, Borland, WordPerfect, and Lotus), who viewed Microsoft's business strategies as suspect at best. Microsoft was quickly making enemies in the industry, a pattern that would complicate its interactions with the government for years to come.

Perhaps not surprisingly, therefore, the flurry of press reports that followed Microsoft's acknowledgment of the FTC investigation speculated about whether the FTC's inquiry would go beyond Microsoft-IBM collusion and turn to Microsoft's purportedly anticompetitive practices. The *New York Times* reported that there were complaints within the industry that Microsoft's "applications software developers have access to improvements or upgrades in those systems [meaning Windows and MS-DOS], giving them an advantage in improving their applications programs." The article also quoted Dick Williams, president and chief executive of Digital Research Inc., which had produced CP/M (a predecessor of DOS) and DR-DOS (a primary early competitor of MS-DOS). Williams accused Microsoft of trying to undermine customers' acceptance of DR-DOS 5.0 in April of 1990 by pre-announcing its own updated and forthcoming version of MS-DOS and falsely asserting that it would soon be released and would incorporate some of the same features—a practice that became known as "vaporware."[4] A follow-up story in the *Seattle Times* speculated that "in a worst-case scenario, an FTC investigation could lead to the *breakup of Microsoft into two companies: one focusing on operations, the other on applications.*"[5] However, other commentators acknowledged that it can be "difficult to distinguish between antitrust activity and Microsoft's legitimate ability to use its broad reach to competitive advantage."[6]

Microsoft denied the prediction of some commentators that the FTC was likely to undertake any broader investigation and maintained that the FTC's investigation was narrow, focused solely on the November 1989 Comdex press release. In an interview, Bill Gates dismissed the suggestion that the investigation would widen, attributing allegations about anticompetitive practices by Microsoft to "jealous competitors seizing an opportunity to discredit Microsoft." Bill Neukom was quoted as dismissing "grousing" by competitors as not related to the FTC's investigation.[7]

Some durable and competing themes thus emerged in the early stages of the investigation—themes that foreshadowed the coming shift at the

FTC from an investigation of collusion to one that instead focused on monopolization. Critics charged that Microsoft wasn't merely an aggressive competitor, but a ruthless one that was seeking to monopolize the market for operating systems and then expand its base into other software applications. It sought to do so, they suggested, by undertaking specific practices to impair the ability of its rivals to compete: withholding from them information they needed to produce programs that would successfully interoperate with Windows, issuing vaporware announcements, and engaging in copycat behavior (that is, emulating software developed by others, but retooling it for the Windows environment). Microsoft's primary response also took shape early on. For years to come, it would consistently charge that its antitrust troubles were largely consequences of sniping by disappointed rivals looking to government to stifle competition rather than promote it and of uninformed hostility from government enforcers. These two competing story lines would reverberate for the next two decades.

Microsoft's protestations notwithstanding, a month later, in April of 1991, the company acknowledged that it had been advised by the Federal Trade Commission that the FTC was widening its investigation beyond the IBM-Microsoft press release to determine whether Microsoft "has monopolized or has attempted to monopolize, the markets for personal computer operating systems, software and peripherals." This expansion of the investigation reportedly came in response to "third-party charges" of Microsoft's monopolization. Bill Neukom was quoted on April 12 as saying that Microsoft was "surprised and disappointed that the inquiry has been broadened"; somewhat in contrast, a day later Microsoft's president, Michael Hallman, told the *Los Angeles Times* that he was "totally disappointed, but not totally surprised." The *Times* also reported that according to "industry sources" complaints from Borland International[8] and Lotus Development Corp.[9] had "sparked the FTC probe."[10]

As developers of applications software, Borland and Lotus were especially concerned with conduct that might give Microsoft's own applications a competitive advantage over their own. But in the world of operating systems, Microsoft faced two principal rivals for control of the PC: IBM, with its OS/2, and Digital Research, which had passed up the opportunity to assist IBM with the development of the first operating system for the PC. By the time of the FTC's investigation, Digital Research, with its DR-DOS, was competing head to head with Microsoft.

Microsoft was also keenly aware of Novell, one of the early players in the development of local area network (LAN) software, which permitted file sharing and printer sharing. Microsoft had first approached Novell to discuss a possible merger in December of 1989, shortly after the Comdex meeting. Although those talks were broken off in January of 1990, they were renewed after Novell announced its intention to purchase Digital Research in July of 1991. When talks between Microsoft and Novell collapsed for a second time in March of 1992, Ray Noorda, the president and CEO of Novell, decided he would cooperate more fully with the FTC's investigation. Indeed, Novell would later emerge as one of the main forces behind complaints about Microsoft within the industry, and the rift between Noorda and Bill Gates would become open and hostile.[11]

The FTC's investigation of Microsoft reached a turning point in the summer of 1991, more than a year after it had begun. Under the laws and regulations that govern the FTC, its staff must first receive formal approval from a majority of the five commissioners before it can issue "compulsory process"—subpoenas in aid of its investigations.[12] The year-long delay in the investigation was no doubt a consequence, in least in part, of the staff's lack of such authority. But that changed on July 31, 1991, when the FTC approved the request. Such compulsory means of extracting documents, including email messages and other kinds of electronically stored information, are important to public enforcement. Whereas private parties can, for the most part, seek information from adversaries and third parties only after they have commenced litigation, the government can do so "pre-filing" as part of its investigation and for the purpose of deciding whether an enforcement action is warranted.

More than a year then passed before it was reported in the press that the FTC's staff was nearing a recommendation to the FTC in the case. A presidential election was upcoming (in November of 1992). Would the government craft a narrow case directed at some of Microsoft's more questionable practices, or would it launch a broad attack on Microsoft's conduct and its business model?

Late 1992 and early 1993 were stressful times for Microsoft, its rivals, and the FTC's staff. Purportedly intense lobbying efforts preoccupied them all and invaded the long hallways of the FTC.[13] Late in September 1992, *Business Week* reported that the FTC's staff was close to concluding its investigation and that it was going to recommend a narrow challenge to halt Microsoft's exclusionary practices, perhaps before the end of that year.[14] According to *FTC:Watch* (an industry newsletter), Mary Lou Steptoe, the acting head of the FTC's Bureau of Competition, forwarded her formal recommendation on the Microsoft investigation to the commissioners in mid December.

She reportedly recommended that the FTC authorize the staff to seek a preliminary injunction under Section 13(b) of the FTC Act to stop Microsoft's DOS licensing practices, particularly its use of per-processor licenses and minimum product licensing commitments. But she recommended against any breakup of Microsoft or any "attack" on "the link between Microsoft's MS DOS system software and the applications programs it writes to run on that system."[15] The *FTC: Watch* story was quickly picked up in the press.[16] In advance of a scheduled meeting of the FTC to consider the recommendation, Microsoft increased its efforts to persuade the FTC that its rivals' complaints were without merit.[17]

The institutional characteristics of the FTC became central to the resolution of the investigation at this stage. The FTC's five commissioners are appointed by the president and their appointments are subject to confirmation by the Senate. No more than three commissioners can be members of the same political party, and the president has the prerogative of appointing the agency's chair.[18] The FTC's status as an "independent" administrative agency also came into play. Although "independent" means that the commission is effectively insulated from direct interference by the Executive Branch, the FTC is subject to congressional oversight. This relationship with Congress invites those seeking to influence the FTC to pursue a two-front lobbying strategy focused on the five commissioners and also on the engaged members of the oversight committee. Indeed, a number of senators had taken specific interest in the investigation of Microsoft, owing perhaps in part to the presence in their states of Microsoft rivals who had briefed them on the nature and impact of Microsoft's conduct. On January 27, 1993, for example, Senator Orrin Hatch of Utah wrote to the FTC's chair, Janet Steiger, supporting the FTC's inquiry into Microsoft's behavior and making a thinly veiled reference to his interest in protecting his state's technology firms, which included Novell and WordPerfect.[19]

When the FTC was called upon to vote to approve or disapprove the recommendations made by its staff—once in February of 1993 and again in July of that year—it was confronted with its own institutional limitations. Not only was it under political pressure to act; owing to a recusal, only four commissioners were eligible to participate in the vote. At its February 5 meeting, Janet Steiger (who preferred the title Chairman) purportedly moved to authorize the staff to file a complaint seeking a preliminary injunction against Microsoft in federal court. According to *FTC: Watch*, the recommendations of the staff focused on two licensing practices: (1) requiring computer manufacturers (OEMs) to pay a royalty on every computer they manufacture and (2) requiring the payment of royalties even on unshipped computers.[20] But the FTC deadlocked, voting 2–2, and the motion failed.[21] The investigation remained open, and the staff turned to "Plan B."[22]

After a second flurry of intense lobbying,[23] including yet another visit from Bill Gates,[24] the FTC reconvened on July 21. Chairman Steiger again moved the commission to act, this time by issuing an *administrative* complaint against Microsoft under Section 5(b) of the FTC Act. This was "Plan B." It illustrated one of the important characteristics of the FTC as an administrative agency: the authority to issue an administrative complaint and to conduct an intra-agency trial before an administrative law judge. In lieu of a petition to a federal court seeking an immediate preliminary injunction, proceeding under Section 5(b) would commit the case to further proceedings within the FTC.[25] In contrast to the February motion, which would have authorized the FTC to commence an action in federal court, an administrative proceeding would delay an assessment by the FTC of Microsoft's conduct until after an administrative trial and, presumably, an appeal back to the FTC. It could thus be interpreted as a compromise that delayed any decision on the merits until a more complete record could be internally developed. For that same reason, however, the administrative route came with a clear cost. With the time necessary to conduct an administrative trial, an appeal back to the FTC, and possible judicial review of a Commission decision by the federal court of appeals taken into account, it would be years before the FTC would be able to mandate any changes to Microsoft's conduct.[26] Awareness of the complications of the administrative option may even have dissuaded Microsoft from seeking any kind of negotiated settlement with the FTC.[27] In fact, it may have emboldened Microsoft, which had reason to believe that if the FTC were to deadlock a second time the investigation would simply come to an end and to believe if the investigation were to continue then no action could be taken against Microsoft for years.

For a second time, the motion failed when the commissioners reached an impasse, voting 2–2.[28] The investigation remained formally open, but it was at a standstill, with no way to break the deadlock apparent. Had the intense lobbying by Microsoft and interested industry participants influenced the outcome of the vote? One commentator wrote: "Had all the high-paid lobbyists had any effect? Yes, in that the FTC staff might have lacked the resources to put together a respectable monopolization case without the help of the lawyers for Microsoft's competitors. No, because in the end, the commissioners voted their philosophical predispositions."[29]

Senator Howard Metzenbaum issued a press release calling for the Department of Justice to assume responsibility for the investigation, and the newly appointed leadership at the Antitrust Division of the Department of Justice contemplated its options. The "simple" ending that Microsoft might have hoped for was becoming less likely.

According to *FTC: Watch*, the Department of Justice formally requested a transfer of the Microsoft investigation files on Wednesday, July 28. The request went to Mary Lou Steptoe, the acting director of the FTC's Bureau of Competition. She informed the commissioners that she intended to comply with the request. According to *FTC: Watch*, Steptoe's communication of her intentions reportedly triggered a heated exchange of memoranda among the commissioners. Commissioner Mary Azcuenaga reportedly moved to formally close the investigation, expressing concern about the precedent of handing over a technically open case file to the Antitrust Division. She also expressed the view that it was "unfair and prejudicial for two federal agencies simultaneously to investigate" the same conduct, adding a comment that "continued inaction on an open matter may create a public perception that the agency is irresolute and inept."[30] Commissioner Deborah Owen purportedly agreed that the investigation should be closed, but opposed the staff's plan to turn over the files: "I believe that the Department of Justice's efforts to second-guess the Commission's decision in this case should be resisted at all costs, as a matter of institutional integrity."[31] Owen later condemned the Antitrust Division's "intrusion into this matter" as "tantamount to political interference in the independent functioning of this agency."[32] Nevertheless, in the absence of a majority of commissioners objecting to the Justice Department's request, a transfer of files from the FTC's Bureau of Competition to the Department of Justice began on July 30, 1993.[33]

By a vote of 4–0, the FTC voted formally to close its investigation of Microsoft on August 20. After the vote, the FTC's secretary issued a "Notice of Placement of Commission Actions on the Public Record in *Microsoft*, File No. 901-0117." For the first time, the FTC publicly acknowledged its indeterminate three-year investigation of Microsoft; it also disclosed the actions that had been taken at the closed meetings on February 5 and July 21.[34] Bill Neukom was notified that the FTC investigation was at an end.[35] Yet as a practical matter the dynamic new head of the Antitrust Division, Anne Bingaman, with not-so-subtle encouragement from two U.S. senators,[36] had broken the FTC's deadlock, declaring herself to be "in effect" the "fifth commissioner" and wresting control of the case from the stymied FTC.[37]

The Antitrust Division's Licensing Case and the 1994 Consent Decree

The transfer of the Microsoft investigation from the Federal Trade Commission to the Department of Justice was unprecedented. Anne Bingaman, who had been confirmed in June of 1993 as the new Assistant Attorney General in charge of the Antitrust Division of the Department of Justice, had been on the job barely a month when she faced the decision whether to ask the FTC to transfer its investigative files to the Department of Justice. Assuming responsibility for the investigation involved complex political and legal issues and posed a risk that the Antitrust Division would again be drawn into the kind of prolonged and combative litigation that characterized its thirteen-year pursuit of IBM from 1969 to 1982. (That case had been abandoned after consuming enormous resources and achieving no benefits.[38])

The decision also presented Bingaman with something of a paradox. The new Clinton administration had promised reinvigorated antitrust enforcement in response to the perceived non-interventionist, free-market policies of the Republican administrations of the past twelve years, and one reason for Bingaman's selection had been a desire to deliver on that promise.[39] Weighing in favor of intervention were the widespread criticism of Microsoft in the industry and the views of two of the FTC's respected commissioners: Chairman Janet Steiger (a Republican) and Dennis Yao (a Democrat and the Commission's sole economist). They had concurred that there was enough evidence to back up those complaints. But Bill Clinton also had promised to support and encourage the growth of the technology sector. Just days after the FTC formally closed its investigation, one commentator wrote that an investigation by the Department of Justice would "raise complex political issues for the Clinton Administration, which has made support for American high-technology companies part of its main agenda."[40] In the magazine *Business Week*, Mark Lewyn and Catherine Yang wrote: "If Justice proceeds, it could reshape a vital industry and redefine antitrust policy for the Information Age. Or the case could once again be caught up in the politics of Washington and Silicon Valley and fall into the time warp of the federal bureaucracy."[41]

Assistant Attorney General Anne Bingaman took up the challenge, and on July 15, 1994, the Department of Justice filed a Complaint and a proposed Final Judgment with the U.S. District Court for the District of Columbia in what would later become known as "The Licensing Case."[42] Augmenting the record amassed by the FTC, the Department of Justice claimed to have "issued 21 Civil Investigative Demands to Microsoft and third parties, reviewed one million pages of documents, ... conducted over 100 interviews [, and] deposed 22 persons, including Microsoft Chairman Bill Gates."[43] The complaint that emerged from its review was clearly somewhat derivative of the FTC's investigation, covering some of the very same conduct that the FTC had scrutinized, but it was narrowly focused on Microsoft's licensing and disclosure practices—specifically its use of "per processor" contracts for licensing MS-DOS and Windows and its use of non-disclosure agreements in connection with its development of Windows 95. The "per processor" contracts required an original equipment manufacturer (OEM) of computers to pay a royalty to Microsoft for each computer sold with a specified class of Intel processor whether or not a Microsoft operating system was included in the computer. The licensing agreements containing these provisions also tended to be long-term (three years or longer).[44]

The combined effect of these contractual provisions was to discourage OEMs from offering competing PC operating systems by raising the costs of doing so. They were "exclusionary."[45] In essence, if an OEM wanted to offer a non-Microsoft operating system on a PC, it would have to pay for two operating systems—a "double royalty" or "tax."[46] This also discouraged software developers from creating alternative operating systems and marketing them to OEMs. In addition, in the words of Herbert Hovenkamp, it "hinders rather than promotes innovation by suppressing the opportunities of smaller rivals who cannot realistically compete to have their operating systems installed on new computers."[47]

Whereas the "per processor" royalty contracts were directed at OEMs, the non-disclosure agreements applied to independent software vendors (ISVs)—that is, developers of software applications meant to run on PC operating systems. Although the complaint acknowledged Microsoft's legitimate purposes in seeking confidentiality with respect to beta versions of Windows, which it had required in the past, it alleged that Microsoft was using a new and more restrictive form of the agreement in connection with its development of Windows 95. These new non-disclosure agreements went beyond requiring confidentiality. They restricted some of the leading ISVs working on applications for the forthcoming Windows 95 from developing applications for any competing PC operating system and any competing technologies.[48]

Invoking the legal standards that had been developed by the courts from *Aluminum Co. of America* to *Aspen Skiing*,[49] the complaint concluded that "Microsoft's exclusionary contracting practices have had the effect of excluding competitors on a basis other than competition on the merits and have thereby allowed Microsoft illegally to perpetuate its monopoly in the

PC operating system market."[50] Pursuant to its agreement with Microsoft, in lieu of any litigation the proposed Final Judgment would be entered as a consent decree (the analog of a negotiated settlement in a private case). Mirroring the allegations of the complaint, the decree prohibited Microsoft from entering into "per processor" licenses, limited the duration of its contracts to one year, and limited the scope of non-disclosure agreements to confidentiality.[51]

In one important respect, however, the decree went beyond the specific allegations of the complaint. Paragraph IV(E)(i) of the decree included a prohibition on "tying" (that is, conditioning the licensing of one product on the licensee's acceptance of a license to another): "Microsoft shall not enter into any License Agreement in which the terms of that agreement are expressly or impliedly conditioned upon ... the licensing of any ... other product." But the decree also included an important proviso: "provided, however, that this provision in and of itself shall not be construed to prohibit Microsoft from developing integrated products." This "integration" proviso might well come into conflict with the prohibition on tying, depending upon how software that combines multiple functions would be viewed. The inherent tension in the language of the decree virtually ensured that the Department of Justice and Microsoft would again differ and return to court.

Under a Watergate-era "sunshine law," the Tunney Act, federal consent decrees such as the one negotiated in 1994 between the Department of Justice and Microsoft are subject to review by federal courts and are to be approved only if in "the public interest."[52] With few exceptions, federal courts generally had demonstrated deference to the government and approved such decrees. But on February 14, 1995, in an unusual turn of events, U.S. District Court Judge Stanley Sporkin declined to approve the proposed Licensing Decree, questioning its scope, its likely effectiveness, and its enforcement provisions and complaining that the government hadn't provided him with enough information to enable him to conduct a public-interest assessment.[53]

Judge Sporkin first addressed two procedural issues: whether two interested third parties would be permitted to intervene and formally participate in the Tunney Act proceedings and the question as to whether an anonymous industry group would be allowed to file an amicus brief with the court.[54] Although he denied the motion to intervene, he permitted both parties and the anonymous amici to submit their views to him for consideration. This decision was consistent with his ultimate view that the Tunney Act's public-interest standard mandated a comprehensive inquiry.[55]

The involvement of these third parties also illustrated the degree of interest and engagement of the industry in the proceedings involving Microsoft. That engagement, which was unusually intense, differentiated the Microsoft antitrust litigation from virtually every antitrust case that had preceded it, save perhaps the breakup of AT&T. Microsoft's critics developed multiple strategies for advocating their views and found multiple access points in the political and legal process for doing so: Congress, the federal agencies, and finally the courts. They also did battle through the press, which followed the cases intently. The lessons learned and the patterns developed during the Licensing Case provided a foundation for even more elaborate efforts to influence the initiation and the management of the 1998 case.

Judge Sporkin concluded that the licensing decree didn't satisfy the Tunney Act's public-interest standard, citing two critical points of disagreement between the court and the parties: the amount of information provided to him in support of the decree, and the scope of his review authority. The government maintained that the district court's review should be confined to the specific allegations of the complaint that it had filed. Sporkin insisted instead that the Tunney Act required him to evaluate the case that *might have* been brought as well as the case that had been brought:

> To make an objective determination, a court must know not only what is included in the decree but also what has been negotiated out, directly as well as indirectly *i.e.*, what is the understanding of the parties as to what, if any, additional action the Government will or will not take with respect to matters that were inquired into, but with respect to which the decree is silent.[56]

With obvious frustration, he declared that "Tunney Act courts are not mushrooms to be placed in a dark corner and sprinkled with fertilizer."[57]

Judge Sporkin also argued that the decree was simply too narrow, in that it might not reach future iterations of Microsoft's operating systems,[58] and that the remedy was unlikely to prove effective, in part because it failed to address other objectionable conduct by Microsoft:

> The decree deals with licensing and non-disclosure practices that the Government found to be anticompetitive and detrimental to a free and open market. What the decree does not address are a number of other anticompetitive practices that from time to time Microsoft has been accused of engaging in by others in the industry. Since a Court cannot shut its eyes to the obvious, it has asked the parties to discuss these widespread public allegations. The Government has refused, and Microsoft has claimed that the accusations are false.[59]

It was at this juncture that Judge Sporkin put himself on a collision course with the court of appeals.

Based on the briefs filed by amici and on a book critical of Microsoft that he had read the previous summer, Judge Sporkin expressed his concerns about three kinds of conduct not addressed in the complaint or the decree: vaporware, Microsoft's use of its dominance in operating systems to impart competitive advantages to its own applications software, and Microsoft's alleged manipulation of operating-system code to impair interoperability of its rivals' programs with Windows.[60] In the decree he made specific suggestions for covering these areas, also suggesting the addition of "an appropriate compliance apparatus" such as the use of an independent "private inspector general."[61] Although the government expressed its willingness to add a monitoring provision to the decree, it and Microsoft rejected all of Sporkin's substantive suggestions.[62]

For the first time in their four years of interaction, the U.S. government and Microsoft found themselves on the same side of the controversy. When Judge Sporkin refused to approve the decree, they jointly and promptly appealed his order to the U.S. Court of Appeals for the District of Columbia Circuit.[63] The confrontation between Judge Sporkin and the Department of Justice revealed the paradoxical nature of the Tunney Act: How could a federal court, in essence, order the executive branch to continue litigating a case that it desired to settle? Could it order the Department of Justice to file a complaint broader than the one it had filed? If it were to do those things, the settlement that had led to the proposed decree might well have to be scuttled. There was no reason to believe, for example, that Microsoft would have agreed to any of Judge Sporkin's proposed additions. Judge Sporkin's view was that he wasn't ordering a broader complaint, but was simply refusing to approve the one submitted. If he lacked the authority to reject the decree on the ground that it was insufficiently supported by the record, the Tunney Act would be toothless. The Department of Justice responded that the court was invading the province of prosecutorial discretion and that Judge Sporkin's reading of the Tunney Act raised serious separation-of-powers concerns.[64]

The court of appeals agreed with the Department of Justice. Concluding that the district court had exceeded its authority, the appellate court roundly reversed Sporkin's decision.

The court posed two questions: Is the district judge entitled to "seize hold of the matter" and "decide for himself" the appropriate response of the executive and judicial branches? Can the district court "interpose its own views of the appropriate remedy" over and above those that the government seeks "as a part of its overall settlement"? The court answered both questions in the negative. Although the Tunney Act didn't envision a mere "rubber stamp," "Congress surely didn't contemplate that the district judge would, by reformulating the issues, effectively redraft the complaint himself." Neither did the statute contemplate a judicial inquiry into the mental processes of the government agency when it negotiated a consent decree. In the absence of a showing of bad faith, "the district court is not empowered to review the actions or behavior of the Department of Justice; the court is only authorized to review the decree itself."[65]

On the penultimate issue, the court of appeals also sided with the government and Microsoft: the district court lacked sufficient grounds to reject the decree as an inadequate remedy for Microsoft's alleged wrongdoing. In Sporkin's view, to be adequate a consent decree, like any effective antitrust remedy in a monopolization case, must "effectively pry open to competition a market that has been closed by defendant['s] illegal restraints."[66] To support its argument that the decree would be effective, the government had presented a declaration from the economist Kenneth Arrow, a Nobel laureate. Arrow, who had been consulted before the filing of the consent decree, was now asked to respond to the lengthy anonymous amicus brief that Judge Sporkin had accepted.[67] Arrow's declaration, in conjunction with the amicus brief, quietly introduced the economic and intellectual framework that has since guided the antitrust analysis of the platform-software industry.

The amicus brief, which called for a breakup of Microsoft, identified two Stanford University economists, Garth Saloner and Brian Arthur, as consultants who had contributed significantly to its preparation. Saloner and Arthur had authored some of the earliest papers on "network effects," a market phenomenon that arguably had shaped the market for operating systems.[68] As two other influential economists would later argue, "the old industrial economy was driven by *economies of scale*; the new information economy is driven by the *economics of networks*."[69]

The theory of network effects recognized that the value of a product to its users can increase the more widely it is used, producing "network externalities" or "network effects." "The key concept is *positive feedback*."[70] Just as a telephone can become more valuable to every user as access to additional users is established, Windows had become more valuable to consumers as it got more popular, as more applications were written for it, and as more information could be easily shared across the "network" of users. At some point, a network can "tip" in favor of one producer. Once that occurs, it can be very difficult for others to contest the market—"new entrants would face daunting barriers to entry."[71] This can be especially true when there is a large installed base of customers, who become "locked in" to the network because the costs of switching out of it can be high. As Arrow explained, these markets are referred to as "increasing returns" markets.[72]

It is important to recognize that network effects and increasing returns are not antitrust violations. They are characteristics of a market. As two commentators observed in criticizing Judge Sporkin's approach to the remedy issue in the Licensing Case, "[n]etwork effects are an inherent part of certain markets, not a 'market failure' for which the law must necessarily correct. The law may need to adapt to network effects, but it should neither ignore them nor attempt to defy them."[73] On the other hand, network effects can render a market more conducive to monopolization in some cases. Arrow and the amici agreed that Microsoft had benefitted from network effects *and* that it had taken actions to further and artificially fortify the barriers to entry that had developed in the market for operating systems, as with its "per processor" licenses.[74] As the court of appeals explained, relying on Arrow's declaration:

> It is undisputed that the software market is characterized by "increasing returns," resulting in natural barriers to entry. Because the costs of producing software are almost exclusively in its design, marginal production costs are "virtually zero." Professor Arrow, the government's consultant and a Nobel-prize winning economist, described the importance of Microsoft's large installed base in an increasing returns market as follows:
>
>> A software product with a large installed base has several advantages relative to a new entrant. Consumers know that such a product is likely to be supported by the vendor with upgrades and service. Users of a product with a large installed base are more likely to find that their products are compatible with other products. They are more likely to be able successfully to exchange work products with their peers, because a large installed base makes it more likely that their peers will use the same product or compatible products. Installed base is particularly important to the economic success of an operating system software product. The value of the operating system is in its capability to run application software. The larger the installed base of a particular operating system, the more likely it is that independent software vendors will write programs that run on that operating system, and, in this circular fashion, the more valuable the operating system will be to consumers.[75]

Arrow and the amici therefore appeared to agree on the critical economic characteristics of the industry. They also agreed that Microsoft's conduct—its use of "per processor" licenses, minimum commitments, and longer-term contracts—contributed to its dominance by raising artificial barriers to entry. Here they also drew from the literature on raising rivals' costs as a means of asserting power over price. Microsoft's conduct imposed significant costs on rivals, who would have to neutralize the incentives provided to OEMs to deal solely with Microsoft.[76] As Arrow's declaration explained, "[t]he most effective and economic point of entry for sales of IBM-compatible PC operating systems is the OEM distribution channel." He argued therefore that "[n]ew operating system software products should have unimpeded access to this channel."

But Arrow and the amici disagreed sharply as to whether the remedies in the 1994 decree were appropriate remedies for Microsoft's violation of the antitrust laws. The amici asked that Microsoft be broken up; Arrow declared that such a remedy was unwarranted. Echoing the legal standard for monopolization rooted in the *Aluminum Co. of America* decision, he reasoned that "[f]or the most part, Microsoft appears to have achieved its dominant position in its market as a consequence of good fortune and possibly superior product and business acumen."[77] The economic rationale for the complaint was to eliminate only the *artificial* barriers to entry erected by Microsoft's conduct. Arrow argued further that "[a] rule penalizing market successes that are not the result of anticompetitive practices will, among other consequences, have the effect of taxing technological improvements and is unlikely to improve welfare in the long run."

Judge Sporkin had found the arguments of the amici and their consultants as to remedy more persuasive than Arrow's arguments. Even if Arrow's affidavit was taken as true, the decree only halted the most obviously offensive conduct; it did nothing to undo its consequences: "Simply telling a defendant to go forth and sin no more does little or nothing to address the unfair advantage it has already gained. In short, given the Government's expert's own analysis of this market, the decree is 'too little, too late.'"[78]

An additional point of difference between the district court and the parties related to the types of monopolization claims permitted under Section 2 of the Sherman Act and the appropriate remedies for each. The government's case focused on conduct that would maintain its monopoly position; the market position that Microsoft had already acquired before it undertook that conduct wasn't the problem. The case for broad remedies is strongest when a monopolist is accused of having achieved monopoly unlawfully. But remedies in monopoly maintenance cases tend to focus on enjoining conduct that helps to maintain the monopoly and undoing the *incremental* degree of power (or incremental insulation from erosion of power) that can be attributed to the wrongful conduct. Correctly isolating and removing the increment can be difficult, however.

Consistent with Arrow's declaration, the government took the amici to task on this distinction, arguing that Microsoft's market position was attributable to its successes and to the characteristics of the market rather than to its exclusionary conduct. The government's concern about Microsoft's licensing practices was "focused primarily on their implications for the future."[79] Whether, and to what degree, Microsoft's monopoly position could be attributed to its anticompetitive conduct, however, became a persistent question throughout all of the *Microsoft* cases, especially those later filed by private parties: How much of Microsoft's market power could be fairly attributed to its wrongful conduct rather than to its presumptively lawful underlying monopoly?

The government's complaint in the Licensing Case alleged only maintenance of a monopoly, not unlawful acquisition of one—a fact that influenced the court of appeals when it reviewed the district court's work. In the court of appeals' view, "the remedies must be of the 'same type or class' as the violations," which circumscribed the scope of the district court's authority to review the remedies proposed in the consent decree. Moreover, it found that a district court cannot refuse to approve a consent decree merely because it prefers some remedies over others. The court reasoned that the "public interest" inquiry didn't require a showing that the remedies selected were the best ones available, and that the district court should defer to the government's predictions as to their efficacy. In the case of most negotiated consent decrees, there has been no trial and hence no findings of fact. Thus, the remedies agreed to probably reflect the government's (and the defendant's) internal assessment of a case's strengths and weaknesses that would become evident only after a full trial.[80]

The court of appeals concluded by adopting a very deferential standard for reviewing government-negotiated decrees. Of course, if the decree "is ambiguous, or the district judge can foresee difficulties in implementation, we would expect the court to insist that these matters be attended to." Otherwise, although a district court judge is "not obliged to accept" a decree that "appears to make a mockery" of the judicial power, "[s]hort of that eventuality, the Tunney Act cannot be interpreted as an authorization for a district judge to assume the role of Attorney General."[81]

But the court wasn't yet done with its work. For the first time in the Microsoft cases, but not the last, it sharply rebuked the district court judge for demonstrating a lack of impartiality, and it granted Microsoft's request that the case be reassigned to another judge on remand. In particular, the court cited Judge Sporkin's open reliance on his summer reading of the book *Hard Drive*, his decision to permit anonymous amici to participate in the proceedings, his acceptance of *ex parte* submissions by those amici and other non-parties, and some specific comments that suggested that he distrusted Microsoft's lawyers and Microsoft.[82] Pursuant to the court's order, on remand the case was reassigned to Judge Thomas Penfield Jackson. In August of 1995, thirteen months after the government and Microsoft agreed to the decree, Judge Jackson approved it—after a twenty-minute hearing—and assumed responsibility for supervising it.[83]

The likelihood that the decree would improve competitive conditions was immediately questioned. The *New York Times* reported the next day that, although "[t]he settlement requires Microsoft to make some changes in the way it licenses software to personal computer producers," it "does not fundamentally affect the way Microsoft does business." The *Times* also reported that the Justice Department's investigation of Microsoft would continue.[84] Several months later, a more comprehensive piece in the *Times* openly challenged Anne Bingaman's prediction in July of 1994 that the decree would give consumers more choice in operating systems: "It has not happened. The practices Microsoft agreed to forgo had already served their purpose. Gates was right when he summed up the effect of the consent decree in one word: 'Nothing.'"[85] The *Times* article went on to catalog the continuing and growing range of concerns about Microsoft's conduct, focusing on the rise of the Internet and the new importance of Internet browser software. What would later become known as the "Browser Wars" had begun, and the Licensing Decree case had done nothing to anticipate or prevent them.[86]

In retrospect, the limited effectiveness of the decree is not surprising. As Kenneth Arrow and the amici had explained, the platform-software industry was characterized by network effects and tipping. As consumers and businesses used Windows more and more, it became more valuable both to them and to Microsoft. At some point, perhaps before Microsoft began using "per processor" licenses, the market had already "tipped" in favor of Windows, which made it very difficult for producers of rival operating systems to seriously contest Microsoft's dominance of the market. The decree, focused as it was on a monopoly-maintenance theory, wasn't intended to dissolve all barriers to new entry, but only to arrest Microsoft's attempts to fortify its monopoly by erecting new barriers. Prohibiting "per processor" licenses wasn't intended to, and in truth could not, seriously alter the structure of the market. It could only achieve the more modest goal of keeping the market from becoming even more difficult to penetrate. Later critics would point to the episode as evidence that only a structural remedy, such as a breakup, could be effective. But at the time, Arrow simply declared that the goals of the decree were modest and that there was reason to believe they could be achieved. The hope was that, by removing the anticompetitive restraints, the decree would "level the playing field and open the market in the future."[87]

The Civil Contempt Proceedings of 1995–1998

For more than two years, tensions continued to grow between the government and Microsoft, in part because of continuing complaints from Microsoft's rivals. During that time, the government shifted its attention away from rivalry among suppliers of PC operating systems (which had dissipated despite the decree) to the emerging field of Internet browsing. Beginning in July of 1995, Microsoft had contractually required OEMs to install its browser, Internet Explorer, with Windows 95. Microsoft had taken this approach when both products were first introduced, shortly after its aborted effort to come to some agreement with Netscape Communications, the pioneer in Internet browsing technologies. Netscape had rejected Microsoft's overture to work together on the browser's future development, a fact that later would be deemed significant in the story presented in support of the 1998 case.

The software code for the first two versions of Microsoft's Internet Explorer browser, IE 1.0 and 2.0, like that of Netscape's Navigator browser, was distinct from the code for Windows. But in August of 1996 Microsoft released IE 3.0, which included both files that updated and replaced files in Windows 95 and files that included software code specific to the browser and code relating to the operating system. This began the process of "commingling" browser code and operating-system code in Windows,[88] a design strategy that Microsoft had previously followed with success when it combined MS-DOS and Windows. The next version of Internet Explorer, IE 4.0, was due to be shipped in October of 1997. Microsoft was going to require OEMs to preinstall it with Windows 95 no later than February 1998.

The upcoming release of IE 4.0 provided the Department of Justice with a possible legal opportunity to deal with the browser problem. As was discussed above, Paragraph IV(E)(i) of the 1994 Consent Decree prohibited Microsoft from conditioning a license for Windows on the licensing of any "other product." The Department of Justice could argue that Internet Explorer was an "other product" and that Microsoft was violating the anti-tying provision of the decree by requiring OEMs to install it with Windows. This approach had the advantage of not requiring the Department of Justice to file a new lawsuit to prove that the bundling violated the antitrust laws; it merely had to show a violation of the decree. The disadvantage of this approach was that it might fail owing to the "integrated products" proviso of Paragraph IV.

By the summer of 1996, Netscape was vigorously advocating intervention by the Department of Justice. It submitted to the Department of Justice a white paper of more than 200 pages, titled "Regarding Recent Anticompetitive Conduct of Microsoft Corporation," that had been prepared by the attorneys Gary Reback, Susan Creighton, and Lisa Davis, with "extensive consultation" from Garth Saloner of Stanford University. The white paper drew significantly from the anonymous amicus brief filed by Reback in the Tunney Act proceedings concerning the 1994 consent decree.[89] By August, it had been reported in the press that Netscape had secured legal counsel and had accused Microsoft of violating the 1994 consent decree by tying sales of Windows 95 to other Microsoft products (specifically Internet Explorer). It also asserted that Microsoft was engaging in other anticompetitive conduct designed to coerce its customers into abandoning Netscape's Navigator browser in favor of the latest version of IE.[90] Microsoft blasted back, calling Netscape's accusations "bizarre" and "irresponsible."[91] Nevertheless, Netscape's complaints led to a revival of the Justice Department's probe into Microsoft's conduct and a new request for information from Microsoft—this time for information having to do with browser competition.[92] Despite Netscape's efforts, however, by October some in the industry were already predicting that Netscape would be "wiped out" in the browser battle with Microsoft.[93]

Changes were also occurring within the Department of Justice. In the fall of 1996, Anne Bingaman, who had presided over the investigation that had led to the Licensing Case and the negotiation of the subsequent 1994 Consent Decree, announced her intention to leave the department. She was replaced by her former deputy, Joel Klein, who had already done extensive work on the Microsoft matter, and who served as the Acting Assistant Attorney General in charge of the Antitrust Division until he was confirmed as its permanent head in July of 1997.[94] By that time, frustrated with what they perceived as the slow pace of the Justice Department's investigation, several Republican U.S. senators asked the Federal Trade Commission to wrest back the investigation of Microsoft from the Justice Department, but the FTC declined.[95]

Although some of the licensing practices prohibited by the consent decree had ended, Microsoft's business model had persisted. It continued to add to Windows things that it viewed as new features, and that rival software firms and the Department of Justice viewed as new programs. Was this "tying" or "integration" under the terms of the Licensing Decree?

Although Judge Sporkin had expressed concern about the efficacy of the consent decree, his diagnosis of its infirmities barely alluded to the nuanced language of the one section that now drew the parties back into court. In a broader sense, however, Sporkin's concerns were significantly vindicated: the consent decree simply did not get at the heart of the competitive problem that Microsoft's business model had created.

On October 20, 1997, the Department of Justice asked the district court to conclude that Microsoft was violating the 1994 consent decree. As a remedy, the Department of Justice asked the court to order Microsoft to stop requiring OEMs to license Internet Explorer as a condition of licensing Windows and to impose a fine of $1 million for each day that Microsoft failed to carry out that order.[96] Lest Microsoft think that this was the only legal action being contemplated, the Department of Justice also announced that it wanted to "make clear" that it was still pursuing "an ongoing and wide-ranging investigation to determine whether Microsoft's actions are stifling innovation and consumer choice."[97]

To support its petition, however, the Department of Justice had to grapple with the seemingly paradoxical language of the decree, which prohibited tying but permitted "integration." The government asserted that Paragraph IV of the consent decree "prohibits Microsoft from conditioning the terms of an OEM's license to distribute the Windows operating system on the OEM also licensing and distributing other Microsoft products." The petition further asserted that "[t]he purpose of that and other provisions of the Final Judgment was to prevent Microsoft from protecting or extending its operating system monopoly."[98] Paragraph V of the Petition charged:

On September 30, 1997, Microsoft released its newest version of Internet Explorer, known as Internet Explorer 4.0. In direct violation of the Final Judgment, Microsoft has required OEMs, as part of their license for Microsoft's Windows 95 operating system and as a condition of receiving that license, to license, preinstall, and distribute Microsoft's Internet Explorer 3.0 browser on their PCs that also have Windows 95 installed.

In contrast to the consent decree's narrowly targeted prohibitions of "per processor" license restrictions and its overreaching non-disclosure agreements, the Justice Department's civil contempt petition thus went to the heart of Microsoft's business model: its ability to expand the capabilities of Windows and condition Windows licenses on the inclusion of other functions that had developed first as stand-alone programs. "If successful," one commentator observed at the time, [the Justice Department's lawsuit] could threaten the key to Microsoft's vast market power: the ability to maintain the dominance of its operating system by constantly incorporating new features."[99]

The Justice Department's decision to invoke the decree may have been conceived as a less risky way to strike surgically at the heart of the case against Microsoft, but it turned out to be a nearly disastrous diversion that failed to produce the hoped-for result. The effort also highlighted some of the doctrinal and institutional questions that complicated efforts to address Microsoft's "integration" model effectively and foreshadowed some of the problems that would arise in attempting to remedy Microsoft's conduct.

First, if one takes the Justice Department's allegations on their face, Microsoft had been in violation of the decree for more than two years when the government filed its motion, in the fall of 1997. If there was a violation of its provisions, it was clearest from July 1995 until August of 1996, when the code for IE and the code for Windows 95 were completely separate and OEMs were bound by their license to install IE along with Windows. Microsoft would then have had a difficult time arguing that IE wasn't an "other product" or that IE was "integrated" into Windows. In fact, when IE was first introduced, Windows 95 was offered to retail consumers both with and without IE. Yet the Department of Justice did nothing at that time to enforce the decree, even though it was well aware of the bundling, and the browser investigation itself lay fallow in the Department of Justice for a year before a new investigation was started.

With the filing of the civil contempt petition, it became clear that the government and Microsoft had drastically different interpretations of Section IV(E)(i) of the decree. Whereas the government charged that Microsoft was engaged in "tying" Windows 95 (a "covered product") to IE (an "other product"), Microsoft responded that it had merely "integrated" IE and Windows. The futility of the compromise struck in Paragraph IV of the Consent Decree was laid bare.

The contempt proceeding also created its own remedy problem. In order for the contempt proceeding to be effective, the Department of Justice had to go beyond simply asking that Microsoft be held in contempt, which the petition sought. It had to specify what behavior would purge the contempt and keep Microsoft from violating the decree in the future.

The Justice Department's approach sounded straightforward: Microsoft must stop "continuing to require, or in the future requiring, OEMs to license any version of Internet Explorer as an express or implied condition of licensing Windows 95 or any Covered Product" as defined in the 1994 consent decree. Behind the simplicity of this request, however, were some difficult questions. What did it mean to say that an OEM would no longer be required to install "any version of Internet Explorer" when IE 3.0, as released, included files that updated Windows 95? Wouldn't OEMs want the updates of Windows? More importantly, if the software code that produced "Internet Explorer" was contained in files or libraries of files that were also used by "Windows," would it be possible to install an operable version of Windows without code for Internet Explorer? Would Microsoft have to "rip out" files that were also necessary to make Windows run? Most fundamentally, however, what would be the boundaries between the two programs if it turned out that they shared some of the same lines of code or some of the same files? Was a separation between "browser" and "operating system" merely a historical artifact, more relevant to how the products were initially developed than to a necessary technical distinction between the two as they were now evolving?

When Microsoft responded to the Justice Department's contempt petition, it emphasized these remedy problems and sought delay. First, Microsoft argued that it couldn't comprehend the Department's generic reference to removal of "Internet Explorer." Removing IE 3.0 from a computer with Windows 95 installed would cause certain Windows 95 features to "break" and would cause certain applications to run poorly on Windows 95 because those applications needed code included in IE 3.0.[100] Second, Microsoft asked for a full evidentiary hearing, with discovery, to explore whether the parties intended the decree to cover the "integration" of the operating system and a browser—a process that probably would extend the hearing process past the date when OEMs would be required to preinstall IE 4.0 along with Windows. By that time, of course, Microsoft would have established a new status quo that would be difficult for a court to reverse.

In response, the Department of Justice disagreed with Microsoft's characterization of the relief's effect and sought to avoid delay, arguing that the court could determine the decree's meaning from the "four corners of the Final Judgment."[101] But the Department's response showed some imprecision in articulating its technical goals and perhaps in the Department's understanding of what was involved in the design of IE and Windows. The Department now said that it wanted only "a simple order" forbidding the forced installation of "the software code" that Microsoft "separately distributes at retail as 'Internet Explorer 3.0.'" Somewhat muddying the request, however, the Department also indicated that it might be enough if the order required "only that Microsoft not compel OEMs to display the IE icon on the Windows 95 desktop or in easily accessible files as a condition of licensing Windows 95." Such relief "could achieve much of the value of complete relief" without raising possible technical problems with

Windows or any application, "because the code on which such software depends could remain."[102]

On December 11, 1997, six days after hearing oral arguments on the petition, Judge Jackson denied it, declining to hold Microsoft in civil contempt. For contempt to be appropriate, he reasoned, Microsoft would have to have violated a "clear and unambiguous term" of the consent decree. Microsoft argued that the government was fully aware of its efforts to integrate IE and Windows at the time the decree was negotiated and that the "integrated product" proviso "was the result of Microsoft's insistence—and the government's acquiescence—that Microsoft would retain complete discretion to decide what features to include in its operating systems, limited only by the antitrust laws generally." In the court's view, this was sufficient to demonstrate "the ambiguity of the term 'integrated product'" and hence Microsoft's conduct couldn't be the basis of a contempt finding.[103] Microsoft had "advanced a plausible interpretation of the term" that supported its position that IE was an integrated component of Windows 95.[104]

Although Judge Jackson characterized Microsoft's interpretation of Paragraph IV as "plausible," in his view it was incorrect. Here Jackson's analysis of the language of the decree intersected with the antitrust law of tying. In defining IE as an "other product," the government had turned to the "independent demand" test that had developed for tying: "All Internet browsers, IE included, currently enjoy independent consumer demand and are regularly licensed and distributed separately from operating systems." Microsoft responded by defining an "integrated product" as "one like Windows 95, consisting of a wide range of features and functions that, although they may also be available separately, have been 'combined' or 'united' together." However, Paragraph IV(E)(i)'s implicit reference to "tying"—a legal term of art—appeared to invoke the legal definition of separate products that the Department of Justice had urged. Jackson concluded, therefore, that, "contrary to Microsoft's claim to absolute discretion to dictate the composition of its operating-system software, it appears not unlikely, as a matter of contract, that Microsoft's 'unfettered liberty' to impose its idea of what has been 'integrated' into its operating systems stops at least at the point at which it would violate established antitrust law."[105]

Although the Department of Justice's request for relief appeared to depend on a finding of contempt, Judge Jackson nevertheless entered a preliminary injunction preventing Microsoft from distributing Windows on the condition that licensees also take IE. Although he was "preliminarily inclined" to agree with the government's view of the decree, Jackson also acknowledged Microsoft's argument that Windows 95 might "break" if IE were unbundled and concluded that "[d]isputed issues of technological fact … abound as the record presently stands."[106] The injunction was to remain in effect until a complete record could be established.

Jackson's preliminary injunction forbade Microsoft from licensing any operating-system software, including Windows 95 "or any successor version," on condition that the licensee preinstall any Microsoft Internet browser software, including Internet Explorer 3.0, 4.0, "or any successor." On its face, this injunction went beyond Windows 95, on which the Justice Department's petition had focused, and would also apply to the upcoming Windows 98.[107] In addition, because of the "complex issues of cybertechnology" involved in finally deciding on the proper application of the consent decree to IE, Jackson appointed a special master, Lawrence Lessig of the Harvard Law School, to receive evidence and to report his proposed findings of fact and conclusions of law on or before May 31, 1998.[108]

Jackson's decision set in motion a flurry of activity. Microsoft immediately appealed his order to the U.S. Court of Appeals for the District of Columbia Circuit. It did not, however, seek a stay of Judge Jackson's order. Instead, to drive home its point that Windows 95 and IE were fully integrated and that Windows 95 would be disabled if IE were removed, it took an audacious step. Seizing on language in Jackson's opinion that his injunction would apply to "all software code" now distributed at retail as IE 3.0 (language echoing that used by the Department of Justice), Microsoft proceeded to "break" the operating system by taking that language literally. That is, it now told OEMs that if they wanted the latest upgrade of Windows 95 without "Internet Explorer 3.0 code" they would have to delete all the files that Microsoft distributed with IE 3.0 at retail, including common files that were needed to permit the newer version of Windows 95 to boot up. In other words, complying with Jackson's order would render the latest version of Windows inoperable. As an alternative, Microsoft told OEMs that if they didn't want IE 3.0 they could license the August 1995 version of Windows, now two years old and no longer the most current version of the operating system. Microsoft's defiant act must have made a lasting impression on Judge Jackson, who later sat in judgment on the Windows 98 case.

Microsoft's literal response to Judge Jackson's order was widely derided in the press, and an incredulous Jackson declared that it had taken him "less than 90 seconds" to "uninstall" Internet Explorer by using Windows' own uninstall feature without rendering Windows inoperable.[109] The response also drew a quick legal response from the Department of Justice in the form of a second contempt motion, this one accusing Microsoft of failure to adhere to the preliminary injunction just entered by Judge Jackson.[110]

The Justice Department's second contempt motion led to another whirlwind round of litigation. First there were further hearings before Judge Jackson relating to Microsoft's compliance with his preliminary injunction. Then Microsoft asked Jackson to revoke his reference to the special master, arguing that the appointment was improper and that Microsoft was entitled to examine the special master to determine whether he might be biased. After Jackson denied that motion on January 14, 1998 (also refusing to stay the proceedings before the special master), Microsoft sought immediate review in the court of appeals.[111] By that time, Lessig had begun taking evidence from the parties on the technical issues involved in whether Internet Explorer should be considered a separate product under the consent decree. But his efforts were halted a month later when the court of appeals granted Microsoft's motion for a stay of the special-master proceedings.

For all the derision heaped upon Microsoft for arguing that it would have to "break" Windows to extract "all the code" distributed with its IE browser, the technical issues were nagging ones that put the Justice Department in a difficult position. To meet Microsoft's arguments about the integration of the operating system and the browser, Justice Department lawyers needed to understand how software programs were written. This required going beyond the simple question whether something Microsoft labeled as "Internet Explorer" was distributed separately from something called "Windows." They needed to appreciate the technical characteristics of software code and design, something that Microsoft and its software engineers already understood. Although the Justice Department had been investigating the browser issue for more than a year, more was learned in deposition discovery for the Lessig hearings and for the hearing on the Department's second contempt motion. The Department also hired an independent software consultant to assist the trial staff and to testify.[112]

But the very process of injecting more technical information into the court proceedings created its own tactical risk. The more deeply the Department of Justice penetrated the technical aspects of software programming, both for purposes of arguing liability and for purposes of designing a workable and effective remedy, the more it risked the criticism that judges were being asked to second guess the decisions of trained software engineers and designers. Courts would probably be uncomfortable with this role and might reject legal arguments that put them in the untenable position of specifying design changes in software. Making the case appear too technical might cause courts to shy away from legal intervention.[113]

On January 21, 1998, shortly before Judge Jackson was expected to rule on the contempt motion for failure to comply with the preliminary injunction, the Department of Justice and Microsoft entered into a settlement based on a concession that would come back to haunt the government both in the court of appeals and throughout the subsequent proceedings. The Department of Justice tried to solve its tactical and technical problems by picking a remedial approach that was simple and easy to understand, but which it also felt would address the competition problem behind the decree's prohibition on bundling. The settlement provided that Microsoft would be in "full compliance" with Judge Jackson's December preliminary injunction if Microsoft gave OEMs the option of installing the version of Windows it had distributed in August of 1996 with IE 3.0. An OEM would then be permitted to modify that version by running the Windows "Add/Remove" utility for Internet Explorer, removing the Internet Explorer icon, and marking a specified Internet Explorer file as "hidden." OEMs opting for this older version of Windows would then get certain files that Microsoft stated would make the older version of Windows the same as the most current one, "with the sole exception of Internet Explorer 4.0 functionality."[114]

The Department of Justice had hinted at the remedy of using the Add/Remove utility earlier in the proceedings (along with the removal of the icon), and it was the approach Judge Jackson had taken in his demonstration of how easily IE could be "removed." The remedy was not, however, the same as the "simple order" that Microsoft be prohibited from requiring installation of the "software code" that Microsoft "distributes at retail as 'Internet Explorer 3.0,'" as the Justice Department had originally proposed. Removal through the Add/Remove utility prevented the end user—at least the average end user who couldn't write software code—from browsing the Internet unless a new browser was installed.[115] It didn't remove all the code shipped with IE, or even all the code related to browsing the Internet. In fact, Microsoft estimated that approximately 90 percent of that code would still remain after the Add/Remove utility was run.[116]

Blocking access to Internet Explorer through the use of the Add/Remove utility was a simple fix, but it disconnected Microsoft's allegedly unlawful conduct from the remedy. The Justice Department charged that Microsoft had compelled its licensees to take a second product, IE, if they wanted Windows. The traditional remedy for such unlawful bundling was unbundling (that is, separation of the tied package), which Judge Jackson had sought. But Jackson's effort to impose the traditional remedy for unlawful tying collided with Microsoft's software engineering choice to integrate the code of Windows and IE. The remedy proposed in the settlement left the compelled product in place but rendered it useless to the average consumer. By settling for this limited remedy, the government had in effect capitulated to Microsoft's decision to commingle IE and Windows code in Windows 95. Whether Microsoft's design decision was in fact technically justified or was merely part of its broader effort to impair competition from Netscape wasn't addressed. As it turned out, the question whether any remedy could be effective if it didn't require a reengineering of the code to reconstitute Windows and IE as distinct products continued to plague all of the litigation efforts against Microsoft.

The January settlement cleared the question of compliance with Judge Jackson's December 11 preliminary injunction, but it didn't decide whether the injunction had been issued properly or whether the appointment of the special master had been lawful. By the time the settlement was entered, those issues were on appeal to the U.S. Court of Appeals for the District of Columbia Circuit, which had decided to hear Microsoft's argument on an expedited basis. This meant that the Licensing Case was headed for the court of appeals a second time. And for the second time that court reversed the decision of the district court.

On the procedural issues, the court of appeals held that Judge Jackson had acted precipitously in granting a preliminary injunction without giving notice to Microsoft that he would decide anything other than the contempt motion. The court also held that Jackson's appointment of a special master had been "either a clear abuse of discretion or an exercise of wholly non-existent discretion."[117]

More important, however, was the court's disagreement with Jackson's interpretation of the consent decree. Like the district court, the court of appeals approached the meaning of Paragraph IV of the decree as an exercise in contract interpretation. The goal was to discern the intentions of the parties. Essential to that task was an appreciation for the source of the anti-tying provision and the reasons for the "integration" exception.

As the court of appeals first observed, the anti-tying provision of the decree had been inserted because of a complaint that Novell had filed in 1993 with the European Union's competition-enforcement agency. In June of 1994, Microsoft, facing probes in both the United States and the European Union, proposed trilateral discussions in the hope that a joint settlement could be negotiated to cover both jurisdictions, thereby eliminating the prospect of inconsistent remedies. Paragraph IV was the product of those negotiations.

Novell, which owned the rights to DR-DOS, had alleged in Europe that Microsoft's use of "per processor" and "per system" licenses effectively conditioned the licensing of Windows 3.11 on the licensing of MS-DOS. Windows 3.11, a competitive response to Apple's Macintosh, provided a menu-driven graphical user interface that was intended to replace the arcane command interface of DOS with something more "user friendly." It was initially offered as a stand-alone product that could be used with any version of DOS, including DR-DOS. Novell's tying complaint thus was focused on preserving the possibility of combining its own operating system, DR-DOS, with Windows 3.11—an option it claimed was being effectively foreclosed by Microsoft's licensing practices. At a minimum, therefore, the decree had to be read to forbid Microsoft from conditioning the licensing of Windows 3.11 on the licensee's acceptance of a license for MS-DOS.

But the tying of Windows 3.11 to MS-DOS was already a dated issue. Windows 95 was a successor to both MS-DOS and Windows 3.11, and it combined their functions into a single package. Paradoxically, while barring any tie between MS-DOS and Windows 3.11, the decree acknowledged Windows 95 as a "covered product," which the court interpreted as acceptance by the government that it was a single, integrated product. For the court of appeals, the issue thus became whether the combination of Windows 95 and IE was more like the combination of MS-DOS and Windows 3.11 (which would constitute a barred tie-in of two products) or more like Windows 95 (an "integrated" operating system that "combines the functionalities of a graphical interface and an operating system").[118]

The court began by rejecting the positions of both parties as too extreme. The government's reading of the anti-tying provision, which emphasized the separate marketing of Windows 95 and IE before they were combined, denigrated the integration proviso. On the other hand, Microsoft's assertion that the integration proviso gave it complete design discretion nullified the anti-tying provision and wouldn't have resolved the Novell complaint, as was intended. The court then set out to offer its own solution based on its own definition of integration:

> ... a simple way to harmonize the parties' desires is to read the integration proviso of § IV(E)(i) as permitting any genuine technological integration, regardless of whether elements of the integrated package are marketed separately. ... [A]n "integrated product" is most reasonably understood as a product that combines functionalities (which may also be marketed separately and operated together) in a way that offers advantages unavailable if the functionalities are bought separately and combined by the purchaser.[119]

Citing the limited institutional capacity of courts to judge the code-writing practices of software engineers, the court ultimately endorsed a very deferential standard that sought to differentiate "tying" from "integration" based upon economic efficiency. It would also be easy for a software manufacturer to meet and difficult for a plaintiff to overcome: "The question is not whether the integration is a net plus but merely whether there is a *plausible claim that it brings some advantage.*"[120] Applying this deferential definition of integration, the court concluded that the Windows 95-IE combination was distinguishable from the combination of MS-DOS and Windows 3.11. Hence it was a protected "integration" under the consent decree, not tying. Microsoft had "clearly met the burden of ascribing facially plausible benefits to its integrated design as compared to an operating system combined with a stand-alone browser such as Netscape's Navigator." Those benefits included permitting applications to benefit from a browser's functionality without requiring the user to separately start and open a browser application, the provision of system-wide services not related to Web browsing (e.g., a HyperText Markup Language reader), and various other OS upgrades.[121]

The court distinguished this kind of beneficial integration from the mere act of "bolting" two products together (which wouldn't necessarily offer any advantages and would therefore be fairly characterized as tying). And it observed that commingling of code alone wasn't sufficient to establish "true integration." But in judging Windows 95 with IE to be an integrated product, it applied a very low threshold, one that was consistent with its strong view that courts weren't institutionally competent to second guess software engineers as to the most beneficial way to write software code.[122] In doing so, the court didn't consider the effects of Microsoft's "integration" on competition, perhaps because it viewed its task as limited to discerning the intentions of the parties to the consent decree.

Although the court of appeals purported to analyze only the intentions of the parties to the 1994 consent decree, its approach to integration undoubtedly had implications for the antitrust analysis of tying in the software context. The court even asserted that its stated understanding of the decree was "consistent with tying law."[123] Tying was *per se* unlawful at the time, so assertions of efficiency justifications were being channeled by defendants into the "two products" element of the offense. As Judge Patricia Wald argued persuasively in her dissent, the majority had so blurred the line between contract interpretation and the application of antitrust law that there appeared to be little for the district court to do on remand, even though the court of appeals had decided the case on the basis of a slim factual record. The court of appeals had not only declared Windows 95 to be an integrated product; it had embraced a test for integration that would make it very difficult for the Justice Department, or any other plaintiff, to prevail on a tying claim targeted at platform software. Indeed, it appeared to foreclose a finding of two products, which would be a necessary prerequisite to such a claim under the formal law of tying. Sorting out the implications of the court's decision, however, would have to await the court of appeals' third opportunity to review the work of the district court in the *Microsoft* cases, and that was three years away.

In the fall of 1997, as government lawyers prepared the civil contempt petition, it must have already been apparent that the 1994 consent decree's language was too internally contradictory to constrain Microsoft's continued expansion of Windows through "integration," especially with respect to its browser. At the same time, the government was becoming increasingly aware that the conduct more clearly barred by the decree, which was targeted at PC operating system rivals now gone from the market, had become largely irrelevant.[124] Microsoft's behavior had changed in character, as had the market. Microsoft had redirected its attention from actual rivals to nascent ones, and was now engaged in a more far-ranging pattern of conduct. Internal documents secured from Microsoft during the continuing investigation that ran concurrent with the contempt proceedings appeared to undermine the arguments it was making in those proceedings to defend its integration decisions. Through integration it wasn't seeking to produce technologically superior products; rather, it was seeking to debilitate a new competitive threat to its monopoly in operating systems from Netscape. Reining in Microsoft would require a new case.

While the civil contempt phase of the Licensing Case was wending its way through the courts, the federal government and a group of states began to prepare new and broader complaints that focused on the next expected iteration of Windows: Windows 98. The Windows 98 cases were filed in May of 1998, just a month before the court of appeals' decision in the civil contempt proceedings. In reaching its conclusion in the contempt proceeding, the court of appeals reduced the decree's anti-tying provision to a pyrrhic victory covering only an already outmoded operating-system product and any very closely analogous products. For all intents and purposes, it had no prospective effect. The decision confirmed what all involved probably suspected: that the 1994 decree was dead. The majority's rationale also cast doubt on the likelihood that any subsequent case challenging Microsoft's integration strategy as an unlawful form of tying would succeed.

Conclusion

The early phases of the *Microsoft* cases established many of the enduring themes that would be maintained by Microsoft and by those who questioned its conduct. The basic economic framework for understanding and analyzing the field of platform software also emerged, as did greater appreciation for the interaction between technological progress and the legal standards that had developed over decades under U.S. and foreign antitrust laws.

The early phases of those cases also exposed some of the institutional complexity of U.S. competition policy. They highlighted structural, political, and operational differences between the two federal antitrust enforcement agencies in the United States. They suggested a role that Congress could play in trying to influence enforcement agency action. They also revealed the many access opportunities that were available to private parties intent on influencing the process of law enforcement. And they featured the first appearances of the American states and the European Union as players that would have to be integrated into the overall enforcement process.

These various factors—substantive, procedural, and institutional—remained on full display as the Microsoft cases entered their third phase: the Windows 98 cases.

3 Bringing the Windows 95/98 Monopolization Case

On May 26, 1995, Bill Gates distributed to his executive staff a now-famous memorandum, "The Internet Tidal Wave," in which he discussed the coming importance of the Internet to Microsoft's business and described how the Internet would transform communications.[1] "The Internet is the most important single development to come along since the IBM PC was introduced in 1981," Gates wrote. Presciently, he predicted a world in which "virtually every PC will be used to connect to the Internet" and recognized the coming importance of using the Internet to transmit video and audio content.[2] Gates also identified a competitive threat from Netscape, whose Internet browser had been commercially available for less than six months[3]:

A new competitor "born" on the Internet is Netscape. Their browser is dominant, with 70% usage share, allowing them to determine which network extensions will catch on. They are pursuing a multi-platform strategy where they move the key API [application programming interface] into the client [the browser] to commoditize the underlying operating system. ... We have to match and beat their offerings. ...

In this chapter we explore the antitrust enforcement response to Microsoft's campaign to "match and beat" Netscape's Navigator browser, a campaign that subsequently became known as the "browser wars." We start with the Justice Department's and the states' investigations and the events leading up to the filing of their complaints in May of 1998. We then describe the themes and theories of their legal case as set out in those complaints. We follow this with the trial phase of the litigation, held before Judge Thomas Penfield Jackson, particularly focusing on Judge Richard A. Posner's failed effort to mediate a settlement of the litigation. We conclude the chapter with a discussion of Judge Jackson's decision, in which he held that Microsoft had violated Sections 1 and 2 of the Sherman Act.

The Federal and State Investigations

A Slow Start

In May and June of 1995, contemporaneous with Gates' "Internet Tidal Wave" memorandum, Microsoft and Netscape held a series of meetings in which Microsoft offered Netscape a "special relationship" if Netscape would abandon its efforts to develop its browser for Windows 95.[4] More specifically, according to notes of one of the meetings taken by Marc Andreessen, the driving technical force behind the development of Netscape's browser, Microsoft offered Netscape "tight integration" with Microsoft's products if the two firms developed a "tight relationship." The key to this relationship, however, was for Netscape to "stay away" from Windows 95.[5] Microsoft's own email messages indicate that Microsoft's basic idea was that Netscape could build on top of Windows 95, but that it had to abandon any efforts to develop the Netscape browser in a way that would compete with Microsoft on the platform (or operating system) level.[6] In an email message, Microsoft put it graphically: It wanted to "suck[] most of the functionality of the current Netscape browser … into the [Windows 95] platform," which it would then control.[7] In return, Microsoft would be willing to make an equity investment in Netscape and to actively participate in Netscape's business, but this would be part of Microsoft's "general strategy" to "love … [Netscape] to death."[8]

Netscape could have dealt with these meetings as a simple business matter, which presumably it did until it became clear in July of 1995 that discussions with Microsoft would be fruitless.[9] But Netscape could also construe Microsoft's overture as a legal problem. Microsoft's approach arguably invited an anticompetitive strategy to divide future markets with Netscape and to make certain that Netscape didn't become a competitor to its Windows operating system. Indeed, the promise of "tight integration" carried with it an implicit threat of "untight" integration with Windows if Netscape balked—that is, a threat to withhold or delay necessary information for interoperating with Windows.[10] This, too, might be anticompetitive conduct.

Netscape thus was confronted with a choice between becoming a participant in illegal activity and becoming a victim. There was a way to avoid either outcome, however. Netscape could threaten Microsoft with antitrust litigation, or it could ask the government to bring an antitrust suit against Microsoft. It chose to do the latter.

Shortly after the June meetings with Microsoft, Netscape's key officers and its antitrust lawyer, Gary Reback, traveled to Washington to meet with lawyers from the Justice Department's Antitrust Division. Although the Justice Department's Windows 95/98 complaint would later characterize the June 1995 meetings with Microsoft as "a blatant and illegal attempt to monopolize the Internet browser market,"[11] Netscape's contemporaneous disclosure of the meetings resulted in no immediate action from the Justice Department.[12]

The Justice Department's failure to seize on Netscape's complaint at the time is understandable. The Department knew the story only from Netscape's side, and that version of the story was based on notes taken by Andreessen. It had yet to discover Microsoft's view, as represented by Bill Gates' "Internet Tidal Wave" memorandum and the email messages related to the Netscape meetings—information that would clarify Microsoft's goal in meeting with Netscape. Further, government enforcers generally receive competitors' complaints with some wariness, particularly if the competitor is itself a dominant firm (as Netscape was, at least for a brief moment). Government enforcers are keenly aware of the self-interest of complaining rivals and of the potential for being misled by competitors whose interests may not be aligned with the public interest.

On the other hand, competitors' complaints can be useful. It is rare for consumers to be immediately aware that they have been harmed by an antitrust violation directed at excluding a rival; consumer injury in such cases is likely to be both diffuse and somewhat speculative. For this type of antitrust violation, the targeted and injured competitor is the first to know that a possible violation has occurred and can serve as an early "trip wire" to identify anticompetitive conduct. In addition, the targeted competitor has a sufficiently substantial economic interest to make it worthwhile to bring a violation to the attention of a government enforcer.

Skeptical or not, the Department of Justice could have begun an investigation of the Netscape meetings to determine whether Netscape's account was accurate. The Department's attention at that time, however, was focused on what appeared to be a different problem with Microsoft. In the summer of 1995 Microsoft was getting ready to launch Windows 95, a highly promoted new version of its operating system. Bundled into Windows 95 was software that would allow users to register for Microsoft's new online service, Microsoft Network (MSN). Established online competitors, such as America Online (AOL), had been complaining to the Justice Department that the bundling of this software with Windows 95 would give Microsoft an unfair competitive advantage in online services, putting the MSN icon directly in front of all Windows users.[13] In June of 1995 the Department had begun a formal investigation, issuing civil investigative demands (CIDs) requiring online services companies, content providers, and Microsoft to produce documents to the Department. Microsoft had moved to quash its CID, arguing that the demands were excessive and burdensome.[14] In July, three days before a hearing on Microsoft's motion, the Department withdrew the CID, announcing that if it were to bring suit it would do so before August 24, the consumer launch date for Windows 95.[15]

In mid July, as Netscape was complaining to the Department, Microsoft made a new product announcement: It would bundle its new Internet browser, called Internet Explorer, into Windows 95. This decision fit into the information Netscape had provided regarding Microsoft's interest in the browser market, and possibly Microsoft's desire to exclude Netscape from that market. The decision to bundle the browser also raised legal questions similar to the decision to bundle the MSN software. The Department responded by expanding its MSN investigation to include the browser.[16]

Despite these investigative efforts, the Department pulled back from litigation. Faced with the August 24 shipment date for Windows, it realized that it would be difficult to convince a court to issue a preliminary injunction to stop a product that had been subject to so much marketing effort.[17] On August 9, 1995, it announced that it wouldn't bring suit to stop the distribution of Windows 95.[18] Although purporting to leave the investigation open, the Department's decision effectively acquiesced not only in Microsoft's inclusion of MSN in Windows 95, but in the inclusion of Internet Explorer as well. Windows 95, and all that it contained, became a fait accompli.

There the matter apparently rested for a year before Netscape's lawyers made another effort to convince the Justice Department to investigate. As we discussed in chapter 2, this time Netscape's arguments were presented to the Justice Department in the form of a white paper that detailed a legal theory that Microsoft's conduct was intended not just to monopolize the browser market, but, more significantly, to maintain Microsoft's monopoly in the market for operating systems.[19] This theory of monopoly maintenance would eventually become the central theory of the litigation to be filed against Microsoft, but commencement of that action was nearly two years away. The Department's immediate response, in September of 1996, was to open an investigation focusing on the browser.[20]

The States' Investigative Effort

In September of 1996, shortly after the Justice Department opened its new Microsoft investigation, the head of Texas' state antitrust enforcement agency, Mark Tobey, became interested in Microsoft's conduct. Tobey's interest wasn't the result of Netscape's efforts to convince a government agency to bring suit; it was provoked by an article that appeared in the weekly magazine *Time*. The article detailed the competition between Netscape and Microsoft and discussed Microsoft's projected release of a new version of Internet Explorer that would be "fully integrated with the computer desktop."[21] In February of 1997, after calling Gary Reback and getting a copy of Netscape's 1996 white paper, Tobey issued Texas' civil investigative demands to Microsoft for documents.[22] Parallel state and federal investigations were thus underway.

No single state would have sufficient resources to initiate and prosecute a monopolization suit against Microsoft. Over a number of years, however, the states had developed a process for pooling resources on major antitrust cases, allowing multiple states jointly to investigate antitrust violations and file suit together. Although no formal guidelines exist for deciding when these multistate investigations are appropriate, the states had adopted a practice of presenting possible multistate cases at semi-annual meetings of state antitrust staff attorneys from around the country to see whether there might be broader interest in the litigation. Tobey presented the early results of his investigation at the April 1997 meeting. Although he received an unenthusiastic reception from the other states at first, as Texas obtained more Microsoft documents and email messages, other states became interested and began to issue their own investigative subpoenas to Microsoft.

At this time the states were not being propelled by the efforts of the private parties—indeed, at least some of the state enforcers were skeptical of Netscape's white paper—but by information revealed in the states' investigations, particularly email messages that Microsoft was turning over to the states discussing how tightly to integrate Internet Explorer with what would become Windows 98. The story these messages told was not of a design decision being driven by technical requirements and innovation, but of a design decision being driven by marketing considerations and a desire to "win[] the browser battle."[23]

Microsoft's email messages spoke of the need to be "leveraging Windows" and of the need to change Microsoft's approach from trying to "copy Netscape and make IE into a platform" to an approach that finds ways "to tie IE and Windows together."[24] They spoke of needing something that will "cut off" Netscape, "something more—Windows integration."[25] Instead of touting the product superiority of an integrated Windows and browser, they had language like this: "It seems clear that it will be very hard to increase browser market share on the merits of IE 4 alone. It will be more important to leverage the OS asset to make people use IE instead of Navigator."[26]

The states became convinced that they had a case to bring.

Forming the Federal-State Enforcement Joint Venture

As the summer of 1997 progressed, both the Justice Department and a group of states continued to discover documents and began to take statements from potential witnesses. Some of the statements were taken jointly, but mostly the federal and state investigations were conducted in parallel.[27] Although an effort was made to coordinate deposition schedules, there was no attempt to divide up the work among the federal and state agencies involved.[28]

At this point there was an uneasy balance between coordination and competition in the investigation, in part reflecting the different institutional positions of the Justice Department and the states. To draw on the language of industrial organization, institutionally the Justice Department has been the dominant firm in antitrust enforcement and the states have been the smaller fringe competitors. In an industrial setting, these roles are related to the relative size and scope of business firms. Larger firms have the comparative advantage of more resources, but may be organizationally slower to act and may be less innovative. Smaller firms lack resources, but may be less wedded to orthodoxy and more willing to take risks and upset consensus. In the industrial world, partnering between large and small firms is a common way to get the advantages of both types of firms. The partnering in the Microsoft litigation to some extent can be seen in these terms. Whether the states would want to partner or to compete—or just to push the Justice Department to act—wasn't clear at this point in the investigation, although there were indications that they were following a prodding strategy.[29] However, it also wasn't clear whether the states would have the capacity to participate actively in litigating a complex monopolization case in a high-technology industry against a well-resourced defendant. Indeed, institutional capacity would be problematic for the states throughout the *Microsoft* litigation.

Institutional roles were not the only factors affecting the investigation. Entwined with the institutional roles were the personal histories of the players involved and the significance of the Microsoft case itself. Joel Klein, who now headed the Antitrust Division, was politically astute and strategically inclined to guard information closely. His political sensitivity led him to see the importance of state enforcers—particularly those from states with Republican attorneys general—as allies in the Microsoft case.

Joint venturing with those states in particular might mute the appearance of partisan political decision making in antitrust enforcement, although, of course, it wouldn't end it. But litigation against Microsoft was also a highly visible affair, potentially the most significant antitrust case the Justice Department could bring. The more widely the information about the investigation was shared, the more likely it would be that the information would become publicly known (accurately or not). Leaks of such information could affect the stock market, provide Microsoft with political ammunition, or simply harm the Justice Department's legal strategies. This gave Klein reason to be guarded in working with the states, which reinforced the natural institutional role of dominant firm that the Department has played.

The states, too, had histories that influenced their approach. As the investigation progressed, New York became more actively involved, and there was some concern about a repeat of New York's recent experience in the merger of Bell Atlantic and Nynex. New York had viewed Bell Atlantic as a likely entrant into its telecommunications market and believed that Bell Atlantic's acquisition of Nynex (which then had a monopoly on telephone service in New York) would eliminate the potential for competition between the two firms, in violation of the Clayton Act. In part because the merger had limited geographic effect, few states were apparently interested in joining New York in an effort to stop the merger. The case was also a legally difficult one, so New York tried to persuade the Justice Department to sue. Joel Klein, then acting head of the Division, decided not to bring suit. The merger went forward, although New York's attorney general had publicly recommended against it.[30]

The decision not to oppose the Bell Atlantic–Nynex merger, made in April of 1997, was fresh in the minds of those involved in the Microsoft investigation. New York's antitrust enforcers didn't want to again be in the position of relying solely on the federal Department of Justice. This time, they would be ready to file their own case if the Department of Justice declined to pursue a case against Microsoft.[31] But the Bell Atlantic–Nynex experience may have had an effect on the Department of Justice too. The decision not to challenge the deal had come as the Senate was considering whether to confirm Klein in the position as head of the Antitrust Division and it drew senatorial criticism on the ground that he might be a weaker enforcer of the antitrust laws than his predecessor.[32] As a result, Klein's nomination was held up for a short time, confirmation not coming until July of 1997.[33] Whether or not Klein actively sought to demonstrate that he was a strong enforcer, he must have known that his enforcement decisions in the Microsoft investigation would be viewed in the light of the charges that had been made during his confirmation hearings, as well as in the light of earlier criticism that the Department of Justice had entered into an ineffective settlement with Microsoft in the 1994 licensing case (a settlement that Klein had successfully defended in argument before the court of appeals).[34]

Institutional Competition and the Decision to File

In chapter 2 we described the Justice Department's effort in late 1997 to use the 1994 licensing decree as a way to stop Microsoft from bundling Internet Explorer into Windows 95. The Justice Department had asked Judge Jackson to hold Microsoft in contempt for violating the decree, using the contempt motion as a "surgical strike" against bundling rather than filing a completely new (and perhaps broader) suit under Section 2 of the Sherman Act. The states hadn't been parties to the 1994 decree, however, and so they weren't involved in the contempt proceedings.[35] Their only enforcement option was to consider filing a new case against Microsoft.

In December of 1997, just as Microsoft was filing its appeal of Jackson's decision in the contempt case, as many as nine states were reported to have met "to coordinate possible antitrust enforcement actions against Microsoft."[36] At the same time, it was reported that the Justice Department had hired the New York lawyer David Boies to assist it in the Microsoft investigation. Boies' exact role wasn't disclosed, but Boies was well known as one of the best trial lawyers in the United States. His hiring was described, somewhat dramatically, as signaling the Justice Department's "stop-at-nothing eagerness to prevail in its high-stakes fight" with Microsoft.[37]

Although it might have seemed odd for the Department of Justice to hire outside legal help, it had done so before on occasion, recognizing that the general decline in government antitrust litigation had left it short on experienced trial lawyers. In economic terms, Boies was the quintessential specialized asset that had to be acquired from the outside. In addition to his extensive trial experience, Boies had the specific experience of having helped to defend IBM in the long-running monopolization case that the Justice Department had pursued in the 1970s and ultimately abandoned. Rather than signaling an intention to bring suit (a decision that the Justice Department hadn't yet made), Boies' hiring confirmed the importance to the Department of making the right decision on whether to bring suit. What Boies brought to that decision wasn't so much antitrust expertise (which the Department already had) as big-case antitrust litigation expertise. Boies could address the question whether the government had a case it could win in court and the question how it might do so.

Windows 98 was scheduled to be shipped to computer manufacturers (original equipment manufacturers, or OEMs) on May 15, 1998. The Department of Justice and the states knew that, despite the 1994 decree and the contempt proceeding, Microsoft had given no thought to modifying Windows 98 so that the OEMs could either remove or hide Internet Explorer.[38] Whatever might be the value of trying to enforce the 1994 decree now, the Department and the states had to do something more—and do it before Windows 98 was shipped to the OEMs—unless they were willing to see an entire new generation of the operating system on the market with an integrated browser.

The period between January and May of 1998 was consequently an intense one for state and federal antitrust enforcers. The most critical decision for the Department and the states to make, of course, was whether to file suit at all. The states, for their part, were not only considering whether to file their own suit, but were also trying to prod the Department of Justice to bring suit, knowing that the Department had far greater resources than they. So it was not surprising to see that an April 1998 newspaper story that Klein "hasn't yet signed off on filing a new case" was followed three days later by a story that the states were circulating a draft complaint and "plan to take action with or without the Justice Department." The story added that "some officials say they fear the department won't follow through with plans to file an antitrust suit" and that the remedies the Department might seek "won't go far enough to address Microsoft's dominance of personal-computer software."[39] Threats to file suit aren't always credible; however, in view of the states' extensive independent investigation of the case plus their development of their own draft complaint, the states' threat couldn't be dismissed out of hand.

Closely intertwined with the question whether to file suit was the question whether a pre-trial settlement was possible. The main focus of the investigation was still on the browser, and there were continuing efforts to reach a settlement on the browser issues. Settlement efforts, of course, are part of nearly every potential lawsuit and are certainly part of almost every antitrust investigation, but the settlement negotiations with Microsoft had their own peculiarities.

One peculiarity of the settlement efforts had to do with to the cyclical quality of the investigation itself. The Department of Justice had been pursuing the same basic legal case, in somewhat different form, since 1995, when it had looked into the bundling of MSN and Windows 95. That investigation had been dropped in the face of the impending launch of Windows 95. Less than two weeks *after* the Justice Department ended the

MSN investigation, it finalized the settlement of the 1994 monopolization litigation. A little more than two years later, the Department was litigating browser integration as a violation of that settlement, and another iteration of the operating system, Windows 98, was on its way.[40] A second settlement was then reached with Microsoft, this one on the Department's motion to hold Microsoft in contempt for violating Judge Jackson's preliminary injunction enforcing the 1994 settlement.[41] A settlement of the current browser claims, if reached, would be the third settlement with Microsoft in four years. It could certainly be argued that the previous settlements had been unsuccessful in dealing with the integration issue, and that Microsoft had gotten the better of the two previous deals. Microsoft also appeared to be committed to defending its integration strategy. There was no reason, therefore, for the Justice Department to expect that it could reach a better settlement the third time around.

Another aspect of the negotiations was their multilateral quality. The settlement negotiations were a mixture of direct discussions between Joel Klein and Bill Gates, between Microsoft lawyers and Justice Department lawyers, and, in its final round, among Microsoft lawyers, Justice Department lawyers, and lawyers representing the states. The negotiations had been unsuccessful to that point, not because of disagreements among the enforcement agencies as to settlement terms, but because Microsoft and the enforcement agencies couldn't agree to terms.[42]

Microsoft had also made an effort to deal directly with individual state attorneys general to convince them not to file suit. This effort bore substantial fruit when Texas' attorney general announced three days before suit was supposed to be filed that Texas—which had played a leading role in the states' investigation and in the joint federal and state efforts—was withdrawing from the litigation because "several officials of Texas' computer industry" were concerned that suing Microsoft might "negatively impact their companies."[43] The Texas attorney general's decision could have been a serious blow to the states' case, but in a multistate enforcement setting the loss of a single state need not derail the joint effort.

A final effort at negotiation came on Friday, May 15, and Saturday, May 16, 1998. Microsoft agreed to hold off shipping the Windows 98 code to the OEMs, scheduled for that Friday. The Department of Justice held off filing suit, which had been scheduled for the day before. The states, at the Department's request, also held off filing their similarly scheduled suit. But the weekend negotiations failed, the truce ended, and on Monday, May 18, the Department of Justice and the states filed their separate complaints, and Microsoft began shipping its code for Windows 98.[44]

The Windows 95/98 Monopolization Case: The Scope of the Complaints

Initial Complaints

The complaints that the Justice Department and the states filed provided a first public glimpse of the governments' anticipated themes.[45] The story was further developed in the testimony of the expert economists, Microsoft's motion for summary judgment and the governments' response, the testimony of other witnesses, the opening and closing statements of counsel, and in the end, the proposed findings of fact and conclusions of law that were submitted by the parties to the court after the close of trial. Outside the courtroom, the parties used press releases, public comments, and an unprecedented (for an antitrust case) level of press coverage in an effort to shape their stories.

The governments' story proceeded on three levels. The first concerned the conduct itself. Although there was some significant agreement on what the conduct was, the government plaintiffs and Microsoft characterized it very differently. The second came in the parties' conflicting portrayals of the markets in which the conduct occurred. Finally, the parties had very different views of the adequacy of the antitrust system itself—that is, different views as to whether antitrust enforcement through government agencies and the courts could timely and effectively police "new economy" industries.

Overarching Themes

The government plaintiffs sought to reduce a fairly complex series of events into an elemental story of classic exclusion.[46] Faced with what Microsoft perceived as a significant threat to its monopoly operating system from emerging rivals, Microsoft first solicited an agreement with one of those rivals, Netscape, to suspend competition. When that invitation to collude was rebuffed, Microsoft embarked on a broad-based effort to eliminate the threat. A twist to the story was the "nascent" state of that competitive threat—neither Netscape's Navigator browser nor Sun Microsystems's Java programming language had yet become an "operating system" capable of competing with Windows.

As presented by the government plaintiffs, Microsoft had been wildly successful in the market for Intel-compatible desktop computer operating systems (PC OS), a market in which its share was persistently above 90 percent. Until the growth of the Internet and the development of Netscape's Navigator Internet browser and Sun's Java programming language, Microsoft's domination of that market had been insulated from competitive challenge by significant barriers to entry, most importantly the existence of numerous applications programs that were compatible only with Microsoft's operating system. Yet, despite its successes, Microsoft had been caught unprepared for the Internet revolution; Netscape and Sun had not. Microsoft sought to play catch-up, first by seeking Netscape's cooperation and then, when that failed, through a two-pronged strategy of marketing its own Internet browser, Internet Explorer, and integrating Explorer more deeply into its dominant Windows 98 operating system. It also embarked on a wide-ranging campaign to arrest the spread of Netscape and Java. In short, Microsoft wasn't content merely to compete with Netscape on the merits of their respective browsers.

As the government plaintiffs set out in their complaints, and especially through the testimony of their first witness in the trial, Netscape's president and CEO, Jim Barksdale, Microsoft perceived a twofold threat to its PC OS monopoly. First, the combination of Netscape's Internet browser and Sun's Java programming language threatened to "commoditize" the operating system. Navigator and Java were both platform-neutral programs—that is, they were designed specifically to interoperate with *any* underlying operating system. In contrast, programs written specifically for Windows could run only on computers that used Windows as their operating system. Second, and more important, Netscape elected to expose Navigator's application programming interfaces (APIs), inviting software programmers to write programs to run on top of Navigator, which was subsequently referred to as a "middleware" program. With the growth of the Internet, Navigator was becoming a delivery mechanism for providing computer users easy Internet access to platform-neutral programs, whether written to Netscape's APIs or in the programming language Java.

This potential for generic operating systems was anathema to Microsoft, which had been highly successful in marketing its proprietary Windows product. Microsoft, the plaintiffs argued, was worried that users, by combining the features of both Netscape and Java, might eventually be able to access non-Windows-compatible programs over the Internet using any kind of computer running any kind of operating system. This would give software developers incentives to develop new operating systems, alternative middleware platforms, and new application programs that wouldn't have to be "Windows compatible," which would then free computer manufacturers from their dependence on Windows and bring Microsoft's domination of PC operating systems to an end. Microsoft thus saw more than just a competitive threat. It saw the possibility of an end to its dominance and its economic lifeline, and ultimately its obsolescence.

Microsoft advanced quite a different story. First, although Windows had no doubt been a success, that success was attributable to Microsoft's innovations and its responsiveness to consumer needs. Microsoft had earned a commanding position in the market because of its superior products. A focal point of this part of its story was Microsoft's defense of the integration of its IE browser into Windows. Microsoft steadfastly maintained that Windows was but a single integrated program and that Microsoft must remain free to serve consumers by adding "functionality" to Windows through "integration." Any effort to restrict its autonomy to develop Windows in response to consumer demand would harm consumers, not serve them.[47]

A second and related major theme of Microsoft's story was that the government plaintiffs' actions had been instigated by Microsoft's rivals and would help them, not consumers.[48] Microsoft correctly observed that the government plaintiffs had relied heavily on information provided by Netscape, Sun, and other firms in formulating their cases. But Microsoft inferred from this a kind of "capture": the government plaintiffs had been manipulated into acting to protect competitors, not competition. Microsoft repeated this theme—that the credibility of the government complaints was undermined by their reliance on the self-interested advocacy of Microsoft's rivals—throughout the course of the U.S. case, and later in Europe.

Third, Microsoft challenged the heart of the government plaintiffs' story by questioning causation—that is, the degree to which any of its conduct actually caused competition to be harmed. It argued, for example, that its actions never foreclosed Netscape from reaching end users, who remained free to download Netscape's browser directly over the Internet. Moreover, in its view, the competitive decline of Netscape was largely attributable to the failings of the product itself and the superiority of IE. In other words, Microsoft argued that it had defeated Netscape through legitimate competitive means, such as a superior product. It also questioned whether Netscape and Sun ever would have developed into a full-blown alternative to its operating system, even if Microsoft hadn't undertaken any conduct directed at forestalling that result.[49]

With these two competing stories shaping their arguments, the parties squared off on the more technical questions: By what conduct, and with what effect, had Microsoft allegedly sought to terminate this nascent competitive threat to a critical part of its business?

The Conduct

The Justice Department's complaint focused on the period from May 1995 to May 1998.[50] Although the complaint began with a broad argument that "new software products" could become "alternative 'platforms' to which applications can be written," and that such platforms might threaten Microsoft's control of the market by functioning across multiple operating systems, the complaint actually discussed only Internet browsers, and their ability to deliver the cross-platform Java programming language, as the potential competitive threat to Microsoft's monopoly in the market for operating systems.[51]

What did Microsoft do wrong? The complaint described six components of an anticompetitive campaign that Microsoft executives had characterized "as a 'jihad' to win the 'browser war'"[52]:

• The May 1995 meeting between Netscape and Microsoft in which, the complaint alleged, Microsoft had attempted to convince Netscape to "divide the browser market."[53] This was the meeting about which Netscape had complained to the Justice Department in 1995, a complaint that had produced no enforcement action at the time.
• Microsoft's decision to invest "hundreds of millions of dollars" to develop Internet Explorer, but to then distribute it "without separate charge."
• The agreements requiring OEMs to preinstall IE with Windows 95, the basis for the contempt motion then pending on appeal.[54]
• Microsoft's intention to tie IE to Windows 98 both technically and contractually by designing Windows 98 so that removal of IE would be "operationally more difficult" than it was with Windows 95 in addition to being contractually forbidden.[55]
• Microsoft's licensing agreements, which did not allow OEMs to modify the initial boot-up sequence or desktop, thereby restricting the ability of OEMs to offer a competing browser to their customers.
• Microsoft's agreements giving a variety of Internet access and content providers (including AOL, AT&T WorldNet, and Disney) various kinds of preferential treatment on the desktop or in the browser in return for their preferential or exclusive distribution and promotion of Internet Explorer.[56]

What was Microsoft's goal? Quoting a Microsoft vice president, the complaint alleged that Microsoft intended to "cut off [Netscape's] air supply."[57] Microsoft could still "breathe" by selling its operating system, but Netscape would suffocate because the only product it had to sell was its browser, which it couldn't charge for and which it could no longer distribute effectively. Microsoft's conduct, this "browser war," the Justice Department alleged, precluded "competition on the merits" between Internet Explorer and other browsers and precluded the emergence of competition with Microsoft's operating system. As a result, the Department of Justice argued, innovation would be hurt, for example, by creating a disincentive for Microsoft's competitors to engage in research and development because they would know that Microsoft could "limit the rewards from any resulting innovation."[58]

The Markets

Central to the plaintiffs' story was that Microsoft was a monopolist in the market for "Intel-compatible PC operating systems worldwide," of which it persistently enjoyed a share in excess of 90 percent. Microsoft vigorously argued against what it saw as a far too narrow market definition, in effect defined by its own product. In its view, the relevant market was far broader and more fluid, and included Apple's Macintosh operating system (Mac OS), as well as operating systems for newer devices, such as personal digital assistants and mobile telephones. The plaintiffs also contended that "Internet browsers" was a second, distinct market, an assertion that Microsoft denied and vigorously contested. As it had done in the 1995 consent decree contempt proceeding, Microsoft insisted that the browser was an integrated feature of the PC OS and that there was no distinct browser market.[59]

Perhaps more stunning was the contrast in portrayals of these various markets. For the governments' part, the PC OS market was portrayed as static, protected by significant entry barriers. Moreover, owing to Microsoft's durable position in that market, innovation was lacking. The result was that the PC OS market had become unresponsive to consumer demand and virtually impenetrable to direct challenge. Hence the only route for a challenger was an indirect one, such as developing a new platform from middleware (e.g., Netscape's Navigator along with Sun's Java programming language).

In contrast, Microsoft's principal economic expert sought to portray the software industry as dynamic and free of impediments to entry. He maintained that "[c]ompetition in the software industry is based on sequential races for the leadership of categories" of software, and that market leaders regularly are leapfrogged by new entrants with "killer applications." In such an industry, no firm can truly exercise market power except in the most fleeting sense. At best, Microsoft's dominance of the market for desktop-computer operating systems would prove to be transitory, unless its products were truly superior and remained so.[60]

The Efficacy of the Antitrust System

The parties also presented dueling views as to the efficacy of the antitrust system for policing competition in new economy industries. Microsoft and critics of the government plaintiffs' case persistently argued that the antitrust system was clumsy and slow, an outmoded tool for evaluating the economics of the "new economy" information age, and that the government plaintiffs' case would inhibit innovation and harm consumers. Microsoft's expert economist argued that the governments' experts misapplied traditional economic thinking to Microsoft because they "relied on textbook theories of competition that do not apply to, or explain the dynamics of, the microcomputer software industry."[61]

The government plaintiffs and their supporters responded that although Microsoft's products might be part of the "new economy," Microsoft's motives and conduct—and the consequences of its conduct—were all too familiar. To the extent that the economics of the software industry presented new conditions, the antitrust laws were adequate to deal with those conditions. Indeed, they helped to explain how Microsoft sought to exclude its rivals. As Joel Klein declared on the day the cases were originally filed:

[N]othing we are doing here will or should prevent Microsoft from innovating or competing on the merits. What cannot be tolerated—and what the antitrust laws forbid—is the barrage of illegal, anticompetitive practices that Microsoft uses to destroy its rivals and to avoid competition on the merits. That, and that alone, is what this lawsuit is all about.[62]

Judge Jackson's Effort to Accelerate the Trial

The federal case and the states' case were filed just as Microsoft was about to ship the code for Windows 98 to the OEMs and a month before its scheduled retail release. In both cases the plaintiffs sought a preliminary injunction to stop the distribution of Windows 98 until the case could be decided.[63]

The cases were assigned to Judge Thomas Penfield Jackson because he was handling the related consent decree and the related contempt proceeding. The plaintiffs anticipated a relatively quick hearing on the preliminary injunction, then perhaps another year of pretrial discovery in preparation for a full trial on the merits.[64] The Department of Justice and the states were still investigating other areas in which Microsoft might have been using similar exclusionary tactics, including streaming video technologies and Java distribution.[65] A preliminary injunction followed by a later trial would have allowed the Department of Justice and the states time to do three things that the pressure to file suit had made difficult: see whether there were even broader claims to be pursued, develop a better understanding of Microsoft's products and the industry, and decide what relief might be effective.

Apparently concerned that a full trial on the merits might devolve into years of "trench warfare" between the plaintiffs and Microsoft, Judge Jackson surprised all of the parties. Four days after the plaintiffs filed suit, Jackson, acting on his own motion and invoking a provision of the Federal Rules of Civil Procedure, consolidated the preliminary injunction hearing with the full trial on the merits and scheduled the trial and the hearing for September—only four months later.[66] Not only did this mean that the plaintiffs would have to prepare for a full trial on short notice; it also meant that there would be no immediate preliminary injunction. Windows 98 would be shipped with an installed and integrated Internet Explorer browser.

The failure to obtain a preliminary injunction turned out to be crucial. The Justice Department's brief supporting its motion for a preliminary injunction had argued that the wide distribution of IE with a new generation of "Windows 98 computers" threatened "irreversibly to 'tip' the market" in Microsoft's favor.[67] Although the market may have already been tipping as a result of Microsoft's previous conduct, the failure to stop shipment of Windows 98 integrated with IE actually spelled the end of any competitive threat that Netscape might have posed to the Windows' operating system. It ensured that IE would be the dominant Internet browser no matter what happened in the litigation. This meant that if the coming litigation were to have any effect beyond being a statement of legal principles, the plaintiffs would have to present a case involving more than just browser integration.

A Failed Mediation Effort

The Trial

For a complex antitrust case, the trial phase was conducted speedily. Testimony ended on June 24, 1999, thirteen months after the complaints were filed and eight months after the trial itself began. This relative speed was due in large part to two decisions that Judge Jackson made. One was to limit the number of witnesses the parties could present: twelve witnesses for each side, with the Justice Department and the states counted as one "side," plus three rebuttal or surrebuttal witnesses for each side. The other was to require the parties to present their witnesses' direct testimony in written form, which meant that live testimony would consist entirely of cross-examination.[68] Even with these limitations, the trial record was large—more than 13,000 pages of trial transcript and more than 1,000 admitted exhibits. Underscoring the trial's broad scope was the length of the proposed findings of fact and conclusions of law that the parties presented to Judge

Jackson—the plaintiffs' proposals ran to nearly 1,000 pages, and Microsoft's to nearly 800.[69]

As the length of the record indicates, the case that Jackson decided was not quite the case that the plaintiffs had described in their initial complaints. By the time the trial ended, the plaintiffs' case had expanded far beyond Microsoft's effort to suppress Netscape's browser. It now included Microsoft's efforts to suppress other competitive threats: Sun's Java technologies, Intel's Native Signaling Processing software and its technical assistance to Sun, Apple's QuickTime software for multimedia playback, RealNetworks' streaming media technologies, and IBM's competing operating system and competing office-productivity applications. Nevertheless, even though the examples of exclusionary conduct had expanded beyond those set out in the complaint, the basic monopolization theory of the original complaint was still in place—that is, that Microsoft sought to maintain its monopoly in operating systems by suppressing any competitive threat to Windows, whether the threat came from browsers or from any other potential platform program (now generically labeled "middleware"). And the basic focus remained on Microsoft's position in the market for operating systems for Intel-compatible PCs, excluding operating systems for servers, for personal digital assistants, or for other types of devices.

Judge Jackson heard final arguments in September of 1999 and issued 412 findings of fact on November 5 of that year. Normally a federal judge trying a case without a jury hands down findings of fact and conclusions of law together in a single opinion. In an extremely unusual (perhaps unprecedented) move, Jackson wrote that he would delay issuance of his conclusions of law, and that they would be delivered "in a separate Memorandum and Order" that would be filed "in due course."[70] His findings of fact, however, left little room for speculation about the likely outcome of the case—Jackson was going to rule in favor of the government plaintiffs.

Jackson's Surprise

Two weeks after issuing his findings of fact, Judge Jackson called the parties into his chambers for a conference. "There are several things I want to take up this afternoon," Jackson said, "one of which I think will come as something of a surprise to you. ... I have prevailed on Richard Posner, the Chief Judge of the Seventh Circuit, to function as a mediator to see whether or not he can get you all playing the same tune."[71]

A surprise, indeed. Commentators suggested that Jackson's decision to delay his conclusions of law would prompt the parties to settle (Jackson later acknowledged that this was his strategy, saying that both sides were "pretty arrogant" and needed to be forced to talk).[72] Still, no one predicted that Jackson would appoint a mediator to facilitate the process, let alone Judge Posner, a highly regarded antitrust authority whom Jackson had never met.[73]

In many ways the Posner appointment looked like a master stroke. Posner had the stature, the intellectual clout, and the ability to address both sides with authority. Although he was considered conservative in antitrust matters, his views had come to represent much of mainstream antitrust thinking, and he could give both Microsoft and the plaintiffs a glimpse into how an appellate court might react to Judge Jackson's findings. Having written extensively on antitrust issues, and having decided many antitrust cases, he was also well positioned to understand the problems of remedy, and to provide the parties a measure of judgment on what might be a sensible and administrable remedy if the case for violation was sound.

Jackson told the parties that the mediation would be "voluntary" and that he was "not going to order it." At the same time, however, he said that he thought it would be a "very useful thing to do." In light of the fact that Jackson had yet to hand down his conclusions of law, and the matter of remedy had yet to be broached, it was clear that neither side had any choice in the matter—unless, of course, they were willing to abandon hope of any favorable decisions from him in the future. Jackson had them boxed in.

The mediation posed some obvious problems. It would take time. Judge Posner would have to familiarize himself with the record and the details of the case, and the parties would need to present their views to him on both liability and remedy. There was a strong potential for institutional disagreement between the Justice Department and the states. Although the states and the Justice Department had collaborated well during the trial, the states had begun their investigation of Microsoft with a concern about the Justice Department's resolve, and had criticized the earlier federal settlements with Microsoft as ineffective. Indeed, one reason that Jackson gave for invoking the mediation process was that there had been "disturbing reports in the press" of disagreements between the Justice Department and the states.[74]

A settlement could also have significant institutional costs. A settlement would mean that there would be no judicial opinion deciding the legal principles applicable to the case. Such opinions are important for providing guidance as to what conduct is permissible. If the government was going to prevail, as seemed likely from the issued findings of fact, a settlement would also mean loss of the deterrent effect that a finding of liability could have. That would be costly for government enforcers, in view of the case's high visibility and the infrequency of government monopolization litigation.

In addition, a settlement might affect the ability of other parties to obtain relief from Microsoft. Proceedings were underway before the European Commission dealing with Microsoft's conduct involving the interoperability of servers with Windows on the desktop, soon to be followed by an investigation of Microsoft's bundling of its media player into Windows. The terms of any settlement might well affect the European Commission's choice of remedies, perhaps leading it to impose more substantial remedies than the United States or perhaps encouraging it to follow the United States' lead. Private actions for damages might also be affected. Such suits had already been filed in the United States, and more seemed likely to follow in light of Jackson's positive findings of fact and his expected conclusions of law. A settlement would mean that Jackson would never enter his conclusions of law—and might even withdraw his findings of fact, if an agreement so provided—with the result that much, or all, of the preclusive effect of Jackson's findings might be lost.[75] To the extent that the government plaintiffs viewed such complementary litigation as an important component of antitrust enforcement, a settlement would be another public benefit lost.

None of these factors necessarily doomed the mediation. Although the mediation would take time, if successful it would avoid a litigated remedy phase and lengthy appeals. The plaintiffs could benefit from a settlement that went into effect immediately, dealing with the competition problems now rather than at some time in the distant future. More importantly, a presidential election was only a year away, and a settlement would remove the opportunity for a new administration's Justice Department to alter the outcome of the litigation. Microsoft, too, might benefit from ending the litigation. The trial had closed with Windows 98, but new versions of Windows were under development and the industry was moving toward greater reliance on servers and networks. At this point, Microsoft had a strong claim to keep the focus on Web browsers and Windows, minimizing the impact of a loss, but a litigated remedy proceeding might bring out additional issues that warranted a broader approach.

Nor were the institutional issues insoluble. In the past, the Justice Department had settled major antitrust cases against dominant firms long into a trial, the 1984 settlement of the AT&T monopolization case being a prime example. Moreover, denying private plaintiffs the preclusive effects of a trial court's findings of fact is a familiar effect of government settlements and generally gives defendants an incentive to settle. Nor would a settlement necessarily hurt the European Commission's case. For example, even after the Justice Department dismissed its monopolization case against IBM in 1982, the European Commission had continued its investigation, and

IBM had agreed to disclose certain interoperability information to its competitors despite the Justice Department's objections to that remedy.[76]

Finally, differences between the Justice Department and the states wouldn't necessarily derail a settlement. Judge Jackson would have to approve any settlement between the Justice Department and Microsoft as being in the "public interest." Once Jackson did that, how likely would it be that the states would convince Jackson that a different remedy was necessary, particularly since he had already indicated his unhappiness with the states' pursuing their own approach?

Thus, despite the unusual difficulties the mediation process faced, a mediated settlement had attractions for all parties. Most important, if Microsoft was serious and the Department of Justice was at least somewhat accommodating, a mediated settlement was possible no matter what the states threatened.

The Mediation Process

Judge Posner wasted no time taking charge of the mediation process, promptly establishing a schedule of weekly meetings—one day with the plaintiffs, the next day with Microsoft—for broad and fact-intensive presentations on liability issues and remedial options.[77] Although the government plaintiffs were well prepared to discuss the liability issues that were the initial focus of the mediation meetings, they were less prepared to engage in discussions about possible remedies for Microsoft's conduct. Having focused almost exclusively on liability for almost two years, they had devoted considerably less time and resources to the thorny question of remedies, and they had yet to decide collectively what remedy they would seek from Judge Jackson, let alone what they would deem acceptable as part of a negotiated settlement with Microsoft.[78]

On January 10, 2000—nearly three months after the mediation began—the Justice Department presented Judge Posner with a fairly well-developed remedy proposal.[79] The Department's proposal rejected conduct remedies, such as disclosure of information (APIs or source code) or restrictions on Microsoft's business practices. Information disclosure, the Justice Department argued, presented difficult problems of definition and timing, and restricting business practices would require ongoing supervision and enforcement. The better solution was a structural one: Microsoft should be broken up.

The Justice Department proposed that Microsoft be split into three separate companies.[80] One would have the soon-to-be-introduced Windows 2000 desktop and server operating systems, one would have the code from

Windows 98 and its successor (Millennium, also known as the "9x code"), and one would have Microsoft's applications software, including Office. All three also would have the rights to Internet Explorer.

The theory behind the proposal was that the "9x company" would provide immediate competition in the market for operating systems for the latest version of Windows. It could be spun off quickly, because it had established development teams; it would provide a product that would be attractive to PC users; and it might go on to develop a new product based on the 9x code (something that Microsoft wasn't planning to do). The applications company, it was argued, might also increase competition in the market for operating systems. No longer interested in maintaining Microsoft's Windows monopoly, the new company might have the incentive to "port" Office (that is, to develop versions of it that would work with competing, non-Microsoft operating systems, such as Linux), or perhaps to develop its own operating system.

Whatever the merits of the Justice Department's proposal, it was an unlikely candidate for a negotiated settlement. And when reports of the proposal appeared in the press, Microsoft issued an immediate and strong public rejection.[81] However, the mediation effort continued, Judge Posner meeting separately with the government plaintiffs and with Microsoft. Posner also engaged in direct discussions with Bill Gates in an effort to learn whether a structural settlement was possible.

Posner soon became convinced that a structural remedy wasn't an attainable goal for the mediation. Not only were there substantive questions about the proposed remedy, but Microsoft's incentive to accept a structural resolution depended in part on predicting what Judge Jackson might do if there were no settlement. At that point, the betting was that Jackson wouldn't order structural relief and that the court of appeals wasn't likely to uphold a breakup even if Jackson ordered it. Why would Microsoft agree to a breakup in the mediation?

With structural relief off the negotiating table and predicted to be out of the case once it returned to the district court, Posner sought to guide the parties toward a settlement based on conduct remedies. Over the course of nearly two months, he produced a series of increasingly detailed proposed consent decrees, taking comments from the parties (at first from the Justice Department and Microsoft, and later from the states too) and deciding which changes to include in subsequent drafts.[82] Posner participated actively in this process, attempting to develop a draft decree that would be acceptable to the parties and would be judicially administrable. This was a delicate and complex process, requiring intensive efforts to persuade each side to move toward a position that would be acceptable to the other. During this entire time, however, Posner acted as an intermediary—he never asked the parties to meet face to face.[83]

One sticking point in the negotiations involved the disclosure of information that would allow competing middleware to interoperate with the Windows operating system. Although the failure to disclose interoperability information had played almost no part in the litigation, there were persistent concerns about Microsoft's ability to manipulate this information to disadvantage competing middleware rivals, and about its ability to discourage the growth of cross-platform middleware that might result in a challenge to Microsoft's dominant position in the market for operating systems. Early drafts concentrated on requiring disclosure of the APIs that enabled Microsoft middleware to run on Microsoft operating systems, but "operating systems" applied only to the PC and "middleware" was confined to programs that exposed "commercially significant APIs" to provide a platform for applications without specifying what level of exposure would be "significant." Later drafts sought to clarify to what type of middleware the requirement would apply.

The drafts also tried to deal with the industry's movement toward greater use of server-PC networks, even though this issue hadn't been addressed in the litigation. Here the effort was to require some disclosure of protocols (the rules that enable desktop computers to interoperate with servers). Such disclosure would help to ensure that competing operating systems for servers, or middleware interoperating with servers, wouldn't be at a competitive disadvantage when those servers linked to PCs running the Windows operating system.[84]

Another sticking point involved bundling—one of the principal issues that had triggered the case against Microsoft in the first place, and one that had proved difficult to resolve in the 1994 Consent Decree. A settlement that failed to resolve the tension between "tying" and "integration" would leave an important concern about Microsoft's business strategy unaddressed and would certainly be considered a failure.

Early drafts provided for a "Technical Committee" to determine whether Microsoft's bundling of "end-user middleware" into its operating system lacked "technological justification." If the "Technical Committee" were to reach that finding, it could fairly be viewed as anticompetitive tying, and Microsoft would be required to offer a "variant version" without the middleware, or with end users' access disabled. Licensing fees for the variant version would be reduced to ensure that it would be a competitive alternative.[85]

The approach of the early drafts exhibited all the problems that had plagued the bundling issue from the beginning. Was any technological justification enough, no matter the anticompetitive effect and no matter how slight the technical advantage? Would removal of end users' access solve the competition problem? Even if end users couldn't access Microsoft's middleware, independent software vendors could still write to Microsoft's middleware APIs, rather than to APIs from competing middleware, and thus the applications barrier to entry would be maintained. And the creation of a "Technical Committee" added new problems. Who would serve on the committee? Would its decisions be reviewable and, if so, by whom and under what standard of review?

A different and perhaps more promising approach, based on a Microsoft proposal, was advanced near the end of the mediation process. Instead of offering a "variant version" with hidden middleware, Microsoft would license its Windows source code to the highest-volume OEMs. The license would be granted only for the purposes of allowing OEMs to disable end-user access to Microsoft middleware and allowing OEMs to "facilitat[e], improv[e], or otherwise optimiz[e]" the interoperation of non-Microsoft middleware with the operating system. Although this proposal included many restrictions, it would have required Microsoft to provide some technical support to the OEMs, and it might have resulted in the OEMs' working with software companies to produce somewhat different versions of the Windows operating system.[86] The proposal also eliminated the cumbersome "Technical Committee." Whether the proposal would be attractive to any OEMs, however, wasn't certain.

Final Efforts

The provision for the licensing of source code was advanced in a draft agreement that Judge Posner circulated on March 24, 2000. On March 26, in an effort to move the parties to settlement, Posner set a final timetable for the mediation process, with specific deadlines for the exchange of any edits by the Justice Department and Microsoft to the March 24 proposal.[87] If an agreement wasn't reached by April 5, Posner warned, he would advise Judge Jackson that he was terminating the mediation.

But what about the states, whose potentially separate position had concerned Judge Jackson when he set up the mediation process? Posner's schedule stated that drafts and memoranda transmitted to the Justice Department were to be transmitted to the states as well—subject to "appropriate measures to insure confidentiality," reflecting a concern about press leaks from the states—and the states were to endeavor to work with the Justice Department to achieve a common position. Although Posner's timetable didn't provide for separate responses by the states to the drafts, it did acknowledge the possibility that only some of the government plaintiffs might reach an agreement with Microsoft by his April 5 deadline. Were that to happen, Posner wrote, he would extend the mediation by an additional week to convince the "nonagreeing party or parties" to join the agreement.

The final timetable well illustrated how the states were marginalized throughout the mediation process, without apparent objection from the Justice Department or Microsoft. Although formally included in the process, the states had been kept at a distance substantively. Drafts had been exchanged mostly between Posner and the Justice Department and between Posner and Microsoft. The states' reactions to these drafts weren't sought until later in the process, and the states' expressed differences with the Justice Department's views were not well received by Judge Posner. As a result, the states' substantive concerns had little influence on the development of the proposed decree.[88]

This approach seemed to be at odds with an underlying assumption of the mediation process: that a settlement negotiation should include all the parties. Certainly the Justice Department preferred having all the states agree to any settlement, thereby thwarting active criticism from its erstwhile partners that the settlement was too weak.[89] Microsoft, too, preferred settling with all the parties rather than settling only with the Justice Department and continuing to litigate with some or all of the states—defendants are always looking for "global peace." In addition, only through a global settlement could Microsoft secure the advantage of one of its conditions for settlement: having Judge Jackson vacate his findings of fact.[90] Microsoft assumed that private plaintiffs would then be unable to use Jackson's findings of fact offensively against Microsoft in any subsequent private suits for money damages. If some of the plaintiffs didn't settle, however, Jackson's findings of fact would become final and would be followed by his conclusions of law, which everyone assumed would conclude that Microsoft had violated federal antitrust laws. This could hurt Microsoft in subsequent private litigation.

In fact, however, the Justice Department and Microsoft were perfectly free to settle without the states—or with only some of them—and to force the remaining states to continue the litigation without the Justice Department's resources. The mediation showed how under-resourced the states were. At best, the states had sufficient resources to add to the Justice Department's efforts, but they didn't have enough resources to supplant those efforts. If the Justice Department was at a technical disadvantage in the mediation relative to Microsoft, the states were even more so.

There was one thing that the states could be counted on doing, however: They probably would object to settlement terms that they viewed as too weak. The states had consistently taken an aggressive position toward Microsoft and would probably continue to do so during the remedies phase of the litigation. Thus, keeping the states on the periphery during the mediation negotiations, while emphasizing the need to have all the parties go along with an agreement, had the potential to magnify the states' power. Not only would it increase the chances that they would object (because they wouldn't be invested in the drafts that were being developed); it also would make it appear that they could veto any proposed agreement that they didn't like. The Department of Justice and Microsoft would still be free to settle if they really wanted to; but if they didn't want to settle, the states would probably have publicly disagreed with the compromises any settlement proposal would necessarily entail. The states would then take the blame for the mediation's failure.

Whether this was a consciously pursued strategy or not, it was how the mediation played out. The Justice Department followed Judge Posner's timetable, submitting its proposal on March 28 and providing the states with copies the next day. On March 31 the states submitted to Posner critical comments on the Justice Department's draft and added three major relief proposals: to expand the types of middleware to which API disclosure would apply, to require Microsoft to port Office to the two operating systems whose market shares "are closest to Microsoft's" (this would have included Linux), and to appoint a Special Master to oversee the decree, with a third-year review in which the Special Master could propose additional remedies, including the divestiture of the Windows operating system.[91]

The states submitted their comments to Judge Posner at 8:30 p.m. Central Standard Time. Three hours later Posner told the states that he regarded the mediation as over. In Posner's view it was obvious that Microsoft wouldn't accept the states' proposals, particularly because of the porting requirement and the proposed scope of required API disclosure. Believing that the states' proposals were sufficiently extreme so as not to be a serious settlement offer, Posner said he wouldn't submit them to Microsoft for its review, because that would improperly place the onus of rejecting them on Microsoft.[92]

Judge Posner made a formal announcement of the end of the mediation the next day, issuing a statement that a settlement would have been in the national interest and expressing his disappointment that after four months the disagreements among the parties were "too deep-seated to be bridged."[93] He praised the efforts of the Justice Department and Microsoft— "I particularly want to emphasize that the collapse of the mediation is not due to any lack of skill, flexibility, energy, determination, or professionalism on the part of the Department of Justice and Microsoft Corporation"— but pointedly did not mention the states.

Did Posner act precipitously in terminating the mediation process when he did? Microsoft's response to the Justice Department's March 28 proposal was yet to be seen, and Posner's own timetable provided an additional twelve days during which any non-agreeing parties might have been persuaded to join an agreement had the Justice Department and Microsoft reached one. Indeed, by that time the parties might have felt that a settlement without the states was nearly as good as one with them and far preferable to no settlement at all.

Whether or not the mediation might ultimately have produced an agreement, blaming the states for its failure assigned more blame (or credit) to them than they were due.[94] As we will see in chapter 4, Microsoft and the Department of Justice eventually did reach a settlement in which some but not all of the states joined. If Microsoft and the Justice Department had wanted to reach a separate settlement during the mediation with Judge Posner in 2000, they could have done so and they could have communicated their willingness to do so to Judge Posner. Perhaps the Justice Department privately preferred to return to the district court, and perhaps Microsoft had made global peace a non-negotiable demand. In any event, Judge Posner abandoned the effort rather than continue to pursue a global or a partial resolution of the claims made by the federal and state governments.

Rendering Judgment

Two days after the mediation ended, Judge Jackson handed down his "conclusions of law." As was expected in view of his findings of fact, Jackson concluded that Microsoft had violated both Section 1 and Section 2 of the Sherman Act.

Monopoly Power

To decide whether Microsoft had violated Section 2 of the Sherman Act, the district court first had to conclude that Microsoft had monopoly power in a defined, relevant market. Judge Jackson's approach to this issue was a straightforward application of familiar antitrust principles.

First, Jackson defined the narrowest realistic market—that for Intel-compatible PC operating systems—on the basis of his findings that there were "no products" to which a significant number of users of Intel PCs could switch to satisfy operating-system functions "without incurring substantial costs" and that no producer was likely to provide a "viable alternative" product "within a reasonably short period of time."[95]

Second, Jackson found that Microsoft had monopoly power in this market. Monopoly power is usually inferred from the structure of the market. Jackson found that Microsoft had a "dominant, persistent, and increasing share of the world-wide market" (more than 90 percent for "the last decade"), and that its share was predicted to climb "even higher over the next few years."[96] That share comfortably exceeded the historic benchmarks used by the courts to infer monopoly power.

Monopoly power also requires the existence of barriers to entry into the monopolized market. The entry barrier here was the existence of software applications programs that ran on Windows, dubbed the "applications barrier to entry." Jackson explained the problem this way[97]: Consumers purchase operating systems in order to be able to run applications programs on their computers. The more applications that run on any given operating system, the more valuable that operating system will be to consumers, and, therefore, the more willing consumers will be to purchase that particular operating system. This is an example of what economists call an "indirect network effect."[98] Independent software vendors (ISVs) have economic incentives to write software that is compatible with the most popular operating system. Perhaps they will later write software for other systems; but perhaps they won't, because "porting" an applications program from one system to another is costly. As ISVs write more software for a particular operating system, consumer demand for that system will then increase, which will lead to the writing of more software for that operating system, which will lead to more demand for that product, and so on—a positive feedback loop, or, as Jackson called it, "the chicken-and-egg problem."

Microsoft's Windows had the most users and the largest number of applications (more than 70,000) of all operating systems for desktop computers. This made it extremely unlikely that a new entrant could break into the market for operating systems—in view of the pre-existing base of applications, consumers wouldn't be likely to desert Windows for a new operating system. After all, how many programs compatible with a new operating system would consumers expect to be offered, either now or in the future? Nor would ISVs be likely to write programs compatible with a new system that lacked an established or a likely base of users. Why would ISVs invest in writing software for a new system that consumers might not adopt? Thus, the network effects, which brought benefits both to consumers and to ISVs, also acted to repel new entry into the market for operating systems.

Jackson backed up the theoretical arguments for monopoly power and barriers to entry with evidence relating to actual marketplace conditions.[99] The evidence showed that OEMs were "uniformly" of a mind that there was no alternative operating system to which they could switch in response to a price increase by Microsoft, and that OEMs believed that the likelihood of a viable alternative in the near future was "too low to constrain" Microsoft's economic power. Neither firms that had tried to compete in the market for operating systems nor firms that were currently competing in that market had been successful. IBM had invested "tens of millions of dollars" to attract ISVs to write software for its Intel-compatible operating system, OS/2, but could attract only 2500 applications "at its peak" and eventually withdrew from the market for operating systems because it couldn't compete effectively with Microsoft. Apple, which supported 12,000 applications, had been unable to present "a significant percentage of users with a viable substitute for Windows." Nor were "fringe operating systems" (such as Linux, an open-source operating system developed by volunteer programmers) able to attract enough applications programs to have much of a competitive impact in the market.[100]

Jackson's findings also rejected Microsoft's argument that constant innovation in the software industry meant that any "category leadership" would be short-lived, perhaps taking place in cycles of two to four years, so that Microsoft couldn't really have any durable monopoly power.[101] Even though the "exponential growth of the Internet" had fueled the growth of server-based computing, middleware, and open-source software, Jackson found that "the fact that these new paradigms already exist in embryonic or primitive form does not prevent Microsoft from enjoying monopoly power today." Consumers weren't turning to these alternatives, nor were they likely to do so at "any time in the next few years." Until they did, Microsoft could set its prices "substantially higher" than it would in a competitive marketplace and then either lower them "in time to meet the threat of a new paradigm" or "delay" the arrival of that new paradigm by "expending surplus monopoly power" in ways that would maintain its monopoly position.[102]

Jackson concluded that Microsoft's market share, the "applications barrier to entry," and the lack of any meaningful competition over a substantial time period established that Microsoft had monopoly power. Still, Microsoft argued that the evidence didn't show that Microsoft had actually behaved like a monopolist, because it hadn't charged "substantially higher" prices for Windows and it continued to innovate. Jackson again rejected Microsoft's position. Finding that it was "not possible with the available data" to say what the monopoly price of Windows might be, Jackson wrote that even if one assumed that Microsoft priced its product below the monopoly price, that would "not be probative of a lack of monopoly power." Network effects would give Microsoft an incentive to set a sufficiently low price to attract more users to its product which would increase the size of the network, thereby "intensify[ing] the positive network effects that add to the impenetrability of the applications barrier to entry." The same would be true with innovation: Microsoft would have an incentive "to innovate aggressively despite monopoly power" because this might "thwart" or "delay" those "potential paradigm shifts."[103]

There is some tension between Jackson's findings on monopoly power and his approach to Microsoft's actual pricing and innovation. On the one hand, Jackson used conventional antitrust analysis to make the seemingly obvious point: that Microsoft was a monopolist, with no significant competition in sight. On the other hand, Jackson acknowledged that Microsoft, as a monopolist in a network industry facing at least nascent threats from new products, might still act in ways that would take account of the potential for competition in the future. Microsoft had incentives to maintain the ubiquity of its operating system and to maintain consumers' willingness to purchase Intel-compatible PCs rather than deserting those PCs for different kinds of computers that might use different operating systems. These incentives led Microsoft to price its product below the monopoly price (somewhat) and to innovate (to some extent). These conclusions would seem to indicate that Microsoft faced at least some competitive pressures and that it reacted to them.

In the end, however, the notion that Microsoft was, in effect, a monopolist without monopoly power was simply too unlikely to accept. Judge Jackson resolved the tension by deciding that Microsoft's arguments weren't sufficient to rebut the plaintiffs' proof of monopoly power—a conclusion he buttressed by pointing to numerous examples of exclusionary conduct that he thought could only be viewed as consistent with the behavior of a monopolist intent on erecting and preserving barriers to entry into its market.[104]

Exclusionary Conduct

As we explained in chapter 1, the second inquiry in a monopolization case focuses on conduct: Has the monopolist maintained its monopoly power in some improper way? Has it engaged in exclusionary or predatory behavior, or, instead, could its conduct be viewed as procompetitive, in the sense that the conduct was industrious, efficient, or supported by legitimate business justifications?

For Microsoft, the central claim of exclusionary conduct involved its comprehensive response to the emergence of Netscape's Internet browser. And that response involved Microsoft's technological and contractual efforts to integrate its Internet Explorer browser into the Windows operating system, as well as a range of additional, supporting conduct.

At the trial, the plaintiffs, consistent with their complaints, attacked the bundling of Windows and IE on two legal grounds: as monopolization under Section 2 of the Sherman Act and as a restraint of trade under Section 1. As we saw in chapter 2, Judge Jackson had previously held that the bundling violated the consent decree entered in the Justice Department's 1994 licensing case against Microsoft. The consent decree had forbidden Microsoft from conditioning a license for one product on taking a license for another—an "anti-tying provision"—but didn't forbid Microsoft from offering "integrated" products. The court of appeals, in an opinion subsequently referred to as *Microsoft II*, had reversed Jackson, but the court's decision was not technically controlling on the plaintiffs' antitrust claims, because, as we noted in chapter 2, the court of appeals' analysis focused on applying principles of contract interpretation to ascertain the intentions of the parties in arriving at the language of the 1994 Consent Decree. Still, the court of appeals had provided some "guidance" to Jackson on how to interpret the consent decree's distinction between separate and hence "tied" products, on the one hand, and "integrated" products, on the other, in the event of further proceedings under the decree. That guidance had taken a deferential view of design decisions that offered a "plausible claim" of "some advantage," leading the court of appeals to indicate that it was "inclined" to view the Windows 95/IE package as a "genuine integration."[105]

Microsoft II therefore appeared to support a finding that the combination of IE and Windows 98 was lawful—which is why Microsoft began its proposed conclusions of law by quoting from that opinion, whereas the plaintiffs didn't discuss the case until nearly the end of theirs.[106] But Jackson decided not to follow the court of appeals' approach. Factually, he viewed IE and Windows as separate products. Legally, he was unwilling to defer to Microsoft's design decisions simply on the showing of *some* benefit to consumers from the integration.

On the factual issues, Jackson pointed out that not only was there demand from a "substantial percentage" of corporate customers for

Windows without any browser, but the decision to "bind" Internet Explorer to Windows (as Microsoft's own documents put it) was taken for an anticompetitive purpose: "to prevent Navigator from weakening the applications barrier to entry." In Windows 95, Microsoft imposed integration through contract by forbidding the OEMs from removing IE, then technically integrated the two programs by commingling code "specific to Web browsing in the same files as code that provided operating system functions." Microsoft's "primary motivation" for this technical integration, Jackson found, "was to ensure that the deletion of any file containing browsing-specific routines would also delete vital operating system routines and thus cripple Windows 95."[107] Windows 98 bound IE even more tightly to the operating system. Microsoft chose not to provide users with an Add/Remove utility that would enable users to "remove" IE, although, as we saw in chapter 2, this utility merely masked IE's functionality and didn't actually remove most of its code. Even when a user chose a different default browser, Windows would override that choice in certain circumstances and launch IE, providing, in Microsoft's own words, "a jolting experience."[108]

Jackson concluded that "no technical reason" justified Microsoft's refusal to license Windows 95 without IE, or its refusal to allow the OEMs to uninstall IE in Windows 98, or its refusal to meet consumer demand for a browserless Windows 98, when "it remains possible" for browsing functionality to be removed without adversely affecting applications running on Windows 98.[109] Jackson pointed out that "[a]s an abstract and general proposition, many—if not most—consumers can be said to benefit from Microsoft's provision of Web browsing functionality with its Windows operating system at no additional charge." Nevertheless, there was "[n]o consumer benefit" to Microsoft's "refusal to offer a version of Windows 95 or Windows 98 without Internet Explorer, or to Microsoft's refusal to provide a method for uninstalling Internet Explorer from Windows 98."[110] Thus, the focus of the court's concern wasn't merely on the fact of Microsoft's tying of IE to Windows, but on the manner in which it did so. Therefore, the fact that "integration" was of some benefit to consumers wasn't dispositive; Microsoft's inability to offer any justification for making IE unremovable underscored the conclusion that its actions were fairly characterized as "tying."

Jackson's departure from the approach of the court of appeals was even clearer when it came to the legal issues, for he flatly rejected the standard that the court of appeals proposed in *Microsoft II* for interpreting the consent decree in deciding the Section 1 tying claim. Calling the court of appeals' approach an "undemanding test" that "appears to immunize" software product designs from antitrust liability, Jackson criticized the appellate court for departing from Supreme Court precedent by not considering the products from the viewpoint of consumer demand and for refusing to balance hypothetical advantages against real anticompetitive effects. Hewing instead to his reading of Supreme Court precedent in the tying area, Jackson proceeded with the analysis that those cases require: (1) the existence of two separate products (consumer demand and industry practice so indicated), (2) the possession of "appreciable economic power" in the market for the tying product sufficient to compel the tie (Microsoft's monopoly position in the market for operating systems surely qualified), (3) a forced purchase of the tied product (consumers couldn't avoid taking IE), and (4) a "not insubstantial" amount of commerce foreclosed (inferred from Netscape's loss of usage share rather than direct proof of lost dollar revenues).[111] Thus, rather than decide the tying claim in the shadow of the court of appeals, Jackson chose the shadow of the Supreme Court: "To the extent that the Supreme Court has spoken authoritatively on these issues, however, this Court is bound to follow its guidance and is not at liberty to extrapolate a new rule governing the tying of software products."[112]

The legality of bundling Windows and IE was relevant both to the plaintiffs' Section 1 restraint of trade case and to their Section 2 monopolization case. In deciding the monopolization case, Jackson viewed the illegal bundling as but one example of Microsoft's effort to exclude Netscape from the distribution channels for browser software—particularly from the most efficient channels, the OEMs and the Internet access providers. This effort to suppress Netscape's threat to the "applications barrier to entry" also included the following:

• the June 1995 meetings between Microsoft and Netscape at which Microsoft tried to keep Netscape from developing a platform-level browser
• restrictions on the boot-up process that prevented OEMs from removing the IE icon from the Windows desktop or from giving users an opportunity to choose a different default browser
• a variety of exclusive or nearly exclusive arrangements with companies that provided Internet access or content (most importantly, an agreement that AOL would use IE to the near-total exclusion of Netscape)
• Apple's agreement to bundle IE with the Macintosh operating system and make IE the default browser, an agreement obtained after Microsoft threatened to cancel development of a new version of Microsoft Office for the Macintosh

• various inducements to software developers and Internet content providers to develop or use IE, such as direct payments or the provision of free software to configure IE-compatible websites
• lower royalty rates for those OEMs loyal to Microsoft's efforts to increase IE's browser share (such as Compaq) and higher royalty rates to those that weren't (such as Gateway)
• the decision to set IE's price at zero by providing it with Windows at no additional cost.

The difficulty with Jackson's approach to the Section 2 claim, however, is that if one looks at each of the acts separately, rather than as part of a pattern, some can be viewed as arguably procompetitive responses to Netscape's challenge. Particularly susceptible to this characterization were acts that resulted in lower prices (for example, the willingness to make IE "free" and various payments to software and website developers) and agreements to grant valuable concessions to certain companies without charge (for example, placing AOL's icon on the desktop). Thus, to some extent, Microsoft bought buyers' loyalty by offering good deals, which would seem to be more fairly characterized as "competitive" conduct than as "anticompetitive" conduct.

Jackson found that these price cuts and concessions were quite costly. From 1995 through 1999, Microsoft spent $100 million each year developing IE and $30 million each year promoting it.[113] Jackson pointed out that, even without an interest in excluding Netscape, Microsoft might very well have decided to give IE away—in 1994, IBM had announced that it was going to include free Web browsing capability in its operating system. But Microsoft went substantially beyond what might be thought of as normal competitive behavior. Microsoft "paid huge sums of money, and sacrificed many millions more in lost revenue every year."[114] This investment, Jackson found, was potentially profitable only because it protected the applications barrier to entry: "Neither the desire to bolster demand for Windows, nor the prospect of ancillary revenues, explains the lengths to which Microsoft has gone."[115] Perhaps consumers benefited in the short run, Jackson implied, but not in the long run.

Jackson saw a similar pattern when he examined Microsoft's efforts to undermine Sun's Java technologies, which Netscape's browser helped to distribute. Sun's idea was that these technologies would provide applications writers with an operating-system-neutral middleware platform to which they could write applications that would work with any operating system—"write once, run anywhere" was Sun's advertised goal.[116]

Microsoft had agreed to distribute Sun's Java technologies, but Jackson found Microsoft's incentives to be fundamentally at odds with Sun's approach. Microsoft wanted to make porting to other platforms more difficult, not easier, and to that end it developed a "polluted" form of Java that it used to deceive software developers. Acting under its agreement with Sun, Microsoft developed its own Java development tools and its own Windows-compatible "Java Virtual Machine," which translated Java code into code that could work with the underlying operating system. On the one hand, Microsoft's tools and JVM were easier for developers to use than Sun's development tools, and they allowed Java programs to run faster on Windows. On the other hand, Microsoft's implementations also meant that Java program developers using Microsoft's tools would unknowingly create applications that wouldn't be compatible with other JVMs and might not be portable, and developers using Sun's methods would produce programs that wouldn't run on Microsoft's JVM.[117]

Jackson found that Microsoft had created this incompatibility with non-Windows implementations intentionally. Worse, Microsoft hadn't informed developers that their use of Microsoft tools would undercut Java's unique cross-platform character and hadn't given developers a choice between faster operation on Windows and portability to other operating systems (something it "easily" could have done by including Sun's methods in its developer tools).[118]

Microsoft also sought wide distribution of its JVM, making a "large investment" in its development, bundling it into IE, offering it free to software developers, and giving developers "costly" technical information and "other blandishments"—all to ensure that developers would produce Java implementations that would rely on Microsoft's Windows-specific technologies rather than on Sun's.[119] As with its decision to provide IE without additional charge, Microsoft might have engaged in some of this conduct even without a commitment to protect the applications barrier to entry, but Microsoft went further in an effort to undermine Java's cross-platform qualities, even attempting to pressure other important technology developers (particularly Intel) not to develop Java-compatible products.[120]

Thus, Microsoft's conduct with regard to Java was another example of its broader anticompetitive effort to maintain its monopoly. Microsoft had "expended wealth and foresworn opportunities" in a way that could be explained only by its expectation that perpetuating the applications barrier to entry would block rivals from entering the market for operating systems for Intel-compatible PCs. Microsoft's conduct was not legitimately competitive, Jackson concluded. It was "predacious."[121]

Consumer Harm

Proof of predatory or exclusionary conduct, done to establish or maintain a monopoly, is sufficient to prove a violation of Section 2. Government plaintiffs seeking equitable relief rather than monetary damages need not prove the extent to which consumers were actually harmed by the conduct. The Sherman Act's legislative judgment is that the harm done to the competitive process by exclusionary conduct—not the harm done to specific competitors—will end up hurting consumers.

Microsoft, however, had consistently argued that there was no proof of harm to consumers. Not only had consumers benefited from Microsoft's efforts, particularly with regard to Internet browsers; the alleged exclusion of Netscape and Java hadn't caused harm, because neither was a real and current threat to Microsoft's position in the market for operating systems. "Predacious" though the conduct might have been, there was no causal link between the exclusionary conduct and Microsoft's continued monopoly position.

Jackson didn't ignore the general gist of Microsoft's consumer-injury or causation arguments.[122] He conceded that Microsoft's introduction of IE at no separate charge benefited consumers by increasing their familiarity with the Internet, reducing their costs, and providing Netscape with an incentive to improve Navigator. Jackson also found that there was insufficient evidence to conclude that either Navigator or Java would have "ignited genuine competition" in the market for operating systems, even in the absence of exclusionary conduct on Microsoft's part. Nevertheless, Jackson found that consumers were harmed in concrete ways. Consumers who wanted browserless operating systems couldn't get them from Microsoft; OEMs that wanted to simplify the boot-up process for their customers were unable do so because of restrictions placed on them by Microsoft; consumers who preferred Navigator were forced either to pay some "substantial price" (acquisition by downloading, degraded system performance, and diminished memory capacity) or to forgo Navigator and stick with IE.

Even more importantly, albeit more speculatively, the court concluded that Microsoft's conduct had an adverse effect on innovation. Even if Navigator and Java might not have become effective competitors to Windows, Microsoft's efforts "hobbled a form of innovation" that would have "conduced to consumer choice" and would have brought about more competition and more innovation. Microsoft's efforts—directed at firms such as Netscape, IBM, Compaq, Apple, and Intel—ultimately conveyed an unambiguous and bold message to any potential innovator in the software industry or the computer industry that Microsoft would use its "prodigious market power and immense profits to harm any firm that insists on [competing] against one of [its] core products." Microsoft had "trammeled the competitive process through which the computer industry generally stimulates innovation" with the result that some innovations "never occur for the sole reason that they do not coincide with Microsoft's self-interest." Microsoft's actions warranted liability under the Sherman Act.

Conclusion

Jackson's decision was a sweeping victory for the government plaintiffs. Although he didn't accept every claim they made, he accepted both the central monopoly maintenance theory under Section 2 and the argument that bundling the browser and the operating system was a violation of Section 1.[123] The question now was how much of his decision would survive appellate review, a question that even Judge Jackson openly raised.[124]

4 Concluding the Windows 95/98 Case: Appeal and Settlement

As was often the case in the *Microsoft* litigation, time was pressing. It was June 7, 2000, more than two years since the litigation was filed. Judge Thomas Penfield Jackson had just entered his final judgment, granting the plaintiffs the remedy they had requested and ordering that Microsoft be broken up.[1] Microsoft would certainly appeal to the U.S. Court of Appeals for the District of Columbia Circuit. That appeal, likely to be followed by an effort to seek review in the U.S. Supreme Court, would further prolong the litigation and defer the implementation of any final remedy for Microsoft's violations of the Sherman Act.

Acutely aware of the potential consequences of further delay in implementing relief in a high-technology industry, the plaintiffs were eager to speed the case along. Microsoft, on the other hand, was just as eager to slow things down.

Adding to the familiar time concern was the uncertainty over the upcoming presidential election, then only five months away. By the time the appeal could be argued, there would be a new administration, whether Republican or Democratic, and the views of a new Antitrust Division with respect to the case might very well be different from those of its predecessor. The longer the appellate review process was extended, the greater was the chance of divergence from the current Justice Department's approach to the case. This gave the plaintiffs an additional incentive to speed up the review process and thereby increase the chances that current enforcement views would be advanced in support of Jackson's decision and remedy. It also provided Microsoft with an added incentive to delay, in the hope that a new administration might view the case with greater skepticism and resolve the case on terms more favorable to Microsoft, perhaps even abandoning it if significant portions of Judge Jackson's decision were reversed.

In this chapter we see how these contending strategies played out. The chapter is divided into four sections. In the first section we describe the failed effort of the Justice Department in June of 2000 to get an appeal directly to the Supreme Court. In the second section we analyze the D.C. Circuit Court of Appeals' subsequent opinion. That court was presented with a number of major doctrinal questions; we focus on five of them: Microsoft's monopoly power, the legality of Microsoft's varied exclusionary practices, the integration of the browser and operating system both as monopolizing conduct under Section 2 and as a tying restraint under Section 1, the court's handling of the intellectual property issues in the case, and the questions of harm and causation. In addition to these doctrinal issues, we review how the court of appeals dealt with Jackson's handling of the litigation, particularly Jackson's troubling decision to provide journalist interviews while the case was still under consideration. In the third section we deal with the remedy issues, considering Jackson's decision to enter his remedial decree without a hearing, the content of that decree and the reasons Jackson gave for breaking up Microsoft into two separate companies, and the subsequent court of appeals' decision to vacate Jackson's order and return the remedy issue to a different district court judge. In the fourth section we discuss how the parties finally settled the case, describing a settlement process that was much different than the failed Posner mediation, the unsuccessful efforts by some of the states to obtain stronger relief, and the content of the settlement decree approved by the newly designated district court judge, Colleen Kollar-Kotelly.

As we will see, Microsoft's strategy to have the D.C. Circuit Court of Appeals consider the case wasn't as successful as it had hoped, for the court ended up affirming the core of Jackson's opinion and upholding the critical parts of the plaintiffs' case. On the other hand, the settlement decree vindicated Microsoft's strategy of delay until a new administration came to power in Washington. Although the Justice Department didn't abandon the case, the settlement decree was narrowly focused and, in the end, didn't disturb Microsoft's monopoly position.

Supreme Court Review

For 71 years, from 1903 to 1974, appeals of federal government civil antitrust cases had gone directly from the district courts to the Supreme Court. Congress enacted this unusual provision in recognition of the importance of government antitrust cases and the need for swift Supreme Court review of those cases, without an intermediate stop in a court of appeals. In 1974, though, Congress, wanting to reduce the burden on the Supreme Court's caseload, had eliminated automatic direct Supreme Court review.

Government appeals would now normally go to the courts of appeals and to the Supreme Court only on discretionary review.

The 1974 act, however, retains the possibility of a direct Supreme Court appeal in government civil antitrust cases where the Supreme Court's "immediate consideration" would be "of general public importance in the administration of justice."[2] Not only did the government plaintiffs in *Microsoft* want to get to the Supreme Court as quickly as possible; they also wanted to avoid the D.C. Circuit Court of Appeals because of that court's earlier decision on product integration in *Microsoft II*. As we discussed in chapters 2 and 3, that decision had endorsed a standard for evaluating product integration that seemed very favorable to Microsoft and which Judge Jackson had rejected as inconsistent with the relevant Supreme Court precedent. The government plaintiffs believed that the decision made the D.C. Circuit Court of Appeals an unfavorable forum in which to review Jackson's treatment of this crucial issue.

Direct review under the 1974 act first requires the district court judge to certify that immediate Supreme Court consideration was "of general public importance in the administration of justice." Even before entering his final remedy order, Judge Jackson had informed the parties that he intended to invite the government to file a motion pursuant to the act and that he was inclined to certify the case for direct review in the Supreme Court.[3] The certification couldn't be made, however, until Microsoft filed its notice of appeal in the court of appeals.

Microsoft filed its notice of appeal on June 13, 2000. Less than an hour later, the D.C. Circuit Court of Appeals took what the Justice Department later characterized as an "extraordinary step." On its own motion, the court entered an order that it would hear the appeal *en banc*—that is, all the eligible circuit court judges would hear the appeal, not just a three-judge panel as was customary before *en banc* review.[4] This was the D.C. Circuit's way of informing all those involved—the parties, Judge Jackson, and the Supreme Court—that it was ready to handle the case quickly and that one potentially delaying step—consideration of the case by a three-judge panel before any possible *en banc* consideration—would be skipped.

Later that evening, the Justice Department nevertheless asked Judge Jackson to certify the appeal to the Supreme Court. Seven days later, Jackson granted the Justice Department's motion and certified the case to the Supreme Court.[5]

In the nearly 30 years since Congress had changed the law dealing with expedited appeals, the Justice Department had invoked the certification provision only twice, each time in connection with a challenge to the decree that had restructured AT&T in settlement of a government monopolization case.[6] Emphasizing the similarities to the AT&T case in terms of relief and national economic importance, and the rarity of requests for expedited review, the Justice Department argued rhetorically that if the Microsoft case didn't qualify for direct review it was "difficult to imagine what future case would."[7]

Microsoft fought Supreme Court review, arguing that the case was complex, that the record was lengthy, that the grounds for appeal were numerous ("a morass of procedural and substantive issues"), and that it would be better to have the court of appeals undertake the necessarily "painstaking review of a lengthy and technologically complex trial record." Supreme Court review, if it were then necessary, would benefit greatly from having the court of appeals "clear out the procedural and factual underbrush."[8]

Nearly three months after Jackson certified the case for expedited review, the Supreme Court denied the request and remanded the case to the D.C. Circuit Court of Appeals.[9] In a two-paragraph dissent, Justice Stephen Breyer posed the competing interests of speed and economic importance against the institutional benefit from having the court of appeals narrow and focus the issues for subsequent review. Although Breyer would have heard the appeal, no other justice joined his opinion; as is customary, the Supreme Court did not provide any reasons for denying the government's request.

The Supreme Court's refusal to hear the case seemed a major tactical loss for the plaintiffs at the time, but things turned out just the opposite. Within two weeks of the remand from the Supreme Court, the court of appeals set a briefing schedule calling for initial briefs of 150 pages for each side (Microsoft would have an additional 75 pages for a reply brief) and scheduling the better part of two days for oral argument, with a specific amount of time set aside for each crucial issue.[10] By contrast, Supreme Court briefs are ordinarily limited to 50 pages and oral arguments to one hour in total. Although the Supreme Court might have expanded those limits somewhat, it was unlikely to have done so to the extent that the D.C. Circuit Court of Appeals did. Microsoft thus received its "painstaking review"—one more painstaking than the Supreme Court probably would have given—before the court it preferred. But it didn't lead to the result that Microsoft had sought.

The Court of Appeals' Decision

Focusing the Appellate Arguments
Despite the extended time the court of appeals scheduled for oral argument, and despite the lengthy briefing that the court of appeals allowed,

both sides still needed to streamline and focus their arguments. The plaintiffs focused their story more on the browser and Java, and less on the wider story of how Microsoft pursued its strategy against Intel, IBM, Apple, and RealNetworks.[11] Not only was this consistent with how the complaint originally framed the case; it also made the case more manageable on appeal. Microsoft tried to direct the argument away from the Section 2 monopolization case and toward the Section 1 tying case, emphasizing the benefits of integration and the court of appeals' decision in *Microsoft II* regarding integrated products.[12]

Microsoft also tried to recast the facts of the case in such a way as to exploit Judge Jackson's approach to his findings of fact. Jackson hadn't provided any citations to the record to support his more than 400 specific findings (an unusual approach in a complex a case in which the parties offered sharply conflicting accounts of the evidence), nor had he expressly attributed any of his findings to lack of credibility of the facts or witnesses (which might have provided a basis for greater deference by the court of appeals, even though credibility issues, particularly with some of Microsoft's witnesses and arguments, had evidently informed his conclusions).

Perhaps hoping that the lack of record citations would undermine the willingness of the court of appeals to accept Jackson's findings (after all, it would be hard for the court of appeals to go through a voluminous trial record to double-check the findings' accuracy), Microsoft constructed a counter-narrative. It portrayed the computer industry as "the envy of the world," characterized by falling prices and "unprecedented levels" of innovation—"the opposite of what one would expect if the industry were under the thumb of an oppressive monopolist." In this story Microsoft was the challenged competitor that had, over the course of the past fifteen years, "survived several inflection points that could have destroyed its operating system business."[13] To support its effort to rewrite the facts, Microsoft included copious references to the testimony presented at trial, but without directly attacking any of Jackson's specific findings of fact as "clearly erroneous."

The plaintiffs, on the other hand, emphasized that Jackson's "detailed findings of fact" were based on "the court's consideration of the entire trial record and its assessment of the credibility of the witnesses' testimony" and demonstrated Microsoft's "extensive campaign" to maintain its monopoly. But the plaintiffs didn't rely solely on the legal presumption of validity that a trial court's factual findings carry. Their brief, like Microsoft's, was studded with references to the trial record, not just to Jackson's specific findings of fact. And they went one better. The plaintiffs had originally provided Judge Jackson with a CD-ROM of their proposed findings of fact, which included hyperlinks from their proposed findings to the trial evidence on which they had relied. In an unusual move, the plaintiffs filed copies of this CD-ROM with the court of appeals, presumably to make it easier for the court to retrace Jackson's steps if it were concerned about whether his findings had adequate record support. This turned out to be a very successful strategy.[14]

Backdrop Issues

Three overall points stand out when the court of appeals' decision is assessed.

First, although the court rhetorically stuck to the legal requirement that findings of fact are entitled to a presumption of validity, to be rejected only if "clearly erroneous," the court wasn't content to rely on Jackson's findings of fact. At the oral argument it was apparent that the judges were quite familiar with the record independent of Jackson's findings. The court's opinion subsequently made this familiarity plain by liberally citing the actual record, in addition to citing particular findings of fact.

Second, although it is always hazardous to predict the outcome of an appeal on the basis of questions asked at oral argument, it is safe to say that no observer at oral argument would probably have predicted a unanimous opinion authored "by the court" rather than by a particular judge, which is ultimately what occurred. Indeed, the questioning revealed that some, but not all, of the judges had substantial concerns about major parts of the plaintiffs' case.[15] The fact that the seven judges on the court were able to arrive at a unified opinion indicates a strong internal effort to reach consensus, perhaps at the risk of complete theoretical consistency.

Third, in view of the complexity of the case, the court acted relatively quickly, handing down its decision just four months after oral argument. Even so, the time interval between argument and decision was almost twice the median time for deciding appeals in the federal system in 2001, another example of the constant tension in the litigation between the perceived need in a high-technology industry to decide matters quickly and the need to take sufficient time to understand the complexities of that industry.[16]

The court of appeals acknowledged the potential importance of the time factor at the very beginning of its opinion. Pointing out that the process had moved quickly in comparison with other important antitrust cases, the court also observed that six years had passed since the first allegedly anticompetitive acts in the case (the 1995 meetings with Netscape), and that "six years seems like an eternity in the computer industry." The passage of time, the court worried, might make conduct remedies "unavailing" because past conduct might now be "obsolete." Remedies directed at structure, on the other hand, faced a distinct and difficult challenge: How can a court determine with confidence what structural changes will be effective in restoring competition to a constantly changing marketplace? Even though forward-looking remedies might, therefore, be a limited option in cases involving high-technology industries, the court suggested that there was still a role for government enforcement, albeit a diminished one—the government could still bring cases to "defin[e] the contours of the antitrust laws." The threat of private damages suits would then remain "to deter those firms inclined to test the limits of the law."[17]

The court also addressed another "matter of note" at the beginning of its opinion: the question of how antitrust should apply to industries in the "new economy." Microsoft had pressed "new economy" arguments on Judge Jackson—particularly the idea that monopoly power had to be evaluated differently for firms in network industries in which the winner faces a constant threat of displacement by new products with even greater consumer benefits—but Jackson had brought those arguments into the traditional construct of antitrust law and economics. The court of appeals pointed out that in network industries there could still be competition "for the field," even if there were no competition "within the field" once the network tipped and a winner emerged, but it also acknowledged that there were conflicting scholarly views regarding how, or whether, to modify antitrust rules to account for the economic structure of "new economy" industries. The court chose not to resolve the scholarly disagreements, however, indicating that it would measure monopoly power and Microsoft's conduct according to traditional antitrust analysis, which seemed fully adequate for the task.

Questions of speed and efficacy had dogged the *Microsoft* litigation from the beginning, of course. After calling these issues "backdrop," the court never developed its observations or even directly mentioned them again. Why did the court include this discussion? Perhaps it served to acknowledge that at least some of the court's members were extremely dubious about the plaintiffs' enterprise, but found themselves with little institutional choice but to work through the facts and deal with the case with which they were presented. Perhaps others found the "new economy" arguments simply overblown and unpersuasive and were themselves confident that the antitrust laws were flexible enough, and their capacity to apply economic reasoning was sufficient, to permit a reasoned resolution of the case. In any event, the court may have been implicitly suggesting that the institutional constraints under which it was operating—the need to respect the fact finding of the trial court, the desire for compromise to reach a unified result in a legitimately contested case, and the press of time—shaped the court's result and helped its members to overcome any misgivings they may have had about how best to apply the antitrust laws to Microsoft.

Monopoly Power

The court of appeals began its monopolization analysis by affirming "in its entirety" Judge Jackson's finding that Microsoft possessed monopoly power.[18] The court agreed with Jackson that the relevant market was that for operating systems for Intel-compatible PCs, concluding that Microsoft's factual argument to the contrary fell "far short" of what was necessary to challenge Jackson's findings as "clearly erroneous." It further concluded that Microsoft's share of that market was "predominant" at over 95 percent, or 80 percent if the Mac OS were included—and observed that "Microsoft challenges neither finding." In the court of appeals' view, Jackson had correctly explained how the applications barrier to entry protected Microsoft's position, because the breadth of current and future applications programs would lead consumers to prefer the dominant operating system even if no consumer used every available application.

Microsoft's principal strategy for challenging the district court's conclusion regarding monopoly power was to cast the traditional structural approach as dated, arguing that current market shares and market structure didn't provide an accurate assessment of monopoly power in "dynamic" software markets.[19] In lieu of structural analysis, Microsoft asked the court to focus on its behavior, arguing that in the long run it had acted like a firm with no such power, constrained to price below the monopoly price and to innovate constantly.

These arguments were at the heart of Microsoft's narrative and the economic case it had presented to both the district court and the court of appeals. The court of appeals, however, kept its focus just where Jackson had: on the short run. The only effective constraint on a monopolist's ability to raise prices is a substitute product that might materialize "in the relatively near future," but Jackson's unchallenged findings provided "no reason" to believe that "prompt substitutes" for the Windows operating system were available. In fact, an analysis of the structure of the market was sufficient to show the existence of monopoly power "even in a changing market."

Moreover, the court of appeals agreed with Jackson that Microsoft's conduct didn't actually demonstrate that it behaved as if it faced significant competition, as Microsoft urged. To the contrary, Microsoft's actual behavior was more consistent with the behavior of a firm that possessed significant monopoly power than with the behavior of one that did not. Microsoft priced its operating system without regard to rivals' prices and took various actions that were rational only on the assumption that it possessed monopoly power. Rather than undermining the inferences to be drawn from the structural evidence, therefore, the direct evidence regarding its behavior reinforced the structural evidence that Microsoft was indeed a monopolist.

Exclusionary Conduct

Somewhat in contrast to the court of appeals' treatment of monopoly power, its approach to analyzing whether Microsoft's conduct was exclusionary diverged from Judge Jackson's approach, even though many of Jackson's ultimate conclusions would be affirmed. First, the court adopted an approach for distinguishing between exclusionary and legitimate acts that it likened to the rule-of-reason approach used under Section 1 of the Sherman Act, an approach not used at the trial and not directly sought by any of the parties. Second, despite making a reference to Microsoft's "pattern" of exclusionary conduct, the court chose to break down Microsoft's behavior into discrete segments, each of which it analyzed individually. Jackson had integrated the story of Microsoft's behavior, showing Microsoft's systemic effort to maintain its monopoly in the market for operating systems. The court of appeals dis-integrated the story, treating each action as relatively discrete and unconnected.

The court's overall approach—drawn, it said, "from a century of case law on monopolization"—required three steps:

• The plaintiff must first prove that the monopolist's conduct has an anticompetitive effect—that is, "it must harm the competitive *process* and thereby harm consumers," not just "one or more *competitors*."
• If the plaintiff proves anticompetitive effect, the burden shifts to the monopolist, which can then offer evidence of a "procompetitive justification," a "non-pretextual claim that its conduct is indeed a form of "competition on the merits," such as "greater efficiency" or "enhanced consumer appeal."
• If the monopolist meets its burden of establishing a procompetitive justification for its conduct, the burden shifts back to the plaintiff, which can seek to rebut the evidence of the justification; if the justification is not rebutted, the plaintiff must show that "the anticompetitive harm of the conduct outweighs the procompetitive benefit."

The monopolist's intent in undertaking the conduct might also be relevant, but only to the degree it "helps to understand the likely effect."[20]

This approach is a familiar one for antitrust, at least in broad outline, for it tracks the "rule of reason" that courts have often used in antitrust cases since the U.S. Supreme Court articulated it in its 1911 *Standard Oil* decision. Indeed, the court of appeals explicitly noted the connection, observing that "[i]n cases arising under §1 of the Sherman Act, the courts routinely apply a similar balancing approach under the rubric of the 'rule of reason.'"[21] By synthesizing prior case law into a single framework rooted in the economic principles of antitrust analysis—competitive effects—the D.C. Circuit Court of Appeals presented a more cohesive framework for resolving monopolization cases than other courts had previously articulated.

Some critics subsequently faulted the court of appeals for likening monopolization analysis to the "rule of reason."[22] They pointed out that detractors of the rule of reason had long maintained that it was an inherently unstructured, vague test that left far too much discretion in the hands of courts and juries to consider a variety of factors and hence resulted in uncertainty—firms couldn't easily predict what would be deemed a "reasonable" impact on competition as opposed to an "unreasonable" one. Such uncertainty, critics have argued, is especially troubling in the case of single-firm conduct, where risk-averse firms might avoid aggressive competitive strategies for fear of falling victim to antitrust challenges. They also worried that "balancing" procompetitive and anticompetitive effects is difficult and is likely to undervalue efficiencies.

As applied by the D.C. Circuit Court of Appeals, however, these criticisms were mostly unfounded. Drawing upon decades of case law and modern economic principles, the court articulated and applied an operable approach to judging the conduct of monopolists, encountering few difficult judgment calls. The difficulty with the court's application of its rule-of-reason approach didn't lie with any uncertainty in judging competitive effects, but with its decision to evaluate individually the effects of and justifications for each specific act challenged by the government plaintiffs, rather than to evaluate the acts collectively. In effect, the court ignored the forest and focused only on the trees.

The limitations of its approach were especially evident in the court's assessment of Microsoft's bundling of IE and Windows. Judge Jackson, in his Section 2 analysis, had viewed the license restrictions and integration of IE as components of a broader effort to exclude Netscape from the most efficient channels of distribution and thereby maintain the applications barrier to entry. The court of appeals, however, looked at each act more narrowly and in isolation, not as a part of a wide-ranging and relentless exclusionary strategy. Indeed, to the court, the issue wasn't even whether the integration of IE into Windows was, itself, an act of monopoly maintenance. Rather, the court broke down Microsoft's design conduct further, examining three separate acts: excluding IE from the "Add/Remove" utility in Windows 98; commingling the code for browser functions in files that also included code for operating-system functions, so that browser code couldn't easily be deleted without undermining the functionality of Windows; and overriding a user's choice of a default browser other than IE in certain circumstances. It then evaluated each act separately.

The first two acts were relatively easy to assess. With respect to the exclusion of IE from the Add/Remove utility in Windows 98, the court observed that the change "reduces the usage share of rival browsers not by making Microsoft's own browser more attractive to consumers, but, rather, by discouraging OEMs from distributing rival products." Similarly, the court concluded that Microsoft's commingling of code "deters OEMs from preinstalling rival browsers, thereby reducing the rivals' usage share and, hence, developers' interest in rivals' application programming interfaces as an alternative to the API set exposed by Microsoft's operating system."[23] The court thus agreed with Judge Jackson's finding that OEMs would want to install only one browser, fearing that having two browsers on a single computer would increase service calls from novice users and would "significantly" increase OEMs' support costs.[24] The court then pointedly observed that Microsoft proffered "no justification" for either the removal of IE from the Add/Remove utility or the commingling of IE and Windows code. Instead, the court found that Microsoft made only "general claims regarding the benefits of integrating the browser and the operating system," claims that it neither specified nor substantiated, and it made no claim that omitting IE from the Add/Remove utility or commingling code "achieves any integrative benefit."[25]

The third act—the default override—presented a closer call. Although this design choice likewise was deemed anticompetitive because it deterred consumers from using a different browser and "protect[ed] Microsoft's monopoly," Microsoft had introduced evidence of "valid technical reasons" to support the override. Departing from Jackson's findings, the court accepted Microsoft's factual argument that in certain circumstances it needed to override the user's choice of a default browser because some of Windows' features weren't supported in Navigator. Although the court represented that it had therefore reached the third step of its rule-of-reason analysis, and that it would have to decide whether the anticompetitive effect outweighed Microsoft's proffered technical justification, it didn't undertake any balancing. In a move that was typical of rule-of-reason decisions under Section 1, it instead concluded that once the burden shifted back to the governments as a result of Microsoft's non-pretextual technical justification, it remained there—the plaintiffs, it observed, "offer no rebuttal whatsoever." Because the government neither rebutted Microsoft's justification for the default override nor introduced further evidence of its anticompetitive effect, the court concluded that "Microsoft may not be held liable for this aspect of its product design."[26]

The court similarly applied its approach to each of the other exclusionary acts of monopolizing conduct that the plaintiffs had attacked. For example, the court readily characterized as anticompetitive a variety of contractual practices that resulted in the contracting party's exclusive or near-exclusive use of IE and Microsoft's JVM to the exclusion of Netscape's Navigator or Sun's JVM. The court also condemned Microsoft's threat to withhold support and updating of Office for the Macintosh unless Apple agreed to bundle IE into its operating system and make it the default browser. Similarly, the court condemned the threats that Microsoft made to coerce Intel to stop developing a fast Sun-compliant JVM. Finally, the court condemned Microsoft's efforts to deceive software developers by not disclosing to them that Microsoft's Java development tools would create programs that weren't fully cross-platform compatible with programs developed with Sun's Java tools. Indeed, the court underlined Microsoft's anticompetitive objective in deceiving the Java developers by quoting a document, not even mentioned by Judge Jackson, in which Microsoft made plain its anticompetitive goal: "Kill cross-platform Java by growing the polluted Java market."[27]

As was true of its assessment of the licensing restrictions and integration efforts, the court's decision to characterize each of these practices as anticompetitive was based on an assessment that each had a "substantial" adverse effect on Netscape's or Sun's ability to gain sufficient usage share to become a platform that could threaten the applications barrier to entry. In so doing, the court was sensitive to the strategic importance of each of the affected channels of distribution, particularly the cost-efficient OEM channel, even though the cumulative market share of the channels foreclosed might not have reached the "roughly" 40 or 50 percent that would have been required to show a Section 1 violation for exclusive dealing.[28] In so holding, the court of appeals was consistent with Jackson's basic approach to explaining how these agreements helped Microsoft maintain its monopoly, thereby violating Section 2.

To the extent that Microsoft advanced a procompetitive justification for these exclusive practices it was to keep developers focused on Windows APIs, "which is to say," the court wrote, that "it wants to preserve its power in the operating system market." This wasn't an "unlawful end" to the court, but it wasn't a procompetitive justification either. In the absence of procompetitive justification, there was nothing to balance against the anticompetitive effects, even if balancing might be practicable. Microsoft's exclusive dealing practices violated Section 2.[29]

The court did not condemn every one of Microsoft's practices as anticompetitive, however. When it came to practices that lowered price or improved a product, the court was less inclined to characterize Microsoft's conduct as anticompetitive. For example, Judge Jackson had found that Microsoft had "expended wealth and foresworn opportunities" in its development and promotion of IE, and that those expenditures could be explained only by Microsoft's expectation that the applications barrier would be preserved and its monopoly position would be maintained. The court of appeals, however, was unwilling to focus on how much profit Microsoft sacrificed. Because offering a customer a good deal was the "hallmark" of competition, there was "no warrant" to condemn Microsoft for offering IE "free of charge or even at a negative price" in the absence of any district court findings of liability for predatory pricing.[30] Similarly, when discussing the development of Microsoft's JVM, which created incompatibilities with programs written for Sun's JVM, the court wrote that a monopolist doesn't violate the antitrust laws "simply by developing a product that is incompatible with those of its rivals" or by providing costly technical support to induce developers to write their Java applications to Microsoft's (incompatible) JVM.[31] Developing an "attractive product" isn't anticompetitive, so those weren't practices that "maintained monopoly" in violation of Section 2.

The Tying Claim

The bundling of the browser with the operating system had been a major issue in the contempt proceedings that had arisen from the 1994 Licensing Decree, and it continued to play an important role in the governments' Windows 98 case, although it was presented as but one component of a far larger strategy. As we have discussed, the court of appeals upheld the district court's conclusion that most of the means that Microsoft used to integrate IE into Windows were acts of monopoly maintenance, in violation of Section 2. Plaintiffs had also argued, however, that the tying of IE to Windows unreasonably restrained trade in an alleged market for Internet browsers, in violation of Section 1. The district court had agreed, citing four specific acts: licensing IE together with Windows 95 and 98 as a bundle at a single price, refusing to permit OEMs to uninstall IE or remove the icon from the desktop, excluding IE from the Add/Remove Program utility, and overriding the user's choice of a default browser.[32] The court of appeals accordingly included a lengthy discussion of the Section 1 tying issue. That discussion, however, differed in important ways from the court's Section 2 analysis, from the earlier court of appeals' decision in *Microsoft II*, from Judge Jackson's handling of the tying claim, and from Supreme Court tying precedent.

Under Section 1, tying has traditionally been analyzed by a *per se* rule under which a defendant will be found to violate Section 1 if it sells two products (a "tying" product and a "tied" product), it has market power in the market for the tying product, it conditions the sale of the tying product on the purchase of the tied product, and the sale affects an appreciable amount of commerce. On its face, there is no place for the defendant to justify the tie as an efficient one. Over time, efficiency justifications crept into the analysis, however, under the guise of the requirement that there be two products. Firms accused of unlawful tying would defend by seeking to show that the two products were really one owing to the efficiencies of integration. If there are two products, however, proof of sufficient market power in the market for the tying product and of substantial effect on commerce in the market for the tied product will make out a violation of Section 1. This will be sufficient to show injury to the competitive process, without the need for any further proof. The inclusion of a requirement of market power could be understood as qualifying the typical facial condemnation associated with true *per se* rules, establishing a "quasi" or modified *per se* standard for tying.

The first thing the court of appeals did, however, was to hold that Judge Jackson should have decided the tying claim under a rule of reason, not under the *per se* rule as Supreme Court precedent dictated.[33] The court of appeals based its decision on two broad arguments. First, the court decided that the Supreme Court's test for determining whether there are two separate products, articulated in the *Jefferson Parish* case, wasn't appropriate for the platform-software market at issue in *Microsoft*. The *Jefferson Parish* test asks whether there is separate consumer demand for each product, but, the court of appeals pointed out, this examines only the current market situation, judging whether consumers *today* have a separate demand for each part of the bundle, or, perhaps, looking at whether other competitors currently offer the products unbundled.[34] An innovative integration, however, may present a consumer with a new choice—a product that isn't yet on the market and which will end future consumer demand for two separate products (the integration of starter motors into automobiles was a good example). Looking at the conduct of competitors in the industry could thus lead to judging innovative product integration by the standard of less innovative firms. Thus, the current approach, the court said, might not give newly integrated products "a fair shake."[35]

The court also argued that applying the *per se* rule to platform-software markets creates an "undue risk" of "deterring welfare-enhancing innovation." Tying in platform software could be different than tying in other product markets because tying may benefit consumers not only by providing an integrated product but also by increasing the value of the platform for makers of complementary software applications. It might turn out that the benefits for complementary software producers can be achieved *only* by providing a consistent, integrated platform, rather than offering the platform either with or without the "tied" product. Certainly a court couldn't say that bundling in such a market is so lacking in "redeeming virtue" that there would be little social loss in condemning all such ties without further inquiry. Rather, a full inquiry into anticompetitive effects and procompetitive justifications is necessary.

Applying a rule of reason to bundling may have been unusual for a Section 1 case, but the rule of reason was what the court had already applied to the bundling issues it had discussed in its Section 2 monopoly-maintenance analysis. One might have thought, therefore, that the court could simply use the same analysis and find that the bundling also violated Section 1. But the court didn't do so. Instead, even though it acknowledged that the facts of the two "substantially overlap[ped]," the court distinguished the Section 1 and Section 2 claims, emphasizing that the Section 1 claim involved some additional issues, such as selling Windows and IE for a single price and the contractual provisions forbidding the OEMs from uninstalling IE or removing it from the desktop, and pointing out that Judge Jackson had neglected to refer specifically to code commingling when discussing tying.

The court of appeals also had the option of relying on its tying discussion in *Microsoft II*. In that decision it had indicated that product integration would be judged leniently under the antitrust laws, emphasizing the judiciary's limited institutional competence to judge product design. It had also maintained that integration would be lawful if there were a "plausible claim" that the integration brought "some advantage"—a standard that, as we noted in chapter 3, Judge Jackson had characterized as "undemanding." The court now backed away from its earlier position, however. Specifically rejecting the panel's disclaimer of institutional incapacity, the court adopted an approach that called on the trial court to engage in a full inquiry into the anticompetitive effects and the efficiency justifications of software design.[36] This marked change in approach from *Microsoft II* was particularly noteworthy because two of the seven members of the *en banc* court had been on the panel that had decided the earlier case.

At first, it appeared that the court might leave matters at that, remanding the case for consideration of the tying claim under a more standard rule-of-reason approach. It even observed that "[i]n light of the monopoly maintenance section [of our opinion], obviously, we do not find that Microsoft's integration is welfare-enhancing or that it should be absolved of tying liability."[37] Nevertheless, the court—not constrained either by the Section 2 discussion earlier in its opinion or by the panel opinion in *Microsoft II*—then wrote expansively about potential efficiencies from tying IE and Windows, even though in its Section 2 analysis it had found no procompetitive justifications for a number of the specific acts associated with the integration.

First, the court suggested that Microsoft could take advantage of economies of scope by bundling IE with Windows, for example, by creating shared library files that would perform operating-system functions and browser functions with "the same lines of code."[38] In its monopoly-maintenance discussion the court had rejected Microsoft's argument that the same lines of code were used for both functions, but the court now chose to delve more deeply into the testimonial record of the trial to support its understanding that various lines of code might have shared functionality.[39]

Second, the court suggested that bundling IE might bring further efficiency gains because IE's application programming interfaces would now be included in Windows, making Windows a "better platform" for software developers. There were other ways to distribute browser APIs, of course—other applications could include browser APIs, OEMs could distribute them, or competing browsers could distribute APIs. The presumption that Windows could be the most efficient vehicle for API distribution, because the APIs would then be available for all developers, is a recognition of the network effects of having a single platform. These network effects, however, would strengthen the applications barrier to entry by enhancing the likelihood that ISVs would write programs using IE/Windows' APIs rather than using APIs from competing cross-platform middleware. In its monopolization discussion the court didn't raise the possible efficiencies of having all APIs in a single platform; indeed, it wrote that Microsoft's effort to focus developers on Windows' APIs wasn't a procompetitive justification.[40] In the Section 1 tying analysis, however, "simplifying the work of applications developers" was seen as a possible consumer gain rather than as a barrier to middleware competition.[41]

The court's opinion did not resolve the question whether tying IE to Windows was unreasonable. Instead, the court remanded the case for further trial, instructing the district court to reevaluate the various aspects of the bundling with regard to its effect on the market for the tied product (browsers). If there had been net harm, the court wrote, the district court "must then consider whether any additional remedy is necessary," although the court didn't indicate what that additional remedy might be.[42] In view of its observations about the possible efficiencies associated with integrating IE and Windows, however, it wasn't clear what issues remained for the district court to decide. Nor was it clear why, after the court's affirmance of the Section 2 claim, the government would want to pursue the Section 1 claim any further.

It is difficult to explain why the court's analysis of the integration of Windows and IE under Section 1 was so different from its analysis of integration under Section 2. The reasons given for distinguishing the two claims are weak. Switching the focus from the effect on the market for operating systems to the effect on the browser market doesn't explain the change in analysis—there is no inherent reason why tying analysis should be limited to effects in the market for the tied product, and the two complementary product markets were closely linked in any event.[43] Nor would considering additional ways in which Microsoft tied IE to Windows make the tying *less* problematic. Perhaps the different analyses are attributable to the court's willingness to accommodate some inconsistencies in the opinion in an effort to secure a unanimous opinion, some members wanting a broad statement of general tying principles while others were more concerned about sticking closely to the facts of the case as presented to the district court.

Whatever the explanation for the seeming inconsistencies in the court's approach to product integration, there is an important common thread between its tying discussion and its general Section 2 analysis—a thread that is inherent in the rule of reason. The rule of reason emphasizes anticompetitive effects and efficiencies. No matter what legal or economic theories the parties use to shape their arguments, in the end the courts are going to be concerned with whether they are looking at business practices that have an anticompetitive effect and an efficiency rationale and with whether their application of antitrust law will end up doing more harm than good if the court incorrectly condemns efficient business behavior. This explains why the court of appeals begins its discussion of tying by mentioning its concern for false positives. Doctrines that purport to set aside efficiency, or to short circuit inquiry into efficiencies, will be applied gingerly. Neither the plaintiffs' presentation nor Judge Jackson's opinion recognized the inevitability of that inquiry or made clear why the decision to bundle the products in a way that excluded Netscape's Navigator (or, more precisely, Microsoft's decision to refuse to offer IE and Windows both bundled and unbundled) lacked an efficiency justification. Jackson clearly felt more constrained by the existing Supreme Court law on tying than did the court of appeals, which was willing to distinguish it. For its part, the court of appeals may have been confident that there was no longer a majority of Justices willing to uphold the *per se* rule for tying and that hence there was no significant risk that its approach would be reversed.

Intellectual Property Issues

There is only one place in the court of appeals' opinion where the court comes close to actually balancing an anticompetitive effect against a procompetitive justification and reaching a "net" result. It comes in the discussion of Microsoft's licensing restrictions forbidding OEMs from removing desktop icons, folders, or "Start menu" entries, altering the initial boot sequence, or altering the appearance of the Windows desktop.[44] As with other aspects of Microsoft's conduct, the plaintiffs argued that Microsoft took these actions to discourage the installation of any competing browser as a way of insulating its operating-system monopoly from the eventual emergence of competition.

Microsoft sought to justify the three licensing restrictions primarily on legal, rather than economic, grounds. It argued that it had the "right to protect against unauthorized modifications in its copyright works," going so far as to assert that the copyright laws gave it the right to prevent OEMs from removing access to IE's browser functionality without authorization: "[I]f intellectual property rights have been lawfully acquired ... their subsequent exercise cannot give rise to antitrust liability."[45] This sweeping argument, if taken seriously, would have meant that the copyright laws gave Microsoft the right to forbid unbundling Internet Explorer from Windows, in effect overriding the antitrust laws.

The court of appeals reacted unfavorably to Microsoft's arguments. For one thing, the court considered the copyright argument only in connection with the boot-sequence and desktop restrictions—hardly the most competitively critical restraints. It didn't even mention the potentially broader application of the argument to the refusal to allow the unbundling of Internet Explorer or the removal of access to it. Even at this reduced level, however, the court sharply rejected the argument: "Microsoft's primary copyright argument borders upon the frivolous." To say that the exercise of lawfully acquired copyright rights cannot give rise to antitrust liability "is no more correct than the proposition that use of one's personal property, such as a baseball bat, cannot give rise to tort liability."[46]

Even though the court rejected Microsoft's broad copyright argument, it went on to consider Microsoft's assertion that it should be able to limit "deleterious alterations of a copyrighted work."[47] The court accepted this argument not so much as a matter of absolute right under copyright law, but more as a matter of judging whether Microsoft was using its intellectual property right "in an unreasonable manner, despite the anticompetitive consequences." It thus weighed Microsoft's interest in forbidding OEMs from installing a shell program that would prevent consumers from ever seeing the Microsoft "desktop," which the court characterized as a "drastic alteration" in the copyrighted work, as against the "marginal anticompetitive effect" that such a provision might have had on the ability of middleware to compete. Thus, the court found that the desktop restriction didn't violate Section 2 of the Sherman Act.[48]

In reality, the court of appeals' balancing approach had little to do with the scope of the actual rights that Microsoft might, or might not, have had in preventing alterations to Windows that would result in a different desktop. Whether copyright law would have considered such alteration an infringement didn't matter and was never shown. Rather, the court carried out an intuitive weighing of the harms to competition and the benefits to Microsoft from being able to impose the restriction. It had no record support for quantifying either effect, however, making its conclusion more an *ipse dixit* than a guide for how such balancing might be done generally.[49]

More curious, and more problematic, is the way the issue of intellectual property was handled generally. "New economy" industries are often heavily dependent on protection of intellectual property. One of the most important issues in applying antitrust law to these industries is how to reconcile intellectual property law—which grants exclusionary rights to encourage the production of intellectual property products—with antitrust law's general condemnation of monopolization through exclusionary practices. Bill Gates subsequently put it this way: "Microsoft is an intellectual property (IP) company. We have no factories of any consequence or natural resources. Indeed, we have no physical assets of any kind that are important to the success of the company. Our products instead consist almost entirely of information we create. ..."[50] One might have thought, therefore, that there would have been more extensive exploration of the conflict between these two legal regimes, one of which promotes exclusion and one of which condemns it.

The court of appeals was able to brush aside Microsoft's intellectual property argument as "bordering on the frivolous" because Microsoft advanced the argument only in an extreme form. Microsoft never made a serious effort to prove exactly what its rights were under various intellectual property laws, even though Judge Jackson had specifically invited it to do so,[51] choosing instead to rely on earlier court decisions of questionable factual and legal relevance to its licensing restrictions.[52] Why Microsoft didn't make its intellectual property claims more central is difficult to say. Perhaps it was because Microsoft didn't want to be put into the position of having to defend the actual scope of its rights to Windows, a complex task under copyright law. Perhaps it was because the plaintiffs' case mostly didn't challenge Microsoft's use of those rights—unlike the European Commission's case (which, as we will see in chapter 6, did challenge Microsoft's withholding of arguably protected information, and in which the scope of intellectual property rights played a more important role).

Whatever Microsoft's tactical reasons for downplaying the intellectual property issues, the court of appeals didn't invest much effort in trying to make a better argument than Microsoft chose to advance. The end result, however, was that the court of appeals' opinion offers little in the way of general principles for how a court should resolve a conflict between antitrust law and intellectual property law.[53]

Causation and Harm

Microsoft argued in the court of appeals that it shouldn't be liable under Section 2 because there was no causal link between its exclusionary conduct and the maintenance of its monopoly, an argument it had unsuccessfully pressed on Judge Jackson. The court of appeals acknowledged that the threats from Netscape and Java were more potential than actual, but that was no reason to absolve Microsoft of liability. Monopolists, the court wrote, do not have "free reign to squash nascent, albeit unproven, competitors at will."[54]

Nevertheless, the court of appeals was cautious in its rejection of Microsoft's argument. The court was willing to say that the plaintiffs had shown a sufficient causal connection between Microsoft's conduct and its maintenance of a monopoly to obtain injunctive relief, but perhaps not enough for the breakup they sought. That remedy would require "confidence" that there had been an "actual loss to competition."[55]

The court of appeals' caution was another result of its reviewing Microsoft's exclusionary conduct piece by piece under the rule of reason, rather than as a systematic effort to protect its durable monopoly position. Judge

Jackson had also found that it was unclear whether Netscape's and Sun's products would have evolved into genuine rivals to Microsoft's operating system, but he had recognized that Microsoft's campaign against Netscape and Sun not only denied consumers certain specific benefits but also conveyed an important lesson to any firm that might seek to challenge Microsoft's most important products. The court of appeals, on the other hand, implied that it wasn't so certain that Microsoft's "squashing" of Netscape and Java ultimately mattered very much to competition. If that had been the case, however, then Microsoft really didn't have as much to fear from Netscape as Gates and all his top executives thought, and as Microsoft's three-year campaign indicated—a view substantially at odds with the normal assumption that businesspeople know more about their business than judges do and wouldn't engage in such lengthy and expensive efforts without good reason.

Two "Side Issues"

In the last part of its opinion, the court of appeals turned to two challenging issues that were unrelated to the merits of the plaintiffs' substantive case against Microsoft: (1) Judge Jackson's failure to include record citations in his findings of fact; and (2) his meetings with journalists during the trial and his public statements about the case before the appeal was taken.

With regard to the first challenge, the court concluded that Jackson's findings permitted "meaningful appellate review" even though the findings were "exceedingly sparing in citations to the record." As we have seen, although the court closely examined the testimony and exhibits presented at trial for itself, the court of appeals didn't appear to be discounting his findings in any way. It judged them under the usual "clearly erroneous" standard, which is deferential to the district court's factual findings. The court pointed out that Jackson had been quoted as wanting to "confront the Court of Appeals with an established factual record which is a fait accompli" so that the court wouldn't make up the facts on its own, as he thought it had in *Microsoft II*, but the court said it took no offense: "We do not view the District Judge's remarks as anything other than his expression of disagreement with this court's decision, and his desire to provide extensive factual findings in this case, which he did."[56]

The second challenge was potentially more explosive and troubling. Immediately after Judge Jackson issued his final order, and before the case was appealed, reports began to emerge of Jackson's private meetings with journalists.[57] By the time the case was argued before the court of appeals, it had become clear that Jackson had met with two reporters while the trial was in progress (embargoing publication of the interviews until after the trial ended), had given interviews to other reporters after issuing his final judgment, and had made public remarks defending his decision in the case before the appeal had been argued. For a judge to give such interviews and public statements while a case is still being considered is more than "extraordinary" (which was how one of the reporters involved characterized it); it is a potential breach of the judicial canons of ethics, and it can provide grounds for disqualification from the case.[58]

Some of Judge Jackson's statements were certainly colorful. He analogized Microsoft's unwillingness to acknowledge its illegal behavior to the similar unwillingness shown by an infamous D.C. drug-dealing gang that was prosecuted for three "brutal" murders: "[T]hey maintained that they had done nothing wrong. ... I am now under no illusions that miscreants will realize that other parts of society view them that way."[59] He analogized Microsoft's situation on losing the trial to Japan's situation after losing the Second World War: neither could dictate "the terms of their surrender."[60] He analogized the need for the remedy he imposed on Microsoft to the efforts of a mule trainer who "took a 2-by-4 and whopped [the mule] upside the head The mule was reeling and fell to his knees, and the trainer said: 'You just have to get his attention.'"[61]

It is difficult to understand why Judge Jackson put so much of his time and effort on the *Microsoft* case at risk. He had used the rules of procedure deftly and creatively to expedite the processing of the case. Jackson's opinions—his findings of fact and conclusions of law—were thorough and were, in many ways, very persuasive. The judge had pulled together a lengthy and complex record in a way that told a clear story of a company intent on suppressing any competitive threat to its dominant position. He told that story within the framework of traditional antitrust economics, concentrating on market definition, entry barriers, and exclusionary practices, while also incorporating the most contemporary economic themes and evidence presented by the parties. His opinions avoided using some of the more colorful language that was often featured in the pleadings or in testimony, such as the remark that Microsoft wanted to bundle IE into Windows without charging for it so as to "cut off Netscape's air supply," or that Microsoft wanted to "pollute Java" through developer tools that would create Java programs only for Windows. He never once wrote that a Microsoft witness wasn't credible, even though such a finding might have further insulated his opinion from judicial review and even though he reportedly held this view, at least with regard to Bill Gates.[62]

Whatever Jackson's motives, his actions and statements were hard to defend. Indeed, the court of appeals, noting that in oral argument counsel for the plaintiffs "all but conceded that the Judge violated ethical restrictions by discussing the case in public," characterized Jackson's "multiple" violations of the judicial Code of Conduct as "deliberate, repeated, egregious, and flagrant."[63]

The real question was what the remedy should be. The judicial Code of Conduct itself has no enforcement mechanism, but federal law requires disqualification when a judge's impartiality "might reasonably be questioned." The court pointed out that although not every violation of the Code of Conduct destroys the appearance of impartiality, Jackson's conduct had crossed the line and disqualification was required: "Rather than manifesting neutrality and impartiality, the reports of the interviews with the District Judge convey the impression of a judge posturing for posterity, trying to please the reporters with colorful analogies and observations bound to wind up in the stories they write."[64]

Finding that Judge Jackson should be disqualified wasn't the end of the matter, however. The court could make the disqualification prospective, replacing Jackson in all future proceedings when the case was remanded. This was the approach the court had taken in 1995 when it had questioned Judge Sporkin's impartiality in the 1994 Microsoft consent decree proceedings and had the remand of the case assigned to a different judge. Or, as Microsoft urged, it could make the disqualification retroactive, vacating the judgment and ordering the entire case to be retried.[65]

Caught between its outrage at Jackson's conduct and its realization that "full retroactive" disqualification would severely penalize the plaintiffs who had nothing to do with Jackson's improper conduct, the court chose a middle course. Noting that the "most serious judicial misconduct occurred near or during the remedial stage," the court decided to disqualify Jackson as of the date he entered his remedy order, but not to vacate his findings of fact and conclusions of law.[66] The court of appeals had reviewed the record "with painstaking care." Having "discerned no evidence of actual bias," it concluded that the findings of fact and the conclusions of law warranted deference and should be upheld. Having acknowledged in its opinion the institutional difficulty that courts face when trying to act expeditiously in cases involving technologically dynamic industries, the court wasn't about to start this case over, more than three years after it had been filed, when it believed that the central finding of a Section 2 violation for monopoly maintenance was sound. Ultimately, the court chose not to let Jackson's indiscretions interfere with the merits of the litigation, but to require that another judge be assigned to handle all future proceedings.[67]

The Remedy

There was one more significant area for the court of appeals to review. Judge Jackson had entered a sweeping remedial order breaking Microsoft into two companies and enjoining it from a wide variety of conduct until the breakup became effective. Microsoft raised questions not only about the substance of the remedy order but also about the process Jackson followed in deciding to enter it. Ultimately, the court of appeals concluded that the process was defective, so it didn't directly rule on the propriety of the structural relief itself. But the court did set out its views on the proper scope of a remedy in the case—views that appeared to set a high bar for structural relief and that influenced the terms of the settlement that the parties ultimately negotiated.

Judge Jackson's Process

The day after he issued his conclusions of law holding that Microsoft had violated the antitrust laws, Judge Jackson held a conference in his chambers to discuss the appropriate process for deciding on a remedy. Jackson expressed uncertainty as to the exact procedure that should be followed, but he was quite clear that he wanted to get the case to the appellate court as quickly as was possible, hoping that the remedy issue could be resolved within sixty days.[68] Although Microsoft strongly urged some form of hearing procedure to examine whatever remedial proposal the plaintiffs might advance, no conclusive decision emerged on what that procedure might be. Instead, Jackson simply entered an order scheduling the dates for the plaintiffs to produce their proposed remedies and for Microsoft to then produce its objections, counter-proposals, and "recommendations for future proceedings." A "hearing on remedies" was scheduled for May 24, 2000, only slightly within Jackson's sixty-day "limit."[69]

On April 28, the Department of Justice and the state plaintiffs filed a proposed final judgment seeking to split Microsoft into two companies and to impose a wide range of restrictions on Microsoft's business practices—restrictions that would be in effect until full implementation of the reorganization. On May 10, Microsoft filed its own proposed judgment, its objections to the plaintiffs' proposal, and a request for discovery and for a remedies "trial" to begin in December, seven months later.[70]

On May 24 the parties appeared before Judge Jackson for the scheduled "hearing on remedies," prepared to argue for the positions they had advanced in their briefs. Once again, however, Jackson surprised the parties. Whatever they might have expected him to order by way of further hearings, Jackson made clear at the very beginning of the hearing that he would decide the merits of the remedy without any further proceedings and that he was inclined to embrace the governments' proposed breakup. Microsoft's protestations that it was entitled to further "due process" were unavailing.[71]

Jackson's willingness to proceed without pausing for what he later called "unnecessary" hearings was consistent with the way he had managed the Microsoft litigation generally. Indeed, in the first contempt proceeding, he had entered a preliminary injunction on his own motion without any further hearings on the questions relevant to the issuance of an injunction, exhibiting limited patience for protracted proceedings. For that failure of process he was later roundly criticized by the court of appeals and reversed.[72] How much more likely would reversal be for failing to hold an evidentiary hearing on one of the most sweeping antitrust decrees ever proposed?

The plaintiffs immediately recognized the problematic nature of Jackson's decision, but decided neither to object nor to raise the issue in the papers they filed two days later. Their objection to the lack of hearings, if denied by Judge Jackson, might only solidify Microsoft's claim of error, and there was little indication that Jackson had any interest in further proceedings, as he made clear when he entered final judgment two weeks later.[73] Certainly it was hard to protest when the judge seemed to be about to award the plaintiffs exactly what they had requested.

Hindsight shows, however, that plaintiffs would have been better served had they been able to make a full record for their proposal, one tested by cross-examination. Whether Jackson would have agreed to such a hearing had the plaintiffs requested one, and how such a hearing would have affected the subsequent court of appeals' decision and the later settlement, are among the great unknowns of the *Microsoft* litigation.[74]

Jackson's Remedial Decree

The substantive provisions of Jackson's final decree had two basic parts. The first was the restructuring of Microsoft. The second was a set of interim prohibitions relating to specific aspects of Microsoft's conduct, to be in effect until the restructuring could be implemented.[75]

The decree's restructuring provisions envisioned breaking up Microsoft into two separate companies. One ("OpsCo") would carry on the "Operating

Systems Business," including Windows and the operating systems for servers and hand-held devices. The other company ("AppsCo") would carry on the "Applications Business," which included everything else that Microsoft did, including software, such as Office and Internet Explorer, and non-software, such as MSN (Microsoft's Internet service) and Expedia (an Internet travel service). The details of the restructuring were to be filled in later in a plan initially to be drafted by Microsoft and due within four months of entry of the decree.[76]

The decree's conduct prohibitions were more detailed than the basic divestiture plan, with nine categories of restrictions that covered broad areas of Microsoft's business and behavior. These were to be interim provisions, in effect either for three years after the divestiture plan was fully implemented or until the expiration of the term of the final judgment (ten years from the date of its entry), whichever came first.

The interim provisions focused on the exclusionary conduct proved during the trial. Various non-retaliation and uniformity requirements were designed to ensure that Microsoft would give equal treatment to its customers (such as OEMs) and to its complementary product providers (such as ISVs). Microsoft was required to license Windows to all OEMs on uniform terms, thereby depriving it of a major tool for rewarding OEMs for loyalty to its products and punishing disloyalty, and was forbidden to enter into exclusive agreements with third parties (such as Internet content providers) to distribute Microsoft middleware to the exclusion of competing products.

One major issue on which the parties had not been able to agree in the Posner mediation process was bundling. The interim decree sought to reestablish the normal market-driven feedback mechanism associated with consumer choice, forbidding Microsoft from "binding" a "Middleware Product" to a Windows operating system unless Microsoft offered an "otherwise identical" operating system in which all means of end-user access could readily be removed, either by OEMs during the installation process or by end users using the Add/Remove utility. This approach was quite similar to the Justice Department's earlier solutions, but with two major differences. First, although the decree didn't require Microsoft to take the "bound" code out of the operating system (a remedy that would have been consistent with Jackson's factual findings on improper commingling of code), the final judgment's anti-bundling requirement was meant to be merely a transitional remedy, ending after the divestiture was effective.[77] At the point, presumably, Microsoft's decision to bundle products into Windows would have to take broader market forces into account. Second, unlike the earlier contempt settlement, the decree provided for a reduction of royalties for

OEMs that removed end-user access. This meant that OEMs would have some financial incentive to offer their customers a choice of middleware, since they would no longer be paying for both Microsoft's product and the competing alternative.[78]

The second important remedy issue on which the parties had earlier been unable to agree was compulsory information disclosure. The interim decree took a broad approach, requiring disclosure of all APIs, "communications interfaces," and "technical information" that enabled interoperability with the Windows operating system running on a PC. Disclosure had to be done in a "timely manner"—for example, when the information was disclosed to Microsoft's applications developers, or when Microsoft used the information in any released software (even if the software wasn't in final form). Compliance with this provision was to be facilitated by the establishment of a "secure facility" at which Microsoft would make Windows' source code and any related documentation available to qualified representatives of OEMs, ISVs, and IHVs (independent hardware vendors) so as to enable them to work with that code to ensure "effective" interoperability.

Why Break Up Microsoft?

Judge Jackson's decision to break up Microsoft was momentous. It certainly wasn't the decision the parties had predicted he would make during the Posner mediation process. Indeed, Jackson wrote in his opinion that he had come to a structural remedy "reluctantly," but that he now thought it "imperative."[79]

Why did Jackson decide to order a breakup of Microsoft? In his opinion entering the decree, Jackson gave two basic answers, one administrative and one substantive.

On the administrative side, Jackson pointed out that Microsoft hadn't conceded that it had violated the antitrust laws and hadn't modified its "business protocol" to change its behavior or to alter what "it may yet do" in other markets in the future. Perhaps more significantly, in his view Microsoft had been "untrustworthy in the past" in terms of complying with court-ordered injunctive relief. Jackson recalled Microsoft's earlier literalist efforts to comply with the preliminary injunction he had issued in the contempt proceeding relating to the 1994 decree—efforts he now characterized as "illusory" and "disingenuous."[80] The implication was that injunctive relief was likely to be contentious and ineffective.

On the substantive side, Jackson pointed out that the provisions of the decree were the "collective work product of senior antitrust law enforcement officials of the United States Department of Justice and the Attorneys

General of 19 states, in conjunction with multiple consultants." Without further analyzing the decree, or even describing its provisions, except to say that the decree was "less radical" than one advocated in an amicus brief filed by four disinterested economists, Jackson simply concluded that the plaintiffs' proposal "appears to the Court" to address the principal objectives of a relief decree in an antitrust case—"to terminate the unlawful conduct, to prevent its repetition in the future, and to revive competition in the relevant markets."[81]

Whether Jackson's confidence in the plaintiffs' expertise was warranted is a good question, one that we explore in chapter 7 in the context of a broader discussion of remedies in monopolization cases. We can say here, however, that the parties' claims about the proposed restructuring were never exposed to courtroom testing, although both sides presented rather extensive briefs, supported with expert affidavits, at the May 24 remedies hearing. Instead, Jackson wrote an opinion in which he provided only sketchy justification for the decree's provisions and dismissed the value of taking evidence regarding the future effects of the plaintiffs' proposal. Not only did these failures provide grounds for the court of appeals' subsequent decision to vacate the decree; the lack of judicial exploration of the reasons for the decree's structural and conduct provisions also would make it easier for a new regime at the Department of Justice, and a new district court judge, to ignore whatever merits the proposal had.

Vacating Jackson's Remedy

Not surprisingly, the court of appeals held that Jackson had erred in not providing a hearing on the plaintiffs' proposed remedial decree. "It is," the court wrote sweepingly, "a cardinal principle of our system of justice that factual disputes must be heard in open court and resolved through trial-like evidentiary proceedings."[82] The court probably was influenced not only by this principle but also by the scope of the relief the plaintiffs sought. It specifically pointed to the disputes over the feasibility of breaking up Microsoft and to the impact of a breakup on consumers and shareholders. Making so significant a decision on such a highly disputed matter without any real exploration of the practicality or effect of the proposed relief was no one's idea of wise policy.

Although the court said that failure to hold a hearing was sufficient reason to vacate the decree, the court also included additional grounds for its decision. For one, Jackson didn't adequately explain how the decree would achieve the requisite objectives of antitrust decrees—that is, terminating the monopoly, denying the defendant the "fruits" of its violation, and ensuring that monopolistic practices will not recur. For another, the court of appeals had now "drastically" altered the district court's conclusions on liability. The new district court judge, therefore, would have to reconsider what the appropriate remedy should be in light of the violations the court of appeals had now upheld.[83]

The court's decision to vacate Jackson's decree because of the changes on liability issues effectively bifurcated the decisions on liability and relief and, paradoxically, somewhat validated Jackson's approach to the remedies phase. Jackson originally wanted appellate review of his liability decisions before he entered a remedial order. When he recognized that this avenue wasn't legally available, he short-circuited the remedies process and thereby minimized the delay in moving the case toward appellate review.[84] Had he taken the time for full hearings at that point, the court of appeals probably would still have vacated whatever order he had entered because it altered the bases for Microsoft's liability. On the other hand, had he been affirmed *in toto* except for his failure to hold a hearing, he would have been in no worse position in terms of time; he would have held the evidentiary hearings after the appeal with the bases of liability confirmed. What was lost in the process, however, was a hearing that might have justified structural relief and that might have diminished the court of appeals' natural skepticism about the wisdom of that approach.

Settling the Case

Regime Change

In vacating Judge Jackson's decree and remanding the case for further proceedings, the court of appeals provided only general directions for what a new remedial decree should require.[85] In view of the changes in the grounds of liability, the district court would have to reconsider which of the conduct restrictions in Jackson's decree were still necessary and whether the "sweeping equitable relief" of a structural remedy would be appropriate. The court of appeals also wrote that in order for the district court to again choose a breakup the plaintiffs would have to demonstrate that Microsoft's exclusionary conduct had actually resulted in the maintenance of its monopoly position in the market for operating systems (something even Jackson hadn't found) and that dividing what had always been a "unitary company" would be feasible. The new decree, the court of appeals cautioned, "should be tailored to fit the wrong creating the occasion for the remedy." Although the court didn't say so directly, the strong message was that the new decree should be narrowed to deal only with conduct that the plaintiffs had proved at trial.

The next steps in the litigation process would not only be affected by the court of appeals' decision, however. The year between Jackson's decision in June of 2000 and the court of appeals' decision in June of 2001 had brought a presidential election and a new Republican administration. The new head of the Justice Department's Antitrust Division, Charles James, was nominated twelve days before the appeal was argued to the D.C. Circuit Court of Appeals and confirmed two weeks before the court handed down its opinion. Although the election didn't affect the positions argued by the Department of Justice before the court of appeals (career lawyers in the solicitor general's office had argued the case on behalf of the Justice Department), it would certainly affect the continuation of the litigation, as the responsibility for that task now clearly fell to the new regime at the Department of Justice. In fact, in an interview before his nomination, James had expressed the view that a common operating system was beneficial for consumers and had predicted that the remedy in the *Microsoft* case would be limited to restrictions on Microsoft's conduct.[86]

At first, the post-appeal maneuverings looked much like a replay of both sides' earlier strategies. The plaintiffs urged a quick return of the case to the district court for the speedy determination of a new remedy decree. Microsoft sought further delay, asking for a rehearing in the court of appeals and then for a stay of the court's mandate pending the filing of a petition for Supreme Court review. Once again, a new operating system was on the horizon—this time, Windows XP. Microsoft intended to ship the final code in August of 2001, and to begin retail sales of Windows XP in October.

The court of appeals chose expedition, denying a rehearing and returning the case to the district court. A new trial judge, Colleen Kollar-Kotelly, was assigned to the case.[87] On August 28, 2001, four days after her selection, Judge Kollar-Kotelly ordered the parties to file a joint status report (in which they would identify "with specificity" the issues that she would have to resolve) and a schedule for whatever additional discovery and hearings would be required. The report was to be filed by September 14.

On September 6, before the Joint Status Report was issued and before there had been any substantive negotiations over a possible settlement, the Justice Department publicly announced two major changes in its litigating posture.[88] First, it would abandon its effort to obtain structural relief. Instead, it would seek an order "modeled after the interim conduct-related provisions of the Final Judgment previously ordered in the case." This meant that conduct provisions designed to be temporary and to supplement structural relief would now have to provide sufficient remedy on their own. Second, the Justice Department wouldn't seek to retry the Section 1 tying claim, which, as was noted earlier, had been remanded for possible reconsideration under the rule of reason. This meant that any final relief was unlikely to include any prohibition against tying separate software products to the Windows operating system; bundling prohibitions would be limited to Microsoft's effort to maintain its monopoly in the market for operating systems. The Justice Department was, in effect, inviting Microsoft back to the negotiating table, and on more favorable terms.

This announcement—the first indication that the remand would diverge from the original case and its remedial goals—was no run-of-the-mill tactical decision. President George W. Bush had been briefed about the Justice Department's review of the case by White House Counsel Alberto Gonzales, and had been told of Charles James' decision the day before it was announced. It was reported that the president had "no objections" to the decision to take these two items off the bargaining table.[89] This wasn't the first time that the White House had been informed about important decisions in the *Microsoft* case, although it may have been the first time that the president was informed.[90] But the decision to inform the president is a good reminder that the case had political importance in addition to its economic effect, and that there could be important consequences to backing away from a breakup of Microsoft.

With a structural remedy and the thorny issue of bundling off the table, the parties arranged to meet at the Justice Department's headquarters in Washington on September 11 to discuss a possible settlement. Because of the events that occurred that day, the meeting wasn't held.

Nine days later the parties filed a Joint Status Report in which Microsoft condemned the Justice Department's proposed conduct remedies as "every bit as radical as the now-discarded proposal to break up the company." The parties still appeared to be far apart, but the post-9/11 atmosphere had some effect. At a hearing on September 28, Judge Kollar-Kotelly, pointing out that a quick resolution of the case was "increasingly significant," ordered the parties to conduct "around the clock" negotiations.[91] She set two deadlines. First, she gave the parties two weeks to come up with a settlement on their own. Should they fail to do so, she would appoint a mediator, a step all the parties had opposed in their Joint Status Report. Second, she set November 2 as a deadline for producing a mediated settlement. If the parties were unable to come to terms, she would then schedule discovery, with hearings on the remedy to begin on March 11, 2002.

When the first two-week deadline didn't produce a settlement, Judge Kollar-Kotelly began the mediation process, but the process was structured very differently from the previous mediation under Judge Posner. She appointed as the mediator Eric Green, a law professor who specialized in mediation rather than in antitrust law. Working under a three-week deadline, Green and a colleague didn't try to draw up their own settlement; instead, they had the parties engage in an "extended series of joint meetings" that included the Justice Department, the states, and Microsoft. "No party was left out of the negotiations," the mediators subsequently wrote. "The bargaining table had three sides."[92]

The mediation process produced a settlement, but the differently structured process and the marathon negotiating sessions were not the only important factors. This time the two main parties—the Department of Justice and Microsoft—were prepared to settle. Not only were the uncertainties in the case far narrower for both sides than they were during the Posner mediation, but the new regime at the Justice Department was showing little interest in obtaining relief beyond stopping the practices specifically addressed in the court of appeals' opinion, as the Department's public withdrawal from structural relief indicated. Although the states weren't marginalized in the negotiations this time, the main parties' willingness to settle deprived the states of the apparent power the parties had given them in the Posner mediation—the power to derail a settlement.

In this more confined strategic context, the states were able to play a modest but constructive role, insisting on the addition of two potentially significant provisions. One was the establishment of an independent three-person "Technical Committee," composed of "experts in software design and programming," to monitor Microsoft's compliance with the decree but not to pass on whether there was technical justification for Microsoft's design decisions (the role assigned to a similarly named body in the course of the Posner mediation). Jackson's decree hadn't established such a support mechanism. In view of the technical nature of the decree and Microsoft's obligations, the addition of this body was a valuable improvement.

The other provision added by the states was the requirement that Microsoft license the protocols that controlled communications between Windows running on a desktop computer and Microsoft's server operating system. Server protocol disclosure had been raised during the Posner mediation and had been required in Judge Jackson's decree, even though no evidence about servers or about any exclusionary use of server protocols had been presented at trial. The theory behind such disclosure was that networks of computers, connected through servers, were playing an increasingly important role in the industry, opening up the possibility that server operating systems could become a new form of "middleware" to which applications writers could write, or on which applications could reside, and which might then become a competitive platform to Windows. Such a development would depend on the ability of servers to interoperate with PCs running Windows. Compulsory protocol disclosure would help to ensure this interoperability, precluding a repeat performance of Microsoft's strategy with respect to Netscape and Sun.

Protocol disclosure was a particularly contentious addition to the settlement, coming at the very end of the negotiations when Assistant Attorney Charles James told Microsoft that the states were insisting on it as a condition for joining the settlement. Although Microsoft agreed, Microsoft's proposed language for the provision was acceptable only to the Justice Department, not to the states.[93] As a result, when the parties appeared before Judge Kollar-Kotelly on November 2, as she had ordered, only Microsoft and the Justice Department had agreed to a settlement. None of the states had joined.

In the three days that followed this hearing, the states intensively reviewed the terms of the settlement among themselves and with industry critics of Microsoft. The states were in a difficult tactical position. A settlement had finally been reached in a notoriously difficult case that the judge wanted the parties to settle. The settlement would be reviewed under the Tunney Act, which governed the entry of Justice Department consent decrees in antitrust cases. Under that statute, the judge would be required to enter the settlement decree if she found it to be "in the public interest." The court of appeals had last interpreted that phrase in the earlier Microsoft licensing case, deciding that a judge had the discretion to disapprove only decrees that "make a mockery of judicial power" or are ambiguous or might be difficult to enforce.[94] It seemed unlikely that the states could convince the judge that the proposed settlement satisfied that test. If the judge did decide that the settlement met the public interest standard, how likely was it that the states could successfully argue for a different decree in their own case, particularly in view of the litigating resources that would be required for such an effort? Could the states really litigate these issues against Microsoft on their own?

Under the pressure of acceding to the inevitable, the joint venture among the states broke down. A group of nine states, led by New York, negotiated separately with Microsoft for a few changes in the decree's language, particularly in the protocol-disclosure provision, then announced that they would sign the agreement.[95] The remaining nine states and the District of Columbia still refused to join.

On November 8, 2001, the federal case and the case brought by the states, which had been consolidated shortly after being filed in May of 1998, were formally severed. Judge Kollar-Kotelly set up a two-track schedule, one for the Tunney Act proceedings reviewing the settlement that had been reached by the Justice Department and the "settling states" and the other for hearings on a remedy proposal to be submitted by the non-settling "litigating states."[96] Those states would now be put to the test.

The Terms of the Settlement

The settlement to which the Department of Justice, Microsoft, and nine states agreed took a "checklist" approach to the remedy, focusing mainly on preventing a recurrence of the conduct that had been proved at trial by addressing most but not all of the specific actions that had been reviewed by the court of appeals and found to be monopolizing conduct.[97] Included in the settlement were provisions governing dealings with OEMs (general non-retaliation, a requirement of uniform licensing terms, the lifting of certain licensing restrictions on the boot-up process and on icon displays), provisions restricting exclusive deals with various complementary product providers, and provisions forbidding retaliation against software and hardware developers for developing certain competing products. These provisions related either to Windows or to middleware products, and all of them had exclusions and provisos of varying clarity—for example, allowing Microsoft to enforce "any intellectual property right" (not otherwise limited) in a dispute with a software developer over the developer's support of competing software, or allowing OEMs to provide desktop shortcuts for non-Microsoft middleware so long as the shortcuts didn't "impair the functionality" (not otherwise defined) of the user interface.[98]

Compulsory disclosure of APIs and communications protocols wasn't on the checklist of conduct reviewed by the court of appeals, but it had been part of remedy demands from the beginning of the case through the Posner mediation to the Jackson interim decree. Despite the announced intention to seek a decree modeled after the Jackson interim conduct decree, the settlement pared back Microsoft's obligations from what they had been in Jackson's decree, restricting the API-disclosure provision to interoperation between Windows and Microsoft middleware rather than all Microsoft applications and delaying the disclosure obligation to later beta versions of the Microsoft products. The settlement decree also created a new set of exceptions to Microsoft's disclosure obligations relating to various "security" issues, including anti-virus security, digital rights management, and authentication and authorization, allowing Microsoft to limit licenses of these security-related technologies to firms that are "authentic" and "viable."[99]

The settlement of the bundling issue followed the pattern originally set in the settlement of the licensing contempt case: permit OEMs to hide the Microsoft program's functionality from consumers by removing end-user access.[100] The hope was that this would eliminate the disincentive OEMs had for installing a competing middleware program, the disincentive being the increase in support costs that comes from consumer confusion when the OEM provides two or more programs that do the same thing.

But the settlement had some further elaborations that made it questionable whether OEMs would exercise this option and offer non-Microsoft middleware. First, the settlement permitted Microsoft to provide end users with a mechanism to "enable" access to the hidden Microsoft middleware, which could lead again to consumer confusion over having similar programs. Second, the settlement allowed Microsoft, beginning two weeks after the consumer first booted up a PC, to automatically sweep away the desktop icons and shortcuts provided by the OEM, replacing them with Microsoft's, so long as the user confirmed the alteration. Third, in contrast with the Jackson decree, there would be no reduction in royalty rates if the OEM disabled access to Microsoft middleware so that it could install a competitor's offering. This meant either that the OEM would be paying more if it offered competing middleware or that the competing middleware company would have to license its software without royalties.

The remedy not chosen in the settlement was to require Microsoft to offer an unbundled version of Windows. The court of appeals had found that Microsoft's commingling of browser-functionality code with operating-system code violated Section 2 and lacked any technical or efficiency justification. Even under the checklist approach to remedy, the settlement could therefore quite properly have required Microsoft to "un-commingle" the browser code. Nevertheless, requiring unbundling might have required a costly redesign of Windows—a cost the government plaintiffs had acknowledged when they proposed the original decree to Judge Jackson requiring only the hiding of end-user access, although at the time they also said that unbundling might be appropriate. There was also the technical problem of specifying exactly what code constituted "the browser" in a way that would enable Microsoft to comply with an injunction that required that such code be removed from Windows without disabling it.

Whatever the problems of unbundling, the real question was whether leaving middleware code and APIs in the operating system would affect competition. The theory of the plaintiffs' case had been that middleware was competitively important because ISVs could write programs to interoperate with potentially cross-platform middleware, thereby lowering the applications barrier to entry that helped protect Microsoft's monopoly in the market for operating systems. Objectors to the settlement argued that leaving middleware code in the Windows operating system, even with end-user access disabled, would only perpetuate the applications barrier to entry. ISVs could still write to the APIs exposed by that middleware, and, in view of the ubiquity of Windows and the bundled middleware APIs, competing middleware producers would find it difficult to persuade ISVs to do otherwise. Cross-platform middleware would still be unlikely to emerge.

The Justice Department's argument against requiring unbundling didn't dispute the objectors' views about the effects of leaving middleware APIs in the operating system.[101] Instead, the Department focused on what had been shown at trial. Microsoft had been found liable because it denied OEMs the ability to hide end-user access to IE through the Add/Remove utility. Although commingling code was another way in which Microsoft had prevented OEMs from removing access to IE, the basis of liability was still the "presence, from the user's perspective, of the product." Hiding end-user access was sufficient to avoid potential confusion of end users, thereby removing the OEMs' disincentive to install rival middleware. Rather than try affirmatively to lower the applications barrier to entry (the promise that Netscape had presented and that Microsoft had extinguished), the settlement should be "based on the facts proven by plaintiffs at trial."

The term of the settlement decree was five years, with a possible one-time extension of the decree for "up to two years" if Microsoft engaged in a "pattern of willful and systematic violations." No specific penalties were set out for failures to comply with the decree (for example, a broader set of remedies that the plaintiffs could invoke if compliance efforts were inadequate[102]), nor were there any criteria by which the plaintiffs could measure the effects of Microsoft's efforts (for example, reports on the growth of competition in operating systems or in middleware). A contempt proceeding, the traditional remedy for non-compliance, was possible, of course, but the Justice Department's inability to hold Microsoft in contempt of an earlier antitrust decree had shown how difficult that approach would be. In view of Microsoft's past strategy of delay, the settlement raised the question whether Microsoft would simply try to play the clock out until the decree expired, complying with the settlement's affirmative requirements as slowly as it could.

Competing Remedies

The litigating states' remedy decree, presented to the district court within a month of the announcement of the settlement agreement, set the stage for competition between remedy proposals.[103] Their proposed decree called for a ten-year term, sought the appointment of a special master to monitor Microsoft's ongoing compliance, and provided various penalties for non-compliance, including civil fines and potential compulsory licensing of Windows' source code.

Although the litigating states didn't call for Microsoft's restructuring (the states had earlier abandoned that goal), their proposal went substantially beyond the relief agreed to in the settlement in three important ways:

• Microsoft would be required to offer, at a reduced license fee, an unbundled version of Windows from which all middleware code could be "readily removed."

• Microsoft would be required to auction a license to port Office to operating systems other than Windows or Macintosh, along with all necessary technical information.

• Microsoft would be required to license without fee the source code for Internet Explorer and any improvements Microsoft would make to it during the term of the decree (an "open source" license).

The litigating states' proposals grew out of their belief that the negotiated decree would prove too easy for Microsoft to evade and was unlikely to lower entry barriers or stimulate the competition that would replace the middleware threat that Microsoft had suppressed. But the litigating states' ambitions for more effective relief brought them up against some familiar problems and some new ones. Judging whether to unbundle all "middleware" (a much broader category than just the browser) would require a level of technical specification and understanding that might lead the judge to be concerned that she was being cast in the role of software designer, a role that had made the court of appeals apprehensive in *Microsoft II*. Adding to technical uncertainty was the predictive nature of the remedies the litigating states sought. Would unbundling really lower the applications barrier to entry, or would it merely hobble Microsoft and harm consumers? Would porting Office to another operating system really help that system to compete better? What would be the effect on innovation if Microsoft were forced to give up Internet Explorer and get nothing in return? Who would then invest in browser innovation?

The litigating states now had the burden of addressing these questions. They would have to prove that their proposals were manageable, were consistent with the court of appeals' decision, and carried out the goals of antitrust remedies as articulated in the prior case law: to unfetter the market from anticompetitive conduct, to terminate the illegal monopoly, to deny the defendant the fruits of its violation, and to ensure that no practices remain that might result in future monopolization.[104] The states had some hope of arguing that their proposals were consistent with the language used in prior cases, but the technical and predictive issues and the court of appeals' focus on the specifics of Microsoft's conduct were powerful forces pushing the district court to take a more modest approach toward relief than the states sought.

The evidentiary burden on the litigating states was also greater than the Justice Department's burden in the parallel Tunney Act proceeding to review the settlement agreement. The Tunney Act required soliciting public comment on the Justice Department's settlement (the Department received more than 32,000 comments on the *Microsoft* case, a record number; it received only about 600 comments on the AT&T breakup), but the "public interest" legal standard for judging the settlement was an easy one to meet under circuit case law, and Judge Kollar-Kotelly needed only one day of hearings to make the determination.[105] By contrast, the litigating states had the burden of affirmatively proving that their proposed decree would advance the multiple goals of relief that the court of appeals had set out. Meeting that evidentiary burden eventually required 32 trial days, the states and Microsoft calling more witnesses than Judge Jackson had permitted the parties to call when the case was originally tried on the merits.[106]

The two proceedings put Judge Kollar-Kotelly in a position unprecedented in the history of antitrust enforcement. She had two proposed remedy decrees before her in technically separate cases that involved the same defendant and the same legal and factual issues. As a legal matter she was free to treat the two decrees differently (their merits were being reviewed under different legal standards), but as a practical matter it would be surprising if she entered very different decrees in the two cases. Not impossible, but highly unlikely.

On November 1, 2002, a year after the settlement was announced, Judge Kollar-Kotelly simultaneously handed down her decisions in the two cases—two extensive opinions in which she meticulously reviewed the provisions of both proposed decrees.[107] In the Justice Department's case she entered the proposed settlement decree with only one minor change, retaining jurisdiction to act at her own discretion to issue further orders to carry out the judgment. In the litigating states' case she rejected every major proposal save one—requiring Microsoft to appoint a more independent compliance officer, similar to a provision that had been in Judge Jackson's decree but which wasn't in the settlement—and entered a decree that was virtually identical to the settlement decree she entered in the Justice Department case. To the very limited extent that she was dissatisfied with terms in the Justice Department settlement (for example, she called the provisions on automatic launching of non-Microsoft middleware one of the proposed settlement decree's "more obvious weaknesses"), she solved the problem by approving the settlement decree's provision as still being within "the reaches of the public interest," but then modifying the litigating states' decree to conform to her view of a more appropriate provision.[108] Microsoft, bound by both decrees, would be required to follow the litigating states' decree to the extent that it imposed any stricter obligations.

Four interrelated factors led Judge Kollar-Kotelly to take a highly negative view of the states' proposals. She concluded that the states' proof fell substantially short in many places; that many of the remedies were designed to benefit rivals and hurt Microsoft; that much of the effort to expand relief went beyond the case presented at trial and affirmed on appeal; and that a short-lived decree would be better in this fast-paced industry than a lengthy effort to oversee the redesign of Microsoft's products.

The judge's handling of the unbundling provision offers a good example of the difficulties the states faced in convincing her to adopt their proposed remedies. First, the unbundling provision hinged on a distinction between "middleware" and "operating system" that was difficult to define in a clear way and that went beyond the trial's evidentiary focus on browsers. More significantly, the judge also found that the economic evidence supporting code removal was "grievously inadequate." The litigating states presented only one economics expert to testify on the economic effects of all their remedy proposals (testimony that, in the court's view, was vital to the states' case), but the states' expert didn't testify in support of unbundling code.[109] This meant that the states had no economics testimony to show how unbundling middleware was necessary to "unfetter" the market and prevent the recurrence of monopolizing conduct.

By contrast, the court credited evidence presented by Microsoft that the proposed unbundling remedy would cause significant harm. Not only would the effort to unbundle code make ISV software more complex and more time consuming to develop; it would also place an enormous burden on Microsoft. As Bill Gates testified, even for only ten different removable middleware programs, Microsoft engineers would have to develop operating systems with more than a thousand different combinations while ensuring that each combination would perform effectively and without degradation.[110]

The end result of the states' proposal, Judge Kollar-Kotelly feared, would be the fragmentation of the Windows platform. In a competitive market, of course, there might be different operating systems, with different features; there would be no uniform operating-system platform. After hearing the remedies' evidence, however, Judge Kollar-Kotelly became convinced of the value of a single operating system with a consistent set of APIs to which ISVs could write compatible programs. In place of this model of the market for operating systems, she wrote, what the plaintiffs sought was a "balkanized" Windows and "a drastic remodeling of a product with over 95 percent of the market." Even had the states presented sufficient evidence to support their proposal, she said, she would have been "appropriately reluctant" to order this complete redesign of Windows, placing the court in the role of scrutinizing Microsoft's subsequent software-design decisions.[111]

Judge Kollar-Kotelly's concern that the litigating states' proposals were designed to burden Microsoft and to help its rivals rather than consumers came out even more clearly in the court's review of other proposals. Proposed broad API disclosure, Judge Kollar-Kotelly found, "would likely provide other software companies with the equivalent of the blueprints" to Windows, permitting them to offer "clone" products that would provide the same functionality as Windows. She agreed with Microsoft's economics expert that this was really "an 'intellectual property grab' by Microsoft's competitors"—a "windfall" for competitors who could avoid investing in creating "something new."[112] Similarly, she viewed the porting of Office as something sought just to benefit Red Hat Linux (a distributor of the Linux operating system), by relieving it of the "burden of developing its own office productivity suite."[113] And royalty-free licensing of Internet Explorer would expropriate the value of Microsoft's investment in the browser and diminish incentives for innovation. It was "the most transparent" intellectual property grab by Microsoft's competitors.[114]

Porting and an open-source IE, two of the states' most significant remedies, foundered on another aspect of Judge Kollar-Kotelly's decision. The judge took the court of appeals' decision to require that the relief ordered in the cases hew closely to the grounds for liability affirmed by the court of appeals. In her view, the proposals to port Office and to transform IE into an open-source browser, however, ignored the theory of liability of the original case, which had nothing to do with conduct that "directly hindered" other operating systems' ability to compete with Windows. "It is well recognized," the judge wrote, "that the theory of liability of the case concerns Microsoft's response to cross-platform applications, not operating systems."[115] Microsoft's conduct was directed at the applications barrier to entry. "It is difficult," she concluded, "to understand what role the bolstering of particular operating systems [through porting Office] will play in redressing anticompetitive conduct directed at middleware."[116]

The idea that the only appropriate remedy in the case should be directed at middleware seems curiously misplaced. Conduct directed at middleware wasn't a competitive problem for its own sake in the plaintiffs' monopolization case, but was of concern because it maintained the applications barrier to entry into the market for operating systems. Although porting and the royalty-free licensing of IE might have been unwise remedies if they wouldn't have improved competitive conditions in the market for operating systems, it is hard to see why they were legally improper remedies if the goal of the remedy was to foster market conditions that might allow for competition in operating systems—that might address the *consequences* of Microsoft's unlawful conduct.

Judge Kollar-Kotelly's reluctance to accept remedies that went beyond the exact facts of the case, however, didn't prevent her from approving the protocol-disclosure provision proposed in the Justice Department settlement decree. Recognizing that the protocol-disclosure provision was the most "forward looking" provision of the settlement, because it applied to server operating systems that hadn't been involved in the original litigation at all, the judge was still willing to approve the requirement because it would "likely prove beneficial to the development of middleware platforms." Placing this squarely within the type of facts proved at trial, she was able to conclude that protocol disclosure was consistent with the task before the court, which was "to *remedy* Microsoft's antitrust violations," not to make "general changes to the lawful aspects of Microsoft's business."[117]

"Imposing a remedy in this case isn't unlike trying to shoe a galloping horse," Judge Kollar-Kotelly observed. This led her to stick with the five-year term in the settlement decree, rather than the ten-year term the litigating states sought. The decree might be "forward looking," but who could predict in 2002 what the market might look like by 2012? No, by the time the settlement decree's five-year term was up "the market will have long since sent the horse to pasture in favor of more advanced technology."[118]

How wrong the judge turned out to be. In 2012—ten years after entering her decree—Microsoft still had more than 90 percent of the market for desktop-computer operating systems, and the browser was still an important software application.[119]

The Court of Appeals' Review

When the court of appeals reviewed Judge Jackson's decision in 2001, it expressed skepticism as to whether any remedy could be effective in the case. But Judge Kollar-Kotelly's extensive hearings and opinions, and the existence of a settlement to which Microsoft and the Justice Department had agreed, put the court of appeals in a different position in November of 2003, when it heard arguments on her decisions two years after the settlement agreement was announced. The court of appeals didn't have to decide whether the remedy decrees would actually be effective. Giving deference to Kollar-Kotelly's findings of fact—as it had earlier given deference to Judge Jackson's—it needed only be sure that she hadn't abused her discretion.[120]

Massachusetts was the only litigating state to appeal Judge Kollar-Kotelly's refusal to enter the states' proposed decree. Its appeal was argued before six of the seven judges who had heard the government plaintiffs' original appeal. They unanimously affirmed Judge Kollar-Kotelly on every point.

The court of appeals' treatments of two critical issues illustrate its ready acceptance of Kollar-Kotelly's decision. On the unbundling proposal, the court of appeals approved the judge's refusal to order the removal of code despite the court's own earlier finding that Microsoft's commingling of browser code and operating-system code had constituted monopolizing conduct. The court of appeals applauded Kollar-Kotelly's decision to require only that end users' access to middleware be blocked, because that remedy went to the "heart of the problem" without "intruding" into the design of Windows: "We say, Well done!"[121]

The court of appeals also accepted Judge Kollar-Kotelly's characterization of the proposal to order royalty-free licensing of Internet Explorer, agreeing that it appeared to be intended to benefit "specific competitors" (in this case Apple, which at the time didn't have access to the current version of IE) and, therefore, that it probably was inappropriate. The court acknowledged that this remedy might also lower the applications barrier to entry, noting that the states' economic expert had so testified, but it nevertheless concluded that Judge Kollar-Kotelly was within her discretion to refuse to impose this "drastic" remedy, limiting herself to other ways to reduce the applications barrier to entry, such as opening up OEM distribution channels to rival middleware.

The court of appeals also upheld Judge Kollar-Kotelly's decision to accept the Justice Department's settlement decree in the Tunney Act proceeding.

Two industry groups whose members included Netscape and Sun Micro-systems had intervened to file the appeal (the parties to a settlement, of course, have no interest in appealing a judge's decision to approve that settlement).[122] The court of appeals reversed Judge Kollar-Kotelly's decision to deny intervention, but then proceeded to affirm the entry of the decree as "in the public interest," applying the "narrow" standard for review that it had articulated in the earlier litigation involving Microsoft. Most of the issues were the same as in the litigating states' appeal; to the extent that the intervenors objected to provisions that were only in the settlement decree (the Technical Committee, for example), the court readily approved the judge's decision to accept them. The intervenors made only passing reference to the porting proposal (Massachusetts didn't raise it at all in its appeal), but they didn't discuss its merits, and, therefore, said the court, it wouldn't do so either.

Conclusion

With the court of appeals' decision approving Judge Kollar-Kotelly's decisions on remedy, the government plaintiffs' antitrust suits against Microsoft appeared to have come to an end. From the point of view of competition policy, however, the approval of the settlement was not the end of the matter at all, for it remained to be seen whether the remedies agreed to could be implemented quickly, whether they could be administered easily, and whether they could be effective. Indeed, however difficult the issues of substantive antitrust law may have appeared, designing an effective remedy was even harder. We will return to this issue in chapter 7, where we will discuss the challenges of designing effective remedies in monopolization cases more broadly. That discussion awaits an account of the efforts of the other institutional actors in the antitrust system—private parties and government agencies outside the United States—to call Microsoft to account for its actions.

5 Private Litigation in the United States

In the wake of the governments' cases against Microsoft, the firm faced more than 200 civil actions by private parties alleging they were injured by its conduct. The most easily predicted of these cases were filed by Netscape and Sun, the two most prominently identified targets of Microsoft's conduct in the governments' cases. But the governments' cases in the United States, and their counterpart in Europe (discussed in chapter 6), also generated cases by RealNetworks and Novell and a significant settlement with IBM. Although IBM never filed suit, it was identified as an injured party in the U.S. government's case. In addition, many class action suits were filed in state and federal courts on behalf of various classes of consumers and state entities—among them school districts that had purchased Windows-based PCs. Most of these consumer cases alleged "overcharges"—higher prices for Windows resulting from Microsoft's perpetuation of its monopoly in operating systems.

In this chapter we will not attempt to provide a comprehensive account of all of the cases filed against Microsoft. Our more modest goal is to use some of the principal private cases to illustrate and examine the primary features of the U.S. private antitrust system as revealed through the *Microsoft* cases. Particular attention is paid to the cases brought by Microsoft's competitors, and eventually settled, and to the class actions. To help provide a context for those discussions, we begin by explaining some essential features of the U.S. system of private antitrust litigation, highlighting those that provide specific incentives to encourage private litigation. We then turn to "multi-district litigation," the federal courts' mechanism for coordinating and consolidating the pretrial processing of multiple related claims, and how it affected the private *Microsoft* cases. With that foundation in place, we then turn to a more specific examination of the so-called competitor cases and to the class actions and their outcomes.

An Overview of the Private Antitrust Enforcement System in the United States

Uniquely in the world, U.S. antitrust law not only authorizes but actively facilitates private lawsuits by individuals and firms injured by antitrust violations. Section 4 of the Clayton Act, which has its roots in one of the original provisions of the Sherman Act of 1890, is the foundation of the private enforcement system. It creates a "private right of action," authorizing suit by "any person who shall be injured in his business or property by reason of anything forbidden in the antitrust laws," and permits the successful civil plaintiff to recover "threefold the damages by him sustained, and the cost of suit, including a reasonable attorney's fee."[1]

Although virtually all systems of competition law in the world authorize governments to enforce their substantive provisions, only some of these systems include private rights of action.[2] The U.S. system's added provision that prevailing plaintiffs can recover treble damages, attorneys' fees, and the costs of suit differentiate it from virtually every other system of competition law in the world today.[3] Outside the United States, private suits for violations of competition law are a relatively new and still developing practice, and treble damages are virtually unknown. Typically, the losing party is required to reimburse the winning party for its attorneys' fees and other costs of suit. (Attorneys' fees and costs tend to be far more modest outside of the United States, owing to differences in the procedures used to resolve cases before courts and in the litigation cultures of various nations.)

Treble damages and attorneys' fees thus are two signature features of the private right of action under U.S. antitrust law, and together they help to implement some important congressional policy choices. First, in establishing the private right of action, Congress recognized that public enforcement of the federal antitrust laws alone would not be adequate for policing and deterring anticompetitive conduct. The solution was to recruit "private attorneys general" to supplement public enforcement. By harnessing the self-interest of the injured, the public interest in promoting competition would better be served. The private right of action thus directly supports the goals of detection and deterrence.

Second, private antitrust lawsuits also serve a distinct compensatory function. Section 4 empowers injured persons, whether individuals or businesses, to recover for the harms they have suffered as a consequence of antitrust violations. As the Supreme Court observed in 1982, "the lack of restrictive language reflects Congress' 'expansive remedial purpose' in enacting § 4: Congress sought to create a private enforcement mechanism that would deter violators and deprive them of the fruits of their illegal actions, and would provide ample compensation to the victims of antitrust violations."[4]

In two influential 1977 decisions and one 1983 decision, however, the Supreme Court significantly limited the scope of Section 4. First, in *Brunswick Corp. v. Pueblo Bowl-O-Mat, Inc.*, it narrowed the type of "injury" that can qualify for challenge under Section 4 to "*antitrust* injury," which it defined as "injury of the type the antitrust laws were intended to prevent and that flows from that which makes defendants' acts unlawful."[5] In a second decision (*Illinois Brick Co. v. Illinois*), the Supreme Court restricted the right of recovery under Section 4 to "direct" as opposed to "indirect" purchasers, which significantly limited the availability of the treble damage remedy and increased federalist tensions in the antitrust remedial system.[6] Once barred from federal court, indirect purchasers—often consumers— elected to pursue their antitrust actions under state antitrust laws in state courts, which were more receptive to their standing and their claims. In 1983, the Supreme Court further constrained the reach of Section 4 in *Associated General Contractors of California, Inc. v. California State Council of Carpenters*. After acknowledging that "[a] literal reading" of the language of Section 4 "is broad enough to encompass every harm that can be attributed directly or indirectly to the consequences of an antitrust violation," the Court went on to hold that Congress didn't intend so broad a scope. Quoting from and building upon *Illinois Brick*, the Court reasoned that "[a]n antitrust violation may be expected to cause ripples of harm to flow through the Nation's economy; but 'despite the broad wording of § 4 there is a point beyond which the wrongdoer should not be held liable.'" To help identify that point, it drew upon the common-law tort principle of "proximate cause" and articulated a multi-factor test for evaluating the remoteness of claimed injuries linked to antitrust violations. Plaintiffs asserting injuries far removed from the defendant's conduct were barred from bringing suit.[7] Together these three decisions have limited both the scope of the private right of action and the range of compensation available under U.S. antitrust law.

Third, *treble* damages and attorney's fees together provide added incentives for the injured to detect and prosecute violations—and a disincentive for potential offenders to pursue conduct that violates the antitrust laws. Congress assumed that the typical private antitrust case probably would pit an individual or a small firm against a far larger firm or several firms. In contrast to the power of government, the parties and legal counsel who initiate private claims would need additional incentives to justify the challenging task, and the financial risk, of confronting corporate power. As a matter of economics, treble damages also can be understood as an accommodation to the likelihood that not every antitrust violation will be detected and prosecuted. In that event, single damages probably would be inadequate to deter unlawful conduct. The absence of government authority in the United States to recover civil fines from antitrust offenders further supports this economic rationale for treble damages.[8] In civil cases, the only source of monetary deterrence is the private treble-damages remedy. In the absence of an expectation that all violations will be detected, some multiplier is economically necessary to provide deterrence.

Treble damages and attorney's fees are but two of the features of U.S. antitrust law that provide incentives to initiate private antitrust litigation under Section 4. The federal antitrust laws also facilitate such actions by suspending the Clayton Act's four-year statute of limitations pending a related federal antitrust action (and for an additional year after it is concluded), which extends the permissible period in which to file a private suit. In addition, the Clayton Act authorizes private plaintiffs to offensively use the findings from a previous public prosecution in subsequent private cases. Together, Section 5 and common-law preclusion doctrine can reduce the burden of proof for a private plaintiff suing a defendant who has already been the target of a successful criminal or civil public enforcement action, diminishing the costs of subsequent litigation and eliminating the potential for inconsistent results. In some cases the follow-on plaintiff may even be totally excused from reestablishing liability. The only issues to be litigated will be causation, the amount of damages, and the propriety of other remedies.

This reduction of burden for such "follow-on" or "complementary" private actions can itself be a significant incentive to private parties interested in seeking compensation for injuries revealed through public enforcement actions. In contrast to a plaintiff who initiates an entirely new antitrust challenge, a follow-on plaintiff need not reestablish common claims through the often time-consuming and costly process of discovery and trial, and should be virtually immune in many cases from motions to dismiss and for summary judgment related to liability. As we shall see, however, over time—and in the *Microsoft* cases—the courts have read Section 5 and preclusion narrowly, depriving them of some of their effectiveness as aids to private plaintiffs. Moreover, because few government cases are tried through to judgment, and because the organized plaintiffs' antitrust bar no longer awaits the conclusion of government cases to initiate complementary, private cases, it is unlikely that the promise of preclusion plays a significant role today in promoting the initiation of private actions.

A final and more general feature of American law that can facilitate private antitrust civil actions is the class action. Under Federal Rule of Civil Procedure 23, a single party can initiate an action and seek to represent a class of similarly situated and similarly injured persons. The typical class action is characterized by widespread though individually modest harms. In such cases, the aggregate damage done can be considerable, but the individual harms are far too insubstantial to warrant initiation of individual civil actions. By allowing a single injured party to sue as the representative of a broader class of similarly injured people or firms, the class action empowers plaintiffs and independently promotes both deterrence and compensation.[9] The class action, however, has become increasingly controversial since assuming its current form in 1966. Precisely because it can facilitate litigation on behalf of expansive classes, class actions can be complex, can be costly, and can threaten alleged wrongdoers with very large damage awards—which will be trebled in antitrust cases. There is also no limit to the number of separate class actions that can be filed against the same defendant in connection with a single course of allegedly anticompetitive conduct. As a consequence, class actions have been the focus of aggressive criticism from defendants, from commentators, and from some courts. The critics fear that the device can be too readily abused to coerce defendants into settling less meritorious cases, and that this will lead to windfall recoveries and to over-deterrence of legitimate conduct.

All these incentives to initiate private antitrust challenges—treble damages, attorneys' fees, costs of suit, an extended limitations period, preclusion, and class-action procedures—influenced reactions to the initiation of the public Windows 98 cases discussed in chapters 3 and 4. The more than 200 private civil actions filed in both state and federal courts throughout the country revealed and tested the state of the law with respect to such issues as standing, causation, damages and other remedies, class-action certification and settlement, and the scope of preclusion. After more than ten years of litigation, however, all of the private cases were either settled or dismissed. Although a few cases went to trial, only one was submitted to a jury; and that jury deadlocked, leading to a verdict for Microsoft. It is likely that Microsoft eventually will pay more than $5 billion to settle all the private claims. Microsoft also agreed to expand its cooperation with some of its competitors, give away free software, or facilitate the purchase of hardware and software.

Yet Microsoft never agreed to significantly alter the business model that had first drawn the attention of public enforcers and had played a significant part in triggering the avalanche of cases against it: its strategy of "integrating new functionality" into Windows. Microsoft was persistent in maintaining that the conduct remedies imposed in the settlement of the government cases were fully adequate and required no supplementation in the private cases. As one commentator observed, Microsoft instead used "its cash horde to free itself of legal burdens, and in the process develop working relationships with companies that in the past it often sought to hobble."[10]

MDL No. 1332

The Judicial Panel on Multidistrict Litigation (often referred to simply as "the Panel") was created by Congress in 1968 in response to the electrical equipment antitrust cases of the early 1960s. Made up of seven sitting federal judges designated by the Chief Justice of the United States, it remains the principal institution for managing repetitive, related litigation in the federal courts. It is authorized to transfer multiple, related civil actions filed in different federal district courts to a single federal district court and consolidate them for coordinated pretrial proceedings.[11] It can order such consolidation when doing so would serve "the convenience of parties and witnesses and will promote the just and efficient conduct of such actions,"[12] a standard that is often met in private antitrust cases. Groupings or "clusters" of related cases are thereafter assigned a distinct docket number and are referred to as multi-district litigation (MDL) proceedings. Since 1968, of the nearly 400,000 civil actions that have been consolidated into more than 2,300 MDL proceedings, approximately 300 have involved antitrust claims.[13] The two threshold questions posed by any matter before the Panel are *whether* to transfer and consolidate and, if that is to be done, *where* the MDL proceeding should be constituted and before which judge.

Microsoft and some of the plaintiffs in the first wave of private cases spawned by the 1998 government prosecutions successfully invoked the MDL statute in December of 1999 to create MDL No. 1332. On April 25, 2000, in response to their motions, the Panel transferred 27 civil actions against Microsoft from 17 federal districts to Chief Judge J. Frederick Motz in the federal district court in Baltimore, Maryland for coordinated pretrial proceedings.[14] Each of the cases had been commenced, in whole or in part, on behalf of customers of Microsoft, and they alleged a variety of violations of federal and state law. Some of the cases had been initiated in federal court; others had been initiated in state court and then been removed to federal court by Microsoft.[15]

MDL 1332 alone eventually expanded to include 117 cases—a significant proportion of the civil cases filed around the country after the commencement of the government cases against Microsoft. At one point, the MDL court reported that an additional 73 cases that weren't removable remained in state courts, including 27 that were consolidated in California alone.[16] MDL 1332 included six cases filed by Microsoft's rivals (BeOS, Burst.com, Netscape, Sun, RealNetworks, and Novell) that were transferred in 2002. There were also numerous consumer class actions and individual and class actions filed by local governments, school districts, and other public entities. MDL 1332 wasn't closed until 2010, a decade after the MDL proceeding had begun.

Whereas the District of Columbia Circuit Court of Appeals had the final word on the governments' cases, as a consequence of MDL 1332 Judge Motz and the U.S. Court of Appeals for the Fourth Circuit managed and decided many of the private Microsoft cases. Judge Motz issued numerous opinions addressing indirect purchaser and other standing issues, class certification, class-action settlement, and two significant interpretations affecting the scope of preclusion and the operation of the statute of limitations under the Clayton Act. Likewise, between 2002 and 2007, the Court of Appeals for the Fourth Circuit issued seven substantive decisions, some affirming and some reversing his rulings. In this chapter we will examine some of the most important of these decisions; we will also examine others that remained outside the MDL proceedings. We will conclude the chapter with some thoughts about the relative costs and benefits of a system that facilitates multiple, related antitrust proceedings such as those faced by Microsoft.

The Competitor Cases

As we discussed in chapter 4, Microsoft, the Justice Department, and nine of the states that had joined in the 1998 government cases reached a settlement in November of 2001. Until that time, the Microsoft rivals on which the governments' cases had focused—Netscape and Sun—remained on the sidelines. Although they enthusiastically supported the public prosecutions and provided evidence and witnesses to the government, they did not play the more active role of litigants. That quickly changed after the governments settled with Microsoft.

Two months after the settlement was announced, AOL Time Warner, which had acquired Netscape in 1999,[17] commenced its own case against Microsoft. Shortly thereafter, Sun Microsystems did likewise. These two most obvious targets of Microsoft's anticompetitive campaign claimed billions of dollars in damages from Microsoft. Both cases were transferred to Judge Motz, where they joined MDL 1332.[18]

Although the availability of treble damages no doubt provided a significant motive for Netscape and Sun to sue, they also sought to rectify the shortcomings of the governments' case and the perceived weakness of the governments' settlement. As we described in chapter 4, the governments' settlement focused narrowly on prohibiting Microsoft from again engaging in the specific conduct that the D.C. Circuit Court had found unlawful. It did little, however, to remedy the continuing competitive consequences of that conduct. Through their respective suits, Netscape and Sun sought to counteract the effects of Microsoft's conduct more specifically—in effect, to augment the settlement that had been reached by the government. To do so, they would also need to succeed where the government had failed in proving all of the claims in its case. The governments' failure to prove the existence of a distinct "browser market," for example, was a primary reason for Netscape to pursue its own case. "In some ways," one journalist reported, "the Netscape lawsuit is trying to achieve what the government failed to do … at trial, such as proving Microsoft tried to extend its Windows Monopoly to the browser market."[19] Such a finding would fortify its argument that any effective remedy would have to include some kind of court-ordered unbundling of Windows and IE—an injunction forcing Microsoft to decouple IE from Windows, perhaps through the sale of a version of Windows that didn't include an integrated browser.[20] For Sun, the goal was to force Microsoft to include genuine Java—not the "polluted" Windows-only version developed by Microsoft—in Windows. This became known as the "must-carry remedy." Judged by these remedial goals, the two cases ultimately failed.

The Complaints

Microsoft's assault on Netscape and Sun had been a focal point of the governments' Windows 98 case and the district court's findings of fact. As we discussed in chapters 3 and 4, Microsoft perceived the success of "middleware" (specifically Sun's Java programming language and Netscape's Internet browser) as an unfolding threat to its operating-system monopoly. Through a variety of contractual, technological, and other means, it sought to squelch that threat. Although the D.C. Circuit Court had reversed some of the district court's specific conclusions, it largely upheld its findings with respect to this central narrative of the governments' case.[21]

Not surprisingly, Netscape's complaint largely reasserted the central allegations and theories of the governments' case—theories that Netscape (aided by its lawyers and economists) had developed and had advocated for years. The opening paragraph of the complaint quoted the district court's conclusion that "Microsoft's illegal acts 'inflicted considerable harm on Netscape's business.'" The avowed goal of the lawsuit was "to prevent further injury to Netscape, to restore competition lost in the market for Web browsers, to foster competition in the market for operating systems, and to receive treble damages compensation for the harms inflicted upon it by Microsoft." In seven counts based on federal and state law, the complaint thereafter sought to build upon the governments' successful claims and to revive their less successful claims—specifically those of illegal tying of IE and Windows and of attempted monopolization of the browser market. Moreover, in addition to treble damages, costs, and attorneys' fees, the complaint prayed for "injunctive relief sufficient to prevent further antitrust injury to Netscape and to restore competition lost in the market for Web browsers, and to enable middleware platforms to compete with Intel-compatible PC operating systems."[22] This prayer for relief—an obvious, implicit criticism of the government settlement—hinted at Netscape's interest in pursuing an "unbundling" remedy like that pressed by the non-settling states. As one commentator observed, "one option" would be "forcing Microsoft to release a version of Windows without its own 'middleware' products such as a Web browser, media player or instant messenger."[23]

Sun's complaint similarly sought to both build upon and supplement the governments' case, but Sun's legal entanglement with Microsoft long predated the governments' case and was broader in scope than Netscape's. Before the governments' antitrust cases were filed in 1998, and long before Sun filed its own antitrust case against Microsoft, Sun had sued Microsoft in a California federal court, alleging breach of a 1996 Technology License and Distribution Agreement (TLDA), trademark and copyright infringement, and unfair competition under California law. This earlier California litigation, though it didn't assert any federal antitrust claims directly, echoed themes that were further developed in the governments' antitrust cases and laid the foundation for Sun's later antitrust claims, which were filed after the governments' cases were settled.

The California cases focused on Microsoft's alleged distortion of the intent behind the TLDA, which licensed Microsoft to develop its own version of Java. One important proviso of the agreement was that Microsoft maintain Java's cross-platform character. To that end, the agreement also included some specific restrictions on Microsoft's development activities to ensure that it wouldn't transform Java into a Windows-specific platform. When Microsoft failed to adhere to those restrictions, Sun sued, challenging Microsoft's efforts to instead create a "polluted" Windows-only version of Java. The California cases were resolved in January of 2001 with a $20 million payment to Sun and Microsoft's agreement to phase out distribution of its version of Java, but the settlement agreement specifically reserved Sun's right later to assert antitrust claims arising from the same conduct or from related conduct.[24]

Sun's initial antitrust complaint against Microsoft, filed in March of 2002, was later amended twice. The Second Amended Complaint, filed in November of 2003, included thirteen separate counts. In addition to claims that Microsoft had maintained a monopoly in the market for operating systems for Intel-compatible PCs that had been found in the governments' cases, it alleged unlawful tying of IE to Windows and an illegal attempt to monopolize the market for Internet browsers, as did the Netscape complaint. But it also went much further. Additional counts complained of attempted monopolization of the market for operating systems for workgroup servers, tying of the Windows workgroup-server operating system to Windows, tying of certain Web server software to the Windows workgroup-server operating system, and monopolization of the alleged market for office-productivity suites. The server-related claims were similar to those being asserted in the European Commission, and those related to office productivity echoed some of the original claims brought by American states.

Sun's complaint also introduced some new theories that focused more particularly on Java, alleging that Microsoft had attempted to monopolize what Sun called the market for "general purpose, Internet-enabled, distributed computing platforms"—software, such as Java, that facilitated the development of programs designed to be disseminated via the Internet. This claim was prompted not only by Microsoft's effort to distort cross-platform Java, but also by its introduction in February 2002 of "Visual Studio .Net," a Windows-tooled middleware programming product that constituted Microsoft's competitive response to Java. The complaint included a distinct claim that Microsoft had unlawfully tied .Net to both Windows and its workgroup-server operating system.[25]

In addition to the Netscape and Sun cases, RealNetworks commenced its own action in the federal district court in San Jose, California on December 18, 2003. Less directly linked to the U.S. government cases, RealNetworks' complaint nevertheless drew upon some common economic ideas, such as network effects and the applications barrier to entry, to explain Microsoft's power in the market for desktop-computer operating systems. It also reiterated some of the principal assertions regarding Netscape and Java. But its focus was more closely related to the case that had been initiated against Microsoft by the European Commission, which focused on RealNetworks' main product—media players—although here too it drew analogies to Netscape and Java. According to the complaint, just as Netscape had pioneered the Web browser, RealNetworks had developed digital and streaming media technology, including media player software that exposed its APIs. As cross-platform middleware, RealNetworks' media player also threatened Microsoft's OS monopoly. And just as Microsoft had responded to Netscape by emulating its Internet browser and then incorporating its own browser into Windows, Microsoft emulated RealNetworks' media player and then incorporated its version—Windows Media Player—into Windows.[26]

In November of 2004, Novell became the last of Microsoft's major competitors to commence an antitrust action against Microsoft. Although it reiterated and sought to build upon many of the allegations in the governments' and the competitors' cases, Novell's case focused more on Microsoft's Office suite of office-productivity software, not on Internet-related products, because Novell was primarily focused on word processing software and spreadsheet software. Thus, although Count I of its complaint alleged monopolization of the "Intel-Compatible Operating Systems Market," Counts II–V were all expressly directed at monopolization and attempted monopolization of alleged markets for word processing and spreadsheet applications. Although Count VI, the final claim, was interpreted by the Court of Appeals for the Fourth Circuit as also relating to the market for operating systems, it alleged more generally that Microsoft had entered into exclusionary agreements that unreasonably restrained trade in violation of Section 1 of the Sherman Act.

Nevertheless, Novell sought to link Microsoft's competitive strategies directed at office-productivity software with the economic theory of the governments' cases, arguing that Microsoft's conduct with respect to WordPerfect, which Novell owned from 1994 to 1996, was designed to protect its Windows monopoly. Much as the governments, Netscape, and Sun had argued that Microsoft perceived cross-platform middleware as a threat to the applications barrier to entry that had evolved and had protected Windows' dominance, Novell argued that its office-productivity software was perceived by Microsoft as a threat for the very same reasons. A platform-neutral office-productivity suite that exposed its own APIs and shared files with Office could facilitate more competition in the market for operating systems.

Novell's complaint also presented a fascinating history of software development that predated the rise of the Internet and the related events involving Netscape and Sun. It alleged that, in response to Microsoft's introduction of Microsoft Office in the early 1990s, the rival software developers WordPerfect Corporation and Borland had agreed to cooperate with each other in creating their own "suite" of office-productivity software. WordPerfect Corporation made WordPerfect (one of the pioneering word processing programs, and a very successful one), and Borland made Quattro Pro (one of the earlier and more successful spreadsheet programs). In mid 1994, Novell acquired WordPerfect Corporation and secured the rights to Quattro Pro and to GroupWise (an email program) in order to assemble its own suite of office-productivity programs, "PerfectOffice," which it intended to use to challenge Microsoft's Office.

According to its complaint, an essential component of Novell's strategy—and one of the principal reasons Microsoft viewed it as a threat—was its commitment to "OpenDoc," which Novell described as "an 'open-source' standard for cross-platform linking and embedding." Novell further alleged that "OpenDoc allows users to view and edit information across applications, directly in competition with Microsoft's" alternative, proprietary standard. Novell also developed "AppWare," a software-development tool that, like Java, exposed its APIs, making it possible to write programs that would work with PerfectOffice regardless of the operating system. According to Novell:

This Novell portfolio of OpenDoc, AppWare, and WordPerfect software posed a competitive threat to Microsoft's operating system monopoly similar to that described in the Government suit. ... Like the Netscape-Java combination, the combination of WordPerfect, a popular application, with the system neutral Open-Doc protocol and AppWare development environment, threatened Microsoft's operating system monopoly.[27]

Novell accused Microsoft of trying to squelch this threat by significantly impairing the functionality and hence the marketability of Novell's products, largely by withholding technical information that would permit them to interoperate fully and effectively with Windows 95. Novell also alleged that Microsoft sought to exclude Novell's office-productivity applications from the most effective channels of distribution, especially computer manufacturers, by requiring such OEMs to license Office as a condition of licensing Windows and by prohibiting the installation of competing office-productivity software. Finally, Novell accused Microsoft of manipulating its "Windows-compatible certification" program to force Novell and others to utilize Windows-specific technologies that degraded the performance of their products and, when Novell refused to do so, by refusing to certify its products as "Windows compatible."[28] Novell concluded its lengthy complaint by alleging that the collective impact of Microsoft's conduct was to delay, raise the cost of, and otherwise interfere with Novell's product-development and sales efforts, suppressing innovation, foreclosing consumer choice, and damaging competition.[29] For a variety of unique reasons, as we shall see, Novell's claims were among the most procedurally complex claims made in the competitors' suits, presenting issues of standing, limitations, and assignment of rights. The one claim that eventually reached trial on its merits resulted in a deadlocked jury and no verdict. On appeal, the surviving remnant of Novell's case was dismissed in 2013.

Resolving the Competitors' Cases

The cases initiated by Netscape, Sun, and Novell produced three important decisions from the U.S. Court of Appeals for the Fourth Circuit. The first—the "must-carry" remedy—focused solely on Sun and concerned its effort to require Microsoft to distribute Java with all copies of Windows and IE. The second determined the degree to which the plaintiffs could preclude Microsoft from relitigating the 412 distinct factual findings that had been made by Judge Jackson in the governments' cases. It was broader in scope and implication than the Sun must-carry appeal, and involved both rival and class-action plaintiffs. The third, like the first, concerned issues unique to one party, in this instance Novell. Collectively, the three decisions largely favored Microsoft and significantly constrained the competitor plaintiffs' efforts to seek both compensation and remedies that would supplement those secured by the governments' settlement.

Recall that the D.C. Circuit Court, in endorsing an essential predicate of the governments' cases, had concluded that Microsoft perceived Sun's Java as an emerging threat to its operating-system monopoly. As middleware that could run on any kind of operating system and that exposed its own APIs, Java rendered operating systems more of a "commodity." And, as was noted above, that threat was amplified by Netscape's Internet browser, which provided a cost-effective means of disseminating Java.

In its follow-on complaint, Sun alleged that Microsoft had pursued an "embrace and extend" strategy to quell that threat. First, in 1996, it embraced Java, licensing it from Sun. It then "extended" Java, reengineering it into a Windows-only platform. Then, by exploiting the ubiquity of

Windows and widely distributing its own altered version of Java, Microsoft extinguished Java's true potential as cross-platform software.[30] By the time Sun initiated its separate antitrust litigation, it also added to these allegations Microsoft's efforts to destroy Java's primary channel of distribution: Netscape's browser. Judge Motz later explained: "While ... deliberately fragmenting the Java platform to make it less attractive for developers and users, Microsoft also successfully embarked upon a campaign to destroy Sun's channels of distribution for Java."[31] The final piece of the strategy was Microsoft's introduction in early 2002 of its own competing programming product, .Net, which together with the governments' settlement prompted Sun to file its antitrust suit.

With the decline of Netscape's fortunes and the failure of Sun's effort to secure Microsoft as a partner in the development and dissemination of unadulterated Java, Sun was in need of an alternative strategy for distributing Java. Ironically, its best option was now Microsoft. Securing that alternative thus became a major goal of Sun's antitrust action against Microsoft.

In the fall of 2002, in the course of the MDL proceeding, Sun asked the district court for a preliminary injunction requiring Microsoft to distribute Java with every copy of Windows and IE. This became known as the "must-carry" remedy. Early in December of 2002, several weeks after the conclusion of a three-day hearing, Judge Motz announced his intention to grant the motion, agreeing with Sun that "[t]he 'must-carry' remedy ... is designed to prevent Microsoft from obtaining future advantage from its past wrongs and to correct the distortion in the marketplace that its violations of the antitrust laws have caused."[32] In January of 2003, after additional hearings, Judge Motz delivered the remedy that Sun had hoped for. Commencing 120 days after entry of the court's order, Microsoft was enjoined: "from distributing the Windows PC Operating System or Microsoft Web Browser unless ... Microsoft incorporates and distributes in each copy of its Windows PC Operating System and Microsoft Web Browser, without modification and as the Default JRE [Java Runtime Environment], the JRE Software delivered to Microsoft by Sun prior to the effective date of this Order. ..."[33] With Judge Motz's Order, Sun had realized one of the principal goals of its suit against Microsoft. But its victory was short-lived.

In June of 2003, the Court of Appeals for the Fourth Circuit reversed Judge Motz's Order, effectively ending Sun's hope for a must-carry remedy. In an opinion authored by Circuit Judge Paul V. Niemeyer, the court concluded that Sun had failed to satisfy one of the long-standing prerequisites for a preliminary injunction: immediate and irreparable harm. Whereas Judge Motz viewed the must-carry injunction as necessary to preserve Sun's market position pending a full trial on its allegations, the Court of Appeals instead concluded that there was no immediacy to the threat.[34]

A critical point of disagreement between Judge Motz and the Court of Appeals for the Fourth Circuit involved the notion of "tipping." As explained by Sun's economist, Dennis Carleton, and as embraced by the district court, competition in the emerging middleware market for general-purpose Internet-enabled distributed computing platforms was "for the field." Owing to network efforts, it was likely that at some point the field would "tip" in favor of one or another platform. Thus, although Sun was in fact the current leader in the market, Microsoft's tactics, including the introduction of .Net, could lead to a tipping away from Java in favor of .Net. The district court concluded that the injunction was necessary to preserve the status quo and prevent this tipping, which would be the fruit of Microsoft's unlawful conduct, not of any superior Microsoft product. If it occurred, the consequent monopolization would be all but irremediable by the courts.

The court of appeals rejected that conclusion through a combination of imposed procedural hurdles and pointed criticism of the district court's reasoning. It began by emphasizing that the standard for issuing a "mandatory" injunction—a court order that affirmatively requires new conduct, in contrast to a "prohibitory" injunction, which merely prohibits specified actions—is exacting. It then divided the test for issuance of a preliminary injunction into two parts. First, certain "conditions precedent" had to be established:

> In sum, preliminary injunctions are extraordinary interlocutory remedies that are granted in limited circumstances and then only sparingly. The limited circumstances amount to the demonstration of a need to protect the status quo and to prevent irreparable harm during the pendency of the litigation to preserve the court's ability in the end to render a meaningful judgment on the merits. If that need is not presented, then a preliminary injunction should not be considered.

If such a need is demonstrated, according to the Fourth Circuit, a district court should proceed to balance four factors: the likelihood that the plaintiff will suffer irreparable harm, the likelihood that the defendant will suffer harm as a result of the injunction, the plaintiff's likelihood of succeeding on the merits, and the public interest.

In the court's view, the alleged threat of tipping was a "future harm" that "was not sufficiently immediate and therefore too speculative." Sun therefore had failed to establish the initial condition for a mandatory injunction—immediate and irreparable harm—and it was unnecessary to undertake a weighing of the relative burdens of an injunction on Sun and Microsoft. The court also rejected Sun's claim of present harm from the alleged market distortion caused by Microsoft's conduct, concluding that it was "defined at too general a level to warrant the relief ordered," particularly since the district court hadn't undertaken any effort to define the purported market for "general purpose, Internet-enabled distributed computing platforms."

The court's "two-step" sequential approach was rigidly formalistic and can be faulted on a number of grounds. First, and glaringly, the burden on Microsoft of carrying Java would have been light in comparison with the threat that faced Sun. Microsoft had already been carrying original Java and later would carry its own, altered version, so inclusion of the Java code in Windows and IE would have involved little if any additional effort on its part. Thus, had the court utilized a more integrated approach that fused the "conditions precedent" with the weighing of impact, it could have more readily balanced the relative harm to Sun and Microsoft and it might have reached a different ultimate conclusion.

Second, the court's announced standard for granting relief imposed an unusually heavy burden on plaintiffs seeking any kind of preliminary injunction, especially a "mandatory" injunction, revealing an unspoken yet strong and largely unexplained bias against preliminary injunctions. Quoting language from previous Fourth Circuit cases, the court described preliminary injunctions generally as "*extraordinary* remedies" that involve "the exercise of *far-reaching power*" and hence should only be ordered "*sparingly* and in limited circumstances." It then declared, with little additional support, that "application of this *exacting* standard of review is even *more searching* when the preliminary injunctive relief ordered by the district court is mandatory rather than prohibitory in nature."[35] Even its exaggerated distinction between "mandatory" and "prohibitory" injunctions seems debatable at best—the line between the two may not always be pronounced and is unlikely to be significant in many circumstances. Indeed, in Sun's case it is arguable that there was no "prohibitory" injunction that could have preserved the status quo and that the mandatory injunction being sought was far less invasive than a prohibitory injunction that might have ordered Microsoft to immediately cease distribution of its own altered version of Java. The court of appeals thus seemed to approach the case decidedly predisposed to denying motions for preliminary injunctions—an approach that is uncommon among other courts. Reliance by one federal circuit on such a uniquely demanding standard illustrates how the choice of a transferee court in MDL proceedings can affect the ultimate outcome of transferred cases.

More deeply, the court's approach implicitly rejected one of the central assumptions of the D.C. Circuit Court's opinion in the government cases: that Section 2 must be read to protect nascent sources of competition as well as fully mature sources. Throughout the *Microsoft* cases, Microsoft and its critics argued that the courts were poorly equipped to make decisions on Internet time—they were simply too slow, and markets would correct themselves more quickly than courts could. Yet when the district court in Sun's case tried to anticipate and respond to that possibility by acting early enough to make a difference, the court of appeals reversed, claiming that the harm was too remote. By the time tipping is evident, however, action by a court probably will come too late to preserve the competitive status quo and permit the court to order meaningful relief should it conclude that a violation has occurred. The Court of Appeals for the Fourth Circuit embraced a standard, therefore, that when satisfied would almost certainly come too late to be effective in cases involving illegal efforts to smother new competition, especially in technology industries.

It is no response to this paradox to argue that the D.C. Circuit Court also emphasized the need for adequate evidence of causation—that is, of links between the violation, the harm, and the remedy. To the extent that causation is a requirement of any antitrust case, it is relevant to the ultimate disposition of the case on the merits. As the Court of Appeals for the Fourth Circuit itself seemed to acknowledge, one of the essential purposes of a *preliminary* injunction is to preserve the court's ability to remedy a violation if one is found after a full trial on the merits. In this instance, Judge Motz had the better sense of how to balance protection of nascent competition and concerns about causation. That balance is best struck when the court, faced with significant evidence of a violation, uses the preliminary injunction to preserve the viability of a competitive threat that, once eliminated, will be beyond its power to recreate. This was surely a lesson of the collective *Microsoft* cases, which in the end were impotent to restore Netscape and Sun to the position of potential they had before Microsoft commenced its anticompetitive campaign.

In a later section of its opinion, the Court of Appeals for the Fourth Circuit approached the law of monopolization in a similarly rigid fashion. Sun had sought its preliminary injunction on the basis of Count 1 of its complaint, which alleged that Microsoft sought to maintain its operating-system monopoly. As the court put it, this raised a seemingly paradoxical question:

"The essential question arises therefore about how a preliminary injunction entered to regulate conduct in an emerging and undefined market [i.e., the alleged market for general-purpose, Internet-enabled distributed computing platforms] preserves the court's ability to render meaningful judgment on the merits of Sun's claim that Microsoft monopolized the market for worldwide licensing of Intel-compatible PC operating systems, a market that by definition does not involve middleware." In the appellate court's view, the district court solved this "two-market problem" by adopting from Sun a discredited theory: that Microsoft was seeking to use its operating-system monopoly to "leverage" its way into the emerging middleware market for general-purpose Internet-enabled distributed computing platforms, where its market share was still quite small. In the court's view, which was well supported in the case law, "monopoly leveraging" couldn't constitute a stand-alone Section 2 violation unless the leveraging rose to the level of threatening attempted monopolization of the second market. As a result, the Court of Appeals for the Fourth Circuit concluded that the district court erred when it relied on a monopolization count that concerned Microsoft's operating-system monopoly to issue a preliminary injunction designed to preserve competition in a different "market" that hadn't been defined fully and in which Microsoft's current market share was far too small to satisfy a valid claim for attempted monopolization.

But here again the Court of Appeals for the Fourth Circuit approached its task very rigidly, implicitly rejecting some of the essential economic theories that pervaded the *Microsoft* cases. The "tipping" theory urged by Sun and endorsed by the district court was integral to the theory of network effects endorsed in the government cases to establish Microsoft's monopoly power in the market for PC operating systems. Moreover, the D.C. Circuit Court had no problem recognizing that Section 2 of the Sherman Act protects nascent competition from exclusionary behavior, even though at the moment of exclusion that threat may not be fully formed and immediate. Microsoft itself certainly viewed Java and Netscape together—as middleware—as a sufficiently concrete threat to its operating-system monopoly to warrant a concerted effort to drive them from the market. And even though the D.C. Circuit Court rejected the government's claim that Microsoft attempted to monopolize a distinct market for Internet browsers on the ground that it didn't define the market adequately, it upheld the monopolization claim on the ground that Microsoft's elimination of a potential threat to its own monopoly was actionable even though that threat hadn't yet been fully realized and even though it had taken shape in a seemingly different "market."

The court of appeals' focus on leveraging theory, therefore, was an exercise in misdirection. Preserving Java's viability as middleware, as the district court had attempted to do, preserved it as a threat to Microsoft's operating-system monopoly, both directly as a nascent platform itself and indirectly to the extent it was cross-platform middleware and could generate incentives for others to develop new operating systems. There was thus no disconnection, as the Court of Appeals for the Fourth Circuit seemed to conclude, between the requested injunction and the allegations of the complaint with respect to the market for operating systems. In the end, the Court of Appeals for the Fourth Circuit simply erected hurdle after hurdle before Sun's case, making it very unlikely that the victim of a well-conceived exclusionary strategy in an emerging market could ever secure the intermediate protection needed to permit the court to fully evaluate the alleged monopolist's strategy. In doing so, it unnecessarily constrained the Sherman Act's capacity to shield new and innovative competitors from exclusionary attacks from incumbents—at least in the Fourth Circuit.

Sun and its fellow Microsoft rivals suffered yet another setback from the Court of Appeals for the Fourth Circuit just six months after the must-carry ruling, but this one divided the court and had far more wide-ranging implications for the many plaintiffs in MDL 1332.

As we noted at the beginning of this chapter, Section 5 of the Clayton Act permits subsequent private plaintiffs to use the findings of fact from a previous successful government prosecution to establish their own *prima facie* case. Subsequent plaintiffs also can avail themselves of the common-law doctrine of collateral estoppel or "issue preclusion" to prevent the relitigation of facts tried and found against a common defendant from the earlier case.[36]

Judge Jackson's disposition of the government *Microsoft* cases included 412 distinct findings of fact, but, as we learned in chapters 3 and 4, not all of his conclusions of law were affirmed on appeal. A critical issue in the subsequent cases became, therefore, whether and to what degree the private plaintiffs could invoke collateral estoppel to preclude Microsoft from relitigating Judge Jackson's factual findings in light of the reversal of some of his conclusions of law.[37]

In August of 2002, a group of plaintiffs in the MDL proceedings that included a consumer class, but also Netscape, Sun, Burst.com, and Be Incorporated, moved Judge Motz for an order precluding Microsoft from relitigating 356 of the 412 findings entered by Judge Jackson. Consistent with the purposes of preclusion doctrine, these plaintiffs sought to use the vigorously contested results of the government cases to significantly limit their burden of reestablishing Microsoft's antitrust liability. Judge Motz responded by granting much of the motion, concluding that Microsoft would be precluded from relitigating 350 of Judge Jackson's findings of fact.[38]

The parties clashed sharply, however, on the import of the D.C. Circuit Court's reversal of some of the district court's conclusions of law and on the standard to be used in determining the scope of preclusion. As to the first point, Judge Motz was persuaded by the plaintiffs' argument that "many of the facts underlying the tying, attempted monopolization, and exclusive dealing claims [which were legally rejected in various ways] underlie the monopoly maintenance claim [which was affirmed] as well and, therefore, should be given preclusive effect." The second issue—the standard to be used to define the scope of preclusion—turned out to divide not only the parties, but the district and appellate courts.

As Judge Motz observed, the plaintiffs and Microsoft appeared to agree that traditionally preclusion would be accorded only to findings that were "necessary to the prior judgment." But whereas Microsoft urged the court to interpret "necessary" as "indispensable," the plaintiffs argued that they needed only show that a specific factual finding was "supportive" of the prior judgment. In a critical portion of his ruling, Judge Motz sided with the plaintiffs:

To adopt [Microsoft's proposed rule] … would be to frustrate the accomplishment of the goals of efficiency and economy that the doctrine [of estoppel] is designed to further. The requirement that a finding have been necessary to a prior judgment serves the important purpose of "prevent[ing] the incidental or collateral determination of a nonessential issue." … But that purpose cannot be permitted to override the doctrine of collateral estoppel itself, and it is sufficiently served by requiring that a specific finding be supportive of the prior judgment.[39]

Microsoft appealed, and once again Judge Niemeyer wrote the opinion of the Court of Appeals for the Fourth Circuit reversing Judge Motz. Just as he had approached the must-carry appeal by first delineating a narrow role for mandatory preliminary injunctions, Judge Niemeyer again began by establishing a limited role for offensive collateral estoppel under a demanding standard:

In sum, the doctrine of offensive collateral estoppel or offensive issue preclusion may be *used cautiously* to preclude a defendant from relitigating a fact actually found against the defendant in prior litigation when the fact was *critical and necessary* to the judgment in the prior litigation, so long as the plaintiff using the fact could not have easily joined the prior litigation and application of the doctrine would not be unfair to the defendant. The *caution that is required* in application of offensive collateral estoppel counsels that the criteria for foreclosing a defendant from relitigating an issue or fact be *applied strictly.*[40]

As was true of Niemeyer's opinion on must-carry, the language of this collateral estoppel decision seemed to hint at an unspoken hostility to the plaintiffs' claims that went beyond the immediate issue before the court. Indeed, the standard endorsed by the court was unreceptive to plaintiffs' assertions of collateral estoppel and likely to impose the significant costs of relitigation on them and the legal system, contrary to the very purposes of preclusion doctrine—a point that had been expressed by Judge Motz and that was made again by Circuit Judge Roger L. Gregory, who dissented from the court's interpretation of "necessary." The court's directions on remand further evidenced an extremely limited view of preclusion. It sternly instructed the district court that "it must take care to limit application [of collateral estoppel] to facts that were necessary to the judgment *actually affirmed* by the D.C. Circuit," seemingly suggesting that only the "12 specified acts of anticompetitive conduct" described by the court would satisfy that instruction.[41] This approach, by narrowly focusing on the alleged exclusionary conduct at issue, thoroughly ignored the continued relevance of the extensive predicate findings made by Judge Jackson with respect to the markets involved and the economics of platform software. In doing so, the court also overlooked the conceptual distinctions that separate issue and claim preclusion. For a second time, the Court of Appeals for the Fourth Circuit had reversed Judge Motz and dealt a significant blow to the private plaintiffs who sought to build upon, but avoid having to fully replicate, the government cases.[42]

The third decision of the Court of Appeals for the Fourth Circuit affecting the competitor cases involved only Novell. As was noted above, after Novell's case was transferred from Utah and consolidated with the other cases in MDL 1332, Microsoft moved to dismiss all of Novell's six claims on procedural and statute-of-limitations grounds. It argued that Novell lacked standing to assert Counts I and VI of its complaint, which concerned the market for Intel-compatible PC operating systems, because it didn't compete in that market. In addition, pointing to the Clayton Act's four-year statute of limitations, it urged the court to dismiss Counts II–V, which concerned alleged markets for word processing and spreadsheet software, as coming too late. Novell had commenced its action in November of 2004, even though it had sold its interest in WordPerfect and Quattro Pro in March of 1996—more than eight years earlier. A critical question with respect to these middle four counts was whether the filing of the U.S.

government case in May of 1998 "tolled" (that is, suspended) the statute of limitations pursuant to one of the provisions of the Clayton Act. If not, they were time barred.

Judge Motz denied Microsoft's motion with respect to standing, but granted it with respect to the statute of limitations. Because the denial of a motion to dismiss is normally not appealable, Microsoft asked Judge Motz to certify the standing question for appeal under the provisions of 28 U.S.C. §1292, which he did. Microsoft then petitioned the Court of Appeals for the Fourth Circuit to hear its appeal. When the court agreed to do so, Novell cross-appealed the dismissal of its four claims on statute-of-limitations grounds. In the end, therefore, the appeals court reviewed the district court's disposition of both motions and, in October of 2007, affirmed both of Judge Motz's rulings.

Microsoft's standing argument was based largely on a single principle from the Supreme Court's decision in *Associated General Contractors of California, Inc. v. California State Council of Carpenters*: that plaintiffs cannot suffer antitrust injury, and cannot therefore sue for damages, in markets in which they are neither consumers nor competitors. Microsoft argued on the basis of this language that because Counts I and VI were directed at the market for operating systems, in which Novell didn't compete, Novell lacked standing to pursue them. The Court of Appeals for the Fourth Circuit agreed with the district court, however, that Microsoft's reading of *Associated General Contractors* and its proposed "bright line" test was simplistic. Although the status of a plaintiff as a consumer or a competitor of the defendant is relevant and may tend to demonstrate its standing, it wasn't a necessary precondition of standing. Indeed, in this case such a formalistic rule would necessarily denigrate the central theory of Novell's complaint, which echoed the allegations of the governments' case with respect to Sun and Netscape: that Microsoft directed its actions *outside* the relevant market for PC operating systems in order to protect it from future competition *inside* that market. Another way to comprehend the point is that the standing analysis should focus on whether the plaintiff posed a competitive threat, not on whether it was a current "competitor."

In the view of the Court of Appeals for the Fourth Circuit, *Associated General Contractors* required a more flexible and searching analysis that included consideration of whether the injury was of the type Congress sought to redress under Section 4 (i.e., competitive as opposed to individual injury) and consideration of causation (the link between the defendant's alleged acts and the plaintiff's injuries). *Associated General Contractors* also calls for consideration of the relative directness or remoteness of the injuries, whether there are more direct victims, and whether it will be difficult to determine and apportion any damages. Interpreted in this way, *Associated General Contractors* can be viewed as a synthesis of the principles developed in *Brunswick Corp. v. Pueblo Bowl-O-Mat* and *Illinois Brick*, although it goes further.

As the district court had done, the Court of Appeals for the Fourth Circuit concluded that Novell satisfied all of the *Associated General Contractors* conditions for standing. In echoing the government's allegations that Microsoft acted to fortify the barriers to entry into the market for PC operating systems, Novell clearly alleged an injury to "competition." And Microsoft's internal documents left little doubt that its conduct caused Novell's injury—indeed the court observed that Microsoft's conduct was intended to do so. Novell supported its allegation that "Microsoft specifically targeted its products for destruction as a means to damage competition in the operating-system market" with several internal Microsoft documents, including one from Bill Gates. After noting the relevance of such "specific intent" evidence to proving causation, the court explained:

For example, Microsoft Chairman Bill Gates specifically suggested waiting to publish critical technical specifications of Windows 95 until 'we have a way to do a high level of integration [between Microsoft Office and Windows 95] that will be harder for [the] likes of ... WordPerfect to achieve.' ... Otherwise, Gates noted, '[w]e can't compete with ... WordPerfect/Novell.' ... Additionally, Novell proffers the following email from senior Microsoft official Jeff Raikes to investor Warren Buffett:

> If we own the key 'franchises' built on top of the operating systems, we dramatically widen the 'moat' that protects the operating system business. ... We hope to make a lot of money off these franchises, but even more important is that they should protect our Windows royalty per PC.

... The "moat" protecting Windows to which Raikes refers is the applications barrier to entry; the email therefore supports Novell's assertions that its products were directly targeted.[43]

Similarly, the court concluded that Novell had satisfied the three remaining *Associated General Contractors* requirements: directness, absence of more direct victims, and potential problems in determining and apportioning damages. Again, the evidence that Microsoft specifically targeted Novell favored a finding that its injuries were direct and that there was no other plaintiff better situated or more likely to challenge that conduct. Finally, and in contrast to the typical overcharge cases involving direct or indirect purchasers, only Novell could sue for the exclusionary damages it suffered, so concerns about the kind of duplicative recoveries and difficult apportionment decisions that can arise when both direct and indirect purchasers seek recovery were unwarranted.[44] Novell's claims concerning the market for PC operating systems therefore could rightfully be maintained.

Microsoft's statute-of-limitations argument was more focused and more successful. Section 5(i) of the Clayton Act suspends the tolling of the four-year statute of limitations for private actions when a related government action is filed, provided that the private action is "based in whole or in part on any matter complained of" in the government's case. In Microsoft's view, Section 5's tolling suspension provision was unavailable to Novell because the government's case focused solely on the PC operating-system and browser markets, whereas Counts II–V of Novell's complaint concerned word processing and spreadsheet software. Novell argued in response that its claims concerning the markets for office-productivity software were so closely related to the governments' previous claims regarding the market for PC operating systems and the market for browsers that Section 5's test was satisfied.

The Court of Appeals for the Fourth Circuit again agreed with the district court, in this instance affirming its conclusion that Microsoft's motion should be granted. Relying in part on a "different markets" rule, it concluded that subsequent antitrust claims, to satisfy Section 5's proximity requirement, should involve injuries alleged in the same markets that were the subjects of the governments' case. Otherwise, the balance struck by the statute between facilitating related claims and honoring the goals of the statute of limitations—providing predictability and certainty to defendants while avoiding prolonged antitrust litigation—would be undone. Under that test, Novell's allegations with respect to the markets for office-productivity software didn't sufficiently overlap with the government's claims and hence couldn't benefit from Section 5's tolling provision. They were time barred. Although Novell argued that Microsoft pursued the same exclusionary strategy with respect to its the office-productivity software that it had pursued with respect to Netscape and Java, it couldn't persuade the court that the two markets were related enough to trigger tolling: "After tarrying with these claims for more than eight years, Novell cannot now resurrect stale causes of action, and Microsoft is entitled 'to the comfort of repose.'"[45]

Novell thereafter returned to the district court with its claims narrowed to Counts I and VI. Those counts focused on the market for PC operating systems, which had been at the focus of the governments' case. But it faced a renewed charge by Microsoft that when it had sold its interest in the PC operating systems DR DOS and Novell DOS to Caldera, Inc., in 1996, it had also sold the right to bring claims for any injuries suffered in the market for

PC operating systems between 1994 and 1996. Although Judge Motz had rejected Microsoft's assertions earlier in the case, he reconsidered them on remand.

Early in 2010, Judge Motz reversed course, dismissing Novell's final two claims and seemingly bringing to an end Novell's case and with it the decade-long MDL 1332. Anticipating the possibility that the Court of Appeals for the Fourth Circuit might disagree, however, Judge Motz also ruled in the alternative on the parties' cross-motions for summary judgment on the merits. He concluded that a reasonable jury could find for Novell on Count I (its claim that Microsoft monopolized the market for Intel-compatible PC operating systems), but that there wasn't sufficient evidence in the court's view to support Count VI (which alleged violations of Section 1 of the Sherman Act in connection with Microsoft's allegedly exclusionary agreements with distributors, resellers, and OEMs).[46]

In an unpublished and hence non-precedential opinion issued in May of 2011, a divided Court of Appeals for the Fourth Circuit concluded that Novell could still proceed on one claim. Because it hadn't conveyed the right to assert claims related to its office-productivity applications, it could present to a jury its claim that Microsoft had sought to impair Novell's ability to compete in the market for office-productivity software in order to fortify its monopoly in the market for PC operating systems.[47] In late 2011 that single claim was tried to a Utah jury. When it deadlocked, unable to deliver a verdict, Judge Motz, who had been designated as the trial judge given his familiarity with the private *Microsoft* cases, dismissed Novell's case. On appeal, in perhaps the last appellate decision to relate to the embattled software industry of the 1990s, the Tenth Circuit affirmed, concluding that Microsoft's decision to discontinue sharing certain of its Windows APIs with Novell didn't meet the legal requirements of being "anticompetitive."[48]

Settling the Competitors' Cases

The harsh reality of the D.C. Circuit Court's conclusions in the governments' cases for Microsoft, combined with the hurdles erected by the Court of Appeals for the Fourth Circuit for the private competitor-plaintiffs, seemed to propel all of the private parties toward settlement. Microsoft surely understood that, despite the D.C. Circuit Court's narrowing of the scope of its liability, it stood adjudicated as a monopolist, and it likely had significant exposure for damages to the immediate targets of its unlawful conduct. To the extent Microsoft's rivals had felt emboldened by the D.C. Circuit Court's decision, however, that confidence probably was eroded by the Court of Appeals for the Fourth Circuit. In contrast to the mixed reception it received in the D.C. Circuit Court, Microsoft had won some important victories in the Fourth Circuit that had strengthened its hand and diminished the plaintiffs' hopes of any quick, easy, and bankable resolution of their claims. Microsoft and the plaintiffs also must have appreciated that the plaintiffs still faced two additional challenges, one legal and one strategic. As a matter of law, they still faced the formidable task of proving specific dollar damages that could be linked to Microsoft's conduct. Strategically, all of the rivals remained largely captive to the Windows world and needed to find a way to coexist with, if not cooperate with, Microsoft. Continued warfare was an increasingly inadvisable strategy.

In May of 2003, AOL Time Warner was the first of the major competitor plaintiffs to reach a settlement, which it and Microsoft publicly valued at $750 million. According to the official Microsoft press release describing the deal, in addition to resolving the antitrust suit filed by AOL Time Warner, the two firms had agreed to "collaborate on long-term digital media initiatives that will accelerate the adoption of digital content." The press release downplayed the $750 million payment, instead emphasizing the range of cooperation that was anticipated, much of which involved licenses for the use of Microsoft technology. Microsoft granted AOL a "long-term, non-exclusive license" to Microsoft's "entire Windows Media 9 Series digital media platform, as well as successor digital rights management software." It also "provided AOL a royalty-free, seven-year license to use Microsoft's Internet Explorer technologies with the AOL client," and mutual promises were made to "explore ways to establish interoperability between AOL and MSN Instant Messenger networks." The "Browser Wars" thus ended with a whimper, at least insofar as AOL was concerned. Netscape's own browser was, for all intents, abandoned by AOL (later to be resurrected as Mozilla Firefox).

In April of 2004 Microsoft also agreed to pay Sun almost $2 billion—though not just to settle Sun's antitrust claims. The parties specified that $700 million was being paid to settle Sun's antitrust claims, and that an additional $900 million was being allocated to the settlement of patent issues. Like the Netscape agreement, however, the Sun settlement went beyond the payment of damages and royalties and involved what appeared to be a long-term commitment to future collaboration. While proclaiming that the two companies would "continue to compete hard," the agreements also provided for cross-licenses to each other's technologies, Microsoft agreeing to make a $350 million "up-front" royalty payment to Sun and Sun agreeing to pay royalties to Microsoft when Microsoft's technology was incorporated into Sun's server products. The Microsoft press release announcing the settlement described the agreements as including technical collaboration and an agreement by Sun to sign on to the Microsoft Communications Protocol Program established pursuant to its settlement of the government cases, as well as Microsoft's support for Java, Windows certification of Sun's Xeon servers, and future collaboration between the two firms on Java and .Net. (Sun's complaint had portrayed .Net as Microsoft's competitive response to Java.) The last of the agreement provisions to be listed in the press release was the settlement of the antitrust claims. The agreement terminated the U.S. case. According to the press release, Sun, in effect, also agreed to cease advocating its complaint before the European Commission, "satisfied that the agreement ... satisfy the objectives it was pursuing in the EU actions pending against Microsoft."[49]

Press reports indicated that the settlement came after a year of negotiations that had been initiated by Scott McNealy, Sun's CEO.[50] Before his efforts to broker a peace accord with Microsoft, McNeely had been widely viewed as "the leader of the anti-Microsoft camp in Silicon Valley." Critically, the agreement came nine days after the European Commission's decision (discussed in the next chapter) that Microsoft had violated European competition laws and should be fined $605 million. The European case was the result of a complaint that Sun had filed against Microsoft in Europe in December of 1998, and Sun had remained one of the principal protagonists pressing the European Commission to act against Microsoft.

Two factors seem to have been especially influential in securing the Sun settlement. "After two decades of inflamed criticism," one commentator observed, "many here in the technology sector have come to accept the slowly acquired reality that the legal system can do little to resolve their quarrel with Microsoft." Further, the commentator noted, "[m]any of the Valley's leaders acknowledged that Sun's stunning rapprochement with its longtime rival was a simple acknowledgment of the reality of Microsoft's overwhelming power and its deep pockets."[51] But a changing business climate also seemed to be in play. McNeely and Microsoft's CEO Steve Ballmer both spoke of complaints from customers frustrated by the costs of managing the incompatibility that arose from the feud between the two companies. Commenting on the statements McNeely and Ballmer made when announcing the settlement, one *New York Times* commentator wrote: "From the point of view of Microsoft and Sun executives the new alliance was the natural consequence of new Internet technology that forced them together. The war over differing standards for operating computers no longer makes sense. ..."[52] Moreover, Sun (which was under severe pressure to address its failing financial situation) announced significant layoffs and cost-cutting measures the same day that the settlement with Microsoft was announced. (Early in 2010, in a deal that was itself the subject of intense antitrust scrutiny in the United States and Europe, Sun was acquired by Oracle Corporation.)

After AOL Time Warner and Sun had both settled with Microsoft, the remaining competitor cases were also resolved. In November of 2004, with the assistance of Eric Green of Boston University (a mediator who had also participated in the settlement negotiations between Microsoft and the government in 2001), Microsoft reached a settlement with Novell for $536 million. The agreement resolved all claims related to Novell's NetWare (a software server product) and to its other currently owned products. But in contrast to the Netscape and Sun settlements, there was no promise of continuing business cooperation.[53] Novell also agreed to discontinue its participation in the competition-law case that was under appeal to the European Court of First Instance. Also, as we noted above, the settlement didn't cover Novell's antitrust claims arising out of its ownership of Word-Perfect in 1994–1996. Microsoft and Novell disagreed about the value of those claims, which became the subject of the final antitrust case in the *Microsoft* MDL proceeding.

The same day that the Novell agreement was announced, Microsoft separately disclosed that it had reached a "settlement" with the Computer & Communications Industry Association (CCIA), an industry trade group whose membership at the time included a number of Microsoft's principal rivals, among them Sun, AOL Time Warner, and Oracle. CCIA wasn't asserting any claims against Microsoft, but it had been one of Microsoft's most visible and vocal antagonists and had aggressively advocated the pursuit of Microsoft under U.S. and EU antitrust laws. It had also intervened in the Tunney Act proceedings after the governments' 2001 settlement, opposing the negotiated consent decree and supporting the non-settling states in their effort to secure additional remedies.

Under the terms of the settlement, Microsoft agreed to join CCIA and to "compensate CCIA for certain legal-related expenditures it has incurred, in some cases over the past decade, and provide substantial institutional support for new and important policy undertakings." Although the specific amount paid wasn't disclosed by the parties, press reports indicated that it was nearly $20 million. Several weeks after the announcement of the settlement, the *Financial Times* reported that CCIA's president would receive $9.75 million of the total amount as a personal payment approved by CCIA's board.[54] A subsequent report in the *Wall Street Journal* indicated that the amount had been "overstated" and that the president was to receive a "bonus" of $2 million and a pay increase from $200,000 to $500,000 a year.[55] For its part, CCIA agreed to stand down. In the United States it wouldn't seek review in the U.S. Supreme Court of the D.C. Circuit Court's approval of the government settlement, and in Europe it would no longer participate in the continuing proceedings begun in late 1998 and would drop a separate complaint, filed with the European Commission in 2003, that was directed at Windows XP.

Collectively, the Netscape, Sun, Novell, and CCIA settlements manifested a substantially changed litigation strategy at Microsoft. After eluding the threat of Judge Jackson's breakup order, but suffering a significant defeat on liability in the D.C. Circuit Court of Appeals, Microsoft seemed to turn away from the "scorched earth" litigation strategy that had characterized its years under the legal supervision of William Neukom. Microsoft's new General Counsel, Brad Smith, appeared to have new marching orders and a more diplomatic approach. He embarked on a deliberate and measured effort to extricate Microsoft from its labyrinth of antitrust litigation through negotiation.

More particularly, with CCIA's agreement not to pursue an appeal of the governments' settlement, Microsoft had purchased an end to the six year-old U.S. government litigation. Massachusetts lost its appeal to the D.C. Circuit Court in June of 2004, and by November had indicated that it wouldn't seek Supreme Court review of its effort to secure additional remedies. But, as we noted in chapter 4, the court of appeals had also concluded that it had been an error for the district court to deny intervenor status to CCIA and another trade group, the Software & Information Industry Association. Although the deadline for filing a petition with the Supreme Court had already passed for the SIIA, CCIA had sought and received an extension of time to file. It used the threat of a petition effectively as a bargaining chip. CCIA's settlement with Microsoft, therefore, closed the final door on the litigation with the states and the Department of Justice and allowed the negotiated consent decree to move into its implementation stage.[56]

The Netscape, Sun, Novell, and CCIA settlements were also important components of a settlement strategy targeted at the continuing proceedings before the European Commission. As we shall explore in greater depth in chapter 6, these four firms and RealNetworks were the principal complainants to the EC, which had concluded in March of 2004 that Microsoft had violated European competition laws. When the Novell and CCIA settlements were announced, Microsoft's appeal of that decision was still pending before the Court of First Instance ("CFI"—now the "General Court") and Microsoft was awaiting an interim decision from that court on its motion to stay the EC's order pending the appeal. Although the four settlements didn't alter the EC's record in the case, which the firms had helped to generate, the settlements required them all to relent from their active support of the case. As the *Financial Times* reported, with settlements secured between Microsoft and all four of "the Commission's original five allies," RealNetworks alone remained "on the field of battle." The *Financial Times* dubbed the deal with CCIA "an historic truce."[57]

Microsoft openly expressed hope that the settlements would improve its prospects for reaching a settlement with the European Commission before the CFI ruled on the appeal. So far, a settlement had proved elusive. Microsoft also hinted at a desire to isolate RealNetworks and perhaps thereby pressure it into agreeing to a negotiated resolution of its U.S. litigation and a withdrawal of its support for the EC's case. Indeed, at a press conference held after the Novell and CCIA settlements, Brad Smith candidly acknowledged his strategy:

[T]his case represents an important milestone in our reaching agreement with the competitors that have been active in the European proceedings. In our minds there were five entities that were very broadly involved in the European case. We have now reached agreement with four of them. ... That really leaves only one entity that at least in our minds has been involved in a very broad way, and that is Real Networks. It means that Real Networks is now really standing alone in terms of continuing with the litigation path in Europe and elsewhere.[58]

Smith's prepared statement was revealing in another way, probably not intended. Reflecting one of the principal themes that had been repeated by Microsoft throughout the governments' cases—that the governments' and competitor cases were banal efforts to substitute government intervention for true competition—he lauded the combined settlements as an effort to restore the industry to a better equilibrium that wouldn't require government intervention:

We believe that this sends a strong message that we and other companies in our industry do have the capacity now to sit down face to face and resolve the kinds of thorny antitrust issues that in the past were left instead to the government to resolve. We think that's important in Europe as well as in the United States and elsewhere and we're very pleased with this type of additional progress.[59]

From the perspective of antitrust law and policy, however, "sit down face to face" resolution of antitrust issues among rivals is an inherently risky business that may compromise the public interest in competitive markets rather than serve it. An alternative interpretation of the settlements was that Microsoft had outlasted and bought off its rivals using the very monopoly profits it had fought so hard to protect through illegal means. Relatedly, in the view of the *Financial Times*, the settlements served as a reminder of the importance of public enforcement of competition laws: "The circumstances that led to the withdrawal of its [the European Commission's] allies reenforces the importance in competition policy of having a regulator who cannot be bought off by a wealthy company."[60]

For CCIA, the settlement was perhaps a sign of institutional resignation. The limited government settlement in the U.S. cases surely must have seemed like a consolation prize after CCIA's years of vociferous confrontations with Microsoft in the press, in the courts, and before government agencies. As we noted above, the firms in the vanguard of the effort to turn the attention of public antitrust enforcement agencies on Microsoft had probably lost faith that the legal system was up to the task of significantly altering the competitive playing field—Microsoft really had become an unchallengeable force, at least in its operating-system and office-productivity strongholds. CCIA also knew that its work was largely done in Europe, where the Commission's case awaited review by the courts. It was time for CCIA to follow the lead of some of its most significant members and move beyond anti-Microsoft advocacy, extracting one final measure of solace from what was for it a significant "compensation" package.

Microsoft continued its efforts to resolve all of its antitrust disputes. In March and April of 2005 it announced additional settlements with Burst. com and Gateway,[61] and in July it announced a more significant settlement with IBM. Both Gateway and IBM could find specific support for their claims in Judge Jackson's findings of fact in the governments' cases. Jackson found that "[a]mong the five largest OEMs, Gateway and IBM, which in various ways have resisted Microsoft's efforts to enlist them in its efforts to preserve the applications barrier to entry, pay higher prices than Compaq, Dell, and Hewlett-Packard, which have pursued less contentious relationships with Microsoft."[62] Microsoft's press release on the settlement with Gateway acknowledged Jackson's specific findings in regard to Gateway as the basis for its decision to pay Gateway $150 million over four years to support the development, marketing, and advertising of new Gateway products designed to work with "Microsoft's next-generation operating system and productivity software."[63]

Jackson had further found, with respect to IBM, that "[w]hen IBM refused to abate the promotion of those of its own products that competed with Windows and Office, Microsoft punished the IBM PC Company with higher prices, a late license for Windows 95, and the withholding of technical and marketing support."[64] Although IBM never filed suit against

Microsoft, its claims were potentially substantial, because they related not only to the higher prices it paid to license Windows but also to Microsoft's efforts to impede IBM's development of its own operating system (OS/2) and its own suite of office-productivity software (SmartSuite). The settlement therefore consisted of a cash payment of $775 million and a $75 million credit toward the future licensing of Microsoft software.[65]

In October of 2005, nearly a year after the Novell and CCIA settlements, Microsoft came to terms with RealNetworks, the last of the "big five" competitors identified by Brad Smith in his 2004 press conference. RealNetworks, a pioneer in digital media, had been founded in early 1994 by Robert Glaser, who had previously been employed by Microsoft. From RealNetworks' perspective, Microsoft was both a foe and a necessary ally in the competitive struggle with Apple's popular iTunes music service. Perhaps more than RealNetworks' desire to resolve antitrust claims, competition in digital media markets—especially from iTunes—appeared to be what transformed these "one-time antagonists into allies."[66]

The RealNetworks settlement consisted of three distinct agreements collectively valued at $761 million. In the first, RealNetworks agreed to drop all of its antitrust claims against Microsoft "worldwide," including its private treble-damages litigation in the United States and its complaints and advocacy directed at Microsoft before the European Commission and the Korea Fair Trade Commission. According to Microsoft's press release, in return RealNetworks received a "$460 million up-front cash payment" and "a series of technology licenses and commitments under which [it obtained] long-term access to important Windows Media technologies that will enhance Real's media software solutions."[67] In two additional agreements, together valued at $301 million, the firms also agreed to a "wide ranging digital music collaboration" that included Microsoft's promotion of Rhapsody (RealNetworks' subscription-based digital online music service) and Microsoft's agreement to offer RealNetworks' digital games along with its own.

According to the Microsoft press release, the agreements also included "a variety of assurances regarding the design of the Windows operating system, including Windows Media Player, and access for Real to a broad range of Windows platform technologies," including a pledge to "work together to enhance the functionality and performance of Real's software products and services on the Windows operating system." More specifically, they included several provisions that sought to address the challenges RealNetworks faced in gaining access to the Windows desktop after Microsoft began bundling its Windows Media Player with Windows, and anticipated the next iteration of Windows (Vista).[68] According to Brad Smith, "the agreement ensures that Microsoft can innovate and that other media players can compete in a broad marketplace."[69]

Perhaps more than anything in the previous settlements with Netscape, Sun, Novell, and CCIA, the RealNetworks settlement sought to redress some of the competitive harm caused by Microsoft's exclusionary conduct—which may explain why it took longer to negotiate. In seeking to secure additional concessions from Microsoft, RealNetworks may have benefited from aspects of both the U.S. cases and the European cases. Recall that the government had failed to prove the existence of a browser market in the U.S. cases. Although that failure hadn't precluded Netscape and Sun from trying to prove that such markets existed for them, Microsoft could use the governments' loss to argue that Netscape and Sun still faced an uphill battle in their litigation. Microsoft was also in a good position to argue, as it did in many of the private cases and the Tunney Act proceedings, that the remedies it had negotiated with the government in the consent decree were appropriately calibrated to the scope of the violations found and that no additional remedies were justified. Although RealNetworks would have to establish the existence of a "media player market," it didn't face an earlier, adverse ruling on that issue. To the contrary, the European Commission had concluded that a distinct market existed for media players and that Microsoft's conduct damaged competition in that market. Thus, RealNetworks may have been in a better position than either Netscape or Sun to negotiate measures that, in effect, augmented the consent decree in the U.S. cases and were specific to media players.

From the point of view of competition, only the RealNetworks settlement augmented in any significant way the conduct remedies to which Microsoft had agreed in its settlement with the government plaintiffs. With respect to the other competitor settlements, at least the appearance of cooperation replaced years of heated competition. Microsoft's dominance of the markets for operating systems and office-productivity software not only remained intact; it may have become even more entrenched, more durable, and more obvious.

The Non-Competitor Cases and Class Actions

As we noted at the outset of this chapter, the government cases against Microsoft triggered the filing of more than 200 private antitrust cases in numerous state and federal courts throughout the country. In addition to the competitor cases already discussed, these cases included consumer class actions, actions by various state and local governments, and actions by foreign firms and individuals.[70] Many were transferred and consolidated with the other cases in MDL 1332. Those that couldn't have been filed in federal court, and hence couldn't be removed there, remained in the state courts in which they had been commenced.

Like the competitor cases, these cases presented some difficult issues of causation and measurement of damages. More so than the competitors' cases, however, they collectively confronted the courts with some of the most common and yet most complex procedural issues that distinguish private antitrust litigation in the United States today. Why, for example, should a successful government enforcement action trigger so many cases in so many jurisdictions, both state and federal?

The answer to this question probably begins with Microsoft. Few firms in the world today market products that touch as many lives in as many ways as do Microsoft's. In the period we are considering here, the ubiquity of Windows-based computers meant that the effects of its conduct, and hence the collective response to it, would be widespread. Moreover, Microsoft's success contributed to the widespread response to its illegal conduct—it presented an undeniably attractive target for litigation.

Second, although the D.C. Circuit Court reversed some of Judge Jackson's findings and conclusions, the core of the governments' antitrust challenge to Microsoft was significantly upheld on appeal—Microsoft was an adjudicated monopolist that unquestionably had broken the nation's antitrust laws. Follow-on private plaintiffs thus had reason to believe that they could benefit from reliance on specific factual findings, an already well-developed economic theory, and a sound legal basis. None had to construct its own case against Microsoft from scratch.

A third component of the answer no doubt lies in the collective impact of the incentives built into the U.S. private litigation system. As we noted at the outset of the chapter, the provision of treble damages, attorneys' fees, and costs in Section 4 of the Clayton Act, along with the preclusion features of Section 5 of the act, were specifically designed to encourage civil suits by the victims of antitrust violations. The availability of class actions was also integral to the number and variety of private suits that followed the governments' cases. Class actions are ideally suited for redressing "negative value" suits—cases in which illegal conduct has many victims but each victim's harm is too small to justify an individual lawsuit. No single consumer of Windows could have justified initiating an antitrust challenge against Microsoft; the cost of prosecution would obviously and greatly outweigh the individual value of any likely recovery. The collective redress facilitated by the class-action device provides what may be the sole feasible means of securing compensation and deterrence in the case of such negative value injuries, and that characteristic of the U.S. class action was on full display in the *Microsoft* litigation.

Finally, the division of cases between state and federal courts vividly illustrated the combined impact of the Supreme Court's 1977 *Illinois Brick* decision, which precludes indirect purchasers (often consumers) from suing in federal court, and its 1989 decision in *ARC America*, which upheld the authority of states to permit indirect purchasers to do so under state antitrust laws.[71] It also illustrates the interdependence of indirect purchasers' rights and the class action.

Precisely because *Illinois Brick* barred them from federal courts, consumers have sought redress in state courts. Owing to differences in state antitrust law and common law, such cases can proliferate on a state-by-state basis in response to conduct that has widespread effects, as was the case with Microsoft. And there is no legal equivalent of a Judicial Panel on Multidistrict Litigation with authority to consolidate suits filed in different states rather than in federal court. Moreover, by their nature, actions by indirect purchasers tend to be class actions, because indirect purchasers are often consumers and their individual injuries are often too small alone to warrant initiation of a lawsuit, especially a major undertaking like an antitrust action. State-by-state proliferation of indirect-purchaser cases is further encouraged, therefore, by class-action laws, which demand that the claims of the members of a class be significantly related. Class actions brought on behalf of the consumers of a single state under that state's antitrust or related law may be easier to certify than nationwide class actions, which may require reconciling variations in the laws of different states and may include both direct and indirect purchasers. This is especially true because, although a majority of states now support indirect purchasers' rights, a minority of states follow *Illinois Brick*. Indeed, litigation against Microsoft provided the vehicle for resolving the status of indirect purchasers' rights in a number of states that had yet to confront the choice of following or rejecting *Illinois Brick*.

In the remainder of this chapter we focus on three issues that arose in the private class-action litigation against Microsoft and were frequently intertwined: the right of indirect purchasers to sue and the related question of statutory "standing," class-action certification, and the class-action settlement process. Many of these cases sought "overcharges"—the alleged difference between the competitive price of Windows and the price that was paid as a result of Microsoft's anticompetitive conduct. The inherent merit of the many class actions commenced against Microsoft remains subject to serious question—it was going to be very difficult to prove measurable overcharges caused by the elimination of merely nascent competition. Yet the absence of any provisions for civil penalties in the United States meant that the only monetary penalty that could be imposed on Microsoft in the United States would have to come from private litigation, so it may have had an important and enduring deterrent effect.

Indirect Purchasers and Antitrust "Standing"[72]

Stating the rule of *Illinois Brick* is deceptively straightforward: Section 4 of the Clayton Act doesn't authorize suits by indirect purchasers seeking to collect overcharges from one or more antitrust offenders. Indirect purchasers can still seek injunctive relief, and there are some other exceptions to the basic rule; however, as it has been interpreted since 1977, *Illinois Brick* creates a nearly *per se* ban on civil antitrust suits by indirect purchasers in the federal courts.

Illinois Brick had immediate and broad implications for the private right of action under federal antitrust laws. In the Supreme Court's view, its holding followed logically from the Supreme Court's 1968 decision in *Hanover Shoe, Inc. v. United Shoe Machinery Corp.*, which barred antitrust defendants from defeating claims by *direct* purchasers on the ground that the direct purchasers had "passed on" any overcharges to *indirect* purchasers.[73] It also relied on some critical assumptions about how best to calibrate the antitrust right of action to make it reasonably administrable and to secure deterrence. The Supreme Court was especially concerned with the possibility that defendants sued by plaintiffs at multiple stages of a distribution chain could face duplicative damage awards and with the possibility that allocating damages among such plaintiffs would be a daunting task for courts.

Ironically, however, the larger systemic consequences of *Illinois Brick* were greater complexity, increased costs, and increased administrative burdens on the courts owing to the independent role of state antitrust laws and courts. Microsoft thus faced, and was forced to navigate, the complicated federal-state system that had developed over the previous three decades. It sought to remove from state to federal court as many of the cases filed in state court as it could in order to facilitate their consolidation into MDL 1332.[74] And when removal wasn't possible, it sought to combine multiple cases filed within the same state—notably California, where about thirty cases were eventually combined in a state equivalent of MDL proceedings. And wherever feasible, it sought to persuade state courts and the federal

MDL court to follow *Illinois Brick* and dismiss indirect purchasers' claims outright.

Although not unique in this respect, Microsoft's experience illustrated the extent of this arguable splintering of antitrust enforcement authority and its practical impact on the implementation of the private right of action. More now than perhaps at any other time in U.S. antitrust history, defendants charged with serious antitrust wrongdoing may be forced to manage their defense in multiple jurisdictions, state and federal, before multiple fact finders, in cases initiated by multiple public enforcement agencies and private plaintiffs. Such a system imposes potentially enormous costs and risks; deterrence might be promoted, but in an unmeasured and untargeted fashion. Microsoft's experiences fully illustrated the consequences and costs of such a fractured competition policy system.

It is easy to understand why Microsoft would aggressively pursue dismissal of cases brought by indirect purchasers. First, motions to dismiss cost little and have a potentially enormous payoff. As a threshold question, the right of indirect purchasers to sue can be raised promptly by a motion to dismiss and, if successful, result in termination of the litigation. Microsoft filed many such motions advocating the rule of *Illinois Brick* for states in which the question hadn't yet been settled. It pursued the argument in state courts in those cases that couldn't be removed, and in federal court for those that had successfully been removed (despite removal, such cases are still controlled by state law). To illustrate the strategy and evaluate its success, we profile just a sampling of the many decisions spawned by the "*Illinois Brick* problem." We will begin with the *Comes* litigation from Iowa, but we will also examine the treatment of the issue by Judge Motz and the Court of Appeals for the Fourth Circuit in MDL 1332.

The *Comes* litigation, which proceeded over a period of seven years, is a self-contained series of lessons on the most challenging procedural issues that characterize indirect-purchaser antitrust litigation in the United States today. The litigation included three visits to, and three substantial opinions from, the Iowa Supreme Court to determine the right of indirect purchasers to sue under Iowa's state competition law, the propriety of class certification, and the scope of preclusion. The *Comes* litigation also included an early test of the Class Action Fairness Act of 2005: Microsoft sought to remove the case from state court to federal court following its passage by Congress.[75]

Comes v. Microsoft Corp. followed a now-familiar pattern of proceeding through years of motion practice, discovery, class-action assessment, and finally, well into trial, settlement. More broadly, the *Comes* litigation illustrates many of the features of private follow-on U.S. antitrust litigation that have spawned controversy and criticism. From the plaintiff's perspective, it illustrates how—despite the incentives built into the antitrust system to encourage and facilitate follow-on private compensatory litigation—defendants can take full advantage of the numerous procedural hurdles erected by the courts to prolong and increase the cost of antitrust litigation. And that is so even in cases of established antitrust liability. On the other hand, the litigation illustrates the ultimate power of those same incentives to produce an advantage for the doggedly persistent plaintiff and the unpredictable and substantial nature of litigation costs for antitrust defendants (even though they may well have meritorious defenses) in follow-on cases.

The case for overcharges in the *Microsoft* class-action cases, let alone the question of how to allocate them among various levels of purchasers, was attenuated, at best. How might a plaintiff prove an "overcharge," a monopoly price, let alone one that could be attributed to Microsoft's conduct? As a general matter, to prove that a firm is charging a monopoly price, it is necessary to prove a benchmark price, the price that would prevail in a competitive market. But a monopoly price that results from successful competition isn't an *unlawful* monopoly price. To establish an unlawful "overcharge," therefore, it could be argued that but for Microsoft's conduct the price for Windows would have fallen in response to the competitive pressures that Microsoft's conduct eliminated. But the theory of the governments' case was that Microsoft squelched a nascent *future* competitive threat. It would be difficult to prove that a future threat would have exerted downward pressure on the price of Windows and, if so, that it could be quantified. In the alternative, one could argue that Microsoft's conduct allowed it to further increase its price, above the price it had been charging, owing to its "legitimate" success. In that event, the plaintiffs would have had to directly link some portion of the Windows licensing fee to Microsoft's illegal conduct—an illegal monopoly profit *increment*. No matter how the issue was approached, the plaintiffs would have to prove some kind of benchmark price and demonstrate a difference that could be causally linked to Microsoft's unlawful conduct. That was going to be a challenge.

Comes v. Microsoft Corp. was filed under Iowa's antitrust laws in early 2000 as a class action on behalf of all "end-user licensees of Windows 98" living in Iowa. Because virtually all of the class members became Windows licensees through the purchase of Intel-based personal computers that came equipped with Windows, they were indirect purchasers of Windows. And as was true of most of these indirect-purchaser class actions, the plaintiffs sought recovery of "overcharges," alleging that Microsoft "knowingly, flagrantly, and with impunity licensed its Windows 98 operating system for Intel-based personal computers without regard to competition, at a monopoly price in excess of what Microsoft would have been able to charge in a competitive market."[76]

Microsoft responded with a motion to dismiss the complaint under *Illinois Brick*, relying both on the policies behind the decision and on Iowa law, which included a directive that Iowa courts "harmonize" their interpretation of Iowa's competition law with parallel federal antitrust laws—a common feature in the antitrust laws of many states. The Iowa district court granted the motion, but the plaintiffs appealed. In the first of several decisions in the case, a divided Iowa Supreme Court reversed the district court's decision to dismiss the complaint. The narrow issue on appeal concerned the proper interpretation of Iowa's Competition Law, which had been revamped in 1976, a year before *Illinois Brick*. In contrast to *Illinois Brick*, which interpreted Section 4 of the Clayton Act, the Iowa Supreme Court found nothing ambiguous or limiting in the language of Iowa's private right of action: "[a] person who is injured … by conduct prohibited under this chapter may bring suit." It created a right to sue "for *all* consumers." Microsoft urged in response that the court should read the private right of action in light of the Iowa statute's "harmonization" provision that the Iowa Competition Law should be "construed to complement and be harmonized with the applied laws of the United States which have the same or similar purpose." The Iowa Supreme Court rejected the argument, however. Under *California v. ARC America Corp.*, it was settled that federal antitrust law didn't preempt state law. Hence it was permissible for state antitrust laws to supplement federal law. More importantly, the Iowa Supreme Court emphasized that the harmonization provision was directed at the *substantive* commands and prohibitions of the state's antitrust law, not the *remedial* question of who can sue, which illustrated an important way in which state law might supplement federal law. Also, with remedial supplementation, there was no real possibility of doctrinal "conflict" between federal and state law, something that might present a greater concern.

The Iowa Supreme Court went beyond the express language of the statute, however, and directly addressed what had emerged as the principal policy difference dividing federal and state courts on the question of indirect purchasers' rights. *Illinois Brick*'s effective ban on consumer antitrust suits seemed anomalous in view of the U.S. Supreme Court's assertion two years later in *Reiter v. Sonotone Corp.* that the Sherman Act was a "consumer welfare proscription." The question presented in *Reiter* was whether consumer injury resulting from an antitrust violation qualified as injury to "property" as required by Section 4 of the Clayton Act. The Supreme Court concluded that it did. In examining the legislative history of the provision, the Court observed that "[c]ertainly the leading proponents of the legislation perceived the treble-damages remedy of what is now § 4 as a means of *protecting consumers from overcharges* resulting from price fixing."[77] States that rejected *Illinois Brick* focused on this anomaly: How can a law intended to protect consumers accomplish its goal if it bars them from suing? The Iowa Supreme Court majority concluded that it could not:

> In order for us to agree with Microsoft that the harmonization statute requires us to prohibit suits by indirect consumers, we must accept the fact that real victims-those who purchase goods and pay the overcharge-cannot recover. This result would overwhelmingly defeat the purpose of the Iowa Competition Law. Consumers in this state are best protected by permitting all injured purchasers to bring suit against those who violate our antitrust laws.[78]

As was true of the *Comes* litigation in Iowa, the follow-on suits against Microsoft provided the vehicle for settling the status of indirect purchasers' rights in many other states. Like the Iowa Supreme Court, courts in Nebraska, Tennessee, and Vermont concluded that indirect purchasers had the right to sue under their respective state antitrust laws. But Microsoft prevailed in many other states, including Colorado, Connecticut, Hawaii, Indiana, Kentucky, Maryland, New Hampshire, Ohio, Oklahoma, and Rhode Island, all of which elected to follow *Illinois Brick*.[79] In these jurisdictions, Microsoft was successful in terminating some of the class-action litigation.

Today, according to one recent survey, the rule of *Illinois Brick* has been rejected as a matter of state antitrust law in more than 35 states. In those states, both direct and indirect purchasers can sue for damages arising out of violations of antitrust law, although in some of those states only the state is authorized to bring suit on behalf of indirect purchasers.[80] Even though the *Microsoft* cases were responsible for settling the question in a number of these jurisdictions, the larger challenges of managing multiple related lawsuits remain. To the degree that cases filed in state court cannot be removed, future defendants probably will continue to face the high costs and the duplication associated with the regime that the U.S. Supreme Court created in *Illinois Brick* and *ARC America*, because consumers have identified a state-court, state-law counter-strategy for overcoming the limitations imposed by *Illinois Brick* on federal antitrust actions.[81]

Microsoft also litigated the question of indirect purchasers' rights successfully before Judge Motz and the Court of Appeals for the Fourth Circuit, but there it was presented in a different context. Most of the 64 cases pending before Judge Motz had originally been filed in *federal* courts, then transferred to him as part of MDL 1332. For these federal plaintiffs, *Illinois Brick* was settled law. Thus, in contrast to the many state cases, these plaintiffs weren't challenging *Illinois Brick* outright, but instead were seeking to tailor their complaint to fall outside its scope. First, they argued that they were in fact "*direct* purchasers" because, even though they had purchased their Windows-based computers from OEMs, they had agreed to the terms of Microsoft's software license when they had first booted up their computers and accepted its terms. In addition, they argued that they fell within two of the recognized exceptions to *Illinois Brick*: (1) their claims extended to injunctive relief and hence weren't limited to "overcharges" and (2) Microsoft effectively "controlled" the OEMs from which they had purchased their computers. Early in 2001, Judge Motz rejected all three arguments and certified his ruling for immediate appeal to the Court of Appeals for the Fourth Circuit.[82]

In an opinion delivered by Judge Niemeyer (who, as was noted above, authored several of the Fourth Circuit's opinions in the private competitor case appeals), the court affirmed. But, as the district court had done, it went beyond simple reliance on *Illinois Brick* to incorporate the U.S. Supreme Court's later standing decision in *Associated General Contractors* as an alternative ground for dismissing the plaintiffs' claims. It thus viewed the "right to sue" as an issue distinct from "standing."

As Judge Motz had done, the Fourth Circuit rejected the plaintiffs' effort to work around *Illinois Brick*.[83] Critical to their attempt to do so was the plaintiffs' focus on Microsoft's use of a licensing scheme, rather than a true sales model, and their plea for overcharges. Microsoft had one form of license for OEMs and a second for end users: the "End-User Licensing Agreement" (EULA), which a consumer purchasing a Windows-based computer had to accept independently in order to use any Microsoft software pre-installed by the OEM from which the computer was purchased. The EULA also provided that Microsoft would refund the value of its software to an end user who declined to accept the terms of the EULA. The plaintiffs argued that the EULA thus created both direct contractual and economic relationships between end users and Microsoft, and that hence *Illinois Brick* wasn't a bar to their claims for overcharges.[84]

The court of appeals rejected the argument, concluding that, although Microsoft licensed rather than sold its software, the plaintiffs licensed it indirectly through OEMs and retailers as part of the purchase of computers. This interpretation of their status was reenforced by the plaintiffs' effort to recover overcharges, which could be determined only by engaging in the kind of pass-on calculations that *Illinois Brick* sought to preclude. In contractual terms, the rights conveyed by the license were "offered" by Microsoft and "accepted" directly by consumers, but they were *paid for* only indirectly through the OEMs from whom consumers purchased computers with software pre-installed.

The court also rejected plaintiffs' efforts to emphasize the injuries they suffered other than overcharges. Plaintiffs claimed "direct injuries" from suppression of competitive technologies, from the restrictive terms of the licensing agreements, and from degraded computer performance. But in the court's view all these alleged injuries were derivative of the claim of overcharges, and so were similarly barred by *Illinois Brick*.[85]

In the alternative, the court found that the plaintiffs lacked "standing" to assert these claims under the five-factor analysis established in *Associated General Contractors*, the factors being a lack of causal connection between an antitrust violation and the harm alleged, whether the harm was of a type Congress sought to redress, the directness of the injury, the presence of more direct victims, and any difficulties likely to be encountered in apportioning damages.[86] Although (like the Fourth Circuit) some courts have viewed analysis under *Associated General Contractors* as distinct from *Illinois Brick*, these factors are obviously a fusion of the concerns raised by the Court in *Illinois Brick* and *Brunswick Corp. v. Pueblo Bowl-O-Mat*, with an added emphasis on common-law concepts of proximate cause.

In the end, however, here too Microsoft was successful in narrowing the scope of the private cases against it through hard-fought invocation of *Illinois Brick*. When Microsoft prevailed, many consumers were left without any means of effective redress—if one assumes that, had they been permitted to continue, they could have established some basis for claiming that overcharges attributable to unlawful conduct had been passed on to them. The settlements negotiated in every single one of the surviving indirect-purchaser overcharge class actions, however, may illustrate two points often made by critics of the *Illinois Brick* repealers and of class actions in general: that once such cases are permitted to go forward few defendants can incur the risk of permitting them to proceed to trial and that, regardless of the cases' ultimate merits, defendants face enormous pressures to settle.

A Primer on American Class-Action Practice and Class Certification in the *Microsoft* Cases[87]

The many class representatives and their lawyers locked horns with Microsoft repeatedly over one of the most complicated and contentious issues in the world of litigation in the United States: "class certification," an issue that was further complicated by the law of indirect purchaser rights. The use of class actions in the federal courts is controlled by Rule 23 of the Federal Rules of Civil Procedure, which took its current form in 1966. Many states have modeled their own class-action rules on its provisions. Although the general rule in American litigation is that each party to a lawsuit can represent only its own interests, Rule 23 permits an individual or a single entity to sue as the "representative" of a larger "class." Authority to serve as a class representative, however, is contingent upon "certification" of a class by the court.

A requirement of most class-action rules in the United States is that common issues among the individual members of the class "predominate" over individual issues. If that isn't the case, a class action can devolve into many individual trials, losing the value of aggregation of claims. Also essential in a class action is that the plaintiff present a sound theory of collective harm and a reasonably reliable methodology for calculating it. Especially in indirect-purchaser antitrust litigation, the burden of fulfilling these requirements almost invariably requires the participation of expert economic witnesses, who are asked to establish both a basis for calculating class-wide damages and a method for dispensing them to parties at various levels of the distribution chain. The reliability (and hence the admissibility) of such testimony is often hotly contested, because exclusion of the expert's testimony may, as a practical matter, defeat class certification.

The division of direct and indirect purchasers between federal and state courts almost ensures that the process of certifying classes will be especially demanding in antitrust cases. In the *Microsoft* cases, that difficulty was amplified by the complexity of the causation and damage issues posed by the private class actions. If Sun and Netscape represented only "nascent" threats to Microsoft's operating-system monopoly, how could even their total exclusion have immediately harmed consumers with higher prices? Perhaps it could be shown that the mere threat of future competition modulated Microsoft's pricing, so that elimination of that threat resulted in higher prices. Under any theory, if Microsoft possessed a monopoly *before* it undertook its campaign to eliminate that threat, it was also necessary to demonstrate whether and to what degree, if any, its actions to maintain that monopoly either incrementally augmented that monopoly or insulated it from erosion in a way that contributed to the maintenance of supracompetitive prices. Finally, if consumers were being overcharged, who was paying the overcharge? As we have noted, the typical Windows end user acquires a license as part of a package of computer and software that it purchases from a manufacturer or a retailer of computers. To what extent did the manufacturers and retailers bear the cost of any overcharge? To what degree did they "pass it on" to consumers?

The potentially difficult task of measuring and allocating overcharges among direct and indirect purchasers was one of the reasons why the Supreme Court, in *Illinois Brick*, barred indirect purchasers from suing in the first place. These issues emerged and greatly influenced the class-certification wars that erupted between Microsoft and the various class representatives. Thus, although the right to bring suit as an indirect purchaser and the right to bring suit as a representative of a *class* of indirect purchasers seemed to be distinct issues, the interdependence of the two became apparent. For purposes of class certification, the class representatives were expected to present common proof of damages for the indirect-purchaser classes they sought to represent. They would thus have to address the very issue that troubled the Supreme Court in *Illinois Brick*—how "pass-on" would be proved on an individual basis or a class-wide basis—in order to satisfy the requirement of class certification that common issues predominate over individual ones.

Even when Microsoft was unsuccessful in barring indirect purchasers from suing by invoking *Illinois Brick*, it initially met with some significant success in opposing class certification by relying on analogous arguments. In two states, Maine and Michigan, courts concluded that, for some of the very same reasons the Supreme Court had barred indirect purchasers from suing in *Illinois Brick*, representatives of the class of indirect purchasing consumers couldn't satisfy the predominance requirement for class-action certification. One roughly contemporaneous study of class certification in indirect-purchaser actions argued on the basis of these and similar decisions that the state-level *Illinois Brick* repealers should be abandoned in favor of a more uniform application of *Illinois Brick* by state courts.[88]

One of the most important early victories for Microsoft was the *A&M Supply Co. v. Microsoft Corp.* litigation in Michigan, decided in 2002. The *A&M* case was the first Microsoft-related state action pertaining to indirect purchasers in which the issue of class certification reached a court of appeals.[89] After a lengthy analysis, the Michigan appellate court concluded that the trial court had erred in granting the plaintiff's certification motion, largely because the class representative hadn't presented a method for calculating "actual damages" (pass-on), which in turn meant that common issues wouldn't predominate over individualized ones.[90]

But a counter-trend had already emerged. In California, in August of 2000, a Superior Court had certified two classes of indirect purchasers in a consolidated case. Microsoft opposed certification, focusing largely on the predominance requirement. Specifically, Microsoft argued that pricing differences, changes in the computer industry, variation in the channels of distribution for its products, and the fact that its products represented only a fraction of the cost of a typical computer all suggested that individualized issues of proof would overwhelm the common ones. In a comprehensive decision that would reverberate for years, Judge Stuart R. Pollak rejected those arguments. He found in California's rejection of *Illinois Brick* a broader policy directive that the problems of apportioning damages aren't "insuperable." In contrast to the courts that were comfortable with the "inconsistency" of authorizing indirect-purchaser suits but denying motions to certify indirect-purchaser class actions, the California court instead sought to reconcile its application of the standards for class certification with the goals of its state *Illinois Brick* repealer.[91] This was a common characteristic of later courts that followed the same path.

The California and the Michigan and Maine certification decisions thus became rival, antagonistic precedents for later cases. Microsoft pressed other courts to embrace what it considered the good sense of the *A&M* decision, and that of similar decisions in Michigan and Maine, in counterpoint to plaintiffs' urging that courts follow the lead of California.[92] But as litigation across the country progressed, Microsoft's victories in Maine and Michigan increasingly appeared to be outliers. As one court observed in 2003, "[e]very state, with the exception of Maine and Michigan, that has a repealer statute has granted class certification to indirect purchasers seeking redress against Microsoft for antitrust violations. The very same pass-through and overcharge arguments that Microsoft makes here, have been rejected by a large majority of courts considering the issue."[93] Ironically, the "market" for class certification had "tipped" irretrievably against Microsoft.

Again, the *Comes* litigation is instructive. After the Iowa Supreme Court's reversal and remand of the Iowa trial court's initial decision declining to recognize indirect-purchaser standing, the court certified two classes of purchasers and Microsoft again appealed to the Iowa Supreme Court. This time in a unanimous opinion, the court affirmed. As in many of the other state *Microsoft* cases, much of the attention of the parties and the court focused on the "predominance requirement" as it related specifically to the harming of indirect purchasers. The Iowa Court found, however, that the questions of liability that were common to the class—whether Microsoft was a monopolist, whether it engaged in anticompetitive conduct, and whether its conduct violated the Iowa Competition Law—were themselves sufficient to establish predominance. It also found predominance in its more particular examination of the fact of injury and the measurement of damages, relying in large part on the testimony of the plaintiff's expert, Jeffrey K. Mackie-Mason, who had also testified for the class representatives in the California, Massachusetts, Minnesota, and Wisconsin cases against Microsoft. Mackie-Mason's affidavit asserted that Microsoft's alleged violations of Iowa competition law were "susceptible to common proof on a formulaic basis." Refusing to delve any further into the merits of these assertions at the class-certification stage in order to resolve differences on the basis of contradictory evidence, the court, relying in part a decision from North Dakota, affirmed the certification order.[94]

What explains this seemingly abrupt change of direction toward allowing class certification? Though some critics have questioned the actual dollar value of indirect-purchaser litigation, as well as the likely incremental contribution they can make to securing deterrence, courts were certainly uncomfortable with the apparent inconsistency of granting indirect purchasers "rights" yet depriving indirect purchasers of any effective means of enforcing those rights, especially in states that had repealed *Illinois Brick* by statute for purposes of their state antitrust laws. Since many indirect purchasers will be consumers, and since their claims will probably be too small to warrant individual lawsuits, the class action provides the only procedural means for even potentially realizing the purpose of those rights. In this sense, Microsoft's experience with indirect-purchaser class-action certification illustrates the interdependence of elements of the private antitrust enforcement system. Indirect purchasers' rights are of little value in the absence of an effective class-action device. More broadly, it can be argued that providing rights without any hope of remedies is contrary to longstanding principles of law, that it erodes public confidence in the judicial system, and that in the broadest sense it undermines the perception of rule of law.[95]

It is worth observing, however, that since the period 1999–2005, when Microsoft faced the issue of class certification, federal courts in particular have become increasingly demanding of putative class representatives in antitrust cases and in general. Whereas the *Comes* court could confidently reject Microsoft's argument that each member of the plaintiff class should be required to demonstrate some kind of concrete passed-on harm on the ground that it "asks the court to make a class certification ruling based on the merits of the case, something we have uniformly rejected,"[96] more recently federal courts, including the U.S. Supreme Court, have openly invited inquiry into the merits when it is necessary to fulfill the trial court's obligation to conduct a "rigorous analysis" before class certification. These decisions have shifted the focus of concern from safeguarding the rights of class members to safeguarding the interest of defendants in remaining free from what they argue is the coercive power of class certification, specifically the pressure to settle that can follow from reliance on a lenient standard of certification.[97] Although it is too soon to tell whether these more recent developments in the federal courts will influence state courts, one wonders whether the various plaintiffs in the *Microsoft* cases would be as successful today in seeking certification.

Settling the Class-Action Cases

In contrast to settlements in typical litigation, class-action settlements must be reviewed and approved by the court. In return for the right to represent a class, parties to class actions thus surrender some of the autonomy that individual litigants enjoy. Under the current version of Federal Rule 23(e)(2), for example, courts are required to hold a hearing after receipt of a motion for approval of a class-action settlement and can approve the settlement only after a finding that it is "fair, reasonable, and adequate."

The final phase of Microsoft's litigation of the various class actions involving alleged overcharging of indirect purchasers, therefore, consisted of negotiating class-action settlements in state and federal courts throughout the country, then seeking court approval. A significant settlement was reached with a group of plaintiffs in the federal MDL litigation. Another settlement resolved the nearly 30 cases in the consolidated California litigation. Microsoft ultimately reached settlements with state class-action plaintiffs in 20 states.[98] Although some trials began, none of the more than 200 private cases against Microsoft ever reached a conclusion on the merits after trial, with the exception of the Novell case. Of the cases that weren't dismissed, every one was settled.

By their nature, all settlements resolve claims between the plaintiffs and the defendants. In effect, the parties declare that they no longer wish to litigate. That nature is evident in the class-action settlement context, as well, but it leads to complications and reveals how courts in practice influence the class-action settlement process. First, in contrast to non-class settlements, the approval process mandated by Federal Rule 23 provides an opportunity for interested parties to lodge their objections. This feature of federal practice is also typical of parallel state rules and permits objections to be expressed by unnamed class members, by interested non-parties, or by the court. Second, courts are generally reluctant to reject settlements for a number of reasons, not the least of which is the disquieting prospect of directing parties who have declared a truce to continue litigating. In practice, however, courts with concerns about class settlements urge the parties to renegotiate and resubmit the settlement, often with some specific guidance as to the initial settlement's perceived shortcomings. This capacity to influence the settlement terms is more than just a simple power to approve or disapprove a settlement; it is one of the primary powers of the approving court.

For the most part, the *Microsoft* settlements proceeded without objection, or with little objection. Some, however, were hotly contested, and a number required appellate review. In some cases, non-parties sought to intervene for the purpose of objecting to various aspects of the settlement. And in a number of cases Microsoft objected to the attorneys' fees being sought by plaintiffs' counsel.[99] Here we will focus on two of the contested settlements: one before Judge Motz in the MDL 1332 proceeding and the other in the California state litigation.

On November 21, 2001, a group of plaintiffs in the MDL 1332 litigation and Microsoft announced that they had reached a settlement of more than 100 of the pending class-action suits. The proposed Settlement Agreement sought to resolve claims on behalf of a "Nationwide Settlement Class," "defined generally as persons and entities who have acquired licenses for Microsoft operating system or applications software in the United States since January 1, 1985." The class was created specifically for purposes of the settlement and, according to the district court, could potentially encompass 100 million possible claimants. This practice of using "settlement classes" to resolve putative class-action litigation before certification of a class was approved in principle by the U.S. Supreme Court in 1997, but all Rule 23 requirements for certification of a class other than trial-management concerns must be satisfied before a court can approve a settlement-only class.[100]

The proposed Microsoft settlement was highly irregular, however, in that it didn't provide for any payments to the class members. Citing difficulties in identifying more than just a small percentage of the individual class members, as well as the cost of administering any payment or voucher-based settlement to such a large class, the plaintiffs urged the court to embrace a "*cy pres* only" settlement. (*Cy pres* awards have long been used in class actions to dispose of any residue that remains after reasonable efforts to distribute the settlement fund to class members have been exhausted. The remaining funds are awarded to the "next best" purpose, such as an eleemosynary or public interest organization whose work is related to the goals of the laws being enforced in the class action.) Under the Settlement Agreement, an independently run "eLearning Foundation" would be created and initially funded by Microsoft. The avowed purpose of the foundation was to help close the "digital divide" through a grant program that would provide hardware and software to the nation's neediest public schools, covering kindergarten through high school. Microsoft committed to an initial payment of $400 million for technology acquisitions, technical support, and professional development for a period of five years, and a potential additional payment of $100 million in matching funds for contributions made to the foundation by other donors. In addition, Microsoft agreed to provide at least 200,000 refurbished computers per year for the five-year term of the settlement agreement, to provide Microsoft software to the schools at no cost, and to provide free training and support. In return, the members of the nationwide class would release Microsoft from all claims against it—a prospect that drew the ire of state attorneys general and class representatives in some of the other states where cases were pending, especially California.[101]

Pursuant to Rule 23's requirements for court approval, the settlement was submitted to Judge Motz for review and was challenged by a wide range of objectors, including certified and putative class representatives in pending state class-action suits and the attorneys general of a number of states. In the end, Motz refused to approve the deal that had been struck.

Judge Motz saw no problem with using a *"cy pres* only" remedy in a case in which the number of claimants and the costs of administering individual claims made them uneconomical. More serious were the potential conflicts of interest within the defined class: between direct and indirect purchasers, between indirect purchasers in *Illinois Brick* repealer states and those in non-repealer states, and between certified and uncertified classes. Motz also noted the variations in state laws applicable to various class members. But here too he concluded that these issues wouldn't preclude approval. Many of the "conflicts" would arise only if individual claims were involved, pitting various class interests against each other for their share of the settlement fund; no such conflicts would arise with a *"cy pres* only" approach. Moreover, Motz noted that objectors could opt out of the settlement (although Microsoft retained the option itself of scuttling the settlement if too many class members exercised that right). Finally, Motz concluded that, although considerations of comity might favor state-by-state resolution, "the federal court is an appropriate forum for forging a constructive solution to a multijurisdictional problem of national scope." Perhaps revealing something of his own view of the superiority of the MDL proceeding over individual state adjudication, he concluded that "[c]omity does not require tolerance of economic balkanization and litigation chaos."[102]

Although Judge Motz didn't find sufficient cause in these three arguments to deny the motion for preliminary approval of the settlement, other grounds proved more persuasive. "As a procedural matter," he concluded, although the record was adequate to assess the *value of the settlement*, it was inadequate to determine the *value of the claims*—an essential component for evaluating the "adequacy" of any class-action settlement. Whereas the experts proffered by the parties had established a range of values for the settlement—from $700 million to $1.6 billion (a range based on the benefits it would bestow on the schools, not on the actual costs to Microsoft, which were probably much lower)—there was widely conflicting evidence as to the value of the claims that had been asserted against Microsoft. The expert retained by the objecting California plaintiffs estimated the range of damages to the national class before mandatory trebling to be from $10.3 billion to $18.9 billion. The "upper level of the overcharges" estimated by the MDL plaintiffs' expert fell within that range, but the court noted that "he believes his upper level estimate might not be recoverable." In contrast, Microsoft's expert, consistent with Microsoft's view that there hadn't been any overcharges attributable to the conduct that had been challenged as anticompetitive, didn't offer an independent assessment of damages. Instead, he criticized the work of the plaintiffs' experts, arguing that with some changes in the assumptions their models would yield a range from zero to, at most, $200 million. The court also observed that business organizations, not individual consumers, might hold roughly 85 percent of the claims, posing additional challenges to estimating the value of "consumer" harm.[103] Without a basis to estimate the reasonable value of the claims, Judge Motz concluded that he couldn't evaluate the adequacy of the settlement and therefore could not approve it.

Moreover, Judge Motz concluded that "as a substantive matter" the proposed funding for the charitable foundation was deficient in two ways. First, the fund was simply not enough to have a significant effect on the technology deficiencies of needy schools. A more "troublesome" consequence of the level of funding posed something of a paradox. A number of objectors had argued that the hardware and software programs, as they were to be structured, could themselves have anticompetitive effects. Although the Settlement Agreement was, on its face, "platform neutral," and although it included a non-discrimination provision that prohibited the foundation from favoring Microsoft software or hardware running Microsoft software in awarding grants, in practice it was very likely to have the anticompetitive effect of dislodging Apple from the education industry (the industry in which it had historically been strongest), thereby facilitating a further expansion of Microsoft's dominance.[104]

As we noted above, rather than simply rejecting the settlement, Judge Motz suggested to the parties some specific ways in which the agreement might be revised to address his concerns—for example, by relying on an "all cash" fund that could be used with greater autonomy by grantees.[105] Judge Motz's invitation wasn't accepted, however. After his rejection of the proposed nationwide settlement, Microsoft declared that it would "return to litigation," although for the most part it turned to the painstaking task of settling the class-action overcharge cases one by one.[106]

In January of 2003, just over a month before a scheduled trial date, Microsoft and the California state class-action plaintiffs announced that they had reached a $1.1 billion settlement of more than twenty class actions that had been filed in various California courts and consolidated pursuant to California's analog to the federal MDL statute. After five more months of negotiation, the settlement agreement was finalized and submitted to the court for approval.[107] The agreement provided for "consumer vouchers" that represented "direct compensation for the alleged overcharges," and for a *cy pres* remedy designated for California public schools serving low-income households. The *cy pres* distributions were to be funded from the residual of the Consumer Vouchers. The trial court approved the settlement in July of 2004, and an appeal was taken by an objector limited to the *cy pres* plan.[108]

The California Court of Appeals affirmed, rejecting the objector's arguments that the public schools were ineligible to receive *cy pres* awards because they weren't specifically mentioned in the California *cy pres* statute, which specified only "nonprofit organizations or foundations" and "child advocacy programs." In the court's view, the statute applied only in the absence of express settlement-agreement provisions. The objector also argued that, wholly aside from the California statute, the trial court had abused its discretion by failing to consider alternative distributions. That argument, too, was rejected. The sole question at the class settlement approval stage was whether the *cy pres* distribution *actually negotiated by the parties* satisfied the "fair, adequate, and reasonable" standard, not whether some alternative might be preferable.[109] The court concluded that the *cy pres* distribution also furthered the compensatory purposes of the settlement, because the class as a whole would benefit, albeit indirectly, from the school program, "by insuring that a new generation of computer literate children will enter the work force full trained to make the best use of computer technology." It also aided the goal of deterrence through disgorgement if ill-gotten gains.[110]

After nearly a decade of litigation, Microsoft ultimately reached settlements in cases filed in nineteen states and the District of Columbia. Of the federal cases, MDL 1332 had dwindled down to its final two cases: an indirect-purchaser class action from Arizona (*Daisy Mountain Fire District v. Microsoft Corp.*), which was also later settled, and the *Novell* litigation. Several private cases also are pending in Canada.

Conclusion

The private treble-damages litigation triggered by the government cases engaged the many plaintiffs, Microsoft, and the courts for more than a decade. Collectively, it illustrates on a grand scale some of the most controversial features of the American antitrust system, and some of the recurrent doctrinal and procedural challenges. As we have noted, maintaining a divided system in which indirect purchasers are barred from federal court yet are permitted to pursue their claims in many state courts encourages the filing of multiple related lawsuits, leads to forum shopping, to duplication of effort, and to challenging questions about class certification, and makes settlement a more complicated task.

In the end, it is difficult to assess the costs and benefits of these cases, both for the parties and, more broadly, for the institutions charged with deciding them—the federal and state courts. As we have noted, all of the cases that were not dismissed were settled.. For the most part, Microsoft negotiated truces with its competitors and offered consumers small and widely dispersed cash rewards and coupons. It agreed to almost no additional modifications to its business practices.

Were the compensation and the deterrence realized by the private cases, especially the many class actions, reasonably calibrated to the offenses committed—did they yield "efficient" compensation and deterrence? This is a fair question. At best, any "calibration" seems crude. In addition, it is difficult to estimate the institutional costs of the system, which also need to be accounted for on any system-wide balance sheet. Substantial resources were expended in numerous courts over many years in efforts to resolve these cases. Society, too, shares the cost of a system that produces hundreds of related and overlapping civil suits and uncertain benefits. In chapter 7 we will explore their remedial value more extensively.

6 Antitrust as a Global Enterprise

The most profound development in antitrust law at the close of the twentieth century was not its engagement with the business of the information and technology age, but its expansion into a global enterprise. As late as the 1980s, robust antitrust enforcement was the concern of a relatively small group of jurisdictions led by the United States, the European Union, Germany, Canada, and Australia.[1] But with the fall of the Soviet Union in the early 1990s and other global political and economic developments, more and more nations turned away from centrally planned economies. These nations sought instead to develop or strengthen their reliance on markets. Throughout the former Soviet Union, in nations formally under its influence, and in many others throughout Africa, Asia, and South America, this greater reliance on markets spawned acute interest in the previously underdeveloped field of "competition policy." By the end of the first decade of the twenty-first century, the International Competition Network, a virtual organization created by sixteen enforcement agencies in 2001 to link together the competition-policy enforcers of the world, had more than 100 jurisdictions as members.[2]

Microsoft's encounter with the antitrust system coincided with this crucial period in the continuing evolution of this global enforcement community. Facing investigations and prosecutions in several countries, Microsoft became a test case for the system's capacity to judge the conduct of a dominant firm that crossed many borders. Although enforcement actions were focused primarily in the United States and the European Union, significant cases were also brought in Korea and Japan, and investigations proceeded in a number of other countries. As one sign of the changed times, in 2008 and 2009 the press reported that investigations of Microsoft were underway in China, Taiwan, and Russia.[3]

In this chapter we will focus primarily on the European Commission's case against Microsoft, which was opened in December of 1998 shortly after the commencement of the U.S. government cases in the U.S. District Court for the District of Columbia. To provide some context for understanding the European litigation, we begin the chapter with a comparative overview of the competition-policy systems and prohibitions of the United States and the European Union. In the second section of the chapter we review and analyze the European Commission's decision in the case and the European Court of First Instance's sweeping affirmance of that decision.[4] In the third section we discuss the U.S. Justice Department's surprisingly harsh and public criticisms of the European litigation and its reaction to a proceeding that the Korea Fair Trade Commission brought under Korean competition law.

A Comparative Overview of U.S. and EU Competition Law

As we have discussed, Section 2 of the Sherman Act is the principal federal statutory provision that addresses the conduct of a single firm. It prohibits not only "monopolization" but also attempted monopolization and conspiracy to monopolize. These terms were drawn from the common law as terms of art, although the Sherman Act's drafters assumed that their meanings would evolve over time. As was true at common law, and as we discussed in chapter 1, Section 2 of the Sherman Act doesn't prohibit "monopoly." By its terms, "monopolization" contemplates some kind of active conduct. The mere possession of monopoly power, even the charging of supra-competitive prices, therefore isn't an offense under Section 2, despite its adverse economic consequences. In interpreting Section 2, the courts instead developed a "power plus conduct" formula that looks to whether a firm is a monopolist, or is in a position to become one, and whether its conduct can fairly be characterized as "predatory" or "exclusionary" rather than merely competitive (or even aggressively competitive). Although often presented as two distinct elements of an offense, in truth power and conduct can be highly interdependent.

Like the Sherman Act, the Treaty of Rome, which established the predecessor of today's European Union in 1957, included a prohibition of single-firm conduct—but it didn't follow the U.S. model of drawing on language and processes of common law.[5] Instead of "monopolization," Article 102 prohibits "abuse" of a "dominant position."[6] Also in contrast to Section 2 of the Sherman Act, Article 102 specifies four broad categories of conduct that might constitute "abuse" instead of leaving the task of specification completely to the courts. The potential offenses listed include "exploitative" as well as exclusionary conduct. Thus, in theory, though rarely in practice, the European Commission could challenge the mere exercise of monopoly power (that is, charging prices that are by some measure too high, as with "price gouging")—something that couldn't be done under U.S. antitrust laws

Despite these important differences, Article 102 shares Section 2's framework for evaluating exclusionary conduct: it focuses on power ("dominance") and conduct ("abuse"). But here again the two jurisdictions tend to diverge, though only to a degree. Although there is a wide range of conduct that would be similarly permitted and condemned under both laws, Section 2, as interpreted by the U.S. Supreme Court, is generally perceived as more permissive—and that is true with respect to both elements of the framework. Section 2's power requirement tends to require a higher degree of market power than Article 102's requirement of dominance, sometimes expressed simply as a very high market share. Similarly, U.S. courts have defined "predatory" and "exclusionary" quite narrowly, whereas Article 102's notion of "abuse" has been interpreted more broadly. Thus, although virtually any conduct that would violate Section 2 in the United States is also likely to violate Article 102, the converse is not true. Despite a common conceptual framework, conduct that could violate Article 102 might escape condemnation under Section 2 of the Sherman Act. Although agreement is far more common than conflict, from time to time this difference has caused some tension between U.S. and European enforcers, and it did so in the *Microsoft* cases. As we shall see, however, those differences were magnified by political changes in the United States—changes that illuminate the continuing role that ideological divergence can play in explaining differing attitudes toward the enforcement of prohibitions of dominant-firm conduct.

It is important to appreciate, however, that, for a number of reasons, the EU's "abuse-of-dominance" formulation is by far the more prevalent model in the world today for identifying anticompetitive single-firm conduct. First, with the fall of the Soviet Union, membership in the EU became an important priority for a number of countries in Eastern and Central Europe, and for other countries interested in someday joining the EU. Conformance to the EU's laws, including its competition laws, was a prerequisite to eventual membership and an important reason to follow the lead of Article 102 in framing national competition laws. There was also a phase of competitive "antitrust imperialism" from the early 1990s until the beginning of the 2000s, when many nations were drafting their own competition laws for the first time. During this period the United States and the European Union vied for leadership in the world of competition policy, each proselytizing for its own substantive standards and institutional systems, sometimes through technical assistance programs. The end result was the emergence of a global template that combines features of both. For example, although the EU's "abuse-of-dominance" approach is by far the predominant model for addressing single-firm conduct, many jurisdictions have followed the U.S. example of including a stand-alone merger control provision in their competition laws in addition to the prohibition of anticompetitive single-firm conduct. Under EU law, by contrast, the Merger Regulation is linked to and derivative of Article 102's prohibition of abuse of dominance. There was no distinct prohibition of anticompetitive mergers.

Second, the Sherman Act's common law approach of specifying offenses very broadly and leaving specification to courts would be alien to and hence ill-fitting as a model for civil-law systems. It is constructed upon the assumption in common law that the legislature generally outlines the scope of the law and the courts develop specific standards over time. The EU model, which includes a greater degree of legislated specification, is arguably more adaptable to both common-law and civil-law systems.

Third, and perhaps most directly relevant to the resolution of the *Microsoft* cases, in the decade that followed institution of the U.S. *Microsoft* cases, a series of U.S. Supreme Court and appellate court decisions, an explosion of critical commentary, and a change of administrations in Washington collectively moved the content of U.S. law in a decidedly more permissive, non-interventionist direction. That direction, and the assumptions it reflected about the relative costs and benefits of unchecked single-firm conduct and of government intervention, were perceived as too permissive by many other jurisdictions and hence limited the utility of the U.S. example around the globe. The EU's approach seemed to strike the better balance. The *Microsoft* cases thus contributed in significant part to a worldwide debate about the proper scope of the prohibitions applicable to single-firm conduct.

To this point we have sketched some of the similarities and differences between the substantive law of unilateral conduct in the United States and the European Union. Competition policies are implemented, however, by institutions, and the institutional arrangements for doing so can be quite varied depending upon the general framework of a jurisdiction's approach to government regulation of the private sector. As we noted in chapter 2, in the United States authority to challenge violations of antitrust law ("infringements" of "competition" law in the nomenclature of the EU) is dispersed and includes private litigation. In the European Union it is more centralized, although more recently there have been efforts to encourage National Competition Authorities to accept responsibility for a more significant share of enforcement responsibility. There have also been efforts to promote a limited system of private enforcement.

Two characteristics of the European Commission's system for deciding cases of alleged competition law infringements played important roles in the EU cases against Microsoft, and distinguished them procedurally from the U.S. Justice Department's case: how the EC responds to complaints from private parties and how it reaches decisions as to whether the subject of such a complaint has indeed infringed EU competition laws. In both ways, the institutional distinctiveness of the European Commission and its Directorate General for Competition ("DG Competition" or "DG Comp") affected the course of the European Microsoft investigation and prosecution.[7]

In the European Union, the European Commission can commence a new matter on its own initiative or in response to market information provided by private parties or other competition authorities, such as National Competition Authorities. In addition, a private party with a "legitimate interest" can submit a more formal "complaint" to the Commission alleging an infringement of the competition laws.[8] The Commission is required to perform at least an initial assessment of a properly constituted formal complaint, but it isn't obliged to carry out a complete investigation or to initiate proceedings against the subject of the complaint. It has wide prosecutorial discretion in responding to it. Thus, the Commission can reject a complaint on the merits if it concludes that there hasn't been any infringement of EU competition law. But it might also decide not to pursue a complaint because it doesn't warrant the necessary commitment of time and resources, as might be the case if the alleged infringement doesn't involve the public interest or because it doesn't pose a competition problem with an EU-wide dimension. As was true in the EC *Microsoft* cases, EC-initiated investigations and actions on formal complaints aren't mutually exclusive, can arise in parallel, and can be consolidated.

Another distinguishing feature of the EC's framework is its recognition of "interested third parties." In the United States, interested parties can informally approach the government enforcement agencies, advocate investigations, and otherwise offer their views throughout proceedings, as Netscape and a number of other firms and groups did in the initial U.S. investigation. Once litigation has formally been initiated in the courts, they can also formally "intervene" to become parties themselves. In the EU, in addition to formal complainants, the Implementing Regulation authorizes natural or legal persons to "apply to be heard and show a sufficient interest." If the EC concludes that the necessary showing has been made, it can formally acknowledge interested third parties and can invite them to submit their views in writing and perhaps to participate in oral hearings. Firms that are the subject of investigation also have certain rights to respond to the submissions of interested third parties.[9]

If, on the basis of its initial assessment, the EC concludes that a matter merits further investigation, it will "open proceedings," a more active stage of investigation. This more formal step, however, doesn't necessarily indicate that the EC will pursue a case of infringement, but it triggers a more formal and in-depth investigation, one that can take several years. As is true of the initial assessment phase, the investigative phase of a proceeding can conclude with a decision to close the investigation. As it did in the *Microsoft* case, however, it can also lead to a Statement of Objections (SO), which is analogous to an administrative complaint in the United States. The issuance of a Statement of Objections triggers specific procedures that include the subject's right to respond, and it leads to a preliminary decision by the EC, a hearing, and ultimately a final decision. Commission decisions can be appealed to the General Court (known as the "Court of First Instance" at the time of the *Microsoft* case) and ultimately to the European Court of Justice. A Statement of Objections might also lead to "Commitment Procedures," essentially a negotiated settlement that requires the target to make certain "commitments" to address the competitive concerns. Commitment Procedures are similar in nature to the process in the United States that can lead to a consent decree, and was attempted unsuccessfully in the EC *Microsoft* case.[10]

The European Commission's Case against Microsoft

On December 10, 1998, seven months after the U.S. government cases were commenced in Washington, Sun Microsystems applied to the Commission for the initiation of proceedings against Microsoft. A little more than a year later, in February of 2000, the Commission also began its own independent investigation of Microsoft's conduct. Distinct case numbers were initially assigned to the two matters. On August 1, 2000, the Commission formally initiated proceedings in the Sun case and sent Microsoft its first Statement of Objections; a year later, it did so in its own case, and at that time it joined the two proceedings into what became viewed collectively as the European Commission's *Microsoft* case.[11]

Sun's complaint focused on an issue that wasn't directly addressed in the U.S. cases until the remedy stage: "interoperability." The charges focused both on the interoperability of desktop computers (what the Commission described as "client PCs") running Microsoft Windows with workgroup servers running non-Microsoft operating systems (client PC to server) and on the interoperability of workgroup servers running Microsoft's server operating systems with other servers running non-Microsoft operating systems (server to server).[12] Sun claimed that Microsoft abused its dominant position in client-PC operating systems by "reserving to itself information that certain products for network computing, called work group server operating systems, need to interoperate fully with Microsoft's PC operating systems."[13]

The Commission's self-initiated investigation focused on Microsoft's integration of its Windows Media Player (WMP) into its Windows operating system for desktop computers. It thus had more in common with the U.S. case, which had focused on Microsoft's similar decision to integrate its Internet Explorer browser into Windows. When the Commission decided to initiate proceedings in the media player investigation, it issued a second Statement of Objections to Microsoft that combined the interoperability issues raised in Sun's complaint with the integration issues posed by its own. After Microsoft responded to the two SOs, the Commission undertook an investigation that began first with Microsoft's customers, and then broadened to look more generally at the market. A Supplemental Statement of Objections followed in August of 2003.[14]

"Interested third parties" also played a significant role in the Commission's proceedings. As we noted in discussing the U.S. private competitor cases in chapter 5, the group included some easily predictable firms, such as AOL/Time Warner (which owned Netscape), RealNetworks, and Novell, but also included Lotus Corporation and a number of trade associations, some of which had been formed by Microsoft's rivals and some of which represented Microsoft's views.[15] These interested parties submitted a significant amount of information to the Commission and were permitted to answer to Microsoft's responses to the various Statements of Objections.[16]

After a three-day oral hearing in November of 2003, and a number of submissions that Microsoft made in response to the Commission's evidence and views, the Commission and Microsoft engaged in a last-minute effort to settle the case. The Competition Commissioner, Mario Monti, participated in those negotiations, but he ultimately rejected Microsoft's commitment offers as inadequate, particularly as they affected future integration decisions. Monti, an economist by training, had also been responsible for fortifying the Commission's capacity to undertake more sophisticated economic analysis in response to three judicial reversals of Commission merger challenges in 2002. The *Microsoft* case thus became something of a test of his efforts to improve the economic analysis that undergirded the Commission's competition-related decisions.[17]

On March 24, 2004, the Commission issued a lengthy decision concluding that Microsoft had abused its dominant position in violation of Article 102. The Commission ruled decisively against Microsoft on both Sun's complaint about server interoperability and its own concerns about the tying of WMP to Windows. To remedy its violations of Article 102, the Commission ordered Microsoft to disclose the information necessary to facilitate interoperable server products and to offer a version of Windows for client PCs that didn't include WMP. Notably, it didn't seek to enjoin Microsoft from continuing to sell its integrated version of Windows and WMP. It also fined Microsoft nearly €500 million.[18]

Competition Law and Platform Software

As a preliminary matter, the European Commission addressed and rejected a common component of the narrative Microsoft advocated both in the European Union and in the United States: that competition law is too crude a tool for judging the technologies of the "new economy."

Recall from earlier chapters that Microsoft had urged the courts in the United States to approach the antitrust analysis of platform software and related markets with caution. In its view, these markets are uniquely dynamic, quickly evolving, and subject to disruptive technological upheavals, and thus traditional methods of antitrust analysis are prone to error. More concretely, Microsoft urged diminished reliance on "structural" evidence, such as market share, as a basis for inferring market power. Owing to the dynamism of these markets, it argued, market share could at best offer a static snapshot that would probably overstate Microsoft's market position. New technologies could "leap-frog" over Microsoft in the near future. In lieu of traditional structural indicators, it urged the Commission to require the government to produce more "direct" measures of market power.[19]

The European Commission rejected this argument, as had the Court of Appeals for the D.C. Circuit. Quoting the D.C. Circuit's opinion and work by the American economists Michael Katz and Carl Shapiro, the Commission stated that traditional antitrust methods and standards were adequate to assess Microsoft's power and the effects of its conduct. Although that analysis should be informed by the economic characteristics of new economy industries, the Commission reasoned, those characteristics didn't justify a wholesale abandonment of current antitrust standards. Indeed, the Commission found, the nature of new economy industries might, contrary to Microsoft's assertions, suggest the need for greater concern:

The specifics of any particular industry (be it "hi-tech" or "old economy") must of course be taken into account when analysing issues of market definition and market power. Differing characteristics will undoubtedly have an influence on the specific assessments that are reached. This, however, does not mean that no antitrust analysis could be applied to "new economy" markets. In fact, the specific characteristics of the market in question (for example, network effects and the applications barrier to entry) would rather suggest that there is an increased likelihood of positions of entrenched market power, compared to certain "traditional industries."[20]

Properly informed, both jurisdictions thus agreed that the standards of competition law enforcement were adequate to the task of understanding and judging Microsoft's power and the effects of its conduct.

Industry Characteristics

The first step in the European Commission's analysis was to examine the characteristics of the software industry. Once again, the Commission found broad common ground with the U.S. agencies and courts. Three especially important characteristics were network effects, the applications barrier to entry, and interoperability. These three characteristics largely explained why Microsoft had become so dominant in platform software and also pointed the way to understanding the strategic nature of its challenged conduct. The core of the economic theory behind the EC's case, therefore, was neither new nor novel. The EC's economic reasoning shared a view of the industry that had first been articulated to the U.S. agencies and courts a decade earlier in the Licensing Case we discussed in chapter 2.

Recall that the central theory behind the U.S. cases was that Microsoft perceived a threat to its monopoly in desktop-computer operating systems from middleware, especially Netscape's Internet Browser and Sun's Java programming language. To squelch that threat, it undertook a wide variety of acts to prevent middleware from either evolving into a competing operating system or facilitating the emergence of competing operating systems.

Much as had been found in the U.S. case, the EC found that network effects and the applications barrier to entry were characteristics of the market for operating systems for desktop computers that were essential to an understanding of Microsoft's dominance. But the U.S. cases had focused primarily on the relationship between the desktop-computer operating system and middleware. The EC's case examined the relationship between operating systems for desktop computers and those for servers—a dimension not explored in the U.S. cases until the negotiated remedy stage. The EC found that the desktop-to-server relationship, however, exhibited some of the very same interdependencies that were evident in the desktop-to-middleware market and posed some of the same threats to Microsoft, provoking analogous anticompetitive responses.

As had the U.S. authorities and courts, the Commission noted the "dependency" of application programs on access to the Application Programming Interfaces (APIs) of operating systems. When exposed, APIs allow programs, including middleware, to call on the operating system for various functions. The relationship between APIs and programs establishes what users experience as "compatibility" of programs and operating systems. As the Commission explained, "[a]n application that uses a given API to access a service provided by a given operating system cannot run on an operating system that provides an equivalent service through a *different* API." This in turn explains the need to "port" application programs—to adapt them for use with multiple operating systems that use different APIs.[21] But the economic incentive for software developers to port programs to other operating systems was limited as they became increasingly invested in writing programs to Windows' APIs, another indication of the impact of network effects.

Going beyond the U.S. cases, however, the Commission also made extensive findings about the rise and the evolution of network computing and digital streaming media. One of the virtues of networks is their ability to use "distributed applications"—programs that can be accessed from a common network resource, such as a server, by multiple computers that, together with the server, make up a "distributed system." For such a networked system to function properly there must be "interoperability between the various pieces of software running on different physical machines of the network." And for interoperability to be realized there must be standardized protocols for "interconnection and interaction."[22] As was true of APIs, the Commission found that without access to Microsoft's communication protocols non-Microsoft servers couldn't interoperate smoothly with client PCs and servers using Microsoft's server operating system.[23]

As a consequence of network effects, the applications barrier to entry, and issues related to interoperability, Microsoft's dominance in the computing world of 1998 was well established. Even if Microsoft hadn't acted to protect its position, the prospects for competition probably were limited, owing to the importance of smooth interoperation between client PCs running Windows and applications programs, middleware, alternative platforms, and server operating systems. Competitive vitality in each of these areas had become heavily dependent on Microsoft's willingness to share various kinds of information that facilitated compatibility and interoperability, especially its APIs and its server communication protocols.

The Theories of the Case

Whereas the U.S. case was constructed around Microsoft's wide-ranging responses to actual and perceived future competitive threats to its monopoly in client-PC operating systems, the European Commission's case was at once narrower and broader.[24] Like the U.S., the EC focused on Microsoft's response to another form of middleware: streaming media players, such as RealNetworks' RealPlayer and Apple's QuickTime. That response, however, consisted mainly of the technological and contractual binding of its Windows Media Player to Windows, as had been done with IE and Windows. The broader range of conduct related to impeding the development of middleware that was integral to the U.S. case wasn't evident in Europe. On the other hand, in investigating Sun's complaint, the Commission's case examined Microsoft's response to the rise of network computing. At the heart of Sun's complaint was its assertion that Microsoft had wrongfully refused to disclose the information that was needed to allow its Solaris operating system for servers to work as "seamlessly" with Windows-based client-PC operating systems and other Windows software as Microsoft's own operating-system software for servers. This refusal to share interoperability information, Sun asserted, constituted an abuse of Microsoft's dominant position in the market for client-PC operating systems and gave Microsoft a significant competitive advantage in the market for workgroup-server operating systems that wasn't based on the merits of its own products.[25]

The Commission's findings also revealed a pattern of conduct that saw Microsoft first cooperate with its rivals, then emulate them, then turn against them. This had been an oft-repeated refrain from participants in the industry—that Microsoft's strategy was to "embrace, extend, and extinguish" the desirable Internet-related technologies first developed by its rivals.[26] Recall from chapter 3 that in the U.S. cases, the court found that Microsoft first sought to acquire Netscape, but when its offer was rebuffed it continued to develop its own Internet browser, Internet Explorer. It then embarked on a wide-ranging strategy to impede the distribution of Netscape's browser. In chapter 5, we examined Sun's similar assertions with respect to Microsoft's treatment of Java.

As had been true of its relationship with Netscape, Microsoft had first embraced and supported RealNetworks. Like Netscape, RealNetworks was a pioneer in developing technologies to exploit the potential of the Internet. Going beyond the mere ability to play audio and video files on a desktop PC, RealNetworks anticipated the potential for streaming audio and video content over the Internet and developed software that would facilitate transmission, receipt, and playback. Although in the early 1990s Microsoft began to incorporate multimedia playback capabilities into Windows, Real-Networks was the first to commercially develop software for streaming digital media over the Internet, initially through its RealAudio player in 1995. As the Commission found, Microsoft first included the RealAudio player as part of Internet Explorer in Windows 95. And in 1997 it entered into an agreement with RealNetworks to jointly develop streaming media technologies. But later that year it acquired another streaming media company, and in May of 1998 it announced the release of "the Microsoft Media Player." Microsoft Media Player evolved into the Windows Media Player. As it had done with IE, Microsoft then deeply integrated WMP into Windows as a non-removable component, eventually withdrawing support for Real-Networks' formats and for Apple's QuickTime media player.[27] Microsoft also initially embraced and supported but then emulated and ultimately withdrew support for non-Microsoft server operating systems, especially those of Novell and Sun. Here, too, other firms were the pioneers; Microsoft only followed later.[28]

Collectively this meant that, although the range of conduct at issue in the EC's cases arguably wasn't as sweeping as that examined in the U.S. case, characterizing the EC's case simply as one involving two discrete acts—the tying of WMP to Windows and the refusal to supply server-related interoperability information—ignored the larger context in which Microsoft acted. In truth, Microsoft's conduct was more far-ranging, complex, and persistent, as it had been in the United States.

Assessing Dominance

To evaluate Microsoft's conduct, the European Commission first laid out extensive findings of fact, many of which paralleled the original findings of the U.S. district court in the governments' prosecutions of Microsoft. Then, drawing upon its own previous decisions as well as those of the European courts, it defined the contours of the abuse-of-dominance offense under Article 102—the legal framework under which it would evaluate Microsoft's market position and conduct.

The Commission's analysis followed the traditional framework used in the United States and the European Union, first assessing power ("dominance") and then conduct ("abuse"), but also giving consideration to anti-competitive effects and justifications. Although the basic approach in the two jurisdictions is very much alike, the Commission's decision revealed some important differences between the U.S. and the EU.

The Commission defined "dominance" as "a position of economic strength enjoyed by an undertaking which enables it to prevent effective competition being maintained on the relevant market by affording it the power to behave to an appreciable extent independently of its competitors, its customers and ultimately of the consumers."[29] The traditional way to establish "monopoly power" in the U.S., or "dominance" in the EU, is to define a relevant market, calculate market shares, and infer market power from "high" market shares and other structural market characteristics, such as the number and capacity of other firms and conditions of entry. More direct measures can also be considered; in the U.S. those included the fact that Microsoft set its prices for Windows without considering any rivals' prices and Microsoft's pattern of exclusionary conduct, which wouldn't have been rational if Microsoft didn't possess monopoly power.[30]

As a prerequisite to its evaluation of dominance, therefore, the EC first applied the framework established in its 1997 Commission Notice on the Definition of the Relevant Market to define three markets that were relevant to the assessment of Microsoft's conduct: the markets for client-PC operating systems, workgroup-server operating systems, and streaming media players. In accordance with the Notice, it looked at demand-side substitutability (the range of products or services regarded as substitutable or interchangeable by consumers, with a product's or a service's price, characteristics, and uses taken into account) and supply-side substitutability (the ability of suppliers to switch production in response to "small and permanent changes in prices" to meet demand for the relevant products/ services "in the short term without incurring significant additional costs or risks in response").[31]

As had the courts of the United States, the Commission readily concluded that "client PC operating systems" constituted a distinct relevant market for antitrust purposes. The Commission found that there was a decided lack of "realistic substitutes" for Windows on client PCs and that supply-side substitution was very unlikely, especially owing to the applications barriers to entry.[32] That left the question of Microsoft's dominance.

In contrast to the aggressive stance Microsoft had taken throughout the U.S. proceedings, where it vigorously contested both the existence of a relevant market for Intel-compatible PC operating systems and its alleged dominance in that market, Microsoft conceded both points in its response to the Commission's supplementary Statement of Objections.[33] The Commission nevertheless went on to make detailed findings to support its conclusion that Microsoft was not only dominant in the market for client-PC operating systems but "overwhelmingly" dominant[34]:

Very large market shares, of over 50%, are considered in themselves, and but for exceptional circumstances, evidence of the existence of a dominant position.

Market shares between 70% and 80% have been held to warrant such a presumption of dominance. Microsoft, with its market shares of over 90%, occupies almost the whole market—it therefore approaches a position of complete monopoly, and can be said to hold an overwhelmingly dominant position.[35]

Note that in the Commission's view a 50 percent market share could be enough to establish "dominance." Under traditional U.S. law, it wouldn't be sufficient to support a finding of "monopoly power" for purposes of the offense of monopolization. To find a violation of Section 2 for a firm with a 50 percent market share, a U.S. case would have to proceed on the theory of "attempted monopolization," which would also require evidence of specific intent to monopolize and a dangerous probability of monopolization.[36] Hence U.S. law and EU law differ in theory on how to assess single-firm power, but not in ways that mattered with respect to the alleged market for client-PC operating systems in the *Microsoft* cases. Microsoft's market share, which consistently exceeded 80 percent no matter how it was measured, easily supported the traditional inference that it was a "monopolist" in the U.S. and a "dominant firm" in the EU.[37] That conclusion wasn't affected in either jurisdiction by the inclusion or the exclusion of Apple's small share of the market for client-PC operating systems.[38]

Although the Commission found that Microsoft's very high share warranted a "presumption of dominance," it didn't rest its conclusion of dominance simply on calculations of market share. It next observed that Microsoft "enjoyed an enduring stability and continuity to its market power." This was so regardless of the evolution of Windows through various versions, partly owing to the impact of network effects and the "various levers" Microsoft used to promote "migration towards new versions" of Windows.[39]

The Commission then turned to a detailed examination of the economics of platform software. As had been true in the U.S. proceedings, the defining characteristics of platform software—network effects, the applications barrier to entry, and interoperability—played important roles not only in defining the relevant market but also in assessing Microsoft's market power. As the Commission explained, "the more popular an operating system is, the more applications will be written to it and the more applications are written to an operating system, the more popular it will be among users." Quoting Bill Gates' testimony before the U.S. District Court in the states' remedies case, the Commission observed that such indirect network effects created a "positive feedback loop" whose benefits Microsoft fully recognized. As a result, it was exceedingly unlikely that a substitute operating system attractive to users would develop:

Although in theory possible, it would be extremely difficult, time-consuming, risky and expensive to develop an alternative client PC operating system, with *a priori* no application able to run on it, because users are very unlikely to buy an operating system without a wide range of applications already available, tested and used by other people. Therefore, for a new operating system product to enter the client PC operating system market, it would be necessary that such a product is either able to support a critical mass of existing Windows-dependent applications, or a comparable critical mass of applications already written for the new platform.[40]

This finding lent additional support to the inference of dominance drawn from Microsoft's market shares.

The Commission further observed that "[i]n essence, the dynamic between the Windows client PC operating system and the large body of applications that is written to it is self-reinforcing. In other words, applications developers have a compelling economic incentive to continue writing applications for the dominant client PC operating system platform (that is to say, Windows) because they know that the potential market will be larger." Again citing to the U.S. District Court's findings of fact, the Commission concluded that "the 'positive feedback loop' protects Microsoft's high market shares in the client PC operating system market from effective competition from a potential new entrant. The term 'applications barrier to entry' has been coined to describe this phenomenon." That applications barrier to entry, the Commission found, "enables Microsoft to behave to a very large extent independently of its competitors, its customers and ultimately of consumers."[41]

As had the courts of the United States, the Commission thus concluded that, owing to a variety of measures, Microsoft indeed was "dominant" in the market for client-PC operating systems. But the Commission didn't find merely that Microsoft was dominant; it concluded that Microsoft's dominant position "exhibits extraordinary features" that made it especially dominant. Those features included durable high market shares, network effects, and significant barriers to entry. Windows had become, in the Commission's view, the "*de facto* standard operating system product for client PCs."[42]

The Commission also concluded that there was a distinct market for "work group server operating systems," and that Microsoft held a dominant position in that market too. Again the Commission looked at both demand-side and supply-side substitutability, beginning with an examination of functionality—that is, the tasks that various types of server operating systems performed. It distinguished workgroup-server operating systems from "high end" or "enterprise" servers and from fringe or "edge" servers that perform specialized and limited tasks. The differentiating characteristics of workgroup servers and enterprise and "edge" servers included the importance of interoperability with client PCs. Workgroup servers performed tasks such as filing and printing for small to medium-size networks; more "high end" servers carried out "mission-critical tasks," such as support for large databases where interoperability among servers wasn't as critical. The Commission found that the need for interoperability between workgroup-server operating systems and client PCs supported the view that they were distinct from other kinds of server operating systems. Indeed, it highlighted the unique function of workgroup-server operating systems as the heart of distributed networks consisting of servers and multiple client PCs.[43]

Microsoft vigorously contested these findings, but the Commission systematically rejected its arguments, relying in large part on two kinds of evidence. First, the Commission conducted a "market enquiry"—a survey of users of servers. Although Microsoft objected to the use of the inquiry, in the Commission's view its results, along with statements taken from Microsoft customers, suggested that differentiation of tasks and workloads supported the view that workgroup-server operating systems were a distinct relevant market.[44] Here we can observe some interesting institutional differences between the tools that were available to the U.S. Department of Justice and the methodologies that were at the disposal of the European Commission. The authority to undertake a market inquiry is typically associated with administrative agencies. Thus it is something that the Justice Department would not typically do, especially in the context of an enforcement action, although it would routinely interview and take evidence from industry participants, including both customers and rivals. Second, the Commission looked at Microsoft's marketing and pricing practices with respect to its various server operating systems. Again it concluded that Microsoft's own behavior supported the conclusion that workgroup-server operating systems constituted a distinct relevant market. Microsoft marketed different versions of its server operating systems at significantly different prices, considering its customer's different functional needs, workloads, and available hardware.[45]

The Commission then considered supply-side substitutability. Noting Microsoft's failure to respond fully to the concerns it had expressed in its Supplementary Statement of Objections, the Commission concluded that producers of operating systems for client PCs, as well as for enterprise and "edge" servers, were unlikely to enter into the production of workgroup-server operating systems in the foreseeable future, and that this lent further support to the conclusion that the market for workgroup-server operating systems was a distinct relevant market:

[O]ther operating system vendors, including in particular vendors of server operating systems, would not be able to switch their production and distribution assets to work group server operating systems without incurring significant additional costs and risks and within a time framework sufficiently short so as to consider that supply-side considerations are relevant in this case.[46]

With the relevant market defined, the Commission turned to the question of dominance, again commencing the inquiry with an analysis of Microsoft's share of the market for operating systems for workgroup servers. But determining Microsoft's share of that market proved to be more of a challenge than determining its share of the market for client PCs. In lieu of the kinds of simple sales measures that were used for client PCs, the Commission turned to two proxies: shipment and revenue measures from third-party sources in the software industry and its own Market Inquiry. After an extensive review of the various available data, it concluded that Microsoft's share of the market for workgroup-server operating systems, viewed in conjunction with the "weak position" of its principal rival and "limited presence" of others, was sufficient to warrant a presumption of dominance:

The Commission has examined a variety of data in order to measure Microsoft's market share. ... All these data sets confirm that Microsoft holds by far the leading market share—in every measure, it has a share of at least 50%, and for most measures, its figures are in the 60-75% range. Such market shares are consistent with a presumption of dominance in the work group server operating system market according to the caselaw. ...[47]

As in its evaluation of the market for client-PC operating systems, however, the Commission didn't rely solely on market-share evidence. Also looking at conditions of entry, it found important parallels between the market for client-PC operating systems and that for workgroup-server operating systems. Microsoft argued that the latter didn't exhibit the kind of network effects that were so important in the former. But the Commission concluded that, in addition to external evidence, Microsoft's own internal communications suggested the contrary: that the "positive feedback loop" played a "similar role in server operating system markets to the one it plays on the client PC operating system market."[48]

The Commission also pointed to several other factors that contributed to barriers to entry that fortified Microsoft's dominance. It found additional indirect network effects at work in connection with the availability of information-technology technicians skilled in servicing specific work-group-server operating systems (a factor that customers would consider in selecting an operating system) and in connection with the importance of customer expectations about the long-term viability of a platform, taking into account such factors as the likelihood of continued vendor support and continued platform development. Moreover, in the Commission's view, Microsoft's practice of withholding interoperability information created an additional and "artificial" barrier to entry.[49]

Finally, the Commission looked to the importance of commercial and technical "associative links" between the market for client-PC operating systems and that for workgroup-server operating systems—links that further supported its conclusion that Microsoft held a dominant position in the latter market. Here the Commission's analysis appeared to diverge from the more compartmentalized approach typically taken under U.S. law. The Commission observed that

an isolated analysis of the competitive conditions on the market for work group server operating systems—ignoring Microsoft's overwhelming dominance in the neighbouring client PC operating system market—fails to deliver an accurate picture of Microsoft's true market power. Indeed, Microsoft's dominance over the client PC operating system market has a significant impact on the adjacent market for operating systems for work group servers."[50]

Relying on an earlier decision that had been affirmed by the Court of First Instance and the European Court of Justice, the Commission reasoned that

there are substantial direct and indirect network effects, not only within each of the two different markets for client PC and work group server operating systems, but also between the two markets. The exploitation of those network effects with a view to leveraging its quasi-monopoly from the client PC operating system market to the work group server operating system market is at the root of the identified abuse of refusal to supply. ....[51]

The third and last of the relevant markets defined by the Commission was the market for streaming media players. In the United States, the D.C. Circuit had concluded that the governments had failed to prove the existence of a distinct market for Internet browsers; the Commission certainly wouldn't want to meet the same fate when the European courts reviewed its decision. In contrast to its approach to the markets for client-PC and workgroup-server operating systems, however, the Commission's purpose in defining the market for streaming media players wasn't to demonstrate Microsoft's dominance. Instead, it was related directly to the charge that Microsoft had unlawfully "tied" its Windows Media Player to Windows. To assess whether that conduct had any anticompetitive effect, it needed to define the relevant market for the tied product.

Microsoft responded much as it had in the United States with respect to browsers, arguing that the ability to stream media was a "functionality" that it had added to the client-PC operating system, not a distinct "product." It based that conclusion on its view that "no client PC would be shipped without substantial multimedia functionality, including the capability to play audio and video content streamed over the Internet."[52] The ability to stream digital media, in its view, was now an integrated feature of the operating system, and hence media players were not a distinct "product."

The Commission roundly rejected Microsoft's position, however, concluding not only that streaming media players were a distinct product, but that only certain players provided significant competitive constraints on Microsoft. The Commission found that playback-only devices and software weren't substitutable by consumers for streaming media players. Moreover, it concluded that only streaming media players based on proprietary, not licensed, third-party technologies and intellectual property provided competitive constraints on Microsoft's Windows Media Player. It also noted that "to develop, innovate and promote a new media player including codecs [algorithms for compressing and decompressing digital files], formats, DRM [digital rights management] and media streaming technology requires significant investments in terms of research, development and promotional efforts." This meant that the prospects for new entry were very limited, which lent further support to the view that a limited set of streaming media players constituted a distinct relevant market.[53] Finally, the Commission found that indirect network effects were significant and tended to erect barriers to entry for would-be new entrants, explaining that "[c]ontent providers and software developers look to installation and usage shares of media players when deciding—under resource constraints—on the basis of which technology to develop their complementary software."[54] Therefore, the Commission concluded that, owing to their unique characteristics and functions, a lack of realistic substitutes, and barriers to entry, "streaming media players" constituted a third relevant product market.

Refusal to Supply Interoperability Information
With the relevant markets defined and Microsoft's dominance in two of them established, the European Commission turned to defining "abuse" and applying that definition to Microsoft's conduct. It began by noting that, although "dominance" alone isn't an offense under EU competition

laws, "an undertaking enjoying a dominant position is under a special responsibility not to engage in conduct that may distort competition." This notion of a "special responsibility" arguably reveals an attitudinal divergence between the U.S. and the EU with regard to their respective policies toward dominant firms, one that could make a difference in the outcome of close cases, although the degree of any divergence probably has been exaggerated.[55]

As the D.C. Circuit had done to define the "exclusionary conduct" component of the U.S. offense of monopolization, the Commission looked to its case law to define "abuse." As the U.S. courts also had done, the Commission identified two characteristics that distinguish abusive conduct—competition on some basis *other than* the merits and anticompetitive effect:

> The concept of abuse [relates] to the behaviour of an undertaking in a dominant position which is such as to influence the structure of a market where, as a result of the very presence of the undertaking in question, the degree of competition is weakened and which, through recourse to *methods different from those which condition normal competition* … , *has the effect of hindering the maintenance of the degree of competition still existing in the market or the growth of that competition.*[56]

As is also the case under U.S. law, application of this general definition of abuse is further informed by tests that address specific kinds of potentially abusive conduct. In this instance, the Commission looked to previous decisions regarding both refusals to supply and tying. Refusals to deal—to supply or purchase goods or services—are among the most difficult kinds of unilateral conduct to judge under competition laws. First, the law generally favors competition over cooperation, so when a firm refuses to deal with one of its rivals it would appear to be engaging in laudable, procompetitive conduct, not in suspect conduct. Some courts and commentators also have argued that imposing liability for refusals to deal with rivals can inhibit incentives to innovate for both the dominant firm and its challengers. A dominant firm's incentive to innovate might be diminished if it fears being ordered to share the fruits of its efforts with its rivals. Conversely, the incentives of its rivals to innovate may be stunted if they believe that they can gain access to the dominant firm's innovations through actions by agencies or by courts. Finally, liability for a refusal to deal can lead to challenging remedial issues. If a dominant firm is ordered to deal with its rivals, agencies or courts may have to establish the terms of dealing and provide some oversight for an extended period. These administrative and remedial challenges can be greatest when the firm currently doesn't offer for sale or license the "product" that is the subject of the refusal.[57]

Further complicating the question was the fact that Microsoft's refusal to supply involved intellectual property rights. Microsoft asserted that it had invested "billions of dollars" in developing its software, and that intellectual property rights were "meant to protect" that investment. If the Commission were to force Microsoft to disclose protected information, "future incentives to invest in the creation of more intellectual property" would be "eliminated." More specifically, Microsoft argued that it had copyright and patent rights that allowed it to prevent Sun from implementing the requested protocols in Sun's products, and that trade-secret law also gave it the right to refuse to disclose the currently secret protocol specifications that Sun wanted.

Although the general rule, under both U.S. and EU law, has long been that "undertakings are ... free to choose their business partners," the European Commission drew on a line of cases indicating that refusals to license intellectual property rights might violate Article 102 in "exceptional circumstances."[58] Microsoft argued that exceptional circumstances could be found only if three conditions were met: "(i) supply of the information is essential to carry on business; (ii) the refusal is likely to eliminate all competition; and (iii) the refusal is not objectively justified." But the Commission declined to endorse a fixed test based on "an exhaustive checklist of exceptional circumstances." Instead, it concluded that "the Commission must analyse the entirety of the circumstances surrounding a specific instance of a refusal to supply and must take its decision based on the results of such a comprehensive examination."[59] This approach was arguably analogous to the framework that the D.C. Circuit had applied, focusing the Commission's inquiry on the effects of Microsoft's refusal to supply and its proffered justifications.

The Commission began its analysis of the competitive effects of the refusal to supply by examining whether the information was "indispensable" for doing business in the market—that is, whether there was "no realistic actual or potential substitute" for the information. It reasoned that Microsoft's refusal to disclose interface information had to be evaluated in light of two "key elements" of its findings: that "Microsoft enjoys a position of extraordinary market strength on the client PC operating system market" and that "interoperability with the client PC operating systems is of significant competitive importance in the market for work group server operating systems."[60]

The European Commission noted that, as had been the case with Internet browsers in the United States, Microsoft was a late entrant to the market for workgroup-server operating systems—a market that had initially been

developed by UNIX vendors and Novell, firms that had a "distinct technological lead" by the time Microsoft entered. Microsoft nevertheless benefited from the establishment of networks and workgroup servers because
of its dominance of the market for client-PC operating systems:

> The value that their [the initial developers of work group operating systems] prod-
> ucts brought to the network also augmented the client PC operating systems' value
> in the customers' eyes and therefore Microsoft—as long as it did not have a credible
> work group server operating system alternative—had incentives to have its client
> PC operating system interoperate with non-Microsoft work group server operating
> systems. While entering the work group server operating system market, pledging
> support for already established technologies was important in gaining a foothold
> and the confidence of the customers.[61]

But Microsoft's incentives, and hence its strategy, changed when it established a toehold of its own in the market. The Commission explained:

> Once Microsoft's work group server operating system gained acceptance in the mar-
> ket, however, Microsoft's incentives changed and holding back access to informa-
> tion relating to interoperability with the Windows environment started to make
> sense. … Microsoft then engaged in a strategy of diminishing previous levels of
> supply of interoperability information. This disruption of previous levels of supply
> concerns elements that pertain to the core tasks that are expected from work group
> server operating systems, and in particular to the provision of group and user admin-
> istration services.[62]

This change of policy became more pronounced as Microsoft released
different versions of its own server operating systems and began to expand
its own share of the market for workgroup-server operating systems. Hence,
the Commission documented Microsoft's "rapid rise to dominance" in that
market as well as the growing profitability of its workgroup-server operating systems. Critically, that rise—and the precipitous decline of its rivals
and difficulties faced by would-be new entrants—wasn't attributable to
the superiority of Microsoft's products, in the Commission's view; rather,
it was attributable to the interoperability advantage Microsoft had secured
through its refusal to supply necessary interoperability data.

The importance of interoperability was supported by the Commission's
Market Enquiry, by statements from customers, and by Microsoft's internal documents: "Various sources of evidentiary material such as Microsoft's
own marketing documents, reports by industry analysts and customer
evidence show that interoperability with the Windows environment has
played a key role in driving the uptake of Microsoft's work group server
operating systems."[63] The Commission rejected Microsoft's alternative view

that its products were superior and that the decline of its rivals' fortunes were attributable to their own failures as unsupported by the evidence.[64] Indeed, as had been true in the U.S. cases, Microsoft's internal documents contradicted its litigation positions and probably undermined its credibility. The Commission cited a 1997 speech in which Bill Gates had told the Microsoft sales force "What we are trying to do is use our server control to do new protocols and lock out Sun and Oracle specifically. ... Now, I don't know if we'll get to that or not, but that's what we are trying to do."[65] The Commission therefore concluded that "Microsoft's behaviour risks eliminating competition in the work group server operating system market, due to the indispensability of the input that it refuses to supply to its competitors."[66]

In the U.S. case the government plaintiffs weren't required to prove that consumers had been harmed by Microsoft's conduct, but Article 102 specifically provides that the Commission can prove an abuse of dominance by showing that the dominant firm's conduct had limited "technical development to the prejudice of consumers." The Commission thus pointed out that Microsoft's refusal to supply the requested interoperability information had locked consumers into a "homogeneous Windows solution at the level of work group server operating systems," thereby impairing their ability "to benefit from innovative work group operating system features brought to market by Microsoft's competitors." Constrained prospects for marketing innovations to consumers, in turn, impaired the incentives of rivals to continue developing workgroup-server operating systems. This was in contrast to what had happened when Microsoft had shared interoperability information, which had allowed Microsoft's rivals to compete vigorously and to deliver innovations.[67]

Microsoft responded that imposing a duty to deal would inhibit *its* incentive to innovate. But here the Commission differentiated again between interoperability information and the broader features of a workgroup-server operating system. The only incentive to innovate that might be impaired by an order to supply interoperability information would affect communications protocols—that is, interoperability information. As the Commission had earlier emphasized, Microsoft wasn't being asked to share Windows source code. More importantly, the principal focus of innovation was at the level of server operating systems. Even if the imposition of a duty to deal might impair Microsoft's incentive to innovate as to interoperability information (and that was doubtful—Microsoft would still have an interest in improving the smooth interoperation of its own operating systems for client PCs and for workgroup servers), that impairment would pale in comparison with the loss of incentive to innovate at the level of server operating systems that would follow from permitting it to refuse to supply. To the contrary, imposing a duty to deal would greatly enhance the incentives of all firms to innovate, promoting robust competition among various suppliers of workgroup-server operating systems. Imposing a duty to deal with respect to interoperability information would simply neutralize the non-merits competitive advantage that Microsoft was able to secure through its refusal to supply.[68]

Microsoft also asserted that there was a lack of evidence of harm to consumers. The Commission rejected this argument, citing, ironically, the representations Microsoft had made in the U.S. remedy proceedings in support of the importance and the likely effect of the Communications Protocol Licensing Program to which Microsoft had agreed in the settlement of the U.S. case. In the United States, Microsoft had asserted that protocol disclosures would *promote* product diversity and consumer choice. If disclosure promoted consumer choice, then, the European Commission reasoned, surely Microsoft's failure to disclose similar information had *restricted* choice. Further, the Commission pointed out that under European case law it isn't necessary to show that an abuse of dominance "directly" prejudices consumers. Article 102 can also reach abuses that "indirectly" prejudice consumers by "impairing the effective competitive structure in the market." In other words, harm to consumers can be fairly inferred from significant harm to the competitive structure of the market.[69]

Having found anticompetitive effect and harm to consumers, the Commission turned to Microsoft's justifications. Microsoft argued that its refusal to supply was "objectively justified" because the information Sun sought was protected by intellectual property rights, and that it had no incentive to foreclose competition in any event. Again, the Commission found Microsoft's arguments and evidence unpersuasive.

With regard to intellectual property, Microsoft argued that it was "self-evident" that it was objectively justified in refusing to license intellectual property rights that were meant to protect the "billions of dollars" it had invested in research and development. This broad argument was similar to the one Microsoft had unsuccessfully made in the U.S. case to justify its refusal to allow alterations to its copyrighted Windows program, and the Commission likewise rejected it.[70] Such a rule, which was contrary to prior European case law in any event, would give primacy to intellectual property rights over competition law by effectively immunizing refusals to license from scrutiny under Article 102.

The Commission acknowledged that intellectual property rights are intended to protect the "moral rights" of authors and inventors to their work and to ensure that they are rewarded for their investments of money and creative effort. But the Commission also pointed out that an "essential objective" of intellectual property law is to stimulate creativity "for the general public good." This meant that the Commission had to take account of the effects of the refusal to license on competitive conditions in the market and on innovation, both with regard to Microsoft's incentives to innovate and with regard to the ability of Microsoft's competitors to innovate without the requested disclosure. Once it was shown that Microsoft's refusal to license harmed competition, the Commission reasoned, Microsoft's refusal couldn't be objectively justified "merely by the fact that it constitutes a refusal to license intellectual property." Microsoft's argument about incentives to innovate also ignored the interdependence of intellectual property rights and antitrust in promoting innovation. Intellectual property rights and antitrust laws are complementary, working together to encourage innovation.[71]

Once again the Commission explained that non-disclosure adversely affected competitors' incentives to innovate. Any disincentive to innovate that might result from requiring Microsoft to license its interoperability information (something that the Commission had concluded was dubious) would affect only the development of communication protocols, whereas disclosures would tend to provide robust incentives to innovate in the far more competitively significant market for workgroup-server operating systems. Disclosure would incentivize both Microsoft and its competitors to innovate in this market, and "the competitive landscape would liven up." To the Commission this meant that the "positive impact on the level of innovation of the whole industry (including Microsoft)" outweighed the possible negative effect that forced disclosure might have on Microsoft's incentives to innovate.[72]

Microsoft's second justification was that it lacked an incentive to foreclose competition in the market for workgroup-server operating systems because it couldn't increase its profits by leveraging its market power from the market for operating systems for client PCs into a second market, as the Commission had charged. This argument was based on what is known as the "single monopoly profit" theory, which was originally developed to refute the notion that a dominant firm, through tying, could secure additional profit beyond what it is able to get by selling the tying product alone at its profit-maximizing price. As one commentator has explained, the theory posits that "there is a single profit-maximizing price for a package of complementary goods that cannot be enlarged simply by bundling the goods together."[73]

As the Commission explained, however, the theory applies only when the two products involved are "perfectly complementary with fixed ratios." In other words, they are always used in fixed proportion, like pairs of shoes (right and left) or shoes and laces. In that circumstance, a dominant firm cannot increase its profits by tying. There is a unique profit-maximizing price for a pair of shoes when sold by the dominant firm. But in the Commission's view the requisite conditions weren't present with respect to Microsoft's refusal to supply, since client-PC operating systems and workgroup-server operating systems will often be purchased in different amounts, at different times, by different customers—a conclusion that Microsoft conceded.[74]

The "single monopoly profit" theory also doesn't take into account the possible adverse effects of the conduct on the dominant firm's power in the market for the primary product (here, PC operating systems). There are network effects *between* PC operating systems and server operating systems. Microsoft's refusal to supply could be used to fortify its dominance in the market for client-PC operating systems, insulating it from erosion. Thus, its incentive to refuse to supply interoperability information went beyond any benefits it might secure from anticompetitive leveraging of its power into the market for workgroup-server operating systems; it further entrenched its monopoly in PC operating systems.[75]

The Commission found that Microsoft's conduct was consistent with these anticompetitive incentives, not with the "single monopoly profit" theory. The facts strongly indicated that the lack of interoperability information significantly impaired the ability of Microsoft's rivals to compete and, as the Commission had specifically found, resulted in Microsoft's rise to dominance in the market for workgroup-server operating systems. In addition, contrary to its assertions based on the "single monopoly profit" theory, Microsoft had used the denial of interoperability information to insulate its dominance of the market for client-PC operating systems from competition. The "single monopoly profit" theory therefore provided no "objective justification" for Microsoft's refusal to supply.[76]

Bundling the Windows Media Player

The second infringement of Article 102 with which Microsoft was charged was its bundling of the Windows Media Player into Windows. This conduct raised issues similar to those raised by the tying of Internet Explorer and Windows, which was litigated in the U.S. case. Although the European Union doesn't explicitly use the labels *"per se"* and "rule of reason," the European Commission's approach to the bundling issue (like its approach to interoperability) ended up being quite similar to a rule-of-reason analysis, though perhaps administered with some decided skepticism.

The Commission's analysis began with a test for tying that was almost identical to the one traditionally used to administer the qualified *per se* rule in the United States:

Tying prohibited under Article 102 of the Treaty requires the presence of the following elements: (i) the tying and tied goods are two separate products; (ii) the undertaking concerned is dominant in the tying product market; (iii) the undertaking concerned does not give customers a choice to obtain the tying product without the tied product; and (iv) tying forecloses competition.[77]

Although this test makes no mention of efficiencies (the principal difference between a *per se* rule and a rule-of-reason approach under U.S. law), the Commission went on to state that it would also consider Microsoft's justifications for the tying and that it would show that any justifications "do not prevail" over the anticompetitive effects of tying. However labeled, this type of approach is the essence of a "rule of reason."

After applying each of the elements of the test, the Commission concluded that Microsoft's tying was anticompetitive and it rejected Microsoft's justifications. As a preliminary matter, however, the Commission had been urged by Microsoft to take notice of the U.S. consent decree and to go no further. In its view, the decree had the "practical effect" of unbundling Windows and WMP, so "any additional antitrust remedy on the Commission's part would therefore be unnecessary." This was ironic. In the United States, Microsoft had touted its "victory" on the tying claim when the district court's independent finding of *per se* liability had been overturned by the court of appeals and remanded for evaluation under the rule of reason. Supporters of the U.S. case argued in response that Microsoft's "integration" strategy nevertheless had been addressed as a component of the government's monopolization case and had been condemned, so that, in effect, its "tying" had been banned. Without conceding the legal point, Microsoft now pointed to the negotiated decree's provisions prohibiting Microsoft from barring access to non-Microsoft middleware and urged the Commission to abandon any further inquiry into its bundling strategy. But the Commission rejected this view, noting that the U.S. courts had never formally resolved the independent tying claim. Foreshadowing its views on remedy, the Commission associated a tying violation involving software with a remedy of code removal (that is, untying)—something that the U.S. decree didn't require. Hence, the Commission declined to presume that Microsoft's "tying" had been fully addressed and remedied by the U.S. proceedings.[78] The Commission's analysis proceeded, therefore, in the framework it had set out for tying—and it reached the same conclusion as had the U.S. District Court, even after taking into account Microsoft's proffered justifications: Microsoft's tying was anticompetitive and hadn't been objectively justified.

In 190 additional recitals and more than 60 additional pages of analysis, the Commission methodically applied four criteria for assessing tying.

First, were Windows and WMP distinct products? The answer was Yes. The Commission pointed to the existence of independent vendors of media players and distinct consumer demand, as well as to Microsoft's practices of offering its media player for non-Microsoft operating systems and using distinct licensing agreements. Although Microsoft argued that the Commission's focus on historic consumer behavior risked ignoring the argued efficiency benefits of its integration of WMP and Windows, the Commission responded that, despite that integration, there remained independent consumer demand for streaming media players. Microsoft also pointed to the practices of other vendors of operating systems who, like Microsoft, bundled streaming media players with their operating systems. But here, too, the Commission rejected the argument that operating systems and media players had lost their identities as distinct products. Microsoft's focus on other vendors of operating systems failed to take account of independent suppliers of streaming media players and of vendors of operating systems who didn't bundle their own media players but used media players supplied by other software firms. Critically, the Commission also pointed out that even when other vendors of operating systems included media players in their operating systems, unlike Microsoft they didn't make them unremovable. Its restriction on "untying" was an essential component of Microsoft's behavior that often got lost in the technical legal and economic debates about "tying." Microsoft didn't merely tie its own middleware to Windows; it made it impossible to remove. That had been true of Internet Explorer, and it was true of WMP. Though it was true, as Microsoft argued, that consumers wanted streaming media capability in their operating systems, it didn't follow that such capability had to be provided by Microsoft's WMP and no other media player. Any "efficiency" associated with the simple act of bundling could also have been achieved through integration with non-Microsoft media players. The Commission concluded, therefore, that streaming media players and operating systems were two distinct products that were "susceptible to be tied."[79]

Second, did Microsoft possess a dominant position in the market for the tying product, Windows? Again the Commission answered Yes. As the Commission had already concluded, Microsoft held a dominant position in the market for client-PC operating systems. In repeating that finding, the Commission reiterated that Microsoft had tied WMP to Windows and had made it unremovable.[80]

Third, were customers given a choice in purchasing the tied product, WMP, when they purchased Windows? No. Both technologically and contractually, Windows was licensed only with WMP included, and it wasn't removable. Here again the Commission was direct in expressing its differences with the negotiated resolution in the United States: "Removal of end-user access does not restore the choice of Microsoft's customers as to whether to acquire Windows without WMP. ... There are no ready technical means to un-install WMP." Under EU law, it didn't matter that customers didn't specifically "pay" for WMP or that they could in theory decline to "use" it.[81]

Fourth, did the tying of WMP to Windows foreclose competition? Yes. In what became perhaps the most contested element of the tying claim, Microsoft argued that the facts couldn't sustain a finding of harm to competition under the standards that had been articulated by the European courts. It argued that the Commission "must do more than merely show that Microsoft distributes Windows only together with WMP," pointing to the ready availability of alternative streaming media players for free and alternative means of distributing media players, such as downloading, to show that its bundling didn't really exclude competitors. This argument had historically been precluded under the *per se* approach taken in the United States, which assumed that tying arrangements had an adverse impact on competition if they affected a substantial amount of commerce, but the Commission readily admitted that further inquiry was warranted.[82]

Even after taking Microsoft's various arguments into account, however, the Commission concluded that Microsoft's tying of WMP to Windows harmed competition in the two ways in which tying has traditionally been viewed as anticompetitive: it deprived consumers of their ability to freely choose among competing media players and it denied other producers of media players access to both OEMs and end users, network effects playing an important role in explaining the impact of Microsoft's practice.

Obviously Microsoft, with its dominance of the market for client-PC operating systems, could achieve nearly ubiquitous distribution of WMP by tying WMP to Windows. And Microsoft itself had touted the advantages to consumers of an OEM's pre-installation of a media player. To achieve equally efficient access, vendors of non-Microsoft media players could contract directly with OEMs, but such agreements couldn't counteract the advantages that flowed to Microsoft. An OEM would have to incur additional installation, support, and testing costs for providing a second media player, all of which created a disincentive for OEMs to do so. Paralleling the findings in the U.S. case with regard to browsers, the Commission further found that alternatives to the OEM channel, such as free downloading via the Internet, were less efficient for consumers. Microsoft's tying, therefore, had effectively impaired its rivals' access to the most effective means of distributing media players (OEMs), had imposed higher costs on consumers, and had disrupted the interplay of supply and demand by artificially restricting consumer choice.[83]

Network effects again amplified the effects of Microsoft's distribution advantage. Like Internet browsers, "media players constitute platform software." As a result, "[c]ontent providers and software developers look to installation and usage shares of media players when deciding—under resource constraints—on the basis of which technology to develop their complementary software." Because of Windows' dominance and Microsoft's tying of WMP to Windows, independent software vendors had an overwhelming incentive to code their media content for WMP; here again interoperability played an important role. The Commission explained:

> Once complementary software is encoded in the proprietary Windows media formats, it can only be played back on independent vendors' media players if Microsoft chooses to license its technology. In the absence of format and codec interoperability, the compatibility of content and applications with a specific media player constitute in their own right significant competitive factors. They help drive popularity of the media player which, in turn, drives uptake of the underlying media technology, including supported codecs, formats (including DRM) and media server software.[84]

This gave rise to network effects, which also provided a basis for the Commission's objection to any U.S.-style remedy of simply limiting end users' access to WMP without removing code:

> Through tying WMP, Microsoft thus creates a positive feedback loop reminiscent of the one that propelled Windows to its quasi-monopoly position in the client PC operating system market. The possibility for OEMs to hide end-user access to WMP will not alter this mechanism. As long as the WMP *code* is present, content streamed from the Web or applications running on the client PC are able to call upon this code—whether end-user access is removed or not.[85]

In an effort to document these anticompetitive effects, the Commission turned to its own Market Inquiry, to Microsoft's internal documents, and to third-party data. It found clear-cut before-and-after evidence of the changes in Microsoft's usage share of streaming media players. Before Microsoft tied WMP to Windows, RealNetworks' RealPlayer had been the market leader; afterward, WMP became quickly ascendant over RealPlayer and Apple's QuickTime, and the trend continued to favor WMP.[86] To Microsoft's argument that RealPlayer remained a strong competitor and hadn't been fully excluded from the market, the Commission responded firmly that mere survival wasn't enough:

> Under Microsoft's 'last-man-standing' foreclosure rule, a dominant company would actually be given the time to achieve the very objective of tying. But at that point, Microsoft could no longer be subjected to any meaningful antitrust remedy because providing for the formal conditions of a level playing field would not be sufficient to overcome the externalities ... which tend to insulate network markets once they have tipped.[87]

Next the Commission turned to Microsoft's asserted procompetitive justifications for tying. Microsoft first argued that bundling WMP with Windows was efficient because it reduced transaction costs. While agreeing that bundling reduced transaction costs for consumers, the Commission concluded that Microsoft "fail[ed] to differentiate between the benefit to consumers of having a media player pre-installed along with the client-PC operating system and Microsoft selecting the media player for consumers." The reductions in transactions costs could have been achieved by permitting OEMs some autonomy in selecting the media player to be bundled with Windows. That would have left competition to produce the best streaming media players unfettered and would have permitted OEMs to differentiate their own products to meet consumer demand. It was, in short, easy to imagine an equally efficient alternative to the distribution model Microsoft had fashioned—one in which bundling would be more responsive to consumer demand: "Nothing about potential transaction efficiencies for consumers requires the pre-installation to be undertaken by Microsoft, let alone by Microsoft's exclusive and irreversible bundling of WMP with Windows."[88]

The Commission also questioned Microsoft's assertion that bundling produced gains in the efficiency of distribution. While doubting that such gains were significant or that they would be passed on to consumers, the Commission concluded that "such savings cannot possibly outweigh the distortion of competition" that resulted from Microsoft's bundling. Microsoft responded that if it were precluded from bundling it would be put at a competitive disadvantage relative to its non-dominant rivals, who would remain free to integrate streaming media capabilities into their operating systems. But in response to this argument the Commission reiterated that, owing to the adverse effects on competition of some dominant firms' conduct, dominant firms may not always be permitted to pursue the same conduct that small rivals are allowed to pursue.[89]

Next the Commission turned to Microsoft's argument that bundling resulted in efficiencies from having WMP as a standardized platform for content applications. Microsoft didn't provide evidence that the integration of the code for Windows and WMP led to superior technical performance, a point the Commission noted. Rather, Microsoft argued that if a PC operating system included media APIs, developers wouldn't have to "reinvent the wheel" each time they wanted to implement functionality. Even if this were true, however, to embrace that as a true "efficiency" would be to endorse the anticompetitive consequences of tying in a network industry:

> [Our view] would only be different if one held that—as developers would prefer a standardised platform—Microsoft's leveraging of its dominance into the market for media players would spare the industry possible ambiguity as to the outcome of the competitive race among competing media players, thereby generating net efficiencies. Such an argument ... would have the Commission not only condone the extension of the applications barrier to entry through tying, but make it the cornerstone for the justification of tying and the possible domination by Microsoft of ... [the media player] market. Under Community competition law an undistorted competition process constitutes a value in itself as it generates efficiencies and creates a climate conducive to innovation. ... A justification relying on Windows' historic success in the client PC operating system market—and not on the merits of media players—can therefore not have a place within such a system.[90]

Microsoft's final argument was that it had no incentive to foreclose competition. It challenged the view (a major component of the U.S. case) that it perceived middleware as a nascent threat to its dominance of the market for client-PC operating systems. As the U.S. courts had done, however, the Commission found that middleware that exposed its APIs was, either alone or in combination with other middleware, a sufficiently serious threat to Microsoft's dominance of the market for PC operating systems that Microsoft had "incentives to foreclose third party media players through tying."[91]

The European Commission concluded that Microsoft's tying of WMP to Windows constituted an "abuse of dominance" that hadn't been objectively justified. Tying gave Microsoft a significant competitive advantage in the market for streaming media players and interfered with the competitive process. Barriers to entry were enhanced, and innovation was impaired. Consumer choice, and its value as a feedback mechanism for competition, had been diminished. More broadly, the Commission concluded its discussion of Microsoft's liability for the bundling infringement with observations strikingly similar to the concluding paragraph in Judge Jackson's findings of fact in the U.S. Microsoft case:

> To maintain competitive markets so that innovations succeed or fail on the merits is an important objective of Community competition policy. ... Microsoft's tying of WMP ... sends signals which deter innovation in any technologies which Microsoft could conceivably take interest in and tie with Windows in the future. Microsoft's tying instils actors in the relevant software markets with a sense of precariousness thereby weakening both software developers' incentives to innovate in similar areas and venture capitalists' proclivity to invest in independent software application companies. A start-up intending to enter or raise venture capital in such a market will be forced to test the resilience of its business model against the eventuality of Microsoft deciding to bundle its own version of the product with Windows.[92]

The Decision of the Court of First Instance

The European Commission adopted its decision on March 24, 2004, more than five years after Sun's complaint had been lodged. On June 7, 2004, in accordance with European Union law, Microsoft applied to the Court of First Instance (now called the General Court) for an annulment of the decision, reasserting many of the points it had urged on the Commission. Microsoft's pleas for annulment focused on the two primary claims of infringement—refusal to supply and tying—as well as on the Commission's remedies (which we will discuss in chapter 7).

On September 17, 2007, in a lengthy decision, the Court of First Instance dismissed Microsoft's application to annul the Commission's decision in all but one relatively minor respect.[93] On virtually all points of contention, the CFI, after stating the arguments on both sides, agreed with the Commission's analysis of the applicable case law and with how the Commission had marshaled the evidence to support its conclusions. A month later, Microsoft announced that it had elected not to appeal the decision to the European Court of Justice and declared itself in "full compliance" with the Commission's 2004 decision.[94]

Two procedural matters affected the CFI's decision. The first was the standard of appellate review. The Commission claimed that, because its decision rested on "complex technical and economic assessments," only "limited review" was appropriate. Microsoft countered that the CFI should undertake a "searching inquiry" of the Commission's decision. The CFI largely agreed with the Commission that review should be limited to "manifest error," but not without qualification: it would undertake a limited but discerning review, though not necessarily the "searching" review requested by Microsoft.[95]

The second procedural matter was the allocation of the burden of proof between the parties. The CFI wrote that, whereas the Commission bore the initial burden of proving "the existence of the circumstances that constitute an infringement of Article 102," it was up to Microsoft, not the Commission, to "raise any plea of objective justification and to support it with arguments and evidence." At that point the burden "to show that the arguments and evidence relied on by the undertaking cannot prevail and, accordingly, that the justification put forward cannot be accepted"[96] would shift back to the Commission.

As is often the case with appellate review, the defined scope of the CFI's review authority and the allocation of the burden of proof can influence the parties' arguments and the CFI's approach to reaching its decision. In many respects that was true of the CFI's decision in the *Microsoft* case. Microsoft had to show that the Commission's assessments were "manifestly incorrect," a high bar that it was unable to clear. It also retained the burden of establishing its own "objective justifications," and in attempting to do so it again stumbled, as it had in the Commission proceedings.

The CFI's decision was organized around the two claims of infringement of Article 102: refusal to supply and tying. It raised three major issues. First, had the Commission used appropriate legal standards in evaluating the claim of refusal to supply in the presence of Microsoft's assertion of intellectual property rights and in evaluating the tying claim with respect to WMP and Windows? Second, and more broadly, was the Commission correct in its evaluation of competitive harm, or was the harm highly speculative? Third, had the Commission struck the appropriate balance between Microsoft's incentive to innovate and the incentives of other industry participants?

As we noted in our discussion of the Commission's decision, the treatment of refusals to supply is one of the most contentious policy issues in present-day competition law. Microsoft argued, as it had before the Commission, that its conduct didn't fit within any of the limited and specific "exceptional circumstances" that had previously been articulated by the courts to justify imposing a duty to license intellectual property for a refusal to supply. Even if it did, Microsoft argued, under the standard set forth in that case law its refusal was "objectively justified" solely because it involved a refusal to license intellectual property rights.

After dispensing with some preliminary issues, the CFI turned to the legal standard for judging refusals to supply. Recall that the Commission acknowledged the "exceptional circumstances" standard and the relevance of "indispensability" set out in earlier cases, but rejected Microsoft's argument that the particular circumstances identified in previous decisions should be viewed as limiting circumstances (in effect, the *only* "exceptional" circumstances). The CFI embraced an approach more like the formalistic one advocated by Microsoft, but it still reached the same result as the Commission, finding no error in the Commission's articulation and application of the law. From previous case law, the CFI synthesized four requirements for when "exceptional circumstances" might make a refusal to license intellectual property an abuse of dominance: a violation will be found if (1) "the refusal relates to a product or service indispensable to the exercise of a particular activity on a neighbouring market," (2) the refusal excludes "any effective competition on that neighbouring market," and (3) the refusal "prevents the appearance of a new product for which there is potential consumer demand"—(4) unless the refusal is "objectively justified."[97]

The CFI noted, however, that in the Commission's view the specific circumstances previously found to have been "exceptional," although present in the *Microsoft* case, might not be viewed as the only ones ever to be deemed "exceptional," and that other important circumstances were present that might justify imposing a duty to deal on Microsoft.[98] The CFI stated that it would be necessary to consider these additional circumstances only if the Commission had failed to satisfy the already well-established criteria, as Microsoft claimed.[99] But the specific wording the CFI used in articulating the legal test—"the following circumstances, *in particular*, must be considered to be exceptional"—appeared deliberately chosen to express inclusion and not necessarily to imply exclusion of other circumstances that might be presented.[100] This approach could be faulted for injecting uncertainty into the standard, but it also avoided formalistic rigidity and preserved needed flexibility to adapt to future circumstances. Indeed, the standard articulated was itself an illustration of how flexibility over time permitted the law to evolve through different cases and factual circumstances.

The CFI then proceeded to review at length the Commission's analysis of the indispensability of Windows' communication protocols to other vendors of server operating systems and the effect of the refusal to supply on competition. It rejected Microsoft's assertion that the Commission had used an inappropriate standard for judging interoperability and found that the Commission had correctly concluded that Microsoft had been able to establish the "de facto standard for work group computing" owing to "the very narrow technological and privileged links that Microsoft has established between its Windows client PC and work group server operating systems, and… the fact that Windows is present on virtually all client PCs installed within organisations."[101]

With respect to competitive effects, the CFI rejected Microsoft's assertion that the Commission had relied on an incorrect legal standard. Microsoft sought to fault the Commission for requiring only a "risk" of the elimination of competition, arguing that in the case of intellectual property a stricter standard of competitive harm was warranted, one that would require proof that it was "likely to eliminate competition." It further asserted that that likelihood should rise to the level of a "high probability" that the refusal to supply would eliminate "all competition." Characterizing Microsoft's complaint as "purely one of terminology" and "wholly irrelevant," the CFI pointed out that application of Article 102 doesn't wait for the time when there is "no more, or practically no more, competition on the market." Requiring the Commission to wait until the elimination of competitors was "sufficiently imminent" before being able to take action "would clearly run counter to the objective of that provision, which is to maintain undistorted competition in the common market and, in particular, to safeguard the competition that still exists on the relevant market."[102]

Applying that standard, the CFI concluded that the Commission's findings weren't manifestly incorrect. Microsoft's refusal to supply interoperability information provided it with an "artificial advantage." Because Microsoft had prevented its competitors from achieving a "sufficient degree of interoperability with the Windows domain architecture," consumers' decisions as to what workgroup-server operating systems they would purchase were "channeled towards Microsoft's products." That effectively disabled the demand-side preferences of consumers as a normal market feedback mechanism and "discouraged [Microsoft's] competitors from developing and marketing work group server operating systems with innovative features, to the prejudice, notably, of consumers."[103]

The CFI then considered whether Microsoft's refusal had precluded the introduction of a "new product." Microsoft urged the CFI to construe this requirement narrowly, arguing that the Commission had shown only that the information would have allowed competitors to develop their existing products. In what appeared to be an implicit endorsement of the Commission's argument that the CFI shouldn't read the relevant previous cases literally as defining the only exceptional circumstances, the CFI took a broader view of the "new product" requirement:

[T]he circumstance relating to the appearance of a new product … cannot be the only parameter which determines whether a refusal to license an intellectual property right is capable of causing prejudice to consumers within the meaning of Article 102(b) EC. As that provision states, such prejudice may arise where there is a limitation not only of production or markets, but also of technical development.

Since the Commission's findings regarding the limitation on technical development weren't "manifestly incorrect," the CFI concluded that the Commission had met the "new products" part of the test.[104]

Finally, the CFI considered Microsoft's assertion of objective justification. As we have already noted, here the burden rested squarely on Microsoft. Microsoft again argued that its intellectual property rights, by themselves, constituted an objective justification for its refusal to supply, and urged that imposing upon it a compulsory duty to license would impede its incentives to innovate. In strong language it argued that the Commission had adopted a "new test"—and one that was "legally defective" and a "radical departure" from the case law—when it had purported to weigh the relative impact of a duty to license on Microsoft's incentive to innovate against the industry-wide incentives that would result from forced licensing. Microsoft derided this "balancing test," arguing that "dominant undertakings will have less incentive to invest in research and development, because they will have to share the fruits of their efforts with their competitors." It also argued that the test was "vague" and would have "unforeseeable consequences."[105]

As the Commission had done, the Court of First Instance roundly rejected the notion that the mere presence of intellectual property rights alone can satisfy the burden on a dominant firm of proving an "objective justification" for a refusal to license. Reiterating the general legal framework it had earlier set forth, however, it also noted that a refusal without "exceptional circumstances" couldn't constitute abuse. But here the Commission had adequately established such circumstances. At that point, Microsoft could no longer stand simply on the claim of intellectual property rights.

The CFI also rejected Microsoft's harshly worded attack on the Commission's alleged "balancing" of innovation incentives. In establishing exceptional circumstances, the Commission had supported its view that Microsoft's refusal to supply would impair its rivals' incentives to innovate. The burden then shifted to Microsoft to support its assertion that imposition of a duty to license would impair its own incentives. The CFI found no error in the Commission's conclusion that Microsoft had failed to do so. Microsoft had "merely put forward vague, general and theoretical arguments," and the Commission's opinion had refuted them. Hence, Microsoft's attack on "balancing" was misplaced—no balancing had occurred. There was evidence to support the assertion that rival incentives had been impaired, but none to support Microsoft's argument that its own had been damaged.[106] The first part of Microsoft's plea to annul the Commission's decision with respect to its refusal to supply was dismissed.[107]

As had happened in its defense of the charges against it in the United States, Microsoft seemed to lose credibility before the Commission by misstating or overstating its position with respect to interoperability information. For example, it appeared to take mutually inconsistent positions at different times, at first refusing to acknowledge the existence of distinct "interoperability information" and then asserting that it had fully disclosed all the information necessary to permit seamless interoperability of non-Microsoft server operating systems with Windows PCs. It also argued at times that whatever interoperability information it had declined to disclose was proprietary and was protected from disclosure by its intellectual property and trade-secret rights. These at times conflicting arguments were further undermined by the fact that the U.S. settlement had included negotiated provisions for the disclosure of interoperability information.

The second infringement of EU law was the tying claim. Although Microsoft repeated many of the arguments it had first urged on the Commission with respect to each of the traditional elements of the tying claim, its principal arguments consisted of an attack on the Commission's theory of competitive harm and a defense of its integrative business model for operating systems.[108]

First, Microsoft claimed that the Commission had used a "new, speculative, argument with no basis in law, in order to establish the existence of a foreclosure effect."[109] The CFI disagreed, characterizing Microsoft's arguments as "unfounded" and as "based on a selective and inaccurate reading" of the Commission's decision. The Commission hadn't *merely assumed* a foreclosure effect; it had "examined more closely the actual effects which the bundling had already had on the market for streaming media players and also the way in which that market was likely to evolve." Its conclusions hadn't been based on a "new or speculative theory, but on the nature of the impugned conduct, on the conditions of the market and on the essential features of the relevant products." The Court concluded that the Commission's findings were "based on accurate, reliable and consistent evidence which Microsoft, by merely contending that it is pure conjecture, has not succeeded in showing to be incorrect."[110]

Microsoft also argued that the Commission had "failed to take sufficient account of the advantages flowing from the 'architectural concept' of its operating system."[111] This argument was addressed to the "two products" element of tying, as well as to Microsoft's case for "objective justification."

It was, in many ways, the core of Microsoft's narrative: that it should remain unfettered by competition law to evolve Windows freely, adding new "functionality" as dictated by engineering capabilities and consumer demand as it perceives it. Platform software, it argued, shouldn't be designed by antitrust enforcement agencies or courts, but by engineers and consumers, and Microsoft shouldn't be prevented from adopting the same architecture as its principal rivals. Also inherent in the argument was the assertion that, as with the refusal to supply, the Commission's approach to tying would inhibit innovation incentives.[112]

Again, however, the CFI rejected Microsoft's arguments as insufficient to overturn the Commission's findings. Although it agreed that technology industries can be subject to "constant and rapid evolution," so that what may appear to be separate products may evolve into a single product, it also observed that despite the integration of media players in some client-PC operating systems there remained ample evidence that streaming media players continued to maintain a separate as well as an integrated existence in the market. This was true when one looked at consumer demand, the existence of independent developers and vendors of streaming media players, and Microsoft's own marketing conduct and internal documents. Also significant was Microsoft's lack of support for its argument that it had technical reasons for integrating WMP into Windows, and that in effect it was evolving Windows to create a superior operating system. As had been true in the U.S. proceedings, the CFI found that Microsoft's assertion that integration was "dictated by technical reasons" was "scarcely credible."[113]

The formalism of asking whether there are "two products" or one in tying analysis has been faulted by commentators for many years. Indeed, in the United States the "two products" requirement had often been seen as a back-door way of introducing considerations of efficiency, a strategy necessitated by the constraints of the *per se* rule, even in its qualified form. It would arguably be superior, therefore, for an analysis of tying to focus, as do all analyses of exclusionary distribution practices, more on the anticompetitive effects of the practice and its justifications. Adding the label "tying" adds little if anything to the substantive analysis. As a result, adherence to the traditional framework is at best a distraction and at worst obfuscates the central economic questions in an analysis of tying, leaving the impression of formalistic and technical legal rules—analytical boxes to be checked off one by one. Even in the absence of a tradition of any kind of *per se* rule against tying, the contortions necessary to consider efficiency arguments were evident in the continued reliance on the "two product" requirement by the Commission and the CFI.

Microsoft's integration strategy was also the centerpiece of its defense that its decision to bundle WMP into Windows was "objectively justified." The CFI explained:

Microsoft submits that the main justification for its conduct is that the integration of new functionality into operating systems in response to technological advances and changes in consumer demand is a core element of competition in the operating system business and has served the industry well for more than 20 years. The integration of streaming capacity into Windows is one of the aspects of its 'successful business model' and has contributed to the increasing use of digital media. Supported on this point by [others], Microsoft claims that the Commission made a manifest error of assessment by not sufficiently considering the real benefits flowing from the integration of new functionality into the Windows operating system.[114]

The CFI rejected these arguments by pointing to the "precise scope" of the infringement that the Commission found. The problem wasn't that Microsoft offered an integrated version of Windows and the Windows Media Player, but that it offered "only a version of Windows in which Windows Media Player is integrated." Offering a dis-integrated version of Windows as an alternative would have allowed either end users or OEMs to install the media player of their choice while preserving Microsoft's "business model" of offering an integrated product.[115] Indeed, in emphasizing the failure to offer an unbundled version, the CFI and the Commission were in accord with the decisions of the District Court and Court of Appeals in the U.S. *Microsoft* case, holding that it was not simply Microsoft's bundling, but its failure to allow OEMs or end users to *remove* Internet Explorer that constituted monopolizing conduct in violation of Section 2 of the Sherman Act.

The CFI also dismissed the rest of Microsoft's asserted justifications. Standardizing the Windows Media Player platform might have advantages for software developers, but those advantages "cannot suffice to offset the anticompetitive effects of the tying."[116] There was no proof that integration led to superior performance or that Windows operated faster with integrated media functionality (an "unsupported" assertion, according to the CFI). In regard to Microsoft's argument that requiring it to offer different versions of Windows (with and without a media player) would lead to a "fragmentation" of the Windows platform, the CFI noted that the argument was "inconsistent with Microsoft's own business practice," which has been to offer a number of versions of Windows, not all which are interchangeable. The CFI concluded: "Microsoft has not demonstrated the existence of any objective justification for the abusive bundling of Windows Media Player with the Windows client PC operating system."[117]

Reactions to the CFI's Decision

The Court of First Instance's decision triggered a great deal of critical analysis and commentary in the broader competition-policy community. An article in the *Financial Times* characterized the decision as a "stinging defeat" for Microsoft, adding that "[t]here was no mistaking the winners and losers."[118] Another press report described the CFI's opinion as "an unexpectedly clear endorsement" of the Commission's 2004 decision, noting that the work of former Competition Commissioner Mario Monti had been vindicated. The victory also raised the international profile of the Commission, potentially increasing its role as a global leader in the policing of abuses by dominant firms. A former U.S. Department of Justice official was quoted as suggesting that the decision would "help solidify the commission's role as the regulator of the world." Commissioner Neelie Kroes, who succeeded Monti shortly after the 2004 decision of the Commission, became the beneficiary of a major Commission victory, although she was then charged with the challenging task of implementing the Commission's remedies.[119]

Critics focused on various aspects of the case for infringement, voicing objections to the analysis of both refusals to supply and tying. Three principal themes surfaced, echoing the arguments that had been expressed as part of Microsoft's primary narrative: the evidence of anticompetitive effect was weak, the decision would undermine incentives for firms to innovate, and the standards used to judge Microsoft's conduct were "uncertain." Some focused on the likely long-term impact of the decisions, arguing that they would deter aggressive competition and innovation in the technology sector.[120] But the decisions also had defenders and some who were critical also noted that at least some of the decision's conclusions appeared sound. Others still found fault with both the U.S. approach and the EU approach, concluding that the U.S. approach was too permissive and the EU approach too interventionist.[121]

Collectively, the criticisms seem to have been exaggerated, especially with respect to the hostility directed at tying in software markets and the prediction that the decision would interfere with "incentives to innovate." The economic theories that undergirded the case were sound. There was little if any doubt that Microsoft had achieved a durable position of dominance in a distinct (for antitrust purposes) market for client-PC operating systems. It was also widely accepted that Microsoft's position was amplified by network effects and by barriers to entry. Neither was there much genuine debate about whether tying could ever be anticompetitive, and it was well settled in the law that refusals to supply might under some circumstances be anticompetitive, even under the very narrow U.S. approach.[122] In addition, there was the inclusion in the U.S. consent decree of a negotiated duty to license communications protocols to facilitate server interoperability, even though the U.S. case hadn't included a claim of refusal to supply. That inclusion evidenced a wide consensus, noted by the district court judge in the United States who had handled the implementation of the consent decree, that facilitating interoperability was necessary to the future competitive vitality of the industry. Moreover, among the various critics, it was hard to identify any arguments that hadn't also been made by Microsoft in the United States, in Europe, or in both. Microsoft had surely had its "day in court," but it hadn't been able to rebut what was consistently revealed in its internal documents: that its strategy in response to new competition had *not* been focused on competing on the merits. Indeed, Microsoft had been consistently unable to support its technical and economic justifications with sufficient evidence of its own. Critics could frequently be faulted for simply rearguing many of Microsoft's theories without fully crediting the evidence and facts found that undermined or contradicted them outright.

It is worth noting that the "uncertain standards" criticism aimed at the European Commission and the Court of First Instance is a criticism not limited to the EU and may betray an inherent tension between civil and common-law systems. The desire for specificity in legal commands is expressed in civil-law systems in part through legislative particularity as to prohibited conduct. That tradition is reflected to some degree in Article 102, which, in contrast to Section 2 of the Sherman Act, goes beyond a general proscription and includes some specific exemplars of potentially anticompetitive conduct. But the provisions of Article 102 are interpreted over time by the Commission and the courts in a fashion that is analogous to the common-law tradition, advancing case by case, informed by new circumstances and new economic learning. The standards the CFI articulated in *Microsoft* for refusals to supply illustrate that very development, with the court synthesizing earlier decisions to state a rule applicable to a new set of facts and circumstances.[123] To students of the common law, this is a natural and unexceptional process. A degree of uncertainty is a premise of the common-law system, accepted as part of the normal process of doctrinal evolution, despite the common law's professed commitment to *stare decisis*. Better-specified standards can be faulted as being unable to adapt over time. Generally, the "uncertainty" wanes with greater experience and additional decisions, although a change of course can and regularly does inject a new round of uncertainty. "Certainty" was a characteristic of the *per se* rule used in the United States for many offenses and for many years, but despite its clarity it has largely been abandoned because of its inflexibility and its propensity to over-deter.

Global Antitrust Enforcement and U.S. Reactions

By the time of the European Commission's decision in *Microsoft*, the leadership of the U.S. Justice Department's Antitrust Division had shifted from the Democratic administration of Bill Clinton, which had filed and litigated the U.S. case, to the Republican administration of George W. Bush, which had settled it. The Republican administration may not have been as favorably disposed to the case, but the Justice Department's reaction to the European case was quite extraordinary, harsh, and public (as was its reaction to a subsequent case brought in Korea). These public and undiplomatic responses to the exercise of legitimate concurrent jurisdiction for competition matters risked inflaming relationships between U.S. and foreign competition authorities and undermining the credibility of U.S. enforcement officials abroad. Quite obviously, efforts to defend the limited remedies accepted by the Department of Justice in settlement of the U.S. litigation were perceived as American advocacy on behalf of a successful American firm.

In tone and content these public statements also revealed a significant change of enforcement philosophy, at least at the Justice Department—a change that opened a wider rift between the United States and other enforcers around the world with regard to the basics of the analysis of exclusionary conduct by monopolists. Presented as the "views of the United States," the Justice Department's statements suggested greater international divergence than in fact existed. As eventually became clear, the Bush Justice Department's very constrained conception of impermissible single-firm conduct was viewed by many within the American antitrust community as non-interventionist in the extreme. That non-interventionist character came into greater focus in 2008 when the Justice Department was unable to secure the approval of the Federal Trade Commission for its proposed "Section 2 Report" and again when that report was withdrawn by the first appointed head of the Antitrust Division in the Democratic Obama administration.[124]

The first public response occurred when the European Commission issued its decision on March 24, 2004. Although the EC's case didn't focus on the Internet browser wars that were at the center of the U.S. cases, it did focus in part on Microsoft's analogous conduct with respect to streaming media players. To remedy the tying of Windows Media Player to Windows, the EC ordered "unbundling." Microsoft was required to prepare a version of Windows that didn't include Windows Media Player, although it was also permitted to continue to sell a bundled version, so that choices about whether to bundle a media player with Windows and, if so, which one to include, would again be driven by OEMs and consumers rather than by Microsoft. The EC also imposed a significant fine for Microsoft's refusal to supply interoperability information and for tying.[125]

The U.S. Justice Department's prompt and public response chastised the European Commission for both components of its remedy. Recall that in its decision the EC had expressed its view that the U.S. remedy's approach of hiding end users' access to middleware without removing the code was inadequate. The Justice Department now responded, defending its settlement as providing "clear and effective protection for competition and consumers."[126] It touted the U.S. settlement's approach of simply prohibiting "anticompetitive manipulation of icons and default settings" as superior to the EC's choice of requiring an unbundled version, which it derisively labeled "code removal." Echoing a persistent theme of the narrative that Microsoft had advocated throughout the litigation in the United States and in Europe, the Justice Department also characterized Microsoft's addition of Windows Media Player to Windows as a "product enhancement" and maintained that "[i]mposing antitrust liability on the basis of product enhancements and imposing 'code removal' remedies may produce unintended consequences."

Although the Justice Department's choice of words—"may produce unintended consequences"—could fairly be read as no more than a mild rebuke, the full context conveyed a deeper level of disapproval. The Justice Department's implication that the European Commission's decision would preclude product enhancements and the characterization of its remedy as demanding "code removal" challenged the EC's finding of liability as well as its choice of remedy. The critique of the remedy, however, ignored a significant feature of the EC's remedial order: it permitted Microsoft to continue producing a bundled version of Windows and Windows Media Player alongside an unbundled version on the theory that the market, not Microsoft, should judge the desirability of integration.

"Sound antitrust policy," the Justice Department's statement continued, "must avoid chilling innovation and competition even by 'dominant' companies. A contrary approach risks protecting competitors, not competition, in ways that may ultimately harm innovation and the consumers that benefit from it." These general principles seem unobjectionable; but again the implicit message was obvious: the European decision was inconsistent with them. The Justice Department went on to proclaim that "[t]he U.S. experience tells us that the best antitrust remedies eliminate impediments to the healthy functioning of competitive markets without hindering successful competitors or imposing burdens on third parties, which may result from the EC's remedy." This was at best a patronizing coda to what could only have been understood in Brussels as a stinging rebuke that echoed Microsoft's own views.[127]

In reality, the Justice Department was simply refusing to accept the European Commission's conclusions that Microsoft's conduct had severely impaired competition and undermined market-wide incentives to innovate. Yet it cited no evidence of its own to support either its assertion that the Commission's remedy would hinder Microsoft or that the U.S. approach would produce superior results. It also ignored important differences in the course of the two cases. Whereas the U.S. case resolved the tying claim only in the context of monopolization, the European Commission had fully assessed the claim of tying, considering both the Commission's evidence of adverse competitive effects and all of Microsoft's defenses, which it found wanting. This made it appear that the U.S. Department of Justice was simply rearguing the points that Microsoft had unsuccessfully urged on the Commission.

In a revealing passage, the assistant attorney general also criticized the magnitude of the European Commission's fine. But in doing so he expressed a different philosophy about the principles that should inform enforcement efforts directed at dominant-firm conduct, one that may better explain why he elected to respond so publicly and critically to the EC's decision:

While the imposition of a civil fine is a customary and accepted aspect of EC antitrust enforcement, it is unfortunate that the largest antitrust fine ever levied will now be imposed in a case of unilateral competitive conduct, the most ambiguous and controversial area of antitrust enforcement. For this fine to surpass even the fines levied against members of the most notorious price fixing cartels may send an unfortunate message about the appropriate hierarchy of enforcement priorities.

Besides ignoring standard competition-policy concerns that inform the amount of fines, the passage is revealing of the assistant attorney general's non-interventionist philosophy with respect to single-firm conduct. In his view, "unilateral competitive conduct" is the "most ambiguous and controversial area of antitrust enforcement" and hence warrants very limited and cautious policing. But at that point two jurisdictions—the United States and the European Union—had concluded that Microsoft *had* engaged in anticompetitive conduct that had not been justified. Although in many circumstances refusals to deal with rivals and technological tying might warrant a cautious approach to antitrust enforcement owing to their possibly ambiguous welfare effects, there was nothing so subtle or "ambiguous" about the effects of most of Microsoft's conduct. To the contrary, the facts as proved in both the United States and Europe established a brash and far-ranging plan to eliminate competition through exclusionary means. Hence, to the degree the Justice Department was concerned that in the future the decision would have a chilling effect on ambiguous conduct in other contexts, its concerns were based on the speculative premise that the European Commission's decision couldn't and wouldn't be well understood as dependent on its facts. It is more probable that the Justice Department's concern revealed an underlying and continuing disagreement with the legal standards that had been used and the conclusions that had been reached in both jurisdictions. The new leaders of the Justice Department simply didn't believe in the case against Microsoft, or at least didn't believe in much of it.

Building on its criticisms of the European Commission, the Department of Justice subsequently lashed out at the Korea Fair Trade Commission in December of 2005 when the KFTC ordered Microsoft to revise its marketing of Windows in Korea. The Korean case, initiated in 2001 in response to a competitor's complaint, focused on the alleged tying of Windows Media Player and Windows Messenger to Windows. After a lengthy investigation, the KFTC concluded that Microsoft had abused its dominant position in violation of Korea's Monopoly Regulation and Fair Trade Act in three ways: tying its Windows Media Service to the Windows Server operating system, tying Windows Media Player to the Windows PC operating system, and tying its instant-messaging program to the Windows PC operating system.

To remedy these violations, the KFTC imposed a fine on Microsoft of 32.5 billion *won* (equal to about 33.5 million U.S. dollars at the time) and ordered a number of changes in Microsoft's operating systems for servers and for desktop computers. First, it ordered Microsoft to unbundle Windows Media Service from the Windows Server operating system. Second, with regard to the tying of Microsoft's instant-messaging software and Windows Media Player to the Windows PC OS, it ordered Microsoft to produce two versions of Windows—one with both Windows Media Player and its instant-messaging software stripped out and one that would include two new features to be developed: "Media Player Centre" and "Messenger Centre," which would permit consumers to more readily access and download the media players and the instant-messaging software of their choice. This unique remedy probably was designed in response to the perceived short-comings of both the U.S. Justice Department's attempt and the European Union's attempt to address anticompetitive tying by reestablishing competitive conditions driven by market preferences.[128]

As it had done in response to the European Commission's decision, the Antitrust Division of the Department of Justice again responded harshly and publicly. Expressing no disagreement with the substantive analysis of Microsoft's conduct or its consequences, the Justice Department's press release focused on remedy, criticizing the KFTC much as it had scolded the EC:

The Antitrust Division believes that Korea's remedy goes beyond what is necessary or appropriate to protect consumers, as it requires the removal of products that consumers may prefer. The Division continues to believe that imposing 'code removal' remedies that strip out functionality can ultimately harm innovation and the consumers that benefit from it. We had previously consulted with the Commission on its Microsoft case and encouraged the Commission to develop a balanced resolution that addressed its concerns without imposing unnecessary restrictions. Sound antitrust policy should protect competition, not competitors, and must avoid chilling innovation and competition even by 'dominant' companies. Furthermore, we believe that regulators should avoid substituting their judgment for the market's by determining what products are made available to consumers.

And again the Justice Department revealed its defensiveness, insisting that its own decree was a superior approach:

Addressing Microsoft's exclusionary conduct, the United States' final judgment provides clear and effective protection for competition and consumers. Microsoft is prohibited from preventing computer manufacturers and end users from choosing alternatives to software like Windows Media Player and Windows Messenger. The United States continues to be active in its enforcement of Microsoft's compliance with the judgment, and this work has resulted in substantial changes to Microsoft's business practices.[129]

This criticism of the KFTC failed to acknowledge the unique features of its remedies. Whereas the KFTC ordered Microsoft to unbundle its Windows Media Service and its Windows Server operating system, its remedy for the tying of Windows Media Player and instant messaging to the Windows PC operating system the KFTC was a novel one that had yet to be tried in other jurisdictions. Like the European Commission, it ordered Microsoft to produce two versions of its PC operating system, but required the bundled version to include a "Media Player Centre" and a "Messenger Centre" so that consumers would be able to more readily download "competing media players and instant messengers."

Although the Korea Fair Trade Commission could be faulted for foisting a choice upon consumers that some might not have wanted, it had devised a remedy that would reduce the transaction and switching costs associated with accessing alternative media players and instant-messaging software. This might tend to neutralize any undeserved competitive benefit Microsoft possessed by virtue of its monopoly control of the desktop and its reliance on integration, replacing it with competition on the merits. Not content to ignore the installed base of customers with bundled software, the remedy also called for Microsoft to provide Media Player Centre and Messenger Centre via CD or Internet updates, so all Windows users would benefit from the newly accessible alternatives. Rather than condemnation, this original, creative, and relatively non-invasive remedy for Microsoft's conduct warranted at least careful consideration and perhaps praise. The KFTC implicitly recognized that neither the European approach nor the American "hands-off software design" approach was working to reinvigorate competition impaired by Microsoft's conduct.[130]

The 2007 decision by the European Court of First Instance also was met with public criticism from Bush administration antitrust officials. As had been true of the Justice Department's response to the European Commission's 2004 decision and the Korea Free Trade Commission's 2005 decision, it again defended the relief it had negotiated in the U.S. consent decree, arguing that it was adequate and effective to address Microsoft's conduct, seemingly regardless of any differences in the conduct challenged in the United States and elsewhere. However, this time the criticism focused more squarely and explicitly on the standards used to judge the legality of Microsoft's conduct. It accused the CFI of being more concerned with Microsoft's rivals than consumers: "We are ... concerned that the standard applied to unilateral conduct by the CFI, rather than helping consumers, may have the unfortunate consequence of harming consumers by chilling innovation and discouraging competition." In what had evolved into more of a full-throated endorsement of Microsoft's position on the merits, the Justice Department sought to differentiate U.S. standards from European standards, proselytizing on behalf of the perceived superiority of the former and criticizing an arguably caricatured and simplified version of the latter:

In the United States, the antitrust laws are enforced to protect consumers by protecting competition, not competitors. In the absence of demonstrable consumer harm, all companies, including dominant firms, are encouraged to compete vigorously. U.S. courts recognize the potential benefits to consumers when a company, including a dominant company, makes unilateral business decisions, for example to add features to its popular products or license its intellectual property to rivals, or to refuse to do so.[131]

The implicit criticism was transparent: U.S. laws protect consumers, whereas European laws worry more about competitors and hence are prone to capture by rivals of dominant firms. The European Commission and the Court of First Instance had been taken in by Microsoft's competitors, unable to tell the difference between legitimate complaints and complaints from firms trying to hobble their dominant competitors.

The Antitrust Division's attacks on the European Commission and the Korea Free Trade Commission during the Bush administration revealed a significant shift in viewpoint at the U.S. agency from the time the U.S. Microsoft cases were filed. It built upon both spoken and unspoken assumptions about the likely incidence and consequences of error in enforcing antitrust standards against single firms, taking into account strong presumptions about the institutional limits of antitrust enforcement agencies and courts. These views were embodied in the Justice Department's 2008 Section 2 Report, which, as we noted earlier in the chapter, was issued without the support of the U.S. Federal Trade Commission.

With another change of administration in January of 2009, the perception of divergence with respect to the standards for judging single-firm conduct that grew during the eight years of the Bush Justice Department began to dissipate, and along with it public criticism of the European Commission's efforts to apply its competition laws to Microsoft. In December of 2009 the European Commission reached a settlement with Microsoft in a distinct case that, like the U.S. case, focused on Microsoft's integration of its Internet browser, IE, into Windows. With the Section 2 Report withdrawn, and with explicit assertions that a new direction in enforcement would be pursued, a still-new assistant attorney general released the following statement:

The Department of Justice's Antitrust Division commends the efforts of the European Commission and Microsoft Corporation, which have announced that they have reached a comprehensive settlement resolving their disputes under European competition law. As we understand it, the settlement is based on measures to enhance competition and is designed to preserve industry participants' incentives and ability to compete going forward. A settlement that helps to clarify obligations under European law allows the industry to move forward. The Department is committed to continuing its strong and cooperative relationship with the European Commission to promote competition policy that protects consumer welfare.[132]

Conclusion

As we noted at the outset of the chapter, one of the most profound changes in competition policy and enforcement at the turn of the twenty-first century was its full-scale globalization. Microsoft's encounter with antitrust enforcement, therefore, wasn't limited to the laws and institutions of the United States. As a global firm, it was subject to global scrutiny under multiple enforcement regimes with varied procedural and substantive features. The consequences included years of litigation and the commitment of substantial resources to simultaneously navigating multiple investigations and enforcement actions on several continents. When considered along with the combination of public and multiple private actions in the United States, Microsoft's experience was perhaps unique in the history of antitrust enforcement at the time. To some degree, of course, Microsoft's experience was an accident of timing. Microsoft faced this still-developing global system during a time of emergence and change.

In this more complicated world of global antitrust enforcement by multiple enforcers, discussions about "convergence" and "divergence" have become commonplace. Without a doubt, the long-term view exhibits an extraordinary degree of convergence that would have been unimaginable as recently as the late 1980s. Similarly, the degree of agency-to-agency cooperation continues to increase. Nevertheless, with multiple enforcers proceeding under different procedural and substantive standards, some divergence isn't surprising and is unlikely to dissipate completely. Indeed, in the United States it is common for federal courts of appeals to be in conflict with other federal courts of appeals, reaching significantly different conclusions in similar antitrust cases. Critics of the European *Microsoft* case have often emphasized what they view as the more interventionist features of the European system of enforcement of competition policy. That criticism shouldn't obscure the far more significant fact that the European case shared a common and substantial economic core with the U.S. case, which led to largely similar legal conclusions.

7 The Challenge of Remedy

On December 28, 2007, Netscape announced in a blog entry that AOL would be discontinuing its support for Netscape's browser, which AOL had acquired in 1999 for $10.2 billion. On March 1, 2008, AOL officially pulled the plug. Netscape didn't live to see its fourteenth birthday.[1]

The report of Netscape's death in 2008 was greatly exaggerated, however. Netscape had actually died in May of 1998, less than a year before it was acquired by AOL. As we have already seen, Judge Thomas Penfield Jackson declined to rule on the plaintiff governments' request to preliminarily enjoin the distribution of Windows 98 bundled with Internet Explorer in favor of combining the preliminary injunction hearing with trial on the merits. As a result, a new generation of "Windows 98 computers" was produced, placing Microsoft's browser and its browser icon on the desktops of millions of computer users. It would be another three years before any relief would be granted for Microsoft's various efforts to exclude Netscape, and by then it didn't matter—IE dominated the marketplace. The slow progress of the litigation had permitted the market to tip in Microsoft's favor.

To be even more precise, however, Netscape didn't completely die in 1998. Instead, it sowed the technological seeds for a competing browser by making its code into open source, a project it had begun even before it was acquired by AOL. In 2003 AOL spun off the development of this open-source software to the newly created Mozilla Foundation, which AOL supported financially, and Mozilla then developed an independent browser, Firefox. Firefox and Netscape (based on the same underlying code) began releasing versions with features that weren't available in Internet Explorer, thereby gaining users. By 2007, 60 percent of users in one survey rated Firefox as the best browser. Only 11 percent rated IE as the best. By May of 2008—ten years after the monopolization cases were filed against Microsoft—Firefox accounted for about 18 percent of all browser use in the United States, but IE accounted for nearly 75 percent. More important, Microsoft also retained more than 90 percent of the market for desktop-computer operating systems, the market that Microsoft had illegally monopolized according to the findings of the district court eight years earlier.[2]

Although some of the new browser competitors talked of a "second browser war" that would be won by innovation rather than "monopolistic muscle," monopolistic muscle was hardly out of the picture.[3] On January 17, 2009, after a complaint from Opera (a browser company with less than 1 percent of the market), the European Commission announced that it had sent a Statement of Objections to Microsoft outlining its "preliminary view" that Microsoft's tying of Internet Explorer to the Windows' operating system was an abuse of dominant position in violation of Article 102 TFEU.[4] At the same time a trade association filed a second complaint, alleging that Microsoft was refusing to disclose interoperability information "across a broad range of products," including its office-productivity software. The Commission announced that it would be investigating that complaint as well.[5]

From an antitrust standpoint these developments in the markets in operating systems and browsers look particularly disheartening. After a decade of global antitrust enforcement against Microsoft, some of the very same competition issues that prompted the effort remained unresolved—the public enforcement agencies and Microsoft had come full circle to once again examine the same products and the competitive consequences and justifications of the same "integration" business model—and Microsoft still held its monopoly position in the market for operating systems.

The challenge that these developments pose to antitrust is not primarily a challenge of legal doctrine, however. Despite dire predictions to the contrary, the competition laws of various jurisdictions proved equal to the task of judging the effects of Microsoft's conduct. Courts on both sides of the Atlantic—indeed, relatively conservative courts—all agreed that Microsoft's conduct had violated the antitrust laws. Rather, the challenge was to identify effective and administrable remedies.

How should we assess the remedies that were imposed in the *Microsoft* litigation? If the competitive landscape didn't look much different a decade after the initial government cases were filed in the United States, does this mean that the remedies were a complete failure? And no matter how we assess the remedies' record, what lessons for the future can we draw about the remedies that jurisdictions around the world imposed on Microsoft?

We take up these questions by first putting the question of remedies into a broader theoretical framework. We then examine, in three sections, the outcome of the remedies actually imposed in the *Microsoft* litigation. We review the 2002 negotiated settlement of the government cases in the United States, the remedies imposed in the European Commission's cases (including the 2009 case involving browsers), and the remedies that consumers and business rivals obtained in private litigation. We then assess the extent to which the remedies that were imposed globally in the *Microsoft* cases—fines, private damages awards, and conduct decrees—achieved the three policy goals of antitrust remedies: deterrence, compensation, and remediation. In the final section of the chapter, we discuss some lessons learned from the *Microsoft* remedy effort, focusing on remedial goals, benchmarking, the appropriate place of conduct and structural remedies, the use of compliance incentives and civil fines, and the need for greater attention to mechanisms for compliance and transparency.

We conclude the chapter with six specific lessons drawn from our broader discussion: that remedial goals should be set early on, that remedial decrees require articulated goals and benchmarks, that structural remedies should not be abandoned, that conduct decrees should rely more on incentives for reaching remedial goals and less on commanding particular actions, that accountability and transparency in remedies should be increased, and that antitrust's comparative advantage is in designing remedies with incentives for competition, not in predicting future events.

A Theoretical Framework

Courts and commentators have generally advanced three policy goals for antitrust remedies: deterrence (specific and general), compensation, and remediation. Specific deterrence aims to ensure that the antitrust violator will not commit the violation again in the future; general deterrence aims to induce others not to commit similar offenses. Compensation involves requiring the antitrust violator to pay injured parties an amount sufficient to compensate them for their losses. Remediation is more complicated.[6] Remedial decrees are restorative rather than retributive—they are intended to restore the competition that was lost by the defendant's violation, rather than to impose a penalty or a monetary judgment on the defendant for past conduct. Properly calibrating deterrence or assessing monetary injury is difficult enough. The task of restoring competition by means of a decree by a court or an administrative agency is even more challenging, because it involves difficult questions of prediction and institutional competence.

In a case involving the acquisition of a monopoly the intuitively appropriate remedy is dissolution of the monopoly, but in the typical case involving unlawful maintenance of a monopoly the defendant is presumed to have possessed some degree of lawfully acquired monopoly power before the challenged conduct occurred. In monopoly-maintenance cases the violation comes from adding to that power or insulating it from erosion, and courts and agencies must address this question: Should the remedies be limited solely to the "incremental" monopoly power (the power added or the power insulated from erosion) that can be causally linked to the challenged conduct, or should the remedy go farther and impose more intrusive changes to ensure that competition can thrive, particularly in cases where a monopolist engages in systemic anticompetitive behavior to maintain its monopoly?

Limiting remedies to the incremental portion of the defendant's power is a difficult task. It assumes that the increment can be isolated, that causation can be shown, and that the remedies can be calibrated merely to neutralize the effects of the challenged conduct. Further, if the burden of proving the increment is on the plaintiff, and if it is difficult to satisfy, remedies in monopoly-maintenance cases may under-deter, because dominant firms know that their underlying monopoly power—that which gave them the power to injure competition—is insulated from remedial measures. Solving this problem of monopoly-maintenance cases, and allocating the burden of proof, greatly affects the remedy chosen, and it did so in the *Microsoft* cases.

Assessing the remedies in the *Microsoft* litigation also requires putting the question into an institutional framework. As we have seen, Microsoft was subject to litigation brought by government enforcement agencies and by private parties in numerous jurisdictions around the world. Each of these jurisdictions had somewhat different legal instruments available for remedying Microsoft's violations. The U.S. government enforcers couldn't seek monetary penalties, because they had chosen to sue civilly. (There are no civil penalties in the U.S. antitrust system.) The European Union, however, could impose monetary fines. On the other hand, whereas U.S. government enforcers could seek structural remedies (perhaps even the breakup of Microsoft), the EU's power to obtain structural relief was uncertain at the time. Private compensatory remedies were poorly developed in Europe, but such remedies were well developed in the United States, where treble damages and attorneys' fees were available to successful plaintiffs. In chapter 8 we will explore the costs and benefits of this institutional diversity as it affected the question of remedies. For present purposes, it is sufficient to note that any assessment of the remedies should be global.

The Government Cases in the United States

Implementing the Settlement Decree

The negotiated settlement decree entered in 2002 in the U.S. government cases chose a conduct remedy rather than a structural one. That is, the decree required Microsoft to do or stop doing certain things in the future rather than altering Microsoft's ownership or organization in a way that would change its incentives with regard to future conduct, thereby changing the dynamics of the marketplace.[7]

As we discussed in chapter 4, two of Judge Jackson's reasons for choosing a structural approach were his fear that Microsoft wouldn't willingly comply with the conditions of a conduct decree and his concern that constant monitoring by the government and the judiciary would be necessary to ensure that Microsoft was living up to its obligations. A further concern was that a conduct decree would necessarily impose a variety of technical obligations whose monitoring would require expertise that government enforcers lacked.

As it turned out, Judge Jackson's concerns about compliance weren't borne out with regard to most of the provisions of the settlement decree. Contrary to the expectations of many critics of the settlement, most provisions of the decree were implemented without serious violations, although, as Judge Colleen Kollar-Kotelly (who supervised the decree) noted, there were complaints about "virtually every aspect" of the decree—complaints that often required considerable time to investigate and resolve.[8]

Nevertheless, Judge Jackson's concerns weren't entirely misplaced. One area of the decree that proved particularly troublesome, for many of the reasons that Jackson predicted, was the compulsory licensing of the communications protocols for connecting servers with desktop PCs.[9] From the simple matter of Microsoft's refusal to use Adobe Acrobat to image the necessary documentation for the protocols (Microsoft wanted to use its own HTML format for the documents, a format which had "usability" problems[10]) to the more serious matter of accurately documenting all the protocols, the protocol-disclosure project proved enormously difficult and extremely slow.

Microsoft initially undertook the obligation to document the protocols, but in January of 2005 it became clear that it wouldn't complete the documentation within any reasonable period of time. At this point the Technical Committee, the expert three-person group set up to monitor compliance with the decree, undertook a one-year project to assist Microsoft.[11] Microsoft agreed to cooperate with the Technical Committee, but by the end of the year Microsoft reported to the court that it wouldn't be able to complete its part of the project until July of 2006—six months late and only 16 months before the decree itself was scheduled to terminate.

In January of 2006 the Justice Department and the states complained to the court that Microsoft had fallen "significantly behind" in responding to technical issues with regard to the protocols already documented, stating that Microsoft needed to "dramatically increase" the resources devoted to the project.[12] The backlog of technical issues, the plaintiffs reported, "grows day by day," and the number of technical issues identified by the Technical Committee staff "is not declining."[13] Microsoft responded that the technical documentation required by the decree was of a "magnitude, scope, and complexity" that necessitated a "substantial—and ongoing—undertaking." It was having difficulty "finding and hiring competent employees with the necessary experience in and training for these highly specialized tasks"—a surprising admission coming from one of the world's leading technology firms.[14]

By May of 2006 the government plaintiffs had lost their patience. In a joint status report filed with the district court, the plaintiffs stated that the parties' efforts to ensure satisfactory technical documentation of the protocols had reached a "watershed" and that Microsoft's performance in documenting the protocols and resolving technical issues had been "disappointing." A new approach was needed under which Microsoft would rewrite "substantial portions" of the technical documentation it had produced, on which it had already spent a lot of time. Because a significant amount of time would be required to redo the documentation, the plaintiffs reported that Microsoft had consented to a two-year extension of the part of the decree that related to licensing the communications protocols, extending the expiration of those provisions to November of 2009. Microsoft also agreed that it wouldn't oppose a further extension of the protocol provisions, if that proved necessary, for up to an additional three years, bringing the potential end date of the communications protocol section of the decree to ten years from the date of its initial entry—the farthest-off date that had been specified in Judge Jackson's original decree for all of his "interim" conduct remedies.[15]

In October of 2007, with all of the decree's provisions except for protocol disclosure due to expire the following month, some of the state plaintiffs filed a motion to extend the entirety of the states' decree another five years, until November 12, 2012. (The states' decree was virtually identical to the decree entered in the Justice Department's case.) This motion was opposed not only by Microsoft but, in an unusual turn, by the Justice Department as well, which filed an amicus brief supporting Microsoft's position that all the provisions except those for protocol disclosure should lapse as originally scheduled.[16]

In a surprising development, Judge Kollar-Kotelly rejected the shared view of the Justice Department and Microsoft and agreed in principle with the states, granting a two-year extension of the full decree (not the five years the states had sought), until November 12, 2009. Her opinion explaining the extension of the decree was quite critical of Microsoft and its compliance efforts. In her view, the various component parts of the decree were designed to work together, so Microsoft would have to be in compliance with all the provisions of the decree in order for the decree to have a chance of achieving its goal of lowering the barriers to entry into the market for operating systems for desktop computers. Microsoft's "inexcusable delay" in complying with the protocols-disclosure requirements, she wrote, "deprived the provisions of the Final Judgments the chance to operate together as intended [and] is entirely incongruous with the original expectations of the parties and the Court."[17]

In April of 2009 the parties agreed to another extension—this one for 18 months, to May 12, 2011. Although Microsoft was making progress in documenting the protocols, the extension was needed to give the plaintiffs enough time to examine Microsoft's documentation and to have a "reasonable degree of confidence" that further extensions would not be necessary.[18]

In December of 2009 the plaintiffs pronounced Microsoft's protocol documentation "substantially complete." This didn't mean, however, that the documentation was finished—there was still "much work left to do."[19] Six months later, the parties set out a "final plan" for resolving all technical issues (at that point there were more than 1,000 still unresolved, some of which had been open for more than six months).[20] Once again, though, the effort fell behind when more technical issues than had been expected (more than 6,000) were uncovered at the end of 2010.[21] In anticipation of the termination of the decree in May of 2011, however, the Technical Committee stopped submitting new technical problems as of January 1, 2011. By the time of the last report to the court, fewer than 500 documentation issues remained unresolved. At that point, the plaintiffs pronounced the documents to be "of sufficient completeness and quality" so as to be "available for use by third parties" within the meaning of the decree: "Accordingly, Plaintiffs believe is it appropriate to allow the Final Judgments to expire on May 12, 2011."[22] And so the final judgments expired—nine and a half years after they were originally entered.

The Decree's Effect

On February 9, 2005, Judge Kollar-Kotelly held a conference in her chambers to discuss the progress of compliance with the decree. Present were counsel from the Department of Justice, the states, and Microsoft. As of that date, the decree's term was supposed to be nearly half over.

After discussing a number of technical matters, Judge Kollar-Kotelly raised the "broader picture" issue: "What if any effect," she asked, "has this [decree] had on the marketplace generally?"[23] Counsel for the Justice Department responded:

It is a question we ask ourselves relatively frequently, but don't have a particularly good answer for. I think part of the reason for that, is there's been, as far as we're able to observe in the marketplace, no demonstrable change in the operating system market.

That is, Microsoft continues to have a large share in that market. And [for] the [protocol] licensees that are developing products so far ... [w]e haven't seen them out in the marketplace in the same way that we saw Navigator coming in and potentially threatening that dominance on the platform.

Counsel for the litigating state plaintiffs added this:

According to the published data, Microsoft still has plus 90 percent of the Web browser market, so the market shares are at very high, monopoly levels still. And from what we can determine, no OEMs have actually incorporated Firefox [then a newly released open-source browser] into the product that they sell. These are mostly downloads by consumers.[24]

Counsel for Microsoft responded:

[T]he rationale of the decree ... was not to somehow hinder Microsoft or to limit its ability to compete, or ensure that its market share declined. It was instead to eliminate those issues that the Court had concluded amounted to a violation of section 2, and to go beyond that and create additional opportunities for third parties to compete effectively with Microsoft.

That has been accomplished, I believe. ... The question of whether third parties take advantage of those opportunities, how effectively they take advantage of those opportunities, and whether Microsoft can compete on the merits and continue to be successful are all questions that it seems to me the marketplace has to answer as opposed to a court.

So I think measured by that yardstick, I think the decree has been a success.[25]

Judge Kollar-Kotelly agreed with Microsoft, at least in part. The purpose of the decree was to "eliminate" barriers to entry, thereby creating opportunities for new competition; it wasn't to generate that new competition. Whether or not companies in the marketplace chose to take advantage of the incentives provided in the decree, the judge said, "I think Mr. Rule [counsel for Microsoft] is correct, the Court does not control [this]." The decree identifies barriers to entry and gets them "eliminated." "Then we'll see what happens," she said, "and I have a feeling it's going to be a long-term process in terms of actually measuring what happens in the marketplace."

Two and a half years later, in August of 2007, when it looked as though all the provisions of the decree except for protocol disclosure were about to expire, the court once again broached the question of the effectiveness of the decree, and once again the parties provided the court with their views. The Justice Department and the settling states found some "encouraging" indications of competition in the markets for middleware and operating systems and cautioned that the decree's purpose was "re-invigorating competitive conditions that Microsoft had suppressed," not "slicing off some part of Windows' market share." Still, they concluded that it "remains to be seen" whether any particular current product will play a role in challenging Windows' monopoly position: "It is not possible to assess whether these developments will ultimately result in substantial long-term competition in the market for operating systems running on Intel-compatible PCs."[26]

The states that hadn't joined the negotiated settlement were less sanguine. They pointed to a number of indicators of failure: the high market shares that Microsoft continued to maintain in operating systems and browsers, the small number of licenses that had been entered into so far under the protocol-licensing provisions, and the continuing unwillingness of OEMs to preload browsers other than Internet Explorer. They concluded that the "key provisions" of the decree had had "little or no competitively significant impact."[27]

Once again, however, Judge Kollar-Kotelly took a self-described narrow view of the remedy and her role. The "key" to the remedy was to focus on ending restrictions on middleware that might potentially threaten to erode barriers to entry in the market for operating systems. This would be done by enforcing the provisions of the decree aimed at stopping specific anticompetitive conduct. Thus, "The goal of the remedy was not ... extinguishing Microsoft's monopoly position ... or reducing its market share by a particular amount."[28]

This was the last time the parties addressed the effectiveness of the decree in court. By 2011, when the decree terminated, Microsoft had come into compliance with its terms, but whether that compliance restored competition either in middleware or in operating systems seems doubtful. In the final Joint Status Report to the district court, Microsoft noted that 49 companies had taken licenses under the protocol-licensing program (fewer licenses than had been reported a year earlier) and that 24 were shipping products using the licensed technology. To the extent that the purpose of the licenses or the products had been reported, most were for media streaming. Only six general server licenses were reported, and no company had used the protocols to develop a server operating system that could offer the middleware challenge that the decree hoped for.[29]

It isn't clear whether the lack of popularity of these licenses was attributable to cost and terms or whether it was a result of server software firms' choosing instead to use industry-standard protocols or to develop their own protocols.[30] Nevertheless, if the idea behind the protocol-licensing program was that server-side competitors needed access to Microsoft's technology to ensure interoperability between servers and the Windows desktop, the paucity of actual licensing indicates that either the remedy was misplaced or the program's effectiveness was thwarted by Microsoft's delays and the difficulties of implementation.[31]

Structure, or Conduct?

In view of the probability that the negotiated conduct decree entered by Judge Kollar-Kotelly had, at best, inconclusive results, it is important to ask whether Judge Jackson, the Clinton Justice Department, and the litigating states were correct that structural relief would have been more effective at spurring new competition for operating systems. Specifically, would the decree that Judge Jackson entered at the conclusion of the original liability trial have achieved better results than the conduct decree, even if it is assumed that the evidence was sufficient to warrant structural relief?

Jackson's decree called for breaking Microsoft into two companies, one of which would have Microsoft's operating systems and one of which would have the applications. How this would have diminished Microsoft's monopoly power in the market for operating systems is the obvious question. Creating an operating-system company and an applications company would split Microsoft apart, but the day after the reorganization Microsoft would still be the operating-system monopolist.

The government plaintiffs' argument for why the breakup would bring competition to the market for operating systems turned out to be similar to the one it advanced at the liability trial. The theory was that the Applications Company would become the "new Netscape" and that Microsoft Office would perform the middleware function that Netscape's browser had threatened to perform in 1995, thereby restoring the competition that Microsoft had suppressed.[32] Office was then one of the most important programs for workers in the "knowledge industry" (a "killer app," in the lingo of the day). It exposed application programming interfaces, and developers were already writing to it. Once Office was severed from Microsoft, the new Applications Company would have no interest in maintaining a monopoly in operating systems. Its incentive would now be to expand its own market share by porting Office to other operating systems. The mere possibility that the Applications Company could be enticed to port Office might even spark new interest in developing alternative operating systems. In the end, market incentives might lead to the emergence of cross-platform operation of Office. Evidence at trial had already shown how important Office was to another operating system, Apple's operating system for the Macintosh. If it had been worthwhile to port Office to the Mac, might it not be worthwhile now to port Office to other operating systems?

The particular focus of hope in this scenario was that the new Applications Company would port Office to Linux, an open-source operating system that hadn't seen much use with desktop computers (it was doing better on servers, whose users were more technically oriented).[33] The plaintiffs' theory was that Microsoft had no current incentive to port Office to Linux, because doing so would undermine its monopoly in operating systems by making Linux more of a fully operational substitute for Windows. (Microsoft argued that porting Office to Linux would be "very time-consuming and expensive" and would make "no business sense."[34]) After a spinoff of Office, though, the new owners of the Applications Company would have no such hesitation. Corel had already ported its far less popular WordPerfect office-productivity suite to Linux. If Office were ported, however, many more users might be willing to adopt Linux, which would make Linux a far more effective challenger to Microsoft's position in the market for operating systems.

The theory for creating a separate Applications Company, with new market-driven incentives, actually fit well with one of the goals of antitrust relief: restoring competitive conditions to what they would have been in the absence of the anticompetitive behavior. Nothing could restore Netscape, but Office looked like a pretty good substitute, perhaps even a better candidate for being more truly cross-platform middleware than Navigator ever was. The new Applications Company would have impressive financial resources (far greater than Netscape's ever were), skilled employees, and network ubiquity.[35] The new Applications Company would also control the dominant Internet browser—Internet Explorer itself—which it might then develop for cross-platform use, further strengthening competition in the market for operating systems.

As plausible as this scenario might sound, it was just that: a scenario. The market incentives that the Applications Company would presumably have might, or might not, lead to a cross-platform Office, which might, or might not, provide a greater constraint on the Operating System Company's efforts. The plaintiffs didn't propose to force competition on the market. They only proposed to force Microsoft apart. Who knew what would happen after that?[36]

Unfortunately, these critical questions of prediction were never explored outside the parties' papers. The plaintiffs took a rosy view of how things would work out—"the proposed reorganization" would "lower the entry barriers Microsoft unlawfully raised, enhance competition, and foment an explosion of new innovation that will benefit consumers."[37] Microsoft, on the other hand, predicted impending catastrophe—the structural remedy would cause "profound damage to Microsoft and its ability to deliver quality software products" and might even lead to the destruction of its "entire business."[38]

A remedies hearing would have exposed both sides' claims to some testing and to further explication, both of which would have provided useful details about the approach to remedy that the plaintiffs were advancing—details that might have helped inform subsequent proceedings. That opportunity was lost, however, when Judge Jackson simply entered the remedy without further hearing, in an opinion in which he provided only sketchy justification for the decree's provisions and dismissed the value of taking evidence pertaining to the future effects of the plaintiffs' proposal.[39] Not only did these failures provide grounds for the court of appeals' subsequent decision to vacate the decree; the lack of judicial exploration of the reasons for the decree's structural and conduct provisions made it easier for a new regime at the Justice Department, and a new district court judge, to ignore whatever merits the proposal had.

Remedies in Legal Time

The conventional wisdom from the beginning of the case was that changes in technology would outpace the legal process, which would be at an inherent disadvantage in constantly trying to catch up. As was said at the time, the industry was moving on "Internet time" while the government was moving on "legal time."[40] Critics often pointed to the ultimately abandoned thirteen-year monopolization suit against IBM. Begun in 1969, it was dropped by the Justice Department in 1982 because the market for mainframe computers had changed so greatly that the case was effectively rendered moot. The validity of this viewpoint was reinforced by Microsoft's frequent introductions of new products, which always seemed to come as the government was contemplating the next step in its legal challenge. New-product introductions didn't stop with the entry of the remedial decree. Windows XP gave way to Vista and then to Windows 7, and Windows 2000 Server was succeeded by Longhorn, further complicating enforcement of the remedial decree.[41]

The remedies process shows, however, that the conventional wisdom was oversold. As it turned out, prosecutors and courts had more time than they thought they had to design and implement more effective and more durable remedies to deal with Microsoft's monopoly power. Judge Kollar-Kotelly had predicted that by 2008 "the market will have long since sent the horse [the operating system] to pasture in favor of more advanced technology," but her own questioning of the decree's effects showed how wrong that prediction was even during the decree's initial period. Indeed, in a fundamental way, major components of the computer technology involved in the litigation remained stable long after the early 1990s, when Microsoft gained monopoly in the market for operating systems.[42] Windows 98 and its successors have incorporated new features, but the functionality of PC operating systems and browsers hasn't been replaced by any "more advanced technology."

Internet time hasn't run quickly, but legal time has. The original decree was set to expire before it could have any effect on the market. Moreover, although Judge Jackson's decision to accelerate the trial and combine it with the preliminary injunction hearing had put the case on a faster track, an unintended consequence was that no remedies were in place during the pendency of the trial. The court of appeals then stayed Jackson's interim remedies order, with the result that no remedies were ordered until November of 2002, when the settlement decree became effective—more than four years after the case was filed.

At the beginning of the *Microsoft* case, prosecutors had the insight that interoperable applications formed a barrier to entry that stood in the way of Microsoft's competitors in the market for operating systems. When it came to the settlement decree, however, government prosecutors didn't focus adequately on how those barriers had strengthened in the four years since the litigation began. Microsoft had increased the ubiquity of Windows and its main applications—the Internet Explorer browser, the Windows media player, and Office—and had been able to control migration to new versions of Windows by maintaining backward compatibility with earlier versions while removing them from the marketplace. As the feedback loop of consumer and producer behavior was reinforced, it became ever more difficult to overcome the applications barrier to entry and create a competitive network with adequate appeal to consumers and independent software vendors (ISVs). Competition with Windows became increasingly problematic.

In this context, not only were the "forward-looking" remedies of disclosure of application programming interfaces (APIs) and communications protocols unlikely to provide adequate incentives to consumers, ISVs, or OEMs to change their behavior and choose or design non-Microsoft products; they may actually have served to reinforce Microsoft's operating-system monopoly. The disclosure and licensing remedies assured applications writers that they could continue to make use of code in the Windows operating system when designing their applications. Indeed, one of the reasons the Justice Department gave for not ordering code removal was that ISVs had continued to design software that relied on Windows' code; forced removal would disrupt their business.[43] As the court of appeals wrote when reviewing the litigating states' remedy proposals in 2004, "[l]etting a thousand flowers bloom is usually a good idea," but not when it comes to the desktop-computer operating system.[44]

In 2002, Charles James, the head of the Antitrust Division who negotiated and entered into the settlement agreement with Microsoft, appeared before Congress to support the settlement. He testified that the prohibitions in the settlement "had to be devised keeping in mind that Microsoft will continue for the foreseeable future to have a monopoly in the operating systems market."[45] This was a candid admission of the Justice Department's limited ambitions in the Microsoft settlement. The Justice Department understood the court of appeals' decision as affirming liability only on narrow grounds and assigned significant weight to the fact that the case was one of maintenance, not acquisition, of monopoly. The Justice Department therefore accepted Microsoft's monopoly, holding out, at best, a long-range hope of restoring the "competitive potential of middleware" by making sure that non-Microsoft middleware and servers would interoperate well with Windows. What James didn't acknowledge in his testimony, but what subsequent events have shown, was how unlikely it would be that consumers, ISVs, or OEMs would want to use or design a platform that would replace Windows.

Only major structural change in the industry could have altered the incentives felt by consumers and by the industry substantially enough to create a serious challenge to Microsoft's dominance of the market for operating systems for desktop computers. But by the end of the government litigation, no party was willing to advocate such a remedy. The decree entered by Judge Kollar-Kotelly put some constraints on Microsoft's conduct, but the Windows operating system would continue into the twenty-first-century as a monopoly. Microsoft was required to give access to Windows on reasonable and non-discriminatory terms, but only for the limited term of the settlement decree.

The European Cases

The European Commission's 2004 Remedy Order

The remedies the European Commission imposed in its 2004 decision differed in many ways from the remedies in Judge Kollar-Kotelly's decree. The differences stemmed from the different remedial powers in the two jurisdictions, the differences in the cases tried in the United States and in Europe, and, in the tying area, a disagreement as to what might be the best approach to remedy.

First, the European Commission fined Microsoft €497 million (approximately $605 million at the time). No fines were ever imposed against Microsoft in the United States—the case was brought as a civil case, and there is no provision in the Sherman Act for civil fines.

Second, the Commission imposed two affirmative conduct remedies for the two infringements, one for the bundling of the Windows Media Player (WMP) into the operating system and one for the refusal to supply interoperability information relating to Microsoft's operating systems for workgroup servers. Both remedies were forward looking and were designed to restore competition.[46]

With regard to bundling, Microsoft was ordered to offer a "full-functioning" version of Windows without the Windows Media Player "within 90 days," although it was still permitted to offer a bundled version of Windows as well. In making this decision, the Commission rejected Microsoft's argument that removing the WMP code from Windows would "undermine the integrity of the operating system" and cause a "breakdown" in its functionality. The Commission also rejected the U.S. approach of simply hiding end-user access to the media player, arguing that without code removal content providers would still be able to write to the embedded Windows Media Player, thereby perpetuating the competitive disadvantage that Microsoft had imposed on competing media players.[47]

For the interoperability remedy, Microsoft was ordered to make the interoperability information it had previously withheld available "within 120 days" and to license the use of that information on "reasonable and non-discriminatory terms" for the purpose of "developing and distributing work group server operating system products." The Commission indicated that "reasonable terms" meant that pricing couldn't reflect the "'strategic value' stemming from Microsoft's market power" either in the market for PC operating systems or in the market for operating systems for workgroup servers.

The third remedy was injunctive. Microsoft was ordered to refrain from "repeating" the two infringements and from engaging in "any act or conduct having the same or equivalent object or effect." Although the Commission provided some further guidance for what acts might have effects "equivalent" to that of the illegal tying, in general the wording of this injunctive provision was far shorter than the complex provisions of the decree entered in the United States. This brevity, however, probably was due to the fact that the Commission's case focused on only two of Microsoft's business practices and to the fact that the Commission was placing greater reliance on the two affirmative remedy orders to redress Microsoft's violations.

Similarly to the U.S. settlement decree, the Commission established an expert monitoring mechanism, the Monitoring Trustee.[48] The Monitoring Trustee was given responsibility to advise the Commission on Microsoft's technical compliance with the Media Player and interoperability orders. Microsoft was required to give the Trustee full access to its technical information and to pay the Trustee's costs and compensation.

The Court of First Instance (now called the General Court) upheld the fine and the Commission's remedial orders.[49] In the court's view the fine wasn't excessive or arbitrarily set (Microsoft had argued that it should have been set at zero), the unbundling order was proportional to the infringement (particularly since Microsoft was still allowed to offer a bundled version of Windows and the Media Player), and the scope of the protocol-disclosure order was consistent with the interoperability information that Microsoft had refused to supply.

The Court of First Instance rejected the appointment of the Monitoring Trustee, however. (That was the only significant aspect of the Commission's decision with which it disagreed.) The CFI pointed out that the Monitoring Trustee would be more than an expert appointed to advise the Commission (something the Commission had the power to do), but would be independent of the Commission; that the Trustee would have broad power to act on its own initiative, without any time limit; and that the cost of its services was to be borne by Microsoft. The CFI held that the European Commission's investigative and enforcement powers didn't extend that far.

The Unbundling Order: Compliance and Effect

Nearly a year passed before Microsoft began shipping an unbundled version of Windows to OEMs, and even more time passed before the product was available to European consumers. First there was disagreement as to the name for the unbundled product. The European Commission vetoed Microsoft's first choice—Windows XP Reduced Media Edition—and eventually rejected nine names suggested by Microsoft before deciding to call it Microsoft Windows XP Home Edition N, the N standing for "Not with Media Player."[50]

Competitors then complained that the initial version had technical problems because Microsoft had deleted certain registry settings when removing the media player. Microsoft didn't deny that the new version didn't work well (in fact, Microsoft planned to say as much on the packaging for the product), but, in an apparent replay of its approach to Judge Jackson's initial order to offer Windows without Internet Explorer, it maintained that the problems were "a direct result of having to comply with the commission's order," which required the removal of 186 Media Player files.[51] Microsoft quickly agreed to restore the registry settings.

The most important deficiency in the unbundling requirement wasn't of Microsoft's making, however; it was attributable to the European Commission. The original order forbade Microsoft to offer a bundled version at a discount, but it didn't forbid charging the same price for the bundled and unbundled versions. Consequently, Microsoft set the same price for the version of Windows with the Windows Media Player and the version without it, arguing that, because the Windows Media Player was available for free downloading, it couldn't charge more for its inclusion in Windows. With identical pricing, OEMs had no incentive to offer the unbundled version to its buyers, and retail purchasers had no incentive to buy it unless they *really* didn't want the Windows Media Player. When the unbundled version finally became available, Dell announced that it wouldn't offer it to its customers; Hewlett-Packard said that it would offer it, but expected few takers because of the lack of a price differential.[52]

By April of 2006, when Microsoft's appeal was argued before the Court of First Instance, the European Commission was admitting that its remedy had failed in the marketplace because there was no price difference. Indeed, according to Microsoft's counsel, not one order had been placed by any OEM for the unbundled version of Windows XP, and only 1,787 copies had been ordered by computer stores across Europe (which amounted to 0.005 percent of all sales of Windows XP).[53] Although Microsoft argued that consumers simply didn't want an unbundled version of Windows, there is no way of knowing whether a reduced-price unbundled version would have been more successful.

Protocol Disclosure: Compliance and Effect

The interoperability information that the European Commission required Microsoft to disclose was similar to the protocol information that the U.S. decree required be disclosed, except that it involved protocols for communicating between servers rather than between servers and desktop computers.[54] Like the Department of Justice and the states, the European Commission had difficulty getting Microsoft to comply. Compliance with the European order was further complicated by disputes over whether the royalties Microsoft sought were reasonable, as required in the Commission's order.

The Commission's order required disclosure "within 120 days," but Microsoft didn't meet that deadline. In November of 2005, nearly sixteen months after the deadline, the Commission reviewed Microsoft's efforts and concluded that it was "virtually impossible" to develop interoperable software for workgroup-server operating systems from the technical documentation that Microsoft had developed so far. The Commission then set out three "Pricing Principles" for determining whether any non-nominal licensing fees for the protocols would be considered reasonable and not the result of Microsoft's market power: the protocols had to be of Microsoft's own creation, not simply ones taken from the public domain, the protocols had to be "innovative" in the sense that they couldn't be "obvious to persons skilled in the art," and the licensing fees had to be consistent with the market valuation for "comparable" technologies.

The Commission also decided that Microsoft should be fined for its failure to comply with its previous order. Finding that Microsoft's proposed fees were commercially substantial and that Microsoft hadn't shown adequate justification for the rates, either in terms of the innovative quality of the non-patented protocols or the comparability of pricing of the patented ones, the Commission decided to start fining Microsoft €2 million per day (about $2.6 million at the time) if Microsoft wasn't in compliance with its order within a month.[55]

The Monitoring Trustee (who served until the CFI's 2007 decision) subsequently reviewed Microsoft's documentation. The Trustee concluded that a November 2005 version of Microsoft's technical documentation was "not fit for use by developers, totally insufficient and inaccurate for the purpose it is intended, namely to develop work group server operating system products able to viable [sic] compete with Microsoft's own products."

Subsequent revisions of the technical documentation fared no better. A December 2005 version failed to fix the "serious deficiencies" found in the November version. A March 2006 version was "fundamentally flawed in its conception, and in its level of explanation and detail." Later documentation submissions were only partially revised versions of earlier ones.[56]

In July of 2006 the Commission imposed penalties for Microsoft's failure to make adequate disclosure of the interoperability information.[57] It imposed a €280 million fine (about $350 million) for non-compliance for the period from December 2005 to June 2006 and then increased the daily fine from €2 million to €3 million (about $3.8 million a day at the time) if Microsoft wasn't in compliance within a month of the decision. The Commission imposed these fines for Microsoft's inadequate disclosure, leaving for later decision the question whether there should be an additional fine, dating from December of 2005, if the Commission determined that Microsoft's licensing fees weren't "reasonable."

Despite the threat of large daily fines, it was another fifteen months before Microsoft was in compliance with its obligations. In October of 2007—three and a half years after the Commission's initial decision—the Commission announced that the interoperability information "appears to be complete and accurate to the extent that a software development project can be based on it." The Commission also announced that Microsoft had changed its licensing rates from an initial rate of 5.95 percent of net revenues for a worldwide license of all the protocols (including patented protocols) to 0.4 percent of net revenues for a patent license and a one-time payment of €10,000 (about $14,000) for the rest of the protocols.[58] The new rates, the Commission said, were now reasonable and non-discriminatory, as it had originally required. In addition, to satisfy open-source competitors operating under licenses that permitted copying and redistribution of software code, Microsoft agreed to publish "an irrevocable pledge not to assert any patents it may have over the interoperability information against non-commercial open source software development projects."[59]

In February of 2008 the Commission reviewed the royalties Microsoft had been charging between June 2006 and October 2007 for licensing the non-patented protocols to determine whether they were reasonable.[60] Adhering to the "Pricing Principles" originally set out in its decision of November 2005, the Commission began with the innovativeness of the protocols. In a 69-page annex to its decision, the Commission listed all the protocols, along with an assessment of their innovativeness, and concluded that "166 out of 173 protocol technologies disclosed" were *not* innovative. The Commission then compared the protocol-licensing fees with the fees for comparable technology provided by Microsoft and other companies, and concluded that such technology was often provided royalty-free. The Commission accordingly concluded that Microsoft's licensing fees for the period hadn't been "reasonable." The result was an additional €899 million fine, subsequently reduced on appeal to €860 million (about $1.35 billion).[61]

As with the unbundling order, however, it is difficult to tell what effect the disclosure order had on competition in the market for workgroup-server operating systems. In its 2005 decision reviewing Microsoft's compliance, the Commission pointed out that Microsoft's share of the market for workgroup-server operating systems had "continued to grow" since the Commission's 2004 violation decision. In its 2008 decision imposing fines for unreasonable royalty rates, the Commission noted that no firm seeking to develop a competing operating system for workgroup servers had yet taken a license under the program; the only licenses taken had been for products that didn't directly compete with Microsoft's server operating system.[62] In fact, the Commission noted, Microsoft's share of the market for workgroup-server operating systems had increased in 2006 and in 2007.[63]

Perhaps Microsoft's high royalty rates affected competitors' willingness to license the protocols, as the Commission's opinion implied. Nevertheless, the Commission didn't venture a clear finding on why licenses hadn't been taken, and it hasn't followed up with any studies to determine the effectiveness of its order or the impact of the royalty rates it approved.

Europe Makes Another Try at Remedy

A month before the European Commission entered its order fining Microsoft for setting unreasonable royalty rates, it opened two new proceedings against Microsoft. The first, echoing a component of the U.S. cases, questioned Microsoft's tying Internet Explorer to Windows. The second concerned alleged refusals to disclose interoperability information for a broad range of products, including Office and a number of server products. As the Commission noted, both cases involved the "principles" of its 2004 decision that "must be respected by dominant companies."[64] Each of the cases also provided the Commission with an opportunity to improve on the remedial approaches taken in its original decision.

The Commission chose to proceed formally only on the browser complaint. In January of 2009 it filed a statement of objections asserting its "preliminary view" that the tying was an abuse of dominant position in violation of the treaty. Although Microsoft initially disputed the charge, it was in a difficult legal position owing to the Commission's earlier decision involving the media player tie-in and owing to Microsoft's concession in the Court of First Instance that it had a dominant position in the market for PC operating systems. The only real question was what the remedy should be.

Microsoft first said that it would sell Windows 7 in Europe without any browser (something it had resisted doing in the United States), but the Commission objected: "Rather than more choice, Microsoft seems to have chosen to provide less."[65] Instead, the Commission wanted Microsoft to provide a "ballot screen" in Windows that would allow consumers to choose from among several browsers. After "extensive negotiations" Microsoft agreed to the Commission's approach (subsequently called a "choice screen"). Microsoft also agreed to give OEMs and consumers a way to switch IE on or off in Windows 7 and not to retaliate against any OEM that loaded a different browser as the default.[66]

Institutionally, the Commission's approach to remedy was a significant departure from the one it took in its 2004 decision. Rather than proceed through the full hearing process to a final decision, with a time-unlimited remedy, the Commission settled its case under its relatively new "commitment" procedure, with Microsoft committed to a binding remedy for a term of five years, subject to enforcement for breach.[67] In a sense, the Commission's decision was more like the Justice Department's consent-decree settlement of its case against Microsoft, similarly limited to five years (although the Justice Department's decree ended up lasting nearly ten).

Substantively, the Commission also took a very different approach than it had in 2004, choosing neither of the two remedies it had used for the bundling of the media player. It didn't impose a fine (although a fine would have been even more appropriate than in the 2004 decision, which had specifically found bundling to be a violation), and it didn't require Microsoft to offer versions of Windows with and without Internet Explorer. The lack of a fine was the price for achieving a resolution through negotiation—Microsoft said it wouldn't agree to a ballot screen unless the case was settled without a fine.[68] The Commission's decision not to pursue another unbundling requirement recognized that the 2004 approach with respect to Windows Media Player and Windows was a dismal failure that should not be repeated.[69]

The remedy the Commission chose instead was an amalgamation of solutions to the bundling problem that had been tried elsewhere. Like the U.S. Department of Justice and the settling states, the Commission, in order to give OEMs and consumers the option of choosing browsers other than Internet Explorer, accepted the approach of equating "removal" of IE with hiding the browser icon to the consumer but without deleting the underlying code. The ballot screen was similar to the approach that the Korea Fair Trade Commission had taken two years earlier in its case against Microsoft for bundling Windows Media Player into Windows and bundling Windows Media Server into its server operating system.[70] This approach provided an easier means for consumers to select competing software products through Windows.[71]

Although the ballot-screen approach appears to be an improvement over earlier approaches to the bundling issue, it isn't clear how much of an improvement it will turn out to be as a remedy for Microsoft's illegal bundling.[72] The Commission did impose a requirement that Microsoft report periodically on implementation of the commitment, including data relating to use of the choice screen. The commitment also gave both parties the right to review the agreed-upon solution in two years if market circumstances change or the choice screen has "manifestly failed to provide consumers with an effective choice among browsers in a reasonable way."[73] Still, the commitment decision made no provision for making these reports public, nor did it include any mechanism for outside technical support to check on Microsoft's compliance or to deal with technical problems as they arose.

That compliance probably would be problematic was certainly predictable from all other enforcement efforts in the *Microsoft* litigation, and the browser commitment has proved to be no exception. In February of 2011, a little more than a year after the commitment decision was taken, Microsoft distributed an update of Windows 7 without the necessary software for showing the browser choice screen. This failure apparently went undetected for nearly seventeen months, until the European Commission received reports and informed Microsoft, which then quickly fixed the problem and offered to extend the commitment by fifteen months.[74] The Commission, after determining that more than 15 million users had been affected by Microsoft's failure, concluded that, although the violation was "negligent" rather than intentional, the violation was "serious." Accordingly, the Commission fined Microsoft $733 million (approximately 1 percent of its turnover for 2011–2012) while continuing to field complaints from "third parties" about Microsoft's compliance, including problems with Windows 8, the next iteration of Windows.[75] This was a too-familiar replay of Microsoft's earlier compliance problems in the European Union and in the United States.

Of course, compliance isn't the same as effectiveness. Before accepting Microsoft's commitment, the Commission did some "market testing" of various iterations of the proposal with industry firms, but it engaged no independent experts to assess the different ways that the choice screen could be arrayed so as to overcome consumer inertia and aversion to downloading new software programs.[76] Nor did the Commission indicate that it had investigated whether the efforts in the United States or Korea had been successful in increasing consumer choice or competition in the browser market; in fact, there is no indication that the Commission was even aware that its choice screen bore a close resemblance to the remedy the Korea Fair Trade Commission had imposed two years earlier.

As with the U.S. litigation, the question of effectiveness cannot be fully answered without knowing what the goals of the remedy are. The European Commission's browser case focused on competition in the browser market, not on dealing with Microsoft's dominant position in the market for operating systems. If we take market share as one measure of that competition, we see that IE's market share in Europe was already decreasing in the year before the institution of the ballot screen (it was below 50 percent) while that of Google's Chrome was increasing. Both trends continued after the institution of the choice screen (even though for part of this period the choice screen wasn't presented to a large number of users)—IE's share decreased and Chrome's increased. But Firefox's and Opera's shares also decreased, both in the pre-ballot-screen period and the post-ballot-screen period. Thus, it is difficult to tell whether changes in market share were due to the choice screen or whether other factors were equally or more important.[77]

The European Commission's willingness to accept a commitment from Microsoft rather than proceed to a fully litigated decision and a potentially harsher penalty probably reflects some degree of "Microsoft fatigue" at the Commission, as well as the fact that the Competition Commissioner at the time, Neelie Kroes, was reaching the end of her tenure and was looking to "close that dossier" on Microsoft.[78] Indeed, Microsoft fatigue seems particularly apparent in the way the Commission handled the interoperability case against Microsoft that was opened on the same day as the browser case. When the Commission announced the formal commitment in the browser case, it also announced that Microsoft had agreed to publish interoperability information on its website. Without setting out the exact contents of this information, and acknowledging that the commitment was "informal," the Commission stated that it would "carefully monitor the impact of this undertaking on the market and take its findings into account in the pending antitrust investigation regarding interoperability."[79] With this informal resolution, the Commission seems to have closed the books on

Microsoft's abuse of its dominant position in the market for PC operating systems.

Private Litigation

In chapter 5 we discussed the private treble-damages litigation brought against Microsoft in some detail. In this section, focusing on the remedial aspect of private litigation, we highlight the extent of the litigation and the amounts that private litigants recovered in settlement of their claims.

Microsoft estimates that 220 private cases were ultimately filed against it in the United States for the conduct involved in the U.S. government and European Union litigation.[80] Consumer class actions accounted for 182 (more than 80 percent) of the private suits. In addition, individuals filed thirty cases, and state attorneys general filed two cases seeking damages on behalf of their citizens. Settlements were eventually reached in twenty states and the District of Columbia. Only two cases were tried before a jury; one was dismissed after the jury couldn't agree, the other was settled during the trial.[81]

Settlements of the consumer suits typically provided vouchers to class members that could be redeemed for cash after the purchase of a personal computer and/or of personal-computer software. In contrast with settlements in some other consumer class actions, however, consumers weren't required to purchase anything from the settling defendant, Microsoft. Microsoft estimated that the maximum value of the vouchers would be $2.7 billion. It has predicted that the actual cost of the settlements will be between $1.9 billion and $2 billion, because not all of the vouchers are likely to be redeemed.[82]

As we discussed in more detail in chapter 5, the two competitors central to the browser wars, Netscape and Sun, both brought private antitrust cases. Microsoft settled Netscape's suit for $750 million. Sun's complaint, which included allegations related both to the U.S. government litigation and to the ongoing proceeding in the European Commission, was settled for $700 million.[83]

Microsoft also entered into settlements with BeOs and IBM, two competing sellers of desktop-computer operating systems that had been harmed in part by Microsoft's effort to maintain the applications barrier to entry. BeOs's suit was settled for $23.25 million. IBM, which had a more substantial claim relating to its attempt to market an operating system called OS/2, never filed suit, but Microsoft paid IBM $775 million in satisfaction of IBM's potential antitrust claims.[84]

Original equipment computer manufacturers were the direct purchasers of the Windows operating system. If Microsoft, a monopolist, was overcharging for Windows, presumably the OEMs would have a claim for damages. No OEMs, however, brought suit for overcharges. However, substantial evidence introduced at the government trial indicated that Microsoft pressured OEMs in various ways in the course of its effort to exclude Netscape, sometimes retaliating when the OEMs didn't go along. Two OEMs pressed damages claims against Microsoft for this conduct. One of them was IBM, whose claims were included in the $775 million settlement. The other was Gateway, whose claims were settled, without the filing of a suit, for $150 million.

Two competitors in the markets involved in the European Commission's case asserted claims under the Sherman Act for damages. Novell's claim related to exclusion from the workgroup-server market, in which it had been a major participant with its NetWare server operating system. Novell settled its server claim for $536 million, but the settlement also included Novell's agreeing to withdraw from participating in the European Commission's case and agreeing not to participate as an intervenor in Microsoft's appeal to the Court of First Instance.[85] The other competitor was RealNetworks, whose media player was the focus of the Commission's tying complaint. Microsoft settled that claim for $460 million. As in the Novell settlement, Real agreed to withdraw from participating in the European Commission proceeding and from participating in the Korea Fair Trade Commission's investigation of the bundling of Microsoft's Windows Media Player into the Windows operating system.[86]

One excluded competitor filed a private antitrust suit outside the United States. In 2004, Daum Communications, a major Korean Internet portal company, sued Microsoft in Korea for 10 billion *won* ($8.8 million) for bundling Instant Messenger and Windows. Daum had also complained to the Korea Fair Trade Commission, which subsequently found that Microsoft's bundling violated the Korea's antitrust law. In 2005 Microsoft settled Daum's suit for $10 million.[87]

The amounts that Microsoft paid out in settlement of private claims are set out in table 7.1.

Assessing the Remedies in *Microsoft*

We have now seen how governments and private parties in various jurisdictions struggled with the challenges of remedying Microsoft's monopolizing conduct. In this section we turn to an assessment of the extent to which

Table 7.1

Private settlements, in millions. (Consumer settlements based on Microsoft FY 2013 estimated total. Some corporate settlements include technology licenses, not separately valued.)

Consumer class actions	$1900.0
IBM	$775.0
AOL (Netscape)	$750.0
Sun	$700.0
Novell	$536.0
RealNetworks	$460.0
Gateway	$150.0
BeOS	$23.3
Daum Communications (Korea)	$10.0
Total	$5304.3

Table 7.2

Government fines for violations of competition law, in millions.

Europe	$605.0
Japan	$0.0
Korea	$33.5
United States	$0.0
Total	$638.5

the remedies actually imposed in the *Microsoft* cases—fines, private damages awards, and conduct decrees—achieved the policy goals of deterrence, compensation, and remediation.

Fines

The fines Microsoft was assessed for violations of competition law are set out in table 7.2. As the table shows, the European Commission's civil fines were large, whereas no fines were imposed in the U.S. litigation.[88] In the United States the federal government's authority to impose fines is limited to criminal cases, and a significant Section 2 criminal case hasn't been pursued since 1940.[89] However, many states have authority to impose civil penalties for antitrust violations. Although the complaint the states filed against Microsoft in 1998 sought the "maximum" penalties under state law, the states never pursued such penalties actively during the relief proceedings.[90]

The purpose of imposing a fine is deterrence. The economic theory of optimal penalties argues that a fine should be set at an amount that will "deter inefficient offenses, not efficient ones."[91] This means that the penalty should equal the net harm to persons other than the offender multiplied by an amount that accounts for the probability that the offender will be caught and convicted.[92] In theory, if the gain from the violation exceeds the social cost (that is, if the violation leads to efficiencies that outweigh the harm), a rational business firm should commit the offense and pay the penalty; if the gain is less than the social cost (and therefore less than the penalty), a rational business firm will not commit the offense.

Although the economic theory of optimal penalties is straightforward, applying it in monopolization cases is problematic. First, it assumes that the total harm from anticompetitive conduct can be quantified. What is the monetary value of the harm that Microsoft caused, for example? Once we get beyond the possible overcharge for Windows (and, perhaps, for workgroup-server operating-system software), how would we measure the damage from the impairment of rivals' incentives to compete and from lost innovation—a harm that was emphasized in both the U.S. cases and the European cases? The multiplier would be equally difficult to calculate. Although one might make a rough guess as to the probability of successful detection and prosecution for cartels, for which fines are now common, the calculus is much more difficult for monopolization or abuse of dominance, in view of the low numbers of cases actually brought and the highly contested nature of the legal doctrines involved. This means that in a case such as that against Microsoft the multiplier would have to be substantially greater than one.

The European Commission, however, doesn't follow the theory of optimal penalties. Instead it uses a combination of economic impact and fault-based factors. In setting the €497 million penalty for Microsoft's two substantive violations of the Treaty, the Commission proceeded as follows: First it assessed the gravity of the offense, characterizing Microsoft's two violations as "very serious," in part because of their possible effects on other markets that might develop in the future. Next it found that Microsoft's behavior was "particularly anti-competitive in nature," with "significant impact" on markets that are "strategically important" to the information technology sector and affecting the entire European Economic Area. These factors led the Commission to set the basic fine at €165,732,101.

The Commission then doubled this amount to ensure "sufficient deterrent effect," noting that Microsoft was "currently the largest company in the world by market capitalization" and that its resources and profits were "significant." Finally, the Commission increased that amount by another 50 percent to reflect the "long duration" of Microsoft's infringements (five years and five months), yielding, after some rounding, €497,196,304.[93]

Was that the "right" number? Microsoft argued in the Court of First Instance (CFI) that the fine was excessive—indeed, that it should have been zero because the Commission's legal theories were novel—but the CFI upheld the Commission. In response to Microsoft's claim that the Commission had set the basic fine arbitrarily (the Commission didn't indicate in its decision how it chose the figure), the CFI explained the calculation: the basic number was 7.5 percent of Microsoft's European Economic Area turnover in PC and workgroup-server operating systems for the fiscal year 2003. This approach was good enough to allow the CFI to conclude that the Commission wasn't acting arbitrarily, but neither the Commission nor the CFI explained why a fine should be calculated on the basis of sales revenue or why 7.5 percent was the correct percentage. The CFI also upheld the doubling of the base fine to ensure deterrence, not because of Microsoft's size but because it expected that Microsoft would continue to maintain its dominant position "over the coming years," which would yield "other opportunities" to engage in the leveraging behavior the Commission had found abusive.[94]

Whatever the "optimal" level for Microsoft's fine might have been, it might at least be argued that a fine of more than $600 million was sufficiently large to get Microsoft's attention, even if it wasn't as large as the $10 billion fine that one commentator argued should have been imposed to "make even Microsoft … think twice about committing a similar offense in the future."[95] The argument for the specific deterrent effect of the initial fine in *Microsoft*, however, is undercut by Microsoft's subsequent behavior. It was 3½ years before Microsoft was in compliance with the interoperability requirements the Commission ordered, and the Commission considered it necessary to impose additional fines for Microsoft's failure to comply with the terms of the 2004 order and, later, the 2009 commitment decision. As table 7.3 shows, the compliance fines totaled $2.4 billion, four times the amount Microsoft was originally fined for its two abuse-of-dominance infringements.

Nor did the CFI's affirmance of the Commission's 2004 decision and the $605 million fine get Microsoft to reconsider its principal business model, which casts further doubt on the specific deterrent effect of antitrust

Table 7.3

Compliance penalties imposed by European Commission, in millions.

2006	Failure adequately to disclose protocols	$350
2008	Setting unreasonably high royalty rates for protocols[a]	$1350
2013	Violation of Internet Explorer choice screen commitment	$733
Total		$2,433

a. as reduced by General Court

liability in this case. Microsoft continued to rely on integrating IE and other stand-alone programs, such as media players, into the operating system. Microsoft's decision not to change the designs of Windows and IE might well have resulted in the imposition of further monetary penalties had the Commission not been willing to enter into the commitment decision in 2009, settling the browser case without requiring Microsoft to pay any further fines.

One possible implication of the theory of optimal deterrence is that the value to Microsoft of its Windows monopoly, and the value of its integration strategy to the maintenance of that monopoly, far exceeded any fine Microsoft could expect from enforcement authorities for additional analogous actions. Indeed, the willingness of the European Commission to give Microsoft a free pass with a commitment decision only underscored the wisdom—from Microsoft's point of view—of violating the law until it was told to stop.

Private Suits for Damages

Private suits for damages have two primary purposes: to compensate those injured by antitrust violations and to deter future violations. They can also lead to remediation, although often that is not their primary goal. From the perspective of optimal-penalties theory, any money paid out to plaintiffs, just like money paid to the government in the form of a fine, makes an antitrust violation less profitable and hence makes such a violation less likely. Deterrence becomes optimal when the total of the payouts is equal to the product of the harm caused by the violation and an amount that accounts for probability of successful detection and prosecution.

Microsoft's payouts in private litigation, shown in table 7.1, certainly were substantial in an absolute sense. Settlements of suits by end users probably will amount to approximately $1.9 billion; settlement payments to injured competitors amounted to approximately $3.4 billion. Microsoft also had to absorb what probably were very substantial litigation costs, including the fees charged by attorneys and by expert witnesses, and had to endure the disruption of its daily business caused by its efforts to meet its discovery obligations. Nevertheless, although the settlement values were quite large, and presumably acceptable to the plaintiffs, it is difficult to tell to what the extent these settlements significantly advanced either the compensatory function or the deterrent function of private suits for damages.

From the point of view of compensating for antitrust injury, it isn't clear whether Microsoft ever caused consumers financial harm by charging above-market prices for Windows. Whether Microsoft was selling Windows above a competitive price, and if so by how much, was never a subject of litigation in the original government litigation.[96] Perhaps Microsoft was overcharging, or perhaps it was sacrificing current profits to ensure the ubiquity of Windows on desktop PCs. Consumers did recover substantial sums of money, but they have been compensated without having had to prove the amount of the overcharging or the extent of the damages in court.

The compensation story is also clouded by the fact that most of Microsoft's settlements with competitors weren't just straight payments but involved other terms. For example, some of the value of the settlements involving RealNetworks and Novell amounted to "hush money," because the settlements required the plaintiffs to withdraw as intervenors in the proceedings before the European Commission and the Korea Fair Trade Commission. Such payments aren't compensatory for antitrust injuries, and in addition they undercut deterrence by depriving decision makers of the views of those who were harmed by the antitrust violation. On the other hand, some of the settlements included licenses to use Microsoft technology. To the extent that these licenses had value but were provided royalty-free, that would add to the compensatory value of the settlement.

With regard to deterrence, it would be rash to conclude that paying out $5.3 billion to settle the antitrust claims would have no deterrent effect. The question, though, is "How much deterrent effect?" Were the penalties excessive (greater than the harm to society multiplied by an amount that accounts for the likelihood of detection and successful prosecution), or too little?

There are three reasons to doubt that the $5.3 billion in payouts was "too much" in terms of deterrence. First, the settlement didn't actually cost Microsoft $5.3 billion. Damages awards, even treble-damages awards, are tax-deductible unless there has been a criminal conviction (in which case only one-third of the damages award is deductible).[97] Although it is difficult to know exactly how much Microsoft paid in after-tax dollars, there is some indication in Microsoft's financial reporting that its after-tax cost may have been about 30 percent less than the nominal settlement amount.[98] Second, these settlements were for damages to U.S. markets under U.S. law; they were the only financial penalties that Microsoft incurred for its conduct in the United States. To assess under-deterrence or over-deterrence, we would have to add in the $633 million in fines that were imposed outside the United States and somehow calculate the harm that Microsoft caused in all jurisdictions in which it operated (in most of which it wasn't financially penalized at all). Third, optimal deterrence assumes some multiplier of the penalty to take account of the fact that not every violator is successfully caught and prosecuted. As was noted above, a substantial multiplier would have to be applied in order to achieve optimal deterrence. We know that in cartel cases not every violation is caught, even though fines have been high, prosecutions frequent, and legal rules clear. How much more so in monopolization cases, where prosecutions are infrequent and the legal rules make it difficult for the government to prevail?

The safest conclusion to reach in assessing the collective effect of the monetary recoveries in private suits for damages in *Microsoft* is that they were compensatory in a rough, but unproved, way (understood, perhaps, as payment for likely future harm), and that they were likely to have some deterrent effect, but far less than would be viewed as theoretically optimal to deter Microsoft from socially harmful behavior, even when added to the substantial fine that the European Union imposed on Microsoft for its two abuse-of-dominance infringements.

Conduct Decrees

Conduct decrees have as goals both deterrence and remediation. Both in the United States and in Europe, the enforcement authorities attempted to bind Microsoft to decrees that would keep it from repeating the offending behavior that had been proved in their respective cases and would require Microsoft to take steps to facilitate competition in the markets affected by its conduct. These decrees were both "negative" and "mandatory," prohibiting Microsoft from certain specified acts and mandating that it undertake others.

The form of the U.S. Justice Department's detailed decree was a product of many forces. One concern was that in the absence of detailed provisions Microsoft could easily evade the goals of the decree by pursuing alternative strategies, not specifically prohibited, that could achieve the same results. The decree was a classic effort to block off the "untraveled roads" as well as the "worn one."[99] After all, as we discussed in chapter 2, the Justice Department's attempt to enforce the 1994 Licensing Decree to preclude Microsoft from tying IE to Windows was frustrated by the decree's competing provision that permitted "integration."[100] Microsoft's aggressive position with regard to that earlier decree created a lasting impression that the company couldn't be trusted to abide by a vaguely worded or ambiguous decree.

The European Commission took a very different approach. Its prohibitory decree in the 2004 case was the essence of simplicity—Microsoft was forbidden from engaging in "any act or conduct having the same or equivalent object or effect." So far, it appears, this order has gone unremarked, neither drawing a complaint from the Commission nor leading to any different conduct from Microsoft.

To some extent the forms of the decrees in the two jurisdictions have to do with the different litigation emphases in the two proceedings. The U.S. case was a relatively broad one; the browser bundling was but one component. The European case was more closely focused on two discrete issues. Indeed, although the European Commission's prohibitory decree was generally vague, the Commission ended up being very specific and interventionist with regard to two specific orders: to unbundle the Media Player and to provide interoperability information.

Despite the different scopes of the litigation in the two jurisdictions, the remedial aspirations of the two decrees turned out to be somewhat similar, having rather narrow goals. Their approaches to taking on a regulatory burden were different, however, reflecting the different histories and traditions of the two jurisdictions.

In the United States, antitrust remedies have often been criticized as too weak and as "Pyrrhic victories" for antitrust enforcers. The tradition of such criticism dates back to the earliest days of U.S. antitrust enforcement, when Louis Brandeis criticized the relief obtained in the original *American Tobacco* monopolization litigation.[101] Historically, however, U.S. antitrust enforcers haven't been hesitant to propose the strongest remedy—dissolution—although courts have generally been hesitant to accept it.[102] What U.S. authorities have been hesitant to propose are decrees that require continuing intervention and supervision.

Over time, in the United States, the idea has developed that the "supreme evil" of antitrust remedies is "regulatory decrees" in which judges are asked to oversee, perhaps for indefinite periods of time, aspects of the business behavior of firms that have violated the antitrust laws. U.S. antitrust laws express the political preference for private choice over government control;

regulatory decrees run counter to that preference. As the Supreme Court's 2004 majority opinion in the *Trinko* decision put it, it is better to withdraw antitrust remedies completely if "effective remediation" would require a court to "'assume the day-to-day controls characteristic of a regulatory agency.'"[103]

This distaste for government intervention has intensified over time, and it certainly shaped the debate about the appropriate remedies for the *Microsoft* case. One of the major concerns in crafting various remedy proposals was to avoid the kind of invasive regulatory enterprise associated with the district court's administration of the decree settling the *AT&T* monopolization case. In that case the parties had agreed to a restructuring of AT&T that included prohibiting the local Bell operating companies from entering long-distance telephone markets. Almost from the entry of the decree, however, the operating companies sought to avoid this line-of-business restriction, eventually inundating the court with requests for waivers. The judge's ongoing oversight of the industry eventually earned him the title of "communications czar," a pejorative political description that persisted for almost fifteen years. Eventually Congress passed the Telecommunications Act of 1996, vacating the decree to which the government and AT&T had agreed and substituting for it statutory obligations intended to open local telephone markets to competition.

The cautious approach to government intervention also reflects the litigation context in which these problems are handled. Antitrust litigation is inherently backward looking, based on a "crime/tort" model in which the government plaintiff proves illegal behavior and then seeks, as a remedy, some form of corrective action. Despite this desire to ensure competition in the future, however, proof at trial must demonstrate that a defendant's actions caused some violation in the past. Inevitably, remedy must be connected to what the government proves—it is difficult for a court to remedy what hasn't been shown at trial. Thus, in *Microsoft* the court of appeals, when remanding the case for reconsideration of the remedial decree, cautioned the district court judge that the remedy "should be tailored to fit the wrong creating the occasion for the remedy."[104]

The need to connect remedy to wrong is a pragmatic reflection of a court's institutional limitations, but it is also a reflection of a deeper political judgment. Litigation requires the government to prove that the law was violated, which is a constraint on arbitrary government conduct in bringing suit. Tying the remedy to what was proved at trial further limits government action because the government cannot use litigation as an occasion to impose its arbitrary view of economic ordering on a defendant. After all, neither federal antitrust regulators nor the judges before whom they appear are elected officials, constrained by the electoral process.

The political judgment of what judicial conduct is permissible can change over time. Thus, courts in the United States have, at various times, expressed more willingness than current courts to allow remedial orders that impose affirmative obligations on the firms that have violated the antitrust laws.[105] The breadth of the permitted remedy may well reflect shifting views of the utility of government intervention and of the abilities of government enforcement agents to handle the regulatory task.

The experience in the *Microsoft* litigation, however, both in the United States and in Europe, shows that this fear of regulatory decrees is exaggerated. A review of the experience in both jurisdictions shows that conduct decrees can be enforced, although perhaps with some patience, so long as the enforcement agency is willing to devote at least modest resources to policing the decree (modest, at least, in comparison to litigation). Of course, the success of such decrees also depends to some degree on the willingness of the offender to cooperate in good faith.

The Technical Committee set up under the U.S. consent decree was critical to this enforcement effort in the United States, particularly in its involvement with the problem of protocol documentation. Before the decrees, Microsoft's communications protocols had been developed solely for internal use, and their documentation was haphazard. It took some time, however, for the enforcement agencies to recognize that they couldn't rely on Microsoft to come up with usable protocols for other firms. The result was an increasing reliance on the independent efforts of the Technical Committee both to test the documentation and to eventually assist in writing it. The evolution of the Technical Committee's role was a pragmatic solution to the asymmetry between Microsoft, government enforcers, and the court when it came to technical abilities, understanding, and information. In effect, the parties created an *ad hoc* regulatory agency that was subject to some loose judicial oversight, thereby solving the dilemma of giving regulatory responsibilities to courts that have found them institutionally difficult to discharge.

The European Commission's experience in supervising its decree also shows that a more interventionist approach can achieve useful results. Particularly dramatic in this regard is the Commission's review of Microsoft's pricing policies for the protocols it was required to license. The United States took a negotiation approach to the protocols documented under its program, relying in part on licensee complaints and discussions with

Microsoft to get Microsoft to reduce its royalties. The Commission, on the other hand, came up with a more directive approach to valuing the protocols, eventually publishing a review of the innovativeness of all the non-patented protocols. The result was that the Commission ultimately required Microsoft to license the server-to-server protocols for 0.4 percent of revenues for patented protocols and €10,000 for the rest, far lower than the U.S. rate of 4 percent of net revenues.[106]

The real problem with the decrees, however, was deeper than the technical challenge of requiring affirmative disclosures of sensitive corporate information (the APIs and protocols) to potential competitors. The question was whether the required disclosures mattered competitively. In a sense, the European Commission was on firmer footing here than the U.S. enforcers, because the disclosures it required were of a type that the Commission had already found to have mattered competitively. In the United States, the protocol disclosures were "forward looking"; server-to-desktop links had played no part in the liability phase of the trial. Even so, the disclosure remedy seems not to have made much competitive difference in either jurisdiction. This indicates that the real problem wasn't the implementation of a detailed conduct remedy, but the choice of an appropriate and effective one.

Remedy Lessons from *Microsoft*

In this last section of the chapter we explore five areas in which the experience in *Microsoft* offers lessons for crafting better remedies in the future.

Goals

One of the most significant questions that the *Microsoft* litigation poses is whether antitrust enforcers should know what remedy they want before they file suit. Should enforcers take the view that "if you can't fix it, it ain't broke?"

In the U.S. litigation, the Department of Justice and the states did have some specific remedies in mind when they filed their complaints. Although there is no requirement that specific remedies be pled, government enforcers included in their original complaints a requirement that Microsoft include with Windows both Netscape and Internet Explorer (a "must distribute" requirement), but only for three years; the states also asked that Microsoft be required to share certain interoperability information. The conduct part of the remedy that was finally submitted to Judge Jackson was much more detailed, however, and made no mention of the requirement to distribute (which, as we discussed in chapter 5, Sun unsuccessfully sought with respect to Java in its private litigation with Microsoft).

Neither government complaint sought a structural remedy, and such a remedy wasn't really developed until after the government plaintiffs had succeeded in the liability phase of the litigation. The proposed restructuring of Microsoft was based on the assumption that conduct remedies wouldn't suffice to restore competition and would be difficult to enforce, and that a more fundamental approach to spurring competition was needed to address Microsoft's systemic anticompetitive behavior. But if that was the case, why did it take until the end of the litigation for the plaintiffs to reach this conclusion?

Between the filing of the complaint and the plaintiffs' ultimate remedial proposal, the plaintiffs learned a substantial amount about Microsoft and its business practices. Once the litigation broadened beyond the bundling of Netscape into Windows, the initially proposed remedy seemed inadequate to address the competition problem.

Should government enforcers have had their ultimate remedy more definitively fixed before filing suit? On the one hand, it seems inevitable that plaintiffs will refine their case as they learn more in the course of the litigation process. It may be that early notions of the scope and nature of the conduct and the competitive problems it has generated—and hence the most appropriate remedy—will necessarily be misdirected and ill-informed in many cases; it would be unfortunate if government antitrust enforcers were locked into a remedial posture too early in the litigation. This is particularly true of technology markets, in which the products and practices can be complex and technological change can shorten the time within which prosecutors need to act (as happened to the government plaintiffs when they were filing their initial complaints against Microsoft). On the other hand, monopolization cases are resource-intensive. Having some relatively clear idea of a remedy before bringing suit would seem to be a good way both to avoid mistakes in instituting such litigation (why bring a case if you can't accomplish anything?) and to help shape the litigation so that the evidence presented at trial demonstrates the need for the remedy that government enforcers seek. After all, in the words of an earlier Justice Department enforcer, the decree is the "*raison d'etre* of the whole lawsuit, for it is the only thing that binds the parties to the litigation and affords relief to an aggrieved public."[107]

Perhaps the clearest thing that the *Microsoft* litigation teaches about the crafting of remedies is that a better balance should be struck between having a good idea of the ultimate goal of the litigation and maintaining some flexibility to learn from the course of the proceedings. What is less clear is whether the balance was adequately struck in the *Microsoft* case. Ultimately the plaintiffs failed to prevail in their effort to secure court-ordered structural relief. Perhaps they would have been more successful if they'd had such a remedy clearly in mind earlier in the proceedings and then constructed the litigation accordingly.

Goals and Benchmarking

Once remedies are imposed, they tend to take on a life of their own. Enforcers need to pay attention to whether the remedies are being carried out, and the monopolist needs to comply. Ultimate goals get lost because the question becomes one of compliance rather than one of effectiveness; rarely, if ever, do remedial decrees include provisions designed to measure their effectiveness in achieving any stated goals. The tendency to focus on compliance rather than effect was in evidence in the *Microsoft* litigation both in the United States and in Europe (although the district court judge in the United States did express some concern over the effectiveness of the remedies she had ordered pursuant to the governments' settlement—a concern that played some part in her willingness to grant extensions of the decree). This tendency for remedies to continue for their own sake, perhaps beyond the time when they are needed, has led to a strong policy in the United States to limit their duration. Such a policy hasn't yet been clearly felt in Europe; the European Commission's 2004 remedial order has no express ending date, although the 2009 commitment relating to the browser is limited to five years.

More important than setting end dates for remedial decrees, however, is establishing goals for the remedies in the first place. The need for goals is another aspect of the importance of having some relatively clear idea of the desired remedy when filing a case. In the *Microsoft* litigation one can tease out certain goals in the remedies imposed in the United States and in Europe, but these goals are more related to the exact relief ordered (e.g., providing consumers with Windows both with and without the Media Player) than to more substantial competition goals (e.g., jump-starting competition by giving consumers a reason and an easy way to choose a competing media player rather than the Windows Media Player).

Further, if the goals of the remedy aren't clear in the beginning, they are more readily subject to subsequent reframing, particularly if a different political administration takes over the case. In *Microsoft* this reframing began during the settlement phase, when lawyers in the Bush administration's Antitrust Division stated that the "key to the proper remedy" was to "end Microsoft's restrictions on potentially threatening middleware" and "restore the competitive conditions created by similar middleware threats." This narrow focus on the middleware threat, rather than on Microsoft's broad effort to maintain its monopoly in operating systems, was subsequently repeated by the D.C. Circuit Court of Appeals in reviewing the litigating states' remedy proposals and by Judge Kollar-Kotelly in assessing the effectiveness of the remedies.[108]

It is difficult to imagine that the Justice Department that litigated the case and sought a decree breaking up Microsoft would have said that the goal was limited to "protect[ing] consumers by protecting competition in middleware."[109] The originally proposed structural remedy—establishing a stand-alone Applications Company—wasn't designed to create competition in middleware for its own sake, but to restore the middleware threat that Netscape had posed to Microsoft's monopoly in desktop-computer operating systems. Dealing with that monopoly was the real "key to the proper remedy."

Connected to the failure of the remedy decrees in *Microsoft* to set out clear goals is the failure of the decrees to set benchmarks for measuring success in achieving those goals. For example, if one were to articulate a modest goal in the U.S. case of lowering the applications barrier to entry, one could then try to establish benchmarks for determining the extent to which disclosure of application programming interfaces and of communications protocols had reduced entry barriers, perhaps by examining the extent to which cross-platform applications had increased in the market. Nothing of the sort was ventured, however.

Not only does benchmarking offer a way to measure the effectiveness of a decree; it also offers a different approach to crafting these decrees in the first place. Both the United States and Europe chose "command-and-control" remedies—the enforcement agencies chose a specifically defined remedy, and Microsoft was required to comply. Another approach would have been to set the goals for the remedy and give Microsoft more control over how to reach those goals. That might have avoided some of the information asymmetry problems inherent in ordering a monopolist to design a product or manage its business in a particular way. Take the bundling of the Media Player: why not provide market-share benchmarks for competing players and then task Microsoft with the responsibility of identifying means to get consumers (or OEMs) to install them? Microsoft was quite successful in getting users to take Internet Explorer rather than Netscape, often by providing financial incentives but also through contractual and technological means. Why not let Microsoft do the same for the competitor it had excluded, subject to penalties for failure? An effort to mirror the defendant's conduct in this way might be more successful in restoring the competition that had been lost.

Structural Remedies

A structural remedy was the path not taken—more accurately, the path sketched but not taken. The question is whether *Microsoft* will now be seen as proof that it is a path that shouldn't be taken. This may have been one possible implication of the U.S. court of appeals' decision to vacate the restructuring decree and its direction that any relief ordered on remand be "tailored to the wrong." Although the court didn't expressly rule out structural relief in the case, it appeared to be implying that a plaintiff seeking structural relief would have to satisfy a very demanding burden of proof to justify it.

The standard view of restructuring is the one Judge Learned Hand expressed when the Department of Justice sought to dissolve the Aluminum Company of America after finding that it had monopolized the market in aluminum ingots: "Dissolution is not a penalty but a remedy; if the industry will not need it for its protection, it will be a disservice to break up an aggregation which has for so long demonstrated its efficiency."[110]

Although Hand's view is often seen as a conservative one in terms of remedy—just because a defendant violated the prohibition on monopolization is no reason to force its reorganization—it is actually better understood as suggesting an affirmative approach to remedy. That is, the question is not whether the firm "deserves" dissolution, in the sense that there is a clear causal connection between the conduct that led to the suit and the defendant's ability to maintain its monopoly. Rather, the question should be how best to "unfetter the market" so that competition is possible. To paraphrase Judge Hand, does the *market* need dissolution "for its protection"?

The remedy question, then, should be an instrumental one. Tailoring is most appropriate to the criminal law, in which principles of proportionality ("the punishment should fit the crime") are particularly apposite.[111] In monopolization cases, however, the tailoring principle should be viewed pragmatically, cautioning courts and enforcers of the dangers of straying too far from the case proved at trial. Indeed, its invocation underscores the need for government enforcers to decide early on that structural relief is appropriate so that the basis for such relief can be presented during the liability phase of the proceeding. But tailoring can easily result in too narrow an approach to the restorative goal (rather than the retributive goal) of antitrust remedies. This is particularly so in cases, such as *Microsoft*, that involve systemic behavior with broad-ranging international effects.[112] In such cases, remedies that stop at the specifically prohibited conduct will tend to under-deter and are unlikely to succeed in spurring on new competition. The offender in an abuse-of-dominance case or a monopoly-maintenance case must know in advance that by violating the law it is putting at risk its underlying monopoly (however that monopoly was acquired), if that is what it takes to bring competition to the market.

The structural remedy proposed in *Microsoft* was actually quite consistent with this pragmatic approach to restoring competition in the market and with the theory of monopoly maintenance the government plaintiffs pursued at trial. In contrast with what some economists had proposed, the government plaintiffs didn't seek to break Microsoft into a number of vertically integrated operating-system companies. Rather, the plaintiffs proposed a structural solution to replacing the competitive potential that Netscape had offered and Microsoft had suppressed. Setting up a new Applications Company was thus a structural remedy that might have presented Microsoft with a real threat to the maintenance of its operating-system monopoly.

Structural relief can present extreme challenges in implementation, of course. Although the governments' proposed approach in *Microsoft* was a product of much internal deliberation, the exact implementation of the plan was never spelled out and the plan's effects were inevitably speculative. This means that the modern case for structural relief, imposed by judicial decree rather than by settlement, remains untested. It does not mean that structural relief should never be used.

Incentives for Compliance and Civil Fines

The *Microsoft* case provides support for adding civil fines to Section 2 of the Sherman Act, a remedy that the European Commission and the states often impose in antitrust cases.[113] Because criminal prosecutions under the Sherman Act are today confined, as a matter of prosecutorial discretion, to cartel price fixing, the federal government's lack of authority to impose any financial sanction for monopolizing means that private remedies are the only source of monetary deterrence for a Section 2 violation. As we discussed above, even though the private recoveries and the European Union's fines were substantial in *Microsoft*, it is unlikely that the total amount reached the optimal level. Civil fines would increase deterrence, with the added benefit of not being tax-deductible by the offender (as private damages payments are).

Having the option of a civil fine also offers administrative benefits and could help reorient antitrust decrees away from the detail of the command-and-control approach toward an incentives-based approach. In complex cases such as *Microsoft*, in which the government is inevitably at a disadvantage in prescribing the "untraveled roads," consent judgments will necessarily be incomplete contracts, with ambiguities in language and changes in circumstances that are bound to lead to future disputes. Civil penalties, on the other hand, are cheap to decide and easy to administer.[114] Further, a defendant that is fined (enough) has an incentive to fix its business practices so as to avoid the imposition of another financial penalty in the future. Rather than relying on a detailed court injunction to tell the defendant exactly what it can and cannot do, civil fines would rely on the defendant to figure out how to stay out of trouble.

Civil fines could also work as a complement to a remedial decree rather than as a substitute. With a little imagination, it might be possible to "unfetter" the market and restore competition by creating incentives that would reduce the fine if certain benchmarks were reached. The crudest benchmark might be reducing a defendant's market share (although this might have problematic incentive effects for the defendant and its competitors), but other ways could be imagined to measure the competitive vitality of a market. Such an approach would diminish command-and-control regulation of a defendant's behavior, focus the parties (the government and the defendant) on increasing competition rather than just on avoiding acts covered by a court decree, and provide incentives for compliance.

Using money's incentivizing effects as a remedial tool might be an unusual use of civil fines, but it is not without precedent in remedial decrees in antitrust cases. In the case of a merger, for example, the parties may be required to spin off assets or license technology in a way that will stimulate new competition to make up for whatever competition may be lost in the merger. Such decrees also often contain "crown jewel" provisions that require divestiture of important assets if the decree isn't complied with. In this way, "crown jewel" provisions and civil penalties create financial incentives for compliance. Similar approaches might prove effective in cases of monopolization.

Although adding civil fines to U.S. law may sound promising, the history of the European Commission's decree shows that civil fines aren't a remedial cure-all. The Commission imposed substantial fines on Microsoft for its Article 102 violations, then imposed even more substantial fines for failing to comply with some rather specific conduct directives. Nevertheless, it is hard to say that the counter-factual would have been better—the directives but no civil fine. More likely, it would have been better to write the conduct requirements more in terms of competition benchmarks than in terms of specific behavior. We will probably never know the exact amount of additional deterrence a civil fine will buy, but we do know that incentives matter. Giving a violator economic incentives to remove artificial impediments to competition might make a conduct decree more effective.

Compliance and Transparency

An important institutional innovation in the U.S. decree was the Technical Committee. That committee was originally envisioned as a monitor of compliance that would mediate complaints and technical disputes.[115] Over time, however, it became more active in the actual technical work, assisting Microsoft in complying with the decree, developing and testing Microsoft products, and working on documentation to the point that it assumed primary responsibility for documenting particular protocols. By the end of the decree's administration, the Department of Justice was describing the Technical Committee's work as "Herculean." Judge Kollar-Kotelly called the institution of the committee "ingenious."[116]

The Technical Committee differed in important ways from the use of a Special Master, the earlier approach to dealing with the technical issues associated with compliance.[117] Its technical assistance went far beyond a Special Master's judge-like role (which focuses on taking testimony, supervising discovery, and making recommended findings to the district court judge), and its staffing far exceeded what Special Masters are able to get. (The Technical Committee eventually employed about fifty engineers and hired outside consultants to assist it, all paid for by Microsoft.) Judge Kollar-Kotelly concluded that the Technical Committee was a "model for monitoring" that she would "heartily recommend and ... would use again."[118]

The second important innovation in the U.S. decree was the requirement of periodic public reporting. From the beginning of the enforcement stage of the proceedings, Judge Kollar-Kotelly required periodic Joint Status Reports. That was a direct consequence of her insistence that the settlement decree be amended to allow her to retain jurisdiction during its pendency. The Joint Status Reports were prepared by the U.S. Department of Justice, the litigating states, and Microsoft, each party writing its own submission. Each report was then followed by a court conference so that the judge would be aware of how compliance was progressing and could question the parties about it. The Department of Justice also posted the reports on its website, thereby allowing the public to obtain information about the progress of compliance (or the lack thereof).[119]

Although this transparency was admirable, it wasn't complete. Because of confidentiality concerns, the judge permitted the parties to describe their compliance and monitoring efforts in "general" terms. Further, the settlement decree itself had various confidentiality requirements regarding the Technical Committee's work, requiring it to report only to the plaintiffs and leaving any subsequent disclosure up to the plaintiffs (although the judge did require the plaintiffs to include in the Joint Status Report the number and type of complaints that the Technical Committee received).

Confidentiality concerns are important, of course, but they can be used excessively to shield from public view the data necessary to evaluate a remedy's effectiveness. Indeed, Microsoft's periodic reports to the European Commission under the browser commitment aren't public at all. Not only does this interfere with accountability; it makes it harder for other government enforcement agencies to learn what sister agencies are doing and to use that learning in crafting their own remedial decrees. Surely it would have been useful, for example, for the European Commission to have known how effective the Korea Fair Trade Commission's ballot screen had been before it instituted its own version of that remedy.

Conclusion

In this chapter we have reviewed the wide variety of remedies imposed in the *Microsoft* litigation. These remedies include prohibitions on Microsoft's exclusionary conduct, requirements that Microsoft disclose technical specifications in order to encourage the growth of middleware products that might ultimately lower the applications barrier to entry and perhaps allow other operating systems to challenge Windows' dominance, and specific directives to redesign or market products in a way that would increase consumer choice. In Europe, large fines were imposed on Microsoft for its two violations of the treaty and for its subsequent failure to comply with the remedies the Commission ordered. In the United States, Microsoft paid large amounts to settle claims from purchasers of its Windows operating system and from some competitors that were targets of its exclusionary conduct.

How did each option measure up to the goals of antitrust remedies—deterrence, compensation, and restoration of competition? Our review showed that the options chosen had various deficiencies, both individually and collectively. Private monetary recoveries were compensatory, but to what extent purchasers actually had been injured was never clear. Monetary penalties for violation were imposed only in Europe, not in the United States. If monetary penalties should be based on economic harm multiplied by an amount that accounts for the probability of successful detection and prosecution, the likely conclusion is that the monetary penalties were too low for optimal deterrence. Some of the conduct requirements, including unbundling the media player, were outright failures, some (e.g., protocol disclosure) were painfully slow in being implemented, and the effect of some others (e.g., the ballot screen for browsers) is still uncertain. If the purpose of all these remedies was to restore a degree of competition to the market for operating systems, or even to get firms to introduce middleware products that would have the potential to lower the applications barrier to entry into the market for operating systems, or even to bring competition to the markets for certain middleware programs (the browser or the media player, possible goals of the EU cases if not the U.S. cases), our conclusion is that the remedies didn't succeed, at least not in any measurable way.[120]

Even if the remedies chosen weren't ultimately successful, they achieved some small successes. Prohibiting Microsoft from discriminating in royalties among the OEMs deprived Microsoft of a significant lever with which to punish "disloyal" OEMs. Google complained about how Microsoft designed its desktop search functionality in Windows; the government plaintiffs, working with the Technical Committee, got Microsoft to change its design to ensure that users and OEMs would have a choice of search engines. Documenting the protocols at least opened up the possibility of greater interoperability with desktop computers and Microsoft servers, perhaps preventing Microsoft from hiding code that would make interoperability more difficult. The European Commission's effort to ensure reasonable royalty rates for the protocols forced Microsoft to lower its royalty rates dramatically in Europe and, subsequently, in the United States. Rivals that were excluded by Microsoft's conduct, and end users who were harmed, received some compensation for their injuries. Institutionally, the parties and the U.S. district court solved the difficult problem of obtaining compliance with the technical aspects of the decree by developing a privately financed hybrid regulatory agency, the Technical Committee. Forcing a competitor, particularly Microsoft, to share information with potential competitors was never going to be easy. But ultimately the task got done.

We draw six important lessons from this story.

First, remedial goals should be set early, even if they are merely preliminary. Government enforcers learn as litigation progresses, but they shouldn't take on a significant monopolist such as Microsoft without having a fairly good idea of what they want to achieve through litigation.

Second, remedial decrees should have goals and benchmarks that measure success in achieving these goals. Compliance with a decree isn't enough (unless, of course, that is the government's goal). Goals and benchmarks remind the parties of what they want to achieve and provide a transparent means of measuring success for the parties and the public.

Third, structural remedies shouldn't be abandoned. The surest way to restore competition is to change a monopolist's incentives. Sometimes only restructuring a monopolistic firm will achieve that. An unfortunate consequence of the district court's decision to forgo hearings on the governments' structural proposals and the governments' willingness to accept that decision without objection was that a complete record to test the wisdom of the proposed structural relief was never made.

Fourth, conduct decrees should rely more on providing incentives to reach remedial goals and less on commanding particular actions. Monopolists that have been shown to be successful in excluding competitors should be given incentives to reverse the process and *include* competitors. If the U.S. Department of Justice had authority to impose civil fines, it could seek a court decree that would reduce those fines as remedial goals are met. Even without this authority, the Department of Justice could seek a court decree that would impose "crown jewel" penalties for the failure to reach the required goals. Civil fines also have deterrent effect, but to have such effect they must be sufficiently large. To a highly successful firm such as Microsoft, fines that appear to be "substantial" may in fact be quite insubstantial if the benefits of perpetuating the conduct are far greater.

Fifth, there should be more accountability and more transparency in the remedy phase of monopolization cases. Both accountability and transparency are important for evaluating the effectiveness of the chosen remedies. Both foster learning by doing, helping enforcers and judges to develop better remedies in the future.

Sixth, the *Microsoft* litigation reminds us that antitrust lawyers and judges are poor futurists. During the litigation, most of them thought that the pace of technology was moving so fast that imposing remedies on Microsoft was, in the words of Judge Kollar-Kotelly, "not unlike trying to shoe a galloping horse." However, antitrust lawyers and judges do have a comparative advantage when it comes to designing institutions that can create incentives for competition. There never was a "silver bullet" remedy for Microsoft's antitrust violations, but at least the lessons from *Microsoft* can show us how to do better next time.

8 In Praise of Institutional Diversity

On June 27, 2001, the chairman of the House Judiciary Committee, Representative F. James (Jim) Sensenbrenner, introduced a bill to establish an Antitrust Modernization Commission that would investigate and study "issues and problems relating to the modernization of the antitrust laws." Among the subjects deserving of study, Sensenbrenner said, were the question of how antitrust enforcement should be modified in the global economy and the question of the proper role of the state attorneys general in antitrust enforcement.[1] A day after Sensenbrenner introduced his bill, the Court of Appeals for the D.C. Circuit handed down its decision in Microsoft's appeal of the governments' Windows 95/98 case.

The timing of the two events was coincidental, but the connection was not. Sensenbrenner's bill was a response to the growing criticism of how the antitrust laws were being enforced against Microsoft, and, specifically, concern about the role that enforcers other than the Justice Department were playing in the Microsoft litigation. Indeed, nine months before Sensenbrenner introduced his bill, Judge Richard Posner—whose earlier effort to mediate a settlement in the federal and state governments' *Microsoft* case had been unsuccessful—presented a paper examining the application of antitrust law in the "New Economy." Posner argued that the problem didn't lie with antitrust doctrine, which was "supple enough," but rather on the "institutional side" of antitrust. Enforcement agencies and courts lacked "adequate technical resources" and didn't "move fast enough," Posner argued, and those problems were exacerbated by the overlapping authority of multiple enforcers: "No sooner does the Antitrust Division bring a case, but the states and now the European Union are likely to join the fray, followed at a distance by the antitrust plaintiffs' class-action bar." One reform that Posner urged was that the states be forbidden to bring antitrust suits unless they had been injured as purchasers.[2] As Posner noted, the critique wasn't limited to the role of the states, but was also squarely aimed at the

European Union. Implicit and sometimes explicit was the argument that these other jurisdictions were poorly equipped to apply antitrust in an economically informed way.

Critics of the institutions of antitrust enforcement would appear to have a point. The collective *Microsoft* antitrust litigation was a complex, often uncoordinated effort undertaken by a variety of public enforcement agencies and private parties, with different views and incentives, seeking to convince different courts in different jurisdictions to adopt rules controlling the competitive behavior of a single U.S. firm and to impose varying and potentially conflicting remedies on that firm. Could this possibly be the most effective way to run a modern system of antitrust enforcement, one ready to cope with the competition problems of the twenty-first century?

Closer reflection, however, reveals that the *Microsoft* litigation actually makes the case for this institutional diversity. We don't claim that the system is working perfectly, of course. As we have noted, cooperation among various enforcement agencies turned to discord in a number of ways as the collective efforts against Microsoft continued. Rather, our claim is that *Microsoft* itself demonstrates that the outcome of today's institutional structure is likely to be superior to what a more centralized and less diverse system of enforcement would produce. Indeed, some of what was viewed as "discord" can be viewed as positive signs of healthy dialogue and checks and balances at work.

This chapter is divided into four sections. In the first section, we describe the origins of our current institutional system and how it has evolved in the United States, in Europe, and internationally. In the second, we describe how diversity in this system is currently managed, both within the United States and internationally. In the third section, we make the general case for a diverse and decentralized system of antitrust enforcement. We rest our argument on two propositions. The first is that institutional decentralization fosters policy diversity and innovation, maximizes enforcement resources, and mirrors some of the essential attributes of our constitutional structure. The second is that diversity allows for competition in law enforcement, and that competition can help keep enforcement agency discretion in check and produce better antitrust enforcement results. In the fourth section, we apply our general arguments to the *Microsoft* case, examining the public and private parties' worldwide litigation and remedies efforts. We show that to a large degree our general arguments in favor of institutional diversity and competition are borne out by the record. Indeed, the *Microsoft* litigation makes the case that that we are better off with our current system of decentralized and diverse antitrust enforcement than we would be with more centralized antitrust enforcement authority.

Origins and Evolution of the Modern System of Antitrust Enforcement

The Enforcement System of the United States

It is a commonplace to observe that, given a blank piece of paper, no one would design the enforcement system that the United States has today. Of course, no one designed that system in a single sitting. It developed organically in the course of pragmatic efforts over more than a hundred years to deal with different problems at different times. Indeed, many of the features that are sometimes the focus of modern criticism were added at times when the existing structure proved inadequate.

One of the most important innovations of the Sherman Act in 1890 was the creation of a system of public enforcement of competition law at the federal level. Before the Sherman Act, enforcement was a common-law enterprise, invoked in state courts by private litigants seeking to avoid contractual obligations by arguing that enforcement of a particular contract would restrain trade and should therefore be void as against "public policy." Important substantive antitrust doctrines were developed in litigation framed this way, particularly the basic ideas as to what types of restraints might be considered "unreasonable." Sporadic private contract litigation, however, wasn't adequate to deal with the increasing power of large business enterprises (often formed through the legal vehicle of a "trust"). This led several states to adopt "anti-trust" legislation in the 1880s, and then led Congress to provide for federal government enforcement of the 1890 Sherman Act's prohibitions through suits in equity to enjoin violations and through criminal prosecutions. As we discussed in chapter 5, the Sherman Act also included a private right of action for treble damages by those injured by antitrust violations.

Government enforcement of the Sherman Act developed slowly. It was not until 1903 that a special division in the Department of Justice was funded to deal with antitrust enforcement. The small number of cases the department filed in the early years led many to view it as an ineffective enforcement agency. Judicial interpretation of the Sherman Act during this time was also thought to have compromised the act's effectiveness. Particularly important was the 1911 decision in *Standard Oil*[3] in which the Supreme Court adopted a general rule-of-reason approach to the Sherman Act that critics believed launched judges on a "sea of doubt" because it left the legality of any particular restraint to be determined more by a judge's predilections than by clear legal rules.[4]

The Clayton Act and the Federal Trade Commission Act were passed in 1914 to correct these perceived substantive and institutional weaknesses. The Clayton Act added certain specific prohibitions to federal antitrust law, dealing, for example, with mergers, tying, and exclusive dealing contracts. The Federal Trade Commission Act established a new administrative agency, the Federal Trade Commission, and gave it authority to prevent deceptive trade practices and "unfair methods of competition." Congress also gave both the Federal Trade Commission and the Justice Department authority to enforce the new Clayton Act's prohibitions.

When added to the existing federal substantive and institutional framework (the Sherman Act and the Antitrust Division of the Justice Department), the Federal Trade Commission Act and the Clayton Act established some spheres of exclusive authority for each federal agency, but also a significant degree of concurrent authority. The Justice Department alone had formal authority to enforce the Sherman Act, including exclusive authority to enforce its criminal provisions. Conversely, the FTC had exclusive authority over matters concerning consumer protection and deceptive trade practices. But the Clayton Act gave both agencies overlapping authority to enforce its provisions and the FTC Act's prohibition of "unfair methods of competition" created a conceptual overlap with the Sherman Act—overlap that became more apparent over many years of enforcement.

Congress addressed this institutional overlap only to a limited extent in the 1914 Federal Trade Commission Act. It gave the FTC power to investigate Justice Department decrees and report back to Congress (a provision specifically intended to monitor the Justice Department "laxity"[5]) and allowed courts in Justice Department cases to appoint the FTC as a "master in chancery" to address remedy issues.[6] As a general matter, however, Congress saw the two agencies as focusing on problems related to competition in different ways, using different procedures. The Justice Department would continue to deal with monopoly "as established fact," litigating in court the legality of a company's practices. The new FTC would engage in preventive regulation, checking monopoly "in the embryo" by stopping unfair methods of competition by a corporation of "no conspicuous size."[7] The statutory language, however, didn't set out these different roles clearly, and Congress paid little attention to the potential for conflict between the agencies, being more concerned with adding a new agency to strengthen the government's enforcement of antitrust measures than with working out the details.

It may be that Congress wasn't particularly concerned with the prospect of overlapping antitrust enforcement authority among multiple enforcers because multiple enforcement already existed when Congress established the FTC. For one thing, Congress had created a private treble-damages remedy in the Sherman Act in 1890. By 1914 the private right of action was considered an important enough aspect of antitrust enforcement that the Clayton Act included provisions intended to strengthen it.[8] For another, state antitrust enforcement, under state antitrust law, was relatively robust at the time. At least 35 states had antitrust laws by 1915, and state enforcers had sued many of the same companies that the Justice Department was suing under the Sherman Act, including the major trusts of the day, sometimes bringing suit before the Justice Department.[9] Congress was well aware of this state enforcement when it was considering the Clayton and FTC Acts. The Senate even vigorously debated an amendment that would have given the states power to bring antitrust suits in the name of the United States when the attorney general failed to do so.[10]

Over time the role that multiple enforcers played in enforcing the antitrust laws in the United States expanded. This is true both for private actions and for state enforcement. For example, for more than 50 years the volume of private antitrust litigation has dwarfed the number of cases that federal government enforcers bring.[11] Indeed, the, Supreme Court has emphasized the role that private litigants play in the antitrust enforcement system by referring to them as "private attorneys general."[12] The role of the states in enforcing federal antitrust law has also grown. In the 1940s the Supreme Court recognized the power of state attorneys general to sue in federal court under federal antitrust law not only for damages that their states incurred as purchasers but also to enjoin Sherman Act violations that damage their states' economies.[13] In 1976 Congress gave state enforcers further statutory authority to sue in federal court for monetary damages suffered by natural persons residing in their respective states as a result of a violation of the Sherman Act.[14]

In the *Microsoft* litigation the states' long-recognized power to seek equitable relief for Sherman Act violations formed the basis for the states' Sherman Act suit and for the claim of some of the states to a remedy different from the one to which the Justice Department and the other states agreed. Although Microsoft broadly attacked the states' power to seek a separate remedy, Judge Kollar-Kotelly rejected Microsoft's arguments, noting that it was "beyond dispute" that the states could bring their own suits for injunctive relief under the federal antitrust laws and could seek the equitable relief that they felt was appropriate, even if they disagreed with the Justice

Department.[15] Although she ultimately rejected the states' effort to augment the remedies that Microsoft had negotiated with the Justice Department and some of the states, the judge never questioned their authority to seek it.

The Enforcement System of the European Union

Europe didn't enter the field of enforcing competition law until 1957, when it adopted the Treaty of Rome, which included the two competition-law provisions that remain in force today (originally denoted as Articles 85 and 86, covering restraints of trade and abuse of dominance, and today renumbered as Articles 101 and 102). These provisions were grounded in the post-World War II effort to create Europe-wide markets free of government and private restraints that would impair the development of a single "common market."[16] When the Treaty of Rome was signed there were only six members of what was then called the European Economic Community, and EEC institutions were just being formed. At that time Germany was the only member state with a full antitrust law, and that law had only just become effective (after years of political opposition).[17]

Lacking the support of strong enforcement by member states, the European Commission initially chose to centralize its authority. It took an expansive view of what affected "trade between the Member States" under the Treaty, thereby narrowing the scope of the member states' exclusive jurisdiction over local matters, and restricted the ability of the member states to apply the treaty's provisions in their domestic courts.[18] Even where the member states could apply the treaty's provisions, they were free to do so only when the Commission hadn't initiated formal proceedings in the particular case under consideration.[19]

Much has changed since those early days. By 2013, the European Union had 28 member states, each with its own internal competition law and its own enforcement authority, and the European Commission had come to embrace the efforts of its member states' National Competition Authorities (NCAs). Under the Commission's 2004 Modernization Regulation, the NCAs have significant power to enforce the competition-law provisions of the Treaty, which the Commission and the NCAs are to apply "in close cooperation."[20] To carry out this more cooperative effort, the Commission has adopted somewhat complex rules for coordinating NCAs' actions and for allocating cases to the competition authority that is "well placed" to act (which may end up being the Commission itself[21]).

Although the NCAs are given substantial responsibility for enforcing EU competition law, member states are less free than U.S. states are to pursue their own approaches to competition law. Member states are forbidden from finding that practices violate domestic law if they are lawful under Article 101.[22] When a member state applies the treaty's provisions to acts that are "already the subject of a Commission decision," its decision cannot "run counter to the decision adopted by the Commission."[23] Once the Commission initiates a proceeding, NCAs are no longer competent to apply the Treaty's competition-law provisions, although there is still some room for applying domestic law and although prior consultation with the member state is required.[24] But even with these restrictions, the NCAs have been very active, bringing many more cases than the Commission itself both for cartel practices and for abuse of dominance.[25]

A more important difference between the European and U.S. antitrust enforcement systems is the underdevelopment of private antitrust enforcement in Europe. Private actions for damages can be brought only in member states' courts, and there is an "astonishing diversity" in the member states' legal regimes relevant to such actions.[26] Many factors have limited the use of private actions in the member states so far, among them the general unavailability of mechanisms for collective litigation (such as class actions), limited discovery procedures, difficult standing and proof requirements, single damages, limited admissibility of expert economic testimony, disapproval of contingency fee arrangements with attorneys, the general rule that the losing party pays the winning party's costs, and a lack of judges educated in competition matters. In 2004 the Commission began an effort to increase private enforcement in member states' courts, hoping that an increase in private litigation would augment the Commission's resources, increase deterrence, promote a "culture of competition," and provide "direct justice" (that is, compensation to those injured by antitrust violations). So far, however, the Commission's efforts have had very limited success.[27]

International Enforcement and the Globalization of Antitrust

Although the first wave of modern antitrust laws came in the immediate post-World War II period (in Japan in 1947, in the United Kingdom in 1948, and in Germany and the European Community in 1957), the most spectacular increase in antitrust legislation began in the 1990s, with the fall of communism. The belief that markets are the preferable mechanism for organizing an economy became widespread, and countries were given an assortment of incentives to adopt competition laws to bolster those markets. The incentives included technical assistance from the United States and the European Union, funding from the World Bank, support for membership in the World Trade Organization, and, for some European countries, the promise of membership in the European Union.[28] By the end of 1996, 70 countries had competition laws of some kind, and 61 percent of those laws had been adopted since 1990.[29] By the early 2000s, the number of jurisdictions with antitrust laws had risen to approximately 85, and by 2010 the number had increased to approximately 110, and both China and India adopted modern competition-law regimes.[30] Thus there arose the possibility of increased antitrust enforcement around the world, by countries at very different stages of development with very different economies, institutional structures, resources, and expertise.

Globalization has also led to an increase in the application of national antitrust law to conduct occurring outside national boundaries. "Extraterritorial" application of domestic antitrust law hasn't only raised the possibility of conflict among jurisdictions; it has also raised the possibility that jurisdictions may use their domestic antitrust law to favor domestic industries over non-domestic competitors whose actions have significant anticompetitive effects within their national borders.

For the United States, extraterritoriality isn't a novel phenomenon. International markets have been important since the earliest days of U.S. antitrust enforcement, as have efforts to apply U.S. law to conduct occurring abroad. Although there was some early dispute about the territorial scope of the Sherman Act, jurisdiction over conduct occurring outside the United States but with effects within the United States has been accepted since 1945, when the *Alcoa* case applied the Sherman Act to a cartel of non-U.S. aluminum producers whose conduct could have affected U.S. commerce.[31] The Justice Department has also had a long interest in stopping international cartels; attempting to do so was a major part of its enforcement program under Thurman Arnold's leadership from 1939 to 1943.

What is new in the United States is the sustained interest since the early 1990s in criminal prosecutions of substantial international price fixing cartels and the high number of cross-border transactions, particularly mergers that the federal and state agencies review.[32] In both areas this has led to more occasions for applying U.S. law to non-U.S. companies for conduct some of which occurs outside the United States.

A parallel development has occurred in Europe. In 1981 the European Commission prosecuted a cartel of producers of wood pulp that included a U.S. export trade association that had been given an antitrust exemption under U.S. law.[33] In 1988 the European Court of Justice upheld the Commission's assertion of jurisdiction in the case, giving the Commission effective control over conduct occurring outside of Europe that affected European markets.[34] One year later the European Commission adopted its first fully articulated Merger Regulation, applicable to mergers with a "Community dimension."[35] The combination of the Merger Regulation and the wood-pulp cartel decision has enabled the Commission to review multinational mergers even if none of the firms were located within Europe. This led to an increase in mandatory pre-merger filings by international corporations simultaneously subject to U.S. and European law and, of course, set up the possibility for conflicting decisions on multinational mergers by the European Commission and by U.S. enforcement agencies.

Despite the increased potential for conflict among diverse institutional enforcers, conflict isn't the only possible outcome. In fact, in some areas a growing consensus on fundamental principles of competition law has emerged. Cartel enforcement is the prime example. During the 1970s, governments outside the United States were often hostile to U.S. antitrust enforcement against non-U.S. companies operating cartels that affected the United States. Over time, however, this hostility has waned. Today most countries strongly favor the prosecution of international price fixing cartels and welcome the U.S. Justice Department's efforts to prosecute non-U.S. companies and their executives. Similarly, a somewhat common analytical methodology has emerged in the merger area, with the result that disputes in particular cases have been rare, although those that have occurred have been well publicized.[36]

Managing Diversity

In light of the possibility that institutional diversity and concurrent enforcement authority can give rise to conflicts among agencies, particularly as transactions and effects cross jurisdictional boundaries, antitrust agencies have adopted a variety of approaches to manage diversity and minimize conflict. These approaches haven't ended conflict, but they have reduced its likelihood.

Efforts within the United States

Whatever the possibilities for conflict between the Federal Trade Commission and the Department of Justice that Congress failed to address when it established the FTC, the two agencies have most often avoided major confrontations by dividing their responsibilities. Before 1950, for example, the Justice Department rarely filed suit under the Clayton Act's provisions dealing with mergers or exclusive dealing, despite the grant of dual jurisdiction in 1914, while the FTC filed a substantial number of complaints involving both practices. On the other hand, the Justice Department necessarily handled all Sherman Act criminal prosecutions (as we have already noted, it has exclusive authority to represent the United States in criminal matters), while both agencies handled non-criminal pricing conspiracies (with the FTC being slightly more active).[37] It was not until 1938 that the FTC and the Justice Department entered into an informal agreement to determine which agency should handle a particular investigation, an agreement not formalized until 1948.[38]

In the modern era the division of responsibility has been most important in merger enforcement. In 1976 Congress required merging parties to provide pre-merger notification to both federal agencies simultaneously, relying on the agencies themselves to determine which mergers each would investigate but providing no explicit statutory directives.[39] This led the agencies to improve the existing liaison procedures—an effort that has proved problematic at times despite ongoing efforts to agree on a "clearance" method for allocating cases efficiently. Public "turf battles" between the two agencies have occasionally broken into public view.[40]

By contrast, state enforcement agencies don't divide up enforcement responsibilities among themselves or with the federal agencies. Instead, even though each state is legally independent, the states have developed mechanisms for cooperating in multistate investigations and litigation. Indeed, as a general matter, the most significant state antitrust cases since the 1980s have been brought as multistate cases involving the cooperative efforts of varying numbers of state enforcement agencies, depending on the interest of each individual state in the particular matter as well as on the resources that individual states have available at the time.

The organizational vehicle for cooperation among state enforcers is the National Association of Attorneys General (NAAG). Through its central office in Washington, NAAG has helped to coordinate the states' efforts in investigation, litigation, lobbying, and training.[41] In addition, the states, through NAAG, have formalized some of the relationships that have evolved to handle multistate merger enforcement, joint state and federal merger enforcement, and joint state and federal criminal investigations.[42] As a result there are numerous examples not only of multistate cooperative effort, but also of cooperation among groups of states and the federal enforcement agencies, particularly in the area of merger enforcement.[43] Open conflict has been rare.

Just as the relationship between the Department of Justice and the Federal Trade Commission doesn't always work smoothly, these formal and informal mechanisms don't guarantee a lack of conflict. As the *Microsoft* litigation itself shows, sometimes state coalitions can degenerate in the course of litigation as states (or groups of states) pursue unique theories of liability or seek their own remedies.[44] In addition, states have the ability to file suit on their own without regard to what other enforcers choose to do. This can lead a state to file suit even though the federal government has also sued the same defendant on similar grounds, or has settled a suit with the same defendant, or has decided not to sue the same defendant.[45]

Private litigants engage in similar collaborative efforts with government enforcers. Private enforcers often bring litigation after a government suit has been filed, often called follow-on or complementary litigation; much of the private Microsoft litigation was of this variety. This type of litigation makes use of earlier government efforts and furthers the deterrence goal of government enforcement. It is also becoming increasingly frequent for private and government enforcers to investigate a particular practice at the same time, which results in the sharing of investigative information, joint litigation for damages, coordinated settlements, and even, on occasion, the filing of separate suits against the same defendant.[46] Of course, as with federal and state enforcers, private litigants don't always agree with the views of other enforcement agencies. They remain free to bring suits that government enforcers decline, leaving the courts to decide whether the private litigants are correct in their view of what constitutes a violation of the antitrust laws and to determine appropriate remedies for violations.[47]

International Efforts

On the international level, coordination is now managed in a number of formal and informal ways.

Formally, the European Union manages the relationship between the European Commission and the countries that are members of the EU through the European Competition Network, which it established by regulation in 2004.[48] The Commission's view of this collaborative effort, however, is more limited than the U.S. approach, applying only to cooperation among "two or three" of the national competition authorities, after which the Commission is to handle the matter exclusively.[49] The Commission doesn't work jointly with national authorities on prosecutions in the way that federal enforcement agencies work with state attorney generals' offices. The European Union has thus created a more formally hierarchical network, in contrast to the flatter, informal network that functions in the United States and reflects the constitutional role of federalism.[50]

A number of countries have also signed formal bilateral cooperation agreements that increase the ability of the involved jurisdictions to coordinate investigations and exchange information in competition-enforcement matters.[51] Some of the agreements have included a requirement of "positive" comity, that is, giving the local jurisdiction the opportunity to pursue a matter before another jurisdiction acts. This principle has been used on occasion in U.S-EU merger enforcement, where the United States has decided it didn't have to act because the European Commission was acting and vice versa.[52]

There is also a substantial amount of informal "pick up the phone" cooperation among enforcers in many jurisdictions, and it allows much greater coordination of enforcement actions.[53] This coordination has been particularly strong in cartel enforcement. Enforcers from a number of jurisdictions often carry out simultaneous raids on corporate offices in various countries. Such raids often are followed by multijurisdictional leniency negotiations for firms that have decided to cooperate with prosecutors and by cartel prosecutions in a number of the involved jurisdictions.[54]

International coordination also was advanced by the establishment of the International Competition Network in 2001. The ICN isn't a traditional bricks-and-mortar international agency with a headquarters and an independent staff; rather, it is a virtual organization designed to bring enforcement agencies together to share enforcement experiences, undertake studies of various competition policy questions, provide additional training to build expertise and agency capacity, and develop non-binding recommendations on "best practices" that individual authorities will then have the option to adopt or not. Membership in the ICN is limited to governmental antitrust enforcement agencies, but it receives substantial input from non-governmental organizations and from private lawyers who serve as advisers. The result has been a variety of reports setting out "guiding principles" and "recommended practices" for merger notification and review (an issue of particular concern to international businesses faced with multijurisdictional filing requirements), manuals relating to "good practices" in cartel enforcement, and a movement to enunciate substantive legal rules.[55]

The General Case for Institutional Diversity

Today's antitrust enforcement system is highly developed, diverse, and decentralized. This diversity is now managed in a way that reduces conflict and promotes cooperative outcomes, but this management comes at a cost and cannot eliminate all conflict. Are the benefits of institutional diversity sufficient to outweigh the costs of dealing with multiple, overlapping jurisdictions and the costs of occasional conflicts? Should we retain the present model of decentralized antitrust enforcement, or would we be better off if we were to move toward more centralization in the institutions of antitrust enforcement?

The case for decentralized antitrust enforcement rests on two propositions. The first is that decentralization itself offers certain benefits: it fosters policy diversity and innovation, it maximizes enforcement resources, and it mirrors our federal constitutional structure. The second is that decentralization allows for competition in law enforcement, guarding against prosecutorial default and political capture. The result of both is better enforcement than would be produced by a more centralized system.

Decentralization and Competition Policy

The first major benefit of decentralized enforcement agencies is policy diversity. Policy diversity is more likely with decentralized enforcement because different agencies will probably reflect different interests and constituencies, along with different institutional approaches. Different agencies can also develop different specializations (whether by knowledge of different industries or different remedial approaches), which can then provide comparative advantage in dealing with particular competition problems. True, different policies can be hashed out internally in a single agency, but "not invented here" and other bureaucratic obstacles can transform diversity into unwelcome dissent and reduce the chances that different policies will emerge and be adopted. Structuring a system that makes policy diversity more likely also reduces the risk that antitrust violations will go undetected or unremedied.

In the United States the institutional design was intendedly diverse. Operational control over the Antitrust Division and the Federal Trade Commission is structured differently (a single head for the former, five commissioners for the latter), and the two agencies determine policy direction separately. As a division of the Department of Justice, the Antitrust Division is a part of the executive branch and hence is more closely tied to the attorney general and to the White House and to the goals of other cabinet-level agencies. The Federal Trade Commission, as an "independent administrative agency," is separate from the executive branch and subject to congressional oversight.

This diversity has produced some important differences in enforcement interests. In recent years, for example, the Federal Trade Commission has been very active in intellectual property issues; the Department of Justice has relegated them to a much lower priority.[56] The two agencies have also disagreed over the proper approach to single-firm conduct. After joint hearings that were expected to lead to a joint report on the federal agencies' views of single-firm conduct, the Justice Department unilaterally issued a report in 2008 setting out its approach. Three of the four sitting FTC Commissioners publicly disagreed with the Justice Department's report and issued their own formal statements.[57] Merger enforcement can also differ. For example, the rate of merger enforcement by the Justice Department fell during the Bush administration and has risen during the Obama administration, but the rate of merger enforcement by the FTC stayed relatively steady during the Bush and Obama administrations.[58] Even the different structures of the two agencies can matter. The FTC's multiple-commissioner model provides a legitimate way for dissenting commissioners to air their disagreements over cases that the FTC has chosen not to bring, whereas the option of public dissent isn't available to Justice Department officials.[59]

Many have argued not just that decentralization can produce diversity in policy, but also that institutional diversity is important for producing and testing innovations in government policies. The argument, developed during the 1930s in the context of a debate over the desirability of allowing the states to experiment with legislation to cure the ills of industrialization and the Great Depression, was most famously articulated by Justice Louis Brandeis in 1932: "It is one of the happy incidents of the federal system that a single courageous state may, if its citizens choose, serve as a laboratory; and try novel social and economic experiments without risk to the rest of the country."[60]

Policy diversity and innovation may be particularly important in antitrust enforcement, a field in which views of what constitutes optimal antitrust policy necessarily shift over time. Not only does antitrust enforcement reflect political values that are subject to change (views on corporate size and economic concentration being important examples), but the economic theories that support antitrust are also subject to constant empirical testing and reevaluation. We shouldn't expect the social science of economics to be more fixed than the natural sciences of physics and biology, which rely on experimentation and are subject to evolution. Neither should we expect antitrust enforcement to converge on an unchanging policy equilibrium. Diversity in the institutions of antitrust enforcement helps to test orthodox views and is an important mechanism for ensuring the continuing evolution of antitrust policy.[61]

A second important benefit of decentralization is that it can increase the resources available for enforcement. Different agencies are likely to face different budgetary constraints, even within the same system of government and certainly if they are in different governmental systems. They may also have different champions in the budgetary process. Having different agencies involved in enforcement can mean that there will be more capacity to initiate antitrust enforcement at any given time, or that through collaboration more resources can be brought to a given task than any single agency might be able to muster. In the U.S. system, for example, the Department of Justice and the Federal Trade Commission have different amounts budgeted for their antitrust-enforcement missions.[62] States' enforcement budgets vary both in absolute amounts and in the ways in which states fund their enforcement efforts; occasionally, separate federal funding has been made available to augment state resources.[63]

A third benefit of decentralization is its consistency with constitutional structure. Today's enforcement system grows out of the structural aspects of our political system. Although state governments' antitrust enforcement and even states' antitrust laws probably could be preempted by Congress, efforts to centralize antitrust enforcement in the federal government would have to contend with the politics and the structure of federalism, and such efforts would have ramifications for areas beyond antitrust (for example, regulation of financial institutions and of the environment). Indeed, even though the Antitrust Modernization Commission began with a mandate to assess the proper role of the states in antitrust enforcement, its final recommendations for changes in state enforcement practice were very limited, in part because it recognized that "principles of federalism and practical political concerns" counseled in favor of deference to state interests.[64]

Beyond constitutional principle, however, federalism offers some distinct benefits to antitrust. Because the states have historically had an independent role in articulating competition policy, their views can increase support for antitrust policy, leading courts to be more attentive to antitrust arguments in cases of strong local concern. Local enforcement agencies can also provide greater understanding of local markets (supermarkets or hospitals being good examples) than a central agency might have, and such understanding may lead to better enforcement decisions. The result can be more effective antitrust enforcement—a point that has come to be appreciated in Europe, where the European Commission has increased the role of member states' enforcement agencies.

The political immutability of decentralized antitrust enforcement is even clearer on an international level. When the U.S. economy changed after the Civil War, and business conduct began affecting many states, the obvious solution was to use the power of the federal government to deal with national economic problems. That approach was taken in areas as diverse as fraud, railroad regulation, and antitrust. But such an approach isn't available on an international level. With the failure of the effort to give the World Trade Organization some jurisdiction over transnational antitrust matters, there is little choice but to continue the current pragmatic networking effort to connect independent national agencies—an effort that tries to combine the virtues of diversity with those of cooperative mechanisms.[65]

Decentralization is not without costs. First, there are the transactions costs in coordinating action and dividing responsibility among agencies. Second, diversity can impose costs on the businesses that are subject to different enforcement approaches. Compliance costs may increase if multiple enforcers have different views of competition policy. Different enforcement views might lead companies either to adapt to the most interventionist agency's approach or to vary their business practices from jurisdiction to jurisdiction in order to stay within the law.[66] Third, decentralized enforcement can invite "forum shopping." With a single enforcer, parties must present all their arguments to a single decision maker around whom they can't do an end run. If there are multiple enforcers, parties can look for a more sympathetic enforcer to consider their cause.

Although each of these points has some merit, perhaps the most worrisome is the concern about "forum shopping"—that is, the concern that a complainant will look for an agency that is more favorably disposed to its point of view than to a public-interest view of antitrust policy. This could be of particular concern in an antitrust case, because the complainant might be a losing competitor trying to get the government to bring it the success that the market has denied. Of course, a single agency can be captured as well. Sectoral regulation is usually done by a single agency, and that is where we have been most concerned about capture. As a general matter, however, agency capture has been of lesser concern in antitrust, in part because the enforcement agencies aren't in charge of any one industry and in part because the agencies are very aware of the potential for capture and have shown an ability to discount complaints so as to be certain that they aren't protecting competitors when taking action. If anything, having multiple enforcers might reduce the possibility of capture. Agency officials concerned about capture can check their enforcement views with agencies that have decided not to go forward with a suit; and agencies that are willing to be captured run a greater risk of exposure if other agencies decline to bring suit.

Decentralization and Institutional Competition

Will decentralization result in *better* antitrust enforcement, or is it just likely to produce *more* enforcement? Critics argue that diverse policies and multiple enforcement agencies will lack the coherence that centralized enforcement can produce, leading to excessive enforcement and bad results—that the result will be a race to the bottom, not a race to the top. We disagree.

In our view, the check on bad policy diversity and the incentive for good enforcement come from the process of institutional competition in a decentralized enforcement system. Institutional competition constrains abuse by enforcement agencies, and incentivizes good behavior, in much the same way that market competition does with regard to business firms. True, government agencies don't compete in the same way that businesses do. Nevertheless, we can identify four ways in which competition among government institutions can check what might otherwise be self-interested behavior, leading, instead, to enforcement action that serves the broader public interest.

The first way in which institutional competition can check enforcement abuse is through yardstick competition, which occurs when one agency's performance is used to measure that of another agency. The idea is a familiar one in the context of regulating public utilities: regulatory agencies have compared the rates and performance of different firms as a way to test whether requested rates are "just and reasonable" and should be approved.[67] In the antitrust area, the legislators who fund the enforcement agencies and, ultimately, the voters who elect the legislators must make judgments about the quality of enforcement agencies' decisions. These judgments are very difficult to make, however, even for professional observers. Yardstick competition, by providing comparisons of enforcement performance, can help decision makers to form more accurate judgments, thereby disciplining or rewarding antitrust enforcement agencies for poorer or better performance.

The second check can come from regulatory competition. The idea here is that jurisdictions seek to attract mobile factors of production so as to improve the economic welfare of their citizens. One way to do this is to provide attractive regulatory regimes.[68] Applying this theory to antitrust, we can see both general and specific aspects of antitrust enforcement that can make economies stronger or weaker, and more or less attractive to investment. For example, antitrust rules can protect competitors or instead provide a more open market system that protects competition, can favor consumer welfare or producer welfare, can give manufacturers a free hand in arranging their distribution systems or instead protect discount retailers from termination for price cutting, and can be permissive or intolerant of cartel activity. Regulatory competition provides pressure to adopt whichever of these approaches works better and produces economic benefit for the citizens of a particular jurisdiction.

The third way that competition checks enforcement agency behavior—particularly the behavior of dominant agencies—is maverick competition. In the industrial world, a maverick is a firm with some incentive to deviate from the consensus within an industry—a firm that is "an observably disruptive force."[69] Economists have pointed out that monopoly firms have incentives to protect the status quo and to avoid disruptive technologies that will undercut their current products. In the world of government antitrust enforcement, dominant enforcement agencies may similarly favor the conventional approach; non-dominant enforcement agencies can provide similar disruptive force. For example, developing countries can remind enforcers in developed countries that antitrust law can have distributive effects that developed countries might ignore. Private enforcers suing for damages on behalf of injured consumers can remind public enforcers that consumer welfare means paying attention to practices that injure actual consumers. Dominant agencies will not necessarily respond to maverick enforcers, but the existence of mavericks at least provides some external prod that may lead dominant agencies to consider approaches that they otherwise might not have.

The final disciplining force that comes from enforcement agency competition is competition over the norms of antitrust enforcement. Norms are the consensus views of behavior that a particular group believes to be correct. Scholars have long pointed out that social norms extend beyond strict legal requirements to encompass customs and standards that groups adopt and apply to themselves and which help to control the behavior of the members of the group.[70]

From the very beginning of antitrust law in the United States there has been a tradition of vigorous policy debate over the propriety of various enforcement norms.[71] This debate in part is a result of the open-textured language that Congress consciously chose when enacting the Sherman Act in 1890, but it also is a consequence of the fact that political views regarding the central values of antitrust law—our concerns about monopoly, concentrated economic power, and the role of the state in the economy—are constantly changing.

At any particular time, the norms of antitrust enforcement can be shaped by this policy debate. The report of the Antitrust Modernization Commission, for example, can be seen as a way to articulate and shape current enforcement norms, even though the report resulted in no changes in U.S. antitrust legislation. Similarly, the effort of the International Competition Network is consciously directed at articulating "best practices" in various enforcement areas in the context of an international legal regime that lacks any transnational antitrust enforcement agency. In these cases and others, antitrust enforcement agencies, along with interested scholars and lawyers, contend over the correct approach to antitrust rules and enforcement practices in an effort to gain legitimacy for their views. Some views get marginalized; others become the consensus norms, to be tested through actual enforcement practice.

The theoretical benefits of institutional competition aren't necessarily realized in every aspect of today's antitrust system. Yardstick competition could be very important, but it depends on whether those who oversee institutional performance actually compare different results, as state regulatory agencies often do.[72] Regulatory competition doesn't apply within the U.S. federal system, either between the Antitrust Division and the Federal Trade Commission or between the federal agencies and the states, but it could be operative on the international level. Maverick competition can be particularly important where smaller agencies operate within a larger national system, as is the case in the United States. Norms competition is internal within the world of antitrust policy making, but this competition can matter when enforcers need to convince other decision makers— courts, for example—that their policies are correct.

Nevertheless, there are good examples of each type of competitive effect. Yardstick competition is implicated when congressional oversight hearings separately examine the records of the two federal enforcement agencies.[73] Regulatory competition is a way of understanding the general spread of antitrust enforcement in the 1990s, as well as the increasing intolerance of cartels shown by enforcers in jurisdictions such as Europe and Japan. Policy makers saw that antitrust law generally, and cartel enforcement specifically, could lead to more robust economies with lower prices, to the advantage of both producers and consumers. Many countries wanted the economic benefits of these policies. Maverick competition has come from state antitrust enforcers (as when the Reagan administration cut back on merger enforcement in the 1980s) and from the Federal Trade Commission (as when several of its commissioners perceived the Justice Department's Section 2 Report as radically non-interventionist). And norms competition has been apparent in many areas—notably in merger enforcement, an area in which the federal agencies have consciously used the Horizontal Merger Guidelines to advance their policy views both nationally (particularly in the absence of any legislative changes in substantive merger law for more than 60 years and no Supreme Court involvement for more than 30) and internationally (the U.S. agencies have been quite successful in moving other jurisdictions much closer to U.S. analytical approaches).[74]

It would be Panglossian to say that the competitive process in government enforcement always drives enforcement to the "right result," as it would be to say the same for competition in product markets. Market failures will always occur. But it is important to recognize that even if competitive forces don't always work, and even if the potential benefits of institutional competition aren't always realized, institutional monopoly lacks any of these competitive checks. This further reinforces our view that the default position should be institutional decentralization, with diverse enforcement institutions allowed to manage the system in a way that achieves the most effective combination of competition and collaboration, just as is done in the industrial sector.

Microsoft and Institutional Diversity

The *Microsoft* litigation provides an important test case for evaluating the theoretical arguments for and against institutional diversity, both within the United States and across different jurisdictions. As we noted at the outset of this chapter, the collective enforcement effort directed at Microsoft triggered calls in Congress for institutional reform. The litigation produced a high degree of policy competition and took advantage of the strengths (or overcame the weaknesses) of enforcement agencies with different institutional capacities. On the other hand, the record of coordination among enforcement agencies was mixed; at least for a while, there was some discord among various enforcement agencies, both in the United States and between the Justice Department and non-U.S. agencies. In the end, however, it is hard to imagine as successful an outcome to the *Microsoft* litigation had enforcement been centralized.

The Litigation
The virtuous story was on display from the very beginning of the litigation, when the Federal Trade Commission deadlocked in its original investigation and the Department of Justice then decided to continue it. Without a competing enforcement authority, the antitrust investigation of Microsoft's behavior might have quickly come to an end.

Two years later, when the Department of Justice began its investigation of the bundling of Internet Explorer into Windows, the states were also pushing ahead with their own investigation. Here again, but on the states' side, the existence of multiple enforcers was critical. Political pressure forced Texas (the state that had initiated the investigation) to withdraw, but other states involved in the investigation were able to continue it. As for the actual decision to file suit, it is possible that neither the Justice Department nor the states would have filed alone—the former out of caution, the latter for lack of resources. Filing together, however, solved those problems.

The complaints that the states and the Justice Department filed against Microsoft were quite similar, even though the states and the Justice Department didn't coordinate with regard to their contents, but there were some potentially important differences. The states' complaint included a count directed at Microsoft's conduct involving its dominant word processing program, Word, and sought relief that the Justice Department didn't request relating to interoperability between the browser and the Windows operating system. The exigencies of time and Judge Jackson's trial orders forced the states to abandon their somewhat separate substantive foray against Word (an effort that they never resumed after the trial), but their focus on interoperability with Windows was a continuing concern in the litigation and at the relief stage and was part of the final consent decree.

At the trial itself, the federal and state enforcers did a good job of managing diversity, combining their resources in an effort that produced a substantial victory for the antitrust enforcement agencies. That joint effort continued through the appeal, the D.C. Circuit upholding the basic monopolization case that the plaintiffs had brought. The differences on remedy, hinted at in the original state complaint, didn't emerge again until the very end of the litigation, when, after a change of administrations in Washington brought a negotiated settlement, some of the states tried unsuccessfully to persuade Judge Kollar-Kotelly to impose a remedy stronger than the one that the Justice Department and some of the states were willing to accept in settlement of the litigation.

During the litigation the states were criticized for their conduct during the Posner mediation process. Having the states at the negotiating table was said to have led to the failure of the mediation, the implication being that the mediation would have produced a settlement had the states not been involved. It was this experience that led some to urge that states no longer be allowed to engage in antitrust enforcement.

Criticism of the states in the Posner mediation doesn't make the case for more centralized enforcement, however. For one thing, in the Posner mediation the states lacked the power to derail any settlement that the other two parties might have wanted. The later mediation during the Bush administration, and the settlement agreement it produced, showed that the Justice Department and Microsoft were perfectly capable of reaching an agreement without the states' consent when both sides wanted to do so. Thus, the states weren't to blame for the breakdown in the mediation process. For another, the criticism of the states' position assumes that settlement was the appropriate resolution of the litigation at that point. The states were less sure, advancing the position that there was public benefit in having the district court issue an opinion applying antitrust law to Microsoft's conduct. Subsequent events show that the states had a point. There is a benefit in having one of the most important antitrust cases ever brought fully resolved in the courts, and the court of appeals' decision in the case has had an important influence on the development of antitrust law. If the states' participation actually made settlement more difficult, that might be viewed as a positive benefit of diverse antitrust enforcement rather than a cost.

The European side of the litigation adds further support to the arguments in favor of decentralization. In 1998, with the Justice Department's resources committed to the problem of the exclusion of the browser, Sun couldn't have convinced the department to expand its efforts to include the interoperability problem on the server side. Instead, Sun filed a formal complaint with the European Commission, which that commission's rules required it to consider. In this way the existence of multiple enforcers significantly expanded the public resources available for antitrust enforcement, bringing antitrust attention to an aspect of Microsoft's behavior that wasn't encompassed in the U.S. investigation.

Of course, Sun might have been engaged in forum shopping, looking for a jurisdiction more favorable to its claims than the United States. The usual antitrust policy concern with forum shopping—that it might lead to protecting ineffective competitors from stronger rivals—might be exacerbated in the international context if the ineffective competitor is an in-state company and the stronger rival is an out-of-state company, In *Microsoft*, however, there were no European competitors to protect. Sun, and later RealNetworks, were as "out of state" as Microsoft in Europe. The Commission's incentives in this case, if there were any, would have been to protect European consumers, but protecting consumers is a proper goal of antitrust policy. To the extent that the Commission's enforcement decision created out-of-state spillovers, these spillovers would be to the benefit of consumers in other jurisdictions, again perfectly consistent with appropriate antitrust policy and the recognition that the conduct of U.S. firms that operate globally will necessarily affect consumers outside the United States.

Coordination among agencies is another potential source of costs and benefits from decentralized enforcement. Although coordination between the European Commission and U.S. enforcement authorities is now routine in merger and cartel cases, it hasn't been routine in monopolization cases, and there is no indication that the Commission coordinated its *Microsoft* investigation with the U.S. Department of Justice.

The reasons for the lack of coordination in *Microsoft* aren't clear. It may be that abuse-of-dominance cases are "one-off" affairs, with unique factual settings requiring intensive investigation. Or perhaps it can be traced to the different views about single-firm conduct that Europe and the United States had during the Bush years, although this wouldn't explain the lack of coordination in the early phases of the U.S. and EU investigations of Microsoft, when enforcement positions were more closely aligned.

Whatever the reasons for the lack of coordination, one lesson of the *Microsoft* litigation is that antitrust enforcement would benefit from increased coordination in dominant-firm investigations. Government enforcers are always at an informational disadvantage in antitrust investigations. Exchanging information across jurisdictions can help all investigators understand the monopoly firm's conduct (much as, in the United States, the federal government and the states benefited from exchanging information). Information exchanges will not always prevent jurisdictions from taking different positions that reflect their views, nor should they, but early coordination might make it more difficult for disappointed competitors to forum shop. Pooling of knowledge across countries might also allow enforcement agencies to focus more clearly on the international effects of the remedies they are considering, perhaps leading to more effective remedies (or, at least, helping to avoid inconsistent ones).

Remedies

The remedies aspect of the litigation demonstrates a different play of diverse policy views, institutional strengths, and political support. On the positive side, it is clear that the range of remedies would have been far narrower had only one jurisdiction been involved. The United States rejected code removal as a way of dealing with the technological bundling; Europe and Korea both ordered it, without any apparent technical problems in its implementation. Europe and Korea eventually chose a form of "must-carry" regulation in an effort to remedy browser bundling; the U.S. Department of Justice abandoned that approach early in the litigation (after including it in its original complaint), and, as we discussed in chapter 5, Sun was unsuccessful in its own effort to secure that remedy from the U.S. federal courts. There would have been no fines imposed on Microsoft without the European and Korean cases; on the other hand, damages recoveries for market exclusion and overcharges were possible only under U.S. law.

Combining the financial penalties imposed by all jurisdictions probably increased worldwide antitrust deterrence and achieved (or perhaps over-achieved) antitrust enforcement's goal of compensating those injured by antitrust violations.

The most difficult aspect of the remedies imposed on Microsoft was the requirement for protocol disclosure. Mandatory disclosure not only presented technical issues (treated similarly in the United States and the European Union), but also presented a policy problem with regard to setting the royalties for licensing the protocols. In the United States, rate regulation is generally considered antithetical to antitrust remedies; the Europeans have a more interventionist approach. Nevertheless, even the U.S. enforcers needed to consider the royalty rates Microsoft would be allowed to charge; ordering protocol disclosure would have been useless if Microsoft were permitted to charge rates that discouraged competitors from using the protocols.

U.S. enforcers dealt with the royalty through negotiation with Microsoft, so it is difficult to tell how they ended up deciding that Microsoft's rates were, in fact, reasonable, but the European Commission dealt with rates more openly. The Commission made clear that its goal was to make sure that potential competitors would have access to the protocols, and not to be so concerned with whether Microsoft was getting a sufficient reward to incentivize innovation. As we explored in chapter 6, in its view protocol disclosure would create more, not less of an incentive to innovate in server operating systems. With this goal, the Commission's more activist approach was plainly more successful than that of the Justice Department.[75] Rates were far lower for the European protocols than the U.S. protocols. In addition, Microsoft's pledge not to enforce any intellectual property rights against nonprofit open-source users should have aided the firms that presented the strongest competitive challenge to Microsoft. Diversification thus led to potentially more effective remedies.

Enforcement diversity also produced gains in the U.S. remedy proceedings. The states that negotiated the settlement along with the Justice Department were able to secure two significant remedy additions to the settlement decree. One was the establishment of the Technical Committee to assist in monitoring compliance with the decree; the other was the requirement of communications protocol disclosure. Judge Kollar-Kotelly, who subsequently wrote that the Technical Committee was "one of the most successful aspects of the Final Judgments, because it has been invaluable in facilitating the Plaintiffs' enforcement efforts," described the disclosure requirements as "the cornerstone of the Court-ordered and Court-approved remedies and, as the Final Judgments' most forward-looking provision, ... the basis on which the parties and the Court aspired to have the applications barrier to entry broken down over time."[76] It is unlikely that either of these provisions would have been in the decree without the states' participation.[77]

The ongoing administration of the consent decree also benefited from multiple enforcers. All of the state plaintiffs participated in the administration of the decree (even those that had originally opposed the settlement), along with the federal government, extending the resources devoted to monitoring the decree. More important, when Microsoft continued to delay complying with the protocol-disclosure requirement, it was the states that convinced Judge Kollar-Kotelly to extend the termination date of the decree until she could be certain of Microsoft's compliance. In so doing, the states performed the important "backstop" function that multiple enforcers can provide.

A review of the remedies, however, also shows that the potential benefits of diversity were somewhat muted. Although the debate about remedies in the United States provided a rich range of possibilities, the government plaintiffs were ultimately rather conservative in their choices, and even, in some ways, in the restructuring proposal itself (for example, not breaking Microsoft into three competing companies as some suggested). Certainly the plaintiffs' eventual unwillingness to pursue a structural remedy after the U.S. court of appeals' decision, whatever the legal or tactical reasons for that choice, limited the experimental value of diverse enforcement.

There is a second way in which the remedies part of the litigation failed to live up to the experimental possibilities that multiple enforcement can provide. As we discussed earlier, the remedies chosen in each of the jurisdictions lacked clearly articulated goals or observable benchmarks. The lack of any testable hypotheses makes it difficult to say which of the "experiments" were good ones and which were not.

A particularly obvious example of the non-experimental quality of the remedies decisions is the European Commission's agreement to accept Microsoft's commitment to provide a ballot screen as a way to deal with browser integration. Although Korea had implemented a similar remedy, there is no indication that the European Commission inquired as to whether the Korean remedy had had any positive effect on competition. There may have been innovations in remedies, but inquiries into their effectiveness have yet to be undertaken.

The Benefits of Institutional Competition

Of the four ways in which government institutional competition can benefit the public interest, two were involved in the *Microsoft* litigation: maverick competition (from the states and Korea) and norms competition.

The states first adopted a maverick role in the 1980s, in a deliberate effort to act as a prod and as a counterweight to the Reagan administration's shift toward a less interventionist antitrust policy. The *Microsoft* litigation, however, is an unusual example of the states' willingness to carry out a sustained effort to alter the actions of the U.S. Department of Justice, the dominant institutional enforcer. The states had some success in this effort, mostly involving remedy issues, but the litigation also showed how difficult it is for a maverick to become a full substitute for the dominant enforcer (as the non-settling states unsuccessfully tried to do by offering their own approach to remedies).

Korea's maverick role was a new role for Korea and an unusual one for a relatively small non-U.S. enforcement agency. In imposing its ballot-screen remedy, the Korea Fair Trade Commission chose an affirmative remedy that other agencies had avoided. Once Microsoft acceded to that remedy, it was easier for the European Commission to impose a similar remedy, even if the Commission didn't self-consciously follow the KFTC's lead.

The *Microsoft* litigation also triggered robust norms competition regarding the proper approach to evaluating dominant-firm behavior. This area had been relatively dormant since the 1970s, when some commentators and legislators had advanced "no-fault" monopolization legislation to break up firms in certain highly concentrated industries. Even though the litigation and settlement of the monopolization case against AT&T, more than 15 years earlier, was politically contested, that case didn't arouse much debate over whether AT&T had acted improperly in suppressing competition from providers of long-distance telephone service. *Microsoft* was different from the outset, however, with its dueling narratives over the proper application of antitrust law to high-technology network industries. Over the course of the litigation, the parties contended in the courtroom, and commentators contended outside the courtroom, over the antitrust norms that should be applied to Microsoft. With the change from the Clinton administration to the Bush administration, this debate became sharper—the Bush Justice Department took a more critical and public stance toward the enforcement decisions in Europe and Korea.

Eventually the debate over Microsoft spilled beyond the confines of the specific litigation. As we noted at the outset of this chapter, Congress established the Antitrust Modernization Commission in 2001 largely for the purpose of examining the Microsoft enforcement effort, but the commission went much further in examining the state of antitrust law. After the European Commission initiated a review of its own standards for the behavior of dominant firms, in 2006, the Federal Trade Commission and the Department of Justice followed suit and held joint hearings to consider appropriate policy regarding single-firm behavior generally. In 2008 the Department of Justice, pointedly without the FTC's concurrence, issued a report summing up its view on enforcement.[78] Similarly, in 2009, the European Commission provided "guidance" on its enforcement priorities regarding dominant-firm behavior—views that differed to some extent from those expressed by the Justice Department.[79] Academic commentators continue to debate the appropriate standards for judging monopoly conduct, and official U.S. enforcement views changed again in 2009, with the Justice Department withdrawing the Section 2 report issued by its predecessor and perhaps moving back toward the economic approaches that underlay the *Microsoft* case that the Justice Department brought more than a decade ago.

The *Microsoft* litigation thus supports the view that maverick competition and norms competition can affect the behavior of the dominant enforcement agency, acting to check its conduct somewhat, and can incentivize the production of good competition policy. It is less clear whether the two other kinds of enforcement competition—yardstick competition and regulatory competition—affected the *Microsoft* litigation much. Yardstick competition requires someone to apply the measure. It is difficult to find a federal or state body that has taken a close look (or any look) at comparative enforcement efforts in the *Microsoft* case. Nor is it clear that governments (or enforcement agencies) can or do use monopolization law to compete for mobile sources of capital. Yardstick or regulatory competition may be important in other areas of antitrust enforcement, but they weren't apparent in *Microsoft*.

Conclusion

The present diverse system of antitrust enforcement in the United States starts with many pages of history. In view of the peculiarities of the history and the unplanned nature of the enforcement institutions, it is easy to make the resulting system appear to be chaotic, but it is not. In operation, enforcement agencies often cooperate, even if they also compete and even if one agency has no warrant to tell another what it must do. As a rule, the system works; instances of conflict, which do occur, are exceptions.

The arguments for a diverse and decentralized system of antitrust enforcement go beyond history and the steps that agencies have taken to manage the system in which they operate. There are good theoretical arguments for why decentralization produces benefits for antitrust enforcement: it can encourage policy diversity and experimentation, it can expand resources devoted to investigation and enforcement, and it can shadow the decentralized federal government structure into which it fits. The system is further supported by the processes of institutional competition that multiple enforcement creates—processes that can help check enforcement abuses and give agencies positive incentives to produce good results.

The benefits predicted by theory are borne out to a large degree in the *Microsoft* litigation. Looking at the litigation from its earliest genesis at the Federal Trade Commission to its most recent conclusion in Europe, it is hard to imagine a better result had one agency been in charge. Multiple agencies, with different strengths, different legal instruments, and different policy views, were necessary to produce the benefits to competition law that the *Microsoft* litigation produced. There were many aspects of the litigation and remedy to criticize, as our earlier chapters indicate. But our diverse system of antitrust enforcement isn't one of them.

9 Lessons from the *Microsoft* Cases

Microsoft has now entered the third decade of its engagement with the global system for enforcing competition policy. As we noted in chapter 1, that engagement has been almost unique in its scope and duration and has been uniquely revealing of the content and characteristics of that system. While distinctive in some ways, however, Microsoft's experience also is predictive of the future direction of antitrust enforcement, particularly for firms with dominant market positions in multiple jurisdictions. Such firms can expect global scrutiny when their conduct has a significant potential to affect competition adversely. International complexity, both substantive and institutional, is now the norm for these enterprises, inviting an assessment of this still-evolving system's strengths and weaknesses.

In this closing chapter, we consider what lessons such firms and the larger antitrust community might draw from the collective "*Microsoft* cases." To do so, we return to the questions we posed in the first chapter, seeking to answer them in light of our examination of the law, the economics, the institutions, and the remedies that influenced the resolution of the *Microsoft* cases. We will also revisit some of the competing strands of narrative that vied for supremacy among the parties and commentators, to assess whether the resolution of the public and private cases tended to support them or to debunk them. In particular, we ask these questions: Were the institutions of antitrust enforcement—the public enforcement agencies and the courts—well suited and capable of accurately judging Microsoft's conduct and doing so in a timely manner? Relatedly, were the substantive antitrust standards up to the task of judging the conduct of a "new economy" firm, such as Microsoft? Were the remedies negotiated with or imposed on Microsoft proportional to its wrongdoing and adequate to compensate the harmed, to redress the consequences of its conduct, and to deter similar conduct in the future?

A fourth question relates to a thread of narrative that emerged as the expiration date of the consent decree in the United States approached and the cases in the European Union concluded. Some critics of the cases suggested that their collective effect was to distract Microsoft from its role as a technology firm and dull its competitive edge. They argued that Microsoft became more cautious as a result of the cases and that innovation suffered; antitrust enforcement had reduced innovation, not promoted and protected it. Under this narrative, the dominant firm is portrayed as a purveyor of innovation and antitrust enforcement as its enemy. In our view, the opposite was the case. Microsoft didn't fall behind its rivals as an innovator because of antitrust enforcement; to the contrary, it invited the attention of antitrust enforcers when it fell behind in the race to innovate, and then responded by using its market power to suppress the disruptive technologies of its more innovative rivals. As we will explain, this provides a very potent lesson for competition policy in the twenty-first century.

Were the Institutions Adequate?

Recall that a major component of Microsoft's narrative on both sides of the Atlantic targeted the competence and effectiveness of the institutions of antitrust enforcement. First, it argued that those institutions were poorly equipped to understand the "new economy" and hence incapable of properly applying the antitrust laws to assess its power and its conduct. Second, summoning the memory of the U.S. government's ultimately abandoned 13-year prosecution of IBM, Microsoft argued that agencies and courts moved too slowly to effectively judge markets that functioned on "Internet time" and were continually evolving. Together these arguments constituted a plea for a laissez-faire policy toward technology industries and an indictment of rudimentary principles of rule of law—Microsoft's power and conduct were simply beyond judging in a timely and accurate fashion. Microsoft's argument extended to the content of antitrust law's prohibitions, which it viewed as outdated.

This narrative proved to be inconsistent with the actual performance of the agencies and courts, however, as well as with the evidence. The laws and the institutions of both the United States and the European Union were capable of grasping the economics of the "new economy," which in fact weren't consistently "new." The multiplicity of institutions examining Microsoft's conduct also illustrated the check-and-balance value of a diverse competition-enforcement ecosystem and created unprecedented opportunities for cooperation and for global, inter-governmental dialogue about antitrust doctrine and remedies in technology industries. Perhaps more so than ever before, the conduct of a single firm triggered a healthy exchange of views within and across jurisdictions.

Unfortunately for Microsoft, upon close examination the features of the new economy that were most significant for the analysis of its conduct tended to undermine, not support, Microsoft's position—they tended to explain its power and its incentives to restrain competition. With ready access to input from economists and commentators, the agencies and the courts thus came to understand these features of the new economy all too well. Network effects amplified Microsoft's power, which was further insulated from challenge by the applications barrier to entry. Network effects also were important in illuminating Microsoft's incentives to pursue anticompetitive strategies, including emulating its competitors' products, integrating them into Windows, and then making them irremovable. This was also true of Microsoft's decision to cease sharing its communications protocols, and of a wide range of other conduct that impaired competition. Similarly, agencies and courts had no problem understanding and accepting the premise of "leapfrog competition"—competition *for* the field, instead of within it—but Microsoft failed to demonstrate that Windows faced any genuine threat of being leapfrogged in the foreseeable future. These findings about the industry were common to the U.S. and EU cases. Lack of judicial comprehension wasn't Microsoft's problem; failure to persuade was.

Microsoft's assertions regarding its intellectual property rights and incentives to innovate similarly appeared to be overblown, which prompted agencies and courts in the U.S. and the EU to reject them as legally and economically unfounded. Again, this wasn't attributable to any institutional lack of capacity to comprehend those rights and incentives, or to a lack of sensitivity for incentives to innovate. Rather, after considering Microsoft's arguments, both jurisdictions concluded that Microsoft's interpretation of the rights provided by intellectual property laws was untenably one-sided and that it denigrated concerns about competition policy.

Overall, therefore, it doesn't appear that a lack of institutional capacity either undermined the antitrust enforcement community's ability to evaluate Microsoft's power and conduct fairly and correctly or that it hindered Microsoft's ability to advocate its best defenses. As we shall also see, neither did lack of doctrinal flexibility.

Microsoft was correct, however, that the system for enforcing competition policy moved too slowly to be effective in the context of quickly evolving technology markets—but not for the reasons it cited. Although the system wasn't too slow to judge Microsoft, it proved too plodding and cautious to protect competition from the effects of Microsoft's conduct.

Combining the specter of the failed *IBM* case with a simplistic presentation of Joseph Schumpeter's theories on innovation, Microsoft argued that events would overtake any enforcement action. In its view, the competitive landscape would evolve on its own owing to the dynamic forces that continually buffeted the software industry—the forces Schumpeter had described as a "perennial gale of creative destruction." "Creative destruction," Schumpeter argued, was the process whereby capitalism spurred on major changes by developing new consumers, new products, new markets, new methods of production and transportation, even new forms of organizations. According to Schumpeter, because of these forces even a monopolist can face intense pressure to remain innovative. This philosophy and its colorful imagery resonated with Microsoft and its experts, who fully embraced it, arguing to the antitrust enforcement agencies, the courts, and the public that at best the firm's dominance was unstable and probably fleeting. By the time competition-enforcement proceedings could be concluded, a new "market" would have already emerged.[1]

Like a number of Microsoft's arguments, this was an exaggerated tale, manufactured for purposes of the litigation and disconnected from its actual experience—and it carried with it a significant measure of irony. First, as to timing, it was clear in the U.S. cases that Judge Jackson had no intention of repeating the IBM experience. Thanks in significant part to a number of procedural techniques he invoked, the merits of the public cases, which were commenced in May of 1998, were effectively concluded with the decision of the U.S. Court of Appeals in June of 2001. For a major American antitrust case, that was extraordinary, even though post-appeal settlement discussions continued into 2002 and remedial proceedings weren't concluded until 2004. Although the European Commission's work didn't move along at an equally brisk pace, it cannot fairly be said that the fact that it took the Commission more than five years to reach a decision was due entirely to its procedures or to administrative inertia. Microsoft surely contributed to any delays. Regardless, in both jurisdictions the facts found with regard to Microsoft's market dominance and its conduct were hardly stale by the time of the final decisions. There had been no transformation of the relevant markets in the interim, as had occurred with IBM in the 1970s. Microsoft retained its dominance of the market for desktop-computer operating systems, and its dominance of the markets for browsers, streaming media players, and server operating systems was increasing. No "creative destruction" had occurred or was imminent.

Microsoft's objection to the sluggish pace of administrative and judicial process can be faulted on two other grounds. First, it is at best inconsistent to maintain that antitrust cases are complex, requiring careful consideration of voluminous technical information about markets and conduct, yet also to demand that they be resolved expeditiously. Careful and hence more accurate assessments of competition challenges may not always lend themselves to quick investigation and resolution, however "quick" is defined. Whereas the movement away from certain, inflexible rules toward more economically informed, more effects-based standards was driven by an interest in reducing the costs of errors, the more demanding evidentiary standards that now prevail aren't costless. Today's antitrust cases often require more information, and hence are more likely to involve additional decision costs, including time and significant input from enforcement institutions with often limited resources and experts, than past antitrust cases. Second, the objection can be faulted for being too narrowly focused on the remedial purposes of antitrust enforcement. The essence of the argument was that markets would outpace the courts, so eventual remedies would be meaningless. But antitrust enforcement actions aren't just about halting and correcting for the effects of the anticompetitive conduct of a defendant. As the D.C. Circuit had pointed out in its *Microsoft* decision, they are also about deterrence. (Some would argue that they are *primarily* about deterrence.) Legal and economic principles that are thoughtfully developed may deter the future conduct of the defendant as well as that of others, and that deterrent effect may begin to take hold even before the case is finally resolved. Indeed, deterrence may have been the most enduring value of the collective *Microsoft* cases.

Moreover, to the extent any Schumpeterian "perennial gale of creative destruction" was blowing, it wasn't enveloping the market for desktop-computer operating systems, except indirectly. Rather, it was stimulating innovation in the more competitive markets for Internet-related middleware (such as browsers and streaming media players) and servers. When Microsoft missed the "Internet tidal wave" and also fell behind in the development of server software, it sought to calm those winds, not to embrace them. As we will discuss further below, Microsoft had often been a reactive innovator, rarely initiating major changes on its own. It repeatedly found itself in the position of having to respond to the more revolutionary initiatives of its rivals. Schumpeter's theories and descriptions of innovation in monopolistic markets thus weren't an especially good fit for the market for desktop-computer operating systems and hence provided a weak response to the case for Microsoft's dominance. By way of contrast, the robust pace of innovation in the complementary middleware and server markets was more consistent with the view that competition provides a more potent spur to innovation than monopoly does. Microsoft's effort to portray antitrust enforcement as an enemy of innovation, therefore, seemed to have the facts backward. Microsoft's behavior in the market for desktop-computer operating systems wasn't consistent with Schumpeter's vision of the insecure and hence innovative monopolist. Therefore, its narrative was a transparent strategy to detract attention from the innovation-impairing consequences of its conduct in other markets, where antitrust had an important role to play in preserving competition.

Microsoft's claim that the course of litigation would be "too slow" proved to be true, but not for Microsoft, which had an interest in seeing the proceedings drawn out as long as possible as its own fortunes waxed and those of its rivals waned. This was especially true while the threat of a court-ordered breakup hung over Microsoft and as it waited for a change of administrations in Washington. Instead, antitrust enforcement proved to be too slow to save competition. Even though the threat was nascent, Netscape and Java together appeared to be forging a pathway to an invigorated and more competitive market, challenging the hegemony of Windows (and Microsoft's business model of marketing integrated software) by demonstrating the potential of middleware. But by the time the case was resolved, the emerging competitive threat of middleware had been dampened and its pace of development had slowed. Netscape had been hobbled and Sun was facing deep difficulties. As we argued in chapters 4 and 5, the hesitancy of the courts to act more quickly to preserve the competitive moment also left fewer viable remedies. Courts cannot raise the dead. As Judge Motz recognized in Sun's effort to secure a preliminary must-carry order in the MDL proceeding detailed in chapter 5, especially in industries characterized by rapid innovation and network efforts, the consequences of tipping are genuine and may be irretrievable if not addressed early on. In such circumstances, courts should be especially protective of "competitive moments" in the form of fledgling rivals threatened by the questionable conduct of dominant firms. This was something that the D.C. Circuit also understood when it noted the importance of shielding even "nascent" competition from exclusionary strategies. As we observed in chapter 6, the European Commission realized it as well. In this respect, the courts may not have fully credited the economics of the new economy, with the consequence that the timeline to decision was "too slow," but that failure worked to Microsoft's benefit.

Were the Legal Doctrines Up To the Task of Judging Microsoft's Conduct?

The *Microsoft* cases were a major contributing cause of renewed attention to the legal and economic standards used to judge the conduct of dominant firms. The "browser war," along with other legal developments in the United States and Europe, led to something of a "standards war" among commentators and public enforcement agencies in various jurisdictions. In the end, a number of jurisdictions adopted new guidelines for assessing dominant-firm conduct, but differences of opinion about how best to strike the balance between intervention and unimpeded reliance on markets stymied U.S. enforcers, and they weren't able to reach consensus.

Some commentators viewed the *Microsoft* cases as a test of the adequacy of legal standards that had been developed in a time of dominant railroads and steel manufacturers to judge the business practices of the Information Age. As we have argued, however, although the software industry had some new economic characteristics, in an economic sense it wasn't entirely different from more traditional industries. Moreover, Microsoft's conduct was hardly "new" in comparison with earlier monopolization cases. Although Microsoft's products and those of its rivals seemed to be on the "cutting edge" of technology, many of its tactics and its anticompetitive strategies were obvious and profoundly traditional, and its defenses were unsupported. Indeed, every public body that investigated Microsoft concluded that it had violated the principles of competition law, and every judicial tribunal faced with the review of agency action agreed that there was a basis for finding a significant violation of law—even if every claim wasn't upheld.

Nevertheless, there were some challenging tests of the applicable legal doctrine. One focus of attention was the law of "tying." In the United States, much of the criticism focused on the vestigial remnants of a once-rigid *per se* rule. In theory, under a true *per se* rule, anticompetitive harm is presumed and efficiency defenses are disallowed. A well-established body of commentary had criticized the *per se* rule on the ground that it overlooked a variety of ways in which the practice might have no effect on competition or might even be procompetitive. Other commentators had responded to the critics, observing that although tying didn't warrant blanket prohibition because it wasn't always anticompetitive, neither was it uniformly neutral or procompetitive. Tying could be anticompetitive under certain circumstances, so the practice might still warrant antitrust scrutiny to evaluate its effects and justifications in specific situations.

As we discussed in chapter 2, very early in the case Microsoft built upon that commentary to argue that its "integration" strategy shouldn't even be analyzed as tying and, if it was, that the *per se* rule was poorly suited to judge the benefits of integration for consumers. But in truth, by the time of the *Microsoft* cases, the U.S. *per se* rule had long since eroded. The Supreme Court had significantly qualified it in the mid 1980s, and four justices appeared to be ready to abandon the *per se* nomenclature entirely. The district court applied the law of tying in its modified form, a quasi *per se* rule that required proof of market power in the market for the tying product and permitted several different avenues for introducing justifications for tying (one of which was the "two products" requirement, which gave Microsoft a way to present and advocate its story of integration and efficiency).

In any event, Microsoft prevailed in its insistence that its integration be judged for both its effects and justifications. Neither in the United States nor in the European Union did prosecutors fail to make any showing of competitive harm, and Microsoft was never denied the opportunity to introduce its justifications for integrating its middleware (IE in the U.S., WMP in the EU) into Windows. The D.C. Circuit concluded that even the limited *per se* rule formally relied upon by the district court shouldn't be applied to platform software, and so reversed the district court's conclusion that Microsoft's tying constituted an independent violation of the Sherman Act. Because settlement followed on remand, there was never any complete rule-of-reason trial of the tying claim in the United States. Microsoft's integration strategy was, however, included in the government's Section 2 monopolization allegations, in connection with which its justifications were fully aired—and then rejected by both the district court and the court of appeals. Similarly, in Europe, which has no formal *per se* rule, the European Commission and the Court of First Instance found significant evidence of competitive harm. There Microsoft had every incentive to defend its integration strategy. Yet its evidence of legitimate technological or business justifications for integration was found wanting. What was left in both jurisdictions was a finding that Microsoft's integration strategy had affected competition adversely and that there was no technological or business justification for it. This wasn't a failure of doctrine and standards; it was a failure of proof—once the burden shifted to Microsoft, it failed to demonstrate that the benefits of its integration strategy were sufficient to ameliorate that strategy's anticompetitive effects.

The critique of tying also suffered from having been constructed on several unrealistically simple and ultimately unsupportable assumptions.

First, Microsoft was never prevented from selling Windows with its own integrated middleware, and it continues to do so today. As we have pointed out, in the United States there was no "unbundling" requirement, and in Europe, although an unbundling remedy was tried, the unbundled versions of Windows and WMP were initially intended to operate alongside Microsoft's preferred and integrated version of Windows. Similarly, the later attempt to facilitate more browser competition through the establishment of a ballot screen didn't affect Microsoft's ability to continue integrating its software.

Second, neither in the United States nor in Europe was the challenge to integration based solely on a simple act of tying—the mere act of selling one product on the condition that the buyer also purchase (or in this case license) a second product. As we have explained, instead the factual and economic inquiry focused on *how* Microsoft "tied" the two products: through integration of the code for both IE and WMP with Windows, and, importantly for both jurisdictions, by electing to integrate the code in such a way that removing Microsoft's middleware would cause Windows to crash. That design choice, which took matters a step beyond a mere conditioned sale, lacked any technical or business justification that Microsoft was able to support. Even if consumers benefited from having a browser or a media player integrated into their operating system, Microsoft wasn't able to show that its making its own middleware irremovable—itself an anti-competitive act—was of any benefit to the consumer. Neither was Microsoft able to show that any such benefits to consumers could be realized only by integrating its own middleware, rather than middleware from some other supplier into Windows. Thus, the way Microsoft chose to integrate IE and WMP had significantly impaired competition from rival middleware by depriving consumers of their ability to express their marketplace preferences for the products they favored, effectively disabling a critical demand-side feedback mechanism of the normal competitive process. Its design choices rendered the market for middleware less responsive to input from consumers (either direct input or indirect input through OEMs).

Third, Microsoft's conduct went well beyond simple tying—especially in the United States. Indeed, especially in light of the D.C. Circuit's decision in the 1994 Consent Decree case, it is difficult to imagine that the U.S. *Microsoft* case would have been prosecuted as vigorously as it was if Microsoft had done nothing more than sold Windows bundled with IE. Recall that in that decision the court accepted Microsoft's argument that "integration" should be differentiated from "tying." As we detailed in chapters 2 and 3, it became clear as the U.S. cases progressed that Microsoft had engaged in a wide-ranging anticompetitive strategy to undermine the promise of middleware, and that product integration was only one component of that strategy.

The critique of tying was constructed upon a pristinely hypothesized and one-sided premise: that unique benefits to consumers flowed from Microsoft's integration strategy. For purposes of the U.S. cases, this critique was narrowly targeted at undermining the *per se* rule. But for broader purposes it was incomplete. Proponents of this view tended not only to discount whether actual evidence supported the imaginable, theoretical benefits of integrating operating systems and middleware, but also to discount or ignore the distinct question of whether consumers benefited at all when middleware was so deeply imbedded as to make it irremovable. More important, critics of the tying claim often denigrated or ignored the evidence of the anticompetitive effects of Microsoft's conduct. Even if Microsoft had proffered more substantial evidence of the benefits of integration, those benefits would have had to be scrutinized in light of the competitive harm.

In the end, therefore, the critique of tying was directed at an illusory target: a theoretically simple case of tying brought under a rigid *per se* rule and exhibiting clear consumer justifications without threat of harm. One could agree completely with the proposition that antitrust law should not condemn tying as so imagined and yet still conclude that Microsoft's conduct was unlawful. And that's what both jurisdictions did.

It is also important to observe that the agencies, courts, and the law all proved able to understand and judge what was a relatively new theory of how tying could be anticompetitive—but again, this wasn't to Microsoft's advantage. The traditional anticompetitive theory of tying focuses on its impact on the market for the tied product (in the *Microsoft* cases, the markets for middleware, such as IE and WMP). Competition from rival producers of the tied product can be impaired or entirely eliminated, and consumers can be deprived of the opportunity either to decline to purchase the tied product or to purchase it from another vendor.

One of the central allegations in the U.S. monopolization claim against Microsoft, however, was that it used tying to insulate itself from competition in the market for the *tying* product, Windows. As we described in chapters 1 and again in chapters 3 and 4, Microsoft, by impairing third-party middleware suppliers, protected its Windows monopoly from nascent competition either from middleware itself (which might have developed into a platform of its own) or from other operating systems (which might have developed in such a way that they would work with non-Microsoft middleware). While this theory of harm marked a new phase in the analysis of tying, it was well supported by both commentators and the analysis in the U.S. courts.[2] The courts again proved able to adapt to new learning, but that didn't work to Microsoft's advantage.

Another focal point of doctrinal criticism was the U.S. court of appeals' reference to the "rule of reason" in connection with its analysis of the monopolization claims against Microsoft. In fact, that reference seemed to set off something of a panic, especially within the Bush Justice Department. Critics of the reference pointed out that detractors of the rule of reason, which is associated with analysis under Section 1 of the Sherman Act, had long maintained that it was a vague and inherently unstructured test that gave courts and juries far too much discretion. As a result, the criticism went, application of the rule of reason led to uncertainty—firms couldn't easily predict what would be deemed a "reasonable" adverse effect on competition as opposed to an "unreasonable" one. It was thought that such uncertainty, in combination with the threat of treble damages, might lead defendants to settle even weak antitrust cases. Further, it was argued that uncertainty of legal standards was especially troubling in a case of single-firm conduct, because risk-averse large firms might avoid aggressive competitive strategies for fear of falling victim to antitrust challenges. That such over-deterrence would chill aggressive competition is a frequent but unsubstantiated charge made by many skeptics of antitrust enforcement. Critics of the rule of reason also associated it with the idea of "balancing" procompetitive and anticompetitive effects—something they characterized as difficult to do, likely to undervalue efficiencies, and therefore inherently prone to error.

"Rule of reason" is simply a catchphrase that describes an insight that is common to all applications of antitrust laws and is rooted in the common-law origins of the Sherman Act. It fairly characterizes the analytical framework used to evaluate the competitive effects of various forms of collusion (including joint ventures and mergers) and exclusion (whether by a single firm or many). That straight-forward insight is that many forms of conduct will be neither unambiguously harmful nor unambiguously beneficial. In such cases, we can simply abdicate responsibility to markets without oversight or else strive collectively to reach reasonable judgments as to whether the effect of some conduct is adverse and therefore not adequately justified. That some judgments in such matters are difficult shouldn't dissuade us from making the best judgments we can in light of reasonably available and reliable evidence.[3]

Criticism of the rule-of-reason approach taken by the D.C. Circuit was especially unfounded. Drawing on decades of case law and on modern economic principles, the court articulated and applied an operable approach to judging the conduct of monopolists, encountering few difficult judgment calls. Like many other narratives that emerged in the course of the *Microsoft* cases, the fear of "rule of reason monopolization analysis" was exaggerated.

It is important to appreciate that when the D.C. Circuit stated its approach to defining exclusionary conduct it had already concluded without reservation that Microsoft was a monopolist. Consistent with the general framework that the Supreme Court has articulated for monopolization cases, proof of monopoly power is often approached as a precondition to consideration of effects and justifications, and the standards for proving such power are demanding.[4] Furthermore, in keeping with the evolution of U.S. antitrust law toward an economically driven, effects-based approach, the court's framework emphasized the centrality of anticompetitive effects and efficiencies. Though there certainly remains room for debate, especially in the context of high-stakes litigation, anticompetitive effects and efficiencies aren't amorphous and undefined terms under today's antitrust laws. As the court proceeded to judge each of Microsoft's challenged practices, it examined evidence of actual effects, as well as effects that could be gleaned from economic reasoning, to judge whether each practice was anticompetitive, procompetitive, or perhaps neutral. None of its findings could have been very surprising to Microsoft, especially in view of the lack of evidence of procompetitive justifications and the extensive evidence of anticompetitive intent (which, the court observed, cast light on probable effects).

As we noted in chapter 4, although the court called for "balancing" when evidence of both harms and benefits has been presented, in only one instance can it be said that the court undertook any such effort. Even then, however, it didn't purport to be balancing effects in the sense of quantifying and comparing harms and benefits to determine which was measurably greater. That such balancing ever takes place under the rule of reason is one of the great myths of American antitrust law.[5] Courts rarely have quantitative evidence of measured effects and efficiencies. Moreover, such a simple comparison approach would be inconsistent with the consumer-welfare focus of U.S. antitrust law. In operation, "balancing" has come to mean reaching a judgment about some conduct's effect on competition on the basis of the evidence—and that is what the court of appeals did in *Microsoft*.

Another doctrinal controversy involved the standards for judging a dominant firm's refusal to supply its rivals. As we discussed in chapter 6, Microsoft's decision first to share interoperability information with rival suppliers of server operating systems and then to deny them such information when it had developed its own server operating system was a critical part of the European Commission's case against Microsoft but wasn't a specific claim in the U.S. cases. As we also discussed in chapter 6 and in chapter 4, even though there was no refusal to supply claim in the U.S. cases, the U.S. consent decree included disclosure provisions designed to promote interoperability. For these reasons, there was shared attention in both jurisdictions to the competitive consequences of the relationship between the market for desktop-computer operating systems (a market that Microsoft dominated) and the still-emerging market for server operating systems.

Although the law of refusal to supply was more settled in the European Union than in the United States at the time Sun complained to the European Commission in late 1998, in 2004, just as the Commission was reaching its *Microsoft* decision, the U.S. Supreme Court issued a decision that significantly constrained the ability of Section 2 of the Sherman Act to reach such behavior. The coincidental juxtaposition of the European Commission's decision in *Microsoft* and the U.S. Supreme Court's decision in *Trinko* provoked comparison. Critics of the *Microsoft* case saw in *Trinko* additional support for a more tolerant and non-interventionist view with respect to refusals to supply and, more generally, with respect to single-firm conduct.

Although the American approach and the European approach to analyzing competition law have converged significantly, the two regimes aren't identical, and the European Commission's decision regarding Microsoft's refusal to supply interoperability information can be viewed as revealing its fundamentally different view of what enforcement of competition law can accomplish. Rather than embrace the philosophical preference for non-intervention that was evident in recent U.S. Supreme Court cases such as *Trinko*, the European Commission showed that it was possible to intervene in an effort to improve the competitive situation. However, the European Commission intervened only after carefully examining the competitive effects of Microsoft's refusal to license interoperability information and finding that the refusal had harmed innovation. Although much was made of this finding as evidence of divergence between the EU and the U.S., the same result was reached through the U.S. consent decree, even in the absence of a claim of refusal to supply in the U.S. case, and both the European Commission and the U.S. district court were able to design administrable licensing regimes in response. Although neither licensing program spurred significant competition in the market for operating systems, the two regimes did increase competitive offerings in other software markets, particularly from open-source software providers, and certainly didn't harm innovation. So here, too, the claims of divergence were exaggerated.

Furthermore, as we discussed in chapter 6, the European Commission's case was structured and decided under the current state of the applicable EU law at the time of the *Microsoft* Statement of Objections. That doesn't mean that it couldn't have been structured in other ways. For example, *Trinko* concluded that a history of past dealing between a dominant firm and a rival would tend to suggest a previously profitable relationship. Hence, withdrawal of that relationship in favor of a change of policy might reflect a willingness to forgo profits in favor of strategic advantage that comes from exclusion. At the least, under such circumstances, the refusal should be supported by legitimate business justifications. And a prior course of dealing can reduce or eliminate concerns about the administrability of an imposed duty to deal. Courts need not create and impose untried conditions of dealing, such as price, but can rely on history. Finally, *Trinko* had relied in part on the presence of a broad regulatory scheme that was available to police exclusionary conduct in reaching its conclusion to limit the scope of Section 2. There was no comparable regulatory scheme covering Microsoft's conduct in Europe. In view of those facts, it is arguable that a prohibition of refusals to supply could be justifiable even under *Trinko*. This scenario is also consistent with what the European Commission had found.

Were the Remedies Adequate?

The collective, global enforcement effort directed at Microsoft revealed how difficult it can be to identify effective remedies for violations of competition law, especially by single dominant firms and especially in technology industries. Microsoft faced nearly every one of the panoply of tools available in antitrust's remedial tool bag: fines, damages, injunctions against continued conduct, mandatory injunctions requiring changed conduct, continuing oversight of some of its conduct, and even (for a while) the threat of a court-ordered reorganization. But there were no benchmarks established at the start of the case whereby any of the measures ultimately ordered or agreed upon could be evaluated. Although compliance is one measure of success, it may only support an appearance of success. In the absence of clear benchmarks and goals, it is difficult to evaluate whether the specific remedies, and hence compliance with them, truly mattered to competition. Nevertheless, it seems worthwhile to consider what the *Microsoft* cases may have taught us about the design of remedies and what criteria we should use to judge their efficacy.[6]

At a minimum, a remedy should terminate any conduct that violates the law. That will generally be a reliable baseline assumption, but there might be exceptions. For example, if the practice has some plausible benefits, it may be preferable to craft a less restrictive alternative remedy that will redress its adverse effects while preserving its benefits, perhaps by imposing conditions on its use. Similarly, a more creative remedy may be required if, under the circumstances, a simple injunction will be too difficult to administer or will have some adverse competitive effects of its own.

More broadly, however, a remedy that does nothing more than enjoin offending conduct will neither prevent repetition of the conduct nor repair any damage done to the competitive process.[7] Indeed, by failing to do more, such a limited remedy may well encourage the same firm or other firms to undertake the same conduct in the future. To be judged "effective," therefore, a remedy also should deter similar future conduct by the same firm or other firms and should restore or establish more competitive conditions. In many jurisdictions, it would also be important to provide a mechanism for compensating the victims of the unlawful conduct.

By these standards, how should we judge the remedies imposed on Microsoft?

For the most part, Microsoft's worst conduct, including its contractual practices and its deceptive and coercive conduct directed at Sun and Apple, appeared to have stopped. At the least, ending those practices removed an impediment to competition in the market for middleware. But the degree is uncertain, as is the lasting effect of these limited remedies—and in the United States all those remedies have now expired. Microsoft's dominance of the market for desktop-computer operating systems remains largely intact. Although competition in the markets for operating systems for other devices (especially mobile phones and tablets) has flourished, that competition doesn't appear to be attributable to the remedies in the *Microsoft* antitrust cases. Ironically, it may even be a result of Microsoft's continued dominance of the market for desktop-computer operating systems, which created incentives for its rivals to seek new avenues for invention.

It is even less clear that the negotiated remedy that most directly addressed the integration of Windows and IE had any significant beneficial effect. Recall that in the United States the courts concluded that Microsoft violated Section 2 of the Sherman Act by making IE irremovable and through other conduct that impaired competition in middleware, yet the negotiated settlement didn't require separation of IE and Windows, as did the European Commission's judgment. The U.S. consent decree did nothing to modify Microsoft's integration strategy. It mandated only that end-user access to IE be hidden, not that IE's code be removed. This resolution may illustrate the exception noted above regarding prohibition of offending conduct. But other options were available that might have had more beneficial consequences and still have permitted Microsoft to integrate IE and other middleware with Windows.

It also seems likely that the significant fines in the European Union and the many settlements in the United States—with the attendant years of litigation costs, possible reputational harm, and litigation distraction—deterred not only Microsoft but also other dominant technology firms. As we argued in chapter 5, however, the private "overcharge" actions in the United States were of questionable merit and proved too difficult for the courts to evaluate in a timely and cost-effective way. They may, therefore, suggest a possibility of "over-deterrence." However, since in the United States public enforcers lack any authority to impose civil fines, these private suits may well have provided the most important source of deterrence, even though the settlements were poorly calibrated to the harm Microsoft had caused. However difficult it may be to judge the deterrent value of the collective remedies imposed on or agreed to by Microsoft, Windows remains a highly profitable product and a dominant one. If Microsoft's conduct prolonged Windows' dominance by even a single year, its investment in litigation costs was well spent and the specific deterrent value for Microsoft may have been slight.

Perhaps the greatest challenge for any remedy is to restore the market to where it was before the conduct occurred or, perhaps more controversially, to jump-start competition in a market that has been damaged in order to improve incentives for more competition. The market can then be left to evolve, with competition not fettered by the offending conduct. From this perspective, we draw three lessons from the *Microsoft* cases. None of these observations counsel for "regulating" markets; rather, the lesson here is that true confidence in markets and their outcomes may suggest the need for restorative and rehabilitative measures after a period of anticompetitive distortion.

First, competition-enforcement agencies and courts should strive to preserve "competitive moments." As we argued in chapter 5 and in the present chapter, if the wheels of antitrust enforcement moved too slowly in any dimension in the *Microsoft* cases, it was with respect to preserving rivalry before it was effectively vanquished. Timidity in the use of status-quo-preserving preliminary relief, such as temporary restraining orders and preliminary injunctions, can allow such moments to pass. And they cannot be easily recreated, especially if new competitors have been damaged beyond repair or have exited the market. The "balance of equities" should be struck in favor of protecting such emergent competition, especially when tipping is a genuine threat, the justifications for the dominant firm's conduct appear suspect, and the burden of preliminary relief on the dominant firm is relatively small.

The standard refrain to this view, often repeated by defendants in U.S. antitrust litigation, is that the antitrust laws are intended to "protect competition, not competitors."[8] Though this slogan may serve as a valuable guiding principle in competitive markets, it shouldn't be accepted uncritically when invoked by a self-interested dominant firm urging it as an immutable article of faith to immunize its conduct from antitrust scrutiny. As one court has correctly observed, "in a concentrated market with very high barriers to entry, competition will not exist without competitors."[9] The slogan assumes a false dichotomy. In the context of public enforcement, it also has been invoked in support of the criticism that agencies aren't able to differentiate valid claims of illegitimate exclusion from the whining of rivals facing legitimate though aggressive competition by their dominant competitors. Agencies, however, aren't so easily taken in. And in both the United States and Europe, there are courts to check any possible instances of such agency capture. Although courts certainly can be mistaken in their judgments, any continued insistence that the *Microsoft* cases were simple illustrations of government being captured by a dominant firm's competitors is unsupportable.

Second, markets function best when the ability of consumers to make informed choices about their competitive options is unimpaired. The interaction of supply and demand to produce efficient market outcomes assumes as much. This simple maxim is the foundation for consumer-protection laws that prohibit deception and fraud, and for many regulations that mandate disclosures of truthful information about product characteristics. It is also at the heart of antitrust regimes committed to protect consumers' welfare. As the U.S. Supreme Court has recognized, conduct that renders markets "unresponsive to consumer preference" is "not consistent with this fundamental goal of antitrust law."[10] When such conduct is found, remedies should be targeted at restoring the damaged mechanism.

In myriad ways, Microsoft sought to insulate its products from the test of the marketplace rather than subject them to competition on the merits. This was true of Microsoft's IE and WMP middleware, and it was true of Windows. The negotiated remedy in the United States did little to reestablish consumers (including OEMs) as the drivers of demand beyond prohibiting some of Microsoft's most coercive design and contracting practices.

In this respect, the solutions proposed and tried by the Korea Fair Trade Commission and later by the European Commission had some under-appreciated aspects. Both the KFTC and the EC tried to restore the role of consumer-driven decision making in the market, and both tried to do so without unduly interfering with Microsoft's ability to offer its own products in competition with those of its rivals. Even if consumers continued to prefer Microsoft's products, this creative effort to reempower consumers was an important example for future cases involving similar conduct and similar consequences. The goal isn't a pre-determined quota for each rival, but a return to consumer-driven allocation of market share.

Nevertheless, as we have discussed, these efforts faced withering criticisms from some commentators and from U.S. antitrust authorities. Critics caricatured any remedy that required Microsoft to alter Windows as software engineering by amateurs, charging that courts and enforcement agencies were poorly equipped to design software—a task they said was best left, unfettered, to software firms like Microsoft. This was another exaggerated criticism heaped on an illusory issue. True, agencies and courts shouldn't pretend to be software designers. But they didn't have to be software designers in order to judge the results of a software firm's practices. The U.S. Department of Justice, the states, and Judge Jackson didn't have to be software engineers to understand that Microsoft had designed IE to be irremovable or that the commingling of code meant that if IE were fully removed then Windows would be disabled. Likewise, the Korea Fair Trade Commission and the European Commission didn't have to undertake the design work to know whether the ballot-screen options they demanded provided simple mechanisms that consumers could use to express their preferences for competing products. Software design can be judged by its performance, and that can include whether its features facilitate, inhibit, or leave untouched competition on the merits.

Third, as we have already noted, no court can resuscitate a hobbled or vanquished competitor. When conduct is deemed anticompetitive because it fortifies or raises barriers to entry, effective remedies should include steps to dismantle the barriers and facilitate easier entry. Perhaps the most prominent example of this approach in the Microsoft cases was mandated disclosure of interoperability information, required under the U.S. consent decree even though, in contrast to the European cases, there were no claims of refusal to supply. The parties and courts in both jurisdictions readily understood that this was the most forward-looking of the remedies, because it would redirect competition from exploitation and elevation of barriers to entry toward competition on the merits of the product offerings of Microsoft and its rivals. In truth, however, again it isn't certain whether these measures were effective in realizing their stated goals.

The most dramatic remedial proposal—structural relief that would have reorganized the company into two parts—remained untried, and the record remained insufficient to allow its wisdom or its likely effectiveness to be judged. Markets are about incentives, and structural relief is more effective than court injunctions at altering incentives. It was thought that separating Microsoft's operating-system and applications businesses would diminish or eliminate impediments to entry and fortify incentives for competition in the markets for middleware and operating systems. Although the theory seemed sound, the proposal was largely an economist's construct. Microsoft had always been an integrated firm, so reorganizing it in the hope of altering its incentives was a gamble that could have had severe and hard-to-predict consequences for the industry.

Did Antitrust Enforcement Dull Microsoft's Innovative Edge?

A final strand of narrative emerged as the *Microsoft* cases were coming to a close. Although some of its elements had long been a part of the story line that Microsoft had advocated, it added a distinct, "post-*Microsoft*" epilogue, and it raised a concern that will continue to confront antitrust enforcers in the technology sector: how best to analyze the strategies and counter-strategies associated with the emergence of disruptive technologies.

In this narrative, Microsoft is portrayed as an innovating dominant firm. Its rivals, unable or unwilling to keep pace with it, sought the protection of government antitrust enforcers, who, by seeking to impose liability on Microsoft for its innovations, are portrayed not only as inept and ill-informed, but as enemies of innovation. Beyond that, some critics of the cases have argued that antitrust enforcement hobbled Microsoft—that by inhibiting it from competing aggressively, antitrust enforcement dulled its overall capacity for innovation in the aftermath of the cases.

As was true of Microsoft's efforts to portray its conduct as innovative, the premise of this closing plot twist is inconsistent with the facts found in the various cases. Antitrust enforcement didn't hobble Microsoft; Microsoft got into antitrust trouble when it fell behind its rivals and tried to use its market power to exploit the characteristics of the industry to slow its rivals and buy time to catch up. As Bill Gates had acknowledged, Microsoft had been caught unprepared for the "Internet tidal wave." The same was true with respect to the development of server operating systems, as was found in the EC's case. When the "Internet tidal wave" hit, Microsoft lost its footing. Its emerging rivals, which had recognized the Internet's potential, began to design software to fully exploit it—first browsers, distributed programing language, and media players, and later search engines.

The cases against Microsoft, therefore, cannot fairly be viewed as misguided efforts to impose liability on a dominant but innovative firm. They were prompted not by any "innovative" product strategy, but rather by Microsoft's all-out counter-strategy to preserve its Windows monopoly by impeding competition from its more innovative rivals. If Microsoft was hobbled, it was hobbled by competition, by complacency of a kind long associated with monopolists, and by a lack of foresight—not by antitrust enforcement. It was caught flat on its feet when other firms brought new technological capabilities to the market.

The introduction of disruptive technologies will continue to generate tensions between new firms and incumbents, especially when the latter are dominant. As was true in the *Microsoft* cases, an important question for enforcers will be whether the dominant firm is the purveyor of the disruptive innovation (which might counsel for self-restraint) or whether its rivals are the purveyors. If this threshold issue can be evaluated correctly, government enforcement will be a valuable friend and supporter of innovation, not its enemy.

Conclusion

When Microsoft rose to prominence, in the 1980s, it was accompanied by IBM and Intel. Although they were influenced by the innovations of Xerox, Apple, and other companies, these three firms sat together at the center of the personal technology universe and apart from most other firms in terms of dominance. IBM had attracted the attention of antitrust enforcers long before the advent of the personal computer, and Intel would later be chastised by the Federal Trade Commission and by other companies (including its principal rival, Advanced Micro Devices) for seeking to maintain its position of dominance through anticompetitive means. Today, the center of the technology universe is a more complex place, occupied by a group of extraordinarily successful companies, each associated with a particular segment of the technology marketplace but all both interdependent and in competition to varying degrees. Microsoft and Intel remain, now accompanied by Apple, Amazon, Facebook, and Google.[11] Each of these companies has been a subject of scrutiny under antitrust and consumer-protection laws for various reasons and in various parts of the world. That scrutiny probably will continue, owing to some of the very same market characteristics that may have provided Microsoft with the incentives to fortify its monopoly position not through innovation and the superiority of its products but through the exercise of market power.

This is neither surprising nor historically unusual. To a significant degree, the cutting-edge industries of the day have always drawn the attention of antitrust enforcers. This was true of the railroads and of the steel, oil, and staple-product industries of the turn of the twentieth century, and it was true of the large grocery and retailing business of the mid twentieth century. Viewed in a larger historical context, therefore, technology industries aren't being singled out and "targeted" for any kind of "special" treatment. They have drawn attention to themselves because of their success and their prominence, and in some instances because of abusive practices intended to secure or maintain their prominence. Also, as was once true of the railroads and of the oil industry, the technology industry today is driving development and economic progress. Thus, the attention it is receiving is appropriate, so long as enforcement is properly directed at anticompetitive collusion and exclusion and is attentive to the need to preserve true efficiencies and incentives for innovation.

Today's developing industries sometimes combine breakthrough technologies and new capabilities with new methods of distribution and sale. The field of competition can be global. The products, the services, and the business models can be complex, dynamic, and exciting to study. The products can be used by millions if not billions of consumers. And the negative effects of anticompetitive conduct can include erecting or fortifying barriers to new and path-breaking competition. Some of the most promising and potentially game-changing technological developments today are outside of the highly visible world of consumer technology. Breakthroughs in industrial software and in new methods of manufacturing probably will transform the global economy in this still-new century. And more traditional industries—especially those now undergoing consolidation and transformation, such as transportation, telecommunication, and the various media-related industries, such as the music, book, and video content industries, should not be overlooked. As has always been true of competition policy, enforcement efforts must strive for balance. It would be a mistake to simply take a pass on technology, relying on platitudes like those served up during the *Microsoft* cases (for example, that a field is so fast moving or so dynamic that intervention can never be justified). Deterrence of egregious conduct must be maintained, and that can happen only with the credible threat of measured antitrust enforcement against demonstrably or predictably anticompetitive strategies. Competition-enforcement agencies will need the resources to remain educated about these changing industries and to maintain their capacity to bring the occasional, but essential, "big case."

More broadly, from the perspective of competition policy, the *Microsoft* cases teach that those who make competition-enforcement policy must continue to be attentive to the behavior of dominant firms. As one commentator has persuasively argued, exclusion is a "core competition concern" that should not be relegated to secondary status behind cartels.[12] We find no reason in the collective experience of Microsoft to doubt that proposition or to question whether the antitrust laws and institutions are capable of continuing to facilitate progress by protecting competition and the competitive process.

Appendix

Chronology of Microsoft Antitrust Cases and Related Events[1]

• June 1990: Just over ten years after its founding, Microsoft becomes the subject of a Federal Trade Commission investigation into its cooperative relationship with IBM. The investigation widens to include Microsoft's licensing and other practices in connection with Windows.

• January 1993: William Jefferson Clinton is sworn in as president of the United States. Promising to bring renewed vigor to federal antitrust enforcement, his selection to head the Antitrust Division of the U.S. Department of Justice, Anne K. Bingaman, is confirmed by the Senate in June.

• July 1993: After the FTC twice deadlocks on whether to issue a complaint against Microsoft, the Antitrust Division of the Department of Justice asks the FTC to transfer its investigative files to the Antitrust Division, which then takes up the investigation. The FTC formally closes its own investigation in response.

• July 1994: After another year of investigation, the Department of Justice negotiates the first consent decree with Microsoft relating to its Windows licensing practices ("the Licensing Decree").[2]

• February 1995: The federal district court assigned to review the Licensing Decree under the Tunney Act (a Watergate-era statute that mandates federal court approval of certain antitrust consent decrees) rejects it on the ground that it isn't in the "public interest."[3] Within months, the district court's decision is reversed by the U.S. Court of Appeals, which also orders that Judge Stanley Sporkin, who reviewed and rejected the decree, be removed from the case.[4] On remand, the case is reassigned to Judge Thomas Penfield Jackson, who approves and enters the decree.[5]

• October 1997: The Department of Justice accuses Microsoft of violating the anti-tying provisions of the1994 Licensing Decree and petitions the federal court to hold it in civil contempt for conditioning the right to license Windows 95 on its licensees' agreement also to license its Internet browser, Internet Explorer (IE), and for prohibiting licensees from disaggregating Windows and IE. Judge Jackson denies the petition to hold Microsoft in civil contempt, citing the ambiguity of the relevant provisions of the consent decree, which prohibited tying but permitted Microsoft to develop "integrated" products. The court nevertheless preliminarily enjoins Microsoft from conditioning the licensing of Windows on the inclusion of IE pending a complete trial on whether doing so violated the decree.[6] Microsoft files an appeal.

• May 1998: The Department of Justice, twenty states, and the District of Columbia file two complementary antitrust actions against Microsoft in the federal district court in Washington. The cases are assigned to Judge Thomas Penfield Jackson.[7]

• June 1998: Windows 98 is shipped. Separately, the court of appeals reverses the district court's preliminary injunction in the Licensing Decree appeal because of lack of adequate notice and because it was based on an erroneous reading of the tying and integration provisions of the consent decree. In the court's view, Microsoft successfully demonstrated "facially plausible benefits" of integrating IE and Windows, which satisfied the provisions of the consent decree. The court reverses Judge Jackson's order and, although its reading of the decree leaves little room for an alternative interpretation, it remands. The remand prompts a dissent from a panel judge who would have left application of the decree to the district court.[8]

• Fall 1998–summer 1999: Judge Jackson conducts a bench trial (a trial without a jury) on the governments' cases against Microsoft.

• December 1998: In response to a complaint from Sun Microsystems, the European Commission opens an investigation into whether Microsoft abused its dominant position in desktop operating systems by refusing to supply Sun with the interoperability information necessary to allow its server operating system to work with desktop computers running Windows.

• November 1999: Judge Jackson issues the district court's findings of fact, but delays issuing its conclusions of law.[9] It is clear from the findings of fact that the court will rule against Microsoft. In one last effort to settle the case, Judge Jackson appoints Richard A. Posner, a highly regarded antitrust authority and judge of the U.S. Court of Appeals for the Seventh Circuit as a mediator to help resolve the case. Focusing on the difficulty of identifying a court-imposed remedy in the case, an editorial in the *New York Times* in late November concludes with this sentence: "Perhaps the odds of finding a remedy acceptable to Microsoft and the government remain low, but they are far higher with Judge Posner than without him."[10]

• February 2000: The European Commission broadens its investigation of Microsoft to include whether Microsoft unlawfully tied its Windows Media Player to Windows.

• April 2000: After Judge Posner's effort to mediate a settlement collapses, Judge Jackson promptly issues his conclusions of law and rules in favor of the governments on nearly all of their allegations against Microsoft.[11]

• June 2000: As a remedy for its violations of federal antitrust laws, the district court orders that Microsoft be broken into two companies and requires Microsoft to prepare a plan for divestiture. The court stays its order of divestiture pending an appeal and imposes interim remedies, which are later also stayed pending appeal.[12]

• August 2000: The European Commission sends its first statement of objections to Microsoft based on its investigation of Sun's complaint, alleging that Microsoft's refusal to disclose interoperability information to vendors of competing server operating systems was an abuse of dominance.

• September 2000: The U.S. Supreme Court refuses to hear Microsoft's direct appeal from the district court and instead remands the case to be heard by the U.S. Court of Appeals for the District of Columbia Circuit.[13]

• January 2001: George W. Bush is sworn in as president of the United States. In the months that follow, new leadership at the Antitrust Division takes charge of the *Microsoft* case after Microsoft's appeal is briefed and argued by the previous administration.

• January 2001: An opinion by District Court Judge J. Frederick Motz in Baltimore recounts that 61 private antitrust cases against Microsoft—some filed in federal court and others filed in and then removed from state courts around the country—have been transferred to him to be consolidated with three other cases for pre-trial coordination. Seventy-three cases deemed unremovable remain in state courts.[14] Over time, more than 200 private antitrust cases are filed against Microsoft in state and federal courts throughout the United States. Eventually, 117 cases are transferred and consolidated for pretrial processing before Judge Motz in a single multidistrict proceeding, MDL 1332.

• June 2001: Although the district court's holding on liability is largely affirmed by the *en banc* and unanimous U.S. court of appeals, the court reverses some of the court's more controversial liability conclusions, including the tying claim, as well as the court's breakup order. And for a second time the D.C. Circuit orders that a federal district court judge (this time Judge Jackson) be removed from the case.[15]

• August 2001: The European Commission issues its second statement of objections to Microsoft, this one alleging that Microsoft's tying of Windows Media Player to Windows is an abuse of dominance.

• September 2001: Under new leadership, the Department of Justice announces that it will not pursue the tying claim on remand and that it will no longer seek the breakup of Microsoft.[16]

• November 2001: The Department of Justice, nine states, and Microsoft reach a settlement of the Windows 95/98 case filed in 1998 and craft a new consent decree, which is then submitted to the federal district court for approval pursuant to the Tunney Act.[17]

• January 2002: AOL Time Warner, which has acquired Netscape, files suit against Microsoft for antitrust violations related to the government suit filed in 1998.

• March 2002: Sun Microsystems similarly files suit against Microsoft for antitrust violations.

• November 2002: With one reservation regarding its own continuing jurisdiction, the district court per Judge Colleen Kollar-Kotelly conditionally approves the settlement of the Windows 95/98 case under the Tunney Act, rejecting the objections of nine non-settling states and the District of Columbia. Massachusetts alone appeals the court's decision to deny the non-settling states' request for additional remedies. A five-year consent decree goes into effect.[18]

• May 2003: AOL Time Warner settles with Microsoft for $750 million.

• August 2003: Following additional investigation, the European Commission sends Microsoft its third statement of objections, combining the allegations of its previous two and alleging that Microsoft is abusing its dominant position by refusing to supply interoperability information and by tying. At Microsoft's request, an oral hearing is conducted November 12-14, 2003.

• March 2004: The European Commission rules that Microsoft violated European competition laws, fines it the equivalent of $605 million, and orders Microsoft to offer a version of Windows without Windows Media Player and to disclose the communications protocols necessary to facilitate interoperability between Windows-based desktops and network servers utilizing non-Microsoft operating systems. Microsoft appeals to the European Court of First Instance.[19]

• April 2004: Microsoft settles with Sun for $1.6 billion and an agreement to undertake cooperation.

• June 2004: The U.S. Court of Appeals for the District of Columbia Circuit rejects Massachusetts' appeal seeking additional remedies and approves the 2001 settlement involving the Department of Justice, nine states, and Microsoft.[20]

• July 2004: Microsoft is notified by the Japan Fair Trade Commission that the non-assertion of patent provisions in Microsoft's agreements with computer manufacturers are inconsistent with Japanese competition law. To remedy the violation, the JFTC requires Microsoft to nullify the provisions and to notify computer manufacturers that it will not seek to enforce them.[21]

• November 2004: Microsoft settles with its rival Novell for $536 million and with the Computer Communications Industry Association, an industry trade group that had actively supported the pursuit of Microsoft under the antitrust laws and had intervened in the Tunney Act proceedings to settle the governments' cases.

• July 2005: Microsoft settles with IBM for a cash payment of $775 million and $75 million in software.

• October 2005: RealNetworks, whose complaints about Microsoft's integration of Windows Media Player into Windows led to one portion of the European Commission's investigation and case against Microsoft, settles its own antitrust claims with Microsoft for $761 million.

• December 2005: The Korea Fair Trade Commission concludes that several of Microsoft's marketing practices violate the Korea Monopoly Regulation and Fair Trade Act. In February of 2006, it orders Microsoft to pay a fine equivalent to $33 million and to modify its operating systems for servers and those for desktop computers. Microsoft appeals the decision.

• May 2006: The Department of Justice and Microsoft announce that they have agreed to extend some of the provisions of the five-year 2001 consent decree (which took effect in November of 2002) for an additional two years, through November of 2009. The district court approves the extension proposal in September of 2006.[22]

• July 2006: The European Commission, frustrated with Microsoft's lack of progress in complying with its 2004 orders regarding the disclosure of technical data, again fines Microsoft.[23]

• January 2007: Microsoft announces that only two private antitrust class actions related to the governments' cases remain pending in the United States. It reports that it has secured dismissals of cases in sixteen states, won denials of class certification in two, reached final settlements in seventeen, and reached preliminary settlements in the final two.

• September 2007: The European Court of First Instance rejects virtually all of Microsoft's appeal of the European Commission's March 2004 decision that it violated European competition laws by tying its Windows Media Player to the Windows PC operating system and by its refusing to provide rivals in the market for workgroup-server operating systems with the interface information necessary for their products to interoperate with Windows. With the exception of a relatively minor remedial point, the

European Court of First Instance also concludes that the European Commission's remedies were appropriate.[24]

• November 2007: With the exception of certain provisions previously extended by mutual agreement of the parties through 2009, the bulk of the 2002 consent decree in the United States is set to expire. Some states request an extension of nearly all of the remaining provisions of the decree, but the Department of Justice formally opposes the extension, indicating that in its view the standards for an extension that were set out in the decree haven't been met.

• January 2008: Over the objections of the Department of Justice, Judge Kollar-Kotelly agrees to further extend the bulk of the 2002 consent decree at the request of the states so that nearly all of its provisions will continue as a whole until November of 2009.[25]

• February 2008: The European Commission fines Microsoft €899 million for non-compliance with its March 2004 decision.[26]

• September 2008: The Japan Fair Trade Commission issues a Hearing Decision finding that Microsoft's use of non-assertion of patent provisions in its Windows licensing agreements with original equipment manufacturers is an unfair business practice in violation of Article 19 of Japan's Antimonopoly Law. Microsoft is ordered to end use of the provision.[27]

• January 2009: The European Commission issues a statement of objections to Microsoft concerning the tying of Internet Explorer to Windows, initiating a new case against the company for abusing its dominant position in Europe.[28]

• January 2009: Barack H. Obama is sworn in as president of the United States.

• April 2009: The U.S. Department of Justice, seventeen states, and the District of Columbia announce that they have reached agreement with Microsoft to extend certain provisions of the 2002 consent decree that settled the 1998 case for an additional 18 months, through May of 2011.[29] In accordance with the agreement, the U.S. District Court enters its Second Modified Final Judgment on April 29.[30]

• December 2009: The European Commission announces a settlement with Microsoft of its browser case, accepting Microsoft's commitments to offer users a wider choice of browsers.[31]

• May 2011: The final judgments and consent decree in the governments' *Microsoft* cases expire.

• June 2012: Europe's General Court upholds €860 of the €890 million in penalties imposed by the European Commission against Microsoft for its failure to comply with the Commission's 2004 decision and order.[32]

• March 2013: The European Commission fines Microsoft an additional €561 million for failing to comply with its 2009 commitments to offer users a choice of browsers.[33]

• September 2013: The U.S. Court of Appeals for the Tenth Circuit rules in favor of Microsoft, dismissing the sole remaining claim brought by Novell in the last of the Microsoft cases in the United States related to the events of the 1990s that gave rise to the *"Microsoft* cases."[34]

Notes

Chapter 1

1. For a concise account of the development of Microsoft Corporation with a focus on the personal history of its founder, Bill Gates, see Ken Auletta, *World War 3.0: Microsoft and Its Enemies* (2001), 140–159. An official corporate account of the history of Windows ("A History of Windows: Highlights from the First 25 Years") is available at http://windows.microsoft.com.

2. The government didn't formally seek to enjoin the shipment of Windows 98, although that might have been the inescapable result had the court entered the order it sought and Microsoft failed to comply. The government explained as follows.

... What the United States seeks is an Order during the pendency of this litigation enjoining Microsoft:

1. from enforcing restrictive agreements which prevent OEMs [original equipment manufacturers], ISPs [Internet service providers], and ICPs [Internet content providers] from choosing which browser or browsers they will distribute or promote, including any restrictions on the right of OEMs to remove Microsoft's browser or to implement the OEM's own screens or boot-up sequence;
2. from distributing bundled versions of its operating system and its browser at a single price unless Microsoft provides a practical way of removing Internet browser functions and provides OEMs who do not wish to license the Microsoft browser an appropriate deduction from the royalty fee; and
3. from distributing a bundled version of its operating system and its Internet browser unless Microsoft treats Netscape's browser the same as its own with respect to inclusion in and removal from the operating system.

Memorandum of the United States in Support of Motion for a Preliminary Injunction, in *United States v. Microsoft Corp.*, 87 F. Supp.2d 30 (D.D.C. 2000) (Nos. 98-1232 and 98-1233) (filed May 18, 1998) (http://www.usdoj.gov).

3. Statement of Assistant Attorney General Joel I. Klein, Filing of Antitrust Suit Against Microsoft, May 18, 1998 (http://www.usdoj.gov), at 1.

4. The Sherman Act thus addressed a long-standing tension in American culture: if private power can threaten the integrity of public power, should public power be used to mitigate the effects of private power, and, if so, can it do so effectively? One commentator has offered this more general observation: "The American political system is designed to prevent abuses of public power. But where it has proved less vigilant is in those areas where the political meets the economic realm, where private economic power comes to bear on public life. We seem loath as a society to acknowledge the historical coincidence of the two, even though historians ... have persuasively described our history as an ongoing contest between public and private power. We like to believe that our safeguards against concentrated political power will ultimately protect us from the consequences of accumulated economic power. But this hasn't always been so." Tim Wu, *The Master Switch: The Rise and Fall of Information Empires* (2010), 300.

5. For an in-depth discussion of the broader history of the idea of "private attorneys general," see William B. Rubenstein, "On What a 'Private Attorney General' Is—And Why It Matters," 57 *Vand. L. Rev.* 2129 (2004).

6. See, e.g., *Bell Atlantic Corp. v. Twombly*, 550 U.S. 544, 559 (2007) ("the threat of discovery expense will push cost-conscious defendants to settle even anemic cases"). For an examination of how constraints on antitrust standards of liability imposed by the Supreme Court in private cases can affect public enforcement, see Howard A. Shelanski, "The Case for Rebalancing Antitrust and Regulation," 109 *Mich. L. Rev.* 683 (2011). For an examination of the U.S. antitrust system from an institutional perspective, see Daniel A. Crane, *The Institutional Structure of Antitrust Enforcement* (2011).

7. In the United States, antitrust law takes its name from the interstate trusts that developed in the U.S. economy in the 1880s. Elsewhere in the world, antitrust law today is referred to more generically as "competition" law. We will use the terms interchangeably in this book.

8. *Standard Oil Company of New Jersey v. United States*, 221 U.S. 1 (1911).

9. For a more complete explanation of the historical evolution of the rule of reason, see Andrew I. Gavil, "Moving Beyond Caricature and Characterization: The Modern Rule of Reason in Practice," 85 *S. Cal. L. Rev.* 733 (2012).

10. The Supreme Court formally acknowledged this distinction between the first two sections of the Sherman Act in *Copperweld Corp. v. Independence Tube Corp.*, 467 U.S. 752 (1984).

11. The trust was a legal device that facilitated the coordination of production and pricing of goods across industries like oil, whiskey, railroads, and sugar. The trust agreement delegated to a trustee the authority to determine industry wide output and pricing. Without effectuating a formal merger, therefore, it permitted rivals to in effect act as one, as a monopoly, through collusion among themselves. Its inven-

tion has been credited to Samuel C. T. Dodd, an attorney for the Standard Oil Company, who first used the device to organize the Standard Oil Trust in 1882. See Ron Chernow, *Titan: The Life of John D. Rockefeller, Sr.* (1998), 226–227. Before the development of anti-trust laws, these trusts were viewed as a method of providing legal legitimacy under state incorporation laws to what were in effect industry-wide cartels. For a more complete history of the development of the trust device and of congressional responses to it in the form of the Sherman Act, see Herbert Hovenkamp, "Antitrust Policy, Federalism, and the Theory of the Firm: An Historical Perspective," 59 *Antitrust L. J.* 75, 79–87 (1990). For a contemporary account, see F. J. Stimson, "Trusts," 1 *Harv. L. Rev.* 132 (1887).

12. The trusts were also faulted by contemporary critics for their lack of business ethics and harsh treatment of their workers. For a classic example, see Upton Sinclair, *The Jungle* (1906), which portrays the sanitary and working conditions of the members of the Beef Trust.

13. As Hans Thorelli observed in his enduring study of the adoption of the Sherman Act, "There can be no doubt that the Congress felt that the ultimate beneficiary in this whole process was the consumer, enjoying a continuous increase in production and commodity quality at progressively lowered prices. The immediate beneficiaries legislators had in mind, however, was in all probability the small business proprietor or tradesman whose opportunities were to be safeguarded from the dangers emanating from those recently-evolving elements of business that seemed so strange, gigantic, ruthless and awe-inspiring. ... Perhaps we are even justified in saying that the Sherman Act is not to be viewed exclusively as an expression of economic policy. In safeguarding rights of the 'common man' in business 'equal' to those of the evolving more 'ruthless' and impersonal forms of enterprise the Sherman Act embodies what is to be characterized as an eminently 'social' purpose. ..." Thorelli, *The Federal Antitrust Policy: Origination of an American Tradition* (1954), 227. See also William L. Letwin, *Law and Economic Policy in America: The Evolution of the Sherman Antitrust Act* (1965). Additional studies reflecting varying perspectives of the Sherman Act's origins and purposes include Robert H. Bork, "Legislative Intent and the Policy of the Sherman Act," 9 *J. L. & Econ.* 7 (1966); Robert H. Lande, "Wealth Transfers as the Original and Primary Concern of Antitrust: The Efficiency Interpretation Challenged," 34 *Hastings L. J.* 65, 93–96 (1982); James May, "Antitrust in the Formative Era: Political and Economic Theory in Constitutional and Antitrust Analysis, 1880–1918," 50 *Ohio St. L. J.* 257 (1989); Rudolph J. R. Peritz, *Competition Policy in America 1888–1992: History, Rhetoric, Law* (1996).

14. For example, if a monopolist is currently earning an additional profit of $1,000 from charging supra-competitive prices, it might be willing to spend almost all of those profits to hinder the entry of a new rival whose entry threatens to dissipate that profit by returning price to the competitive level. Perhaps the new entrant requires approval from a local zoning board to build a new facility to compete with

the monopolist. To protect its ability to earn the $1,000, the monopolist might be willing to spend almost all of it to oppose the zoning approval.

15. For a discussion of the relationship between Section 1 and Section 2, see *Standard Oil Company of New Jersey v. United States*, 221 U.S. 1, 60–62 (1911).

16. See generally Jonathan B. Baker, "Exclusion as a Core Competition Concern," 78 *Antitrust L. J.* 527 (2013).

17. *United States v. Aluminum Co. of America*, 148 F.2d 416, 427, 430 (2d Cir. 1945).

18. See, e.g., *United States v. United States Steel Corp.*, 251 U.S. 417, 451 (1920) ("the law does not make mere size an offense, or the existence of unexerted power an offense").

19. *Verizon Communications Inc. v. Law Offices of Curtis V. Trinko, LLP*, 540 U.S. 398, 407 (2004) (quoting *United States v. Grinnell Corp.*, 384 U.S. 563, 570–571 (1966)).

20. The Court expanded on this rationale in its 2004 *Verizon* decision: "The mere possession of monopoly power, and the concomitant charging of monopoly prices, is not only not unlawful; it is an important element of the free-market system. The opportunity to charge monopoly prices—at least for a short period—is what attracts 'business acumen' in the first place; it induces risk taking that produces innovation and economic growth. To safeguard the incentive to innovate, the possession of monopoly power will not be found unlawful unless it is accompanied by an element of anticompetitive conduct." The assumption that the promise of monopoly prices is necessary to provide a sufficient incentive for rivals to compete, however, may lead to an unnecessarily permissive attitude about monopoly. It is debatable, for example, whether the lure of "monopoly prices" in fact is the incentive that drives most firms to compete aggressively, especially in industries in which the promise of monopoly is at best remote. It appears that the promise of some incremental measure of profit, as perhaps by securing a larger share of the market or realizing greater economies of scale, is sufficient to spur competition. For additional discussion of this point, with specific reference to the Court's *Trinko* decision, see Andrew I. Gavil, "Exclusionary Distribution Strategies by Dominant Firms: Striking a Better Balance," 72 *Antitrust L. J.* 3, 42–43 (2004).

21. The phrasing comes from Judge Hand's opinion in *United States v. Aluminum Co. of America* (148 F.2d at 430): "A single producer may be the survivor out of a group of active competitors, merely by virtue of his superior skill, foresight and industry. In such cases a strong argument can be made that, although the result may expose the public to the evils of monopoly, the Act does not mean to condemn the resultant of those very forces which it is its prime object to foster: *finis opus coronat*. The successful competitor, having been urged to compete, must not be turned upon when he wins." Hand's expression of the idea that monopoly obtained by "skill" should be protected can be traced to Section 2's very limited legislative history. See 21 *Cong. Rec.* 3151–3152 (1890) (statements of Sens. Kenna and Hoar). Senator Hoar

actually used the phrase "superior skill and intelligence," and distinguished such acts from what he viewed as the common-law definition of unlawful monopoly: "the sole engrossing to a man's self by means which prevent other men from engaging in fair competition with him." Id. See also *United States v. E.I. du Pont de Nemours & Co.*, 351 U.S. 377, 390–391 and n. 15 (1956) (discussing limited legislative history of Section 2). The distinction was also acknowledged by William Howard Taft, who authored one of the earliest monographs on the Sherman Act: *The Anti-Trust Act and the Supreme Court* (1914).

22. Four prominent examples of the competing line of cases are *Brooke Group Ltd. v. Brown & Williamson Tobacco Corp.*, 509 U.S. 209 (1993) (predatory pricing); *Verizon Communications Inc. v. Law Offices of Curtis V. Trinko, LLP*, 540 U.S. 398 (2004) (refusals to deal in a regulated industry); *Weyerhaeuser Co. v. Ross-Simmons Hardwood Lumber Co.*, 549 U.S. 312 (2007) (predatory overbuying); and *Pacific Bell Telephone Co. v. linkLine Communications, Inc.*, 555 U.S. 438 (2009) (price squeeze claims in a regulated industry).

23. *Lorain Journal Co. v. United States*, 342 U.S. 143, 150 (1951).

24. *Aspen Skiing Co. v. Aspen Highlands Skiing Corp.*, 472 U.S. 585, 605 (1985) (footnote omitted).

25. Id. at 605, n. 32 (quoting Phillip Areeda and Donald Turner, *Antitrust Law*) and n. 33 (quoting Robert Bork, *The Antitrust Paradox*).

26. *United States v. Microsoft Corp.*, 253 F.3d 34, 59 (D.C. Cir. 2001). The D.C. Circuit's formulation of the law of monopolization is discussed at greater length in chapter 4.

27. *Standard Oil Company of New Jersey v. United States*, 221 U.S. 1 (1911); *American Tobacco Company. v. United States*, 328 U.S. 781 (1946); *United States v. United States Steel Corp.*, 251 U.S. 417 (1920); *United States v. Aluminum Co. of America*, 148 F.2d 416 (2d. Cir. 1945); *United States v. E.I. du Pont de Nemours & Co.*, 351 U.S. 377 (1956); *In re IBM Corp.*, 687 F.2d 591, 593 (2d Cir. 1982) (granting petition for writ of mandamus ordering dismissal of case pursuant to stipulation of dismissal reached by the Department of Justice and IBM in government's § 2 case); *Am. Tel. & Tel. Co. v. United States*, 552 F. Supp. 131 (D.D.C. 1982), *aff'd mem.*, *Maryland v. United States*, 460 U.S. 1001 (1983) (approving dismissal pursuant to settlement between Department of Justice and AT&T).

28. On the level of enforcement of Section 2 of the Sherman Act, which covers single-firm monopolization, see William E. Kovacic, "The Modern Evolution of U.S. Competition Policy Norms," 71 *Antitrust L. J.* 377, 448–460 (2003) (discussing modest level of Section 2 enforcement over time, with a focus on trends across various presidential administrations). On the uneven history of success of Section 2 prosecutions, see William E. Kovacic, "Designing Antitrust Remedies for Dominant Firm Misconduct," 31 *Conn. L. Rev.* 1285 (1999) and William E. Kovacic, "Failed

Expectations: The Troubled Past and Uncertain Future of the Sherman Act as a Tool of Deconcentration," 74 *Iowa L. Rev.* 1105 (1989). For a classic discussion of the role of popular support for antitrust enforcement, see Richard Hofstadter, "What Happened to the Antitrust Movement?" in *The Paranoid Style in American Politics and Other Essays* (1965), 188. See also Jonathan B. Baker, "Preserving a Political Bargain: The Political Economy of the Non-Interventionist Challenge to Monopolization Enforcement," 76 *Antitrust L. J.* 605 (2010); Jonathan B. Baker, "Competition Policy as Political Bargain," 73 *Antitrust L. J.* 483 (2006).

Chapter 2

1. See, e.g., Jim Erickson, "Microsoft Practices Target of Federal Probe," *Seattle Post-Intelligencer*, March 13, 1991; Lawrence M. Fisher, "Microsoft in Inquiry by F.T.C.," *New York Times*, March 13, 1991. See also Jim Erickson, "When Microsoft Plays Hardball: Fair or Foul? Federal Probe Shines Spotlight on Computer Giant," *Seattle Post-Intelligencer*, March 16, 1991.

2. See Carla Lazzareschi, "IBM, Microsoft Admit FTC Probe on Software Investigation," *Los Angeles Times*, March 13, 1991 (quoting William Neukom).

3. For a purported, detailed account of these events, see Stuart Taylor Jr., "What to Do with the Microsoft Monster," *Am. Law.*, Nov. 1993.

4. Microsoft released Windows 3.0 in May of 1990.

5. Paul Andrews, "Can Microsoft Just Do It?" *Seattle Times*, March 18, 1991 (emphasis added). See also Taylor, "What to Do with the Microsoft Monster" ("a few industry leaders, notably Steve Jobs, ... have called for breaking Microsoft up by splitting its operating and applications software divisions into two companies").

6. Erickson, "When Microsoft Plays Hardball."

7. Fisher, "Microsoft in Inquiry by F.T.C." (quoting William Neukom).

8. Borland's most successful programs at the time included Turbo Pascal (which facilitated computer programming using the Pascal language) and Sidekick (a desktop organizer that included a calculator, a calendar, and a directory of contacts). By acquiring other firms, Borland also offered Paradox (a database program) and Quattro (a spreadsheet program designed to compete with Lotus' popular 1-2-3).

9. Lotus was an acknowledged pioneer in the development of spreadsheet programs and was very successful with 1-2-3.

10. Carla Lazzareschi, "FTC Has Widened Its Probe, Microsoft Says," *Los Angeles Times*, April 13, 1991. Public critics of the government investigation also emerged by this point. See, e.g., T. R. Reid and Brit Hume, "Trust-Busters on Microsoft's Trail Are Following Wrong Scent," *Chicago Tribune*, April 28, 1991; Evan I. Schwartz, "Don't Persecute Microsoft for Doing Things Well," *Business Week*, April 29, 1991.

11. See, e.g., Wendy Goldman Rohm, *The Microsoft File: The Secret Case Against Bill Gates* (1998), 121–122. See also Mark Lewyn and Richard Brandt, "Novell vs. Microsoft: What's Behind the Hate," *Business Week*, Sept. 27, 1993 (detailing the failed merger negotiations between the two firms and Novell's subsequent decision to materially encourage the FTC's investigation of Microsoft).

12. 15 U.S.C. § 49.

13. For a detailed later account, see Taylor, "What to Do with the Microsoft Monster." See also Rohm, *The Microsoft File*, 109–118; *FTC: Watch* No. 383 (Feb. 8, 1993), 2.

14. Kathy Rebello, Mark Lewyn, and Evan I. Schwartz, "Did Microsoft Shut the Windows on Competitors?" *Business Week*, Sept. 28, 1992. In the same article, it was also observed that at the time Bill Gates didn't have any powerful government connections and had contributed very little to politicians (all to Democratic congressmen).

15. *FTC: Watch*, No. 380 (Dec. 21, 1992), 9. The FTC is authorized to seek a temporary restraining order or a preliminary injunction in a federal court under Section 13(b) of the FTC Act, 15 U.S.C. § 53(b). See also Kenneth G. Elzinga, David S. Evans, and Albert L. Nichols, "*United States v. Microsoft*: Remedy or Malady?" 9 *Geo. Mason L. Rev.* 633, 635 (2001):"Within the FTC, there was a difference of opinion about whether to proceed against Microsoft. The Bureau of Competition recommended that the Commission challenge Microsoft's use of per-processor licenses and minimum commitments. But the Bureau of Economics refused to endorse this recommendation. Neither bureau recommended action on claims that Microsoft leveraged its position in operating systems to gain advantages in applications software. The FTC's general counsel recommended further investigation of this issue, but the Commission decided not to do so."

16. See, e.g., Paul Andrews, "Microsoft Injunction Sought: Alleged Antitrust Practices Are Targeted," *Seattle Times*, Dec. 9, 1992; Mark Lewyn, Kathy Rebello, and Paula Dwyer, "The FTC vs. Microsoft: The Software Giant May Be Forced to Change," *Business Week*, Dec. 28, 1992. According to Stuart Taylor, the Bureau of Economics didn't join in the recommendation. Taylor also reported that the focus of injunction would be to bar Microsoft from using blanket CPU licenses, from using tying in the DOS market, and from purposely creating incompatibilities. Taylor, "What to Do with the Microsoft Monster."

17. In mid January, Neukom confirmed by letter to Commissioner Azcuenaga that Microsoft was making several confidential submissions to the FTC in advance of personal meetings to be held in Washington on February 2, 1993, just in advance of the FTC's scheduled February 5, 1993 vote on the staff recommendation. See letter of transmittal from William H. Neukom, Vice President for Law and Corporate Affairs, Microsoft Corporation, to Commissioner Azcuenaga (Jan. 19, 1993) in re File No. 901-0117.

18. 15 U.S.C. § 41.

19. He wrote: "[M]y focus is on the critical technology represented by America's software industry, and the corresponding importance of full, free, fair, and open competition to its growth and success. This aspect of our economic philosophy is especially important to my state, Utah, which is home to one of the country's most vibrant software creation activities, according to a recent report by *Business Week*." Letter from Senator Orrin G. Hatch to Hon. Janet Steiger, Chairman, Federal Trade Commission, Jan. 27, 1993.

20. *FTC: Watch* No. 383 (Feb. 8, 1993), 1–2.

21. According to several sources that were later confirmed by the FTC's official closing announcement, Chairman Steiger and Commissioner Dennis Yao (the FTC's sole economist) voted for the motion; Commissioners Deborah Owen and Mary Azcuenaga voted against it. Commissioner Roscoe Starek III was recused. *FTC: Watch* reported that "[Commissioner] Azcuenaga expressed doubt that Microsoft's practices are anything more than legal volume discounts" (No. 383, Feb. 8, 1993, 1).

22. According to one account, after the February vote "the Commission did ask the Bureau of Competition to further investigate alleged incompatibilities between Windows 3.1 and DR DOS. Microsoft's competitors, particularly Novell, continued to lobby for action. Novell owned both DR DOS and Netware. Netware was the most popular operating system for network server computers but faced competition from Microsoft's new Windows NT Server operating system. Once again, the Bureau of Competition recommended action, the Bureau of Economics dissented, and the Commission deadlocked in July 1993." Kenneth G. Elzinga, David S. Evans, and Albert L. Nichols, "*United States v. Microsoft*: Remedy or Malady?" 9 *Geo. Mason L. Rev.* 633, 636 (2001).

23. The June 7, 1993 *FTC: Watch* (No. 391) reported that "a fierce lobbying campaign has broken out among the commissioners" and that Commissioner Dennis Yao was trying to persuade Commissioner Azcuenaga to switch her vote. In addition, according to *FTC: Watch*, there was discussion of whether Microsoft had used its position in the OS market to unfairly disadvantage competitors in the market for applications software, whether Microsoft deliberately hid features from applications developers to hamper development of competing products, and whether Microsoft deliberately misled competitors about its plans for future products.

24. According to *FTC: Watch* (No. 394, July 19, 1993, 2), Bill Gates visited the FTC two days before the FTC was scheduled to discuss the option of initiating an administrative complaint against Microsoft. *Business Week* confirmed the report in an article published on August 2, 1993, detailing the conduct of the meeting and describing the "air" as "frosty." According to another commentator, "[t]he Gates visits capped a week in which lobbyists for Microsoft's largest competitors had been clogging the

halls of the FTC doing what one calls 'dog and pony shows' for each of the commissioners." Taylor, "What to Do with the Microsoft Monster."

25. 15 U.S.C. § 45(b).

26. The July 19, 1993 *FTC: Watch* reported that an administrative complaint might take "years to litigate" and might lead to uncertainty in the industry, a concern for Commissioners in considering their vote on the second, administrative option.

27. "Why," Taylor asked in "What to Do with the Microsoft Monster," should Microsoft give an inch? Another 2-to-2 vote would be a victory that it could (and later did) hail as a glorious vindication. Besides, Microsoft's lawyers were well aware that the FTC may be institutionally incapable of litigating a big, rich company into submission, so hobbled is the agency by scant resources, by jurisdictional limitations, and by the commissioners' chronic inability to resolve major administrative complaints in under five to seven years. Microsoft had every reason to believe it was almost home free."

28. As had been the case in February, Chairman Steiger and Commissioner Yao voted in favor of the motion and Commissioners Owen and Azcuenaga voted against it. Commissioner Starek was recused.

29. Taylor, "What to Do with the Microsoft Monster." Whereas "philosophical predisposition" might have explained the opposition to the two enforcement motions, it was simplistic to conclude that the positions of Janet Steiger and Dennis Yao were similarly mere products of "philosophical predisposition." Moreover, other commentators critical of the investigation argued that it "stalled ... for good reason." Julie Pitta, "Nature Abhors a Monopoly," *Forbes*, July 6, 1992. The *Forbes* article argued that with the coming of the "second generation of desktop machines" (32-bit instead of 16-bit), Microsoft's future market share "won't be anything like the more than 90% stranglehold it has on operating systems for 16 bit IBM-compatible personal computers" and asked "Who are the contenders for control of the operating systems of the 1990s?" It answered that the competitors included IBM, AT&T (Unix), and Sun. Yet it later acknowledged that Microsoft "may continue to dominate in operating systems at the low end of the market, such as for home computer buyers."

30. *FTC: Watch* No. 395 (August 2, 1993), 1–2. See also Stuart Taylor Jr., "Microsoft Probe, the Sequel: Justice Dept. Seeks FTC Files on Software Giant," *Legal Times*, August 2, 1993.

31. Id.

32. *FTC: Watch*, No. 396 (Sept. 6, 1993), at 1. Stuart Taylor reported in "Microsoft Probe, the Sequel" that Bingaman made courtesy calls to all four commissioners and that Owen responded angrily.

33. In an interview with the *Legal Times*, Bingaman said she saw a distinction "between cases in which the FTC has affirmatively declined to act based on a decision that there is no actionable conduct ... and a 2-2 split in which ... you have a decision by default in effect." Taylor, "What to Do With the Microsoft Monster."

34. In full, the notice read as follows:

1. At a closed Commission meeting on February 5, 1993, Chairman Steiger moved that the Commission authorize the Commission staff to file a complaint in an appropriate federal court seeking a preliminary injunction, under Section 13(b) of the Federal Trade Commission Act, to ban Microsoft from engaging in exclusionary tying practices and from the deliberate creation of nonfunctional incompatibilities between its own and competitors' operating system software in order to harm competitors, and to remedy Microsoft's practices with respect to existing per processor elements of current DOS license provisions. The motion failed for lack of a majority. For the record, Chairman Steiger and Commissioner Yao voted in the affirmative on the motion; Commissioner Azcuenaga and Commissioner Owen voted in the negative; and Commissioner Starek was recused.

2. At a closed meeting on July 21, 1993, Chairman Steiger moved that the Commission—having reason to believe that Microsoft Corporation has violated Section 5 of the Federal Trade Commission Act and Section 3 of the Clayton Act—issue an administrative complaint against Microsoft Corporation. The motion failed for lack of a majority. For the record, Chairman Steiger and Commissioner Yao voted in the affirmative on the motion; Commissioner Azcuenaga and Commissioner Owen voted in the negative; and Commissioner Starek was recused.

35. Letter from Donald S. Clark, Secretary, FTC, to William H. Neukom, August 20, 1993 (advising of closing if investigation by a vote of 4–0).

36. See letter from Hon. Howard M. Metzenbaum, Chairman, Senate Subcommittee on Antitrust, Monopolies and Business Rights to Janet Steiger, Chairman, FTC (July 13, 1993) (encouraging referral to Department of Justice if deadlock cannot be broken). See also letter from Hon. Orrin G. Hatch to Janet Steiger (July 21, 1993) (urging referral to Department of Justice in the event of another deadlocked vote). Stuart Taylor reported that Bingaman personally reviewed and approved the letter in advance. Taylor, "What to Do with the Microsoft Monster."

37. Mark Lewyn and Catherine Yang, "How Microsoft Wound Up in Justice's Lap," *Business Week*, Sept. 27, 1993, quoting Anne Bingaman, the Assistant Attorney for Antitrust, as saying "We, in effect, could act as the fifth commissioner."

38. For a critique of the government's litigation against IBM, see Franklin M. Fisher, John J. McGowan, and Joen E. Greenwood, *Folded, Spindled, and Mutilated: Economic Analysis and U.S. v. IBM* (MIT Press, 1983).

39. See Catherine Yang, "Annie Gets Her Antitrust Gun: Microsoft Could Be the First Target for Justice's Anne Bingaman," *Business Week*, August 23, 1993.

40. John Markoff, "Microsoft Confronts Its Success," *New York Times*, August 23, 1993. In the same article, Markoff also identified Novell as "the leader in a campaign within the industry against Microsoft," noting that it has "hired several law firms, economists, and public relations people as part of its effort."

41. Lewyn and Yang, "How Microsoft Wound Up in Justice's Lap."

42. Complaint, *United States v. Microsoft Corp.*, Civ. Action No. 94-1564 (SS) ("Licensing Case Complaint") (http://www.usdoj.gov); Final Judgment, *United States v. Microsoft Corp.*, Civ. Action No. 94-1564 (SS) (http://www.usdoj.gov).

43. *United States v. Microsoft Corp.*, 56 F.3d 1448, 1451 (D.C. Cir. 1995).

44. Licensing Case Complaint, ¶¶ 23–24. The Complaint also alleged that "in fiscal year 1993, "per processor" agreements accounted for an estimated 60% of Microsoft's MS-DOS sales to OEMs and 43% of Windows sales to OEMs." Id. at ¶ 26.

45. As Herbert Hovenkamp has observed, Microsoft's "per processor" licensing practice was "somewhat more akin to exclusive dealing than tying" and "had the effect of raising the costs rival operating systems faced." He concluded, therefore, that it was "exclusionary." Hovenkamp, *The Antitrust Enterprise: Principle and Execution* (2006), 266.

46. The government's complaint alleged that "Microsoft's practices deter OEMs from entering into licensing agreements with competing providers of operating systems, discourage OEMs who agree to sell non-Microsoft operating systems from promoting those products, and raise the price of computers sold with competing operating systems, thereby depressing the demand and restricting the output of these products." Licensing Case Complaint, ¶ 28. This was later explained by Joel Klein and Preeta Bansal: "The practical effect of this license was to impose a "tax" on manufacturers' use of competing operating systems—the computer manufacturer had to pay two licensing fees for using any operating system other than Microsoft's—and thus to diminish the viability of actual or potential competitors to Microsoft. The anticompetitive impact of the per-processor license was increased by Microsoft's practice of using it in long-term licenses with large minimum purchase commitments, thereby locking in PC manufacturers to Microsoft and impeding development and marketing of competing operating systems." Klein and Bansal, "International Antitrust Enforcement in the Computer Industry," 41 *Vill. L. Rev.* 173, 174–175 (1996).

47. Hovenkamp, *The Antitrust Enterprise*, 267. For an argument that Hovenkamp's assessment of the "per processor" royalty practice is flawed because it focuses solely on the licenses' likely anticompetitive effects while ignoring potential efficiency justifications, see Richard A. Epstein, *Antitrust Consent Decrees in Theory and Practice* (2007), 77–78. Epstein's arguments, however, are largely theoretical and speculative and don't appear to be supported by any evidence regarding Microsoft's actual use of the "per processor" license.

48. Licensing Case Complaint, ¶ 34. ("The terms of these non-disclosure agreements would preclude developers at these companies from working with operating-system companies, other competitors of Microsoft, and competing technologies for an unreasonably long period of time.")

49. See the discussion of monopolization standards in chapter 1.

50. Licensing Case Complaint, ¶ 35. The complaint went on (¶¶ 36–38) to detail how the practices "harmed competition, consumers and innovation" in a variety of ways.

51. *United States v. Microsoft Corp.*, 1995-2 Trade Cas. (CCH) ¶ 71,096 (D.D.C. 1995) (entering Final Judgment). Section IV of the Judgment addresses "Prohibited Conduct." Paragraph A limited the duration of licensing agreements to one year. Paragraphs C and D prohibited "per processor" licenses, substituting a preference for "per copy licenses." Paragraph K limited the scope and duration of non-disclosure agreements.

52. 15 U.S.C §§16(b)–(h). Section 16(b) provides that "[a]ny proposal for a consent judgment submitted by the United States for entry in any civil proceeding brought by or on behalf of the United States under the antitrust laws shall be filed with the district court before which such proceeding is pending. ..." Section 16(e)(1) provides that "[b]efore entering any consent judgment proposed by the United States under this section, the court shall determine that the entry of such judgment is in the public interest." The public-interest portion of the statute was significantly amended in 2004, in part in response to the perceived weaknesses of the statute as revealed through the settlement of the 1998 *Microsoft* litigation in 2001 and the subsequent Tunney Act-related appeal, which we discuss in chapter 4.

53. In support of his conclusion, Sporkin issued an initial memorandum opinion and a supplemental opinion a month later. See *United States v. Microsoft Corp.*, 159 F.R.D. 318 (D.D.C. 1995) (February 14, 1995 Memorandum Order) (http://www .usdoj.gov); *United States v. Microsoft Corp.*, 1995-1 Trade Cas. ¶ 70,928 (D.D.C. 1995) (Supplemental Order of March 14, 1995) (http://www.usdoj.gov).

54. The I.D.E. Corporation ("IDEA"), represented by Jeffrey S. Jacobovitz, moved to intervene under Rule 24 of the Federal Rules of Civil Procedure. The Computer & Communications Industry Association (CCIA) also moved to intervene, or in the alternative to participate as an amicus curiae. Represented by a Silicon Valley attorney named Gary Reback, an anonymous group also moved to submit an amicus curiae brief in order to oppose the entry of the negotiated decree. *United States v. Microsoft Corp.*, 159 F.R.D., at 324. As Judge Sporkin explained in his supplemental order of March 14, 1995, "IDEA Corporation's primary reason for participation was to express its belief that the decree should provide for reimbursement of prepaid royalties paid under past licensing agreements with Microsoft. The objections of the [anonymous amicus firms] ... are not only much broader, but also those companies have not suggested that the decree encompass the remedy proposed by IDEA."

United States v. Microsoft Corp., 1995-1 Trade Cas. (CCH) ¶ 70,928 (D.D.C. 1995) (Supplemental Order of March 14, 1995) (http://www.usdoj.gov).

55. *United States v. Microsoft Corp.*, 159 F.R.D., at 328–329.

56. Id. at 332.

57. Id. at 333.

58. Id. The court of appeals would later make the following observation on this point: "The district court understandably questioned the government as to why the decree did not forbid Microsoft from using the alleged anticompetitive licensing practices with respect to all of Microsoft's operating systems (in particular, Windows NT products). But the government explained that Windows NT products do not have "a significant share of a relevant market at this time." *United States v. Microsoft Corp.*, 56 F.3d 1448, 1461 (D.C. Cir. 1995).

59. 159 F.R.D. at 334.

60. As the court of appeals would later recount, Sporkin revealed at a September 1994 status conference that he had read *Hard Drive: Bill Gates and the Making of the Microsoft Empire*, a 1992 book by James Wallace and Jim Erickson, and asked the government's lawyers whether they had investigated its charges, particularly its account of Microsoft's use of vaporware to impair competition. *United States v. Microsoft Corp.*, 56 F.3d 1448, 1452–1453 (D.C. Cir. 1995).

61. Specifically, he asked the following:

(2) Why the proposed consent decree should not be amended to include:

(a) A provision that would clearly state that the consent decree applies to all operating systems commercially offered by Microsoft;

(b) A provision barring Microsoft from engaging in the practice of "vaporware" i.e., releasing misleading information concerning the status of the introduction into the marketplace of new software products;

(c) A provision establishing a wall between the development of operating systems software and the development of applications software at Microsoft;

(d) A provision requiring disclosure of all instruction codes built into operating systems software designed to give Microsoft an advantage over competitors in the applications software market;

(e) A provision establishing an appropriate compliance apparatus (e.g., private inspector general, business practices officer or compliance officer) to ensure compliance with the decree;

(g) [sic] In the event Microsoft chooses not to pay I.D.E. Corporation the damages that it seeks, a provision that would avoid costly litigation. For example, allowing this Court to refer the matter to a Special Master.

159 F.R.D. at 326–327, n. 15. The idea of a monitoring device would later resurface when the question of remedies was again posed in the Windows 98 case along with

another of Sporkin's proposals: erecting a wall between Microsoft's applications and operating systems development.

62. *United States v. Microsoft Corp.*, 159 F.R.D. at 326–327, n. 15. Sporkin's suggestions were similar in part to those made by Stuart Taylor in 1993. Taylor rejected the idea of breaking up Microsoft because it probably would produce uncertain results and certain IBM-style litigation to the death for years to come. His four-part proposed remedy consisted of a ban on CPU licenses that excluded rivals without any clear economic purpose, a ban on tying if efficiencies of integration couldn't be demonstrated, a prohibition on the deliberate embedding of incompatibilities, and documentation of all internal communications protocols. Taylor, "What to Do with the Microsoft Monster." Even closer analogues to Taylor's proposals would later surface in the Windows 98 case.

63. Motion for Expedited Consideration and for Briefing Schedule, *United States v. Microsoft Corp.*, No. 95-5037 (Feb. 16, 1995) (http://www.usdoj.gov). Because both parties jointly appealed, there was technically no "appellee," so the court of appeals permitted the amici in the district court to, in essence, act as appellees to defend Judge Sporkin's decision. See *United States v. Microsoft Corp.*, 56 F.3d at 1455.

64. These arguments were further developed in Sporkin's supplemental order of March 14, 1995 and in a letter from Assistant Attorney General Anne Bingaman responding to that order the same day. Bingaman specifically rejected any suggestion that the Department of Justice and Microsoft had reached any "side agreement" to support the settlement, as Judge Sporkin appeared to imply in his supplemental order. See letter from Anne K. Bingaman, Assistant Attorney General, Antitrust Division, U.S. Department of Justice, to Judge Stanley J. Sporkin (March 14, 1995) (http://www.usdoj.gov). They were also developed further in the briefs filed with the court of appeals.

65. 56 F.3d. at 1459–1461.

66. 159 F.R.D. at 331, quoting *United States v. American Tel. & Tel. Co.*, 552 F. Supp. 131, 150 (D.D.C. 1982), *aff'd sub nom, Maryland v. United States*, 460 U.S. 1001 (1983), which in turn was quoting *International Salt Co. v. United States*, 332 U.S. 392, 401 (1947).

67. See Memorandum of the United States of America in Support of Motion to Enter Final Judgment and in Opposition to the Positions of I.D.E. Corporation and Amici (Jan. 18, 1995) (http://www.usdoj.gov).

68. See, e.g., Joseph Farrell and Garth Saloner, "Installed Base and Compatibility: Innovation, Product Preannouncements, and Predation," 76 *Am. Econ. Rev.* 940, 943 (1986); W. Brian Arthur, "Competing Technology, Increasing Returns, and Lock-in by Historical Events," 99 *Econ. J.* 116 (1989); W. Brian Arthur, *Increasing Returns and Path Dependence in the Economy* (1994). See also Michael L. Katz and Carl Shapiro,

"Product Introduction with Network Externalities," 40 *J. Indus. Econ.* 55 (March 1992); Michael L. Katz and Carl Shapiro, "Network Externalities, Competition, and Compatibility," 75 *Am. Econ. Rev.* 424 (1985); S. J. Liebowitz and Stephen E. Margolis, "Should Technology Choice Be a Concern of Antitrust Policy?" 9 *Harv. J. L. & Tech.* 283, 286–290 (1996) (discussing network externalities, increasing returns and path dependence); David S. Evans and Richard Schmalensee, "A Guide to the Antitrust Economics of Networks," *Antitrust*, spring 1996, at 36. According to one source, the licensing case was "[t]he first government antitrust case to explicitly invoke network effects theory." William J. Kolasky, "Network Effects: A Contrarian View," 7 *Geo. Mason L. Rev.* 577, 581 (1999).

69. Carl Shapiro and Hal R. Varian, *Information Rules: A Strategic Guide to the Network Economy* (1999), 173.

70. Id. Shapiro and Varian continue: "Whether real or virtual, networks have a fundamental economic characteristic: the value of connecting to a network depends on the number of *other* people already connected to it."

71. Id.

72. According to Sporkin, Arrow's declaration "made three main points: 1) that the market is an increasing returns market with large barriers to entry; 2) that the violations set forth in the complaint contributed in some part to Microsoft's monopoly position; and 3) that the decree will eliminate 'artificial barriers that Microsoft had erected to prevent or slow the entry of competing suppliers of operating system software products.'" 159 F.R.D. at 333.

73. Mark A. Lemley and David McGowan, "Legal Implications of Network Economic Effects," 86 *Cal. L. Rev.* 479, 503 (1998).

74. For an additional account of the dueling positions of Arrow and the amici, see Kenneth G. Elzinga, David S. Evans, and Albert L. Nichols, "*United States v. Microsoft*: Remedy or Malady?" 9 *Geo. Mason L. Rev.* 633, 637–638 (2001). See also Mark A. Lemley and David McGowan, "Legal Implications of Network Economic Effects," 86 *Cal. L. Rev.* 479, 501 (1998). ("All of the parties [to the 1994 Licensing Case] seemed to acknowledge the role network effects played in Microsoft's dominance of the operating systems market.")

75. 56 F.3d at 1452.

76. The exclusionary theory of raising rivals' costs was significantly advanced in Thomas G. Krattenmaker and Steven C. Salop, "Anticompetitive Exclusion: Raising Rivals' Costs to Achieve Power over Price," 96 *Yale L. J.* 209 (1986). See also Steven C. Salop and David T. Scheffman, "Raising Rivals' Costs," 73 *Am. Econ. Rev.* 267 (1983); Robert H. Bork, *The Antitrust Paradox: A Policy at War with Itself* (1978), 156 ("By disturbing optimal distribution patterns one rival can impose costs upon another" which can be a means of exclusion.)

77. See Memorandum of the United States of America in Support of Motion to Enter Final Judgment and in Opposition to the Positions of I.D.E. Corporation and Amici (Jan. 18, 1995) (http://www.usdoj.gov) at 29–30 (quoting the declaration of Kenneth Arrow). Seven years later, when the government sought to settle the Windows 98 case, Arrow submitted an affidavit on behalf of an industry group advocating the breakup of Microsoft. The group, known as the Project to Promote Competition and Innovation in the Digital Age ("Pro Comp"), was represented by former Judge Robert H. Bork and former Solicitor General Kenneth Starr and opposed the entry of the 2001 Consent Decree. Its comments, along with Arrow's affidavit, are available at http://www.usdoj.gov.

78. *United States v. Microsoft Corp.*, 159 F.R.D. 318, 334 (D.D.C. 1995).

79. Memorandum of the United States of America in Support of Motion to Enter Final Judgment and in Opposition to the Positions of I.D.E. Corporation and Amici at 30.

80. 56 F.3d at 1460–1461.

81. Id. at 1462. Some commentators praised the court for placing limits on Tunney Act Review. See, e.g., Deborah A. Garza, "The Court of Appeals Sets Strict Limits on Tunney Act Review: The Microsoft Consent Decree," *Antitrust*, fall 1995, at 21. In 2004, however, Congress attempted to reinvigorate the Tunney Act process by broadening the scope of the public-interest inquiry. Subsequent court interpretations, however, have limited the effectiveness of those amendments.

82. 56 F.3d. at 1463–1465.

83. See Steve Lohr, "Judge Clears Antitrust Pact for Microsoft," *New York Times*, August 22, 1995. For the full licensing decree, see *United States v. Microsoft Corp.*, 1995-2 Trade Cas. (CCH) ¶ 71,096 (D.D.C. 1995).

84. Lohr, "Judge Clears Antitrust Pact for Microsoft."

85. According to Ken Auletta (*World War 3.0: Microsoft and Its Enemies*, 2001, 6), "[Deputy Assistant Attorney General Joel Klein] and his colleagues were annoyed that instead of appearing humble when Judge Jackson upheld the consent decree, Gates appeared on CNN's *Larry King Live* the same night and bellowed 'That whole thing really has no effect on Microsoft or how we work. ... What it comes down to is that there is nothing significant that we needed to change, and that just confirms the way we've viewed it all along.' Translated: we won. Justice lost."

86. James Gleick, "Making Microsoft Safe for Capitalism," *New York Times*, Nov. 5, 1995.

87. Memorandum in Support, at 31. For criticism of the 1994 decree's effect, see, e.g.., Michael H. Knight and Nicholas A. Widnell, "Dark Clouds in the Distance? Network Effects and the Approaching B2B Storm," 9 *Geo. Mason L. Rev.* 599, 621

(2001) (arguing that it had little significant impact, either because the market had tipped or because the government decree didn't fix the problem).

88. The extent of the commingling of code is described in Judge Jackson's Findings of Fact. *United States v. Microsoft Corp.*, 65 F. Supp.2d 1, 40–41 (D.D.C. 1999) (¶¶ 158, 161).

89. A year later, Netscape also submitted a substantial "White Paper Update."

90. See Jim Erickson, "Netscape Pushes for Microsoft Probe," *Seattle Post-Intelligencer*, August 21, 1996.

91. Leslie Helm, "Microsoft Calls Netscape's Claims 'Bizarre,'" *Los Angeles Times*, August 23, 1996.

92. After reviewing the brief, Klein asked Phillip Malone of the Antitrust Division's San Francisco field office to "investigate the allegations." Scott McNealy of Sun Microsystems also "pressed Klein vigorously and spent considerable company resources to make the case. If Microsoft was not halted, [he and other Silicon Valley firms] each warned, it would leverage Windows into every new platform and device: the cheap network computers that draw their software from the Internet, handheld devices, cellular phones, cable boxes, PlayStations, pagers, and the servers that process and store digital data." Auletta, *World War 3.0: Microsoft and Its Enemies* (2001), 7.

93. Garth Alexander, "Netscape Losing Browser Battle," *Sunday Times* (UK), Oct. 13, 1996.

94. See "Statement of Attorney General Janet Reno on the Confirmation of Eric H. Holder Jr. and Joel I. Klein" (http://www.usdoj.gov). Bingaman announced her departure in October of 1996; Klein served as Acting Assistant Attorney General until formally nominated to the permanent post in March of 1997 and confirmed in July.

95. Michelle Matassa Flores, "Republicans Challenge Justice Department Probe of Microsoft," *Seattle Times*, June 30, 1997 ("Unhappy with the progress of a federal antitrust investigation of Microsoft, three U.S. senators have asked the Federal Trade Commission to grab control of the inquiry from the Justice Department"); "FTC Rejects Call to Investigate Microsoft," *Computer World*, July 7, 1997.

96. See Department of Justice, Petition by the United States for an Order to Show Cause Why Respondent Microsoft Corporation Should Not Be Found in Civil Contempt, Supplemental to Civil Action No. 94-1564 (D.D.C.) (filed Oct. 20, 1997) (http://www.usdoj.gov). The proposed order also would have required Microsoft to provide consumers with "easy-to-follow instructions" for removing the IE icon from the Windows desktop and to inform consumers that they weren't required to use Internet Explorer, that other browsers would work "without harm to the operation of Windows 95," and that other browsers were "readily available."

97. Department of Justice Press Release, "Justice Department Charges Microsoft with Violating 1995 Court Order" (http://www.usdoj.gov) (quoting Joel Klein).

98. See Petition by the United States for an Order to Show Cause Why Respondent Microsoft Corporation Should Not Be Held in Civil Contempt (Oct. 20, 1997) (http://www.usdoj.gov). See also "Justice Department Charges Microsoft with Violating 1995 Court Order" (press release, Oct. 20, 1997) (http://www.usdoj.gov).

99. Bryan Gruley, John R. Wilke, David Bank, and Don Clark, "U.S. Sues Microsoft over PC Browser," *Wall Street Journal*, Oct. 21, 1997.

100. See Microsoft Corp., Memorandum in Opposition to Petition of the United States for an Order to Show Cause Why Respondent Microsoft Corporation Should Not Be Found in Civil Contempt, Supplemental to Civil Action No. 94-1564 (D.D.C.), 1997 WL 33635512 (Nov. 10, 1997), at 3–6.

101. Reply Brief of Petitioner United States of America (filed Nov. 27, 1997) (http://www.usdoj.gov) at 19. The Justice Department's brief argued that Microsoft's interest in delving into a decree on which Microsoft had commented and supported, and whose review had been "especially substantial and visible," was ironic. Id. at 19–20.

102. Id. at 23. See also 14 and n. 16.

103. Like Judge Sporkin before him, Judge Jackson, in his brief hearing on the decree, didn't focus on the language of paragraph IV. Ironically, his failure to do so was arguably inconsistent with the court of appeals' guidance to the district court in its decision reversing Judge Sporkin's previous rejection of the decree: "A district judge ... is certainly entitled to insist on that degree of precision concerning the resolution of known issues as to make his task, in resolving subsequent disputes, reasonably manageable." *United States v. Microsoft Corp.*, 56 F.3d 1448, 1461 (D.C. Cir. 1995).

104. *United States v. Microsoft Corp.*, 980 F. Supp. 537, 540–541 (D.D.C. 1997). He also declined the government's request to strike some of Microsoft's non-disclosure agreements on the ground that they would impair the court's ability to enforce the consent decree. Id. at 544–545.

105. Id. at 541–543.

106. For Judge Jackson's opinion on the contempt motion, see *United States v. Microsoft Corp.*, 980 F. Supp. 537 (D.D.C. 1997).

107. In its definition of "Covered Products," the 1994 decree included successor versions of Windows 95. See *United States v. Microsoft Corp.*, 1995-2 Trade Cas. (CCH) ¶ 71,096 (D.D.C. 1995) (defining covered products). The Justice Department had referred to "covered products" in framing its request for relief in the contempt petition, but its arguments referred only to Windows 95. See Petition by the United

States for an Order to Show Cause Why Respondent Microsoft Corporation Should Not Be Held in Civil Contempt (Oct. 20, 1997) (http://www.usdoj.gov) at 14 (Prayer II) (requesting order that Microsoft cease requiring OEMs "to license *any version* of Internet Explorer as an express or implied condition of licensing Windows 95 or *any Covered Product*, as defined in the Final Judgment) (emphasis added).

108. For reaction to Lessig's appointment, see David Segal, "Case's 'Special Master' Called a Special Mind," *Washington Post*, Dec. 13, 1997 ("'I know he has a stellar resume and he looks like a man of enormous ability and talent,' [Joel] Klein said. 'But aside from that, I don't know much about him.'").

109. John R. Wilke, "Judge Tells Justice Agency, Microsoft to Argue Contempt Request on Jan. 13," *Wall Street Journal*, Dec. 22, 1997 (reporting that Jackson stated to Microsoft that a court computer technician "took less than 90 seconds" to separate Windows 95 and Internet Explorer and asked why the company couldn't do it as easily). For some examples of reactions to Microsoft's approach, see David Bank and Dean Takahashi, "Microsoft Seeks Alternative Ways to Comply with Court," *Wall Street Journal*, Dec. 19, 19974 (reporting "growing perception" that Microsoft "committed a strategic blunder").

110. See Motion by the United States for Judgment of Civil Contempt And to Enforce Preliminary Injunction (filed Dec. 17, 1997) (http://www.usdoj.gov).

111. In denying the motion, Jackson was particularly critical of Microsoft's attack on Lessig, calling Microsoft's allegations of possible bias "trivial and altogether nonprobative" and continuing: "They are, therefore, defamatory, and the Court finds that they were not made in good faith." *United States v. Microsoft Corp.*, 1998 WL 30147 (D.D.C. 1998).

112. The consultant hired by the Justice Department was Glenn Weadock, who was also an author of how-to books for Windows and PCs. Weadock testified both at the contempt hearing and at the monopolization trial.

113. For examples of cases in which courts had abjured the role of product designer, see *Transamerica Computer v. IBM Corp.*, 698 F.2d 1377, 1382–1383 (9th Cir. 1983) (redesign incompatibility argument); *Cal. Computer Prods. v. IBM Corp.*, 613 F.2d 727, 744 (9th Cir. 1979) (same); *Berkey Photo v. Eastman Kodak Co.*, 603 F.2d 263, 276 (2d Cir. 1979) (predisclosure of innovations argument). In software copyright litigation, however, courts have been less hesitant to explore issues of software design. See, e.g., *Apple Computer, Inc. v. Microsoft Corp.*, 799 F. Supp. 1006 (N.D. Cal. 1992), order clarified, 27 U.S.P.D.2d (BNA) 1081 (N.D. Cal. 1993).

114. See *United States v. Microsoft*, Stipulation and Order (http://www.usdoj.gov), clause 3.

115. See United States' Proposed Findings of Fact, at ¶¶ 15, 16 *United States v. Microsoft*, 980 F. Supp. 537 (filed Jan. 19, 1998) (No. 98-1564) (http://www.justice.gov).

116. See John R. Wilke, "Microsoft Is Again Assailed by Agency, Which Says Firm Thwarts Court Order," *Wall Street Journal*, Dec. 30, 1997 (reporting Microsoft's estimate that 97% of IE code would remain); John R. Wilke and Don Clark, "Judge Rejects Attempt by Microsoft to Remove Special Master in U.S. Action," *Wall Street Journal*, Jan. 15, 1998.

117. The court of appeals' opinion on the contempt motion and preliminary injunction decision is *United States v. Microsoft Corp.*, 147 F.3d 935 (D.C. Cir. 1998).

118. Id. at 946.

119. Id. at 948.

120. Id. at 950 (emphasis added).

121. Id. at 950–951.

122. The court defended its approach and argued that it wasn't being deferential to Microsoft's reading of the decree but rather was concerned about "the limited competence of courts to evaluate high-tech product designs and the high cost of error," which should make courts "wary of second-guessing the claimed benefits of a particular design decision." Id. at 950, n. 13. It later backed away from this view in its consideration of the merits of the Windows 98 case.

123. Id. at 950.

124. In July of 1996, Caldera commenced a civil antitrust action against Microsoft. Caldera had purchased the rights to DR-DOS from Novell, which had acquired them years earlier when it purchased Digital Research, DR-DOS's original developer. Caldera was largely owned by Ray Noorda, the founder and the former head of Novell. When Noorda left the company in 1994, Novell abandoned DR-DOS. Caldera sued Microsoft the day its acquisition of the rights to DR-DOS was complete, but it rejected accusations that it had purchased those rights merely to facilitate the filing of the law suit. See "Novell Founder Noorda Pushes Antitrust Suit Against Microsoft Computers," *Los Angeles Times*, July 25, 1996.

Chapter 3

1. For descriptions of the memorandum's importance to the litigation, see Joel Brinkley and Steve Lohr, *U.S. v. Microsoft* (2001), 7; Ken Auletta, *World War 3.0: Microsoft and Its Enemies* (2001), 55 (discussing the use of the memorandum at trial).

2. "The Internet Tidal Wave" (memorandum from Bill Gates to Executive Staff and Direct Reports), May 26, 1995 (in authors' files), at 1, 2.

3. Id. 4. Netscape Navigator was released on December 15, 1994. See *United States v. Microsoft Corp.*, 84 F. Supp. 2d 9, 29 (D.D.C. 1999) (Findings of Fact ¶ 72).

4. See John Heilemann, *Pride Before the Fall: The Trials of Bill Gates and the End of the Microsoft Era* (2001), 15 (statement of Netscape's president made to Netscape's lawyer).

5. See Marc Andreessen, notes of June 21, 1995 meeting with Microsoft, at 3 ("THREAT THAT MS WILL OWN THE WIN95 CLIENT MARKET AND THAT NETSCAPE SHOULD STAY AWAY") (uppercase in original) (in authors' files).

6. See email message from Dan Rosen (Microsoft) to Bill Gates and others (subject: Netscape meeting), June 22, 1995 (in authors' files) ("We need to understand if you will adopt our platform and build on top of it or if you are going to compete with us on the platform level.")

7. Id.

8. On equity investment and participation, see Andreessen, notes of June 21, 1995 meeting with Microsoft. On general strategy, see email message from Dan Rosen to Bill Gates and others (subject: Netscape), June 14, 1995 (in authors' files).

9. See email message from Paul Maritz to Dan Rosen and others (re: Netscape), July 17, 1995 (in authors' files) (confirming that there was no need to continue discussions with Netscape "at a 'strategic' level"). Although at one time some executives at Microsoft thought that a deal with Netscape was possible, others were less optimistic. See email message from Thomas Reardon (Microsoft) to Brad Silverberg and others (subject: Netscape meeting: reality), June 23, 1995 (in authors' files) ("maybe i am being a dick, but there is no deal here."). This message was forwarded to Bill Gates. See email message from Brad Silverberg to Bill Gates (subject: FW: Netscape meeting: reality), June 23, 1995 (in authors' files) ("not sure i should forward this to you, but i am because i want you to see another perspective of the meeting with netscape so you can be fully informed.").

10. With regard to withholding interoperability information, Andreessen's notes from the June 21 meeting indicate that there was discussion of disclosing important interoperability information relating to one specific Windows 95 API. Microsoft indicated that "we can fix the problem ... [if we have] a special relationship"; otherwise it would take "3 months."

11. See Department of Justice Complaint ¶ 71, *United States v. Microsoft Corp.*, 84 F. Supp. 2d 9 (D.D.C. 1999) (No. 98-1232) (http://www.usdoj.gov) (hereinafter "DOJ Complaint").

12. Heilemann (*Pride Before the Fall*, 15–16) describes the meeting and concludes that Justice Department lawyers took notes "and then promptly forgot about it." For a description of the Netscape-Microsoft meeting and the Justice Department's subsequent investigation by Netscape's lawyer, see Gary L. Reback, *Free the Market!* (2009), 188–194.

13. On the frequency of competitors' complaints about Microsoft, see Steve Lohr, "Gates, the Pragmatist, Walked Away," *New York Times*, May 22, 1995. ("We get complaints about Microsoft all the time. We have become a kind of Microsoft complaints center. And we take them very seriously." —quoting Anne K. Bingaman, head of Antitrust Division) For a discussion of competitors' complaints related to MSN, see William H. Page, "Microsoft and the Public Choice Critique of Antitrust," 44 *Antitrust Bull.* 5, 21–23 (1999).

14. See Viveca Novak and Don Clark, "Microsoft Corp. Broadly Attacks Antitrust Unit," *Wall Street Journal*, June 27, 1995 ("For example, one of the document requests asks the company to produce 'all strategic plans prepared by or for Microsoft by any party and any documents provided by or to the board or top executives of Microsoft concerning predictions as to the future of computers and computer technology.'").

15. See Viveca Novak and Don Clark, "U.S. Withdraws Subpoena to Microsoft," *Wall Street Journal*, July 24, 1995; Edmund L. Andrews, "U.S. Drops Demand for More Microsoft Documents," *New York Times*, July 22, 1995. Microsoft had already begun shipping master copies of Windows 95 to computer manufacturers. Id.

16. For reports of this part of the investigation, see G. Christian Hill and Jared Sandberg, "Justice's Microsoft Investigation Extends to Bundling of Navigation Software," *Wall Street Journal*, July 31, 1995 ("But people familiar with the investigation indicated they may feel the browser issue provides the agency with more and new ammunition. The move shows that the issue of bundling products with Microsoft's dominant operating systems won't go away, and has to be dealt with one way or another.").

17. On the marketing ballyhoo for Windows 95, see, e.g., Don Clark, "Golden Code: Amid Hype and Fear, Microsoft Windows 95 Gets Ready to Roll," *Wall Street Journal*, July 14, 1995. On pressure from software companies and retailers not to stop the launch, see, e.g., "Software Companies Urge Release of Windows 95," *New York Times*, August 8, 1995 (reporting letters sent to Justice Department).

18. See Don Clark, "U.S. Plans No Action Against Microsoft Before Launch of Windows 95 System," *Wall Street Journal*, August 9, 1995.

19. For descriptions of Netscape's white paper, see Heilemann, *Pride Before the Fall*, 17–19; Reback, *Free the Market!* 198–202.

20. See Don Clark and Bryan Gruley, "Microsoft Internet Business Is Focus of Antitrust Probe," *Wall Street Journal*, Sept. 20, 1996; Heilemann, *Pride Before the Fall*, 17–18. There is some disagreement as to the intensity of this investigation. Compare Heilemann, *Pride Before the Fall*, 20 (minimal investigation from 1996 to 1997) with Brinkley and Lohr, *U.S. v. Microsoft*, 5–8 (describing aggressive investigation). Other Microsoft competitors were subsequently involved in trying to convince the Justice Department to bring suit. See, e.g., Heilemann, *Pride Before the Fall*, 88–94 (describ-

ing Sun's $3 million "Project Sherman," a three-month effort in the beginning of 1998 that led to a presentation to the Justice Department by well-respected antitrust lawyers and economists detailing Microsoft's behavior and how it had affected the industry).

21. See Joshua Cooper Ramo, "Winner Take All," *Time*, Sept. 16, 1996, at 56. The impact of the article is discussed in Heilemann, *Pride Before the Fall*, 22.

22. See Brinkley and Lohr, *U.S. v. Microsoft*, 6–7.

23. Email message from Jim Allchin to Paul Maritz (subject: IE and Windows (Jan. 2, 1997) (in authors' files); email from Christian Wildfeuer to Adam Taylor and others (subject: Memphis IEU focus groups report (long mail) (Feb. 24, 1997) (in authors' files). Both of these messages were quoted, in part, by Judge Jackson in his findings of fact, *United States v. Microsoft Corp.*, 84 F. Supp. 2d 9, 51–52 (D.D.C. 1999) (Findings of Fact ¶¶ 166, 169).

24. Email message from Jim Allchin to Paul Maritz (subject: IE and Windows (Jan. 2, 1997) (in authors' files); email from Christian Wildfeuer to Adam Taylor and others (subject: Memphis IEU focus groups report (long mail) (Feb. 24, 1997) (in authors' files).

25. Id.

26. Email message from Christian Wildfeuer to Adam Taylor and others (subject: Memphis IEU focus groups report (long mail) (Feb. 24, 1997) (in authors' files). Wildfeuer's email, for example, noted that focus group participants who used Navigator wouldn't switch to IE if they had to download it, but "once everything is in the OS and right there, integrated into the OS, 'in their face' so to speak, then they said they would use it b/c there would be no more need to use something 'separate.'"

27. For a description of an early joint deposition of Marc Andreessen, see Heilemann, *Pride Before the Fall*, 23–24.

28. Harry First, interview with Stephen D. Houck, New York, Sept. 21, 2004. Houck was head of the New York State Antitrust Bureau when the states began their investigation of Microsoft and signed the states' complaint as counsel for the plaintiff states.

29. For one account of the purported reaction of Phillip Malone (a Department of Justice lawyer) to Mark Tobey's more aggressive approach at Marc Andreessen's deposition, see pages 23–24 of Heilemann, *Pride Before the Fall*. Malone, who was subsequently one of the main Justice Department trial lawyers throughout the litigation, disputes the accuracy of this account.

30. See John R. Wilke and Leslie Cauley, "Justice Department Nod on Pact May Presage More Industry Mergers," *Wall Street Journal*, April 25, 1997 ("In January, Mr.

Vacco recommended strongly against the merger, saying it would eclipse competition in the New York telecommunications market and harm consumers.").

31. First, interview with Houck.

32. See, e.g., John R. Wilke and Bryan Gruley, "Clinton Nominee for Antitrust Chief Gets Tangled in Senate Battles Over Sweeping '96 Telecom Law," *Wall Street Journal*, June 18, 1997. The *New York Times* editorially opposed Klein's confirmation, calling him a "weak antitrust nominee," and urged the Clinton Administration to withdraw his name. "A Weak Antitrust Nominee" (editorial), *New York Times*, July 11, 1997.

33. See "Senate Confirms Joel Klein for Antitrust Enforcement," *Wall Street Journal*, July 18, 1997.

34. The settlement and court decisions involving the licensing case ("*Microsoft I*") are described in chapter 2.

35. Twenty-seven states filed an amicus brief in the court of appeals in support of the Justice Department's effort to enforce the 1994 consent decree. See Brief of Amici States on Behalf of the United States, *United States v. Microsoft Corp.*, 147 F.3d. 935 (D.C. Cir. 1998) (Nos. 97-5343 and 98-5012), 1998 WL 35240327.

36. Don Clark and David Bank, "Up to Nine States Met to Plan Action Against Microsoft," *Wall Street Journal*, Dec. 17, 1997 (specifically mentioning Illinois, Massachusetts, California, Minnesota, Texas, and New York as having been at the meeting).

37. David Segal, U.S. Recruits a Top Gun For Microsoft Showdown, *Washington Post*, Dec. 19, 1997. Charles James, who subsequently headed the Antitrust Division's Microsoft effort in the Bush Administration, was quoted as saying "This is Armageddon ... This is clearly a situation where the department feels that it can't afford to lose, and Boies is as good a trial lawyer as exists in the United States." Id. Joel Klein wouldn't comment on Boies' role and Boies' own description was suitably vague. See id. ("I'll be involved in analyzing issues and helping Justice determine what is the appropriate thing to do."). For background on Boies, see Auletta, *World War 3.0*, 9–12.

38. For evidence of Microsoft's decision not to consider any modifications in Windows 98, despite the broad anti-bundling language of Jackson's preliminary injunction, see Deposition of James Edward Allchin, March 19, 1998 (taken pursuant to Texas Civil Investigative Demand) (in authors' files), 102–104; Deposition of Paul Maritz, April 3, 1998 (taken pursuant to Department of Justice Civil Investigative Demand and Subpoena) (in authors' files), 77–85.

39. John R. Wilke, "States Ready Antitrust Move over Microsoft," *Wall Street Journal*, April 9, 1998. For the earlier story, see John R. Wilke, "U.S. Closes In on New Microsoft Case," *Wall Street Journal*, April 6, 1998. By the end of the month the states were

reported to be ready to join again with the Justice Department. See "States Rejoin Federal Effort In Case Against Microsoft," *Wall Street Journal*, April 30, 1998.

40. The litigation of browser integration as a violation of the 1994 licensing decree is described in chapter 2. The investigation in 1998 also reexamined the 1995 meetings between Netscape and Microsoft, about which Netscape had complained earlier. See John R. Wilke, "U.S. Is Investigating If Firm Tried to Induce Netscape to Split Internet Market," *Wall Street Journal*, April 24, 1998. ("It was like a visit by Don Corleone," [Andreessen] said [of the 1995 meetings with Microsoft]. "I expected to find a bloody computer monitor in my bed the next day.")

41. There had been one additional antitrust investigation against Microsoft between 1994 and 1998, Microsoft's acquisition of Intuit, which Microsoft abandoned in the face of Justice Department opposition. For information on Microsoft's decision on Intuit, see Lohr, "Gates, the Pragmatist, Walked Away." *New York Times*, May 22, 1995.

42. For an argument that Microsoft was using the negotiations as a way of assessing the scope and strength of the case against it, see pages 104–105 of Heilemann, *Pride Before the Fall*. For descriptions of the negotiations, see pages 15–25 of Auletta, *World War 3.0* and pages 99–103 of Heilemann, *Pride Before the Fall*.

43. See Joel Brinkley, "Antitrust Action Against Microsoft Is Called Imminent," *New York Times*, May 13, 1998. The article identified the companies involved in approaching the Texas attorney general as Dell and Compaq. Both were headquartered in Texas at the time and both were major OEMs and "allies of Microsoft." See id. For a description of a meeting with New York Attorney General Dennis Vacco, in which Microsoft's lawyers tried unsuccessfully to convince Vacco that Microsoft wasn't a monopolist because it had only 4% of the worldwide software market, see Brinkley and Lohr, *U.S. v. Microsoft*, 10. Similar meetings were held in many of the other states, to no effect. Id.

44. For descriptions of the final negotiations, see pages 16–17 of Auletta, *World War 3.0* and pages 99–103 of Heilemann, *Pride Before the Fall*. On the states' agreement to delay filing at the Justice Department's request, see First, interview with Houck. On the short delay and subsequent shipment of the Windows 98 code, see John Markoff, "U.S. v. Microsoft: The Company," *New York Times*, May 19, 1998.

45. See DOJ Complaint; Complaint, *New York v. Microsoft Corp.*, 87 F. Supp.2d 30 (D.D.C. 2000) (No. 98-1233) (filed on behalf of 20 states and the District of Columbia) (in authors' files). An amended complaint was filed in July of 1998. See Plaintiff States' First Amended Complaint, *New York v. Microsoft Corp.*, 87 F. Supp.2d 30 (D.D.C. 2000) (No. 98-1233) (in authors' files) (hereafter "States' Amended Complaint").

46. The importance of developing a focused, non-technical narrative was arguably one of the lessons the government drew from previous high profile monopolization

prosecutions. See Andrew I. Gavil, "The End of Antitrust Trench Warfare? An Analysis of Some Procedural Aspects of the Microsoft Trial," *Antitrust*, summer 1999, at 11–12.

47. Microsoft's principal economic expert witness, Richard L. Schmalensee, devoted a significant portion of his testimony to establishing the consumer benefits of Microsoft's integration strategy. See Direct Testimony of Richard L. Schmalensee (1999 WL 34757070) at 102–125. He also argued that consumers had benefited from competition between Microsoft and Netscape. Id. 126–160.

48. See, e.g., "A Case of Trial in Error: The Microsoft Antitrust Lawsuit" (press release, Dec. 7, 1998) (http://www.microsoft.com). ("Microsoft Chairman and CEO Bill Gates told reporters today that the government's antitrust lawsuit benefits Microsoft's competitors, not consumers, and could end up undermining the future of the entire high-tech industry.").

49. See, e.g., Direct Testimony of Richard L. Schmalensee, at 161–171 ("Plaintiffs Have Offered No Reliable Economic Evidence That Consumers or Competition Have Been Harmed by Any Aspect of Microsoft's Conduct.")

50. The standard practice is for the Justice Department and the states to file a joint complaint when they are bringing an antitrust case against the same party, but the states filed a separate complaint in the same court at the same time. Although the two complaints were developed independently, without an exchange of drafts or discussion until very late in the process, the core of the states' complaint was quite similar to that of the federal complaint. First, interview with Houck. We discuss the states' complaint further in chapter 8.

51. See DOJ Complaint, ¶¶ 4, 7–9.

52. See DOJ Complaint, ¶ 10 (quoting Microsoft executives). See also States' Amended Complaint, ¶ 46, at 13.

53. Id. ¶ 14.

54. DOJ Complaint, ¶ 18.

55. DOJ Complaint, ¶ 20.

56. See id. ¶¶ 28–34.

57. DOJ Complaint, ¶ 16, at 5 (quoting a *New York Times* article, which in turn was quoting Paul Maritz, Microsoft's Group Vice President in charge of the Platforms Group). The complaint didn't quote Maritz directly for his "cut off their air supply" remark. At trial an Intel executive testified that Maritz had made the remark at a meeting at Intel; Maritz denied doing so at trial, but testified in an earlier deposition that "it's possible but I just don't recall." See Steve Lohr, "At Microsoft Trial, Accounts Differ on Dealings with Apple," *New York Times*, Jan. 26, 1999.

58. See DOJ Complaint ¶¶ 37, 38.

59. DOJ Complaint, ¶ 2, at 1; ¶¶ 54–55, 57–60, at 15–17. See also *Microsoft*, 253 F3d at 52–53. With respect to the allegation that Web browsers constituted a distinct market, see DOJ Complaint, ¶ 21, at 6 ("Internet browsers are separate products competing in a separate product market from PC operating systems, and it is efficient to supply the two products separately."). See also id. 16–18, ¶¶ 56, 61–65.

60. See Direct Testimony of Richard L. Schmalensee, 17–18. See also id. 30–40. The debate between the governments and Microsoft about the scope and nature of the relevant markets was largely carried on through the expert witnesses. Compare Direct Testimony of Franklin M. Fisher, *United States v. Microsoft Corp.*, 87 F. Supp.2d 30 (D.D.C. 2000) (Nos. 98-1232 and 98-1233), at 22–34 (discussing Microsoft's market power and the reasons therefor) (at http://www.usdoj.gov) with Direct Testimony of Richard L. Schmalensee, 16–101 (Microsoft lacks market power, owing to the "intense" nature of competition in the microcomputer software industry and competition faced by Microsoft from other platforms).

61. Direct Testimony of Richard L. Schmalensee, 100, ¶ 203. See also "Economic Experts Challenge Underlying Assumptions in Government's Case" (Microsoft press release, Oct. 16, 1998) (http://www.microsoft.com) (asserting that "[r]esearch shows direct and unwavering correlation between product quality and market share" and reporting that "[s]everal leading economic experts today told a group of journalists that the government's antitrust lawsuit against Microsoft is depending on theories that are not supported by the realities of the marketplace or by current economic research.").

62. See Statement of Assistant Attorney General Joel I. Klein, Filing of Antitrust Suit Against Microsoft, May 18, 1998 (http://www.usdoj.gov), 6.

63. See Memorandum of the United States in Support of Motion for Preliminary Injunction at 68–69, *United States v. Microsoft Corp.*, 84 F. Supp. 2d 9 (D.D.C. 1999) (No. 98-1232) (http://www.usdoj.gov) [hereinafter Memorandum in Support of Motion for Preliminary Injunction].

64. First, interview with Houck; Heilemann, *Pride Before the Fall*, 109.

65. See David Bank and John R. Wilke, "Microsoft Probe by U.S. Is Expanded to Cover Issues Related to Sun's Java," *Wall Street Journal*, March 17, 1998; John R. Wilke and David Bank, "AOL, MCI Subpoenaed in Microsoft Case," *Wall Street Journal*, Feb. 20, 1998 (reporting inquiry into ISPs and streaming video).

66. See Gavil, "The End of Antitrust Trench Warfare?" at 7.

67. Memorandum in Support of Motion for Preliminary Injunction, at 11.

68. For a fuller exploration of Jackson's procedural decisions, see Gavil, "The End of Antitrust Trench Warfare?" ("What emerges as remarkable is the degree to which the

district court took full advantage of a century of procedural innovations to sidestep the dreary option of protracted litigation.").

69. For the redacted version of the plaintiffs' proposed findings of fact, see Plaintiffs' Joint Proposed Findings of Fact, *United States v. Microsoft Corp.*, No. 98-1232 (TPJ), No. 98-1233 (TPJ) (D.D.C. Aug. 10, 1999) (http://www.justice.gov). For the redacted version of Microsoft's proposed findings of fact, see Microsoft Corp's Revised Proposed Findings of Fact, *United States v. Microsoft Corp.*, No. 98-1232 (TPJ), No. 98-1233 (TPJ) (D.D.C. Sept. 10, 1999) (http://web.archive.org; http://www .microsoft.com/presspass/trial/r-fof/).

70. 84 F. Supp. 2d 9, 12. For reaction to the bifurcation of the findings of fact and conclusions of law, see Joel Brinkley, "U.S. Judge Declares Microsoft Is a Market-Stifling Monopoly; Gates Retains Defiant Stance," *New York Times*, Nov. 6, 1999 ("Antitrust lawyers say they cannot recall another instance in which findings of fact in an antitrust case have been issued ahead of the actual verdict. 'I've been at this for 40 years, and I've never heard of anything like this,' said Stephen Axinn, an antitrust litigator at Axinn, Veltrop & Harkrider in New York.").

71. Transcript of Proceedings Before the Honorable Thomas P. Jackson (Chambers Conference), *United States v. Microsoft Corp.* (No. 98-1232) and *New York v. Microsoft Corp.* (No. 98-1233) (Nov. 18, 1999) (in authors' files) at 1.

72. For a contemporaneous commentator's view of the effect on settlement, see Brinkley, "U.S. Judge Declares Microsoft Is a Market-Stifling Monopoly" (quoting Andrew Gavil). Jackson acknowledged his strategy in an interview with the authors (June 21, 2005, Washington, D.C.).

73. Jackson had discussed the appointment with at least one other person, Judge David Sentelle of the D.C. Circuit Court of Appeals, checking whether there might be a problem in asking a sitting court of appeals judge to be the mediator. Sentelle saw no problem, because Posner sat on a different circuit and wouldn't be involved in reviewing Judge Jackson's decision. See Chambers Conference Transcript, at 9. At the same chambers conference, Jackson informed the parties that he was soliciting an amicus brief from Lawrence Lessig relating to his conclusion of law on technological tying. Coincidentally, Lessig was a former clerk to Judge Posner, a fact that Jackson mentioned to the parties. See id. 10.

74. Judge Jackson cited a *New York Times* story about "divergent views" and "parallel tracks," see id. 3. The *Times* published such a story the day before the chambers conference: Joel Brinkley, "U.S. and State Officials Weigh Microsoft Remedies," *New York Times*, Nov. 17, 1999 ("'There's more tension between the states and Justice on remedies than there was during the trial,' said a senior aide to one of the attorneys general. 'During the trial, we were mostly just passengers, but now there are two different trains running on parallel tracks.'").

75. Section 5 of the Clayton Act provides that in a case brought by the United States a "final judgment or decree" that the defendant violated the antitrust laws is *prima facie* evidence of a violation in any case subsequently brought by private parties. The statute also provides that doctrines of collateral estoppel may be used to preclude parties from relitigating factual matters decided in the government case. The *prima facie* effect does not apply if the government enters into a consent decree before testimony is taken. Although the statute is silent on the effect of the parties' agreement to condition settlement on the withdrawal of a district court's findings, the D.C. Circuit has generally endorsed the practice. See Gavil, "The End of Antitrust Trench Warfare?" at 11. As we discuss in chapter 5, the effect given to Jackson's findings in subsequent private litigation was mixed.

76. For a good review of the outcome of the Justice Department's disagreement with the European Commission over the IBM investigation, see F. M. Scherer, "Microsoft and IBM in Europe," 84 *Antitrust & Trade Reg. Rep. (BNA)* 65 (Jan. 24, 2003). See also "Baxter Urges EC Competition Officials Not to Force Interface Disclosures By IBM," 42 *Antitrust & Trade Reg. Rep. (BNA)* 278 (Feb. 4, 1982) (discussing Assistant Attorney General William Baxter's effort to convince European Commission not to order interface specification disclosure).

77. The mediation process is described in some detail in chapter 21 of Auletta, *World War 3.0.*

78. Five months before the mediation, at a desultory settlement meeting between Justice, the states, and Microsoft, the plaintiffs had provided only an incomplete list of conduct remedies, to which Microsoft didn't agree in any event. Microsoft had been unwilling to discuss a structural remedy at the meeting and the plaintiffs hadn't been prepared to propose one. For a description of the meeting, see John R. Wilke, "Microsoft and Justice Department Met Three Weeks Ago to Seek Way to Settle," *Wall Street Journal,* June 25, 1999.

79. The proposal was put together with only limited assistance from the states, specifically, the advice of the states' outside economics expert, Carl Shapiro, a former chief economist in the Antitrust Division whose scholarly work focused on competition in technology industries. The Justice Department also hired an investment-banking firm, Greenhill & Co., in December of 1999 to advise it on any restructuring plan. See John R. Wilke, "U.S. Hires Investment-Bank Boutique For Advice in Microsoft Antitrust Case," *Wall Street Journal,* Dec. 3, 1999.

80. For an accurate report of the proposal, see John R. Wilke and David Bank, "U.S. Seeks to Break Up Microsoft," *Wall Street Journal,* Jan. 13, 2000. The Department's three-company proposal differed from other restructuring proposals which would have created three identical companies that would compete with each other, commonly called the "clone" approach or the "Baby Bills." See, e.g., R. Craig Romaine and Steven C. Salop, "Slap Their Wrists? Tie Their Hands? Slice Them into Pieces?

Alternative Remedies for Monopolization in the Microsoft Case," *Antitrust Magazine*, summer 1999, at 15.

81. For Microsoft's response, see Wilke and Bank, "U.S. Seeks to Break Up Microsoft" ("'The notion of breaking up Microsoft is an extreme and radical proposal that's not justified by anything in the case and does not reflect the reality of our competitive industry,' the spokesman said."). Also see "Little Progress Is Reported in Antitrust Talks," *New York Times*, Jan. 13, 2000 ("Asked about press reports that the government would seek to break Microsoft into two or three separate companies, Mr. Ballmer said such a move would be 'reckless beyond belief' and would harm consumers."). Betty Montgomery, Ohio's attorney general, was opposed to structural relief as well. See Steve Lohr, "U.S. and 19 States Issue Stinging Reply to Microsoft," *New York Times*, Jan. 26, 2000.

82. Some specific language from Posner's Drafts 16, 17, and 18 is reproduced on pages 350–358 of Auletta, *World War 3.0*.

83. Auletta describes the process on pages 342–344 of *World War 3.0*. He reports that "some of the lawyers on both sides" wondered whether the lack of face-to-face negotiation ended up being a mistake because the parties didn't develop any trust in each other. See id. 361. It should be noted, however, that the parties had participated in face-to-face settlement negotiations both before suit was filed and as the trial was ending, and that these negotiations hadn't produced a settlement either.

84. See Mediator's Draft No. 17 of Settlement Stipulation and Proposed Consent Decree, §§ 2(9) (definition), 3(8) (API disclosure), 4(3) (protocol disclosure) (March 23, 2000) (in authors' files). The protocol provisions would have permitted Microsoft either to publish its protocols or to create a set of APIs in a new operating system that would allow independent software vendors (ISVs) to plug into the operating system and generate protocols "in the same manner" as Microsoft's unpublished protocols. See § 4(3)(b). The middleware obligation was confined to middleware that was "licensed for a positive price," which would have excluded middleware that Microsoft bundled into the operating system at no additional price, such as the media player. This would have kept competing sellers of such middleware at a potential competitive disadvantage, much as Netscape had been disadvantaged.

85. See Mediator's Draft No. 11 of Proposed Consent Decree and Proposed Accompanying Stipulation, §§ 4 (3) (variant version), 4(4) (licensing prices), 5 (Technical Committee) (Feb. 27, 2000) (in authors' files).

86. See Mediator's Draft No. 17 of Settlement Stipulation and Proposed Consent Decree, § 4(1) (March 23, 2000) (in authors' files).

87. The timetable was set out in an email message sent on March 26, 2000 from Judge Posner to Joel Klein (the assistant attorney general in charge of the Antitrust Division), Tom Miller (the attorney general of Iowa), and William Neukom (Microsoft's general counsel) (in authors' files).

88. Attorney General Tom Miller of Iowa subsequently described Posner's view of the states' role as "somewhat reduced" and stated that early drafts of the settlement were provided through Joel Klein rather than directly to the states. Interview with Harry First, Sept. 30, 2005. Also see page 346 of Auletta, *World War 3.0*. ("Posner merely sent copies to Miller of proposals he made to Klein.")

89. Auletta (*World War 3.0*, page 343) refers to the "appeasement accusation" as "the sword the states held over Joel Klein's head."

90. See Mediator's Draft No. 11, § 6 (Microsoft acceptance conditional on the district court's grant of Microsoft's motion to vacate the findings of fact).

91. These provisions were described in a letter from Tom Miller emailed to Judge Posner on March 31, 2000, along with an accompanying draft proposal (titled "Mediator's Draft No. 18/S of Settlement Stipulation and Proposed Consent Decree") (in authors' files). The Special Master provision was § 6 of the proposal; porting was § 4(5).

92. Judge Posner's response to the states' proposals was conveyed in an email sent at 11:20 pm CST on March 31, 2000 (in authors' files). Auletta (*World War 3.0*, page 360) reports that Posner had made a decision to terminate the mediation in the early evening of March 31, even before Microsoft faxed its response to him, and that Posner had telephoned Microsoft and Joel Klein on the evening of March 31 to tell them that the mediation was over. There is no indication in Judge Posner's email, however, that he had already informed Microsoft or the Justice Department of his decision to end the mediation.

93. See "Text of Statement Issued by Judge Posner," *New York Times*, April 2, 2000. Auletta (*World War 3.0*, page 360) reports that Posner's statement originally included a "blistering" denunciation of the states, but that he was persuaded to omit it.

94. Posner has remained determined to blame the states for the end of the mediation. Referring to an article critical of his ending the mediation, see Harry First, "Delivering Remedies: The Role of the States in Antitrust Enforcement," 69 *Geo. Wash. L. Rev.* 1004, 1032–1034 (2001), Posner subsequently wrote the following: "At the last moment, the states upped the ante, making demands that it was plain that Microsoft would never accept. He [First] accuses me of 'impatience' in terminating the mediation when the states unexpectedly escalated their demands (ibid.); yet it was only after four months of almost full-time mediation that, faced with the intransigency and incompetence of the states, I decided the case would not settle, and threw in the towel." Richard A. Posner, "Federalism and the Enforcement of Antitrust Laws by State Attorneys General," in *Competition Laws in Conflict: Antitrust Jurisdiction in the Global Economy*, ed. Richard A. Epstein and Michael S. Greve (2004), 252, 265 n. 7.

95. See *United States v. Microsoft Corp.*, 84 F. Supp. 2d 9, 14 (D.D.C. 1999) (Findings of Fact ¶ 18). For the district court's definition of the functions of an operating

system, see id. 12 (Findings of Fact ¶ 2) ("An 'operating system' is a software program that controls the allocation and use of computer resources [such as central processing unit time, main memory space, disk space, and input/output channels.]).

96. Id. 27–28 (Findings of Fact ¶35). Even had operating systems for the Apple Macintosh been included, Microsoft's share would have been "well above eighty percent." Id. 28.

97. See id. 24–37 (Findings of Fact ¶¶ 30–44).

98. Direct network effects are demand side economies that arise when the benefit of a product to any one buyer increases with the number of other buyers. In a telephone network, for example, consumers directly benefit when multiple users are connected on the same network (they can reach more people). The network effects here are "indirect" because consumers don't benefit directly when multiple users of computers use the same operating system (any single user can run a computer without interoperating with other users) but benefit indirectly—when multiple users adopt the same operating system, more applications programs will probably be available, now and in the future, for the consumer's operating system. See, e.g., Gregory J. Werden, "Network Effects and Conditions of Entry: Lessons from the Microsoft Case," 69 *Antitrust L. J.* 87, 90 (2001); Timothy F. Bresnahan, "Network Effects and Microsoft," Stanford Institute for Economic Research Discussion Paper 00-51, 2001 (http://siepr.stanford.edu), at 3–5. The concept of network effects is explored further in chapter 2.

99. See Microsoft, 84 F. Supp. 2d at 44–46 (Findings of Fact ¶¶ 54, 55).

100. Id. 19–23.

101. Microsoft's economics expert, Richard Schmalensee, developed the category leader argument in his testimony. See, e.g., Direct Test. of Richard L. Schmalensee ¶¶ 72, 129 (arguing that it would take two to four years to attain leadership position in a category of products; the duration could be brief or extended and new platform leadership could come as rapidly as every three years).

102. See *Microsoft*, 84 F. Supp. 2d at 49–51 (Findings of Fact ¶ 60).

103. See id. 51–56 (Findings of Fact ¶¶ 61–66).

104. See *Microsoft*, 87 F. Supp. 2d at 37 (Conclusions of Law).

105. For the court of appeals' discussion of integration in *Microsoft II*, see *United States v. Microsoft Corp.*, 147 F.3d 935, 945–952 (D.C. Cir. 1998).

106. See Plaintiffs' Joint Proposed Conclusions of Law at 56–58, *United States v. Microsoft Corp.*, 84 F. Supp. 2d 9 (D.D.C. 1999) (Nos. 98-1232, 98-1233) (filed Dec. 6, 1999) (http://www.usdoj.gov); Defendant Microsoft Corporation's Proposed Conclusions of Law at 1, *United States v. Microsoft Corp.*, 84 F. Supp. 2d 9 (D.D.C. 1999) (Nos. 98-1232, 98-1233) (filed Jan. 18, 2000) (2000 WL 150760).

107. See *Microsoft*, 84 F. Supp. 2d at 49–50 (Findings of Fact ¶¶ 155, 158 (contracts), 161 (code in same files), 164 (cripple)).

108. Id. 51–52 (Findings of Fact ¶168 (tightly bound), ¶170 (uninstall), ¶171 (default choice), ¶ 172 (quoting Microsoft executive Brad Chase)).

109. For the ease of removing browser functionality, Judge Jackson relied on the testimony of Edward Felten, who developed a prototype browser removal program. See id. 53–55 (Findings of Fact ¶¶ 175–185).

110. Id. 55 (Findings of Fact ¶ 186).

111. See *Microsoft*, 87 F. Supp. 2d at 47–51 (Conclusions of Law).

112. Id. 51.

113. See *Microsoft*, 84 F. Supp. 2d at 43, 45 (Findings of Fact ¶¶ 135, 140).

114. Id. 45 (Findings of Fact ¶ 139).

115. Id. (Findings of Fact ¶ 141).

116. See id. 29 (Findings of Fact ¶¶ 73, 74). For more information on Java, see Mark A. Lemley and David McGowan, "Could Java Change Everything? The Competitive Propriety of a Proprietary Standard," 43 *Antitrust Bull.* 715 (1998).

117. See *Microsoft*, 84 F. Supp. 2d at 105–107 (Findings of Fact ¶¶ 388–390, 394 (incompatibility)).

118. See id. 106 (Findings of Fact ¶ 390 (intended incompatibility)).

119. See id. 107–109 (Findings of Fact ¶¶ 396, 398–401).

120. See id. 109–110 (Findings of Fact ¶ 407 (would develop JVM); ¶¶ 405–406 (Intel)).

121. *Microsoft*, 87 F. Supp. 2d at 44 (Conclusions of Law).

122. Jackson's findings on consumer harm and causation are set out at the end of his findings of fact. See *Microsoft*, 84 F. Supp. 2d at 110–112 (Findings of Fact ¶¶ 408–412). His legal conclusions based on those findings are at 87 F. Supp. 2d at 44.

123. Jackson did reject two important arguments that the plaintiffs advanced, one involving exclusive dealing and one, advanced only by the states, that Microsoft had improperly leveraged its monopoly in the market for operating systems to gain a competitive advantage in the browser market. For the exclusive dealing claim, see Microsoft, 87 F. Supp. 2d at 51–54 (existence of other distribution channels, such as mail and downloading, meant that Netscape was not "actually shut out of the Web browser market," even though these channels were inferior to OEM distribution). For the leveraging claim, see *United States v. Microsoft Corp.*, 1998 WL 614485*26–27 (D.D.C. 1998) (leveraging is a viable claim under Section 2 only if the defendant has monopolized or is attempting to monopolize the second market).

124. See Transcript of Proceedings Before the Honorable Thomas P. Jackson (Chambers Conference), *United States v. Microsoft Corp.* (No. 98-1232). Also see *New York v. Microsoft Corp.* (No. 98-1233), at 13. ("Well, my transcende[nt] objective is to get this thing before an appellate tribunal—one or another—as quickly as possible because I don't want to disrupt the economy or waste any more of yours or my time on a remedy it it's going to come back here.") (statement of Judge Jackson) (April 4, 2000) (in authors' files).

Chapter 4

1. For Jackson's decision entering final judgment and staying part of his remedial order, see *United States v. Microsoft Corp.*, 97 F. Supp. 2d 59 (D.D.C. 2000) (staying structural relief pending court of appeals disposition).

2. The original statute governing appeals in government civil antitrust cases is the Expediting Act of 1903, ch. 544, §§ 1–2, 32 Stat. 823. The act was amended by the Antitrust Procedures and Penalties Act of 1974, 15 U.S.C. § 29.

3. See Transcript of Proceedings Before the Honorable Thomas P. Jackson (Chambers Conference), *United States v. Microsoft Corp.* (No. 98-1232) and *New York v. Microsoft Corp.* (No. 98-1233) (April 4, 2000) (in authors' files) at 11.

4. Of the ten active judges on the D.C. Circuit Court of Appeals at the time, three judges recused themselves from further consideration of the case, leaving an *en banc* court of seven—Chief Judge Edwards, Judges Williams, Ginsburg, Sentelle, Randolph, Rogers, and Tatel. Two of those judges (Williams and Randolph) were on the panel that decided *Microsoft II*; the third judge on that panel (Wald) had retired. For the Justice Department's characterization of the court's order, see Brief for the United States in Response to the Jurisdictional Statement, *Microsoft Corp. v. United States*, 530 U.S. 1301 (2000) (No. 00-139) (filed August 2000) (http://www.usdoj.gov) at 17.

5. Jackson stayed the remainder of his judgment and remedial order on the same day that he certified the appeal. The timeline of the certification process is described in Microsoft Jurisdictional Statement, *Microsoft Corp. v. United States*, 530 U.S. 1301 (2000) (No. 00-139) (filed July 26, 2000) (2000 WL 34016496) at 13.

6. The two previous cases reviewed on expedited appeal were *California v. United States*, 464 U.S. 1013 (1983), and *Maryland v. United States*, 460 U.S. 1001 (1983).

7. Department of Justice Response to Jurisdictional Statement, at 18.

8. See Microsoft Jurisdictional Statement, at 23, 26.

9. The Supreme Court's decision denying an expedited direct appeal is reported at 530 U.S. 1301 (2000).

10. Normal page limits for briefs in the courts of appeals are 30 pages for principal briefs and 15 for reply briefs. The court of appeals' argument schedule for February

26 gave each side 75 minutes for monopoly maintenance and 45 minutes for tying. The schedule for February 27 gave each side 15 minutes for attempted monopolization, 45 minutes for relief, and 30 minutes for conduct of trial and extrajudicial statements.

11. Plaintiffs' brief contained only a short reference to Apple and a brief description of the pressure on "Intel and Others." See Brief for Appellees United States and the State Plaintiffs—Final Version, *United States v. Microsoft Corp.*, 253 F.3d 34 (D.C. Cir. 2001) (Nos. 00-5212, 00-5213) (filed Feb. 9, 2001) (http://www.usdoj.gov) at 29–30, 39–41.

12. Part I of Microsoft's argument in its brief to the court of appeals dealt with the Section 1 tying issue; Part II discussed monopolization. See Brief for Appellant Microsoft Corp., *United States v. Microsoft Corp.*, 253 F.3d 34 (D.C. Cir. 2001) (Nos. 00-5212, 00-5213) (filed Nov. 27, 2000) (in authors' files) at 69–83 (tying) and at 83–114 (monopolization).

13. Id. 16.

14. See Appellees' Brief—Final Version at 6 (noting lodging of CD-ROM). It seems likely that the court of appeals made use of this CD-ROM because there are citations in the court's opinion to parts of the record that are cited in the plaintiffs' proposed findings of fact (with hyperlinks), but which are not cited in the appellate brief or provided in the Joint Appendix that the parties filed with the court. See, e.g., 253 F.3d at 61 (reference to McClain deposition) and at 66 (reference to proposed findings of fact and government exhibit).

15. For contemporaneous reports of the court of appeals argument, see Stephen Labaton, "Judges Voice Doubt on Order Last Year to Split Microsoft," *New York Times*, Feb. 28, 2001 ("The government suffered a second difficult day of questioning in its Microsoft antitrust case today ... "); Peter Spiegel, "Microsoft Judge Worries Prosecutors, Antitrust Case Appeal Panel Member Springs Surprise with Vehement Criticism," *Financial Times*, March 1, 2001 (quoting antitrust professor William Kovacic: "The government has to walk away thinking: We could lose 5-to-2 on any number of issues.").

16. The median time interval from hearing to decision for appeals in all federal courts in 2001 was 2.1 months; in the D.C. Circuit Court of Appeals it was 2.3 months. See Administrative Office of the U.S. Courts, 2001 Judicial Business (http://www.uscourts.gov), table B-4.

17. *United States v. Microsoft Corp.*, 253 F. 3d 34, 49 (D.C. Cir. 2001).

18. Id. 51.

19. For the court of appeals' discussion of the arguments relating to proving monopoly power through direct evidence, see id. 56–58.

20. For the court of appeals' discussion of the required analytical structure, see id. 58–60 (emphasis in original).

21. See id. 58–59 (quoting *Standard Oil Co. of New Jersey v. United States*, 221 U.S. 1, 60 (1911)). For a broader consideration of possible parallels between the government's prosecution of Microsoft and the case against Standard Oil, see John J. Flynn, "Standard Oil and Microsoft—Intriguing Parallels or Limping Analogies," 46 *Antitrust Bull.* 645, 647–652, 725–733 (2001).

22. See, e.g., U.S. Department. of Justice, *Competition and Monopoly: Single-Firm Conduct Under Section 2 of the Sherman Act* (2008) (http://www.justice.gov), 36–38 (implicitly rejecting use of the rule of reason for single-firm conduct); Thomas O. Barnett and Hill B. Wellford, "The DOJ's Single-Firm Conduct Report: Promoting Consumer Welfare Through Clearer Standards for Section 2 of the Sherman Act" (2008) (http://www.justice.gov) at 12 ("Contrary to the suggestion of some courts and commentators, the rule of reason is not the norm for Section 2 analysis—rule of reason is a Section 1 concept and has made its way into discussion of single-firm conduct analysis primarily through its role in tying cases, which, with the notable exception of the Department's Microsoft case, have generally been analyzed under Section 1.").

23. 253 F.3d at 65–66.

24. See id. 64–66. The finding of a "significant" increase in support costs was made by Jackson, see *United States v. Microsoft Corp.*, 84 F. Supp. 2d 9, 49 (D.C.C. 1999) (Findings of Fact ¶ 159). The court of appeals also upheld, as not clearly erroneous, Jackson's finding that Microsoft had commingled operating-system code and browser-functionality code, although the court acknowledged that there was some contradictory evidence on whether Microsoft commingled code this way (there was some testimony that the *same* code provided Web browsing functionality and operating-system functionality). See 253 F.3d at 66.

25. 253 F.3d at 66–67.

26. Id. 67. For the different views on the frequency of the default override, compare Microsoft Appellate Brief at 82 with *Microsoft*, 84 F. Supp. 2d at 52 (Findings of Fact ¶ 171). Jackson made no findings relating to technical justifications for the overrides.

27. 253 F.3d at 76–77.

28. See id. 70–72. On the OEM channel, see id. 64. The plaintiffs didn't appeal Jackson's adverse decision on the Section 1 exclusive dealing claim, although the court of appeals appeared to cast doubt on what it characterized as the "total exclusion test" that Jackson used. See id. 70.

29. See id. 71–72. Note that here the court didn't raise the efficiency justification it subsequently saw when discussing the tying arrangement, that is, the creation of a

single platform with uniform APIs to which software applications developers could write.

30. See id. 68.

31. See id. 75. The court also stated that the Microsoft JVM allowed applications to run faster on Windows than applications written to Sun's JVM.

32. See id. 84–85. The court of appeals noted with apparent interest that the district court had not referred to Microsoft's commingling of IE and Windows code in its findings of fact concerning the Section 1 tying claim, even though it was included in its Section 2 analysis and even though the plaintiffs had requested that it do so. See id. 85.

33. Judge Jackson never wrote that he was applying a *per se* test, nor did the plaintiffs ever mention *"per se"* in their brief. Jackson only stated that there were four necessary requirements for an illegal tie, whether the rule of reason or a *per se* test was applied. See *United States v. Microsoft Corp.*, 87 F. Supp. 2d 30, 47 (D.D.C. 2000). His analysis, however, followed the Supreme Court's approach in *Jefferson Parish Hospital District No. 2 v. Hyde*, 466 U.S. 2 (1984), which commentators have termed a "modified *per se*" approach. Jackson's analysis also didn't consider any efficiency justifications, nor did it require proof of any competitive impact beyond satisfying the requirement that a "substantial volume" of commerce be affected. See *Microsoft*, 87 F. Supp. 2d at 47. For contrasting views on appropriate tying analysis under Section 1, and the application of that analysis to the facts of Microsoft, compare Keith N. Hylton and Michael Salinger, "Tying Law and Policy: A Decision-Theoretic Approach," 69 *Antitrust L. J.* 469 (2001) (favoring approach of Microsoft III to technological tying; "legal standards that excessively discourage technological integration could be quite harmful to the whole economy") with Warren S. Grimes, "The Antitrust Tying Law Schism: A Critique of Microsoft III and a Response to Hylton and Salinger," 70 *Antitrust L. J.* 199 (2002) (preferring Jefferson Parish's modified *per se* approach but approving the attention to factual detail shown in the Microsoft III analysis).

34. See *Jefferson Parish Hospital District No. 2 v. Hyde*, 466 U.S. 2, 19–21 (1984).

35. *United States v. Microsoft Corp.*, 253 F.3d 24, 89 (D.C. Cir. 2001).

36. For the court of appeals' discussion of its institutional capacity to judge product design, see id. 65–67. For the views of the panel in the contempt case, see *United States v. Microsoft Corp.*, 147 F. 3d 935, 952–953.

37. 253 F.3d at 89.

38. Id. 87.

39. For the court's use of the record to support is view regarding shared code, see id. (testimony of Glenn Weadock and James Allchin). Jackson had also found that there

was some code sharing between IE and Windows. When discussing the Justice Department expert's effort to write a program that would remove IE functionality from Windows, Jackson noted that the program did not remove all of the code executed to provide browsing functionality, because "[s]ome of that code ... also supports Windows 98's operating system functionalities." *United States v. Microsoft Corp.*, 84 F. Supp. 2d 9, 54–55 (D.D.C. 199) (Findings of Fact ¶ 183 (testimony of Edward Felten)). Jackson also noted that all Windows-compatible applications (whether written by Microsoft or by independent programmers) share code with the Windows operating system. Id.

40. See 253 F.3d at 71.

41. See id. 93.

42. See id. 95–96.

43. Judge Jackson considered the impact of the tie on the market for operating systems (the tying product), noting that tying causes additional competitive harm when "partial substitutes" are tied. See *United States v. Microsoft Corp.*, 87 F. Supp. 2d 30, 51 n.6 (D.D.C. 2000). The European Commission subsequently considered the impact on the OS market of tying the Windows Media Player to Windows. On the Commission's tying analysis, see chapter 6.

44. "Boot sequence" refers to what occurs each time the end user starts up a computer. The "initial boot sequence" is the first time the end user starts up a computer.

45. Microsoft Appellate Brief at 105. For Microsoft's argument on the boot-up and screen modification restrictions, see id. 102 (citing Jackson opinion dealing with these issues). For Microsoft's broader argument relating to bundling the browser into the operating system, see Reply Brief for Microsoft Corp. at 29, *United States v. Microsoft Corp.*, 253 F.3d 34 (D.C. Cir. 2001) (Nos. 00-5212, 00-5213) (filed Jan. 29, 2001), at 2001 WL 34153358: "By claiming that Microsoft must permit OEMs to make unauthorized modifications to its copyrighted operating systems, plaintiffs seek to deprive Microsoft of its rights under federal copyright law."

46. 253 F.3d at 63.

47. Id.

48. See id. 63.

49. Jackson held that Microsoft presented "no evidence" that the restrictions it placed on the OEMs with regard to altering the Windows program derived from any of the enumerated rights that a copyright holder has under the Copyright Act. In his view Microsoft's actions had nothing to do with protecting the integrity of its artistic work; it had everything to do with suppressing the competitive threat that middleware presented. See *United States v. Microsoft*, 87 F. Supp. 2d 30, 40–41 (D.D.C. 2000).

50. Direct Test. of Bill Gates ¶ 124, *New York v. Microsoft Corp.*, 224 F. Supp. 2d 76 (D.D.C. 2002) (No. 98-1233 (CKK)) (April 18, 2002) (in authors' files).

51. See *United States v. Microsoft Corp.*, 1998-2 Trade Cas. (CCH) ¶ 72,261, 1998 U.S. DIST. LEXIS 14231 at *90 (D.D.C. 1998) (summary judgment).

52. The cases on which Microsoft relied in the district court were *WGN Continental Broadcasting Co. v. United Video, Inc.*, 693 F.2d 622, 625 (7th Cir. 1982), *Gilliam v. ABC*, 538 F.2d 14 (2d Cir. 1976), and *National Bank of Commerce v. Shaklee Corp.*, 503 F. Supp. 533 (D. Tex. 1980). For the court of appeals' discussion of the cases, see *Microsoft*, 253 F. 3d at 63; for Judge Jackson's discussion, see *Microsoft*, 87 F. Supp. 2d at 40 n.2.

53. For further discussion of the intellectual property issues in Microsoft, as well as a suggested approach for dealing with intellectual property defenses to otherwise anti-competitive behavior, see Harry First, "Microsoft and the Evolution of the Intellectual Property Concept," 2006 *Wis. L. Rev.* 1369.

54. See 253 F.3d at 79.

55. Id. 80.

56. See id. 118. The court took the quote from page 230 of Ken Auletta's 2001 book *World War 3.0: Microsoft and Its Enemies*. The court graciously refrained from quoting the next passage in Auletta's book: "Judge Jackson does not hide his contempt for the higher court, saying it is populated by 'supercilious' judges lacking trial experience. 'One of the most frustrating things for judges dealing with the Court of Appeals is the way they thrash through the thickets of legal scholarship. They embellish law with unnecessary, and in many cases, superficial scholarship.'" Id.

57. For the court of appeals' discussion of Jackson's extra-judicial statements and interviews, see *United States v. Microsoft Corp.*, 253 F.3d 34, 107–111 (D.C. Cir. 2001). The exact nature and extent of Jackson's interviews with the press were never definitively established because there was never any formal hearing into the matter. Two written accounts refer to interviews during the trial; only one of those accounts details the extent of the interviews. See Auletta, *World War 3.0*, 405 (reporting three interviews about the case, two of which were during the trial; the third, post-trial, lasted one-hour); Joel Brinkley and Steve Lohr, "*U.S. vs. Microsoft*: Pursuing a Giant; Retracing the Missteps in the Microsoft Defense," *New York Times*, June 9, 2000 (not indicating extent of interviews). For a post-judgment interview, see James V. Grimaldi, "Judge Orders Microsoft Breakup, Calls Company 'Untrustworthy,'" *Washington Post*, June 8, 2000. Jackson subsequently said that he spoke to two journalists "in chambers during the trial" and characterized his discussions with the two journalists as "indiscretions." See Thomas Penfield Jackson, "Microsoft: The Remedies Phase," speech at American Antitrust Institute Conference, June 21, 2005 (hereinafter "AAI Speech"), at 12.

58. For the reporter's characterization of Jackson's conduct, see John R. Wilke, "For Antitrust Judge, Trust, or Lack of It, Really Was the Issue," *Wall Street Journal*, June 8, 2000 (referring to an interview given on the day that Jackson released his final decision). Wilke reported: "'Falsus in uno, falsus in omnibus,' he [Jackson] says, citing a Latin aphorism meaning, 'Untrue in one thing, untrue in everything.' 'I don't subscribe to that as absolutely true,' the judge says. 'But it does lead one to suspicion. It's a universal human experience. If someone lies to you once, how much else can you credit as the truth?'"

59. Auletta, *World War 3.0*, 370 (quoting Judge Jackson).

60. Wilke, "For Antitrust Judge, Trust, or Lack of It, Really Was the Issue," (quoting Judge Jackson).

61. Brinkley and Lohr, *U.S. v. Microsoft* (2001), 278.

62. For Jackson's views of the credibility of some of the witnesses, including Gates, as related in interviews with several reporters, see Brinkley and Lohr, *U.S. v. Microsoft* (2001), at 278; Brinkley and Lohr, "Retracing Missteps" (cited in *United States v. Microsoft Corp.*, 253 F.3d at 109). See also Auletta, *World War 3.0*, 138 (Jackson describing Gates as an "evasive, dissembling, defiant, arrogant" witness).

63. Microsoft, 253 F.3d at 107, 108. The lawyer for the plaintiffs (representing the states) was John Roberts, later to become Chief Justice of the U.S. Supreme Court.

64. Id. 115.

65. Microsoft Appellate Brief at 149. We discuss Sporkin's disqualification in chapter 2.

66. See Microsoft, 253 F.3d at 116.

67. The court also decided two other issues. It reversed Jackson's finding that Microsoft attempted to monopolize the browser market, on the ground that the plaintiffs hadn't proved a relevant market (Web browsers) or barriers to entry into that market. See *United States v. Microsoft Corp.*, 253 F.3d 34, 80–84 (D.C. Cir. 2001). The court also rejected Microsoft's challenge to Jackson's expedited trial procedures, stating that the procedures were "comfortably within the bounds" of a trial court's discretion "to conduct trials as it sees fit." Id. 98. See also 100–101.

68. See Transcript of Proceedings Before the Honorable Thomas P. Jackson (Chambers Conference), *United States v. Microsoft Corp.* (No. 98-1232) and *New York v. Microsoft Corp.* (No. 98-1233) at 13 (stating that his "transcende[nt] objective is to get this thing before an appellate tribunal—one or another—as quickly as possible because I don't want to disrupt the economy or waste any more of yours or my time on a remedy if it's going to come back here") (April 4, 2000) (in authors' files).

69. For Judge Jackson's statements at the chambers conference, see id. 11 ("We might also replicate the procedure at trial with testimony in written form subject to

cross-examination. The more abbreviated the process, the better I think the situation is, but I am open to suggestions); id. 19. ("That's the desideratum. Get it resolved within sixty days.") The schedule was embodied in Jackson's Scheduling Order No. 8, issued April 5, 2000 (in authors' files).

70. The plaintiffs' proposed final judgment and supporting briefs and affidavits are available at http://www.justice.gov; Microsoft's are available at http://cyber.law .harvard.edu/msdoj/. Two of the plaintiff states (Illinois and Ohio) proposed a three-year delay in the reorganization to see whether the conduct provisions of the decree had alleviated "the substantial competitive harms" Microsoft caused; those states otherwise supported the proposed final judgment. See Plaintiffs' Memorandum in Support of Proposed Final Judgment, *United States v. Microsoft Corp.*, 84 F. Supp. 2d 9 (D.D.C. 1999) (Nos. 98-1232, 98-1233) (filed April 28, 2000) (redacted version) (http://www.justice.gov) at A-1–A-2.

71. See Transcript of Proceedings Before the Honorable Thomas P. Jackson, *United States v. Microsoft Corp.* (No. 98-1232) and *New York v. Microsoft Corp.* (No. 98-1233) (May 24, 2000, AM Session) (http://web.archive.org; http://www.microsoft. com/presspass/trial/transcripts/may00/05-24-am.asp) at 5 ("I want to resolve any uncertainty on Mr. Warden's [Microsoft's counsel] part at the outset, however. I intend to proceed to the merits of the remedy today.") (statement of Judge Jackson); id. 38 ("Due process mandates due process and not a rush to judgment.") (statement of John Warden).

72. We discuss the contempt litigation (*Microsoft II*) in chapter 2.

73. For Jackson's opinion entering final judgment, see *United States v. Microsoft Corp.*, 97 F. Supp. 2d 59, 62 (D.D.C. 2000). ("The Court is convinced for several reasons that a final—and appealable—judgment should be entered quickly.") For plaintiffs' awareness of the problem, see email message from Harry First to Justice Department and state attorneys, May 26, 2000 (in authors' files) ("Whether we have a problem, of course, isn't the question. The question is whether there is anything we can do about this without making things worse."). For the approach taken by the Department of Justice and the states, see Memorandum in Support of Plaintiffs' Revised Proposed Final Judgment, *United States v. Microsoft Corp.*, 84 F. Supp. 2d 9 (D.D.C. 1999) (Nos. 98-1232, 98-1233) (filed May 26, 2000) (http://www.usdoj.gov), which details a few suggested changes in their proposed order and argues that Microsoft had not "engaged responsibly" on the issue of process, but could have earlier made clear how much additional time it needed and its reasons for seeking such time. In an interview Jackson gave the day after he accepted the plaintiffs' remedy proposal, he was quoted as saying: "'I am not aware of any case authority that says I have to give them any due process at all. The case is over. They lost.' Besides, he added, 'I'm suspicious that they are just playing for time, hoping they will get to deal with a new administration' that might approach the company with a softer hand." Brinkley and Lohr, "Retracing the Missteps." Jackson later stated that

he believed that whatever he did would not matter because the court of appeals was likely to alter his decision anyway. See AAI Speech at 12.

74. Jackson later pointed out that although Microsoft "desired and expected" an evidentiary trial on remedies "[n]either the DOJ nor the 20 state plaintiffs did." He also pointed out that "equally eminent experts" disagreed on remedy and that "no one's expertise" in predicting future effects would likely be "so clearly superior as to inspire confidence in relying on it." See id. 9–11.

75. The remedy decree is set out at 97 F. Supp.2d 39 (D.D.C. 2000).

76. We discuss the economic theories supporting the proposed breakup in chapter 7.

77. With regard to unbundling browser code, the plaintiffs stated that although a decree "might appropriately require" such a redesign, "the cost of and burden of implementing and enforcing such a provision could be significant." Plaintiffs' Memorandum in Support of Proposed Final Judgment (April 28, 2000) (http://www .usdoj.gov) at 7.

78. The decree specified the following formula for computing the royalty reduction: "[T]he royalty paid ... is reduced in an amount not less than the product of the otherwise applicable royalty and the ratio of the number of amount in bytes of binary code of (a) the Middleware Product as distributed separately from a Windows Operating System Product to (b) the applicable version of Windows." See § 3.g.ii. In a declaration submitted in support of the proposed decree, a government expert witness stated that binary code "correlates with the cost of developing products" (see Declaration of Edward W. Felten at ¶ 91, April 28, 2000, at http://www.usdoj.gov), but the plaintiffs provided no information regarding the likely competitive impact of the royalty reduction.

79. See Microsoft, 97 F. Supp. 2d at 62.

80. Id. We discuss the contempt proceeding in chapter 2.

81. Id. 63. The legal standard Jackson applied to the decree is consistent with the standard that the Supreme Court has articulated. See *United States v. United Shoe Machinery Corp.*, 391 U.S. 244, 250 (1968) (remedy in a Section 2 case must "terminate the illegal monopoly, deny to the defendant the fruits of its statutory violation, and ensure that there remain no practices likely to result in monopolization in the future"). For the economists' amicus brief that advocated the creation of three "clone" companies with identical assets, see Remedies Brief of Amici Curiae Robert E. Litan, Roger G. Noll, William D. Nordhaus, and Frederic Scherer, *United States v. Microsoft Corp.* Civil Action No. 98-1232 (TPJ) (filed April 27, 2000) (http://www .brookings.edu).

82. *Microsoft*, 253 F.3d at 101.

83. See id. 103, 105. The court of appeals also saw Jackson's refusal to hold additional evidentiary hearings as a reflection of his "impatience" with Microsoft's

"intransigence" and cited "the appearance of partiality" as an additional reason for vacating the remedy, adding it to the three others previously given. See id. 117. Jackson subsequently linked Microsoft's stance of "militant defiance, unapologetic for its past behavior" to his decision to require structural relief: "I had no illusions that an order less drastic than that advocated by the government would meet with Microsoft's even grudging submission. ..." (AAI Speech at 11–12). For a similar view from the European Commissioner for Competition, see Neelie Kroes, Q&A at ABA in Washington on April 20, 2007 ("For example there could be a situation in which a dominant company ... has consistently failed to comply with a behavioural remedy despite repeated enforcement action. From this it could be reasonable to draw the conclusion that behavioural remedies are ineffective and that a structural remedy is warranted.").

84. Jackson later stated: "I entered the order calling for Microsoft's bifurcation fully anticipating that the court of appeals would alter it, as the court in fact did." AAI speech, at 12.

85. For the court of appeals' instructions for the remand, see 253 F.3d at 105–108.

86. See John R. Wilke, "Bush's Likely Antitrust Pick Takes Cautious Path," *Wall Street Journal*, Feb. 13, 2001 ("'One thing that is very, very clear is that consumers have benefited by there being a common [software] platform,' Mr. James said in an interview on CNBC last year. 'If Microsoft were to be broken up, you would see divergence of that common platform.' He went on to say that 'at the end of the day, there are going to be conduct remedies' that would fall short of a breakup.").

87. For the court of appeals' decisions, see *United States v. Microsoft Corp.*, 2001 U.S. App. LEXIS 17137 (D.C. Cir. 2001) (denying motion for rehearing); 2001 U.S. App. LEXIS 18715, 2001-2 Trade Cas. (CCH) ¶73,380 (D.C. Cir. 2001) (denying petition to stay its mandate pending Supreme Court decision). The Supreme Court denied Microsoft's petition for certiorari on October 9, 2001—see 534 U.S. 952 (2001). The petition raised only the question whether the court of appeals' disqualification of Judge Jackson also required the court to vacate his findings of fact. On Judge Kollar-Kotelly's appointment, see Stephen Labaton, "Judge Is Assigned to Decide Microsoft Antitrust Penalties," *New York Times*, August 25, 2001. On the shipment of Windows XP, see Steve Lohr, "New Software, New Scrutiny for Microsoft," *New York Times*, July 30, 2001.

88. See U.S. Department of Justice, "Justice Department Informs Microsoft of Plans for Further Proceedings in the District Court" (press release, Sept. 6, 2001) (http://www.usdoj.gov).

89. See John R. Wilke and Ted Bridis, "Regulators Won't Seek Microsoft Breakup," *Wall Street Journal*, Sep. 7, 2001 ("President Bush said yesterday: 'I expect the Justice Department to handle that in a way that brings honor and thought to the process. I respect and hold our attorney general [John Ashcroft] in high esteem and I honor the work that he's done and I'm going to leave it at that.'").

90. There were two reported occasions on which the Clinton White House was informed about the case. One was on the day the complaint was filed (informing the White House Counsel's Office and Council of Economic Advisors). The other was in April of 2000, after the Justice Department had decided on its remedy proposal and shortly before it was submitted to the district court (informing the White House Counsel's Office, Council of Economic Advisors, the Secretary of the Treasury, and the Chairman of the National Economic Council). Jeffrey H. Blattner, The Microsoft Case and the Role of Elected Officials in Antitrust Enforcement (2001) 9 (unpublished manuscript in authors' files).

91. For a description of Judge Kollar-Kotelly's decision, see John R. Wilke, Judge Orders Urgent Talks on Microsoft," *Wall Street Journal*, Oct. 1, 2001. The joint status report is available at http://www.usdoj.gov.

92. See Eric D. Green and Jonathan B. Marks, "How We Mediated the Microsoft Case," *Boston Globe*, Nov. 15, 2001.

93. For a description of the final day of negotiations among the three parties, including the negotiations over protocol disclosure, see John Wilke, "Hard Drive: Negotiating All Night, Tenacious Microsoft Won Many Loopholes," *Wall Street Journal*, Nov. 9, 2001. According to this account, Bill Gates directly approved the protocol-disclosure provision.

94. See *United States v. Microsoft Corp.*, 56 F.3d 1448, 1462 (D.C. Cir. 1995). For the Tunney Act's provisions, see 15 U.S.C. § 16. For an argument that the Tunney Act should not have applied because the settlement came after a full trial and an appeal, see John J. Flynn and Darren Bush, "The Misuse and Abuse of the Tunney Act: The Adverse Consequences of the 'Microsoft Fallacies,'" 34 *Loy. U. Chi. L. Rev.* 749 (2003).

95. The changed language made clearer that the provision would apply to all future Microsoft server products and would include servers connected to PCs via the Internet. See Revised Proposed Final Judgment (redlined version), §§ 3.E, VI.B (http://www.usdoj.gov). The Justice Department described the changes as "clarifications." See John R. Wilke, "Nine States Rebuff U.S.-Microsoft Accord," *Wall Street Journal*, Nov. 7, 2001. New York's negotiator described the protocol changes as ones that "enhanced Microsoft's disclosure obligations in this critical area," although the changes "did not involve many words." See Statement of Jay L. Himes, Chief, Antitrust Bur., Office of the N.Y. State Attny Gen'l, Before Sen. Comm. on the Judiciary, Hearing on the Microsoft Settlement (Dec. 12, 2001) (http://www.usdoj.gov) 12.

96. The nine settling states were New York, Ohio, Illinois, Kentucky, Louisiana, Maryland, Michigan, North Carolina, and Wisconsin. The non-settling states were California, Connecticut, Iowa, Massachusetts, Minnesota, West Virginia, Florida, Kansas, Utah, and the District of Columbia. New Mexico, one of the original litigating states, settled earlier. See "New Mexico and Microsoft Settle Antitrust Case," *New York Times*, July 13, 2001.

97. See Declaration of David S. Sibley, Department of Justice economic consultant (Feb. 27, 2002) (http://www.usdoj.gov), 15, table 3 (listing each provision in proposed final judgment that addressed the specific anticompetitive acts found by the district court and affirmed by the court of appeals). One important variation between the trial and the settlement was Microsoft's conduct involving Java, which the settlement covered only inferentially, at best. See Memorandum of the United States in Support of Entry of the Proposed Final Judgment (Feb. 27, 2002) (http://www.usdoj.gov), 55. Judge Kollar-Kotelly rejected an effort by the non-settling states to include a requirement that Microsoft distribute Java with its Windows operating system. See *New York v. Microsoft Corp.*, 224 F. Supp.2d 76, 260–262 (D.D.C. 2002).

98. See *United States v. Microsoft Corp.*, 2002 U.S. Dist. LEXIS 22864, at *8, *11 (§§ III.C.2, III.F.3) (final settlement decree).

99. See id. *20 (§ III.J.2).

100. See Department of Justice Complaint, *United States v. Microsoft Corp.*, 84 F. Supp. 2d 9 (D.D.C. 1999) (No. 98-1232) (seeking to forbid Microsoft from distributing, at a single price, a version of Windows bundled with IE unless the OEM had the option of deleting the IE icon and "other means by which users may readily use IE to browse the web") (Prayer 2.f.i) (http://www.usdoj.gov). The government plaintiffs had also originally sought to require Microsoft to distribute Netscape with its Windows operating system. See id. 51–52 (Prayer 2.e) (three-year period); States' Proposed Order, Motion for a Preliminary Injunction, *New York v. Microsoft Corp.* (Civ. No. 1:98CV01233) (May 18, 1998), ¶ 2 (requiring inclusion of Netscape browser and "one other commercially available internet browser") (in authors' files).

101. The likelihood that ISVs would continue to write to Microsoft middleware even though end-use access was disabled was raised in Tunney Act objections, along with the argument that unbundling was necessary to lower the applications barrier to entry protecting Microsoft's monopoly in the OS market. See, e.g., Project to Promote Competition and Innovation in the Digital Age (ProComp), Comments to the Proposed Final Judgment in *United States v. Microsoft Corporation*, No. 98-1232, *State of New York, et al. v. Microsoft Corporation*, No. 98-1233, at App. A at ¶ 37 (Declaration of Kenneth Arrow) (Jan. 28, 2002) (http://www.usdoj.gov). Also see Comment of Robert E. Litan, Roger D. Noll, and William D. Nordhaus on the Revised Proposed Final Judgment (Jan. 17, 2002) (http://www.usdoj.gov). For the Justice Department's arguments against unbundling of middleware code, see United States Department of Justice, Response of the United States to Public Comments on the Revised Proposed Final Judgment ¶¶ 229–232, *United States v. Microsoft Corp.*, No. 98-1232 (CKK) (D.D.C. Feb. 27, 2002) (http://www.justice.gov).

102. "Crown jewel" provisions, which require a defendant to give up some additional asset if it is unable to comply with a decree's requirements within a given time, are a familiar part of merger decrees. See Statement of Bureau of Competition

Federal Trade Commission, Negotiating Merger Remedies (April 2, 2003) (http://www.ftc.gov) at 11, 22 n.31 (explaining crown jewel provisions).

103. The litigating states filed an initial proposal on December 7, 2001, and a slightly amended version on March 4, 2002. See Plaintiff Litigating States' Remedial Proposals, *United States v. Microsoft Corp.* 231 F.Supp.2d 144 (D.D.C. 2002) (No. 98-1232), *State of New York v. Microsoft Corp.*, 224 F.Supp.2d 76 (D.D.C 2002) (No. 98-1233) (Dec. 7, 2001) (http://cyber.law.harvard.edu); Plaintiff Litigating States' First Amended Proposed Remedy, *State of New York. v. Microsoft Corp.*, 224 F.Supp.2d 76 (D.D.C 2002) (No. 98-1233) (March 4, 2002) (in authors' files). Microsoft's remedy proposal was the settlement agreement into which it had entered with the Justice Department and the nine settling states. See Defendant Microsoft Corporation's Remedial Proposal, *United States v. Microsoft Corp.* 231 F.Supp.2d 144 (D.D.C. 2002) (No. 98-1232), *State of New York v. Microsoft Corp.*, 224 F.Supp.2d 76 (D.D.C 2002) (No. 98-1233) (Dec. 12, 2001) (http://cyber.law.harvard.edu/msdoj/).

104. This is the standard for an antitrust remedial decree as articulated by the court of appeals. See *United States v. Microsoft Corp.*, 253 F.3d at 103.

105. The Justice Department received 32,392 comments on the proposed final judgment and provided the full text of these comments to the Court on February 28, 2002. US v. Microsoft, 231 F. Supp. 2d 144, 150. Prior Justice Department experts were critical. See Timothy F. Bresnahan, "A Remedy That Falls Short of Restoring Competition," 16 *Antitrust* 67, 69 (2001); letter from Rebecca Henderson, Professor of Management, MIT Sloan School of Management, to Renata Hesse, Antitrust Division, U.S. Department of Justice, Tunney Act Submission Comments on the Proposed *United States v. Microsoft* Settlement 7–8 (Jan. 26, 2002) (http://www.usdoj.gov). The Department responded to 47 comments that it denominated as "critical." For the Department's brief in support of the settlement, see Memorandum of the United States in Support of Entry of the Proposed Final Judgment, *United States v. Microsoft Corp.*, No. 98-1232 (CKK) (D.D.C. Feb. 27,2002) (http://www.usdoj.gov). For the Department's response to the public comments, see Response of the United States to Public Comments on the Revised Proposed Final Judgment.

106. See *New York v. Microsoft Corp.*, 224 F. Supp. 2d 76, 87 (D.D.C. 2002) aff'd, 373 F.3d 1199 (D.C. Cir. 2004). In the remedies proceeding, the states called 15 witnesses and Microsoft called 19. See id. Thirty witnesses testified at the merits trial. See Gavil, "The End of Antitrust Trench Warfare?" at 9–10.

107. See *United States v. Microsoft Corp.*, 231 F. Supp. 2d 144 (D.D.C. 2002) (approving settlement decree); *New York v. Microsoft Corp.*, 224 F. Supp. 2d 76 (D.D.C. 2002) (states' case, entering extensive findings of fact).

108. Microsoft, 231 F. Supp. 2d at 174 (D.D.C. 2002). See Microsoft, 224 F. Supp. 2d at 214 (adding "threats" of retaliation to states' decree); id. 155; (automatic launch

of non-Microsoft middleware); id. 201 (IAP offers during initial boot sequence). In the litigating states' proceeding, Microsoft proposed that Judge Kollar-Kotelly enter the settlement decree.

109. See id. 87, 157. The litigating states' economic expert was Carl Shapiro, who had consulted to the states regarding remedies in the original trial.

110. Id. 158–159.

111. Id. 158.

112. Id. 229.

113. Id. 243.

114. Id. 244.

115. Id. 185.

116. Id.

117. Id. 193 (emphasis in original).

118. Id. 184.

119. For 2012 market share data for PC operating systems, see http://www .netmarketshare.com/operating-system-market-share.aspx?qprid=8&qpcustomd=0 (reporting a 92% share for Windows in a market that included the Mac OS).

120. The court of appeals' affirmance of Judge Kollar-Kotelly's decisions is reported at 373 F.3d 1199 (D.C. Cir. 2004).

121. 373 F.3d at 1210.

122. The groups that sought to intervene for the purpose of filing an appeal were the Computer and Communications Industry Association and the Software and Information Industry Association. See id. 1204.

Chapter 5

1. Section 4 is codified at 15 U.S.C. § 15. Similarly, Section 16 of the Clayton Act, 15 U.S.C. § 26, authorizes private parties to sue for injunctive relief "against threatened loss or damage by a violation of the antitrust laws" and, if successful, recovery of "the cost of suit, including a reasonable attorney's fee."

2. For a survey of the jurisdictions that authorize private rights of action for anti-trust violations and an analysis of their features, see Albert A. Foer, et al., eds., *The International Handbook on Private Enforcement of Competition Law* (2011).

3. It is even unusual under U.S. law. Generally in the U.S., a plaintiff can recover only actual damages and except for a few statutory exceptions, such as antitrust and

civil rights, the "American Rule" is that—win or lose—each party must bear the cost of its own attorney's fees.

4. *Blue Shield of Virginia v. McCready*, 457 U.S. 465, 472 (1982).

5. *Brunswick Corp. v. Pueblo Bowl-O-Mat, Inc.*, 429 U.S. 477, 489 (1977).

6. *Illinois Brick Co. v. Illinois*, 431 U.S. 720 (1977).

7. *Associated General Contractors of California, Inc. v. California State Council of Carpenters*, 459 U.S. 519, 534, 537–538 (1983).

8. For an argument that civil fines should be permitted under U.S. antitrust law, see Harry First, "The Case for Antitrust Civil Penalties," 76 *Antitrust L. J.* 127 (2009).

9. "Group" and "representational" litigation have a long history and deep roots in English common-law practice, but the American class action is somewhat unique in the degree to which it facilitates large-scale litigation. For an excellent general history of the device and its current form, see Stephen C. Yeazell, *From Medieval Group Litigation to the Modern Class Action* (1987).

10. Jonathan Krim, "RealNetworks, Microsoft Settle Suit," *Washington Post*, Oct. 12, 2005.

11. MDL transfers are limited to "pretrial" proceedings. Under the statute, when the pretrial process is concluded, transferred cases must be remanded to their originating ("transferor") court unless they have been "previously terminated," as by settlement or dismissal. See 28 U.S.C. § 1407(a). See also *Lexicon Inc. v. Milberg Weiss Bershad Hynes & Lerach*, 523 U.S. 26 (1998).

12. 28 U.S.C. § 1407(a).

13. For a discussion of the *Electrical Equipment* antitrust cases that eventually led to the creation of the JPML, see Phil C. Neal and Perry Goldberg, "The Electrical Equipment Antitrust Cases: Novel Judicial Administration," 50 *A.B.A. J.* 621 (1964). The complete legislative history of the statute, including a discussion of its historical link to the *Electrical Equipment* antitrust cases, is included in H.R. Rep. No. 90-1130 (1968) and S. Rep. No. 454, 90th Cong., 1st Sess. (1967). For statistics on MDL dockets created, cases transferred, and MDL proceedings terminated, see http://www.jpml.uscourts.gov/.

14. Authority for such transfers within the federal system is established by 28 U.S.C. § 1441.

15. Under 28 U.S.C. § 1441, a case filed in state court that could have originally been filed in federal court can be "removed" by the defendant from the state court where it was filed to the federal court covering the same jurisdiction. Once in the

federal court, the action can be transferred within the federal system to be included in any federal MDL proceedings.

16. See Andrew I. Gavil, "Federal Judicial Power and the Challenges of Multijurisdictional Direct and Indirect Purchaser Antitrust Litigation," 69 *Geo. Wash. L. Rev.* 860, 876 and n. 86 (2001).

17. In November of 1998, six months after the government filed its antitrust case against Microsoft, AOL announced its intention to acquire Netscape for $4.2 billion. (The deal was closed early in 1999.) At the same time, it announced that it had entered into a strategic development and marketing alliance with Sun. At that moment, AOL viewed the combined transactions as critical components of its strategy to transform its AOL Web portal into a center for e-commerce. According to a contemporaneous press report, Microsoft's general counsel at the time, William Neukom, "reiterated the company's view that the deal between AOL and Netscape, and AOL's alliance with Sun, show that the government's antitrust suit against the software giant is groundless." Sandeep Junnarker and Tim Clark, "AOL Buys Netscape for $4.2 Billion," CNET News, Nov. 24, 1998. A year after AOL's acquisition of Netscape, it merged with Time Warner after an antitrust review by the Federal Trade Commission that approved the deal, albeit with some restrictions. See "FTC Approves AOL/Time Warner Merger with Conditions" (press release) (http://www.ftc.gov).

18. Netscape's complaint was filed in the District of Columbia on January 22, 2002 and transferred on June 17, 2002; Sun's complaint was filed in the Northern District of California on March 8, 2002 and transferred on August 9, 2002.

19. Joe Wilcox, "AOL's Netscape Sues Microsoft," CNET News, Jan. 22, 2002.

20. As one account reported, an unbundling remedy had been urged by the nine states that objected to the government settlement and Netscape sought to build upon that suggestion: "One option: forcing Microsoft to release a version of Windows without its own 'middleware' products such as a Web browser, media player or instant messenger." Id.

21. As the court of appeals observed, quoting the district court, Netscape was at the epicenter of the case, because it served as the principal means of distributing Sun's Java to consumers: "In May 1995 Netscape agreed with Sun to distribute a copy of the Java runtime environment with every copy of Navigator, and 'Navigator quickly became the principal vehicle by which Sun placed copies of its Java runtime environment on the PC systems of Windows users.'" 253 F.3d at 74.

22. Complaint, Netscape Commc'ns. Corp. v. Microsoft Corp., Nos. JFM-02CV2090 & 1:02CV00097, 2002 WL 34239419 (D.D.C. Jan. 22, 2002).

23. Joe Wilcox, "AOL's Netscape sues Microsoft," CNET News, Jan. 22, 2002.

24. For a more detailed description of the California litigation, see Sun Microsystems, Inc. v. Microsoft Corp., 188 F.3d 1115 (9th Cir. 1999) and Sun Microsystems, Inc. v. Microsoft Corp., 87 F. Supp.2d 992 (N.D. Cal. 2000). By way of disclosure, Andrew Gavil was Of Counsel to one of the firms representing Sun during portions of its antitrust litigation and worked on limited portions of the case.

25. See Second Amended Complaint, Sun Microsystems, Inc. v. Microsoft Corp., No. C-02-01150 RMW (PVT), MDL No. 1332, 2003 WL 25549149 (D. Md. Nov. 20, 2003).

26. See Complaint, RealNetworks, Inc. v. Microsoft Corp., Case No.03-CV-05717, 2003 WL 23795056 (N.D. Ca. Dec. 18, 2003).

27. Complaint, Novell, Inc. v. Microsoft Corp., No. 2:04CV01045 TS, 2004 WL 2607784, ¶ 51 (D. Utah Nov. 12, 2004).

28. The allegations were summarized in *Novell, Inc. v. Microsoft Corp.*, 505 F.3d 302, 309–310 (4th Cir. 2007).

29. Novell Complaint at ¶ 149.

30. Sun's theory was explained at length in the earlier California litigation and quoted at length by the Court of Appeals for the Fourth Circuit. See *In re Microsoft Corporation Antitrust Litigation*, 333 F.3d at 523. See also *Sun Microsystems, Inc. v. Microsoft Corp.*, 87 F. Supp.2d 992, 995 (N.D. Cal. 2000). In its decision in the governments' cases, the D.C. Circuit Court had also described the conduct directed at Sun. See *Microsoft Corp.*, 253 F.3d at 74–78.

31. *In re Microsoft Corp. Antitrust Litigation*, 237 F. Supp.2d 639, 642 (D. Md. 2002).

32. Id. 646.

33. *In re Microsoft Corp. Antitrust Litigation*, 240 F.Supp.2d 460 (D. Md. 2003).

34. *In re Microsoft Corp. Antitrust Litigation*, 333 F.3d 517 (4th Cir. 2003).

35. *In re Microsoft Corp. Antitrust Litigation*, 333 F.3d at 524–525 (emphasis added).

36. See, e.g., *Parklane Hosiery Co. Inc. v. Shore*, 439 U.S. 322 (1979) (recognizing offensive collateral estoppel).

37. As William Page has observed, Jackson's findings, which focused on Microsoft's monopoly power and exclusionary acts, were of greater value to the rival plaintiffs than to the class-action plaintiffs who were seeking overcharge damages, because Jackson had concluded that it wasn't possible to tell from the available data what the monopoly price of Windows might be. See William H. Page, "Class Certification in the Microsoft Indirect Purchaser Litigation," 1 *J. Competition L. & Econ.* 303, 317–318 (2005).

38. *In re Microsoft Corp. Antitrust Litigation*, 232 F. Supp.2d 534 (D. Md. 2002).

39. Id. at 537.

40. *In re Microsoft Corp. Antitrust Litigation*, 355 F.3d 322, 326–327 (4th Cir. 2004) (emphasis added).

41. Id. (emphasis in original).

42. In *Comes v. Microsoft Corp.*, 709 N.W.2d 114 (Iowa 2006), one of the state indirect-purchaser class-action suits that was also triggered by the government cases, the Iowa Supreme Court reversed the trial court's conclusion that 352 of Judge Jackson's 412 findings of fact should have preclusive effect. Although the trial court properly used a "necessary and essential" standard, it deemed the standard satisfied if a findings of fact "provided a proper foundation" or "proper basis" for the court's conclusions of law. Rejecting this approach as too lenient, the Iowa Court defined the standard this way: "[W]e apply the necessary and essential requirement narrowly, and only preclude those facts vital or crucial to the previous judgment, or those properly characterized as ultimate facts without which the previous judgment would lack support." Id. at 119.

43. *Novell, Inc. v. Microsoft Corp.*, 505 F.3d 302, 317 (4th Cir. 2007).

44. Id. at 317–320. Importantly, the court acknowledged the sometime overlooked proposition that unlawful exclusionary conduct can give rise to both lost profits for the injured rival and overcharges for the consumer that ultimately pays higher prices or receives lower quality goods after the exclusion. Id. at 318 and n. 25.

45. Id. at 322–323.

46. Id.

47. *Novell v. Microsoft Corp.*, 2011 WL 165125 (4th Cir. 2011) (unreported opinion). According to the court, Novell abandoned Count VI of its complaint on appeal, so that all that remained at issue was Count I, the claim that was most closely tied to the governments' cases against Microsoft. Id. at *3 n.7.

48. *Novell, Inc. v. Microsoft Corp.*, 731 F.3d 1064 (10th Cir. 2013), cert. denied (2014).

49. See "Microsoft and Sun Microsystems Enter Broad Cooperation Agreement; Settle Outstanding Litigation" (press release, April 2, 2004) (http://www.microsoft.com).

50. For a more detailed accounting of the settlement process, see Robert A. Guth, "Peace Program: Microsoft, Sun Bury Hatchet," AP Data Stream, April 5, 2004.

51. John Markoff, "Silicon Valley Seeks Peace in Long War Against Microsoft," *New York Times*, April 4, 2004.

52. Id.

53. According to the Microsoft press release (Nov. 8, 2004) (http://www.microsoft .com), "[t]he agreement does not obligate Microsoft to license or otherwise share any of its technology or intellectual property rights with Novell."

54. Tobias Buck, "Critic of Microsoft Received $ 9.75 Million After Deal," *Financial Times*, Nov. 24, 2004. According to the article, the settlement didn't specify how the money paid to CCIA would be disbursed, but Microsoft probably was aware that the CCIA Board intended to award a sizeable portion of it to its president, Ed Black. Later press reports indicated that Nokia withdrew as a member of CCIA in response to the CCIA Board's approval of the settlement and payment to Black. See Dan Gillmor, "Tech Lobbying Group Falls In with the Wrong Crowd," *San Jose Mercury News*, Dec. 1, 2004.

55. Alan Murray, "Political Capital: Microsoft Foe Quits Antitrust Crusade—with Check in Hand," *Wall Street Journal*, Dec. 7, 2004.

56. *Massachusetts v. Microsoft Corp.*, 373 F.3d 1199 (D.C. Cir. 2004).

57. Tobias Buck, "Critic of Microsoft Received $ 9.75 Million After Deal," *Financial Times*, Nov. 24, 2004.

58. Brad Smith, "Microsoft Legal Settlements with the Computer & Communications Industry Association (CCIA) and Novell" (Nov. 8, 2004) (http://www.microsoft.com). See also Jonathan Krim, "Microsoft Placates Two Foes: Settlements Set for Novell, CCIA," *Washington Post*, Nov. 9, 2004 (quoting Microsoft General Counsel Brad Smith as saying he "hopes the settlements will encourage the EU to return to the negotiating table").

59. Brad Smith, "Microsoft Legal Settlements with the Computer & Communications Industry Association (CCIA) and Novell" (Nov. 8, 2004) (http://www.microsoft.com).

60. "MS.dosh Settlement: Microsoft's Pay-offs Show Why Regulators Are Necessary," *Financial Times*, Nov. 26, 2004.

61. Burst.com had a significant patent portfolio focused on audio and video delivery technologies and had sued Microsoft for patent infringement as well as antitrust and trade secret law violations. The settlement consisted of a $60 million payment by Microsoft to Burst and the granting in return of a non-exclusive license to Burst' patent portfolio. See "Microsoft and Burst.com Settle Outstanding Litigation and Enter into Licensing Agreement" (http://www.microsoft.com). In 2010, Burst.com repositioned its product offerings and changed its name to Democrasoft.

62. *United States v. Microsoft Corp.*, 65 F. Supp.2d 1, 18 (D.D.C. 1999) (Finding of Fact 64).

63. "Microsoft and Gateway Lay Foundation for Future Cooperation, Resolve Antitrust Claims" (http://www.microsoft.com).

64. 65 F. Supp.2d at 30 (Finding of Fact 116). For the court's complete discussion of Microsoft's treatment of IBM, see id. at 29–34 (Findings of Fact 115–132).

65. See Microsoft and IBM Resolve Antitrust Issues, July 1, 2005 (http://www.microsoft.com). See also John Markoff, "Microsoft to Pay I.B.M. $775 Million in Settlement," *New York Times*, July 2, 2005.

66. Steve Lohr, "Microsoft Turns Enemy into Ally in Antitrust Settlement," *New York Times*, Oct. 11, 2005.

67. "Microsoft and RealNetworks Resolve Antitrust Case and Announce Digital Music and Games Partnership" (press release, Oct. 11, 2005) (http://www.microsoft.com).

68. Some additional announced features included the following:

• Microsoft will enhance consumers' ability to access Real's software products in simple and straightforward ways, enabling consumers easily to choose their preferred settings for playing media files and managing other media experiences.
• Microsoft will design Windows Vista so that if a user seeks to play a Real media file that has no playback software on the PC, Windows will redirect the user who consents to a web page that enables the user to download the Real software needed to play the Real media file.
• Microsoft and Real will work together to enhance interoperability between Microsoft's Windows Media and Real's Helix Digital Rights Management systems. Microsoft will also enable Real to facilitate the playback of content on non-Windows portable devices and personal computers using Windows Media DRM.
• Microsoft has provided Real contractual assurances ensuring Real broad access to the PC OEM distribution channel.

69. Id.

70. Discussion of the issues raised by claims and cases initiated by foreign plaintiffs is beyond the scope of this chapter. For Judge Motz's consideration of the issues, see *In re Microsoft Corp. Antitrust Litigation*, 127 F. Supp.2d 702, 714–717 (D. Md. 2001).

71. *California v. ARC America Corp.*, 490 U.S. 93 (1989). For a more complete discussion of the issues raised by *Illinois Brick* and *ARC America*, and a proposed solution for the challenges they have created for the U.S. litigation system, see Andrew I. Gavil, "Thinking Outside the *Illinois Brick* Box: A Proposal for Reform," 76 *Antitrust L. J.* 167 (2009).

72. For a comprehensive review of indirect-purchaser issues, see *Indirect Purchaser Litigation Handbook* (2007).

73. *Hanover Shoe, Inc. v. United Shoe Machinery Corp.*, 392 U.S. 481 (1968).

74. For the most part, it was unable to benefit from the enhanced removal provisions of the Class Action Fairness Act of 2005, 28 U.S.C. § 1332(d), which came too late in the litigation process.

75. *Comes v. Microsoft Corp.*, 403 F. Supp.2d 897 (S.D. Iowa 2005).

76. *Comes v. Microsoft Corp.*, 646 N.W.2d 440, 442 (Iowa 2002).

77. Reiter v. Sonotone Corp., 442 U.S. 330, 343 (1979) (emphasis added). The Court didn't have occasion to confront the obvious tension between *Reiter* and *Illinois*

Brick, however, because it viewed Reiter's standing as an indirect purchaser as a distinct issue that wasn't before the Court. Id. at 337, n.3.

78. *Comes*, 646 N.W.2d at 447.

79. For states rejecting *Illinois Brick* in Microsoft-related cases, see *Arthur v. Microsoft Corp.*, 676 N.W.2d 29 (Neb. 2004); *Sherwood v. Microsoft Corp.*, 2003–2 Trade Cas. (CCH) ¶74,109 (Tenn. Ct. App. 2003); *Elkins v. Microsoft Corp.*, 817 A.2d 9 (Vt. 2002). For states following *Illinois Brick*, see *Pomerantz v. Microsoft Corp.*, 50 P.3d 929 (Colo. Ct. App. 2002); *Vacco v. Microsoft. Corp.*, 793 A.2d 1048 (Conn. 2002); *Hindman v. Microsoft Corp.*, 88 P.3d 1209 (Haw. 2004) (unpublished disposition); *Berghausen v. Microsoft Corp.*, 765 N.E.2d 592 (Ind. 2002); *Arnold v. Microsoft Corp.*, 2002–1 Trade Cas. (CCH) ¶73,598 (Ky. Ct. App. 2001) (unpublished disposition); *Davidson v. Microsoft Corp.*, 792 A.2d 336 (Md. Ct. Spec. App. 2002); *Minuteman, LLC v. Microsoft Corp.*, 795 A.2d 833 (N.H. 2002); *Johnson v. Microsoft Corp.*, 834 N.E.2d 791 (Ohio 2005); *Major v. Microsoft Corp.*, 60 P.3d 511 (Okla.Civ.App. 2002); *Siena v. Microsoft Corp.*, 796 A.2d 461 (R.I. 2002). In response to judicial decisions rejecting *Illinois Brick*, some states enacted legislation reestablishing indirect purchasers' rights, although in some instances limiting the authority to assert them to public enforcers or to public entities suing as indirect purchasers, themselves. See Edward D. Cavanagh, "*Illinois Brick*: A Look Backward and a Look Ahead," 17 *Loy. Consumer L. Rev.* 1, 2 n.4 (2004).

80. See Antitrust Modernization Commission, Report and Recommendations 269 (2007) (http://govinfo.library.unt.edu). See also Cavanagh, "*Illinois Brick*: A Look Backward and a Look Ahead" (identifying 30 states that recognize indirect purchasers' rights to sue, 25 of which by statute). In *Comes*, the Court was persuaded that the "trend" among the states was to reject *Illinois Brick*. Its survey identified 36 states and the District of Columbia as having done so at that time. *Comes*, 646 N.W.2d at 448.

81. For a proposed legislative solution, see Gavil, "Thinking Outside the *Illinois Brick Box*."

82. *In re Microsoft Corp. Antitrust Litigation*, 127 F.Supp.2d 702 (D. Md. 2001). The court of appeals denied the plaintiffs' petition for interlocutory appeal in June of 2001. Subsequently, in November of 2004, the district court dismissed the plaintiffs' remaining claims, which were limited to equitable relief, and entered final judgment. Twenty-six of the original 39 plaintiffs on the consolidated complaint then filed the appeal discussed here. In cases initially filed in state court, but successfully removed to federal court and transferred as part of the MDL process, Judge Motz also had to decide whether indirect purchasers had the right to sue under the laws of specific states. See, e.g., *In re Microsoft Corp. Antitrust Litigation*, 401 F. Supp.2d 461 (D. Md. 2005) (indirect purchasers barred from suit under South Carolina antitrust law).

83. For another decision rejecting an attempt to invoke an exception to work around *Illinois Brick*, see *In re Microsoft Corp. Antitrust Litigation*, 168 F. Supp.2d 541 (D. Md. 2001) (rejecting reliance on the "co-conspirator" exception).

84. *Kloth v. Microsoft Corp.*, 444 F.3d 312 (4th Cir. 2006).

85. Id. at 322–323.

86. Id. at 324.

87. The discussion here focuses on the state class-certification decisions. Judge Motz also faced class-certification issues in the MDL proceeding. See *Deiter v. Microsoft Corp.*, 436 F.3d 461 (4th Cir. 2006) (affirming limited certification of a class of direct purchasers).

88. See William H. Page, "The Limits of State Indirect Purchaser Suits: Class Certification in the Shadow of *Illinois Brick*," 67 *Antitrust L. J.* 1 (1999).

89. See *Melnick v. Microsoft Corp.*, 2001–2 Trade Cas. (CCH) ¶ 73,408 (Sup. Ct. Me. 2001) (denying motion for class certification); *A&M Supply Co. v. Microsoft Corp.*, 654 N.W.2d 572 (Mich. 2002) (reversing trial court's decision to grant class certification). See also *Fish v. Microsoft Corp.*, Case No. 00-031126-NZ (Cir. Ct. Mich. 2004) (order denying class certification dated April 8, 2004).

90. *A&M Supply*, 654 N.W.2d, at 601–603.

91. *In re Microsoft I-V Cases*, 2000-2 Trade Cas. (CCH) ¶ 73,013 (Ca. Sup. Ct. 2000).

92. For some examples, see *Howe v. Microsoft Corp.*, 656 N.W.2d 285 (N.D. 2003) (declining to follow *A&M* and *Melnick*); *In re South Dakota Microsoft Antitrust Litigation*, 657 N.W.2d 668 (S.D. 2003) (also declining to follow *A&M*).

93. *In re South Dakota Microsoft Antitrust Litigation*, 657 N.W.2d, at 679. According to one survey published in 2005, of the fourteen state-court decisions on class certification in the various Microsoft cases, only three—the *Fish* and *A&M* decisions in Michigan and *Melnick* in Maine—refused to certify indirect-purchaser classes. Eleven others certified. See William H. Page, "Class Certification in the *Microsoft* Indirect Purchaser Litigation," 1 *J. Comp. L. & Econ.* 303 (2005).

94. *Comes v. Microsoft Corp.*, 696 N.W.2d 318 (Iowa 2005).

95. In a follow-up to his 1999 study of indirect-purchaser class certification in the state courts, Page examined and sought to explain the change of direction in the *Microsoft* cases, which began to more freely certify indirect-purchaser class actions. While acknowledging that some courts were probably unable to overcome the inconsistency of granting the right to sue while refusing to certify, he reasoned that the actual value of the indirect-purchaser cases was very limited. As he had in 1999, he concluded that deterrence should be the primary goal of the private right of action and that the rule of *Illinois Brick* best served that goal. See William H. Page, "Class Certification in the *Microsoft* Indirect Purchaser Litigation," 1 *J. Comp. L. & Econ.* 303 (2005).

96. Id. 325.

97. See, e.g., *Wal-Mart Stores, Inc. v. Dukes*, 131 S.Ct 2541 (2011); *In re Hydrogen Per-oxide Antitrust Litigation*, 552 F.3d 305 (3d Cir. 2008).

98. Settlements were eventually negotiated in Arizona, Arkansas, California, the District of Columbia, Florida, Iowa, Kansas, Massachusetts, Minnesota, Montana, Nebraska, New Mexico, New York, North Carolina, North Dakota, South Dakota, Tennessee, Vermont, West Virginia, and Wisconsin. For the details of the settle-ments, see http://www.microsoft.com/About/Legal/EN/US/ConsumerSettlements/Default.aspx.

99. See, e.g., *Bettendorf v. Microsoft Corp.*, 779 N.W.2d 34 (Ct. App. Wisc. 2009); *In re New Mexico Indirect Purchasers Microsoft Antitrust Litigation*, 149 P.3d 976 (Ct. App. N.M. 2006); *Charles I. Friedman, P.C. v. Microsoft Corp.*, 141 P.3d 824 (Ct. App. Ariz. 2006); *In re South Dakota Microsoft Antitrust Litigation*, 707 N.W.2d 85 (S.D. 2005).

100. *Amchem Products, Inc. v. Windsor*, 521 U.S. 591(1997).

101. *In re Microsoft Corp. Antitrust Litigation*, 185 F. Supp.2d 519 (D. Md. 2002) (2001 WL 34133945). See also "Microsoft Settles Product Pricing Class Action Suits" (press release, Nov. 20, 2001) (http://www.microsoft.com).

102. 185 F. Supp.2d at 526.

103. Id. at 526–527.

104. Id. at 528–529. The court reasoned that Windows-based PCs would necessarily make up the lion's share of the refurbished computer segment of the program, because the program would rely on donations from businesses and government, which overwhelmingly used Windows-based computers. On the software side, the court noted that the "free software" portion of the program had been criticized as "court approved predatory pricing." Id.

105. *In re Microsoft Corp. Antitrust Litigation*, 185 F.Supp.2d 519 (D. Md. 2002).

106. "Microsoft Statement on Court Decision to Not Grant Preliminary Approval of Class Action Settlement" (press release, Jan. 11, 2002) (http://www.microsoft.com). Although a smaller settlement was later reached and approved in some of the direct purchaser MDL cases, there were no other efforts to certify nationwide settlement classes.

107. The facts here are summarized from *In re Microsoft I-V Cases*, 135 Cal. App. 4th 706 (Ct. App. Calif. 2006).

108. Id. at 711–715. For review of a similarly structured settlement, see *Barnhill v. Florida Microsoft Anti-Trust Litigation*, 905 So.2d 195 (Fla. App. 3 Dist. 2005).

109. *In re Microsoft I-V Cases*, 135 Cal. App.4th 706 (Ct. App. Calif. 2006).

110. Id. at 726–728.

Chapter 6

1. The United States and Canada have two of the oldest antitrust statutes of the modern era, both dating back to the late nineteenth century. But laws affecting competition can be traced to much older civilizations. See, e.g., Lambros E. Kotsiris, "An Antitrust Case in Ancient Greek Law," 22 *Int'l Law.* 451 (1988) (discussing prosecution of a cartel of grain dealers in ancient Greece).

2. For information on its membership and activities, see http://www .internationalcompetitionnetwork.org/.

3. The Korean case is discussed later in this chapter. The Japan Fair Trade Commission brought two cases against Microsoft. One was an unfair business practices charge for tying Microsoft Word and Microsoft Excel, resulting in a "recommendation decision" entered against Microsoft in 1998. See JFTC Annual Report on Competition Policy (January–December 1998) (http://web.archive.org) at 8. The other was an unfair-business-practice charge for "dealing on restrictive terms" for requiring Japanese computer manufacturers to agree to a non-assertion of patents (NAP) clause in their Windows licensing agreements. This case resulted in a hearing decision against Microsoft in 2008. An English summary was posted at www.jftc.go.jp. For an analysis of the JFTC's NAP case, see Toshiaki Takigawa, "A Comparative Analysis of U.S., EU, and Japanese *Microsoft* Cases: How to Regulate Exclusionary Conduct by a Dominant Firm in a Network Industry," 50 *Antitrust Bull.* 237 (2005). For investigations in other countries, see "Russia Launches Antitrust Probe of Microsoft," *Washington Post*, June 4, 2009; Dan Nystedt, "Microsoft Faces Taiwan Antitrust Investigation," *Computer World*, August 18, 2008; Mary Jo Foley, "Might Office Be Where Microsoft Gets Socked with Chinese Antitrust Charges?" (http:// www.zdnet.com).

4. The Court of First Instance is today called the General Court. To avoid confusion, we will refer to it by the name that applied during the *Microsoft* cases.

5. The name of the Treaty containing the competition law provisions has changed several times since 1957. For expositional convenience, we refer to all versions as "the Treaty." On the adoption of the original prohibitions in the Treaty, see, e.g., Tony A. Freyer, *Antitrust and Global Capitalism, 1930–2004* (2006), 270–290; David J. Gerber, *Law and Competition in Twentieth Century Europe: Protecting Prometheus* (1998), 336–346; D. G. Goyder, *EC Competition Law* (2003), 24–26. The statutory language of the two articles was drawn from comparable provisions in the European Steel and Coal Treaty of 1951, drafted by Robert Bowie of the Harvard Law School, who was serving as General Counsel to John J. McCloy, High Commissioner for Germany. See Gerber, *Law and Competition in Twentieth Century Europe*, 338.

6. The abuse-of-dominance provision is now Article 102 of the Treaty, which is now called the Treaty on the Functioning of the European Union (TFEU). Article 102 was

originally numbered as Article 86 and subsequently renumbered as Article 82. We will refer to it as Article 102 regardless of the number given in the quoted source.

7. When Sun Microsystems filed its formal complaint about Microsoft with the European Commission, in December of 1998, the procedure for handling private complaints was dictated by Council Regulation 17, the first regulation implementing what were referred to as Articles 81 and 82 of the Treaty at the time of the Commission's decision in its initial Microsoft case. This is reflected in the opening recitals to the Commission's March 2004 decision, which concluded that Microsoft had indeed violated EU competition laws. As part of a substantial modernization effort, Regulation 17 was repealed effective May 1, 2004. The primary focus of that effort, however, concerned abolition of the prior system of notifications and clearances and expansion of the respective roles of national competition authorities and private actions in enforcing EU competition laws. The framework for handling formal complaints was refined, but remains essentially the same as it was during the handling of the Sun complaint from 1998 to 2004. To present a current explanation of that process, the description of EC practice provided here is summarized from four later sources: Council Regulation (EC) No 1/2003 of 16 December 2002 on the implementation of the rules on competition laid down in Articles 81 and 82 of the Treaty (OJ L 1, 4.1.2003) (referred to as the "Modernization Regulation"); Commission Regulation (EC) No 773/2004 of 7 April 2004 relating to the conduct of proceedings by the Commission pursuant to Articles 81 and 82 of the EC Treaty (OJ L 123, 27.4.2004) (referred to as the "Implementing Regulation"); Commission Notice on the handling of complaints by the Commission under Articles 81 and 82 of the EC Treaty (OJ C, 27.4.2004); and DG Competition, Best Practices on the conduct of proceedings concerning Articles 101 and 102 TFEU (2010) (http://ec.europa.eu).

8. Formal complaints from interested private parties are contemplated by Article 7 of Regulation (EC) No. 1/2003 and specific requirements for formal complaints are set forth in Form C, which is included as an Annex to Commission Regulation No. 773/2004.

9. See Implementing Regulation, Art. 13(1)–(2).

10. For a more detailed and specific account of the procedures summarized here, including references to the relevant provisions of the applicable Regulations and Notices, see DG Competition, Best Practices on the conduct of proceedings concerning Articles 101 and 102 TFEU (2010) (http://ec.europa.eu).

11. A Statement of Objections (SO) is an analog to an administrative complaint in jurisdictions such as the United States. The issuance of an SO triggers specific procedures that include the right to respond.

12. "Workgroup server services" are the basic infrastructure services used by office workers. They include sharing files stored on servers, sharing printers, and adminis-

tering user access to network services (such as software applications installed on PCs or servers).

13. Commission Decision 2007/53/EC of 24 March 2004 Relating to a Proceeding Pursuant to Article 82 of the EC Treaty and Article 54 of the EEA Agreement Against Microsoft Corporation (COMP/C-3/37.792—Microsoft), 2007 O.J. (L 32) 23, ¶ 3 (hereinafter "Commission Decision"). The Commission Decision was divided into six parts (1080 distinct paragraphs referred to as "recitals") and a formal summary decision, presented in nine articles. For purposes of presentation and clarity, we refer to the various recitals by their paragraph numbers and the formal decision by article and subparagraph number.

14. See Commission Decision, ¶¶ 4–10.

15. Interested trade associations included the Association for Competitive Technology (ACT), the Computer & Communications Industry Association (CCIA), the Computer Technology Industry Association (CompTIA), the Free Software Foundation Europe (FSF Europe), and the Software & Information Industry Association (SIIA). CCIA and SIAA took anti-Microsoft positions; their membership included Sun, Netscape, and Novell. ACT and CompTIA took pro-Microsoft positions; their membership included Microsoft.

16. See Commission Decision, ¶11.

17. For an analysis of Monti's tenure and his role in the settlement negotiations with Microsoft, see Mark Landler, "A Slayer of Monopolies, One Corporation at a Time," *New York Times*, March 25, 2004.

18. See Commission Decision, ¶¶ 994–1080.

19. *United States v. Microsoft Corp.*, 253 F.3d 34, 57 (D.C. Cir. 2001).

20. See Commission Decision, ¶ 470. See also id. ¶¶ 465–470. The Commission cited with approval Michael L. Katz and Carl Shapiro, "Antitrust in Software Markets," in *Competition, Innovation and the Microsoft Monopoly: Antitrust in the Digital Marketplace*, ed. Jeffrey A. Eisenach and Thomas M. Lenard (1999), 29. Id. ¶ 469, n. 588.

21. See Commission Decision, ¶¶ 37–43.

22. See Commission Decision, ¶¶ 44–51.

23. See Commission Decision, ¶¶ 177–184.

24. The breadth of the U.S. case is described in *United States v. Microsoft Corp.*, 253 F.3d 34, 58 (D.C. Cir. 2001) (in addition to the integration of IE into Windows, case challenged various dealings with Original Equipment Manufacturers, Internet Access Providers, Internet Content Providers, Independent Software Vendors, Apple Computer, Sun Microsystems, and Intel).

25. Although network computing wasn't part of the U.S. case as litigated, the governments' Proposed Findings of Fact noted Microsoft's effort to extend its dominance beyond the desktop: 'Microsoft's entire course of conduct aimed at blunting potential middleware threats has further reinforced the applications barrier to entry by maintaining and expanding Microsoft's ability to influence and control standards in the increasingly important area of network-based computing, and thereby to extend its monopoly power into servers, Internet protocols, and other industry segments." Plaintiffs' Joint Proposed Findings of Fact—Revised, *United States v. Microsoft Corp.*, Civil Action No. 98-1233 (D.D.C. 1999) (http://www.justice.gov), at 6.

26. Intel Vice President Steven McGeady, one of the U.S. government's witnesses in its case-in-chief, testified that Microsoft's Paul Maritz had used the phrase "embrace, extend, and extinguish" to describe Microsoft's strategy with respect to Internet competition in a November 1995 meeting at Intel. See Direct Testimony of Steven McGeady (Nov. 9, 1998), *United States v. Microsoft Corp.*, Civil Action No. 98-1233 (D.D.C. 1999) (http://www.justice.gov) at 54–55. On how Microsoft was accused of continuing to use this strategy in connection with the MIT-developed Kerberos encryption technology, even as the governments' case against it was coming to a conclusion in the trial court, see "Deadly Embrace," *The Economist*, March 30, 2000.

27. See Commission Decision, ¶¶ 126, 302–314.

28. See Commission Decision, ¶¶ 93–100, 587–589.

29. See Commission Decision, ¶ 428, quoting Case 27/76, *United Brands v. Commission* [1978] E.C.R. 207, at ¶ 65. Recall the D.C. Circuit Court of Appeals held that "[t]he Supreme Court defines monopoly power as 'the power to control prices or exclude competition.' *United States v. E.I. du Pont de Nemours & Co.*, 351 U.S. 377, 391, 76 S.Ct. 994, 100 L.Ed.1264 (1956). More precisely, a firm is a monopolist if it can profitably raise prices substantially above the competitive level." 253 F.3d at 51.

30. 253 F.3d at 58.

31. See Commission Notice on the Definition of Relevant Market for the Purpose of Community Competition Law, 1997 O.J. (C 372) 5 (http://eur-lex.europa.eu). The Notice shares a number of core concepts with the U.S. Horizontal Merger Guidelines, although the relevant inquiries into demand-side and supply-side substitutability are framed up in somewhat different ways. See U.S. Department of Justice and Federal Trade Commission, "Horizontal Merger Guidelines" (2010) (http://www.justice.gov), §§ 4, 5, 9.

32. See Commission Decision, ¶¶ 324–342. Expanding on the competitive significance of the applications barrier to entry, the Commission explained: "[T]he demand for ... a new client PC operating system will be small if it is not able to support a large number of applications. A customer will not buy (and an OEM will not distribute) an operating system if no (or very few) applications are able to run on it.

Therefore, any company wishing to switch resources into client PC operating systems would have to simultaneously develop a critical mass of applications that would be able to run on this platform. This is prohibitively expensive and time consuming. ... [N]o company at this time has the technical skills or the financial means to overcome that barrier." Id. at ¶ 340.

33. Id. ¶ 429.

34. Id. ¶ 429. ("The following recitals will show that Microsoft holds a dominant position which exhibits extraordinary features since it controls the quasi-standard of the relevant market in question, and has done so for some time. Microsoft's dominance relies on very high market shares and significant barriers to entry.")

35. Id. ¶ 435.

36. See *Spectrum Sports, Inc. v. McQuillan*, 506 U.S. 447 (1993).

37. "Dominance" and "monopoly power" are legal terms of art and have less meaning as a matter of economics. The economic concept that lies behind these terms is "market power," which is a matter of degree and may not directly correlate to any specific market share. Indeed, market-share evidence is only one kind of evidence— circumstantial evidence—that can be used as part of the assessment of market power.

38. See Commission Decision, ¶¶ 326; 434. See also *United States v. Microsoft Corp.*, 253 F.3d at 52 (affirming the district court's finding that Apple's Mac OS need not be included in the relevant market).

39. See Commission Decision, ¶¶ 436–447.

40. Id. ¶¶ 448–453.

41. Id. ¶ 458–460. The Commission also noted Microsoft's financial performance, attributing some significance to its seemingly high profit margins. Id. 464. In contrast, the U.S. Court of Appeals had been more cautious about attributing significance to evidence of high profit margins in network industries, citing Howard A. Shelanski and J. Gregory Sidak, "Antitrust Divestiture in Network Industries," 68 *U. Chi. L. Rev.* 1, 6–7 (2001). See 253 F.3d at 50.

42. See Commission Decision, ¶ 472.

43. Id. ¶ 383.

44. Id. ¶¶ 348–358. The authority to conduct market inquiries was included in Article 11 of Regulation 17, now superseded by Article 18 of the Modernisation Regulation. See Council Regulation (EC) No. 1/2003 of 16 December 2002 on the Implementation of the Rules on Competition Laid Down in Articles 81 and 82 of the Treaty, 2003 O.J. (LI) 1, Art. 18 (http://eur-lex.europa.eu).

45. See Commission Decision, ¶¶ 368, 382.

46. Id. ¶ 399.

47. Id. ¶ 514. The Commission's complete discussion of its methodology for calculating these shares is contained in ¶¶ 473–513.

48. Id. ¶ 516.

49. Id. ¶¶ 517–524.

50. Id. ¶ 526.

51. Id. ¶ 533. The case on which the Commission relied was its 1992 decision in *Tetra Pak II*, see Commission Decision 92/163/EEC in Case IV/31043—Tetra Pak II, OJ L 72, 18.3.1992, p. 1; Judgment of the Court of First Instance of 6 October 1994, *Tetra Pak v. Commission*, Case T-83/91, [1994] E.C.R. II-755; Judgment of the Court of 14 November 1996 in Case C-333/94 P *Tetra Pak v. Commission* (*Tetra Pak II*) [1996] E.C.R. I-5951.

52. See Commission Decision, ¶¶ 403–404.

53. Id. ¶¶ 407–419.

54. Id. ¶¶ 420, 879.

55. Id. ¶ 542 (citing to Judgment of the Court of 9 November 1983 in Case 322/81, *Michelin v. Commission* [1983] ECR 3461, at ¶ 57).

56. See Commission Decision, ¶ 543, quoting Judgment of the Court of 13 February 1979 in Case 85/76, *Hoffmann-La Roche* [1979] ECR 461, at 91 (emphasis added).

57. Many of the arguments relating to refusals to deal were famously formulated in Phillip Areeda, "Essential Facilities: An Epithet in Need of Limiting Principles," 58 *Antitrust L. J.* 841 (1989), and later influenced the U.S. Supreme Court's analysis in *Verizon Communications Inc. v. Law Offices of Curtis V. Trinko, LLP*, 540 U.S. 398 (2004). But Areeda didn't reject the notion of imposing liability for refusals to deal, as is sometimes suggested. He simply objected to over-reliance on the "essential facility" formulation and proposed ways to focus and limit the application of the doctrine in light of the concerns he articulated. See also Robert Pitofsky et al., "The Essential Facilities Doctrine Under U.S. Antitrust Law," 70 *Antitrust L. J.* 443 (2002).

58. See Commission Decision, ¶¶ 550–553. Cases discussed by the Commission included *Volvo v. Veng*, Case 238/87, [1988] ECR 6211; *RTE and ITP v. Commission*, Case C-241/91P, [1995] ECR 743 ("Magill"); and Case C-7/97, *Oscar Bronner GmbH & Co. KG v. Mediaprint Zeitungs- und Zeitschriftenverlag GmbH&Co. KG*, [1998] E.C.R. 7791.

59. See Commission Decision ¶¶ 554–555, 558.

60. Id. ¶¶ 585–586. The Commission's consideration of competitive effects related to Microsoft's refusal to supply is reflected in ¶¶ 585–708; Microsoft's justifications are in ¶¶ 709–791.

61. Id. ¶ 587.

62. Id. ¶ 588.

63. Id. ¶ 637. As we discussed in chapter 5, in private litigation in the United States, Sun sought a preliminary injunction imposing a "must-carry" duty on Microsoft with regard to Sun's Java. The court of appeals reversed the district court's grant of the preliminary injunction, disagreeing with the conclusion that Sun had sufficiently established a threat to competition that warranted preliminary relief before the market irretrievably tipped in Microsoft's favor. In contrast to the court of appeals' position, the Commission reasoned that "as regards the impact on competition, the relevant criterion for establishing a refusal to supply is whether there is a *risk* of elimination of competition. Immediate elimination of competition is not required. This approach is all the more appropriate in a market that exhibits strong network effects and where therefore elimination of competition would be difficult to reverse." Id. ¶ 622 (emphasis in original). This was entirely consistent with the view that had been expressed by the MDL court in Sun's private case in the U.S. See chapter 5 above.

64. See Commission Decision, ¶¶ 590–665. The Commission also rejected Microsoft's arguments that interoperability information was not "indispensable for its competitors" in the market for workgroup-server operating systems, owing to the availability of three "substitutes": use of open industry standards supported by Windows, the distribution of client-side software on the client PC, and the possibility of reverse-engineering. Id. ¶¶ 666–692. Moreover, the Commission concluded that the U.S. consent decree's Communications Protocol Licensing Program was too narrow and in other ways insufficient to remedy the competitive problems it had identified. Id. 688–691.

65. Id. ¶ 778. (In the original transcript of the speech, this entire sentence is italicized.)

66. Id. ¶ 692.

67. Id. ¶¶ 694–696.

68. Id. ¶¶ 697–701.

69. Id. ¶¶ 702–704. The D.C. Circuit had similarly held: "First, to be condemned as exclusionary, a monopolist's act must have an 'anticompetitive effect.' That is, it must harm the competitive *process* and thereby harm consumers." 253 F.3d at 58 (emphasis in original).

70. Compare the D.C. Circuit's reaction to Microsoft's intellectual property arguments, *United States v. Microsoft Corp.*, 253 F. 3d at 63 (argument "borders upon the frivolous" and is "no more correct than the proposition that use of one's personal property, such as a baseball bat, cannot give rise to tort liability"). We explore these issues further in chapter 4.

71. See Commission Decision, ¶¶ 546–784. With respect to incentives to innovate, the Commission concluded: "on balance, the possible negative impact of an order to supply on Microsoft's incentives to innovate is outweighed by its positive impact on the level of innovation of the whole industry (including Microsoft). As such, the need to protect Microsoft's incentives to innovate cannot constitute an objective justification that would offset the exceptional circumstances identified." Id. ¶783.

72. See Commission Decision, ¶¶ 709–728, 783.

73. Herbert Hovenkamp, *The Antitrust Enterprise: Principle and Execution* (2005), 297. Credit for the early development of the theory is often attributed to the work of Ward Bowman. See Ward S. Bowman Jr., "Tying Arrangements and the Leverage Problem," 67 *Yale L. J.* 19 (1957). For a response pointing out the limits of Bowman's theory, see Louis Kaplow, "Extension of Monopoly Power Through Leverage," 85 *Colum. L. Rev.* 515 (1985).

74. See Commission Decision, ¶ 767.

75. "[B]y strengthening its dominant position in the work group server operating system market, Microsoft effectively reinforces the barriers to entry in the client PC operating system market." Commission Decision, ¶ 769. See also Steven C. Salop, "Using Leverage to Preserve Monopoly," in *Competition, Innovation and the Microsoft Monopoly: Antitrust in the Digital Marketplace*, ed. Jeffrey A. Eisenach and Thomas M. Lenard (1999), 93, 94 (arguing that a monopolist "may attempt a leverage strategy in order to deter or destroy" a new entrant).

76. See Commission Decision, ¶¶ 764–778.

77. Id. ¶ 794. The Commission explained the standard for tying in almost the same terms as had the D.C. Circuit in the U.S.: "There are four elements to a per se tying violation: (1) the tying and tied goods are two separate products; (2) the defendant has market power in the tying product market; (3) the defendant affords consumers no choice but to purchase the tied product from it; and (4) the tying arrangement forecloses a substantial volume of commerce." (253 F.3d at 85)

78. See Commission Decision, ¶¶ 797–798.

79. See Commission Decision, ¶¶ 800–825.

80. Id. ¶ 799.

81. Id. ¶¶ 828–833.

82. With regard to the need for further inquiry into competitive effects, the Commission observed: "There are indeed circumstances relating to the tying of WMP which warrant a closer examination of the effects that tying has on competition in this case. While in classical tying cases, the Commission and the Courts considered the foreclosure effect for competing vendors to be demonstrated by the bundling of a separate product with the dominant product, in the case at issue, users can and do

to a certain extent obtain third party media players through the Internet, sometimes for free. There are therefore indeed good reasons *not* to assume without further analysis that tying WMP constitutes conduct which by its very nature is liable to foreclose competition." Commission Decision, ¶ 841 (emphasis in original).

83. Id. ¶¶ 843–877. The Commission concluded: "alternative distribution channels do not enable media players competing with WMP to match the ubiquitous and guaranteed presence of the pre-installed Windows code on client PCs worldwide." Id. ¶ 877.

84. Id. ¶ 881.

85. Id. ¶ 882 (emphasis in original).

86. Id. ¶¶ 900–944.

87. Id. ¶ 946. Microsoft's principal response to the data on market trends cited by the Commission was typical of the response often proffered by dominant firms accused of exclusionary conduct: their rise and their rival's decline was due to the superiority of their own product and the inferiority of their rivals'. But the Commission concluded that its evidence was "not convincing." Id. ¶ 947.

88. Id. ¶ 957.

89. This is an accepted principal recognized under U.S. law. "Where a defendant maintains substantial market power, his activities are examined through a special lens: Behavior that might otherwise not be of concern to the antitrust laws—or that might even be viewed as procompetitive—can take on exclusionary connotations when practiced by a monopolist." *Eastman Kodak Co. v. Image Tech. Svcs., Inc.*, 504 U.S. 451, 488 (1992) (Scalia, J., dissenting).

90. See Commission Decision, ¶ 969.

91. Id. ¶¶ 971–977.

92. Id. ¶¶ 978, 983. For Judge Jackson's similar finding of fact, see 84 F. Supp. 2d at 112 (¶412), which we discussed in chapter 3.

93. Case T-201/04, *Microsoft Corp. v. Commission*, 2007 E.C.R. II-3601, at ¶¶ 101, 814 (Ct. First Instance) ("CFI Decision"). The one point on which the CFI disagreed with the Commission was the Commission's decision to require a "monitoring trustee" to assist the Commission in monitoring Microsoft's compliance with its remedial order. The CFI held that this was an improper delegation of the Commission's authority. Id. ¶ 1271.

94. See "Microsoft Statement on Compliance with European Commission 2004 Decision" (press release, Oct. 22, 2007) (http://www.microsoft.com).

95. The Court concluded as follows: "However, while the Community Courts recognise that the Commission has a margin of appreciation in economic or technical

matters, that does not mean that they must decline to review the Commission's interpretation of economic or technical data. The Community Courts must not only establish whether the evidence put forward is factually accurate, reliable and consistent but must also determine whether that evidence contains all the relevant data that must be taken into consideration in appraising a complex situation and whether it is capable of substantiating the conclusions drawn from it [citation omitted]." CFI Decision, ¶ 89.

96. Id. ¶¶ 688, 1144.

97. Id. ¶¶ 331–333.

98. Id. ¶ 316–317.

99. Id. ¶ 336.

100. Id. ¶ 332 (emphasis added).

101. Id. ¶ 392.

102. Id. ¶ 561. The D.C. Circuit had expressed a related sentiment: "We may infer causation when exclusionary conduct is aimed at producers of nascent competitive technologies as well as when it is aimed at producers of established substitutes. Admittedly, in the former case there is added uncertainty, inasmuch as nascent threats are merely *potential* substitutes. But the underlying proof problem is the same—neither plaintiffs nor the court can confidently reconstruct a product's hypothetical technological development in a world absent the defendant's exclusionary conduct. To some degree, 'the defendant is made to suffer the uncertain consequences of its own undesirable conduct.'" 253 F.3d at 79 (quoting Phillip Areeda and Herbert Hovenkamp, *Antitrust Law*).

103. See CFI Decision, ¶¶ 649–653.

104. Id. ¶¶ 621–649.

105. Id. ¶ 669–671.

106. Id. ¶¶ 696–701.

107. In the second part of Microsoft's first plea it argued that Sun's request for disclosure did not coincide with the technology it had been ordered to share by the Commission. See CFI Decision, ¶¶ 713–776. In the third and final part it argued that the Commission had acted in derogation of the TRIPS Agreement. But the Commission concluded that both "must be rejected as unfounded." Id. ¶¶ 776, 812. The Court concluded its review of all three parts of the first plea unequivocally: "It follows that the single plea put forward in connection with the first issue must be rejected as unfounded in its entirety." Id. ¶ 813.

108. As it had with respect to the refusal to supply claim, Microsoft also made a technical legal argument about the relative scope and requirements of Article 102's

general prohibition as compared with the specific subsection (d) of Article 102. The Court pointedly characterized Microsoft's arguments as "purely semantic" and declared that they "cannot be accepted." Id. ¶ 850. It further concluded that, "in any event," the Commission's findings satisfied both the general provisions of Article 102 as well as the specific ones of Article 102 (d). Id. ¶ 862.

109. Id. ¶¶ 839, 846.

110. See CFI Decision, ¶¶ 868, 1031–1058 (emphasis added).

111. Id. ¶ 839.

112. The CFI summarized Microsoft's position as follows: "The applicant claims that the integration of media functionality is a 'natural step' in the evolution of those operating systems, as may be seen from the fact that all vendors of operating systems include such functionality in their products. Microsoft is constantly seeking to improve Windows in response to technological advances and to changes in consumer demand, and Windows and other client PC operating systems have evolved over time to support an increasingly wider range of file types. For software developers and consumers, there is no fundamental difference between files that contain text or graphics and files that contain audio or video. In reality, a modern operating system is expected to support both types of files." Id. ¶ 895. See also ¶ 912.

113. Id. ¶¶ 912–944. The D.C. Circuit had similarly found that Microsoft failed to substantiate its assertion that there were any "integrative benefits" associated with its combination of Internet Explorer and Windows. See 253 F.3d at 66–67.

114. See CFI Decision, ¶ 1108.

115. Id. ¶ 1150.

116. Id. ¶ 1151.

117. For discussion of these justifications, see id. ¶¶ 1151–1167.

118. Tobias Buck, "Microsoft Suffers Stinging Defeat," *Financial Times*, Sept. 18, 2007.

119. See Stephen Castle and Dan Bilefsky, "Case May Make EU Legal Arbiter," *International Herald Tribune*, Sept. 18, 2007. See also Molly Moore, "EU Court Rejects Microsoft's Appeal; Judges Uphold $690 Million Fine, Requirement to Share Software Information," *Washington Post*, Sept. 18, 2007 (quoting Microsoft's Brad Smith: "Although the commission's demands cannot be enforced outside Europe, Smith said, the implications of the case will affect 'our industry and every other industry in the world.'").

120. For reactions critical of the CFI's decision, see, e.g., Christian Ahlborn and David S. Evans, "The *Microsoft* Judgment and Its Implications for Competition Policy Toward Dominant Firms in Europe," 75 *Antitrust L. J.* 887 (2009); Arianna

Andreangeli, "Interoperability as an 'Essential Facility' in the *Microsoft* Case: Encouraging Competition or Stifling Innovation?" 34 *Eur. L. Rev.* 584 (2009) (criticizing CFI's approach in *Microsoft* to refusals to supply and urging a return to the "more restrained" position taken in *Bronner* and *IMS Health*); Nicholas Economides and Ioannis Lianos, "The Elusive Antitrust Standards on Bundling in Europe and in the United States in the Aftermath of the *Microsoft* Cases," 76 *Antitrust L. J.* 483 (2009) (criticizing what the authors viewed as the undemanding standard of competitive harm applied by the CFI in *Microsoft* and urging a less formalistic approach to the analysis of tying); Daniel F. Spulber, "Competition Policy and the Incentive to Innovate: the Dynamic Effects of *Microsoft v. Commission*," 25 *Yale J. on Reg.* 247 (2008) (arguing that by focusing "on market outcomes rather than on anticompetitive conduct" the decision "penalizing successful innovators and rewarding their competitors," concluding that "competition policy based on" the CFI decision "diminishes the incentive to innovate").

121. For defense of the CFI's opinion, see, e.g., Pierre LaRouche, "The European *Microsoft* Case at the Crossroads of Competition Policy and Innovation: Comment on Ahlborn and Evans," 75 *Antitrust L. J.* 933 (2009) (arguing that some of the criticisms of the CFI's *Microsoft* decision are "sweeping" and "exaggerated" although not wholly unfounded). See also James F. Ponsoldt and Christopher D. David, "A Comparison between U.S. and EU Antitrust Treatment of Tying Claims against Microsoft: When Should Bundling of Computer Software be Permitted?" 27 *Nw. J. Int'l L. & Bus.* 421, 423 (2007) (faulting both U.S. and EU approaches, concluding that the U.S. approach to tying "offers too little guidance to software manufacturers seeking to avoid liability and unduly discounts potential losses in innovation from excluded competitors" whereas "the EU approach stifles dominant software firm innovation and efficiency because the approach is too rigid and formalistic").

122. See, e.g., Dennis W. Carlton and Michael Waldman, "The Strategic Use of Tying to Preserve and Create Market Power in Evolving Industries," 33 *Rand J. Econs.* 194 (2002) (focusing on the U.S. Microsoft case and making a strong case for how tying can be anticompetitive); Kai-Uwe Kühn, Robert Stillman, and Cristina Caffarra, "Economic Theories of Bundling and Their Policy Implications in Abuse Cases: An Assessment in Light of the *Microsoft* Case," 1 *Eur. Competition J.* 85 (2005) (arguing that a "laissez-faire approach to bundling cannot be justified based on the current status of the economic literature" and concluding that the tying analysis in the EC's *Microsoft* case "stand[s] on more solid foundations" than previous cases in the EU.); Francois Leveque, "Innovation, Leveraging and Essential Facilities: Interoperability Licensing in the EU *Microsoft* Case," 28 *World Competition* 71 (2005) (questioning the degree of impact on consumers and faulting the overall assessment of Microsoft's conduct on innovation incentives as incomplete, but also finding the Commission's case for anticompetitive leverage "convincing"). See also David A. Heiner, "Assessing Tying Claims in the Context of Software Integration: A Suggested

Framework for Applying the Rule of Reason Analysis," 72. *U. Chi. L. Rev.* 123 (2005) (arguing for a deferential rule-of-reason approach to software integration with specific focus on the U.S. *Microsoft* cases).

123. The CFI relied on its decisions in, Volvo, Magill, Oscar Bronner, as well as IMS Health, Case C-418/01, *IMS Health GmbH & Co. OHG v. NDC Health GmbH & Co. KG,* [2004] ECR I-5039].

124. See Competition and Monopoly: Single Firm Conduct Under Section 2 of the Sherman Act (2008) (http://www.justice.gov). A majority of the Federal Trade Commission declined to join in the statement. See "Statement of Commissioners Harbour, Leibowitz and Rosch on the Issuance of the Section 2 Report by the Department of Justice" (Sept. 8, 2008) (http://www.ftc.gov). Chairman William E. Kovacic issued a separate statement. See "Statement of Federal Trade Commission Chairman William E. Kovacic, Modern U.S. Competition Law and the Treatment of Dominant Firms: Comments on the Department of Justice and Federal Trade Commission Proceedings Relating to Section 2 of the Sherman Act (Sept. 8, 2008)" (http://www.ftc .gov). The "Section 2 Report," as it became known, was later withdrawn by the Obama Administration. See Justice Department Withdraws Report on Antitrust Monopoly Law (May 11, 2009) (http://www.justice.gov).

125. We explore the remedy issues further in chapter 7.

126. See Department of Justice, "Assistant Attorney General for Antitrust, R. Hewitt Pate, Issues Statement on the EC's Decision in Its Microsoft Investigation" (press release, March 24, 2004) (http://www.usdoj.gov).

127. The three central ideas in the Justice Department's statement were all echoed simultaneously by Microsoft. An article in the *New York Times* of March 24, 2004 quoted Microsoft's CEO Steve Ballmer for the proposition that "every company should have the ability to improve its products to meet the needs of consumers." Ballmer maintained that the decision would interfere with product enhancements desired by consumers and that the resolution offered by Microsoft to settle the case before the EC's decision was preferable to the one chosen by the Commission. The article also quoted Microsoft Vice President and General Counsel Brad Smith as having criticized the "code removal" remedy as "an approach that in our view will help a small number of competitors—at least that is its theory—at the expense not only of our innovation but at the expense of consumers as well." Smith also accused the Commission of providing an alternative forum for Microsoft's competitors to air their grievances after they had failed to secure more substantial remedies in the U.S. See "Excerpts from Ruling in Europe and Microsoft's Response," *New York Times,* March 24, 2004. See also Steven A. Ballmer, "Global Commerce in the Crossfire," *Washington Post,* March 27, 2004 (editorial by Microsoft CEO criticizing the Commission's decision for "launching an unprecedented challenge to Microsoft's intellectual property rights").

128. For an English-language explanation of the KFTC's *Microsoft* decision that was prepared by the KFTC, see "The Findings of the Microsoft Case" (Dec. 7, 2005) (http://ftc.go.kr). The KFTC's December 2005 decision was followed, in February of 2006, by a written report that detailed the KFTC's theory and findings that Microsoft had violated Korean competition law. Microsoft initially filed an appeal of the decision, but its appeal to the Seoul High Court was dropped in October of 2007 before any decision was reached.

129. See Department of Justice, "Statement of Deputy Assistant Attorney General J. Bruce McDonald regarding Korea Fair Trade Commission's Decision in Its Microsoft Case" (press release, Dec. 7, 2005) (http:// www.usdoj.gov).

130. The KFTC's approach was similar in spirit but less invasive than the "must-carry" remedy that was originally sought by the government plaintiffs in the U.S. Microsoft case. See Sejin Kim, "The Korea Fair Trade Commission's Decision on Microsoft's Tying Practice: The Second-Best Remedy for Harmed Competitors," 16 *Pac. Rim L. & Pol'y J.* 375 (2007) (defending KFTC's reliance on the ballot-screen remedy as a reasonable accommodation of the needs to correct for the anticompetitive effects of Microsoft's bundling without incurring the legal and economic challenges that a "must-carry" remedy would have involved).

131. See "Assistant Attorney General for Antitrust, Thomas O. Barnett, Issues Statement on European Microsoft Decision" (press release, Sept. 17, 2007) (http://www .justice.gov).

132. "Assistant Attorney General for Antitrust, Christine Varney, Issues Statement on European Commission Microsoft Settlement" (press release, Dec. 16, 2009) (http://www.justice.gov).

Chapter 7

1. For information about AOL's discontinuance of support for Netscape, see Tom Drapeau, "End of Support for Netscape Web browsers," Dec. 28, 2007 (stating that AOL's effort by that point had actually dwindled to a "handful of engineers") (http://blog.netscape.com/2007/12/28/end-of-support-for-netscape-web-browsers/). For the purchase price of Netscape, see "America Online Says Netscape Acquisition Has Been Completed," *Wall Street Journal*, March 18, 1999 (value based on AOL share price when transaction closed).

2. Market-share data are reported by Net Applications (http://www.netmarketshare .com). For consumer survey, see Net Applications Newsletter, April 5, 2007 (in authors' files). For 2010 data, see http://www.netmarketshare.com/browser-market -share.aspx?qprid=1 (Firefox's share close to 25%; IE's share about 60%). The market-share data for operating systems includes Apple's operating system for the Macintosh, which wasn't part of the market defined in the governments' cases. This

means that Microsoft's share of the market defined in the litigation was actually over 95%.

3. See Brad Stone, "Open-Source Upstart Challenges the Big Web Browsers," *New York Times*, May 26, 2008 (quoting partner in a firm that had invested in a browser start-up).

4. See "Commission Confirms Sending a Statement of Objections to Microsoft on the Tying of Internet Explorer to Windows" (press release, MEMO/09/15, Jan. 17, 2009) (http://europa.eu).

5. See "Commission Initiates Formal Investigations Against Microsoft in Two Cases of Suspected Abuse of Dominant Market Position" (press release, Memo/08/19, Jan. 14, 2008) (http://europa.eu). The trade association was the European Committee for Interoperable Systems.

6. The U.S. Supreme Court has used a variety of formulations to express the remedial goal of antitrust decrees. Examples: "The relief in an antitrust case must be 'effective to redress the violations' and 'to restore competition.'" It should seek to "unfetter a market from anticompetitive conduct." *Ford Motor Co. v. United States*, 405 U.S. 562, 573, 577 (1972). Relief should "terminate the illegal monopoly, deny to the defendant the fruits of its statutory violation, and ensure that there remain no practices likely to result in monopolization in the future." *United States v. United Shoe Machinery Corp.*, 391 U.S. 244, 250 (1968).

7. There were actually two remedy decrees entered by Judge Kollar-Kotelly, one entered in the Justice Department's case as a result of the settlement (in which nine states joined), and one entered in the states' case after the hearings involving the nine states that didn't agree to the settlement. For the text of the original decrees, see *United States v. Microsoft Corp.*, No. 98-1232 (CKK), 2002 U.S. Dist. LEXIS 22864 (D.D.C. Nov. 12, 2002); *New York v. Microsoft Corp.*, 224 F. Supp. 2d 76, 266–277 (D.D.C. 2002). For a discussion of the process, see chapter 4 above. For expositional purposes, we refer to the decree entered in the settlement.

8. *New York v. Microsoft Corp.*, 531 F. Supp. 2d 141, 158 (D.D.C. 2008) (reviewing complaints). As of October 2005, the plaintiffs and Microsoft had reported 593 complaints, but only 54 of them (approximately 9%) were regarded as "substantial." These figures are compiled from the Joint Status Reports that Judge Kollar-Kotelly required the parties to file every six months in an effort to monitor the enforcement of the decree. See *United States v. Microsoft Corp.*, No. 98-1232 (CKK) (D.D.C. May 14, 2003). Microsoft often joined in these reports. The Joint Status Reports were posted at http://www.usdoj.gov/atr/cases/ms_index.htm. Microsoft posted its own supplemental status reports at http://www.microsoft.com/en-us/news/legal/archive/settlementproceeding.aspx.

9. We discuss the significance of the communications protocols in chapter 4. By contrast to protocol documentation, documenting APIs, as required in the settlement,

occurred with little problem. See Harry First and Andrew I. Gavil, "Re-Framing Windows: The Durable Meaning of the *Microsoft* Antitrust Litigation," 2006 *Utah L. Rev.* 641, 700 n. 257.

10. See Transcript of Hearing, Feb. 9, 2005, *United States v. Microsoft Corp.*, No. 98-1232 (CKK), at 6–7 (statement of Judge Kollar-Kotelly). Microsoft claimed the need to use its own version of HTML for digital rights management reasons; in addition to not supporting sophisticated search techniques, the plaintiffs claimed that the documentation could be read only with Internet Explorer. See Joint Status Report, Oct. 8, 2004, at 4.

11. The Technical Committee's project was to create "prototype implementations" of each task undertaken by the protocols so as to be certain that Microsoft's technical documentation was complete and accurate. See Joint Status Report, Jan. 25, 2005, at 3.

12. See Plaintiffs' Response to Microsoft's Supplemental Status Report on Microsoft's Compliance with the Final Judgments at 2–3 (Jan. 23, 2006) (http://www.usdoj.gov).

13. Id., 3.

14. See Microsoft Corp., Supplemental Status Report on Microsoft's Compliance with the Final Judgments, Civil Action No. 98-1232 (CKK), Jan. 17, 2006 (http://www.microsoft.com), at 5, 8.

15. See Joint Status Report on Microsoft's Compliance with the Final Judgment at 3–6, 7, 10–11, Microsoft, No. 98-1232 (CKK) (D.D.C. May 12, 2006) (http://www.usdoj.gov).

16. For the Justice Department's brief agreeing with Microsoft's position, see Brief of the United States as Amicus Curiae in Opposition to the Motions to Extend the States' Final Judgments, *New York v. Microsoft Corp.*, Civ. Action No. 98-1233 (CKK) (Nov. 9, 2007) (http://www.usdoj.gov).

17. For the district court's opinion granting the extension, see *New York v. Microsoft Corp.*, 531 F. Supp. 2d 141 (D.D.C. 2008).

18. See Joint Status Report, April 16, 2009, at 6.

19. Joint Status Report, Dec. 8, 2009, at 3.

20. See Joint Status Report, June 16, 2010, at 11.

21. See Joint Status Report, April 22, 2011, at 3.

22. See id., 3, 4. Note that during the "extension period," from 2007 to 2011, the states continued to receive and review complaints with regard to the non-protocol aspects of the decree, even though those sections of the Justice Department's settlement decree were no longer being enforced by the Justice Department.

23. Transcript of Hearing of Feb. 9, 2005,16.

24. Id., 23. The lawyer, Stephen Houck, was the only lawyer at the conference who had been involved in the case since its inception. Houck had signed the states' complaint on behalf of New York and had tried the case on behalf of the state plaintiffs.

25. Id., 29–30. The lawyer, Charles "Rick" Rule, had negotiated the decree directly with Charles James. See John Wilke, "Hard Drive: Negotiating All Night, Tenacious Microsoft Won Many Loopholes," *Wall Street Journal*, Nov 9, 2001.

26. See Review of the Final Judgments by the United States and New York Group, *United States v. Microsoft Corp.*, No. 98-1232 (CKK) (D.D.C. Aug. 30, 2007) (http://www.justice.gov), at 8–9. Microsoft filed a separate report arguing that the decree was a "success" for having prohibited Microsoft from engaging in unlawful behavior and for creating mechanisms to "facilitate competition." See Microsoft's Report Concerning The Final Judgments, *United States v. Microsoft Corp.*, No. 98-1232 (CKK) (D.D.C. Aug. 30, 2007) (http://www.microsoft.com), at 2.

27. See California Group's Report on Remedial Effectiveness, *New York v. Microsoft Corp.*, No. 98-1233 (CKK) (D.D.C. Aug. 30, 2007), at 15. For discussion of open-source issues, see id., 10–11.

28. Transcript of Hearing, Sept. 11, 2007, *United States v. Microsoft Corp.*, No. 98-1232 (CKK), at 34.

29. For data on licensee use of protocols, see California Group's Report on Remedial Effectiveness at 11 n. 30, 21 (as of 2007). For further information on the implementation of the protocol-licensing program, see William H. Page and Sheldon J. Childers, "Software Development as an Antitrust Remedy: Lessons from the Enforcement of the Microsoft Communications Protocol Licensing Requirement," 14 *Mich. Telecomm. Tech. L. Rev.* 77, 128 (2007) ("These results would be a catastrophe for a commercial product. They are no less telling for a governmentally supervised program.").

30. See Joint Status Report, Oct. 17, 2003, at 13–16 (availability of alternative protocols); Joint Status Report, Jan. 16, 2004, at 7 (cost and limitations in licenses). A license under the Program initially required an up-front payment of $50,000, which was generally not refundable; this amount was then chargeable against subsequent royalties, if any. See "Microsoft Communications Protocol Program, Program Entry Requirements" (Section C-2) (http://members.microsoft.com); "Microsoft Protocol License Agreement for Development and Product Distribution (Server Software)" (Exhibit C, §1.1) (draft) (http://members.microsoft.com). Microsoft later agreed not to collect any royalties until the government plaintiffs agreed that the documentation was "substantially complete."

31. It may be that the protocol-licensing provision also had a narrower goal, which was simply to prevent Microsoft from altering its current protocols through the

addition of encrypted code that couldn't be reverse engineered. Because any encrypted protocols would have to be available for licensing, encrypting protocols as an exclusionary strategy (that is, for no technical reason) wouldn't be a successful strategy for Microsoft to follow. It isn't possible, of course, to know whether Microsoft might have pursued such an approach in the absence of the decree, or whether the decree kept Microsoft from including undisclosed encrypted code in its protocols.

32. See, e.g., Plaintiffs' Memorandum in Support of Proposed Final Judgment, *United States v. Microsoft Corp.*, No. 98-1232 (TPJ) and *New York v. Microsoft Corp.*, No. 98-1233 (D.D.C. April 28, 2000) (http://www.justice.gov), at 34; Plaintiffs' Reply Memorandum in Support of Proposed Final Judgment, *United States v. Microsoft Corp.*, No. 98-1232 (TPJ) and *New York v. Microsoft Corp.*, No. 98-1233 (D.D.C. (May 17, 2000) (http://www.justice.gov), at 17 (discussing role of Office). For development of the argument for viewing the new Applications Company as performing the role played by Netscape in the mid 1990s, see Declaration of Paul M. Romer, *United States v. Microsoft Corp.*, No. 98-1232 (TPJ) and *New York v. Microsoft Corp.*, No. 98-1233 (D.D.C. April 27, 2000), at paragraphs 20–27 and paragraph 21 in particular (http://www.usdoj.gov); see also Declaration of Rebecca M. Henderson, id. (http://www.usdoj.gov), at paragraph 23 (comparing Office to Navigator).

33. For discussion of porting Office to Linux, see, e.g., Plaintiffs' Reply Memorandum in Support, at 15–19; Declaration of Carl Shapiro, *United States v. Microsoft Corp.*, No. 98-1232 (TPJ) and *New York v. Microsoft Corp.*, No. 98-1233 (D.D.C. April 27, 2000) (http://www.justice.gov), at 10. For general discussion of porting Office and other applications, see, e.g., Plaintiffs' Memorandum in Support, at 33–34; Romer Declaration, at paragraphs 6, 26; Henderson Declaration, at 106.

34. Defendant Microsoft Corporation's Summary Response to Plaintiffs' Proposed Final Judgment, *United States v. Microsoft Corp.*, No. 98-1232 (TPJ) and *New York v. Microsoft Corp.*, No. 98-1233 (D.D.C. May 10, 2000) (in authors' files), at 9–10. See also James V. Grimaldi, "Microsoft Defends Its Practices; CEO Ballmer Sees No Need to Change," *Washington Post*, April 19, 2000 ("'I'll be sort of calculating: Our job is to serve customers and to make money,' Ballmer said. 'There are no customers today for Linux on the client [desktop computer], therefore there is no opportunity to make money. There is nothing in there that looks like a good opportunity for us.'").

35. The new Applications Company would have had an estimated $8 billion in annual revenue and $3 billion in annual profits, far more than many other companies (such as Novell and Adobe) selling software for the PC. See Romer Declaration, paragraph 17.

36. See, e.g., Plaintiffs' Memorandum in Support, 34 (discussing the potential competitive threat of Office and stating "[t]here is, of course, no guarantee that such competition will result"); Plaintiffs' Reply Memorandum in Support, at 16. ("Instead

of forcing immediate entry and competition [in the market for operating systems], the restructuring will enable the market to determine the rate of entry and the form of new competition.")

37. Plaintiffs' Reply Memorandum In Support, at 2.

38. Defendant Microsoft Corporation's Memorandum in Support of Its Motion For Summary Rejection of the Government's Breakup Proposal, *United States v. Microsoft Corp.*, No. 98-1232 (TPJ) and *New York v. Microsoft Corp.*, No. 98-1233 (D.D.C. May 10, 2000) (in authors' files), at 24.

39. We describe the remedies proceedings more fully in chapter 4.

40. For a discussion of the browser competition between Netscape and Microsoft as taking place on "Internet time," and noting the time issues in the governments' case against Microsoft, see Michael A. Cusumano and David B. Yoffie, *Competing on Internet Time* (1998), 322–323.

41. On the application of the protocol-disclosure requirement to Vista and Longhorn, see Supplemental Status Report on Microsoft's Compliance with the Final Judgments, Sep. 5, 2006 (http://www.microsoft.com), at 3–8.

42. See Department of Justice, Exhibit 1, *United States v. Microsoft Corp.*, 87 F. Supp. 2d 30 (D.D.C. 2000) (Civil Action Nos. 98-1232 (TPJ) and 98-1233 (TPJ)) (http://www.usdoj.gov) (93% market share in 1991).

43. Response of the United States to Public Comments on the Revised Proposed Final Judgment, *United States v. Microsoft Corp.*, No. 98-1232 (CKK) (D.D.C. Feb. 27, 2002) (http://www.usdoj.gov), paragraph 232.

44. *Massachusetts v. Microsoft Corp.*, 373 F.3d 1199, 1211 (D.C. Cir. 2004).

45. Statement of Charles A. James, Assistant Attorney General, U.S. Department of Justice, Antitrust Division, Before the Senate Committee on the Judiciary, Concerning the Microsoft Settlement: A Look to the Future, Dec. 12, 2001 (http://www.justice.gov), at 10.

46. For the Commission's discussion of its remedies, see Commission of the European Cmtys., Commission Decision of 24 Mar.2004, Case COMP/C-3/37.792 Microsoft, paragraphs 994–1042 (hereinafter "2004 Decision"). For the Commission's remedial order, see id., articles 2–6.

47. For the Commission's discussion of hiding end-user access, see id., paragraphs 796–798 and 882. We discuss the Justice Department's rejection of requiring removal of IE's code in the settlement, and Judge Kollar-Kotelly's rejection of the litigating states' request for removal of IE's code, in chapter 4.

48. For the Commission's discussion of the monitoring mechanism, see 2004 Decision, paragraphs 1043–1048.

49. For the Court of First Instance's discussion of the remedies, see Case T-201/04, *Microsoft Corp. v. Commission of the European Communities*, 2007 ECR II-03601, at paragraphs 258–266 (interoperability), 1216–1229 (unbundling), and 1326–1367 (fines) (hereinafter "CFI Decision").

50. For discussion of the Commission's difficulties in getting Microsoft to provide an unbundled version, see, e.g., Mary Jacoby, "Microsoft Agrees to Change Name of a Windows Version in Europe," *Wall Street Journal*, Jan. 31, 20054; Josh Brown and Robert A. Guth, "Microsoft Will Alter Windows to Meet EU Regulators' Orders," *Wall Street Journal*, March 30, 2005.

51. Paul Meller, "Rival Calls Microsoft Unready to Carry Out European Order," *New York Times*, March 23, 2005.

52. On the market's reception of the unbundled Windows version, see Josh Brown, "EU's Microsoft Order Has Skeptics," *Wall Street Journal*, April 1, 2005 ("'If there is no difference in price, there will be very little incentive to buy it,' said Ingo Juraske, H-P vice president for Europe.").

53. See Paul Meller, "Microsoft Opens Appeal in Europe," *New York Times*, April 25, 2006; Paul Meller, "Microsoft in European Court Says 2004 Ruling Is a Failure," *New York Times*, April 26, 2006 (quoting the Commission's lawyer as admitting to the court that "I am afraid we cannot say our remedy has had any real impact, as far as we can see").

54. The European Commission's disclosure program was called the Work Group Server Protocol Program; the U.S. program was called the Microsoft Communications Protocol Program.

55. The Commission's discussion of Microsoft's compliance is found in Commission of the European Communities, Commission Decision of 10 November 2005, Case COMP/C-3/37.792 Microsoft (ec.europa.eu). The "Pricing Principles" the Commission applied were developed by the Commission and Microsoft together. See id., n. 122. The Commission assumed at this time that the patented protocol technologies were innovative. See id., paragraph 168.

56. The Commission's subsequent review is found in Commission of the European Communities, Commission Decision of 12 July 2006, Case COMP/C-3/37.792 Microsoft, paragraphs 52, 55, 232.

57. See id. (setting penalties).

58. See press release IP/07/1567 (October 22, 2007) at http://europa.eu. "Net revenues" are the revenues from the products in which the protocols are implemented.

59. Note that one month before the announcement of Microsoft's agreement with regard to open-source licensees, counsel for the litigating states in the United States was telling the district court about the unresolved problems that open-source licens-

ees were having with regard to the U.S. protocol licenses. See Transcript of Hearing of Sept. 11, 2007, at 44. Microsoft had apparently not informed the states that these discussions were preceding in Europe.

60. See Commission Decision of 27 Feb. 2008, Case COMP/C-3/37.792 Microsoft, at http://ec.europa.eu. The fines it imposed were only for the period between June of 2006 and October of 2007 and were only for the protocols available under the non-patent license. The Commission continued to assume that the patented protocols were presumptively innovative. See id., paragraph 132.

61. For the General Court's decision upholding the fine, see Judgment of the General Court (Second Chamber), 27 June 2012, Case T-167/08, *Microsoft Corp. v. European Commission*, at http://eur-lex.europa.eu. In this decision the General Court rejected all of Microsoft's arguments for annulling the fine, including an argument that the fine was disproportional, see paragraph 220. The Court reduced the fine slightly to reflect the time during which the Commission had allowed Microsoft to block its competitors from distributing products developed on the basis of unlicensed protocols, see paragraphs 222–232.

62. See Commission Decision of 27 Feb. 2008, n. 353.

63. See id., n. 355.

64. See Press Release of Jan. 14, 2008, 1.

65. See "Commission Statement on Microsoft Internet Explorer Announcement" (press release MEMO/09/272, issued June 12, 2009) at http://europa.eu.

66. See "Commission welcomes new Microsoft proposals on Microsoft Internet Explorer and Interoperability" (press release MEMO/09/352, July 24, 2009) at http://europa.eu.

67. See Commission of the European Communities, Commission Decision of 16 December 2009, Case COMP/C-3/39.530—Microsoft (tying) (hereinafter "Commitment Decision"), at http://ec.europa.eu. For the Commission's commitment procedure, see Council Regulation (EC) No 1/2003 of 16 December 2002 on the implementation of the rules on competition laid down in Articles 81 and 82 of the Treaty, OJ [2003] L 1, p.1, Art. 9. This procedure didn't come into effect until May 1, 2004, more than a month after the Commission adopted its *Microsoft* decision.

68. See Charles Forelle, "Microsoft Yields to EU on Browsers," *Wall Street Journal*, July 25, 2009 (settlement conditioned on there being no fine).

69. See Kevin J. O'Brien, "Microsoft Browser Offer Fails to Impress Europe," *New York Times*, June 13, 2009 (reporting a spokesman for the Commission as saying that the Commission rejected a browserless operating system because it "did not want to repeat a mistake of the first Microsoft case" when in ordered sale of Windows without a media player).

70. We discuss the Korea Fair Trade Commission's case in chapter 6.

71. The Commission's ballot screen was also a variant of the relief requested in the Justice Department's original 1998 complaint, which would have required Microsoft to distribute Netscape along with Internet Explorer for three years, giving the OEMs the option to delete either or both IE and Netscape. See Department of Justice Complaint ¶ 71, *United States v. Microsoft Corp.*, 84 F. Supp. 2d 9 (D.D.C. 1999) (No. 98-1232) (http://www.usdoj.gov). The Justice Department never pursued this remedy further.

72. For a comparison of the remedies in the two EU *Microsoft* cases, focusing on the relationship between the theories of harm and the remedies utilized, see Nicholas Economides and Ioannis Liannos, "A Critical Appraisal of Remedies in the EU *Microsoft* Cases," 2010 *Colum. Bus. L. Rev.* 346 (2010) (criticizing the choice screen approach because of the "conceptual mismatch between the consumer harm story and the remedy").

73. Commitment Decision, paragraphs 21, 22.

74. See Statement of Microsoft Corporation on EU Browser Choice Screen Compliance, July 17, 2012 (http://www.microsoft.com), in which it is called a "technical error."

75. For the Commission's decision on the violation of the Commitment Decision, see Commission of the European Communities, Commission Decision of 6 March 2013, Case AT.39530—Microsoft (Tying), at http://ec.europa.eu. The fine was €561 million, which the Commission indicated was 1.02% of Microsoft's turnover valued at the EU's published exchange rates, see id., paragraphs 78, 79 and note 88; this would have made the fine the equivalent of $750 million but Microsoft estimated the fine at $733 million. See Microsoft Corp., Form 10-k for Fiscal Year ending June 30, 2013 (www.microsoft.com), at 18. For report of other complaints, see Joaquín Almunia, Vice President of European Commission for Competition Policy, Statement at Press Briefing on Commission's Statement of Objections Sent to Microsoft, Oct. 24, 2012 (http://europa.eu), at 2.

76. The Commission's "market test" refers to the procedure under Article 27(4) of Regulation 1/2003 for seeking comments to proposed commitments adopted under Article 9. The Commission reported when it adopted the commitment that it received nineteen comments "from interested third parties." See Commitment Decision, paragraph 61. It was also reported that before publishing the proposed commitment for comments the Commission had "widely" canvassed Microsoft's rivals and others in the industry. See Charles Forelle and Peppi Kiviniemi, "EU, Microsoft Near End in Antitrust Tussle," *Wall Street Journal*, Oct. 8, 2009.

77. Market-share figures are based on data from StatCounter (http://gs.statcounter .com), which computes market share on the basis of number of page views. Year-to-year comparisons of shares of the browser market were done for March 2009 and

February 2010 (March 2010 being the first full month the ballot screen was available), and March 2010 and February 2011 and March 2011 and February 2012. During the pre-ballot year, IE's share of the market dropped by 7%; in the two post-ballot years its share dropped by 20% in 2010–2011 and 15% in 2011–2012. Chrome's shares increased 277% before the ballot screen, and 121% and 62% in the two years after. Firefox's shares decreased by 1% before the ballot screen, and by 2% and 17% after the ballot screen. Opera's shares fell through the entire period as well, 42% pre-ballot, 1% and 14% post-ballot. Opera was the firm that filed the bundling complaint. Microsoft stated that IE's market share declined even during the period that it had omitted the ballot-choice screen from Windows, a point that the Commission didn't dispute. See Commission Decision of 6 March 2013, paragraph 61.

78. James Kanter and Stephen Castle, "Antitrust Chief in Europe Seeks to Close Cases," *New York Times*, Sept. 23, 2009.

79. See "Commission Accepts Microsoft Commitments to Give Users Browser Choice" (press release IP/09/1941, December 16, 2009) (http://europa.eu).

80. Information about the consumer suits filed against Microsoft is based on email messages to Harry First and Andrew I. Gavil from Rich Wallis, Associate General Counsel of Microsoft, dated August 9, 2007, and June 11, 2008 (in authors' files), and "Mississippi Attorney General Settles with Microsoft" (press release, June 11, 2009) (http://www.ago.state.ms.us). Information on consumer class-action settlements up to May 5, 2007 was posted at http://www.microsoft.com. As of 2013 three private cases were pending in Canada (see Microsoft 10-k for 2013 at 74). In one, the Supreme Court of Canada upheld the right of a class of indirect purchasers of Microsoft operating systems and applications software to bring suit against Microsoft for alleged unlawful overcharges, rejecting the U.S. rule that bars indirect-purchaser suits. See *Pro-Sys Consultants Ltd. v. Microsoft Corp.*, 2013 SCC 57 (2013).

81. See *Novell, Inc. v. Microsoft Corp.*, 731 F.3d 1064 (10th Cir. 2013) (affirming district court's grant of Microsoft's motion for judgment as a matter of law after the jury had hung, 11–1, in favor of Novell), cert. denied (2014); *Gordon v. Microsoft Corp.*, No. 00-5994 (2001 WL 366432) (Minn. Dist. Ct. Mar. 30, 2001) (granting class certification). The *Gordon* case was settled during the trial for $182 million. For an interesting discussion of the trial, belying the skeptical account of jurors' abilities to understand complex antitrust cases, see "*Gordon v. Microsoft*" Observations from the Trial Judge and Selected Jurors (Dec. 17, 2004) (http://apps.americanbar.org).

82. Varying percentages of the unclaimed funds were made subject to a *cy pres* distribution in the form of vouchers to poorer K–12 schools in the particular state. We discuss the *cy pres* settlements in chapter 5. For Microsoft's estimate of the cost of these settlements, see Microsoft Corp., 10-k for 2013, at 74. As of June 2013 Microsoft had made payments of approximately $1.4 billion, "mostly for vouchers, legal fees, and administrative expenses," but Microsoft didn't disclose how much of that amount was for vouchers. See id.

83. See "Microsoft and Sun Microsystems Enter Broad Cooperation Agreement; Settle Outstanding Litigation" (Microsoft press release, April 2, 2004) (http://www .microsoft.com); "AOL Time Warner and Microsoft Agree to Collaborate on Digital Media Initiatives and Settle Pending Litigation" (Microsoft press release, May 29, 2003) (http://www.microsoft.com).

84. See "Microsoft and IBM Resolve Antitrust Issues" (Microsoft press release, July 1, 2005, announcing settlement of all claims except those relating to server products, which IBM was still free to bring) (http://www.microsoft.com); "Microsoft and Be Inc. Reach Agreement to Settle Litigation" (Microsoft press release, Sept. 5, 2003) (http://www.microsoft.com).

85. See "Novell and Microsoft Reach Settlement on Antitrust Claims" (Microsoft press release, Nov. 8, 2005) (http://www.microsoft.com).

86. See "Microsoft and RealNetworks Resolve Antitrust Case and Announce Digital Music and Games Partnership" (Microsoft press release, Oct. 11, 2005) (http://www .microsoft.com); Nick Wingfield, "RealNetworks Has a Microsoft Deal," *Wall Street Journal*, Oct. 12, 2005 (noting agreement to drop out of EU and Korea cases).

87. See Samuel Len, "Daum Sues Microsoft," *International Herald Tribune*, April 13, 2004; "Microsoft, South Korean Firm Reach $30 Million Settlement," *Wall Street Journal*, Nov. 12, 2005 ($10 million of settlement in cash, remainder in other business agreements; Daum also dropped the complaint it filed with the KFTC).

88. Table 7.2 includes the civil fine that the KFTC imposed for Microsoft's bundling practices. See Korea Fair Trade Commission, Microsoft Case (http://eng.ftc.go.kr) (surcharge of 32.4 billion *won*).

89. The criminal case was against the American Tobacco Company. See *American Tobacco Co. v. United States*, 328 U.S. 781 (1946) (affirming conviction of American Tobacco for violating Section 2). In response to Tunney Act comments on its settlement proposal, the Justice Department took the position that it had no authority to order "monetary damages" because the proceeding was an equitable one. The Justice Department also argued that a monetary remedy would be inconsistent with the remedial goals in the case because "punishment is not a valid goal." Response of the United States to Public Comments on the Revised Proposed Final Judgment, *United States v. Microsoft Corp.*, No. 98-1232 (CKK) (D.D.C. Feb. 27, 2002) (http://www.justice.gov) at 15. Compare Howard A. Shelanski and J. Gregory Sidak, "Antitrust Divestiture in Network Industries," 68 *U. Chi. L. Rev.* 1, 96–97 (2001) (arguing that, in view of the difficulties of the various proposed injunctive remedies, the "efficacy and feasibility of monetary remedies" should have been seriously considered).

90. See Plaintiff States' First Amended Complaint, Prayer for Relief ¶ e, *New York v. Microsoft Corp.*, No. 98-1233 (D.D.C. filed July 17, 1998) (in authors' files). The decree that the litigating states subsequently proposed to Judge Kollar-Kotelly, how-

ever, made no claim to civil fines. See Plaintiff Litigating States' First Amended Proposed Remedy, *New York v. Microsoft Corp.*, No. 98-1233 (D.D.C. filed Mar. 4, 2002) (in authors' files).

91. The theory is set out in William M. Landes, "Optimal Sanctions for Antitrust Violations," 50 *U. Chi. L. Rev.* 652 (1983). See also Gary Becker, "Crime and Punishment: An Economic Approach," 76 *J. Pol. Econ.* 169 (1968). The approach is well accepted, at least as a matter of theory—see John M. Connor and Robert H. Lande, "The Size of Cartel Overcharges: Implications for U.S. and EU Fining Policies," 51 *Antitrust Bull.* 983–985 (2006)—although it is highly contested in practice. See Wouter P. J. Wils, *Efficiency and Justice in European Antitrust Enforcement* (2008), 56–59. See also William H. Page, "Optimal Antitrust Penalties and Competitors' Injury," 88 *Mich. L. Rev.* 2151 (1990).

92. See Landes, "Optimal Sanctions for Antitrust Violations," at 656–657. For example, if the harm is $100 and the chances of being apprehended and convicted are one in four, the fine should be multiplied by 4. If the fine were only $100, the rational violator would commit the crime. It would take a fine of $400 to deter the violator from committing the crime; then it wouldn't pay to commit the crime the three other (undetected) times as well as the one detected time.

93. For the Commission's discussion of the fine, see 2004 Decision, paragraphs 1054–1080.

94. See CFI Decision, paragraphs 1299 and 1303 (upholding the fine). For the Court's discussion of Microsoft's arguments, see paragraphs 1326–1367. When the General Court subsequently upheld the Commission's larger €899 million fine for Microsoft's failing to comply with the requirement that the protocol royalties be reasonable, the Court stated that the penalty needed to act as a deterrent, referring in general terms to Microsoft's turnover size and the likely financial benefits Microsoft received from delayed compliance. See General Court Decision, 27 June 2012, at paragraph 220.

95. See Lawrence J. White, "A $10 Billion Solution to the Microsoft Problem," 32 *J. Cyber Rights, Protection, and Markets* 69, 79 (2001).

96. We discuss Microsoft's pricing of Windows in chapter 3.

97. See 26 U.S.C. § 162(g).

98. See "Microsoft to Report Charge Related to Settlement of Class Action Lawsuits" (Microsoft press release, Nov. 20, 2001) (http://www.microsoft.com) (announcing a pre-tax charge of $550 million for settlement of 100 consumer class-action lawsuits and that the settlement would result in a charge of approximately $375 million after taxes).

99. See *International Salt Co. v. United States*, 332 U.S. 392, 400 (1947).

100. We describe the 1994 consent decree and the subsequent enforcement efforts in chapter 2.

101. The phrase dates back at least as far as Walter Adams, "Dissolution, Divorcement, Divestiture: The Pyrrhic Victories of Antitrust," 27 *Ind. L. J.* 1 (1951). For Brandeis' criticism of the *American Tobacco* decree, see Eliot Jones, *The Trust Problem in the United States* (1928), 461–469.

102. For a review of U.S. judicial approaches to restructuring, see Kevin J. O'Connor, "The Divestiture Remedy in Sherman Act, Section 2 Cases," 13 *Harv. J. Legis.* 687 (1976). The European Commission's authority to order structural remedies was only made clear in 2004. See Reg. 1/2003, Art. 7.

103. *Verizon Communications Inc. v. Law Offices of Curtis V. Trinko, LLP*, 540 U.S. 398, 415 (2004) (quoting Phillip Areeda, "Essential Facilities: An Epithet in Need of Limiting Principles," 58 *Antitrust L. J.* 841,853, 1989—"Professor Areeda got it exactly right.").

104. *United States v. Microsoft Corp.*, 253 F.3d 34, 107 (D.C. Cir. 2001).

105. A good example is the decree entered in the Ford-Autolite merger, which not only required Ford to divest the Autolite spark plug manufacturing assets that it was found to have acquired in violation of the antitrust laws but also required Ford to buy half of its spark plugs from the divested plant for five years. This was intended to ensure that the divested company could obtain a foothold in the industry and reestablish its former competitive position. See *Ford Motor Co. v. United States*, 405 U.S. 562 (1972) (upholding order).

106. The Commission specifically noted the 4% U.S. royalty rate (2008 Fining Decision, paragraph 246) and was, perhaps, implicitly critical of the U.S. approach. See id., paragraph 248 ("It is not for the Commission to decide on whether the royalty rates of the [U.S.] MCCP license agreements which have apparently been agreed upon between the Plaintiffs [the United States and the nine settling states] and Microsoft can be considered reasonable in the context of the [U.S.] Final Judgment.") On U.S. negotiations over royalty rates, see First and Gavil, "Re-Framing Windows," at 740.

107. Sigmund Timberg, "Equitable Relief under the Sherman Act," 1950 *U. Ill. L. F.* 629.

108. For the Justice Department's articulation, see Response of the United States to Public Comments on the Revised Proposed Final Judgment, *United States v. Microsoft Corp.*, Civ. No. 98-1232 at 9 (D.D.C. filed Feb. 27, 2002), quoted in *Massachusetts v. Microsoft Corp.*, 373 F.3d 1199, 1243 (D.C. Cir. 2004) and repeated without attribution to the Justice Department in *New York v. Microsoft Corp.*, 531 F. Supp. 2d 141, 156 (D.D.C. 2008).

109. See "Assistant Attorney General for Antitrust, Thomas O. Barnett, Issues Statement on European Microsoft Decision" (press release, Sept. 17, 2007) (http://www

.usdoj.gov). ("The Final Judgment protects consumers by protecting competition in middleware.")

110. *United States v. Aluminum Co. of America*, 148 F.2d 416, 446 (2d Cir. 1945).

111. The U.S. Supreme Court hasn't specified proportionality as a goal of antitrust remedies, but some commentators have argued that proportionality is important in crafting them. See, e.g., William E. Kovacic, "Designing Antitrust Remedies for Dominant Firm Misconduct," 31 *Conn. L. Rev.* 1285, 1312–1313 (1999) ("Remedies should be proportional in the sense that they reflect the dangers of the conduct by which a firm has achieved or sustained a position of dominance"); John E. Lopatka and William H. Page, "A (Cautionary) Note on Remedies in the Microsoft Case," 13 *Antitrust* 25, 26 (1999). ("Indeed, one of our principal points is that a remedy should be proportionate to the violation.") See also Phillip Areeda and Herbert Hovenkamp, *Antitrust Law*, third edition (2007), II ¶ 303 at 37; E. Thomas Sullivan, "Antitrust Remedies in the U.S. and EU: Advancing a Standard Of Proportionality," 48 *Antitrust Bull.* 377, 378, 423 (2003) (observing that "proportionality" is a term not normally employed in the United States). The European Commission adheres to a concept of proportionality in all its remedies, but doesn't exclude the possibility of proportionate structural remedies.

112. See Eleanor Fox, "Remedies and the Courage of Convictions in a Globalized World: How Globalization Corrupts Relief," 80 *Tulane L. Rev.* 571 (2005) (arguing that in a globalized economy, there may be a misfit between national remedies and global harms, leading to remedies that are insufficiently robust to counter transnational violations).

113. See Harry First, "The Case for Antitrust Civil Penalties," 76 *Antitrust L. J.* 127, 132–141 (2009) (detailing civil fines imposed by the European Commission and the states in competition cases).

114. Deborah Majoras, a former chair of the Federal Trade Commission who was a deputy assistant attorney general in the Justice Department and who assisted Charles James in negotiating the Microsoft consent decree, favored the use of civil fines on this ground. See Testimony Before the Antitrust Modernization Commission, March 21, 2006 (http://govinfo.library.unt.edu) at 51-52: "There are also instances in antitrust law where a conduct remedy (because no structural remedy is available) may actually be worse than the conduct that you are trying to avoid for the future. Consequently, there may be some circumscribed instances where we could use civil fine authority. ..."

115. The initial understanding of the Technical Committee's responsibilities is set out in the parties' first Joint Status Report to the court. See Joint Status Report on Microsoft's Compliance with the Final Judgments, July 3, 2003 (http://www.justice.gov), 13–18.

116. For descriptions and praise of the Technical Committee's work, see, e.g., Transcript, Sept. 11, 2007, 32–33 (Kollar-Kotelly); Transcript of Hearing, April 27, 2011,

United States v. Microsoft Corp.,. No. 98-1232 (CKK), at 12–15 (Department of Justice), 30 (Kollar-Kotelly).

117. We discuss the use of a special master in the contempt proceeding involving the licensing decree in chapter 2.

118. Transcript, April 27, 2011, at 30.

119. The order establishing the procedure, filed May 14, 2003, differed from what the parties had proposed in requiring specific reporting of complaints. See Joint Status Report, April 17, 2003, at 8–9.

120. Not all commentators agree with our conclusion. See, e.g., William H. Page, "Mandatory Contracting Remedies in the American and European Microsoft Cases," 75 *Antitrust L. J.* 787 (2009); John E. Lopatka, "Assessing Microsoft from a Distance," 75 *Antirust L. J.* 811 (2009). Others do—see, e.g., Herbert Hovenkamp, *The Antitrust Enterprise* (2005), 300 (describing remedies in the consent decree as "too little, too late"); Carl Shapiro, "Microsoft: A Remedial Failure," 75 *Antitrust L. J.* 739 (2009).

Chapter 8

1. For the original bill proposing the Antitrust Modernization Commission, see H.R. 2325, 107th Cong., 1st Sess. For Sensenbrenner's remarks on introducing the bill, see 80 *Antitrust & Trade Reg. Rep. (BNA)* 614 (June 29, 2001).

2. See Richard A. Posner, "Antitrust in the New Economy" (unpublished draft, August 23, 2000, in authors' files) at 1 and 13. This speech was subsequently expanded and published in 68 *Antitrust Law Journal* 925 (2001). Judge Posner later argued that the states should be stripped of their authority to bring antitrust suits under either state or federal law, or, at least, that the Congress should preempt state antitrust law insofar as it might affect interstate or foreign commerce. See Richard A. Posner, "Federalism and the Enforcement of Antitrust Laws by State Attorneys General," in *Competition Laws in Conflict: Antitrust Jurisdiction in the Global Economy*, ed. Richard A. Epstein and Michael S. Greve (2004), 260–262.

3. 221 U.S. 1 (1911).

4. See *United States v. Addyston Pipe & Steel Co.*, 85 F. 271, 283–284 (6th Cir. 1898) (observing that some common-law judges decide "how much restraint of competition is in the public interest, and how much is not"). See also S. Rep. No. 62-1326 (1913), 11 (expressing concern that the legality of any particular restraint will be determined by a judge's "individual opinion as an economist or sociologist" rather than by the legal standard set by Congress).

5. See 51 *Cong. Rec.* 8845 (1914) (remarks of Rep. Covington). The investigatory provision is codified at 15 U.S.C. § 46 (c). The FTC used this power in its early days,

attempting to prod the Justice Department to enforce previously entered decrees, but these efforts "received slight consideration by the Department of Justice." See Thomas C. Blaisdell Jr., *The Federal Trade Commission: An Experiment in the Control of Business* (1932), 183–258 (investigations of meat-packing, steel, tobacco, oil, aluminum, and radio).

6. The master in chancery provision is codified at 15 U.S.C. § 47. It has been invoked only once, in 1916 by Judge Learned Hand in *United States v. Corn Products Refining Co.*, 234 F. 964, 1018 (S.D.N.Y. 1916), but even in that case the FTC was never required to act because the Justice Department and the defendant agreed to a decree of dissolution. See *United States v. Corn Products Refining Co.* in *Statutes and Decisions Pertaining to the Federal Trade Commission, 1914–1929* (1930). See also William E. Kovacic, "Designing Antitrust Remedies for Dominant Firm Misconduct," 31 *Conn. L. Rev.* 1285, 1317, 1318 and n. 122 (1999).

7. See Marc Winerman, "The Origins of the FTC: Concentration, Cooperation, Control, and Competition," 71 *Antitrust L. J.* 1, 68, 74 (2003).

8. See Act of Oct. 15, 1914, c. 323, § 5, 38 Stat. 731 (making final judgment in an antitrust suit brought by the federal government *prima facie* evidence of a violation in any subsequent private suit; tolling statute of limitations during the pendency of any government antitrust litigation); id. § 16, 38 Stat. 737 (allowing private parties to obtain injunctive relief in antitrust cases).

9. Early state antitrust legislation and judicial interpretations are discussed in, e.g., James May, "Antitrust Practice and Procedure in the Formative Era: The Constitutional and Conceptual Reach of State Antitrust Law, 1880–1918," 135 *U. Pa. L. Rev.* 495, 500–503 (1987) (providing statistics on statutes and enforcement); David Millon, "The First Antitrust Statutes," 29 *Washburn L. J.* 141 (1990). For an example of a federal suit that followed state enforcement, see *United States v. International Harvester Co.*, 214 F. 987 (D. Minn. 1914) (federal suit filed after suits brought by Kentucky and Missouri), appeal dismissed, 248 U.S. 587 (1918).

10. For discussion of the amendment, see 51 *Cong. Rec.* 14,513–14,526 (1914). The amendment failed by a vote of 21–39. The district court decision in *International Harvester* was reprinted for the Senate on the day that the Senate debated the amendment. See S. Doc. No. 63-569 (ordered to be printed, Sept. 1, 1914); 51 *Cong. Rec.* 14,514 (1914).

11. For data on private enforcement, see, e.g., Stephen Calkins, "Perspectives on State and Federal Antitrust Enforcement," 53 *Duke L. J.* 673, 699–700 (2003) (comparing numbers of U.S. government and private case filings, along with private antitrust class actions); B. Zorina Kahn, "Federal Antitrust Agencies and Public Policy Toward Antitrust and Intellectual Property," 9 *Cornell J. L. & Pub. Pol'y* 133, 137 fig. 1 (1999); Richard A. Posner, "A Statistical Study of Antitrust Enforcement," 13 *J. L. & Econ.* 365, 366–371 (1970).

12. For the first such reference, see *Perma Life Mufflers v. International Parts Corp.*, 392 U.S. 134, 147 (1968) (Fortas, J., concurring).

13. See *Georgia v. Pennsylvania Railroad* Co., 324 U.S. 439 (1945) (allowing state to sue as *parens patriae* to enjoin a railroad price fixing conspiracy that allegedly disadvantaged Georgia's economy). States can also sue under the Sherman Act for monetary damages suffered by the state itself as a purchaser. See *Georgia v. Evans*, 316 U.S. 159 (1942) (allowing state to sue for the amount it overpaid as a result of national conspiracy to control asphalt prices).

14. See 15 U.S.C. §§ 15c–15h. For legislative history, see Earl W. Kintner, Joseph P. Griffin, and David B. Goldston, "The Hart-Scott-Rodino Antitrust Improvements Act of 1976: An Analysis," 46 *Geo. Wash. L. Rev.* 1, 18–31 (1977).

15. See *New York v. Microsoft Corp.*, 209 F. Supp. 2d 132, 150–151 (D.D.C. 2002). The Justice Department didn't support Microsoft's motion, but it did argue that only the federal government has the right to seek injunctive relief under the Sherman Act in a "sovereign, law enforcement capacity." The district court didn't address the Justice Department's arguments. See id. 155 n. 28. The Justice Department's memorandum is posted at http://www.usdoj.gov.

16. On the adoption of Articles 85 and 86, see, e.g., Tony A. Freyer, *Antitrust and Global Capitalism, 1930–2004* (2006), 270–290; David J. Gerber, *Law and Competition in Twentieth Century Europe: Protecting Prometheus* (1998), 336–346; D. G. Goyder, *EC Competition Law* (2003), 24–26. The statutory language of the two Articles was drawn from comparable provisions in the European Steel and Coal Treaty of 1951, drafted by Robert Bowie of the Harvard Law School, who was then serving as General Counsel to John J. McCloy, High Commissioner for Germany. See Gerber, *Law and Competition in Twentieth Century Europe*, 338. Although at least some U.S. policy makers were interested in the adoption of deconcentration measures in Germany and Japan after World War II, these measures were eventually abandoned after achieving only limited success. Antitrust outside the United States was thus more an effort to regulate postwar markets and free them from cartel control than it was to dismantle monopoly enterprise. See John O. Haley, *Antitrust in Germany and Japan: The First Fifty Years, 1947–1998* (2001), 48–63; Harry First, "Antitrust in Japan: The Original Intent," 9 *Pac. Rim L. & Pol'y J.* 1, 32–35 (2000) (discussing bifurcation of zaibatsu dissolution and antitrust legislation).

17. See Goyder, *EC Competition Law*, at 28.

18. See Case 56/64, Etablissements Consten, S.A.R.L. v. Commission, [1966] ECR 299, 341 (English Special Edition) (holding that Article 81 applies to agreements "capable of constituting a threat, either direct or indirect, actual or potential, to freedom of trade between Member States"). For areas the Commission reserved to itself, see Council Regulation 17/62 of 6 February 1962, First Regulation implementing Articles 85 and 86 of the Treaty, [1962] OJ L 13/204 [hereinafter Reg. 17/62], art.

2 (negative clearance), art. 4 (notification of agreements seeking [81](3) exemption), art. 9(1) (exclusive power to apply [81](3)). For discussion, see Goyder, *EC Competition Law*, at 438.

19. Reg. 17/62, art. 9(3).

20. Council Regulation 1/2003 of 16 December 2002 on the implementation of the rules on competition laid down in Articles 81 and 82 of the Treaty, [2003] OJ L 1/1 [hereinafter Reg. 1/2003], art. 11(1). See also id., article 15 (cooperation with national courts).

21. The Commission will take a case where the practices involved have competitive effects in "more than three Member States" or the "Community interest requires the adoption of a Commission decision to develop Community competition policy when a new competition issue arises or to ensure effective enforcement." See Commission Notice on cooperation within the Network of Competition Authorities, 2004 O.J. (C 101/43), ¶¶ 14, 15.

22. Reg. 1/2003, art 3. Note that Article 3(2) permits member states to adopt and apply "on their territory stricter national laws which prohibit or sanction unilateral conduct engaged in by undertakings" and that Article 3(3) permits member states to apply national merger laws.

23. Reg. 1/2003, art. 16 (covering "uniform application of Community competition law").

24. See Reg. 1/2003, art. 11(6).

25. For data on activity by National Competition Authorities and the Commission, see http://ec.europa.eu/competition/ecn/statistics.html. For discussion of the early experience of shared enforcement with the National Competition Authorities, see David Gerber and Paolo Cassinis, "The 'Modernisation' of European Community Competition Law: Achieving Consistency In Enforcement," 27 *Eur. Competition L. Rev.* 10 (Part I) and 27 *Eur. Competition L. Rev.* 51 (Part II) (2006).

26. See Denis Waelbroeck, Donald Slater, and Gil Even-Shoshan, "Study on the Conditions of Claims for Damages in Case of Infringement of EC Competition Rules: Comparative Report," 2004 (http://ec.europa.eu), 1. This study, done by the Ashurst law firm for the European Commission, comparatively analyzes the development of damages actions in the legal systems of the 25 member states and provides a detailed analysis of the factors that hinder private enforcement in the EU. Detailed reports on each of the member states are posted at http://ec.europa.eu.

27. For initial discussions, see Commission Green Paper on Damages Actions for Breach of the EC Antitrust Rules, COM (2005) 672 final (Dec. 19, 2005) (reviewing issues involved in increasing private enforcement in Europe); Commission Staff Working Paper, Annex to the Green Paper on Damages Actions for Breach of the EC Antitrust Rules, COM (2005) 672 final, SEC (2005) 1732 (Dec. 19, 2005) (providing

more details). For a review of those efforts and a discussion of possible reasons for the lack of success, see Robert O'Donoghue, "Europe's Long March Toward Antitrust Damages Actions," *CPI Antitrust Chronicle*, April 2011 (describing the Commission as taking "a rather languid course with no clear end-point in sight"). In 2013 the Commission proposed EU legislation to facilitate private damages actions in national courts. See "Proposal for a Directive of the European Parliament and of the Council on certain rules governing actions for damages under national law for infringements of the competition law provisions of the Member States and of the European Union," COM(2013) 404 final (June 11, 2013).

28. For a discussion of the "virtuous competition" for states as buyers of antitrust law, and the incentives that have been offered for adopting a particular approach to antitrust, see Eleanor M. Fox, "Antitrust and Regulatory Federalism: Races Up, Down, and Sideways," 75 *N.Y.U. L. Rev.* 1781, 1799–1800 (2000).

29. See Mark R. A. Palim, "The Worldwide Growth of Competition Law: An Empirical Analysis," 43 *Antitrust Bull.* 105, 109 (1998).

30. This number is an approximation, based in part on the membership of the International Competition Network which in 2011 consisted of competition authorities from 106 jurisdictions. Email message from ICN Secretariat to Harry First, July 25, 2011. This figure doesn't include non-members, such as China.

31. *United States v. Aluminum Co. of America*, 148 F.2d 416 (2d Cir. 1945). For early cases, see, e.g., *United States v. American Tobacco Co.*, 221 U.S. 106 (1911) (agreement involving international market division in sale of tobacco products); *American Banana Co. v. United Fruit Co.*, 213 U.S. 347 (1909) (efforts to suppress export of bananas from Costa Rica; held: not within the jurisdictional reach of the Sherman Act).

32. For a discussion of Thurman Arnold's international cartel program, as well as more recent international cartel prosecutions, see Harry First, "The Vitamins Case: Cartel Prosecutions and the Coming of International Competition Law," 68 *Antitrust L. J.* 711 (2000).

33. See Joined Cases 89/85, 104/85, 114/85, 116/85, 117/85 and 125–129/85, *Ahlström Osakeyhtiö v. Commission*, [1988] ECR 5193. The defendant was the Pulp, Paper and Paper Board Export Association of the United States, formerly the Kraft Export Association, which was exempt from U.S. antitrust law under the Webb-Pomerene Act. See Commission Decision 85/202 of 19 December 1984 in case IV/29.725, Wood pulp, [1985] OJ L 85/1. The period of infringement started in 1974; the Commission started its investigation in 1977 and initiated proceedings in 1981.

34. The Court of Justice did not clearly adopt the U.S. "effects test" for extraterritorial jurisdiction, although the slightly different European approach (which focuses on the place of implementation) does not appear to have restricted subsequent

assertions of jurisdiction. See Goyder, *EC Competition Law*, at 500–502; Richard Whish, *Competition Law*, fifth edition (2003), 436–437.

35. Whether a merger is of "community dimension" depends on the volume of worldwide and Community "turnover" of the undertakings concerned. See Council Regulation 139/2004 of 20 January 2004 on the control of concentration between undertakings, [2004] OJ L 24/1, art. 1(2). On the history of the adoption of the Merger Regulation, see Leon Brittan, *Competition Policy and Merger Control in the Single European Market* (1991), 23–46; Goyder, *EC Competition Law*, at 335–340.

36. The most dramatic examples of conflict in merger enforcement between the U.S. and the EU are the GE-Honeywell and Boeing-McDonnell Douglas mergers; in both the European Commission found anticompetitive effects but U.S. enforcement agencies did not. See Commission Decision 2004/134 of 3 July 2001 in case COMP/M.2220, General Electric/Honeywell, [2004] OJ L 48/1; Commission Decision 97/816 of 30 July 1997 in case IV/M.877, Boeing/McDonnell Douglas, [1997] OJ L 336/16. Compare Statement of Chairman Robert Pitofsky and Commissioners Janet D. Steiger, Roscoe B. Starek III and Christine A. Varney in the Matter of The Boeing Company/McDonnell Douglas Corporation, File No. 971-0051 (July 1, 1997) (http://www.ftc.gov) (separate statement of four FTC Commissioners providing reasons for not opposing merger). Not all disagreements cause controversy, however, nor do all disagreements involve cases where the European Commission acts but the U.S. does not. Compare Commission Decision of 16 October 2002 in case IV/M.2867, UPM/Kymmene/Morgan Adhesives (labelstock), [2002] OJ C 284/4 (clearing merger) with United States v. UPM-Kymmene Oyj, 2003–2 Trade Cas. (CCH) ¶ 74,101 (N.D. Ill. 2003) (enjoining merger as probably violative of Section 7 of the Clayton Act).

37. For enforcement data on the pre-1940 period, see Gilbert H. Montague, "The Commission's Jurisdiction Over Practices in Restraint of Trade: A Large-Scale Method of Mass Enforcement of the Antitrust Laws," 8 *Geo. Wash. L. Rev.* 365 (1940) (FTC and Justice Department).

38. See Report of The Attorney General's National Committee to Study the Antitrust Laws (1955), 376 and n. 53.

39. See 15 U.S.C. § 18a(d) (concurrent jurisdiction).

40. The liaison process, as it operated by the 1970s, is described on pages 193–194 of Robert A. Katzmann, *Regulatory Bureaucracy: The Federal Trade Commission and Antitrust Policy* (1980). The process was formally modified in 1993 (see 65 *Antitrust & Trade Reg. Rep. (BNA)* 746, 1993) and in 1995 (see 68 *Antitrust & Trade Reg. Rep. (BNA)* 403, 1995). For information about an aborted effort to modify the liaison agreement in 2002, see Memorandum of Agreement Between the Federal Trade Commission and the Antitrust Division of the United States Department of Justice Concerning Clearance Procedures for Investigations (March 5, 2002) (http://www.ftc.gov). For

the current liaison agreement, see U.S. Department of Justice, Antitrust Division Manual ch. VII.A, fourth edition, 2008 (http://www.justice.gov). For more recent examples of public disagreements between the two agencies, see Thomas Catan, "This Takeover Battle Pits Bureaucrat vs. Bureaucrat," *Wall Street Journal*, April 12, 2011 (describing disputes over merger clearances, health-care antitrust enforcement, and potential major monopolization investigations).

41. See http://www.naag.org/about_naag.php.

42. See, e.g., National Association of Attorneys General, "Voluntary Pre-Merger Disclosure Compact," reprinted in 4 Trade Reg. Rep. (CCH) ¶ 13,410 (March 21, 1994); Antitrust Division, U.S. Department of Justice, Protocol for Coordination in Merger Investigations Between the Federal Enforcement Agencies and State Attorneys General, reprinted in John J. Flynn et al., *Antitrust: Statutes, Treaties, Regulations, Guidelines, Policies* (2011), 535–543 (governing confidentiality of information, sharing of information, and guidelines for joint investigations and settlements); U.S. Department of Justice, Protocol for Increased State Prosecution of Criminal Antitrust Offenses, reprinted in 70 *Antitrust & Trade Reg. Rep. (BNA)* 362 (March 28, 1996).

43. For examples of joint merger litigation, see, e.g., *United States v. AT&T Inc.*, No. 11-01560 (ESH) (D.D.C. filed Sept. 30. 2011) (DOJ and eight states) (second amended complaint); *United States v. Oracle Corp.*, 331 F. Supp. 2d 1098 (N.D. Cal. 2004) (DOJ and eleven states); *FTC v. Lundbeck, Inc.*, 650 F.3d 1236 (8th Cir. 2011) (FTC and ten states); *FTC v. Tenet Health Care Corp.*, 186 F.3d 1045 (8th Cir. 1999) (FTC and one state).

44. For another example of a disagreement in a state coalition with regard to remedies, see Harry First, "Delivering Remedies: The Role of the States in Antitrust Enforcement," 69 *Geo. Wash. L. Rev.* 1701, 1718 and n. 101 (2001) (separate civil settlements for California and 23 other states).

45. For state and federal suits against the same defendant for the same practices: Compare *New York v. Intel Corp.*, 2011-2 Trade Cas. (CCH) ¶77,711 (D.Del. 2011) (monopolization suit for marketing practices involving x86 microprocessors) (dismissing suit) with In the Matter of Intel Corp., No. 9341 (FTC Oct. 29, 2010) (settlement) (www.ftc.gov). For a state suit after a federal agency settlement, see *California v. Am. Stores Co.*, 872 F.2d 837 (9th Cir. 1989) (state challenge to grocery store merger after FTC settlement had obtained divestiture of 31 to 37 stores; upholding grant of preliminary injunction), rev'd on other grounds, 495 U.S. 271 (1990). For state suits where federal enforcers decided not to sue: See *New York v. Kraft General Foods, Inc.*, 926 F. Supp. 321 (S.D.N.Y. 1995) (after trial, court finds the merger lawful under Section 7); First, "Delivering Remedies," at 1019–1021 (describing successful state suit against hospital "virtual merger" that federal government hadn't challenged); Edward T. Swaine, "The Local Law of Global Antitrust," 43 *Wm. & Mary L. Rev.* 627, 762 (2001) (describing litigation involving collusion in restricting avail-

ability of insurance coverage; case filed by private litigants and state enforcers after Justice Department declined to investigate). For review of the areas of disagreement between state and federal enforcers in the 1980s, see, e.g., Lloyd Constantine, "Current Antitrust Enforcement Initiatives by State Attorneys General," 56 *Antitrust L. J.* 111 (1987).

46. For examples of separate federal and state investigations, with litigation brought by the federal agency, states, and private litigants, see *In re Compact Disc Minimum Advertised Price Antitrust Litig.*, 216 F.R.D. 197, 2003–1 Trade Cas. (CCH) ¶ 74,060 (D. Me. 2003) (approving settlement of resale price maintenance case brought against five record companies by 43 states and territories and by various classes of private parties); Five Consent Agreements Concerning the Market for Prerecorded Music in the United States, FTC File No 971-0070 (May 10, 2000) (complaints and consent orders against five record companies for same conduct) (http://www.ftc.gov). For information sharing between private litigants and public agencies, see, e.g., *In re Visa Check/MasterMoney Antitrust Litig.*, 190 F.R.D. 309, 2001–1 Trade Cas. (CCH) ¶ 72,766 (E.D.N.Y. 2000) (modifying protective order in antitrust action to provide Justice Department access to plaintiff counsel's analysis of discovery materials; Justice Department was bringing its own antitrust action against the same companies); Arthur M. Kaplan, "Antitrust As A Public-Private Partnership: A Case Study of the NASDAQ Litigation," 52 *Case W. Res. L. Rev.* 111 (2001) (describing sharing of information between private plaintiffs and Department of Justice) ($1.027 billion settlement). For separate litigation brought by a private party and the government for the same violation, compare *Sprint Nextel Corp. v. AT&T Inc.*, No. 11-1600 (ESH) (D.D.C. Nov. 2, 2011) (denying, in part, motion to dismiss complaint) (AT&T/T-Mobile acquisition) with *U.S. v. AT&T* (filed Sept. 30. 2011).

47. For examples of private litigation where federal government enforcers take a view contrary to private plaintiffs: Distribution restraints, see *Leegin Creative Leather Prods., Inc. v. PSKS, Inc.*, 551 U.S. 877 (2007) (minimum resale price maintenance subject to rule of reason) (accepting Justice Department argument) (states support plaintiff's view); *Continental T.V., Inc. v. GTE Sylvania, Inc.*, 433 U.S. 36 (1977) (non-price vertical restraints subject to a rule-of-reason analysis; reversing jury award for plaintiff); John J. Flynn, "The 'Is' and 'Ought' of Vertical Restraints After *Monsanto Co. v. Spray-Rite Service Corp.*," 71 *Cornell L. Rev.* 1095 (1986) (discussing lower court unwillingness to find for plaintiffs in distribution cases after Monsanto). On price discrimination, see *United Magazine Co. v. Murdoch Magazines Distribution Inc.*, No. 00 CIV 3367, 2001 U.S. Dist. LEXIS 20878 (S.D.N.Y. Dec. 17, 2001) (denying motion to dismiss claim of discriminatory pricing under Robinson-Patman Act); *Intimate Bookshop, Inc. v. Barnes & Noble, Inc.*, 88 F. Supp. 2d 133 (S.D.N.Y. 2000) (granting motion to dismiss claim of discriminatory pricing under Robinson-Patman Act). The Justice Department takes a highly critical view of the Robinson-Patman Act and its underlying policy, see United States Department of Justice, Report on the Robinson-Patman Act (1977).

48. The formal allocation of responsibility in the Network is set out in Commission Notice on cooperation within the Network of Competition Authorities, [2004] OJ C 101/43.

49. See id. ¶ 12. The Commission envisions the national competition authorities engaging in "parallel action," but endeavoring to "coordinate their action to the extent possible," for example, by designating one of the agencies as the "lead authority." Id. ¶ 13.

50. For discussion of the European hierarchical network approach, see Wolfgang Kerber, "An International Multi-Level System of Competition Laws: Federalism in Antitrust," in *The Future of Transnational Antitrust: From Comparative to Common Competition Law*, ed. Josef Drexl (2003), 269–300.

51. For bilateral cooperation agreements involving the United States, see http:// www.justice.gov/atr/public/international/int-arrangements.html (agreements with 12 governments, as of 2013). For bilateral agreements involving the European Commission, see http://ec.europa.eu/competition/international/bilateral/ (86 agreements, of which eight specifically involve competition law).

52. For discussions of positive comity between the Justice Department and the European Commission, see Goyder, *EC Competition Law*, 508; Rachel Brandenburger, "Twenty Years of Transatlantic Antitrust Cooperation: The Past and the Future" (2010) (http://www.justice.gov), 8–9.

53. See Brandenburger, "Twenty Years of Transatlantic Antitrust Cooperation," 5 (reporting daily phone calls between Justice Department and European Commission enforcers).

54. Simultaneous raids by multiple enforcement authorities investigating price fixing in the air cargo industry have been reported. See *Financial Times*, Feb. 15, 2006, at 9; Paper and Forestry Products (2004) (U.S., EU, Canada, EFTA), reported, Commission press release MEMO 04-123; Copper Concentrate (2003) (U.S., EU, Canada) reported, Commission press release MEMO 03-107; Heat Stabilizers (PVC) (2003) (U.S., EU, Canada, and Japan), reported, Commission press release MEMO 03-33. The Commission's press releases are available at http://europa.eu.

55. For ICN reports, see http://www.internationalcompetitionnetwork.org/library .aspx. The OECD and UNCTAD are also involved in efforts to increase international antitrust enforcement. For a discussion of UNCTAD's role, see Ioannis Lianos, "The Contribution of the United Nations to Global Antitrust," 15 *Tul. J. Int'l & Comp. L.* 415 (2007).

56. For example, in 2002 the FTC and the Justice Department held joint hearings on the patent system and its effect on competition and innovation, but a 2003 report on those hearings was issued only by the FTC—see "To Promote Innovation: The Proper Balance of Competition and Patent Law and Policy" (http://www.ftc.gov)

(critiquing the patent system). A joint FTC-DOJ report wasn't issued until 2007—see DOJ and FTC, "Antitrust Enforcement and Intellectual Property Rights: Promoting Innovation and Competition" (http://www.usdoj.gov). In 2006 the FTC and the Justice Department also disagreed on whether to seek Supreme Court review of an unfavorable decision involving "reverse payments"; the FTC eventually filed its own (unsuccessful) petition seeking review while the Justice Department filed an amicus brief in opposition to review. For further discussion of this case and the divergence in enforcement interest between the FTC and Justice Department, see Harry First, "Controlling the Intellectual Property Grab: Protect Innovation, Not Innovators," 38 *Rutgers L. J.* 365, 391–395 (2007).

57. For the Justice Department Report, see U.S. Department of Justice, Competition and Monopoly: Single-Firm Conduct Under Section 2 of the Sherman Act (Sept. 2008) (http://www.usdoj.gov). For the views of the FTC Commissioners, see U.S. Federal Trade Commission, Statement of Commissioners Harbour, Leibowitz, and Rosch on the Issuance of the Section 2 Report by the Department of Justice (Sept. 8, 2008) (http://www.ftc.gov). Chairman Kovacic issued a separate statement calling for more empirical work regarding the issues raised in the Justice Department's report. (See Modern U.S. Competition Law and the Treatment of Dominant Firms: Comments on the Department of Justice and Federal Trade Commission Proceedings Relating to Section 2 of the Sherman Act at http://www.ftc.gov.) The Justice Department in the Obama administration subsequently withdrew the report, but didn't issue a new one in its place. See "Justice Department Withdraws Report on Antitrust Monopoly Law" (press release, May 11, 2009) (http://www.usdoj.gov). For a fuller discussion, including differences between U.S. and European Commission views on single-firm behavior, see Alden F. Abbott, "A Tale of Two Cities: Brussels, Washington, and the Assessment of Unilateral Conduct," 56 *Antitrust Bull.* 103 (2011). For a less favorable view of the differences between the agencies, see Daniel A. Crane, *The Institutional Structure of Antitrust Enforcement* (2011), 44–46 (arguing that the "squabbling" and "bickering" over Supreme Court positions and the unilateral conduct report diminishes the influence of positions taken by the antitrust enforcement agencies).

58. See Jonathan B. Baker and Carl Shapiro, "Reinvigorating Horizontal Merger Enforcement," in *How the Chicago School Overshot the Mark*, ed. Robert Pitofsky (2008), 247–248 (reporting survey results showing that lawyers involved in merger reviews saw the Justice Department as "more lax" than the FTC and felt that their clients' interests "would be better served" by DOJ review). The authors did a subsequent follow-up study confirming that the FTC merger enforcement was on a "relatively even keel" while Justice Department enforcement rates fell and then rose. See http://lawprofessors.typepad.com/antitrustprof_blog/2012/06/reinvigorated-merger -enforcement-in-the-obama-administration.html.

59. For examples of FTC Commissioner dissent, see "FTC Closes Its Investigation of Genzyme Corporation's 2001 Acquisition of Novazyme Pharmaceuticals, Inc." (press

release, Jan. 13, 2004) (http://www.ftc.gov) (with links to statements by Chairman Muris and Commissioner Harbour, and dissenting statement of Commissioner Thompson); In the Matter of Royal Caribbean Cruises, Ltd./P&O Princess Cruises plc and Carnival Corporation/P&O Princess Cruises plc, Oct. 4, 2002 (http://www.ftc .gov) (with links to FTC Statement and dissenting statement of Commissioners Anthony and Thompson).

60. *New State Ice Co. v. Liebmann*, 285 U.S. 262, 386–387 (1932) (Brandeis, J. dissenting). The idea that state governments, moved by local concerns and knowledge, should be free to experiment without Supreme Court veto had earlier been advocated by Felix Frankfurter. Frankfurter drew on Justice Holmes' dissent in *Truax v. Corrigan*, where the Court had struck down, as a violation of the Due Process clause, a Washington state statute forbidding the granting of labor injunctions. See Felix Frankfurter, *The Public and Its Government* (1930), 49 ("government means experimentation"); *Truax v. Corrigan*, 257 U.S. 312, 344 (1921) (Holmes, J., dissenting) (the Supreme Court should not prevent "the making of social experiments"); see also id. 357 (Brandeis, J., dissenting) ("The divergence of opinion in this difficult field of governmental action should admonish us not to declare a rule arbitrary and unreasonable merely because we are convinced that it is fraught with danger to the public weal, and thus to close the door to experiment within the law.").

61. For discussion of the theory that development of competition law requires continuous learning, see Wolfgang Kerber and Oliver Budzinski, "Competition of Competition Laws: Mission Impossible?" in *Competition Laws in Conflict*, ed. Epstein and Greve, at 31, 37–39. For a full discussion of the argument that pluralism in approaches to competition policy is both inevitable and desirable, see Oliver Budzinski, Pluralism of Competition Policy Paradigms and the Call for Regulatory Diversity, Volkswirtschaftliche Beiträge No. 14/2003, Philipps-University of Marburg (2003) (http://ssrn.com). For a discussion of the development of U.S. antitrust policy, emphasizing "the evolutionary and experimental quality of competition policy making," see William E. Kovacic, "The Modern Evolution of U.S. Competition Policy Enforcement Norms," 71 *Antitrust L. J.* 377, 470 (2003).

62. For example, in fiscal year 2011 the FTC's budget for its competition mission was $129 million; the Antitrust Division's was $163 million. See Antitrust Division, "Congressional Submission FY 2013 Performance Budget" (www.justice.gov), 19; FTC, "2011 Performance Snapshot" at http://www.ftc.gov. For historic data comparing the two agencies, see Crane, *The Institutional Structure of Antitrust Enforcement*, 31.

63. For federal appropriations for state antitrust enforcement, see Crime Control Act, Pub. L. No. 94-503, § 309, 90 Stat. 2415 (1976) (codified at 42 U.S.C. § 3739) ($21 million in "seed money" for distribution to the states to strengthen their antitrust enforcement efforts).

64. Antitrust Modernization Commission, "Report and Recommendations" (2007), 273 (http://govinfo.library.unt.edu). For a review of the Antitrust Modernization

Commission's decisions on state antitrust enforcement, see Harry First, "Moderniz-ing State Antitrust Enforcement: Making the Best of a Good Situation," 54 *Antitrust Bull.* 281 (2009).

65. Although proposals for some sort of international enforcement agency or enforcement process have been made since the end of World War II, including recent efforts to use the World Trade Organization, none has succeeded. See, e.g., Jae Sung Lee, "Toward a Development-Oriented Multilateral Framework on Competi-tion Policy," 7 *San Diego Int'l L. J.* 293 (2006) (discussing failed WTO efforts in the Doha Round); Eleanor M. Fox, "International Antitrust and the Doha Dome," 43 *Va. J. Int'l L.* 911 (2003) (examining alternative models for international antitrust).

66. An example of the possible need for state-by-state compliance decisions is resale price maintenance, where some state antitrust enforcers maintain a strict view of the practice while federal enforcers take a very hands-off approach.

67. See Kerber and Budzinski, "Competition of Competition Laws: Mission Impos-sible?" at 36–37. A regulatory example of the yardstick function was the use of the Tennessee Valley Authority's electricity rates to measure the efficiency and pricing of private electric power companies regulated by state and federal agencies. See Alfred E. Kahn, *The Economics of Regulation: Principles and Institutions*, volume 2 (1971), 104–105. For a general discussion of the theory, see Andrei Schleifer, "A Theory of Yardstick Competition," 16 *RAND J. Econ.* 319 (1985) (application to per-formance of regulated firms).

68. For discussion of the application of regulatory competition to antitrust, see, e.g., Eleanor M. Fox, "Antitrust and Regulatory Federalism: Races Up, Down, and Side-ways," 75 *N.Y.U. L. Rev.* 1781, 1788–1796 (2000) (international competition among antitrust regimes); Frank H. Easterbrook, Antitrust and the Economics of Federalism, in *Competition Laws in Conflict*, ed. Epstein and Greve, at 189 (discussing competi-tion among states relating to economic regulation); Kerber and Budzinski, "Compe-tition of Competition Laws: Mission Impossible?" at 46–49 (discussing whether regulatory competition involving antitrust law is likely). For a useful general review of the theory of regulatory competition, as well as its application in a number of different areas, see *Regulatory Competition and Economic Integration: Comparative Per-spectives*, ed. Daniel C. Esty and Damien Geradin (2001).

69. See Jonathan B. Baker, Mavericks, Mergers, and Exclusion: Proving Coordinated Competitive Effects under the Antitrust Laws, 77 *N.Y.U. L. Rev.* 135, 163 (2002).

70. See, e.g., Robert C. Ellickson, *Order Without Law: How Neighbors Settle Disputes* (1991).

71. For a discussion of the importance of norms in antitrust enforcement, see Wil-liam E. Kovacic, "The Modern Evolution of U.S. Competition Policy Enforcement Norms," 71 *Antitrust L. J.* 377 (2003).

72. William Kovacic has urged competition authorities "in one jurisdiction to benchmark their operational procedures with their counterparts," arguing that "diversification in approaches provides numerous comparative yardsticks by which an agency can evaluate the soundness of its own organizational choices and procedures." William E. Kovacic, "Using Ex Post Evaluations to Improve the Performance of Competition Policy Authorities," 31 *Iowa J. Corp. L.* 503, 513 (2006).

73. For example, both agencies submit separate annual reports to Congress. See FTC, "Performance and Accountability Report Fiscal Year 2011" (http://www.ftc .gov); Antitrust Division, Congressional Submission FY 2013 Performance Budget.

74. William Kovacic makes this point in "U.S. Antitrust Policy: An Underperforming Joint Venture," *Concurrences* No. 4-2011 65 ¶ 5 (2011).

75. The Commission dealt with the incentives issue by finding that nearly all the non-intellectual property protocols were not innovative. Nevertheless, it also substantially reduced the royalty rates for the patented protocols, which it assumed were innovative.

76. *New York v. Microsoft Corp.*, 531 F. Supp. 2d 141, 157, 170–173 (D.D.C. 2008).

77. The states' role in securing the inclusion of the Technical Committee and protocol disclosure was discussed in chapter 7.

78. The issuance of the single-firm conduct report was discussed earlier in this chapter.

79. See Guidance on the Commission's Enforcement Priorities in Applying Article 82 of the EC Treaty to Abusive Exclusionary Conduct by Dominant Undertakings, [2009] OJ C 45/7.

Chapter 9

1. "It is hardly necessary," Schumpeter argued, "to point out that competition of the kind we now have in mind acts not only when in being but also when it is merely an ever-present threat. It disciplines before it attacks. The businessman feels himself to be in a competitive situation even if he is alone in his field or if, though not alone, he holds a position such that investigating government experts fail to see any effective competition between him and any other firms in the same or a neighboring field and in consequence conclude that his talk, under examination, about his competitive sorrows is all make-believe. In many cases, though not in all, this will in the long run enforce behavior very similar to the perfectly competitive pattern." Joseph A. Schumpeter, *Capitalism, Socialism, and Democracy*, third edition (1942), 82–85. For a critical analysis of Schumpeter's views, and a comparison of them to the work of Kenneth Arrow, see Jonathan B. Baker, "Beyond Schumpeter vs. Arrow: How Antitrust Fosters Innovation," 74 *Antitrust L. J.* 575 (2007).

2. For the classic critique of the *per se* rule, see Ward Bowman, "Tying Arrangements and the Leverage Problem," 67 *Yale L. J.* 19 (1957). For an explanation of how tying can be anticompetitive by impairing competition in the market for the tied product, see Michael D. Whinston, "Tying, Foreclosure, and Exclusion," 80 *Am. Econ. Rev.* 837 (1990). See also Michael D. Whinston, "Exclusivity and Tying in *U.S. v. Microsoft*: What We Know, and Don't Know," 15 *J. Econ. Persps.* 63 (2001). For an explanation of how tying can be anticompetitive in the market for the tying product, see Dennis W. Carlton and Michael Waldman, "The Strategic Use of Tying to Preserve and Create Market Power in Evolving Industries," 33 *Rand J. Econs.* 194 (2002). For a critique of the judicial analysis of Microsoft's tying in the U.S. cases, see William H. Page and John E. Lopatka, *The Microsoft Case: Antitrust, High Technology, and Consumer Welfare* (2007), 129–151 (arguing in part that the courts used too lenient a standard in judging the anticompetitive effects of Microsoft's tying of IE to Windows).

3. As Phillip Areeda and Herbert Hovenkamp have observed with respect to the rule of reason, "We cannot realistically hope to know and to weigh confidently all that bears on competitive impact. Nevertheless, we cannot escape this uncertainty either by condemning everything that might possibly impair competition or by validating everything that might possibly serve it. The former violates *Standard Oil*'s mandate and the latter eviscerates the statute. We thus have no choice except to make the best judgments we can, guided by the statutory purpose, our knowledge of the economy, generally accepted economic principles, and the facts of the case." Areeda and Hovenkamp, *Antitrust Law*, third edition (2010), 382.

4. In truth, however, the inquiries into monopoly power and competitive effects aren't discrete and are often interrelated. As the D.C. Circuit itself observed in evaluating Microsoft's monopoly power, evidence of the actual exercise of monopoly power, as with the exclusion of rivals, can suggest both monopoly power and anticompetitive effect.

5. See Andrew I. Gavil, "Moving Beyond Caricature and Characterization: The Modern Rule of Reason in Practice," 85 *S. Cal. L. Rev.* 733 (2012).

6. For an evaluation by a Microsoft executive, see David A. Heiner, "*Microsoft*: A Remedial Success?" 78 *Antitrust L. J.* 329 (2012).

7. As the U.S. Supreme Court succinctly held in *National Society of Profession Engineer. v. U.S.* (435 U.S. 679, 698, 1978), "The standard against which [a remedial order] … must be judged is whether the relief represents a reasonable method of eliminating the consequences of the illegal conduct."

8. The phrase, which originated in the Supreme Court's 1962 *Brown Shoe* decision, was immediately qualified by the Court there, in a decision that enjoined a merger that today would hardly raise any serious concern in view of the low levels of market concentration it produced. *Brown Shoe Co. v. U.S.*, 370 U.S. 294 (1962). In context,

here is how the phrase was used: "Of course, some of the results of large integrated or chain operations are beneficial to consumers. Their expansion is not rendered unlawful by the mere fact that small independent stores may be adversely affected. It is competition, not competitors, which the Act protects. *But we cannot fail to recognize Congress' desire to promote competition through the protection of viable, small, locally owned business. Congress appreciated that occasional higher costs and prices might result from the maintenance of fragmented industries and markets. It resolved these competing considerations in favor of decentralization. We must give effect to that decision.*" (id. 344, emphasis added) The emphasized language was cited for many years to support the view that efficiencies weren't a defense to a merger that appeared to continue an industry "trend toward concentration," a view that is now discredited.

9. *Spirit Airlines, Inc. v. Northwest Airlines, Inc.*, 431 F. 3d 917, 951 (6th Cir. 2005).

10. *NCAA v. Board of Regents of the University of Oklahoma*, 468 U.S. 85, 107 (1984).

11. See "Technology Giants at War: Another Game of Thrones," *The Economist*, Dec. 1, 2012.

12. Jonathan B. Baker, "Exclusion as a Core Competition Concern," 78 *Antitrust L. J.* 527 (2013).

Appendix

1. Several chronologies of events involving Microsoft's encounter with the antitrust laws have been published over the years. For events through early 2001, see Ken Auletta, *World War 3.0: Microsoft and Its Enemies* (2001), xi–xv. For a chronology that focuses more specifically on Netscape, see Michael A. Cusumano and David B. Yoffie, *Competing on Internet Time: Lessons from Netscape and Its Battle with Microsoft* (1998), 337. For a chronology of the investigation and the trial, see Joel Brinkley and Steve Lohr, "*U.S. v. Microsoft*: Pursuing a Giant; Retracing the Missteps in the Microsoft Defense," *New York Times*, June 9, 2000. For a list of *New York Times* articles from 1998 to 2000 see page 337 of Joel Brinkley and Steve Lohr, *U.S. v. Microsoft: The Inside Story of the Landmark Case* (2001). For a timeline of the European Cases, see "Timeline: Microsoft's Battle with EU Regulators," Reuters, March 6, 2013 (http://www.reuters.com).

2. Final Judgment, *United States v. Microsoft Corp.*, Civ. Action No. 94-1564 (SS) (http://www.usdoj.gov).

3. *United States v. Microsoft Corp.*, 159 F.R.D. 318 (D.D.C. 1995). See also *United States v. Microsoft Corp.*, 1995-1 Trade Cas. (CCH) ¶ 70,928 (D.D.C. 1995) (an opinion released one month after Judge Sporkin's original opinion in which he elaborated on the reasons for his rejection of the decree).

4. *United States v. Microsoft Corp.*, 56 F.3d 1448 (D.C. Cir. 1995).

5. *United States v. Microsoft Corp.*, 1995 WL 505998 (D.D.C. 1995).

6. *United States v. Microsoft Corp.*, 980 F. Supp. 537 (D.D.C. 1997).

7. All of the U.S. government filings, as well as the court orders and opinions, are available at http://www.usdoj.gov/atr/cases/ms_index.htm.

8. *United States v. Microsoft Corp.*, 147 F.3d 935 (D.C. Cir. 1998).

9. The U.S. case and the states' case had been consolidated for trial, and Judge Jackson issued a single set of findings to cover both cases. See *United States v. Microsoft Corporation*, Civil Action No. 98-1232 (TPJ); "*New York v. Microsoft Corporation*, Civil Action No. 98-1233 (TPJ), Court's Findings of Fact" at http://www.usdoj.gov.

10. "The Microsoft Referee" (editorial), *New York Times*, Nov. 26, 1999.

11. *United States v. Microsoft Corp.*, 87 F. Supp.2d 30 (D.D.C. 2000).

12. *United States v. Microsoft Corp.*, 97 F. Supp.2d 59 (D.D.C. 2000).

13. *Microsoft Corp. v. United States*, 530 U.S. 1301 (2000). Justice Stephen Breyer dissented, indicating that he would hear the appeal and stating: "The case significantly affects an important sector of the economy-a sector characterized by rapid technological change. Speed in reaching a final decision may help create legal certainty. That certainty, in turn, may further the economic development of that sector so important to our Nation's prosperity."

14. *In re Microsoft Corp. Antitrust Litigation*, 127 F. Supp.2d 702, 704 and n. 1 (D. Md. 2001).

15. *United States v. Microsoft Corp.*, 253 F.3d 34 (D.C. Cir. 2001).

16. "Justice Department Informs Microsoft of Plans for Further Proceedings in the District Court" (press release, Sept. 6, 2001) (http://www.usdoj.gov).

17. "Department of Justice and Microsoft Corporation Reach Effective Settlement on Antitrust Lawsuit" (press release, Nov. 2, 2001) (http://www.usdoj.gov).

18. *United States v. Microsoft Corp.*, 231 F. Supp.2d 144 (D.D.C. 2002).

19. The 2004 decision of the European Commission and related case materials are available at http://ec.europa.eu/competition/index_en.html.

20. *Commonwealth of Massachusetts v. Microsoft Corp.*, 373 F.3d 1199 (D.C. Cir. 2004).

21. "The JFTC Renders a Recommendation to Microsoft Corporation" (press release, July 13, 2004) (http://www.jftc.go.jp).

22. *United States v. Microsoft Corp.*, Civil Action No. 98-1232 (CKK), Modified Final Judgment (Sept. 7, 2006) (http://www.usdoj.gov).

23. Commission Decision of 12 July 2006 fixing the definitive amount of the periodic penalty payment imposed on Microsoft Corporation by Decision C(2005)4420 final and amending that Decision as regards the amount of the periodic penalty payment (Case COMP/C-3/37.792 Microsoft) (http://ec.europa.eu).

24. Case T-201/04 *Microsoft v. Commission* [2007] ECR II-3601.

25. *New York v. Microsoft Corp.*, 531 F. Supp.2d 141 (D.D.C. 2008).

26. "Commission Imposes € 899 Million Penalty on Microsoft for Non-Compliance with March 2004 Decision" (press release) (http://europa.eu).

27. Japan Fair Trade Commission, "Hearing Decision Against Microsoft Corporation" (summary; English translation) (http://www.jftc.go.jp).

28. "Commission Confirms Sending a Statement of Objections to Microsoft on the Tying of Internet Explorer to Windows" (press release, Jan. 17, 2009) (http://europa.eu).

29. "Justice Department Requests Extension of Microsoft Final Judgment" (press release) (http://www.usdoj.gov).

30. *United States v. Microsoft Corp.*, Second Modified Final Judgment, April 22, 2009 (http://www.usdoj.gov).

31. "Commission Accepts Microsoft Commitments to give Users Browser Choice" (press release, Dec. 16, 2009) (http://europa.eu).

32. See "Statement by Vice President Joaquín Almunia following General Court judgment in Case T-167/08 *Microsoft v. Commission*" at http://europa.eu.

33. "Summary of Commission Decision of 6 March 2013 relating to a proceeding on the imposition of a fine pursuant to Article 23(2)(c) of Council Regulation (EC) No 1/2003 for failure to comply with a commitment made binding by a Commission decision pursuant to Article 9 of Council Regulation (EC) No 1/2003 (Case COMP/39.530Microsoft (Tying)) (notified under document C(2013) 1210 final), OJ C 120," at http://eur-lex.europa.eu.

34. *Novell, Inc. v. Microsoft Corp.*, 731 F.3d 1064 (10th Cir. 2013), cert. denied (2014).

Index